Lies and Deceits

Eugene L. Solomon

iUniverse, Inc.
New York   Bloomington

Copyright © 2010 by Eugene Solomon

All rights reserved. No part of this book may be used or reproduced by any means, graphic, electronic, or mechanical, including photocopying, recording, taping or by any information storage retrieval system without the written permission of the publisher except in the case of brief quotations embodied in critical articles and reviews.

This book is a work of non-fiction. Unless otherwise noted, the author and the publisher make no explicit guarantees as to the accuracy of the information contained in this book and in some cases, names of people and places have been altered to protect their privacy.

iUniverse books may be ordered through booksellers or by contacting:

iUniverse
1663 Liberty Drive
Bloomington, IN 47403
www.iuniverse.com
1-800-Authors (1-800-288-4677)

Because of the dynamic nature of the Internet, any Web addresses or links contained in this book may have changed since publication and may no longer be valid. The views expressed in this work are solely those of the author and do not necessarily reflect the views of the publisher, and the publisher hereby disclaims any responsibility for them.

ISBN: 978-1-4401-9809-0 (sc)
ISBN: 978-1-4401-9810-6 (ebook)

Printed in the United States of America

iUniverse rev. date: 12/17/2009

ALSO BY EUGENE L. SOLOMON

The Second Coming

The Jesus Conference

The Conversion of Constantine

The Defining Moment

"The practice of protecting the people from the truth in order to save them from themselves damages the fiber of a society. No society can survive its own hypocrisy."

Charles A. Beard
1878-1948

For Brenda

CONTENTS

Acknowledgments		xiii
Introduction		xv
Chapter One	Colonial America	1
Chapter Two	Revolution And Independence	21
Chapter Three	U.S. Constitution	37
Chapter Four	War Of 1812	66
Chapter Five	Civil War	95
Chapter Six	Capitalism	135
Chapter Seven	Spanish-American War	165
Chapter Eight	World War I	186
Chapter Nine	The New Deal	225
Chapter Ten	World War II	253
Chapter Eleven	Hiroshima	287
Chapter Twelve	The Cold War	315
Chapter Thirteen	Joseph McCarthy	342
Chapter Fourteen	Why They Hate Us	367
Chapter Fifteen	Cuba	406
Chapter Sixteen	JFK Assassination	432
Chapter Seventeen	Martin Luther King Jr.	456
Chapter Eighteen	Vietnam	484
Chapter Nineteen	Watergate	512
Chapter Twenty	Iran	538
Chapter Twenty One	Iran-Contra	560
Chapter Twenty Two	The Gulf War	585
Chapter Twenty Three	Globalization	607
Chapter Twenty Four	September 11	628
Chapter Twenty Five	Today And Tomorrow	654
Epilogue		677
Bibliography		679

ACKNOWLEDGMENTS

It is hard to believe that this four-year research project is completed. I am sure that as time passes new revelations will appear to convince me that I stopped too soon. Special thanks go to Holly and the Florida Atlantic University library staff for putting up with my obsessive requests. First drafts are always a horror to read so I am especially thankful to Jacqueline Gottlieb and Stan Bender for their initial encouragement. Many thanks to Bunky for rescuing me from computer hell every time I pressed the wrong key and trashed everything. Last, but certainly not least, to my loving my wife, Brenda, who is never upset when she finds me still hammering away at the computer instead of being sound asleep next to her.

Eugene L. Solomon
November 2009

INTRODUCTION

"History is not history unless it is the truth."

Abraham Lincoln

"All men are created equal," proudly proclaims our Declaration of Independence. That was America's first big lie.

"We the People," declares our Constitution of 1787. That was America's second big lie.

"Lies and Deceits" in American history is the theme of this book; not just occasional lies and deceits, but a deliberate and constant stream of deception that has plunged our nation into war after war for economic gain.

America is a paradox. The 'American Dream' is about opportunity, justice for all, and personal freedom. America, according to this belief, is about those willing to "pull themselves up by their bootstraps" to provide a better life for our children and future generations. Our economic capitalist system has produced the richest, most powerful country in the world.

However, there is another side to America that is not as glorious. It lurks in the shadows of our past like a nightmare. It is about ambition, greed, and avarice. It is about the displacement of millions of North American Indians who occupied this land before us. It is about the enslavement of four million black Africans, uprooted from their homes and families, and transported to this country in chains to work as slaves to enrich white Americans. It is about constant wars when our national security has never been at risk. It is about America's unrelenting quest for profits and power.

In the 1960s, folk singer Tom Paxton wrote a song called, *What Did You Learn in School Today*. The song includes the following verse:

> I learned that Washington never told a lie,
>
> I learned that soldiers never die,
>
> I learned that our government must be strong,
>
> It's always right and never wrong.

Many people believe that our country is always right and never wrong. They believe it is our patriotic duty to support everything our government does and says. They believe it is patriotic to send our sons and daughters off to war to kill and be killed, to come home without arms, legs, or sight. Today, United States soldiers are, yet again, being killed in wars based on lies and deceits. They are not dying for our country; they are dying for our government and for our business interests. They are dying for the greed of oil and empire. They are dying to cover up the theft of our nation's wealth to pay for the machines of death. And nobody is willing to tell them why we are always at war with someone.

As you read this book, avoid skipping around and selecting topics of personal interest. My experience is that American history can only be understood as a building block, as earlier events in our history bring deeper insight to later events. Finally, this is the work of extensive research, but it is not a work of original scholarship. I have deliberately borrowed from those who have spent their lives researching and analyzing our country's past in far greater depth than I could ever hope to do. I am merely one of their students, and I am indebted to them all for their efforts.

CHAPTER ONE

COLONIAL AMERICA

"When the white man came to this country there were no taxes, no debt, and women did all the work. Why did the white man think he could improve on a system like this?"

Old Cherokee Saying

In a book about lies and deceits in American history it seems fitting to start with Christopher Columbus – a voyager who got lost and stumbled into the Americas by mistake – and then slaughtered its inhabitants. True, his misguided voyages awakened European interest in the North American continent, but when you accidentally stumble upon something that already exists, and you find that it is already occupied by others and you take it by force, is that a discovery?

Europe had long enjoyed a safe land passage to China and India, both sources of valued goods such as silk, spices, and opiates. With the fall of Constantinople to the Ottoman Turks in 1453, the land route to Asia became more difficult. Spain and Portugal, instead, sent explorers sailing around the continent of Africa in an attempt to reach Asia. It was a tedious trip. Columbus thought that since the world was recently proven to be round, why not sail west across the Atlantic Ocean? He was certain he could reach Asia faster that way.

Under the sponsorship of King Ferdinand and Queen Isabella, along with a number of private investors, a deal was struck. In return for bringing back riches, Columbus would receive 10 percent of the profits, governorship over the new-found lands, and the fame that would go with a new title: Admiral of the Ocean

Sea. The terms were generous because nobody really expected Columbus to return alive.

On the evening of August 3, 1492, Columbus departed with three ships. As it turned out, he severely underestimated the circumference of the globe and would land nowhere near Asia, but he was lucky. Instead of finding India, he landed in Barbados on October 12, 1492.

Arawak tribal men and women, naked, tawny, and full of wonder, emerged from their villages onto the island's beaches and swam out to get a closer look at the strange boats. When Columbus and his sailors came ashore, the Arawaks greeted them with food, water, and gifts. Columbus, who kept extensive journals, later wrote of this experience:

> "They brought us many things and willingly traded everything they owned. They were well-built, with good bodies and handsome. They do not bear arms, and do not know them, for I showed them a sword, which they took by the edge and cut themselves out of ignorance. Their spears are made of cane. They would make fine servants. With fifty men we could subjugate them all and make them do whatever we want."

The Arawaks wore tiny gold ornaments in their ears, which excited the eager Columbus. He took some of the natives aboard his ship as prisoners and insisted they guide him to the source of the gold. He then sailed to what is now Cuba, then to Hispaniola (Haiti and the Dominican Republic). There, bits of gold were visible in the rivers and a local chief presented a gold mask to Columbus. This led Columbus to wild visions of gold fields.

On Hispaniola, Columbus built a fort, the first European military base in the Western Hemisphere. He left thirty-nine crew members on the island with instructions to find the gold, while he sailed back to Spain with his prisoners.

His report to the Spanish Court was extravagant. Columbus insisted he had reached Asia and India and that his captive natives were "Indians." The Spanish monarchy was ecstatic and agreed to finance a second expedition, this time with seventeen ships and more than twelve hundred men. The aim of this mission was clear: slaves and gold.

When he returned to Hispaniola, Columbus found all his men dead, killed by the natives. He obstinately searched and searched, but he could not find any gold fields. Knowing that he had to bring back some sort of treasure, he sent his men on a great slave raid. Five hundred Arawak men, women and children, were captured and put in chains. On the return voyage to Spain, two hundred of the natives died; the rest arrived alive and were put up for sale.

Columbus set sail a third time, but this time the goal was gold, not slaves. He landed in the province of Cicao on Haiti, where he demanded that the natives find him gold. The natives had been given an impossible task, as the gold was not there. When the natives fled the punishment that awaited them, they were hunted down and hanged or burned to death. Native resistance was impossible against Spanish armor, muskets, swords, and horses. The Arawaks began mass suicides; infants were killed to save them from the tortures of Columbus and the Spaniards. Within two years, half of the 250,000 natives were dead.

On May 20, 1506, at age fifty-five, Columbus died. At his death, he was still convinced that he had found the route to Asia. Years later, when German map-makers needed a name for this new continent, they chose 'America' because Amerigo Vespucci had written a book describing the New World. Ironically, Columbus never received the honor of having the land named after him, which really is fitting and proper considering the brutality and genocide he exhibited in the Americas.

The true discovery of America belonged to the Native Americans who arrived from eastern Asia in three great migrations thousands of years ago. There is no accurate measure of the Native American population, but estimates place it between two and twelve million, spread out over 500 major tribes. In the east, lived the Mohawk, Oneida, Onondaga, Cayuga, and Seneca tribes. The southeast was home to the Cherokee, Chickasaw, Choctaw, Creek, Natchez, and Calusa. The Plains Indians comprised the Dakota-Sioux, Mandan, Crow, Cheyenne, Pawnee, Arapalo, Osage, Kiowa, and Comanche.

The southwest was home to the Navajo, Pueblo, Hopi, Zuni, and Apache tribes. Most of these tribes would be eradicated by the 'white man's' insatiable hunger for land and wealth.

For almost a century, the English had made sporadic attempts to explore North America and to establish colonies, but always European wars interfered with their efforts. In 1584, Queen Elizabeth approved an expedition headed by Sir Walter Raleigh to explore the possibilities in the New World. If colonization was feasible, England could create permanent military bases there, and use them to launch attacks against Spanish, French and Portuguese shipping. Emigration to America would also be a solution to England's overpopulation and unemployment. When Raleigh returned to England, he was filled with glowing reports.

Despite Raleigh's enthusiasm, there were not enough resources to sustain a colony so far from England. The English Crown, unlike Spain and France, had a limited treasury and was unwilling to finance expensive expeditions without assurances of success. However, things began to change in 1604. Hostilities between England and Spain had been terminated by mutual consent, and it now became much safer to venture across the Atlantic Ocean. By this time, Raleigh's charter rights had reverted to King James I, and the king refused to abandon England's claims to parts of North America. However, Spain made it clear that English encroachment on their territory in the New World would be considered a breach of the peace. James was torn; he did not want to disrupt the peace, but when the French began sending expeditions to America, he saw this as a serious attempt by an enemy world power to carve out a sphere of influence in the New World. James felt he had no choice; he renewed England's focus on establishing colonies in America.

According to English law in the colonial period, a group of individuals could not act as a "corporation" unless they had been granted these privileges by the Crown or Parliament. Towards the end of 1605, a group of English merchants petitioned the Crown for a charter incorporating two joint-stock companies for the purpose of selling land in North America. The creation of the joint-stock company solved the problem of traditional business partnerships.

Instead of each partner being liable for all the debts of the venture, their liability was now limited to their investment. Shares could be sold, thereby attracting capital from many individuals who would otherwise not have participated. America now became a capitalistic venture – profit with limited risk.

King James issued two charters authorizing the formation of the Virginia Company of London, or the London Company, and the Plymouth Company. Each company had identical charters, but different territories in America. The London Company was responsible for "South Virginia," what is now Georgia all the way to New Jersey, and the Plymouth Company was allocated "North Virginia," which later became the New England colonies.

The enticement to invest in either project was the prospect of huge profits. Spain had found fabulous sources of gold and silver in Mexico and Peru, and there was no reason to believe that all this unbounded virgin land in America should not be filled with the same precious metals. Once England's King James became a partner and protector in this venture, finding investors became relatively easy. Most shareholders remained passive investors and stayed comfortably back in England, concerned only with receiving the profits. Others were more adventuresome, and came to America to make sure their laborers did not sneak off with any of the riches. These investors either remained indefinitely in America or commuted back and forth to England.

There was no trouble gathering laborers for the first trip to America. Life was bleak for the common man in England and many were anxious to try something new. There were plenty of incentives to encourage them to leave. Early reports about the New World were enticing. It was thought to be a 'Garden of Eden' where crops were plentiful, the woods abounded with game and animals to feast on, and the fish jumped right out of the water. The new arrivals were assured there was nothing to fear with regard to the Indians.

In December 1606, three ships, the *Susan Constant*, the *Godspeed*, and the *Discovery*, left England for America. The ships arrived in the Chesapeake Bay area with 105 men (39 died at sea). There were thirty-five 'gentlemen', an Anglican minister, a doctor, forty soldiers, and a variety of artisans and laborers. The boats anchored at what is now Jamestown, named after England's king.

But, Raleigh's original reconnaissance report on the land and its population had been cursory and misleading; it had failed to mention that the terrain was swampy and disease-ridden. The river that snaked through the area was nothing more than a swamp that bred mosquitoes by the millions and spread malaria. Nine months later, only thirty-eight of the colonists were still alive. Equally as important, the wrong kind of settlers were sent; soldiers of fortune or 'gentlemen' interested only in precious metals lacked the practical skills necessary to establish a permanent colony. When they could not find gold and silver, they had to fall back on making the land profitable; a back-breaking task beyond their capabilities. They soon learned that capitalism was not for the faint of heart.

The investors back in England, anxious for profits to justify their original investment, sent more laborers to America, but the new arrivals kept dying as fast as they arrived. Starvation, disease, and hostile Indians took their toll. By 1610, there were only 60 settlers left alive in Jamestown. These few remaining men were so discouraged that they abandoned the settlement and set sail for home. However, en route they met up with three incoming ships carrying 400 new recruits, so they turned around and returned, determined to try once again to make this endeavor work.

Over the course of the next nine years, the Virginia Company transported more than 1,700 people to the New World and invested staggering sums of money, but no one had yet figured out how to make a profit. The farming conditions were poor, shortages of food was a major problem, frequent Indian attacks did not help, hurricanes were a menace, and many supply ships from England never reached the colony. But most of all, the settlers failed because they underestimated the hardships and struggles they would face.

However, a miracle saved the day, and that was tobacco. In 1612, John Rolfe, an Englishman living in America, realized that tobacco would grow well in Virginia and sell profitably in England. This was wonderful news since the Jamestown colonists were dying or suffering miserably from their unsuccessful farming efforts. Throughout Virginia and the greater Chesapeake area, the potential cash value of tobacco soon captivated the imaginations of the colonists. They began to plant tobacco in every available clearing.

Exports of tobacco to England rose drastically from 60,000 pounds in 1622 to 500,000 pounds in 1628 and to 1.5 million pounds by 1639. At the end of the seventeenth century, England was importing more than 20 million pounds of colonial tobacco a year. King James damned the diabolical weed, but granted the Virginia Company a tobacco monopoly in exchange for a one-third interest in the business. The first American economic boom was under way.

Excited about their new prospects, the Virginia Company advertised for more labor. When the response was not sufficient to satisfy the demand, the Virginia Company resorted to more villainous means. British judges and prison officials were bribed to deport thousands of convicts and criminals. In addition, the streets of London were full of kidnappers more than happy to cooperate. One moment some innocent person was taking a leisurely stroll, and the next minute he was aboard a ship bound for America.

Once in America, these hijacked young white males became indentured slaves, bound to their master for a period of five years. If they attempted to escape or committed a crime, their term of servitude was increased. They could not marry, leave their place of work, or engage in any occupation without consent. They were severely punished for laziness or neglect of duty. When their weary years of indenture were over, they were free, but, even then, most remained impoverished throughout their lives.

In 1624, the London Company went out of business, as its shareholders lost their desire to continue. King James I died on March 27, 1625 and was succeeded by his son Charles I. Within six weeks, Charles proclaimed Virginia a royal colony and commissioned governors to rule with the advice of an appointed council answerable to the king. A ruling Assembly developed in Virginia along the lines of the British system. It was split into the House of Burgesses and the Governors Council. Every seat was filled by members of five interrelated families, all wealthy Anglican Protestants loyal to England.

****

While the London Company was busy colonizing Virginia, the Plymouth Company was aggressively seeking settlers for the northern part of America.

Pilgrims and Puritans are generally thought of as compatriots. They definitely were not; in fact, they did not even like each other. The Pilgrims wanted a complete separation from the Church of England. Puritans, on the other hand, wanted to remain members of the Church of England, but wanted the Church to return to a more "pure" form of Christianity. For the purposes of this book, they will be considered interchangeably.

The Puritan break with orthodox Catholicism began during the sixteenth century when a great wave of religious change was sweeping across Europe. On October 31, 1517, Martin Luther, a lecturer in biblical studies at the University of Wittenberg in Germany, nailed a piece of paper to the main door of the city's church. Luther's notice was a request to debate a series of theological propositions. The major issue was the Catholic Church's decision to sell indulgences to raise money. These indulgences 'freed' the financial donor of sin – the more indulgences he bought, the more sins he was forgiven – past, present, or future.

Luther's intention was reform; he did not originally advocate breaking away from the established Roman Catholic Church. However, his excommunication as a dangerous heretic in 1521 ruled out any possibility of accommodation or compromise. Luther's protest movement, known as "Protestantism," eventually ignited a conflagration that engulfed all of Europe.

In this new reformation, there would be no pope or controlling authority and no fixed rituals. There would be no priestly confessions or "hail Mary" prayers. The sinner would have to discover the path to absolution through sincere introspection. There would be no fundamental distinction between clergy and laity. Church services would be conducted in the everyday language of the people instead of Latin. Most important of all, salvation would be based on faith, not on merit or the purchase of indulgences. What emanated from Luther's ideas was 100 years of war that ultimately killed one-third of Germany's population.

The early Catholic Church took the words of Jesus very seriously. They glorified the poor and banned outright the concept of interest and money-lending for a profit. However, merchants and entrepreneurs understood that this rigidity was not possible in a highly competitive economy. Credit and money-lending was essential to the economic reality displayed daily in the marketplace. The new Protestant movement recognized that all these restrictions on commerce simply had nothing to do with religious devotion, and they discarded all the biblical, theological, and spiritual arguments against capitalism and opted for pragmatism. Protestants rationalized that their devotion to God and their capitalist aspirations were not in conflict. Instead, they adopted the philosophy that if one works hard and spends little on worldly material goods, surplus capital will accumulate, and this will be a sign of godliness.

The Church of England, or Anglican Church, was established in 1534 when King Henry VIII broke with the Roman Catholic Church because the papal authorities in Rome would not annul his marriage so he could marry another woman. England passed the Act of Supremacy, which declared that the king was now the head of England's Church and the supreme authority over all religious matters. For the Puritans in England, the king had merely replaced the pope, and that would not suffice.

By 1570, Puritans were divided into factions – Presbyterians, Congregationalists, and radical Separatists. The radical Separatists decided to leave England and seek their 'Promised Land' elsewhere. At first, they moved to the city of Leiden in Holland. They remained there for almost twelve years, but finding jobs was difficult because they spoke English instead of the native Dutch. They were also unhappy that their children were adopting Dutch ways and customs and moving away from their English heritage.

In 1617, the Puritan congregation voted to leave Holland. They contacted the Plymouth Company and made arrangements to purchase land in America. This wave of immigrants was quite different from the Anglican Protestants that colonized Virginia. These new arrivals were dissenters in both politics and religion in contrast to the Virginians who were staunch supporters of England's king and the established English Church.

On December 11, 1620, the *Mayflower* delivered the first Puritan settlers to America. They came to the New World to establish a 'visible' society where all civil, social, and religious conduct would be lived according to God's laws, a society where their religious beliefs would permeate family, church, and state. This was not to be a community based on religious tolerance. These evangelical fundamentalists believed they were mandated by God to enforce a strict moral code on all, and that this was the only way to eradicate sin from this world.

During their ocean crossing, the Puritan leaders drew up a social contract designed to secure unity and provide for a future government in their new land. In this Mayflower Compact, the Puritans promised to live in accordance with the principles of the New Testament, to provide financial support for their church, and to obey their church elders. What was remarkable about this contract was that it was not between servant and master, or a people and their king, but between a group of like-minded individuals, with God as a witness and symbolic co-signatory. It is generally thought that the Mayflower Compact introduced democracy into America, but, on the contrary, the intention was to preserve authority in the hands of the self-chosen few.

Unlike the Virginians, whose sole purpose was profit, the Puritans had a fanatical sense of some higher mission. After a 65-day journey, these first Puritans sighted Cape Cod, anchored at Plymouth Harbor, and made their historic landing. They had brought enough supplies to last through the winter, but despite a relatively mild winter, half of the 102 members perished; of the seventeen wives, only three were alive after three months.

In the area where they settled, the climate was cooler than in Virginia and farming had a shorter growing season. The soil was stony and thin, so these Puritans turned their sights to crafts, manufacturing, furs, and fishing. They were as profit motivated as their Virginia counterparts; they just had to adapt to different climatic conditions. They rarely complained about the hardships of their mission, trusting that God sent them to America not because the Lord hated them, but because He loved them. They took pride in being God's new army and dedicated themselves to being "a light upon nations."

Before anyone could be admitted into the Puritan community, he or she had to be certified by a select group of elders. If anyone did not meet the rigid religious and moral standards, they were excluded. Secular entertainments were banned – games of chance, drama, and social parties were considered immoral. The rules were unbending. Women had to be totally subservient; according to scripture they were lustful and prone to be enlisted into the devil's service.

Anne Hutchinson was a devout woman who left her life in England to join the religious experiment taking place in America. Her beliefs, however, differed slightly from the Puritan establishment. More damningly, she, a mere woman, held theological discussions in her house. When she was brought to trial, she was unrepentant and not intimidated. She claimed that her beliefs and interpretations of scripture were as valid as those judging her. She was found guilty of upsetting the tranquility of the community and was banished from the colony. She settled elsewhere, but was clubbed to death by hostile Indians.

The Reverend Roger Williams also had a rebellious spirit. He advocated for the right of every individual to practice religion any way he or she saw fit. He also believed that the Native Americans should be fairly reimbursed for the land the settlers had taken. He was banished from the community for 'wrong thinking.' Williams formed his own community, which he named Providence. Unfortunately, Williams died in poverty. In 1644, Providence became an English colony, majestically renamed Rhode Island and Providence Plantations.

Anne Hutchinson and Roger Williams were the lucky ones. This was an age of horrid cruelty, and rarely was there any mercy. Puritans were accustomed to European 'justice' where ordinary criminals and political dissidents were routinely beheaded, burned, or broken on the wheel. Those who spoke ill of the Lord or the elders or the established religion, were punished by pouring molten metal down their throats or having their tongues ripped out. These Puritans believed that the devil, working through human witches, were the source of all evil. It was not easy to identify a witch, but those who looked or acted differently from the norm were easy targets; mostly they were women who could be accused without sources of defense. In 1692, in the village of Salem, twenty people (14 women and 6 men) were executed as 'witches' and 200 others were imprisoned for wrongful thoughts.

Through hard work and with the help of friendly Indians, the new Puritan colony survived, but it was a slow process. In 1624, they had 124 inhabitants, but only 300 by 1630. The colony never really thrived: as a Separatist settlement it was adrift from mainstream Puritanism, and, therefore, could not recruit from a wider population back home.

The Separatist Puritans may have been a tiny vanguard, but the mainstream English Puritans that followed from 1629 to 1640 constituted a migration. There were more of them, they were financially better off, had greater political and social support, and were highly educated. They left England to establish a 'New England' in America. Their decision was prompted when King Charles I ominously married a Catholic from France rather than a traditional English Protestant.

****

Since colonization was largely privately financed, the religious character of each colony varied depending on the predilection of the financiers and the composition of the early settlers. George Calvert, the First Baron of Baltimore, was a Catholic convert and a large investor in the Virginia Company. He fell in love with the Chesapeake Bay area, but as a Catholic he could not openly practice his faith in the exclusively Anglican Protestant Virginia colony. In 1629, Calvert petitioned his friend and fellow Catholic, King Charles I, for a charter and ten million acres. Charles agreed, in return for 20 percent of the profits.

George Calvert died in 1632, but his son, the Second Lord Baltimore, took over the venture and diplomatically named the area Maryland, after the king's wife. As sole proprietor, Baltimore had powers that can only be called feudal: he could incorporate towns, hold courts of justice, and should he so desire, allow for a variety of religious faiths to worship as they pleased. He also had "full and absolute power to ordain, make, and enact laws," and, in an emergency, he could unilaterally proclaim martial law. The only restriction was that all laws had to be "agreeable to the prevailing laws and customs of England."

The outbreak of the English Civil War in 1642 cast great suspicion on Lord Baltimore's loyalties, and his Protestant enemies seized the colony. Calvert escaped to England, but returned to Maryland in 1644 with his own troops and recaptured the colony. When Charles I was executed in 1649 after a Protestant uprising, Calvert decided it was politically wise to end the religious feuding and he appointed a Protestant governor in Maryland.

After the restoration of the monarchy in England in 1660, Lord Baltimore consolidated his hold on Maryland. It was not to last; more and more Protestants were being elected to the Assembly, which eventually precipitated a clash. The accession of the Catholic James II to the throne in 1685 exacerbated tensions. England's Protestants feared that Catholic England now had plans to persecute them, and on July 16, 1689, they seized the Maryland State House and laid siege to Lord Baltimore's country house, forcing him to flee.

Despite all this political and religious agitation, Maryland developed economically. The new colony learned from the mistakes and successes of Virginia. They planted tobacco, and like Virginia, their economy was built on the backs of indentured servants. When the arrival of indentured servants began to decline, planters began to buy slaves. By 1700, a budding aristocracy in both Virginia and Maryland was completely dependent on its slave holdings.

The leader in promoting colonization of the Carolina area was Sir John Colleton, a Royalist who had fought for King Charles I. England's king was financially and politically indebted to Colleton and agreed to a grant that would discharge his obligation by giving him part of Virginia. The king issued Colleton a charter on March 24, 1663 for "All that Territory or Tract of ground from the

Virginia border southward to Spanish Florida and westward as far as the South Seas."

The new Carolina colony was warm and had rich soil along its many rivers. The first settlers from England arrived in Charles Town (Charleston) in April 1670. Two years later, the colony had 271 men and 69 women. As the population expanded, unrest developed among various religious groups, and the Carolinas were split into South and North Carolina.

****

The proprietary colony of Pennsylvania had a very different history. William Penn was a complex man. He was born in 1644 into a military family, but became a Quaker at the age of twenty-two. The Quakers arrived on the scene in the early 1650s as a nonconformist movement quite different from Anglicanism and Roman Catholicism. It was a loosely organized movement of religious dissenters that believed there was no true church, and they were resigned to waiting for God to reestablish his kingdom. They were so strict in their beliefs that they made the Puritans look promiscuous.

In 1677, Penn and a group of prominent Quakers, purchased and established the colonial province of New Jersey. When constant disagreements could not be resolved, the colony was divided into East and West Jersey. East Jersey became dominated by Scottish Quakers; West Jersey became the home to many English Quakers.

Penn was not happy about this situation and he looked to establish an exclusive Quaker region elsewhere. He knew that the lands behind the Delaware River remained unclaimed and had fertile soil, large deposits of iron ore, coal, copper and other useful minerals, forests of oak, walnut and chestnut, lots of creeks and rivers, a temperate climate, and friendly natives. Penn decided to seek a formal charter for this land from the king.

Penn was fortunate that his father, Sir William Penn, had been an admiral in the Royal Navy and had personal connections with the Crown. The king had borrowed heavily from the elder Penn, and the grant to the younger Penn relieved the king from repaying the debt. The grant permitted Penn to sell land on whatever terms he chose, make all laws, and raise taxes. Penn envisioned a Quaker utopia where a common Christian faith would transcend sectarian differences, but he failed to realize that Quaker beliefs had public repercussions. What does a Quaker pacifist do about defense and security, and how do elected Quaker representatives govern when secular decisions conflict with their religious beliefs?

In 1682, Penn and seventy of his followers landed in Delaware Bay and named their colony Sylvania (King Charles II added the 'Penn' to the proposed name). Twenty-two ships with over 2,000 colonists arrived during the year, and a total of ninety shiploads of settlers landed by the end of 1685. Altogether, 23,000 Quaker settlers came to the Delaware Valley from all over England, principally from the North Midlands, Wales, and London. The London Quakers settled in Philadelphia, which grew to about 2,000 inhabitants within the first two decades.

Most Quakers believed that they could achieve salvation by their own efforts; they did not need a liturgy, a hierarchy of clergy, churches, or church taxes of any type. Instead, the Society of Friends was organized as a structure of meetings - men's meetings, women's meetings, study and business meetings, and even meetings about meetings. Within these meetings, no one led a service; rather, all sat quietly, focusing on their inner light, occasionally standing and speaking to the other Friends. They had leadership figures, specifically the elders and overseers whose duties were to teach and support. Authority, however, resided in the Society itself, manifested by a "rigorous system of collective discipline." This discipline extended from business and law to matters of marriage and dress.

These newly arrived Quakers quickly enraged both the Anglicans and the Puritans. The Quakers denied all existing social conventions. They refused to take their hats off to their superiors, and instead of bowing, they offered to shake hands. They refused to use social titles, but called everyone "Friend" regardless of age or rank. Worse, there was a great deal more equality between the sexes; women were even allowed to preach. The horror of a preaching woman was expressed by Samuel Johnson to his friend,

James Boswell: "Sir, a woman preaching is like a dog walking on his hind legs. It is not done well; but you are surprised to find it is done at all."

****

Unlike Pennsylvania, New York became an English colony by conquest. In 1613, the Dutch East India Company landed in what is now modern Albany and established a trading post. The Company was interested in the fur trade rather than settlements, but their unprofitable venture was abandoned after two years. In 1620, when it appeared that Spain and the Netherlands might again go to war, Dutch interest in the area was revived as a military base against Spanish interests in the New World. In 1624, a group of Dutch settlers was dispatched to the area. The following year a military post was set up on Manhattan Island, then called New Amsterdam. The settlement was 'legalized' by paying the Manhattan Indians sixty guilders (twenty-four dollars in American storybooks).

The Indians, of course, did not understand what was going on. For thousands of years, their tribes lived unchallenged on this land. They revered the beauty and nourishment that nature provided them. The notion that they held title to land - that it was somehow theirs to possess and deny to all others - was plainly absurd to them. How could mere mortals, who passed their short span on earth and soon returned to dust, sell or claim title to land that lived on forever? It would be as foolish as claiming ownership to the sky, sea, moon, or the stars. Land could not belong to any person or people, for the land superseded man. Thus, when the white man came and wanted to purchase title to great expanses of the earth's surface from them, the natives had difficulty fathoming the concept.

The colony of New Amsterdam did not flourish and by 1630 there were only about 300 inhabitants. In 1664, the area was conquered by the English and called New York. It was re-conquered by the Dutch in 1673 and renamed New Netherland, and finally reacquired by the English and again renamed New York.

In 1631, the Dutch became the first Europeans to settle in present-day Delaware. However, within a year, all the settlers were killed in a dispute with the Indian tribes. Twenty years later the Dutch re-established control, but, in 1664, they were forcibly removed by the British. In 1704, the province had grown so large that Delaware became an independent English colony.

The first major Connecticut settlements were established in the 1630s by congregations from Massachusetts that had become dissatisfied with the restrictive nature of church membership. English fishermen settled in New Hampshire in 1623, and became a royal colony in 1679. In 1733, part of Virginia became Georgia and was established as a separate colony because England feared that Spanish Florida was threatening the Carolinas.

As is evident from this very scanty history of colonial America, the one element that was uniform about our original thirteen colonies was its lack of unity and uniformity. This was not a nation; rather it was thirteen separate territories acting independently and without allegiance to one another. It was a hodge-podge of religions, classes, and divisive economic interests.

Each territory had a governor and a legislature composed of the area's wealthiest men. Those who ruled had wide discretionary powers. Land was the key to wealth and power, and unscrupulous deals created vast fortunes. The governor of Virginia, for example, deeded 6,000 acres to each member serving in the legislature to assure their allegiance. William Byrd used his political position to purchase more than 212,000 prime acres for a penny an acre, a fraction of the going price. Henry McCulloh, supervisor of royal revenues, accumulated 1.2 million acres. William Johnson parlayed his social connections into acquiring the second largest private holding of land in the colonies. Opportunities were everywhere for the privileged with money and influence.

Even if you came to colonial America without wealth, there was still a chance for a decent life. This new breed of European immigrant, enticed by all this vacant land and rich soil, ventured westward and staked out promising pieces of land in the wilderness. There was no negotiated contract of sale; they just settled in, built a small home and began farming. They might stay for a few years, sell what they had built for a tidy profit, and move on to other land. These 'illegal' settlers felt no remorse about their actions; after all, the king of England was nothing more than a squatter, usurping the land that really belonged to the Native American Indians. Fortunately for the settlers, the Indians were never united as a nation, so resistance, though fierce, was manageable.

The population of the colonies increased by a million people during the first half of the eighteenth century. The results were stunning. Prosperity spread from the southern plantations to New England's bustling harbors and commercial districts. Boston became the largest seaport and Philadelphia, the largest city. With each passing year, the colonies grew more diverse. The Dutch settled in Brooklyn and the Hudson Valley, Huguenots in Westchester, Scots in New Jersey, and Irish Catholics, Jews, and adherents of every Protestant sect in New York. In Pennsylvania, those of German extraction soon outnumbered those of British origin.

Such a mixture of religious persuasions, aristocrats, laborers, and indentured servants, created tensions and hostilities, but the average colonist was better fed, housed, and clothed than his or her counterpart back in England. The air was clean, and they were less prone to Europe's city-incubated diseases. Taxes were low and any hostility among the different groups was diluted by the commercial vibrancy of the times. Economic opportunity united all in a common passion.

The only limiting factor was the constant shortage of cheap labor. Native American Indians refused to do the white man's work; death was preferable to such a defilement of their heritage and culture. In fact, they died quickly when enslaved. The colonists had to look elsewhere for the solution to the problem, and the solution would soon be forthcoming.

In 1619, a Dutch ship sailed into the Chesapeake area, its captain intent on selling a cargo of black Africans to work in the ever expanding tobacco industry. The human cargo was assembled for inspection like cattle, and a negotiated price agreed upon. The new owner viewed his purchase as an investment, something amortizable over the lifetime of the slave. If profits from the slave's labor exceeded the cost, it would be a good investment; otherwise, it would not. In order to protect this investment, the slave had to housed, fed, clothed, trained, and, of course, kept alive.

The religious immorality of owning slaves was never an issue for the colonists; profit was the sole determining factor. Wealthy elites, including the Puritans, believed that a person's 'station in life' was determined by God; slavery was regarded as nothing more than a personal misfortune. After all, many of the imported slaves had been slaves back in Africa, which was the usual fate of prisoners in tribal conflicts. A victorious African chief would take his captured enemies as slaves and give them out as gifts. With the arrival of Europeans eager to trade guns, alcohol, and merchandise for slaves, African tribes raided other villages and kidnapped thousands for sale. Now these African 'sub-humans' were in Christian lands, where at least they had an opportunity to become 'civilized.'

By the eve of the American Revolution, slavery was legal in all thirteen colonies. Negroes constituted about forty percent of the southern population: half the population of Virginia was black, and in the Carolinas there were two blacks to every white. Forty-two percent of New York households had slaves, more than Philadelphia and Boston combined. The only city with more slaves than New York was Charleston, South Carolina.

Owning slaves became an extremely fashionable sign of wealth and status. The mistress of the house would show off her social position by strolling down Main Street in her newly imported English lace dress accompanied by her 'darkie' and little dog. Slaves were branded like livestock in order to prove ownership and were often exchanged for furniture or livestock. Owners told their blacks how lucky they were not to be slaves on the West Indies sugar plantations where the annual death rate was staggering. Sadly, that was probably true.

From the moment their enslavement began, black Africans fought back. Whenever they could, they revolted. Uprisings began as early as 1657, and occurred up and down the coast. The first major revolt occurred in New York on April 6, 1712. Two dozen black men, many of them recent arrivals from Africa, killed one white man and wounded seven others before escaping into the neighboring forests. Except for six of the blacks who chose suicide, the others were captured within a day. By the next day, the city was in a panic. Seventy black men were arrested. Slave insurrections posed such a threat to the social order that an example "needed" to be set. Some of the captured blacks were tied to a wheel and over a period of hours their bones were crushed until they died. Two others were burned alive. Nineteen were executed. Nobody saw this as 'cruel and unusual' punishment, but, rather, as retribution from a vengeful God.

By 1770, the population of the colonies was more than two million. English ships would leave London with cargoes of glass, shoes, hats, canvas, pewter, iron, and brass utensils, all for sale to the colonists. These wares were usually unloaded in Boston harbor and replaced with local products: wheat and rye, barrels of preserved beef, pork, herrings and mackerel, and thousands of pounds of tobacco. The English ships then sailed southward to Barbados, where some of its cargo was discharged and replaced with sugar. They then began the haul back across the Atlantic. One thing was clear to England. These colonies and the new transatlantic commerce was becoming a vital national asset to be coveted, protected and extended.

Most colonists were descendants of those who left Britain for America, and their allegiance and loyalty was still to the English Crown. They happily thought of themselves as British who, by happenstance, lived in America. Life in the colonies often resembled life back home in England. They shared the British structure of government and were proud to be part of the British Empire. Accents might differ, but English was still the official language. The colonial legal system rested comfortably on England's common law. Towns were named after English hamlets or in honor of an English monarch. Wealthy colonialists flaunted their good fortune and conducted themselves like English aristocrats, which was kind of amusing considering the wild and backward circumstances of the new country.

Obviously, life was hard for those new arrivals without wealth or status. But, despite the hardships, the immigrants poured in. They had an urgent and even reckless desire to seek a better and more productive life. Many were willing to start from scratch in the wilderness. If this meant war with the Native American Indians, as it often did, they would take their chances.

CHAPTER TWO

REVOLUTION AND INDEPENDENCE

> "How is it that the loudest yelps for liberty come from the drivers of slaves?"
>
> England's response to America's call for independence.

By 1732, all thirteen colonies had been formed and were operating independently of one another. Few Americans would have predicted that, within a few decades, their society would be moving towards independence. Most colonists valued their membership in the British Empire and saw no reason to challenge it. The imperial system offered many benefits and few costs. It tied the American colonies into a system of international trade, offered them military protection, gave them a stable political system, and it asked almost nothing in return. Being so far and isolated from England, the colonies were very much left alone. The British Empire was the most successful and freest empire the world had ever seen, and yet, these thirteen colonies of British North America, the jewel in that empire's crown, would soon attempt something that no colonial possession had yet managed to do in human history. They would revolt against the mother country. The British could not understand it, nor could many Americans who wished to remain loyal. What happened?

Many myths surround what transpired between Great Britain and her rebellious colonists. The most popular and most pervasive fiction is that the American Revolution was a tax revolt launched by people who were tired of the burdens of paying for "big government" back in England. However, that was far from the truth. The reasons were far more complicated and devious.

No single date or event marks the beginning of our separation from England, but had there not been a war, separation was still inevitable. An island, like Britain, just could not control the vastness of colonial North America.

Fundamentally, our revolution was fought over a constitutional question. Who was to control the American colonies, Parliament or the colonies' own legislative assemblies? Great Britain's constitution, unlike America's later constitution, was not written down or codified in some authoritative document. The British constitution was a series of statutes, common-law judicial precedents, and individual documents (the most famous of which was the Magna Carta).

Because the British constitution was unwritten, an array of misunderstandings about its principles and terms could emerge, and that is exactly what happened. Britain believed that its governing power rested with Parliament, in partnership with the king. Each member of Parliament represented not merely those who elected him, but all the king's subjects, wherever situated. Thus, even though Americans did not vote for members of Parliament, they were actually represented there, and Parliament could enact legislation on and for their behalf. This upset America's wealthy elites.

Why did these disputes fester for a decade without some compromise or resolution other than war? For one thing, the British did not have the force in the colonies to compel obedience. For another, the British were filled with illusions that the colonies were so different from one another that they could never unite against British rule. In addition to the comfort of British protection against foreign powers, most colonists were loyal English subjects. Being separated from England by the massive Atlantic Ocean, the colonists ignored and avoided many of England's edicts. In the end, the Revolution was a struggle for power. This struggle for power was masked by the issues of taxation, and slogans like "taxation without representation," but all the while the real issue was which side would dictate to the other.

Why did the American colonies matter so much to England and its empire? First of all, colonial purchase of imports stimulated

British manufacturing and increased their exports. Secondly, since most British imports from the colonies were raw materials, the requirement that they be processed in England before domestic use or re-export provided additional employment. Third, imports from the colonies, particularly tobacco and sugar, meant that England did not have to pay Portugal, Spain and Scandinavia for such goods with gold and silver, and, instead, could pay its own subjects for those goods, thereby keeping the money within its own system. Lastly, the colonies were a buffer against France's expansion in North America.

In the French and Indian War of 1754-1763, colonists fought alongside the English against the royal French forces and various Indian tribes allied with the French. European historians refer to this war as the Seven Years' War. There were numerous causes. Both France and England claimed the vast territory between the Appalachian Mountains and the Mississippi River, and from the Great Lakes to the Gulf of Mexico known as the Ohio Country. In order to secure their claims, both European powers took advantage of Native American tribal factions to protect their territorial influence and to keep the other from growing too strong. Religious differences were another major factor. The English feared papal influence in North America, as France's territory in North America was administered by Catholic governors and missionaries. For the predominantly Protestant colonists, French control over North America represented a threat to their Protestant freedoms provided by English law.

The war officially ended with the signing of the Treaty of Paris on February 10, 1763. The treaty resulted in France's loss of all of its North American possessions east of the Mississippi (all of Canada was ceded to Britain) except Saint Pierre and Miquelon, two small islands off Newfoundland. France regained the Caribbean islands of Guadeloupe and Martinique, which had been occupied by the British. The economic value of these two islands was greater than that of Canada because of the rich sugar crops, and the islands were easier to defend. The British, however, were happy with the arrangements, since they already had many sources of sugar. Spain gained Louisiana, including New Orleans, in compensation for its loss of Florida to the British.

In an effort to maintain the new peace, England decided that the former French territories in America would be reserved for the Native American Indians. Therefore, by the Royal Proclamation of October 4, 1763, a line was drawn which, beginning at the Gulf of the St. Lawrence River, connected a series of mountains, in what later became Vermont, to the Adirondacks in New York, down to the Alleghenies in Virginia and Pennsylvania, to the Blue Ridge Mountains in the Carolinas, and to the Great Smokey Mountains in Georgia, with the line continuing to the Florida border. By this Proclamation, the lands west of this line were 'Reserved for the Indians' and colonial settlement was forbidden.

This Proclamation upset the venture-capital colonialists who wanted the freedom to invest and expand wherever they wished. Indeed, it was impossible to prevent them from doing so, and the attempt was abandoned by Britain in 1772. This allowed opportunists to move in and acquire Indian territory, mostly through political maneuvering and outright theft. Indian tribes openly rebelled. In order to maintain order and tranquility, the British government decided that a large army needed to be stationed in the colonies.

Leaving an army of 10,000 men to garrison the new territories and police the frontier was a new departure for Great Britain; heretofore they managed to patrol their empire with a relatively small force. Supporting such a large army in the colonies had horrendous financial implications: the average annual cost amounted to a tenth of England's annual disposable income. How was it to be paid?

The government had a real problem. The French and Indian War had caused England's national debt to balloon. The burden on the British taxpayer was already unacceptably high, and the Crown could not ask for more taxes from its subjects. Wasn't it only fair that the colonists help with the imperial debt, especially since the troops were there to protect them? The colonies had experienced a decade of unprecedented prosperity and now England needed a larger financial contribution. England could accomplish this through more taxes, by raising the price of English exports to the colonies, or by lowering what they were willing to pay for colonial goods. Naturally, all three of these remedies conflicted with the goals of the profit-motivated colonists.

Hardly anyone in colonial America wanted independence. Even as late as the spring of 1776, colonies still called themselves the United Colonies and flew the Grand Union flag of England. Many believed that a war between England and America would be "the most unnatural and unnecessary war" in history. They feared that breaking away from the Crown was a "leap in the dark" that could only result in disaster for the colonialists. Those loyal to England preferred obedience and the status quo. However, the idea of independence was beginning to take hold throughout the colonies. If a survey had been taken, one-third of the colonists were loyal to England, one-third wanted independence, and one-third was undecided.

The war would not just be with our mother country, but within America itself, between the 'Loyalists' who sided with England and the 'Patriots,' who were willing to fight for independence. As with all civil wars, it would be ferocious and bloody. For the colonies, war would be a local conflict, but Great Britain had global concerns. What 'mischief' would France, Spain and the Netherlands cause England once the empire got bogged down with war in the colonies?

Thus, no single issue propelled our nation into revolution. The slogan, "Give me liberty or give me death," did not refer to personal freedom. Liberty, to the wealthy colonists, meant free enterprise. Their argument was simple – free trade meant more trade and that translated into greater American prosperity, which, in turn, would increase colonial purchases of British manufactured goods. Everyone would win as long as the colonists were left alone. However, the pleas of American business were not heard in Britain's Parliament.

England's first action to resolve its financial crisis was to impose the Stamp Act of 1765, which taxed legal documents, newspapers, pamphlets, and even playing cards. The Stamp Act required a fee that affected virtually every aspect of colonial life, from commerce to marriage. Virginia reacted first. A young Patrick Henry rose in Virginia's House of Burgess to read seven resolutions against the Stamp Act. Old-guard English loyalists in the legislature reacted with cries of treason, to which Henry answered: "If this be treason, then make the most of it."

Henry's resolutions were printed and widely circulated throughout the colonies. The reaction was violent in many locales; advocates against the tax, calling themselves the "Sons of Liberty," attacked tax collectors and ransacked their homes and businesses. Britain was shocked by the reaction and unsure of appropriate recourse. They considered taking military control of the colonies, but reconsidered. Instead, in the name of expediency, Parliament repealed the Stamp Act without it ever really taking effect. At that moment, Britain lost its power over the colonies. British rule was doomed.

The stirring slogan, "No taxation without representation," might easily be labeled, "the first American anti-globalization rally." It was a bogus rallying cry issued by the wealthy colonialists who would be paying those taxes. Within the British Empire, 'people' (those without property, women, etc.) never had any political representation. Britain considered all this talk about lack of representation complete rubbish. The American colonists were no different than nine-tenths of the people in the British Empire that had no vote. Parliament was elected by the wealthy property owners on behalf of all the people, and that august assembly represented the entire British Empire including its colonial possessions. Members of Parliament asked: "Who did these Americans think they were? Great Britain was an Empire – where would these ungrateful upstarts be without England?"

Few images in American history are as familiar as that of our nation's earliest patriots, costumed as Indians with blankets and blackened faces, dumping tea into Boston Harbor on December 16, 1773. By the late eighteenth century, Britons everywhere were addicted to tea, and the colonists in the New World were no exception. Americans, at the time, consumed about 6.5 million pounds of tea each year: 2.5 pounds per capita. The only levy on tea was an import duty of about 10 percent, and this was imposed

Lies and Deceits

by British law a full six years before the controversial Boston Tea Party. The tax was mostly irrelevant; colonists easily circumvented it by smuggling the dried tea leaves into the colonies via Holland and France. Only about five percent of consumption was actually declared to the British Crown. Why, then, were Bostonians so riled up by the actions of England's East India Company?

The East India Company was hit hard by England's wars and, by the early 1770s, it was in dire need of assistance from the government. Originally, the Company was forbidden to sell its goods directly to the colonists. Instead, they had to auction merchandise to middlemen, who then shipped the cargo to American wholesalers, who finally sold the tea to local shop owners. In May 1773, Parliament, at the request of the East India Company passed the Tea Act. No new taxes were imposed, but for the first time the Company was allowed to import tea directly from Asia to America without having to split the profits with intermediary merchants. In essence, the price of tea was *cut in half* and was therefore a boom to colonial consumers, but the tea merchants were not happy with the new legislation and they were the ones stirring up the protest movement.

When the new tea shipment arrived in Boston in September 1773, the merchants took action against the "unfair foreign competition" from the East India Company. Ignoring the fact that the colonialists were saving a substantial amount of money, the merchants couched their arguments in the familiar protectionist language of national interest. An editor writing under the pen name "A Consistent Patriot" pointed out that the new legislation would cost honest, hardworking American merchants their livelihood, "just so the East India Company could make more profit." Relying on the ignorance of their audience, these middlemen raised the issue that this was 'taxation without representation' and the first step in a British plot to take over all American commerce.

The colonists viewed the Boston Tea Party as an inconsequential prank; nobody really believed that Mohawk Indians caused this rumpus. But England was aghast at these developments; how dare these upstarts Americans act this way. Were they clamoring for war? If so, they would be taught a lesson they would never forget.

England's Parliament viewed the prospect of war with one of its colonies with dismay and disbelief. The British military was the strongest in the world, while the colonists were a bunch of belligerent ruffians. Parliament believed that instead of complaining, the colonists should be thankful for the opportunities afforded them by being part of the great British Empire. England was correct, the Boston Tea party was a farce; it was all about profits, greed, and avarice, but the public was being mentally prepared for war.

There was a strong feeling in England that the Americans were bluffing; that once they were put to the test of battle, their cause would quickly fall apart. The Continental Congress had no standing army or navy at its disposal and would have to scrape together a force from the ranks of the unemployed, indentured servants, and tenant farmers. Moreover, they had no government, no revenues except what it could coax from its stingy constituent states, no industry to produce the weaponry required to wage a protracted war, no universally accepted currency, and little credit. Its overseas trade was subject to British blockade and seizure. It was surrounded on three sides by British territory from which it could be attacked, and, on the other, the Atlantic Ocean, from which British ships could strike wherever and whenever it wished. In short, if war came, it would be a contest between grotesquely mismatched antagonists.

Getting the colonies to unite for war was no simple task. The Americans were a divided people with no common political center. When problems of governance arose, they looked to their local provincial legislatures and to the elitists that ran the country. Economics rarely drew them together. If a colonist raised tobacco or rice, he shipped it overseas; if he raised grain or milled flour or baked bread, he often dealt in local markets. Many settlers had never ventured farther than their own town. For the most part, their lives would be no different with independence.

The wealthy colonists, on the other hand, had a lot at stake. The key was to convince the lower classes to fight for independence while they reaped the benefits. No better example can be found to argue this point than the French Revolution that began in 1789, six years after our revolution had already been won. You would think there would be major popular American support for a revolution begun by the poor in France to overthrow the wealthy aristocracy. Just the opposite was true. The wealthy colonialists in America now feared that the excesses of the French Revolution might reach American shores and affect their holdings. In both revolutions, America's and French, public opinion was manipulated by the wealthy elites. In our Revolution, they expected their wealth to increase if there was no longer interference from England. When the French Revolution arrived on the scene, they feared that the disorder would be a clear and present danger to their status, wealth, and elitism.

By 1774, the colonies had already experienced the Boston Massacre, even though only three colonists were killed in that test of wills, and on May 5, 1775, the first shots were fired at Concord, Massachusetts. Up until this time, the fighting was not about independence; it was about forcing a wiser policy on the English Parliament. However, on May 10, 1775, all that changed.

Fifty-six of America's wealthiest men met in Philadelphia to decide on a new course of action. From New England came dour John Adams, volatile Paul Revere, and Silas Deane from Connecticut. Virginia sent George Washington, Peyton Randolph, Richard Henry Lee, and Patrick Henry. The Marylanders were headed by future Supreme Court Justice Samuel Chase. Pennsylvania sent Joseph Galloway and John Dickinson. Judicious John Jay and businesslike James Duane led New York's delegation. Christopher Gadsden and Edward and John Rutledge spoke for South Carolina. All these men were rich, white, had substantial economic interests at stake, and had more in common with their brethren back in London than with their own colonists. They were convinced that the opportunity for greater wealth in America was worth the risk of breaking with England, especially if the poor could be convinced to do the fighting and dying.

On June 14, 1775, George Washington, a wealthy Virginian who owned hundreds of slaves, was selected to be commander-in-chief of the colonial forces. He was the ideal choice. Physically, he was a sturdy commanding figure: about six feet, four inches in height with broad shoulders, a narrow waist, and remarkable upper body strength. Some people considered him the finest equestrian they had ever seen. He was the only American with any real military experience, having fought alongside the British in the French and Indian Wars. As the nation's commander-in-chief, he would lead an army of untrained farmers and woodsmen against the most powerful military in the world. When Washington reviewed his 'fighting force,' he called them, "a most dirty and nasty people." The first thing Washington did was to draft his last will and testament, not exactly a sign of supreme confidence.

If George Washington was the father of our country, then Benjamin Franklin of Pennsylvania was our grandfather. Franklin was the son of a Boston candle-maker and the youngest of a dozen siblings. He was the embodiment of the fresh spirit, a man who won his place of eminence without the benefit of inherited wealth, status, or land. His fame and influence stemmed from being the first media mogul of the colonial age. His *Pennsylvania Gazette* was surely the most widely read newspaper on the continent, and his *Poor Richard's Almanac*, issued in three regional editions and featuring Franklin's deadpan drolleries, was a perennial bestseller. He was directly responsible for bringing to Philadelphia such civic amenities as lighted streets, improved police and postal services, a hospital, a subscription library, a volunteer firefighting brigade, an insurance society, a university, and a forum for prominent thinkers to exchange ideas. Among his many inventions were the metal stove and bifocal lenses. His experiments on the little-understood properties of electricity made him the most famous scientist of his day and he was awarded honorary degrees from Harvard, Yale, and Oxford.

Even though war was raging, most of the delegates in this assembled Continental Congress hoped for some sort of eventual reconciliation with Britain. Ben Franklin advocated a unification of the separate colonies, but not severance from Britain. Congress could not make up its mind - it prepared for war while it begged England for peace. As the fighting spread and the losses mounted, the spirit of compromise eroded. In a last ditch attempt to prevent a permanent split with England, Congress sent a petition of grievances to King George, but he considered them unworthy of an answer.

King George was irate, "It is madness; this delusion of the American people. I have an empire to control - if these unruly American colonists get their way, other subjects might also be encouraged to rebel against British authority." In King George's eyes, the colonists were traitors who had to be subdued by force. Using inflammatory words like "traitors" allowed little room for negotiation. It was all a little confusing for the king – war with the colonies would pit Englishman against Englishman – not against some traditional hated foreigner like France or Spain. But King George stubbornly made no effort to diffuse the situation.

Hidden from public knowledge and from the Parliament was that King George suffered from an inherited disease called porphyria, which caused periodic bouts of madness. Some historians have argued that George's erratic behavior during these times was caused by the disease, and had he been able to control his faculties, he would have certainly compromised and avoided war. But King George was out of control, and his 'insane' resolve to destroy the American insurgency became clear when England stopped all trade with the colonies.

On June 7, 1776, Richard Henry Lee of Virginia introduced a resolution in Congress to declare independence, which was tantamount to a declaration of war. Lee's motion, seconded by John Adams of Massachusetts, also urged that Articles of Confederation be adopted to serve as a constitution for the new nation. Congress debated Lee's resolution for two days and then postponed the issue for three weeks. However, it appointed a five-member committee to prepare a preliminary statement on independence during the interim. The declaration committee represented all three geographic sections. In addition to Robert Lee, John Adams, and Benjamin Franklin, Roger Sherman represented Connecticut, and Robert Livingston sat in for New York. When Lee had to return to Virginia, his fellow Virginian, Thomas Jefferson, replaced him. The committee, chaired by John Adams, met for several days and then assigned Jefferson the task of incorporating their thoughts into a first draft.

The tall, handsome, and aristocratic Thomas Jefferson was a substantial slave-owner and knowledgeable on almost every conceivable subject, including botany, agriculture, zoology, chemistry, anatomy, religion, law, politics, history, languages, and literature. He was competent in Latin, Greek, and French, familiar with the classics – Cicero, Demosthenes, Epictetus, and Plato, and had read most of the prominent figures of English literature, including Shakespeare and Milton. He not only designed his own home at Monticello, he invented all sorts of ingenious and labor-saving devices: retractable beds, an indoor-outdoor weather vane, the swivel chair, an adjustable tilt-top table, and a contraption that enabled him to write a letter and make a copy of it at the same time. What set him apart from others was the quality of his mind. It was said that his appearance was "worthy of a God," and "if he was put besides any king in Europe, that king would appear to be his laquey."

In some ways, Jefferson was a mass of contradictions. He thought slavery was an evil institution, but he owned, bought, sold, and bred slaves. He was an elitist who complained bitterly of elites, yet he opposed direct elections on the ground that "a choice by the people themselves is not generally distinguished for its wisdom." He gloried in the violence of revolution, asking, "What country ever existed a century-and-a-half without rebellion? The tree of liberty must be refreshed from time to time with the blood of patriots and tyrants. It is its natural manure."

In religion, Jefferson was a deist, someone who believed in divine providence and Christ's teachings, but not that Jesus was the Son of God. He trembled at the thought that there might be a just God who would punish evildoers, because he rightfully knew that America's institution of slavery and the injustices heaped upon the Native American population would not sit well with a righteous God. However, being politically astute, Jefferson shared these views with only a few close friends and associates. He also understood that religion was a good thing for political tranquility. It kept the masses under control, something about which all the wealthy elitists were quite concerned.

Jefferson's religious views reflected the greatness of his secular mind. He compiled his own bible, arranging selected verses from the books of Matthew, Mark, Luke, and John in chronological order, and then mingled excerpts in order to create a single narrative. His bible begins with an account of the birth of Jesus without references to angels, genealogy, or prophecy. Miracles, references to the Trinity, and the divinity and resurrection of Jesus are excluded. He included all the sayings of Jesus that he thought to be genuine, compiling them for his own devotional purposes in a little book called *The Life and Morals of Jesus of Nazareth*. He arranged these passages about "correct morality and lovely benevolence" in four columns (Greek, Latin, English, and French), side by side. When he eventually retired from public life, he would publish this work as *The Jefferson Bible*.

Jefferson was not a distinguished public speaker. His greatest asset was his pen; he was a virtuoso with written words and memorable phrases. He drafted the initial version of the Declaration of Independence in just three days, using phrases from English philosophers and Virginia's own constitution. As lawyers are inclined to do, Jefferson began his draft by looking for a suitable precedent. Was there a handy document available to justify getting rid of a monarch? Indeed there was: the 1689 English Bill of Rights. In that document, Parliament endorsed the ouster of the despotic James II as the only means to vindicate the "rights and liberties of the people."

The English Bill of Rights, like the Declaration, emerged during a moment of crisis. In 1689, the exiled King James II was raising an army to recapture the throne (he ultimately failed). To keep parliamentary opinion firmly against the old king, the Bill of Rights set forth a long list of grievances against the Crown. Jefferson's draft of the Declaration of Independence follows the same template and, in many cases, recited the same grievances. In Jefferson's draft, there is a sense of betrayal. He said that the Americans had been abandoned by their own kin, and he attacked King George ruthlessly. Not everything that Jefferson wrote was exactly correct. However, Jefferson was writing a persuasive essay, not a balanced assessment of the situation.

Despite Jefferson's enthusiastic draft, he failed to gain the support of Delaware, New York, Pennsylvania, and South Carolina. Connecticut agreed to approve the Declaration on condition that Connecticut remained a "free and independent state." Jefferson criticized delegates who favored retention of ties with Britain and he rejected "the pusillanimous idea that we had friends in England worth keeping." The resistance of South Carolina softened when Congress agreed to remove all references to slavery. Unanimity was important. If certain colonies did not join and remained loyal to Britain, that would give England staging areas for its troops and doom the revolution.

When Congress reconvened on July 2, the voting was unanimous for independence. The question that was not addressed was were these thirteen colonies now a nation, or were they merely thirteen separate British outposts seeking independence from England? Once achieved, would they remain separate and independent of one another? Significantly, the Declaration of Independence never declared that the United States was now a nation. In fact, the very word "nation" was explicitly dropped from the draft and all references instead refer to the separate states. Thus, the very heading of Jefferson's version of the Declaration describes the document as "The unanimous Declaration of the thirteen united States of America" with the words "of the thirteen united" in very small print and the word "united" in lowercase letters. The intent was not to change the character of these thirteen independent states into one indivisible nation. The Declaration twice proclaims that the thirteen colonies are to be "Free and Independent States." Independence was not creating one nation; it was creating thirteen nations pledging to fight together in order to achieve victory, but to never relinquish its separate and distinct governments and individual independence.

Congress devoted the next two days to debating Jefferson's draft. There were at least seven drafts of the Declaration before the final text was approved on July 4. During these debates, Congress trimmed Jefferson's draft by about one-fourth. It deleted what it considered unnecessary words and cumbersome sentences, excised provocative assertions, moderated other passages, and cut statements that would antagonize potential allies. In all, eighty-six changes were made and 400 words were altered or eliminated, including a long passage that blamed slavery in America on King George. What remained was a forceful statement on human rights, listing twenty-five grievances and including the right of the colonies to engage in revolutionary acts. Although the final document is not devoid of feeling, it is a safer and less imaginative document then the one Jefferson originally drafted.

Jefferson was not happy with the changes; he took every alteration as a personal affront. In one obvious example, Jefferson started the second paragraph of the Declaration with: "We hold these truths to be sacred." Franklin slashed out the sentence and substituted: "We hold these truths to be self-evident." Franklin's point was that our rights would come from rationality and the consent of the governed, not the dictates and dogma of any religion.

Few words can capture the boldness of this venture that our Founding Fathers were undertaking. America was just a distant province in the sprawling English empire, but these upstart Americans were about to take on the greatest power in the world. One by one, the delegates affixed their signatures. Everyone who signed the Declaration was committing treason against England. Was this audacity or hubris; divine vision or madness? Benjamin Franklin aptly put it: "Well gentlemen, we will now hang together, or we shall most assuredly hang separately." If the war did not succeed, these men would pay with their lives. True, they had personal motives and would profit most by independence, but their heroism cannot be questioned.

On July 4, Congress ordered the document to be distributed. For what was the point of declaring independence if no one knew about it? The job of printing copies was given to John Dunlap, a 28-year-old Irish immigrant who spent much of that night setting type and running off 200 copies. Over the next two days, copies were sent to all the colonies; one was also sent to England.

The Declaration reached the colonies with a message attached: "We are now citizens of a new country." Soldiers standing in regimental formation listened to their officers read the document, while civilians learned about it from the newspapers. Decades later, the Declaration would be canonized as American scripture, but in 1776 it was generally read once - cheered - and then forgotten.

What Americans thought and felt about the Declaration's "self-evident truths" - that all men "are endowed by their creator with inalienable rights," among them "life, liberty, and the pursuit of happiness" - is not clear. There was no immediate discussion or debate in public about what these claims meant, nor was there any understanding of the contention that all men were "created equal." Nothing special was attributed to these melodic words; hardly anyone believed them. Slavery was living proof that all men were not created equal. People understood these words to mean that all white men were created equal, but even if you were white and free, you knew the words were not true. Economic circumstances separated people into different classes just as much as slavery separated black from white. Those at the top of the heap knew this and those at the bottom knew it as well.

The Declaration of Independence was never intended to proclaim some social revolution. The colonists saw this new document merely for what it was, a statement declaring independence and a justification for war. The document was constructed to sound noble and patriotic, but the words about equality were lies. Revolution and independence were not about equality, but, instead, about economics, and America's power elites intended to keep it that way.

CHAPTER THREE

U.S. CONSTITUTION

"The people who own the country ought to govern it."

John Jay
First Chief Justice of the Supreme Court

With the signing of the Declaration of Independence, a new colonial federation was born. However, unless the war could not be won it would all be meaningless. England sent over 30,000 troops, in addition to 8,000 hired Hessians from Germany, and 30 battleships loaded with cannons. Britain won virtually all the battles, but could not win the war. Late in 1776, after New York and New Jersey were captured by the British, England offered our conquered citizens the opportunity to renew their pledge of allegiance to the Crown – 3,000 citizens accepted, including one of the signers of the Declaration of Independence.

George Washington was no great field commander, but he was the best the colonies had. He fought in all nine major actions against the British and won only three. The war was going so badly that Congress almost replaced Washington as commander-of-the-army, but that would have only made things worse. Washington realized that his major task was to train an army, keep it in the field, supply it, and fill it with promises that they would eventually be paid. By doing his job, he enabled the colonial government to keep functioning until the war was conclusively settled one way or the other.

Washington's army, at no point, totaled more than 60,000 and it was subject to an annual desertion rate of 20 percent. In 1777, an exasperated Washington wrote to the Continental Congress that the number of deserters had become so great that he "he would have to send out half his army to bring back the other half." Washington was always short of everything, but somehow he managed to keep going, writing literally hundreds of letters to state governments, begging for food and supplies. He always remained calm, patient, and reassuring. Fortunately for America, England sent its worst commanders to the colonies, since they expected a quick and decisive end to this upstart rebellion. Washington's generals were not much better than the incompetent English, but at least Washington had the brilliant young Alexander Hamilton at his side.

At the age of twenty, Hamilton became Washington's best executive officer. Hamilton was a man who could be trusted to carry out the most difficult assignment with efficiency and speed. He was brimming with ideas, brave, and absolutely loyal. His function was to transcribe Washington's verbal orders and deliver them to the other generals in the field. Often these generals would resist obeying orders delivered by a young upstart, but Hamilton was an intimidating force. He may have been young and only 5 feet 7 inches, but he stood and walked ramrod straight, and if a general challenged his authority, he fearlessly looked him in the eye and convinced him that disobedience was treason.

While acting as Washington's liaison, Hamilton saw first-hand that the war as it was being fought was hopeless. He realized that Washington's rag-tag army could not win a conventional battle against the stronger, better trained and equipped British. He convinced Washington to change tactics. In order to defeat the enemy, Hamilton proposed that they fight a guerrilla-type war - attack and retreat. The key to victory, according to Hamilton, was to never suffer a major defeat in the field, to always live to fight another day. Time was on their side, according to Hamilton. As long as they could avoid defeat, eventually the British would tire and leave the colonies in disgust. This new defensive strategy did not bolster the morale of Washington's troops, who wanted glory and heroic victories, but it was the only prudent course to pursue. To Washington's credit, he listened to his young aide and adopted these new tactics. Hamilton's strategy changed the course of a war that was doomed to fail.

The war dragged on for eight-and-a-half long years. That America emerged victorious in this war was miraculous under the circumstances and is mostly attributable to British indecisiveness and resolve rather than American brilliance and military prowess. In 1783, Benjamin Franklin and John Adams signed the peace treaty with Great Britain and the war was finally over. There was no magic moment or decisive battle. The war was all about America's determination to hold out long enough to erode Britain's willingness to continue to pay for a war that had begun over economics and money.

In the end, the fight was no longer worth England's effort or expense. It had been the wrong war in the wrong place at the wrong time. Even if Britain prevailed, the agitating problems with the colonies were not going away. However, if England admitted defeat, only their pride would be lost. Few outside of Parliament were interested in the outcome. Certainly, no one from England was volunteering to leave their homeland to fight in the war. Great Britain learned a lesson that is still true today: it is extremely difficult for a superpower to win a protracted war against a committed foe that is defending its homeland and national honor.

In retrospect, the outcome of the war was the best thing that could have happened to both sides. England retreated from what was a relatively unimportant part of the world, rebuilt its army and navy, defeated Napoleon, colonized India and other Third World countries, and became the world's unquestioned preeminent global power. The American colonies, by winning its fight for independence, became able to control its own destiny. However, with the war over, the colonists traded one set of problems for another. They now had to fend for themselves instead of relying on the strength and security of the British Empire.

There is a classic truism about revolutionary movements: It is hard to start a revolution, even harder to sustain it, and hardest of all to win it; but it is only afterward, once the battles have been won, that the real difficulties begin. It was now time to tackle the difficult problem of assembling a permanent government. The fragility of America from its very first days cannot be exaggerated. Unlike the Old World, America was not born out of ancient customs. In most countries, a sense of nationhood arises over centuries, the product of generations of common kinship, common language and myths, and a shared history. America, on the other hand, was born as an artificial collection of states, woven together with the string of precariously negotiated compacts, agreements, charters and covenants. The country did not arise naturally, as in Europe, Persia, or China, but was created rather abstractly, out of the guns of a revolutionary war, and crafted with ink and paper by lawyers and statesmen. America was a theory; it would be held together not by kinship, but by its founding documents.

These new states, like the English colonies they replaced, were dramatically different from one another. Each had its unique characteristics and its own laws and customs. The precise location of the geographical and jurisdictional lines dividing the states were blurred. Each state jealously guarded its own independence, its self-rule, and its sovereignty. Each state had its own army, legislature, functioning courts, taxes, currency, and its own constitution. It is all too often forgotten that before independence, Americans were British subjects as well as citizens of Massachusetts or Virginia or New York. After independence they were no longer Britons, but neither were they Americans yet; they had no united country to attach their loyalties to so they remained faithful and proud members of their sovereign states.

Even before the Declaration of Independence was formally adopted, the Continental Congress had appointed a committee "to prepare and digest the form of confederation to be entered into among these colonies." When such a plan ultimately emerged from the post-independence Congress, it underscored, in word and deed, the sovereignty of each individual state. These Articles of Confederation, as they were called, were America's first constitution, but rather than being a proper constitution, it was really a peace treaty among thirteen separate and sovereign states in which a central government without authority was created. The opening passages of the Articles of Confederation described the arrangement among the states as a "confederation" and a "firm league of friendship with each other" in which "each state retains its sovereignty, freedom, and independence." The intention was for America to be an alliance of sovereign nation-states.

There was no greater testament to the feeble unity of the country than America's governing body: the Continental Congress. After pathetically wandering from Princeton to Annapolis, from Trenton and then to New York where it finally settled, the national legislature could scarcely muster a quorum. It remained a weak and wayward body whose members either did not appear, often had no work when they did appear, or were not listened to when they actually sought to enact policy. At every step, its actions were marked by temporizing, indifference, and hesitation. Governing was impossible: they could not tax or raise money to support an army to repel invaders or suppress internal insurrections. By any standard, America's new government was woefully impotent, and the Articles of Confederation could only be changed if all thirteen states agreed. England watched with amusement; even though they lost the war they were certain that within three years the colonies would come crawling back to the safety and security of the British Empire.

The Articles of Confederation was no mistake. The one thing the colonies feared was a strong central government and the "Articles" was deliberately designed to keep the power in the local governments. However, it now became obvious that if the American experiment was going to succeed, this type of national 'constitution' was not going to suffice, and something completely new was needed. A nation with thirteen separate governments could not work. A strong central government was necessary to maintain an army, negotiate treaties, decide on tariffs and westward expansion, raise taxes, and provide for the nation's overall security. The revolutionary army still had not been paid. Many returned to civilian life with no resources, compelled to beg for handouts. The country had a huge national debt and no steady stream of revenue. The new nation was nearly bankrupt; its currency, if you could call it that, was nearly worthless. Government debts were unpaid and likely to remain so. The new nation of America was a mess.

There were three major challenges that needed to be quickly resolved. First, Britain had closed its ports to American commerce, yet British ships sailed into American harbors bringing goods sorely missed during the wartime years of deprivation. In theory, the United States should have pursued a retaliatory strategy, but the Continental Congress lacked the authority to regulate interstate or foreign commerce. Second, Britain continued to maintain a military presence in Oswego, Niagara, and Detroit. The future of westward expansion was the third major postwar problem. In April 1784, Spain closed New Orleans and the lower Mississippi River to American navigation, thus threatening to align western settlers with Spain. If that happened, control of these regions would be lost to the United States and the possibility existed that the country might eventually split into two or three regional confederations.

A new form of unified federal government was desperately needed to deal with these issues. A monarchy, like England, was ruled out even though it had proven to be the most stable form of government the world had ever known. Plato's *Republic*, written around 380 BC, was one of the most influential treatises written about political theory. Plato's version described a utopian city-state, but even Plato admitted that his concept of such a socialist society was probably not attainable. Plato realized that people want luxuries and fancy food, perfumes and incenses, courtesans and private property, and a military to protect their material possessions. The paradox, according to Plato, is that the rich need the poor to defend the country and protect their riches, or to acquire someone else's riches, but they are afraid to arm the poor because then they might turn on them!

According to Plato, a democracy, *demos krateo*, or "rule of the people by the people" emerges when the impoverished masses are fed up with their lot in life and overthrow the minority of wealthy oligarchs. The 'people' are then in charge. Unfortunately, the people are not knowledgeable about the issues, or the issues are too complicated for them, so they rule by opinion rather than knowledge, which leads to many bad decisions. Plato argued that there was no such thing as a true democracy - there are always unequal classes - students are not equal to teachers, children do not have the same freedom as their parents, the poor do not have the benefits of the rich, and no one ever has complete privacy. To call any system a true 'democracy' was therefore a misnomer.

Plato argued that the whole concept of a democracy was too unwieldy to ever work. It was rule by a licentious, greedy, and ignorant mob unable to discipline their desires. Athens, the prime example of democracy, was a dismal failure. There, 40,000 male citizens were enfranchised to partake in the decision-making process. Each month, about 6,000 of them met in an open-air assembly and suggested legislation on various mundane issues. It was quite chaotic. Democracy, according to Plato, invariably fails and leads to tyranny, the worst of all possible regimes.

Plato also discussed a republic – *res publica*, or "public thing." That was a government ruled by the most worthy enlightened men for the common good of all. This idea of a "republic" seemed to make the most sense to our colonial elitists since it favored men just like them. Democracy was certainly not what our Founding Fathers had in mind. Jefferson and Madison never spoke of democracy in any of their public papers and it was never mentioned in the Declaration of Independence or in any of the state constitutions. James George Cabot of Massachusetts described democracy as the "the government of the worst that would lead to sheer disorder and the destruction of law, peace, and property."

Alexander Hamilton agreed with Cabot: "All communities divide themselves into the few and the many. The first are the rich and well born; the other the mass of the people. The voice of the people has been said to be the voice of God, but no matter how often this has been said, it is not true in fact. The people are turbulent and changing; they seldom judge or determine what is right. Give therefore to the first class a distinct, permanent share in the government. They will check the unsteadiness of the second, and since they are already rich and cannot benefit from any change, they will maintain a good and permanent government that can check the imprudence of democracy."

Debating different theories about the role of government became more immediately relevant when an emerging crisis developed that could not be resolved under the Articles of Confederation. Between 1781 and 1785, the four states that bordered Chesapeake

Bay – Pennsylvania, Delaware, Maryland, and Virginia – became embroiled in disputes over fishing rights, especially the harvesting of crabs and oysters. Tempers flared and threatened to break out into violence among the states, and the federal government was powerless to resolve these disputes.

In early 1786, the thirty-one-year-old James Madison of Virginia, arranged a meeting with representatives from Maryland to deal with these commercial problems. Madison then expanded the meeting to include Delaware, New York, and New Jersey, but still limited the subject to economic issues. With characteristic foresight, Alexander Hamilton, representing New York, seized the occasion to recommend a convention of all the colonies the following year. He worded his recommendation cautiously. He did not want to raise unnecessary alarm about completely abolishing the Articles of Confederation, but that was his intention. He recognized that a new system of government was needed, but he believed that telling the public the truth would only complicate matters.

The fifty-five delegates that attended this Constitutional Convention in Philadelphia were chosen by their state legislatures and were therefore the most prominent men in America. They represented twelve states; Rhode Island refused to send a delegation. The delegates averaged forty-two years of age, with Hamilton and Madison being the youngest at thirty-two and thirty-six, respectively; Franklin was the oldest at eighty-one. Hamilton and twelve others were foreign-born. Washington and Franklin were the only two that lacked a formal education. The others received their college education at institutions such as Princeton (9), Yale (4), William & Mary (4), Harvard (3), Columbia (2), University of Pennsylvania (2), and such British institutions as Oxford (1) and St. Andrews (1).

Eight of the delegates had been signers of the Declaration of Independence. Some had been active in the Revolutionary War as military officers, but most avoided combat and instead served their country as financiers, members of Congress, or as public officials. All were men of extreme wealth and influence. More than half of them were lawyers. They were hardly "demi-gods" as

Jefferson called them, but they were possibly the most enlightened and civilized political body ever assembled. There were notable absences. Jefferson was abroad as minister to France. John Hancock, whose name led the signers of the Declaration of Independence, was missing. The outstanding firebrand, Patrick Henry, refused to attend, warning his fellow slaveholders that if proponents of this new Convention succeeded, "they'll free your niggers."

After electing George Washington as presiding officer, the first order of business was to establish procedure. Each delegation was to have one vote (the more populous states objected, but they let the matter drop). For routine matters, a simple majority would do (seven votes out of twelve); but for major issues, nine votes would be needed to render a decision. Significant substantive changes to the Articles of Confederation required total unanimity. Once these bureaucratic matters were resolved, the delegates got down to the main order of business, establishing a new system of government.

On the morning of May 29, 1787, Edmund Randolph of Virginia rose from his seat and presented what came to known as the Virginia Plan. It was no accident that Randolph, and not Madison, presented the plan. Randolph was the governor of the most populous and powerful state in the Union, and he came from its most politically powerful family. Randolph, an excellent speaker, began cautiously, praising the authors of the Articles of Confederation, many of whom were gathered in the Assembly Room around him, for "having done all that patriots could do in the then infancy of the confederacy." But, Randolph argued, "The Articles of Confederation ought now be corrected and enlarged." As Randolph continued his speech, which lasted the entire day, it became obvious that Randolph was proposing to eliminate the Articles of Confederation.

Among the most radical features of the Virginia Plan was the creation of a new national legislature, or Congress. Representation in this Congress would not be distributed equally among the states, as it had been in the Continental Congress, but would rather be apportioned according to either "quotas of contribution" or "the number of free inhabitants" of a given state. This new Congress would possess the power to "legislate in all cases in which the separate states are incompetent," as well as the ability to veto any law passed by a state that the national legislature considered contrary to the best interests of the country as a whole. This revolutionary step would render the governments of the individual states distinctly inferior to the new 'national' government.

This new national legislature, according to the Virginia Plan, would have two branches, and its members would have very different relationships both to their home state governments and to the people they were supposed to serve. Eligible voters in each state would elect representatives to the first branch, while those in the upper house were to be elected by members of the lower house from a pool of candidates supplied by each of the state legislatures. This concept of a government with a two-house legislature was nothing new. The English Parliament had an "upper" and a "lower" chapter - an elected House of Commons and a hereditary House of Lords – and all thirteen colonies, except Pennsylvania, had two-house legislatures. The Virginia Plan rejected the English notion of a hereditary upper chamber, but, nevertheless, reflected a continuing belief in the traditional English concept of rule by the virtuous few.

Randolph then sketched out his concept for a "national executive." The chief executive, according to the Virginia Plan, would be indirectly elected by the national legislature. Randolph's resolution left open the question of whether the national executive would be a single person or a group of people. Randolph's Plan also called for the creation of a national judiciary with the authority to "examine" every act passed either by Congress or any of the state legislatures. Beyond this role, the judiciary's place in the proposed system was left vague. Randolph finished his presentation by concluding that these "amendments" to the Articles of Confederation should be submitted to the state assemblies for approval. Many of the delegates were stunned by Randolph's proposals, but the issues were now clearly on the table for debate and discussion.

Alexander Hamilton was arguably the smartest man at the Convention. His powerful influence in our nation's early history is a saga of epic proportions. Hamilton was the archetypal self-made man, born on Britain's Caribbean colony of Nevis, he was the second illegitimate son of Rachel Lavien and James Hamilton. His father, an indifferent Scottish drifter, deserted the family when Hamilton was an infant. When Hamilton was eight-years-old, his mother moved the family to St. Croix, a Dutch-controlled sugar island in the West Indies where the slave population was twelve times that of the free population. Hamilton's mother opened a small store and the family eked out a meager living. In the first letter that Hamilton is known to have written, at age ten, he announced his determination to be rich and famous, and to achieve an exalted place in society. He would never lose sight of that goal.

In 1768, when Hamilton was eleven, his mother died of yellow fever, leaving Alexander and his brother penniless. Hamilton went to work for a mercantile firm with business ties in New York. His employer, Nicholas Cruger, and his minister, Hugh Knox, took the young dynamo under their personal tutelage. Recognizing how fortunate he was to have caring benefactors, Hamilton devoured book after book, determined to prove himself worthy of their faith in him. At age 15, parishioners raised money for him to pursue a college education at Princeton, a Presbyterian college in New Jersey. Hamilton sailed alone to New York, but when Princeton refused him admission because he lacked the necessary preparatory schooling, he gained admittance to Kings College, now Columbia University.

Physically, Hamilton was short of stature, handsome, opinionated, combative, and arrogant. When war erupted, he abandoned his studies to become a soldier, recognizing that bearing arms might advance his career. The following year he saw action in New York, retreated across New Jersey with Washington's defeated army, and fought again at Trenton and Princeton. Soon he became General Washington's principal aide.

When he asked his friend, John Laurens, to find him a wife, Hamilton listed the qualifications he required:

> "She must be young and handsome (I lay most stress upon a good shape); sensible (a little learning will do) - well bred - chaste and tender (I am an

enthusiast in my notions of fidelity and fondness); of some good nature - a great deal of generosity. She must neither love money nor scolding, and I dislike equally a bad temper and an economist. In politics, I am indifferent what side she may be of - I think I have arguments that will safely convert her to mine. As to religion, a moderate stock will satisfy me. She must believe in God and hate a saint. As to any fortune she may have, the larger the better since money is the essential ingredient to happiness in this world."

Hamilton found the bride that matched all his specifications. On December 14, 1780, he married Elizabeth Schuyler, daughter of General Philip Schuyler, and thus joined one of the richest and most politically influential families in New York. By this time he was practicing law in New York, having gained admittance to the bar after three months of service instead of the customary two years. With his legal skills and new social connections, he established one of the most lucrative law practices in New York, representing wealthy merchants and large landowners.

In 1782, Hamilton was elected to Congress. Having experienced the war from the front lines, he saw the fatal weakness of a decentralized confederation. Furthermore, he was now in league with commercial interests that did not stop at state lines. Instead, his clients sought profits in global markets. Only a strong national government could advance those economic interests.

There is a saying that the times make the man. That was certainly true of James Madison. Born in 1751 into the largest slave-owning family in Orange County, Virginia, Madison was educated by private tutors before going to Princeton where he studied history, ethics, philosophy, and Hebrew. Scholarly and introverted, he did not fit the mold of a successful politician. Instead he chose a legal career, but was haunted by oppressive doubts as to whether he could ever deliver convincing oral arguments that would persuade a jury. He brooded about his life, coping with emotional woes that included hysterical fears and obsessive anxieties.

Lies and Deceits

Madison made his first foray into public life in December 1774 when he was elected to the local agency created by Virginia's legislature to mobilize its residents against the British. When the Revolution began in 1775, the twenty-four-year-old Madison was given a colonel's commission in the militia, but he never went into battle. In 1776, he left the army and joined Virginia's legislature. There he formed a friendship with Thomas Jefferson that lasted throughout their lives and produced an astonishing exchange of 1,250 letters that survive to this day. It is one of the great correspondences in history.

In 1780, just shy of his thirtieth birthday, Madison was elected to the Continental Congress by the Virginia legislature. Delicate and soft, he was painfully shy and struck most observers in Congress as a mere boy. He certainly did not have a dynamic personality like some of the other political figures of his day. He lacked wit, charm, and oratorical gifts, but he had a great intellect. He was unmarried so in a sense he was married to his post. Politics had become the focal point of his life, his all-consuming passion. He immersed himself in the affairs of Congress and its members, getting to know everyone, winning the trust of his peers, and gaining a reputation for rationality, prudence, and hard work.

The delegates at the Constitutional Convention agreed that all discussions, debates, and notes should be kept secret. Public disclosure of the issues would only politicize the discussions. They considered themselves men of honor who could be trusted to determine what was best for the country. They also did not want their personal finances aired in public. All the participants were sworn to life-long secrecy.

Only one person was allowed to keep notes for posterity and that was James Madison. Each day he took his seat next to Washington and began taking copious notes of the proceedings. He was never absent from the sessions for more than a few minutes so only the briefest of comments went unrecorded. Each evening, following the day's meeting, Madison would painstakingly write out his record from the shorthand notes he had taken. As agreed, Madison's notes were sealed from public view. Only after the passage of half a century would anyone be able to grasp the issues that were so vigorously debated. It is one of the most remarkable facts about our history that the record of the original meanings of our nation's most revered document is so overwhelmingly dependent on the diligence and honor of just one man. Whether Madison, who had his own strong opinions on many of the issues, reported honestly and impartially is an issue that will never be known.

The Convention was truly a remarkable assembly of men. Seven of the delegates had been governors of their native states and no less than twenty-eight had served in Congress. These were men trained in the law, versed in finance, skilled in administration, and learned in the political acumen of their own and earlier times. Moreover, they were men destined to continue public service under the government they had met to construct. They were to become the nation's future presidents, vice-presidents, heads of departments, and justices of the Supreme Court. But most of all, these were men of business and property and the holders of public securities. Their own personal financial interests were at stake. If this new American experiment in government failed, they would lose everything and have to start over. For them this was no intellectual exercise in political theory.

These men of wealth had no intention of handing over any of their power to the unenlightened masses. On this issue there was no dispute: they would establish a government for the people, but not one by the people. According to James Madison, any new constitution must "totally exclude the people in their collective capacity from any share in the government," insisting that the new government had to "protect the wealthy minority against the tyranny of the majority." Most of these Founding Fathers were not religious; Capitalism, not Christianity, defined their natural character. They believed that religion was man-made, but that it was an excellent morality mechanism for keeping the common people from murdering the rich.

The recent Shays rebellion was of great concern to all the delegates. Thousands of Revolutionary Army war veterans had returned to their farms, but were unable to pay the interest and penalties on their pre-Revolutionary loans. Many were imprisoned upon their return home. The vast majority, facing the loss of their farms and livelihood, were now asking if this was the liberty they had fought for. Taking their cue straight from the rhetoric and slogans of the war, they resolved to fight. Disgruntled farmers grabbed pitch-forks and guns, donned their old army uniforms, and started assembling companies of men, drilling for warfare. The chief architect of the rebellion was a much respected officer who had served bravely on the front lines of the war. Daniel Shays had been a former captain in the Continental Army, fought at Bunker Hill, marched at Saratoga, and put his life on the line at Stony Point. He was such a brave and competent soldier that General Lafayette gave him a handsome sword as a token of appreciation, a sword that Shays had to sell to buy necessities for his family.

Shays became the hero of this protest movement. He led 1,100 Massachusetts debt-ridden farmers to the courthouse to prevent seizure of their property for the non-payment of back taxes. A clash of arms ensued. The state militia refused to act; their sympathies were with the rioters. The protest movement quickly found ardent sympathizers in neighboring New Hampshire, Connecticut, and Rhode Island. When judges arrived at the courthouses, furious protesters greeted them with clenched fists and violent insults; the ashen-faced judges swiftly fled. Government officials were terrified by the threat posed by Shays' Rebellion, but there was no money to enlist federal troops to quash the insurrection.

Realizing that the 'national' government was helpless to do anything, Massachusetts Governor James Bowdin raised $20,000 from private donors and put together a force of 4,400 men to confront the rebels. But, the protesters were determined to stand their ground and fight. Wearing sprigs of hemlock in their hats, thus evoking the spirit of 1776, they threatened civil war. Massachusetts appealed to the Continental Congress for additional help. It was a futile gesture. No assistance was coming. A Virginia delegate begged George Washington to ride to Massachusetts to use his immense influence to dispel the rebellion. Washington fired back, "Influence is no government."

Meanwhile, extremism grew. Ominously, many members of the Massachusetts militia broke ranks and joined the insurgency.

The rebellion spread to New Jersey and South Carolina as uprisings swept the countryside. In Pennsylvania, an agitated mob refused to allow the sheriff to auction off cattle confiscated for taxes. Maryland's courthouse was forcibly shut down by angry citizens. In South Carolina, judges fled under a cloud of destruction and plunder. In Virginia, a fulminating mob torched the courthouse, burning all the tax records. With the formal peace treaty with Britain a mere three years old, New Englanders were talking about disunion and the establishment of separate confederacies. Northern provinces began planning their own nation while those in the South openly explored alliances in Europe. When the insurrections were finally put down, Shays fled, but he was captured and condemned to death. On petition, he was pardoned. A broken man, he relocated to New York and lived in poverty until his death in 1825.

To the wealthy elite gathered at the Constitutional Convention, the Shays protest represented the danger of a united armed rabble looking to change places with the rich. Somehow this new constitution they were preparing had to protect the wealthy against the poor malcontents that wanted to take by force what was not theirs. This protection could only come from a strong federal government – one that could put down and intimidate such uprisings. Madison wrote, "In dealing with the dangers of insurrection, I take no notice of an unhappy species of population abounding in some of the states who are sunk below the level of men, but who, in the tempestuous scenes of civil violence, may emerge into a superiority of strength." Hamilton had similar views; "the strong arm of the Union must be available in such crisis as we have recently observed in New England."

While the debates raged on about how much power the federal government should have, the delegates quickly resolved the issue of slavery. South Carolina announced from the outset that any interference with the South's right to maintain slavery would bring an abrupt end to the Convention. Madison spoke bluntly: "No power is given to the general government to interpose with respect to the property in slaves now held by the states." Everyone agreed that adopting a new constitution was more important than a protracted debate about slavery. The result was an unequivocal commitment: the new federal government was barred from taking any action against slavery in the colonies where it presently existed, and there would be no further congressional discussions about the slave issue for the next twenty years. After twenty years, when 1808 finally rolled around, Congress could discuss possible changes in the importation of future slaves. However, even then, under no circumstances could they disrupt the status of current slaves. Those who were already slaves, and their offspring, would be slaves forever. If there was one certainty in this Constitution, it was that slavery would remain legal forever.

There were many different proposals as to how this new government should work, but most wanted something like the English system without the monarchy. New Jersey sought to merely strengthen the Articles of Confederation, but Madison's proposal, based on the Virginia Plan, was finally adopted. It called for three branches of government: a president, a legislative Congress, and a Supreme Court. Madison's plan envisioned the legislature to be "the first among equals." The laws it enacted would be enforced by an executive, and a judiciary would resolve conflicts between the other two branches of government. The Supreme Court judiciary was to be the weakest of the three branches since it was contemplated that most disputes would be handled by the state courts. Surprisingly, nothing was mentioned about the number of justices that would comprise the Court.

Congress was to be the real power in this form of government. It could lay and collect taxes, regulate commerce among the states, declare war, and make all laws deemed 'necessary and proper' for executing its powers. The big problem had to do with the composition of this Congress. The small states wanted representation to be equal, while the larger states thought it ridiculous that little Delaware should have as much say as populous New York, Pennsylvania, Massachusetts, or Virginia. These larger states believed representation should be proportioned by population. Elbridge Gerry of Massachusetts wanted each state's representation to be based on its property values, but the delegates said it was easier to count people than cows, machinery, and fine homes. Benjamin Franklin saved the day by getting the delegates to accept a compromise: a House of Representatives proportioned by population and a Senate where each state would have equal representation.

Many delegates wanted service in this new Congress to be limited to those who met stringent property qualifications, which would limit every phase of the new government to those of wealth. However, Franklin argued that the "Constitution will be much read in Europe, and a great partiality to the rich will not only hurt the esteem of the most liberal and enlightened men there, but discourage the common people from coming to this country."

Determining the size of a state's population then became a contentious issue because it was directly related to the slave question. Obviously, the larger a state's population, the greater its representation and influence would be in the House of Representatives. Southerners considered their slaves as 'property' but wanted them counted as 'people' for the purpose of determining representation. Northerners objected; how could slaves be both property and people? If slaves were counted in determining representation, the South could import millions of additional slaves in order to get greater control in Congress. The solution proposed by John Rutledge of South Carolina and Roger Sherman of Connecticut became known as "The Great Compromise." Three-fifths of every slave was counted as a 'person' for purposes of representation; for all other purposes the slave remained property. As a result, the South with 41 percent of the nation's white inhabitants would have 47 percent of the seats in the House of Representatives. This compromise would remain the law of the land for the next 70 years.

The next issue was the Revolutionary War debts. Most of the war had been fought in the North and great debts had incurred. The northern states wanted the new federal government to assume those obligations. The southern colonies objected; let each state manage its own affairs. Madison worked out a compromise. The southern states would drop their opposition to having the federal government assume the North's war debt, and, in return, the new nation's capital would be relocated from Philadelphia to some southern locale nearer to Virginia and Maryland.

Western expansion was also a hotly debated issue. Many of the delegates were heavily invested in the western lands and they did not want the Convention to make decisions that would adversely affect their plans for developing the area. They also envisioned a time when the western territory would generate new states and the original thirteen colonies would be outnumbered. On the one hand, the delegates favored expansion, but the thought of a major power shift away from the original thirteen colonies was of great concern. Massachusetts proposed that any future representation from the western territory could never exceed the representation from the original thirteen colonies. After a close vote, this idea was discarded as impractical. The issue was left unresolved.

Hamilton was in favor of a strong federal army and navy. "Modern wars spring primarily out of commercial rivalry," he said. "Is not the love of wealth as domineering and enterprising a passion as that of power or glory? Have there not been as many wars founded upon commercial motives as those occasioned by domination? Has not the spirit of commerce, in many instances, administered new incentives to the appetite? Let history answer. Commerce has been for ages the predominant pursuit of England and she has been constantly engaged in wars. In this world-wide and age-long conflict of nations for commercial advantages, the United States cannot expect to become an idle spectator. Even if she wanted to, she could not overcome the scruples of her ambitious rivals."

When the topic turned to the election of a president, many were horrified at the thought of a single chief executive; they wanted nothing that even remotely resembled a monarchy. They wanted to create a powerful executive branch, but not too powerful. The president, under the Articles of Confederation, was largely an honorary position with no powers of appointment or veto, no official military command or direct supervision over executive departments, no personal authority to negotiate or block treaties, no explicit authorization to receive ambassadors, no pardon power, no fixed term of office, no immunity from recall, and no guaranteed salary.

Alexander Hamilton argued that a strong chief executive was necessary; this new president should serve for life and have absolute veto power over the Congress. However, the delegates flatly rejected this proposal. New Jersey wanted the new executive branch to be composed of a rotating committee with limited managerial functions; this was also rejected. James Madison wanted the president to be selected by Congress and to serve a short non-renewable term, but the majority of delegates believed that an election by Congress would be froth with boundless political intrigue. Benjamin Franklin wanted the executive branch to be comprised of three executives serving together, and all three had to be individuals who could afford to serve without pay, which meant that only the wealthy would rule. Some delegates favored selection by the state legislatures. Another suggestion was for each state to choose its most qualified candidate and then Congress would choose among the thirteen candidates.

The delegates from South Carolina voiced strong support for establishing property qualifications for the presidency. At one point, Charles Pinckney floated the figure of $100,000; the equivalent of nearly $2 million in today's economy. In the end, the Convention rejected Pinckney's approach. Anything that made the president look like a king would diminish the document's popularity both in the colonies and abroad. Concerns about presidential dynasties also lurked beneath the question of eligibility. A requirement was adopted that a president had to be a "natural-born citizen," which limited the electorate's choice.

Though seemingly illiberal on this point, their views represented a considerable liberalization of eighteenth-century English practice. Under England's famous 1701 Act of Settlement, naturalized foreigners could never serve in Parliament, or enjoy any office or place of trust, either civil or military. By contrast, our Founding Fathers opened virtually all federal positions - Congress, the judiciary, the cabinet, and the military - to naturalized citizens. In fact, immigrant Americans would account for roughly one-tenth of the membership of the First Congress, a third of the first Supreme Court, four of the nation's first six secretaries of the treasury, and one of its first three secretaries of war. Only the presidency and vice presidency were reserved for those born in the United States and that restriction did not apply to immigrants who were already American citizens as of 1787; men who had proved their loyalty by coming to or remaining in America during the Revolution.

Why did the Founders create this narrow exception? If we imagine a poor boy coming to America and rising through the political system by dint of his own sweat and virtue only to find that he was barred from the presidency, the natural-born rule surely looks anti-egalitarian. In 1787, however, the more salient scenario involved the possibility that a foreign earl or duke might cross the Atlantic with immense wealth and a vast retinue, and then use his European riches to buy friends on a scale that no home-grown citizen could match. Out of an abundance of caution – paranoia perhaps – the Framers barred European noblemen from America's most powerful office.

When everyone finally agreed on a single president, many powers were shifted to the Congress in order to weaken the executive branch. The president would have veto power over congressional acts, but that could be overridden if two-thirds of the members of each house of Congress disagreed with the president's interpretation of the Constitution. The new president would be commander-in-chief of the military and oversee foreign affairs. He could negotiate treaties, appoint ambassadors and federal judges, and choose lifetime members of the Supreme Court, but those actions would have to be approved by Congress. The president was also given the very narrow power of issuing pardons during times of insurrection and rebellion. According to Hamilton, presidential pardons would be "an inducement to rebellious factions to lay down their arms in order to restore tranquility."

Making a 'civilian' the commander-in-chief of the military was something unheard of in Europe, but it showed how concerned the Framers were of the military taking over the government. The delegates next addressed the issue of who would have the power to make war and under what circumstances. Some delegates preferred to give the power to the president, while others, not surprisingly, feared granting such enormous power to one person; they proposed that only Congress should have that power. Reflecting the spirit of compromise that marked the proceedings, Madison urged assigning to the president the power to "repel sudden attacks" when Congress could not act; otherwise, only Congress could declare war, raise and support armies, and maintain a navy. Madison's views prevailed. This ambiguous compromise left the president an opening to employ military force without securing a declaration of war.

The delegates now had to decide on the voting process that would elect the president. A simple direct popular vote was dismissed without discussion. None of the delegates trusted the 'people' to make a wise choice. After much debate, the delegates finally agreed on an Electoral College system. Each state would have electors equal in number to their representatives in the House of Representatives plus their two senators. The system was flawed from the beginning, as it was possible for one candidate to lose the popular vote and win enough electoral votes to be elected. However, the Convention delegates believed this system gave their 'class' the most control over the outcome of the election.

Each elector had two votes, but each had to be cast for a different individual. The candidate with a majority would become president. If no candidate received a majority, the House of Representatives would choose from among the five highest or between the two highest if there was a first-place tie. The candidate with the second highest total would automatically become vice-president. Since the vice-president would have nothing to do as long as the president remained alive, he would preside over the senate, but would only vote if there was a deadlock. The delegates never considered that there might be rival political parties, so they never envisioned a situation where the president and vice-president could be diametrically opposed in their political views. The system would soon prove to be a disaster.

On one matter there was hardly any disagreement. This new government emphasized the expansion of capitalism and the protection of those who were already wealthy. Only rich males

Lies and Deceits

were going to vote. Elbridge Gerry of Massachusetts staunchly proclaimed: "The people cannot be trusted; they are the dupes of pretended patriots." Of our nation's four million male citizens, only 160,000 had enough property to be enfranchised to vote. But, our Framers realized that the situation might change in the future and they wanted to insure, as much as possible, that there could never be a complete transfer of government power by the electorate. A gradual shift could be tolerated and redressed, but there would be no sudden change in power from the elites to the masses. Therefore, the delegates decided that members of the House of Representatives would be chosen every two years, senators every six years, and the president every four years. By spreading the election process over time they hoped to insure a continuity that would guard against any radical changes.

Amendments to this new constitution was purposely made extremely difficult in order to maintain the Framer's original intent. First, an application from two-thirds of the state legislatures was needed to start the process in motion. Then, the application would have to be approved by two-thirds of both houses of Congress. After approval by Congress, the proposed change would have to be approved by three-quarters of the states. Altering this new constitution would be virtually impossible. It can be argued that stability is a good thing, but it certainly is not democracy in action.

Nobody was completely happy with the final Constitution, but they all agreed with Hamilton's appeal to show unanimity. Hamilton then headed a committee to prepare the final document. After all the debates, this should have been easy, but, at the last minute, it was decided that the Constitution should start with a Preamble.

The first draft of the Preamble began by listing the individual states, one-by-one, intending to make it clear that the power of this new government emanated from the state legislatures. But, that first sentence was awkward and if some states decided not to ratify, then their names would have to be deleted. This might encourage other states to stay out of the Union. The best alternative was to group all the states together and describe them by some all-encompassing nomenclature. Gouverneur Morris of Pennsylvania suggested that the Preamble start with the words "We the people." This was quickly rejected. The delegates had labored for months to purposely exclude millions of souls from the legal rolls of humanity; to inject such a term into the document now was considered insane.

However, nobody could come up with anything better. They were pretty sure that everyone would understand that any reference to "we the people" did not mean all the people; it meant only wealthy persons who could vote and hold public office, and certainly not blacks, women, or white males without property. However, against their better judgment it was agreed to adopt "We the people" as the opening phrase. It is hard to tell which was the bigger lie –"all men are created equal" from the Declaration of Independence or "We the people" from the Constitution.

On Sept. 17, 1787, the final version of the Constitution was completed. After four months, thirty-nine delegates from twelve states signed the document. George Washington stepped forward as the first signatory. Whatever its ambiguities and defects, the Constitution corrected the most glaring deficiencies of the Articles of Confederation. It gave the new national government clear authority to handle trade and foreign policy matters and responsibility to protect the nation's security and advance its global interests.

Now the Constitution had to be ratified in its entirety by at least nine of the thirteen state legislatures in order to become effective. The first hurdle was to get the Constitution safely past the Continental Congress. Nothing in the Constitution stipulated that congressional approval was needed, but political realities made such a step impossible to avoid. When the document was presented to Congress, it ignited a firestorm. In three days of furious debate, attempts were made to add amendments prior to sending it to the states.

The concept of a Bill of Rights came from England where such a document had been adopted in 1689 and became one of the fundamental safeguards in English constitutional law. Its purpose was to address the rights of citizens as represented by Parliament against the Crown. Many of our colonial legislatures had already adopted such a document that protected its local citizens, but with the formation of a strong central government, many feared that a federal Bill of Rights was needed. Madison had wanted to incorporate such a Bill of Rights into the main body of the Constitution, and also to insert the Declaration of Independence into the Preamble, but both recommendations had been rejected at the Constitutional Convention. Hamilton argued against a federal Bill of Rights, asserting that such protections were unnecessary since protecting specific rights might imply that any unmentioned rights would not be protected. "Why declare that things shall not be done when there is no power to do them?"

Congress finally sent the proposed Constitution to the states without modification; they simply conceded it was the prudent thing to do. A Bill of Rights would have to wait. After all, the constitutional document as it stood was supported by such luminaries as George Washington and Benjamin Franklin, and while not perfect, it seemed to offer the best hope for a prosperous and secure future.

The state legislatures, however, acting in their own self-interest, were vociferous in their objections to a strong federal government. Federal taxation on top of state taxes drew heavy criticism. Men in Massachusetts complained that there was nothing in the Constitution about religion and that the document had to have some sort of blessing from God. Many states wanted to continue using their local currency rather than some uniform system of paper money. Residents of Maine, then a part of Massachusetts, argued that they were against anything the rest of the residents of Massachusetts favored. Governor George Clinton and his business faction in New York complained that New York was a premier seaport with commercial ties to the entire world, not just the states, and could not be dictated to by fishermen in New England, slave owners in the South, and certainly not by a federal government.

In order to gain the necessary support needed for passage, Hamilton wrote a series of articles urging ratification. In these *Federalist Papers*, as they were called, Hamilton wrote 51 newspaper essays under the anonymous name of *Publius,* a Latin word meaning "to proclaim" or "to bring before the public." He could not publish under his own name because of the oath of secrecy that all the Convention delegates had taken, but everyone knew these articles were written by Hamilton. He was assisted in this endeavor by Madison who wrote twenty-five essays and John Jay wrote five.

In one essay, Madison explained the reasons behind the Constitution's elaborate system of checks and balances:

> "If men were angels, no government would be necessary. If angels were to govern men, neither external nor internal controls on government would be necessary. In framing a government, which is to be administered by men over men, the great difficulty lies in this: you must first enable the government to control the governed; and in the next place, oblige it to control itself."

Some states argued that a new Convention should be convened and the entire document redrafted. However, most believed that would result in endless debate and doom the whole thing. In 1789, New Hampshire became the ninth state to ratify; the other four states made it unanimous. The voting was perilously close. Had there been a switch of ten votes in Massachusetts, or six in Virginia, or two in New York, the Constitution would have been defeated in those crucial states. In 1791, ten amendments that comprise our current Bill of Rights were adopted and became part of the Constitution.

Since its inception, Americans have argued about the best means of nurturing and protecting this Constitution. Throughout most of our history, Americans have proven themselves a remarkably forward-looking people, largely unconcerned about looking back on their past and resolutely, optimistically, looking toward the future. Yet, we have adopted a reverential attitude toward the wisdom of those men who framed our Constitution.

James Madison and his closest friend, Thomas Jefferson, held different views about the reverence of the Constitution. Madison embraced a strict constructionist interpretation of the powers granted under the Constitution. Jefferson was of a different temperament. In a remarkable letter written to Madison just before he returned from France in 1789, Jefferson took up the question of "whether one generation of men has a right to bind another." Jefferson answered in the negative. "The earth belongs to the living; the dead have neither power nor right over it." Applying that belief to the durability and immutability of constitutions, Jefferson asserted that "no society can make a perpetual constitution or perpetual law. The earth belongs always to the living generation."

However much Madison may have respected the intellect of his Virginia friend and neighbor, he was not ready to jettison history and tradition so casually. Responding to Jefferson, he acknowledged that his friend's argument might have some merit in theory, but Madison feared that constant revisions in the form of the government, based on the whims of public opinion in a particular age, would "engender pernicious factions that might not otherwise come into existence." Madison thought it wiser for the Constitution to be firmly rooted in the "prejudices" of those wise men who gathered in Philadelphia in the summer of 1787.

But Jefferson held firm. Writing some 25 years later, he reiterated his skepticism about the permanency of constitutions. "Some men," Jefferson noted, "look at constitutions with sanctimonious reverence, and deem them like the Ark of the Covenant, too sacred to be touched. They ascribe to the men of the preceding age wisdom that is more than human, and consider what they did to be beyond amendment. I knew that age well; I belonged to it, and labored with it. It served its country well, but I know also that laws and institutions must go hand and hand with the progress of the human mind. As that becomes more developed, more enlightened, as new discoveries are made, new truths disclosed, and manners and opinions change with the change of circumstances, institutions must advance also, and keep pace with the times."

The debate the Constitution continues this day: should the Constitution be strictly interpreted in accordance with the wishes the Framers had back in 1787, or is a more liberal interpretation needed for a changing world?

It was not until 1840, a half century after the Constitutional Convention that the posthumous surfacing of James Madison's extensive notes from the Convention emerged. Now, for the first time, the American people could finally read what happened during those momentous months in Philadelphia back in 1787. Of course, by this time most American were no longer interested. It was all ancient history and most of the participants were dead.

What was revealed in Madison's notes was neither divine nor diabolical, but simply an all-too-human exercise in self-interest. Merchants, bankers, plantation owners, land investors, and wealthy lawyers voiced their interests and fears as delegates to the Convention in clear uncluttered language, and drew up plans for a government that would serve their economic interests most effectively. The fifty-three years of silence that followed had the desired effect of transforming our Founding Fathers into myths; their political savvy and common sense became seen as all-surpassing wisdom, and their concern for the people's interests was elevated to universal altruism and self-sacrificing patriotism. With the passage of years and the growing religiosity of the citizenry, it became commonplace to hear that our Framers were divinely inspired in their wisdom and concern for the common man. We now know this was simply not true.

In examining any political phenomena, it is always wise to ask, "Who benefits?" In the case of our Constitution, our Framers made sure that they benefited. The true meaning of the Constitution cannot be understood by its cold, formal, and severe language. Understanding can only come from a careful study of the voluminous correspondence of the period, including contemporary newspapers, pamphlets, and the now-published records of the debates at Philadelphia. Fortunately, the historian Charles Beard undertook this exhaustive study of Madison's notes along with all the relevant secondary sources surrounding that event. In 1913, he published his findings in a controversial majestic work, *An Economic Interpretation of the Constitution*.

Charles A. Beard (1874-1948) is considered one of America's most influential political historians. He published forty-two volumes of history that sold 11.3 million copies during his lifetime. Beard argued that the Constitution was essentially a capitalist document geared to protect wealth and property from any encroachment by the masses. In the closed hot chamber of Philadelphia, there were no theoretical debates about political science or civil liberties; the Constitutional Convention was all about economics. The Founders feared that their true motives would only create incitement and discontent.

According to Charles Beard, the delegates understood that as the country continued to grow, the poor would dramatically outnumber the wealthy. The Constitution had to ensure that these masses never gained control of the country; only a government by the rich and for the rich should control America's destiny. The delegates were not concerned about a Caesar or an absolute ruler; what they feared was the common man.

When Beard's book appeared in 1913, it was banned from many public schools and placed on a "closed and restricted reserve list" in the city's libraries. His book was quite upsetting, especially to America's capitalist class. During one of Beard's speaking engagements at the New York Republican Club, a wealthy industrialist in the audience told him: "Do you know that everyone here despises you?" Beard quickly retorted, "Why should anyone despise a poor professor from Columbia University who is on his way from obscurity to oblivion?" The industrialist replied: "Because you have shown us that the Founding Fathers of our country were just like all of us in this room." On another occasion, ex-President William Howard Taft was asked what he thought about Beard's book. The future Chief Justice of the Supreme Court replied that Beard's conclusions were true enough, "but why did the damn fool have to print it?"

CHAPTER FOUR

WAR OF 1812

"We will be greeted as liberators. It is just a matter of marching in."

Thomas Jefferson
Describing America's invasion of Canada in 1812

After Thomas Jefferson's authorship of the Declaration of Independence, he served in the state legislature, and in 1779 became Virginia's governor. Two years into his governorship, with the Revolutionary War raging throughout the colonies, Virginia was invaded by British troops. Jefferson fled, while his fellow Virginians battled the invaders. It was not a very heroic gesture by the chief executive of the state or by Virginia's proud standards. Popular outrage toward Jefferson swelled in Virginia and there was talk of a legislative inquiry. Embarrassed, Jefferson cloistered himself in his house in Monticello and vowed never to return to public life.

For awhile, Jefferson appeared content living the self-indulgent life of a Virginia gentleman, but in 1782, his wife Martha died following childbirth. On her deathbed, she made Jefferson take an oath never to remarry. Inconsolable, Jefferson plunged into a severe depression. His friends feared he was suicidal. James Madison, one of Jefferson's closest friends, petitioned the Virginia legislature to elect Jefferson. Getting Jefferson away from the haunting memories of his home at Monticello probably saved his life. In 1784, Jefferson replaced the aged Benjamin Franklin as America's ambassador to France. He would remain in Paris for the next five years. In 1787, he sent for his daughter, who was accompanied by Sally Hemings, his fourteen-year-old black slave who would eventually give birth to seven of Jefferson's children.

The first presidential election in America was concluded on January 10, 1789. George Washington ran unopposed and all 69 electors cast one vote for him. The second set of electoral votes were divided among eleven candidates; John Adams received the most, and he became the nation's vice-president. Unlike the monarchs that ruled in Europe with divine favor, Washington and Adams were ordinary citizens. Washington paid rent for his executive residency, which was still temporarily located in Philadelphia, and maintained a staff out of his own private funds. The new president's servants included eight black slaves selected from the 300 he kept at Mount Vernon. Knowing that Pennsylvania law freed any slave residing in that state for six continuous months, Washington made sure that each of his slaves was quietly rotated back home to Virginia every five months.

Washington's first priority was to get the country's finances in order. He appointed the man he trusted most, 32-year-old Alexander Hamilton to be secretary of the treasury and gave him a free hand to put the country on a solid financial footing. Washington made a wise choice. Hamilton thoroughly understood the complexity of the issues. In order for America to become a great economic power it had to emphasize industry and finance rather than agriculture and small farms.

Hamilton wanted to accomplish three things. First, he sought to establish a federal tax system to provide a dependable revenue stream. In conjunction with the revenue issue, he instituted protective tariffs and imposed duties on imports that not only provided additional revenue, but helped build the country's manufacturing economy. Second, he replaced all the revolutionary war debts with new federal bonds based on the full faith and credit of the United States. Finally, he established a central bank modeled on the Bank of England to act as the government's fiscal agent and regulator of its money supply. Once Hamilton's program went into operation, the effect on the economy was extraordinary. Within five years the United States had the highest credit rating in Europe and its bonds were selling at a 10 percent premium. Hamilton's program was setting the foundation for American capitalism, a society based on profit and the pursuit of individual interest.

In 1789, Jefferson accepted President Washington's offer to return to America and become the nation's first secretary of state. The country had changed radically during Jefferson's absence. Hamilton was running the transition from individual colonies to a united nation. Jefferson tried to inject his ideas, but he was no match for Hamilton's perseverance and obstinate determination. Hamilton and Jefferson were totally different in personality, background, and vision. Hamilton, the illegitimate 'bastard' born into poverty, was infuriated by the so-called 'well-born' men like Jefferson who never fought in the Revolutionary War, paid lip-service to the poor, and expressed hypercritical sentiments about equality. According to Hamilton, the poor had to be kept in their place. All men of substance knew that Jefferson was "playing with fire" by encouraging otherwise.

When Hamilton and Jefferson clashed, Jefferson, the nobleman, had no chance against the street fighter. It was obvious that these two men could never co-exist. Jefferson considered Hamilton bourgeois and beneath his aristocratic heritage. When Jefferson realized his role would always be secondary, he resigned. Washington wanted Jefferson to remain in his government, but when he was forced to make a choice, he supported Hamilton. Jefferson retreated once again to his estate at Monticello, but immediately began scheming with Madison to get back into power.

People expected Washington to serve for life, but he set a precedent by resigning at the completion of his second term. Washington's eight years in office provided the nation with the stability that saw it through its new beginnings. He made sure the country focused on solving its internal problems and steered the nation away from foreign entanglements that would divert its resources and commitments. This was not always easy because Britain and France were constantly at war with one another and each side wanted America as an ally, but Washington remained resolute that America should remain neutral. In his famous Farewell Address, he warned Americans not to "implicate" themselves in the vicissitudes of European politics. "Peace not war; commerce not conquest" - these were the foundations that Washington hoped America would be guided by in the future. They were noble words, but America would not listen.

In 1791, two political parties emerged, Federalists and Republicans. Federalists, headed by George Washington, John Adams, and Alexander Hamilton, wanted a strong central government that favored global capitalist interests, long-term economic growth, and neutrality in England's disputes with France. They distrusted the passions and prejudices of the common man, and feared that democracy could readily lapse into chaotic anarchy. Its support came from large commercial landowners and those with banking and business interests, especially in the industrialized northern states.

The Republican Party of Jefferson and Madison, by contrast, distrusted the nation's commercial and financial interests and envisioned a decentralized republic of small farmers and artisans. They advocated a government directly responsible to the will of the people, without the oversight of a ruling class. Hoping to gain a significant advantage from an enlarged electorate, they sought to reduce the property requirements that limited voting rights only to the wealthy.

In foreign affairs, the Republicans supported France's revolution against the traditional monarchy as the pathway to individual freedom. Jefferson would callously quip, "I like a little rebellion every now and then. The tree of liberty must be refreshed from time to time with the blood of patriots and tyrants." He was not concerned that the French reign of terror was guillotining hundreds of wealthy aristocrats. "You must break some eggs to make an omelet," he would sarcastically remark.

After Jefferson and Madison officially formed the Republican Party, Hamilton organized the Federalists into a political party. Although Hamilton found the whole business of political parties distasteful, he recognized that it was the only way for his Federalist political and economic ideas to prevail. This two-party system divided the country into interest groups: north and south; industrial and agrarian; capitalist and labor; rich and poor.

In the presidential election of 1796, each Party was limited to two nominees. John Adams of Massachusetts and Thomas Pinckney of South Carolina represented the Federalists; Thomas Jefferson of Virginia and Aaron Burr of New York were the Republican candidates. Candidates ran as individuals rather than as a team or specifically for president or vice-president, however, everyone understood that Adams and Jefferson headed their respective tickets. Independent candidates, 'favorite sons' supported by their home state were also in the running, but they were not serious contenders. The outcome of this election would determine our nation's second president.

The Electoral College at this time contained 138 members; 70 electoral votes were necessary for victory. When all the ballots were counted, John Adams had 71 votes and was declared the winner. Jefferson came in a close second with 68 votes. Foolishly, twelve Federalist electors voted for 'favorite sons' so Thomas Pinckney only received 59 electoral votes. This made Jefferson the second largest vote-getter and he automatically became vice-president. The Constitution had failed its first test. The two top government positions were held by intense rivals.

With the French Revolution raging, the Federalists took steps to insure that radical insurrection would not reach our shore. In 1798, the Federalist controlled Congress passed the Sedition Act that "punished any person from writing, printing, uttering, or publishing, any false, scandalous, and malicious writing against the government of the United States or the President of the United States, with intent to defame them or to bring them into contempt or disrepute." This law declared war on dissent in complete disregard for the recently passed First Amendment of the Bill of Rights, which guaranteed freedom of speech and the press.

From the start, Jefferson did all he could to undermine the Adams presidency. He spent his four vice-presidential years gathering political strength for the next election. When the time came for the election of 1800, Jefferson and Burr again represented the Republican Party. The Federalists nominated the incumbent John Adams and picked South Carolina's Charles Pinckney (Thomas Pinckney's brother) to 'balance' the ticket.

Lies and Deceits

Aaron Burr, born in 1756, was the youngest of the candidates. His grandfather was an acclaimed New England theologian. His father was president of what is now Princeton College, and his mother was a brilliant diarist. Both parents died when he was three-years-old and Burr was raised by an uncle. Young Aaron was a precocious student and at the age of eleven he met all the entrance requirements to attend Princeton, but the school delayed his entrance until he was thirteen; then they admitted him as a sophomore. Burr graduated with honors at age 16. He was expected to enter the Presbyterian ministry, but religious studies did not suit him. Instead, he decided on law.

Burr joined the Continental Army at the outbreak of the Revolutionary War and became a member of George Washington's staff in 1776. After experiencing defeat after disheartening defeat, he openly criticized Washington as incompetent and argued that Washington should be replaced. Washington was not happy with Burr's opinions and Colonel Burr was soon watching the rest of the war from the sidelines. Displeased by his lack of involvement and chance for further promotion, Burr resigned his commission and returned to private life. He was still only twenty-three years of age.

Upon returning to New York, Burr established a law practice and was soon considered one of the nation's most respected trial lawyers. It was said that he never lost a case in the courtroom. After the war, he and Hamilton would often work together on cases, but eventually they would become bitter enemies which surprised nobody.

Burr was an opportunist and a ladies man. In 1782, he married the wealthy widow of a recently deceased British officer. She was ten years his senior with five children. He immediately acquired a stately mansion overlooking the Hudson River and lived a lavish lifestyle – lots of servants, fine wines, and material luxuries. Throughout his career he maintained a frenetic ambition; an insatiable craving for wealth, power, and acclaim. He was a brilliant but driven personality. In 1791, the New York Assembly elected him to the U.S. Senate. It was a defining moment for him. He found his true vocation; it was not law, it was politics and power.

The presidential campaign of 1800 was one of the vilest, mean-spirited campaigns ever to occur in America. Alexander Hamilton wrote 25 essays under the name "Phocion" denouncing Jefferson as a "coy Caesar" - a coward for not serving in the army and for deserting Virginia when the British invaded his home state. He also attacked Jefferson's extensive slave holdings, hinted at his affair with his black slave Sally Hemings, and attacked Jefferson as an atheist who planned on burning all the bibles in the country once he was elected president. Although none of our early political leaders were known for their religious devotion, atheism was a grave accusation in our avowedly Christian republic.

Jefferson counter-attacked. Adams was accused of having a "hideous bi-sexual character, which had neither the force of a man, nor the gentleness and sensibility of a woman." Adams was called "mentally deranged," and if re-elected he was going to crown himself king. The author of these attacks was not Jefferson himself, but a poison-pen pamphleteer named James Callender who was bankrolled by Jefferson. For his efforts, Callender spent nine months in prison for defaming a sitting president; Jefferson pardoned him immediately after defeating Adams and taking office.

The election was a drawn out and bitterly partisan affair. Each state had its own election day. The election process began with New York in April and ended with South Carolina in early October. It was a tight race right down to the wire. The Republicans owed their victory to many factors, but most important was the Constitution's notorious compromise with slavery whereby the South gained an electoral bonus equal to three-fifths of its slave population. This provision gave Jefferson and Burr the extra votes they needed. Without it, they would have lost.

Jefferson had victory sewed up when the Republicans made a disastrous blunder. Republican electors cast an equal number of votes for both Jefferson and Burr, resulting in each man receiving 73 votes; Adams was third with 65 votes. Republicans celebrated victory and thought the matter closed. What difference did it make that Jefferson and Burr each had the same number of electoral votes – the Republicans had won and Jefferson was president. However, the Constitution provided no means of distinguishing a presidential from a vice-presidential electoral vote. Always the opportunist, Burr was suddenly in a position to claim the presidency, especially if he could make a deal with the losing Federalists.

Burr knew he was playing a dangerous game, but this was completely in keeping with his opportunistic character and personality. His safest course would have been to acknowledge Jefferson as president and assume the responsibilities of the vice-president. Burr was still a young man, just approaching his forty-fifth birthday. Even if Jefferson served two full terms, Burr would only be fifty-three in 1808, and would most likely be the heir apparent – but Burr did not want to wait – and there was no assurance that Jefferson would follow Washington's formula of only serving two terms. Instead, Burr seized the moment knowing that if he failed, he risked political suicide.

Jefferson was furious that Burr would not step aside. Tempers flared, but there was nothing Jefferson could do. The Constitution had failed once again, but the procedure was clear – if no candidate received a majority of the electors, the election had to be decided in the House of Representatives from among the top five candidates. However, if the top two candidates were tied and each received a majority, then the run-off election was just between those two. Each state delegation would caucus and cast one vote. Little Delaware suddenly became as powerful as populous New York.

The Republican Party during this election also gained majority control in both houses of Congress, but the change-over would not take effect until after the presidential inauguration. In the meantime, the Federalist controlled House of Representatives would be in charge of choosing which of the two Republicans would be president. Nine votes from sixteen states would be needed to elect.

The country was in turmoil over what was happening. There was talk of civil war if Burr 'stole' the election. While the country was talking of war, President John Adams was busy. Until the inauguration of the new president, he was still in charge – and so was the Federalist Congress. The whole thing was a constitutional mess.

The Supreme Court at this time consisted of six loyal Federalists; three from the South and three from the North. When Oliver Ellsworth suddenly resigned as Chief Justice, Adams had to act quickly otherwise the new incoming administration would certainly replace Ellsworth with a Republican. Adams convinced Secretary of State John Marshall to accept the position. Marshall agreed and was immediately confirmed by the Federalist controlled Senate.

Adams then secured federal judgeships for two of his brothers-in-law, James Keith Taylor of Virginia and William McClung of Kentucky; and created a new three-judge court for the District of Columbia, appointing his thirty-two-year-old nephew William Cranch, and John Marshall's brother James, to two of the positions. Adams was not finished. He appointed forty-two new federal justices, all Federalists, and had them confirmed within a matter of hours. The Republicans cried 'foul' but it was all legal under the Constitution.

Everyone knew that the election had resulted in a 73-73 tie, but the official results still had to be read into the official record before the balloting in the House could start. All the sealed envelopes were delivered to Jefferson as the presiding officer of the Senate since he was still officially the vice-president. Nobody paid any real attention as Jefferson opened each envelope and went through the formality of reading the results into the record.

When Jefferson opened Georgia's envelope, which contained four electoral votes for him and four for Burr, there was a fatal flaw in the certificate that should have voided Georgia's entire vote. If Georgia's vote was invalidated, Jefferson and Burr would both be reduced to 69 votes; less than the 70 votes needed for a majority. If that happened, the run-off according to the Constitution would be among the top five vote-getters instead of just Jefferson and Burr. With Adams now back in contention, the Federalist controlled House of Representatives would have enough ballots to re-elect him!

Jefferson stared at the Georgia certificate in disbelief. He immediately understood the consequences. Should he call this irregularity to the attention of the representatives in attendance? Was he morally bound to do so? He hesitated for what must have seemed like an eternity. Then he read the Georgia results into the record – four votes for Jefferson and four votes for Burr. Without disclosing that the Georgia vote was invalid, Jefferson declared the election a tie: 73-73.

Nobody realized what Jefferson had done until the session was over. Then there was a big fuss, but the country was already close to civil war over this election. Members of the House from both parties feared the consequences of going back into session to overturn the vote. The delegates realized too late that Jefferson, as one of the candidates, should never have been the presiding officer. Had Chief Justice Marshall presided, the Georgia vote would certainly have been voided.

The voting in the House now commenced. It was agreed that the voting would be continuous and held in closed session - there would be no adjournment until a final choice was made. The first candidate to win nine states would be elected. As the balloting commenced, the vote was 8-6 for Jefferson. And so it remained; ballot after ballot. The delegations from Vermont and Maryland were evenly divided and therefore cast no vote. Neither candidate seemed able to get the needed nine votes. Inauguration Day was less than three weeks away; President Adam's term would end and the Constitution did not specify what would happen if the impasse in the House continued. Who would govern if there was no president?

Burr and Jefferson began making deals with the Federalists – anyone who could swing the election would be rewarded in countless ways. Representative Edward Livingston of New York, a personal friend of Burr, was told he could name his price if New York would change its vote from Jefferson to Burr. Samuel Smith, a Baltimore congressman, was informed he would become secretary of the navy if he could bring Maryland over to Burr. Representative Matthew Lyon, who had the power to break Vermont's tie vote, was told by both candidates, "What do you want Colonel Lyon? Is it office? Is it money? Only say what you want and you shall have it."

All through the afternoon, with a snowstorm raging outside, the House members droned through ballot after ballot with no change. Night fell but the deadlock went on. Candles were brought into the cold drafty chamber; blankets and pillows were carried in for an all-night session. Some of the weary statesmen dozed in their chairs, others sneaked off to vacant rooms between votes for a nap. When a ballot was called, one witness said, it was "ludicrous to see them running into the voting chamber with their night caps on."

The balloting dragged on, day after day, but the battle lines on both sides stood firm. Burr remained in Albany throughout the proceedings, which was probably a big mistake. Meanwhile, Jefferson was politicking in Washington, promising everyone everything, but he was not able to gain that ninth vote.

Fearful that Inauguration Day would dawn with no president, the Republican governors of Virginia and Pennsylvania threatened to send their militia marching on Washington to install Jefferson by force. Federalists in New England vowed to "stop them with all available means." When certain Federalists intimated that they would install their own "president pro temp" on Inauguration Day, Jefferson's allies warned that such "usurpation" would result in a bloody conflict.

The Vermont and Maryland delegations remained tied despite outrageous bribe offers. The next easiest state to deal with was little Delaware, which had only a single representative, the Federalist James Bayard. Our Founding Fathers would have been horrified at the thought that the fate of the presidency hung on the sole representative from the smallest state in the Union.

James Bayard distrusted Jefferson and faithfully voted for Burr on ballot after ballot. But, as the balloting dragged on with no resolution in sight, Bayard became alarmed at the danger of having no president on Inauguration Day. That could lead to chaos and a small state like Delaware depended on a stable federal government for protection. Bayard decided that his main allegiance was to protect the rights of his constituents; Jefferson was better than anarchy. He started dickering for a deal. Whatever Bayard's terms were, Jefferson agreed. Fortunately for the country, the deal was discrete, secret, and deniable, otherwise the result would have been a national disaster.

On February 17, Bayard changed his vote. Jefferson became our nation's third president on the 36th ballot. Burr's career would never recover, but he was still Jefferson's vice-president. You can just imagine how acrimonious that relationship would become. Privately, Jefferson vowed that Burr would never have a peaceful day for the rest of his life.

On March 4, the Republican Jefferson was sworn in by Federalist Chief Justice John Marshall who turned his back on Jefferson during the inaugural ceremony. Standing at Jefferson's side during the administering of the oath of office was Aaron Burr. At that moment it would have been difficult to judge which of the two men Jefferson despised more – John Marshall, his longtime Virginia rival, or Aaron Burr, his running mate who tried to deprive him of the election. John Adams refused to attend the inauguration. Instead, he rode out of Washington at four o'clock in the morning in order to avoid a face-to-face encounter with Jefferson. Two years later, Congress passed the Twelfth Amendment to the Constitution correcting this fiasco. From then on, presidential electors had to cast separate ballots for president and vice-president.

One of the first things Jefferson did as president was attempt to deny the judgeship commissions that Adams had awarded before leaving office. Of the forty-two justices Adams appointed, Jefferson allowed 25 to be granted, leaving 17 appointees unable to take up their positions. Four of these seventeen, including William Marbury took their claims to court. *Marbury v. Madison*, decided in 1803, was arguably the most important case in Supreme Court history. Chief Justice John Marshall upheld Jefferson on a technicality, but established the power of the Supreme Court as a branch of government on a par with Congress and the executive branch.

Shortly after Jefferson was inaugurated, he received news that Spain had ceded the huge Louisiana territory of 530 million acres to France. American business interests feared that Napoleon would now close the New Orleans port, which would curtail trading profits and interfere with their plans for westward expansion. Jefferson sent a special envoy to France to negotiate some sort of arrangement.

Napoleon at the time was fighting a war with Great Britain. He needed money and knew that he could never defend his interests in America. Napoleon surprised everyone by offering to sell the entire territory to the United States for $15 million; three cents an acre. Under the Constitution only Congress could approve such a transaction, but Jefferson, who campaigned on strong states' rights and a weak federal government, did just the opposite. Without the consent of Congress, he immediately agreed to France's proposal. Jefferson gambled that Congress would later approve his action, which they did. It was one the biggest real estate coups of all time.

Though the boundaries of the purchase were vague, suddenly the size of the United States more than doubled. Eventually, the Louisiana territory would evolve into present-day Arkansas, Missouri, Iowa, Oklahoma, Kansas, Nebraska, Minnesota, Louisiana, North Dakota, South Dakota, northeastern New Mexico, northern Texas, and portions of Montana and Wyoming.

Northern speculators seized this new opportunity. Eager to buy as much cheap land as possible in this new territory, they rushed to Washington and began making 'deals' with politicians. By 1850, most of these new territories had formed into states and were admitted into the Union; the investors made a financial 'killing' - but it was the North American Indians that were physically killed off.

"The life my people want is a life of freedom," the great leader of the Lakota Sioux would proclaim. The Indian idea of freedom was centered on preserving cultural and political autonomy, and retaining control of ancestral lands. This was incompatible with America's concept of expansion and progress. Capitalism defined freedom differently - for capitalists freedom entailed the God-given right to expand wherever a profit could be made, even if it was on other people's land. Indian removal, accomplished by fraud, intimidation, and violence, was indispensable to America's idea of economic growth.

Aaron Burr knew that Jefferson was never going to pick him as his running mate in 1804. With eight months remaining in his vice-presidency, Burr decided to run for governor of New York. His plan was to use the New York governorship as a power base to challenge Jefferson for the presidency in the next election.

Alexander Hamilton, who detested Burr, wrote numerous newspaper articles denouncing Burr and his candidacy. Hamilton characterized Burr as dishonest, unprincipled, morally bankrupt, perpetually in pursuit of "permanent power and wealth," and the type of person who would do anything to satisfy his "extreme ambition."

Burr lost the New York election, which he attributed to Hamilton's assaults on his character. Three months later, in a fit of rage, he challenged Hamilton to a duel. Hamilton was duty-bound to accept. Duels were illegal in New York, so arrangements were made for it to take place in Weehawken, New Jersey. Both men were former military men and excellent shots, but it was rare that anyone was ever killed in one of these duels. In most cases neither party was hurt, with the shots intentionally missing. The purpose of a duel was to restore honor, not to inflict bodily harm on your opponent.

Hamilton confided to his friends that he would "throw away his shot" and put the onus on Burr to decide what to do. Hamilton was certain that Burr would never shoot to kill since that would end Burr's political ambitions. On the morning of July 11, 1804, both men took aim and fired. Hamilton's shot hit a branch nowhere near where Burr was standing. Burr's shot pierced Hamilton's heart. Hamilton, our country's dynamic constitutionalist and the man most responsible for our system of government, was dead at the age of forty-nine.

The public was incensed. Burr was indicted for murder in New Jersey and New York, but he fled back to the safety of Washington before he could be arrested. As vice-president, he was immune from prosecution as long as he remained in Washington. Burr's creditors immediately seized his assets in New York and sold his estate. John Jacob Astor bought the property; subdivided it into 400 smaller parcels and made a fortune.

Burr remained in the nation's capital and served out his remaining few months as vice-president. When his term of office expired, he headed west. It did not take long before he was back in the headlines. Newspapers claimed that Burr was plotting to seize New Orleans, loot its banks, invade Mexico, declare war on the United States, and install himself as emperor in the southwestern territories on behalf of Spain. The accusations were outrageous and ludicrous, obviously planted by Jefferson who was obsessed with punishing Burr. The public, as always, believed our president was telling the truth, but it was all a lie.

Jefferson spared no expense or subterfuge in order to capture and punish Burr. Burr became the most famous fugitive of his age. He was hunted down by federal troops and eventually arrested on charges of treason. If guilty, he would be hanged. Burr claimed that his only intention in going west was to find new business opportunities that was ripe for development. He swore that the charges against him were malicious lies, that he was innocent of any wrongdoing, and it was all a plot by Jefferson to persecute him.

Burr was indicted by a Federal Grand Jury, but he was released for lack of evidence (the New Jersey and New York indictments against him for killing Hamilton were never pursued). Jefferson would not relent. Burr was arrested again and brought to trial before the United States Circuit Court in Richmond, Virginia. This time Jefferson was sure Burr would be convicted. Bypassing normal procedures, Jefferson instructed government agents to canvass the country from New York to New Orleans for witnesses and to illegally plunder offices in search of evidence. When the time came for the trial to begin, the government had lined up 140 witnesses to testify against Burr.

Jefferson was elated that Burr was finally going to get his comeuppance and publicly declared Burr guilty "beyond question" - but Jefferson was in for a rude awakening. By a bizarre happenstance, the presiding judge at the trial was none other than Jefferson's old political nemesis, Chief Justice John Marshall. At this time in our country's history, Supreme Court justices were also required to adjudicate circuit court cases. As part of their duties, each justice had to rotate from circuit to circuit and this case just happened to fall into Marshall's normal rotation. Jefferson must have felt that the gods were conspiring against him.

Marshall, the dedicated Federalist, and Jefferson, the leader of the Republicans, were not only bitter political enemies; they were also distant cousins that never got along. Besides their political differences, Marshall had been a combat officer in the Continental Army, while Jefferson's actions as Virginia's governor bordered on cowardice. Marshall and Burr, on the other hand, both served with General Washington at Valley Forge during the brutal winter of 1777. Both men were in Congress at the same time. The two men were not friends, but it was nothing like the animosity that existed between Marshall and Jefferson.

Marshall examined the pre-trial legal briefs and ruled that Burr could be tried for conspiracy, but not for treason. Burr then demanded that the court issue a subpoena requiring President Jefferson to appear as a witness and to produce certain government papers that Burr needed for his defense. Marshall granted Burr's motion, declaring that the president was no different than any other citizen. Marshall would review all relevant government documents and exclude any where national security was at risk. Jefferson refused to comply, claiming executive privilege. It appeared certain that the country was headed for a direct confrontation between the presidency and the judiciary. The tensions eased when Burr settled for the documents and did not insist on Jefferson's personal testimony.

The trial, which many consider the greatest criminal trial in American history, opened in August 1807 amid considerable fanfare. The proceedings from beginning to end comprised a political trial in the most literal meaning of that much overused term. Burr's attorneys included Charles Lee Randolph and Luther Martin – among the most prominent lawyers of the day. The prosecuting attorney was George Hay, the son-in-law of James Madison. He was assisted by William Wirt, a future presidential candidate.

The prosecutors took their orders directly from President Jefferson. The political stakes were high for everyone involved. Despite Jefferson's strong belief in the separation of powers, the president let it be known that "if Marshall should cause Burr to escape, Marshall himself should be removed from office." And Marshall acknowledged that "it would be difficult or dangerous for a jury to acquit Burr, however innocent they may think him."

The government's case was muddy; its witnesses could not agree on exactly what Burr had done or what his intentions were. Other than some hearsay accounts, the government witnesses could not describe a single act of treason. The prosecution's case rested on the allegation that plotting treason was a treasonable act.

The defense contended that the Constitution clearly stated that treason, "shall consist only in levying war" and proof of it required the "testimony of two witnesses to the overt act, or the confession of the accused in open court." Since Burr was not likely to confess, the government needed to produce two witnesses willing to swear that an overt act had actually taken place; it was unable to do so. The jury deliberated for only a few minutes before proclaiming Burr not guilty. Chief Justice Marshall called the whole affair, "the most unpleasant case that has ever been brought before a judge in this or perhaps any country."

Jefferson was livid; he denounced the jury and Marshall, but to no avail. He even proposed a constitutional amendment that would eliminate lifetime tenure for federal judges and authorize the president to remove a judge if two-thirds of Congress concurred. Congress recognized the vindictiveness behind Jefferson's proposals and rejected them.

Burr was free, but wherever he went he was maligned and hated, and creditors hounded him. On June 9, he fled the country and sailed for London. As soon as he arrived, British officials began deportation proceedings. Burr blamed Jefferson for this constant harassment that even reached across the Atlantic Ocean. In 1809, Burr was expelled from England. He sailed to Sweden, then to Denmark and Germany, and finally ended up in Paris. In 1811, the French demanded that Burr leave the country. He returned to

America under an assumed name, arriving unnoticed in Boston on May 5, 1812. A month later he was back in New York City where the fifty-six year old Burr reopened his law practice. His creditors descended on him once again. He remained in New York, but it was a constant struggle to earn a living and keep his creditors at bay at the same time.

When he was seventy-seven years old, Burr married Eliza Bowen Jumel, believed to be the richest woman in America. Burr promptly moved into her enormous Manhattan mansion and began spending her money. This did not sit well with the new bride, and she filed for divorce after a year of marriage. Months later, Burr suffered a major stroke and died. After his death, Burr's daughter sailed for Europe to bring back his personal papers in order to clear his name. On her return voyage the ship mysteriously sunk; she and all her father's papers were forever lost.

By any measure, Jefferson's crusade against Aaron Burr and John Marshall was a debacle. Burr's life and reputation was irreparably ruined and never recovered. Marshall's public standing suffered, but he became immortalized in American history as our nation's leading jurist. Jefferson's libertarian reputation was tarnished, but his image would survive intact.

Jefferson died on July 4, 1826—the very same day that John Adams passed away—it was also the fiftieth anniversary of the Declaration of Independence. Upon his death, Jefferson freed Sally Hemings' surviving children, but not his other slaves—those 100 or more other slaves were auctioned off to pay the enormous debts of his estate.

In 1808, James Madison, who had been Jefferson's secretary of state for eight years, was elected president. The highlight of Madison's presidency came in June 1812, when America seized what it thought would be a great economic opportunity. England was preoccupied in Europe with its war with Napoleon and France. Madison and his Republican counselors figured this was a perfect time to invade British Canada and expand the United States. But first, Madison had to find a pretext for war – telling the public the truth about America's intentions to invade another country for economic reasons was not going to stir up the patriotic passions of ordinary American citizens.

The British Navy at this time was a notorious floating hell. The pay was low, shipboard conditions were miserable, and there was the ever-present risk of being killed in battle by the French. Many British sailors deserted, abandoning the Royal Navy for the rapidly expanding American Navy that offered better pay, better conditions, and less danger. When British commanders boarded American ships in search of British deserters, Madison claimed this was an insult to our national sovereignty; he flamed the war propaganda by declaring that the United States was honor bound to protect its citizens at sea. Congress supported Madison and war was declared, but it was all bogus – we were just looking for an excuse to invade Canada.

England certainly had no reason to go to war with the United States. The United Kingdom had its hands full with France and depended on American supplies to maintain its armies. Any combat in North America would only distract from their fight against the French. Thomas Jefferson, Madison's closest confident, favored war. He openly declared that the Canadians "would welcome America as liberators" and dismissively referred to the conquest of Canada as "a matter of just marching in." When Senator Henry Clay was asked what this war with England was all about, he responded, "Canada, Canada, Canada."

Well, we were not greeted as liberators. The Canadians repelled our attack and soon the fighting shifted to American soil. When Napoleon was suddenly defeated in 1814, British troops were immediately redeployed to America to reinforce their Canadian allies. Within months, President Madison and members of Congress were chased out of Washington and the White House was burned to the ground. Our precious documents, the Declaration of Independence and Constitution were whisked away to safety in the nick of time. Our greedy misadventure could easily have resulted in America becoming a British colonial possession once again, but fortunately for the United States, Britain did not want us back. A peace treaty was quickly signed on February 17, 1815 and all the old borders were restored. American dead totaled 2,260 – a minor

Lies and Deceits

number considering the circumstances. America's first attempt at empire, imperialism, and conquest, was a complete failure.

The War of 1812 was merely a detour in America's drive for expansion. A great cry rose up throughout our land: "Go west, young man!" Settlers surged westward, sparking clashes with Indian tribes. The government's solution was the removal of the North American Indians from their land – first by swindle, then by massacre. Federal negotiators dispensed with negotiations and instead treated the Indians as a conquered people. Such heavy-handed tactics provoked Indian resistance, but to no avail; the ways of the 'white' man were just too strong.

The Cherokees were the largest Indian tribe on the southern frontier of America. Most of their homes were situated along small streams in scattered villages throughout the Appalachian Mountains. Through a series of treaties and several bloody wars, Cherokee land holdings were reduced until the major body of the tribe was concentrated in Georgia and Tennessee. The Cherokees adapted remarkably well to their new circumstances. They established a system of government patterned after our own and began to follow the so-called "civilized pursuits" of farming, cattle-raising, weaving and spinning. By 1827, the Cherokees even had a written constitution similar to ours. Thus, these Indians were neither "savage" nomadic wanderers nor naive political amateurs. The tribes and the U.S. government had agreed to a historic treaty that would preserve their tribal identity, political autonomy and sovereignty.

A number of events culminated in the Georgia-Cherokee crisis of 1829. Gold was discovered in north Georgia on land that was legally the domain of the Cherokee. Georgia adopted a number of repressive acts including a lottery that distributed to whites the lands owned and occupied by the tribes. The Cherokees brought an action in the U.S. Supreme Court seeking to stop Georgia from taking away their land, which had been negotiated in good-faith with the United States government. The Cherokees claimed they were an independent sovereign nation that managed its own affairs and they were not a burden to the State of Georgia or the United States. They asked the Supreme Court for an injunction that would prevent Georgia from driving them off their land and "annihilating" their existence as a political society. Georgia's position was that the U.S. Supreme Court had no jurisdiction; the matter was exclusively a Georgia issue.

Chief Justice John Marshall, writing for the Court, acknowledged the plight of the Cherokee and other Native American tribes, but he rejected their claims. Marshall stated that the Cherokee tribe was not a foreign nation "in the sense of the Constitution" since the 'Indian Territory' was located inside the geographical and jurisdictional boundaries of the United States. Moreover, the Cherokee had acknowledged, in the very treaties in question, that they were under the protection of the United States. Therefore, a better classification for the Cherokee was that of a "domestic dependent nation, resembling that of a ward to his guardian."

The Supreme Court then dismissed the case for lack of jurisdiction, stating that the Constitution was silent on the issue of permitting them to hear disputes involving 'domestic dependent nations.' Marshall wrote, "If it be true that the Cherokee nation have rights, this is not the tribunal in which those rights are to be asserted." But, Marshall left the Cherokee some hope. "The Court might make a different decision about Indian rights in some proper case with proper parties."

The Cherokees returned to the Supreme Court the following year and this time the Court took a different view. Chief Justice Marshall found that the treaty with the United States recognized the national character of the Cherokee and their right of self-government. In addition, the federal government had guaranteed their right to the lands and assumed a duty to protect the integrity of the agreement.

Marshall concluded that the Cherokee nation was a "distinct community occupying its own territory," and that the laws of Georgia had no force. Native American sovereignty could be diminished or eliminated by the United States, but not by any individual state.

The legal victory proved of little benefit to the Cherokee nation. The demand for Cherokee land on which gold had been discovered grew more intense. President Andrew Jackson favored the removal of the Cherokee and other Native American tribes from these valuable lands and refused to enforce the Court's decision. "Well, John Marshall has made his decision, now let him enforce it," said the president.

Jackson's refusal illustrated the problem that occurs when one branch of government refuses to honor the decision of another branch. Jackson was determined to move the Native American tribes westward. In December 1835, the Cherokee tribes were forced to cede all their land to the United States and were driven at gunpoint out of their ancestral homes in Georgia and Tennessee to distant Oklahoma. The journey took more than six months and hundreds of exiled Indians died every day. The very old and very young could not withstand the hardships of the brutal winter, and even the most able-bodied were soon weakened by the relentless blizzards and driving snow. Nearly a quarter of the 15,000 Cherokees died during the relocation. In Cherokee lore, the western trek to Oklahoma is remembered as the "Trail of Tears."

Secretary of War Lewis Cass justified America's actions: "Progressive improvement is inherent in human nature. We are all striving to acquire riches of honor, power, or some other object, and the aggregate of these efforts constitutes the advance of society. But there is little of this in these savages. I wish this progress could be achieved with a smaller sacrifice, but such a wish is in vain. A barbarous people, depending for sustenance on the land alone, cannot live within a civilized community."

Cass met with tribal leaders and promised that if they moved peacefully to new lands across the Mississippi, "the United States will never ask for your land there. This I promise you in the name of your new great father. That part of the country that our president assigns to his red people will be held by them and their children's children forever." The Indians believed the lie – it was a tragic mistake. The United States never kept its pledge – the extinction of the North American Indian followed.

Chief Black Hawk was one of the last holdouts. When he was captured in 1832, he made the following surrender speech:

> "You have taken me prisoner with all my warriors. I have done nothing for which an Indian ought to be ashamed. I fought for my countrymen, the squaws and papooses, against white men who came year after year to cheat us and take away our lands. The cause of our making war is known to all white men. They ought to be ashamed of it. The white men despise the Indians and drive them from their homes, but the Indians are not deceitful like the white man. The Indian does not tell lies; Indians do not steal other people's land.
>
> Black Hawk is a true Indian and disdains to cry like a woman. He feels for his wife, his children and friends. But he does not care for himself. He cares for his nation and the Indians. They will suffer. He laments their fate. The white men do not scalp the head; but they do worse - they poison the heart – they are not to be trusted."

During the early 1800s, Mexico still belonged to Spain and its land was largely unoccupied. The U.S. was rapidly becoming an industrialized giant with no limits, while Mexico remained entrenched in their native traditions. In addition, Mexico did not have the financial resources to overcome the hot arid climate that was not conducive to agricultural abundance. Much of Mexico's landscape was consumed by baking desert plains and barren mountain ranges and it lacked the interlocking navigable waterways that were necessary to facilitate transportation and encourage commerce.

In the summer of 1820, Moses Austin, a bankrupt 59-year old Missourian, asked Spanish authorities for a large land tract that he could promote and sell to American settlers. Austin's request seems preposterous. His background was that of a Philadelphia dry goods merchant, a Virginia mine operator, a Louisiana judge, and a Missouri banker. But early in 1821, the Spanish government gave him permission to settle 300 families in what would later become Texas.

Lies and Deceits

Moses Austin did not live to see his dream realized. On a return trip from Mexico City, he died of exhaustion and exposure. Before he died, his son Stephen promised to carry out his father's dream. By the end of 1824, young Austin had attracted 272 settlers to Texas. The newly independent Mexican government imposed two conditions: settlers had to become Mexican citizens and they had to convert to Roman Catholicism, which was the religion of Mexico. By 1830, there were 16,000 Americans in Texas.

During the next five years, 35,000 Americans, along with their 5,000 slaves, ventured into this area. The vastness of the territory made it impossible for Mexico to control the influx of the American settlers. Differences in language and culture had produced bitter enmity between the American settlers and the native Mexicans. The settlers refused to learn the Spanish language, maintained their own separate schools, and conducted most of their trade with the United States. To reassert its authority over this territory, the Mexican government reaffirmed its constitutional prohibition against slavery, established a chain of military posts, restricted trade with the United States, and decreed an end to further American immigration.

In 1832, General Antonio Lopez de Santa Anna, a Mexican politician and soldier, became Mexico's president. He overthrew Mexico's constitutional government and installed himself as dictator. On November 3, 1835, the Americans in the Texas territory adopted a constitution and organized a temporary government, but voted overwhelmingly against declaring independence. Instead, they hoped to attract the support of Mexican liberals in a joint effort to depose Santa Anna, restore power to Mexico's state governments, hopefully including a separate state of Texas as part of Mexico.

Just in case a peaceful compromise could not be achieved, the American settlers prepared for war and elected Sam Houston commander of whatever military forces they could muster. Soon the ominous news reached the Texans that Santa Anna was marching with 7,000 soldiers to retake the territory. When Sam Houston learned of Santa Anna's plan, he ordered the city San Antonio to be abandoned. But, 150 Texans decided to stay and defend the city. They made their stand at an abandoned Spanish mission called the Alamo.

For twelve days, Mexican forces lay siege to the Alamo. When the fighting was over, virtually all the defenders lay dead. Seven defenders surrendered and were immediately executed; approximately fifteen persons survived. If the Alamo was a military defeat, it was a psychological victory. "Remember the Alamo" became the battle cry for Texas independence.

Volunteers from the American South flocked to Sam Houston's call for reinforcements. On April 21, his army of less than 800 men surprised Santa Anna's army as it camped on the banks of the San Jacinto River. The next day, Houston's army captured Santa Anna and forced him to sign a treaty granting Texas its independence - a treaty that was never ratified by the Mexican government because it was obtained under duress.

Texas had barely won its independence when it decided to become part of the United States. A referendum showed that Texans favored annexation by a vote of 3,277 to 93. The annexation question became one of the most controversial issues in American politics in the late 1830s and early 1840s. The central issue was about the extension of slavery. The admission of Texas to the Union would upset the sectional balance of power in the U.S. Senate. In 1838, former president John Quincy Adams, now a member of the House of Representatives, staged a twenty-two day filibuster that successfully blocked the annexation of Texas. It appeared that Congress had settled the Texas question; it would remain an independent republic.

Presidential politics and constitutional confusion reared its ugly head in the presidential election of 1840. At the Whig Convention, William Henry Harrison was nominated with John Tyler as his running mate. Their opponents were Democratic incumbents Martin Van Buren and Richard Johnson. Harrison and Tyler won by an electoral vote of 234-60. One month after his inauguration, Harrison died. The nation was not only shocked, but confused regarding the process of succession. The Constitution was vague as to whether the vice-president assumed the duties of the presidency or actually became president. Ultimately the situation was settled when it was decided that Tyler was to be president both in name and in fact.

John Tyler considered slavery a necessary and positive good, and he wanted Texas admitted as a slave state. In order to drum up support for his cause, he told the nation that Great Britain was scheming to annex Texas and transform it into a haven for runaway slaves. Sam Houston played along with this ploy by conducting highly visible negotiations with the British government. If the United States would not annex Texas, Houston warned, Texas would seek the support of "some other friend."

Before Tyler's presidential term was up, he unilaterally declared that Texas was annexed and would become part of the United States. Tyler's decision did not require a two-thirds approval vote of the U.S. Senate because it was not a negotiated treaty; he just did it. Texas became the twenty-eighth state and added 389,000 square miles to the size of the United States, even though nobody really knew where the southwestern boundary line ended. In addition to the land, the United States now had 60,000 more white citizens and 15,000 more slaves. Mexico, of course, did not recognize the annexation and considered Texas a rebel province.

In 1844, Democrat James Polk ran for president. He was an avid expansionist and a slave-owning cotton planter from Tennessee. His Republican (Whig) opponent, Henry Clay, called for negotiated treaties with Mexico in order for the United States to expand westward. Polk's position was clear and unequivocal: "Negotiation is bullshit. Elect me and I will give you Mexico; elect me and I will give you Oregon." The election was close; Polk won by 36,000 votes out of the 2.8 million that were cast.

In his first message to Congress, Polk lauded the addition of Texas to the Union. "This accession to our territory has been a bloodless achievement," he said. "No force was used to produce the result. The sword had no part in the victory." These were disingenuous words since Polk's intention was to go to war, capture more Mexican territory, and expand the American empire to the Pacific Ocean.

John O'Sullivan, a noted journalist at the time, called America's imperialist policy our 'Manifest Destiny' – "God has chosen the

United States to spread liberty and civilization to the Pacific Ocean – and beyond. Yes, more, more, more! More until our national destiny is fulfilled and the whole boundless continent is ours." 'Manifest Destiny' aptly expressed America's brash arrogance that we were uniquely virtuous and on a God-given mission to remake the world in our own image. But, the truth was that 'Manifest Destiny' really referred to racism and the exploitation of weaker, dark-skinned, non-Christian peoples.

On January 16, 1846, Polk ordered General Zachary Taylor to position U.S. troops on the Rio Grande border separating Texas from Mexico. The Mexican commander demanded that Taylor and his troops withdraw. Instead of complying, Taylor sent troops across the border to reconnoiter the area and probe the Mexican defenses. On April 24, 1846, a Mexican cavalry contingent opened fire on American troops on the Mexican side of the Rio Grande; eleven Americans were killed and sixty-three were captured.

General Taylor immediately sent a dispatch to Washington that simply announced, "Hostilities have been commenced with Mexico." Polk sent a message to Congress informing its members that "Mexico has invaded our territory and shed American blood on American soil." Declaring that "war exists" between the two countries, Polk asked Congress for a formal declaration of war. On May 13, 1846, after much debate, the House voted to declare war by the overwhelming margin of 174 to 14; the Senate followed two days later with a vote of 40 to 2, with a number of northern senators abstaining. The war was now official.

Polk's approach to Mexico was dictated by the overtly racist attitudes he shared with most of his countrymen. Certain of white Anglo-Saxon superiority, Americans scorned Mexicans as a mixed breed, even below blacks and Indians, "an imbecilic race of men, unfit to control the destinies of that beautiful country." Indeed, Polk found no difficulty justifying war as part of God's plan to take the fertile land from an "idle, thriftless people." He assumed that Mexico could be bullied into submission, or if foolish enough to fight, would easily be defeated.

Congress authorized $10 million for supplies and called for 50,000 volunteers. The enthusiasm for the war was so great that the number of volunteers far exceeded the request. Patriotic songs filled the air, uniforms glittered, and military parades were everywhere. Mexico reacted with anger and disbelief. They never wanted war with America, nor did they ever envision such a state of affairs, but if America wanted war, so be it – Mexico's honor was at stake.

Not all Americans agreed with our government's policy of using war to facilitate economic expansion. When Henry David Thoreau, a writer from Concord, Massachusetts, denounced the war and refused to pay his taxes, he was thrown in jail. His friend and fellow writer, Ralph Waldo Emerson, sympathized with Thoreau's cause, but thought it futile to protest. When Emerson visited Thoreau in jail, he asked, "What are you doing in jail?" Thoreau replied, "What are you doing out there?"

A young congressman named Abraham Lincoln also opposed the war. He introduced his famous "spot resolution," demanding to know precisely the "spot" where Polk believed American blood had been shed on American soil. A few days after his speech deriding Polk, Lincoln voted for a resolution declaring that the war had been "unnecessarily and unconstitutionally begun by the President of the United States." Polk labeled such criticism unpatriotic and was giving comfort and aid to the enemy, but opponents of the war claimed there was a higher patriotism than the slogan, "our country, right or wrong." True patriotism, they argued, was based on principles that far transcended America's quest for power and wealth.

America at this time was a country with twenty-eight states, but the major industrial and banking interests wanted more territory for expansion. Capitalism is dependent on economic growth and Mexico had all this barren land adjacent to our border that extended all the way to the Pacific Ocean. Since Mexico would not sell us the land, we opted to take it by force. The Mexican army was no match for America's superiority in guns and equipment, and their military leadership could not compare with the likes of Zachary Taylor, Stonewall Jackson, Winfield Scott, Jefferson Davis, Robert E. Lee, and Ulysses S. Grant.

The Treaty of Guadalupe Hidalgo, signed on February 2, 1848, ended the war and gave the U.S. undisputed control of Texas and ceded to the United States the present-day states of California, Nevada, Utah, and parts of Colorado, Arizona, New Mexico, and Wyoming. Mexico lost about half its national territory.

Ulysses S. Grant, then a young army officer, recalled in his *Memoirs*, "I was bitterly opposed to the measure of grabbing all this land from Mexico, and to this day I regard that war as one of the most unjust wars ever waged by a stronger nation against a weaker nation. We had no claim on Mexico. Texas had no claim beyond the Nueces River and yet we pushed on to the Rio Grande and crossed it. I am always ashamed of my country when I think of that invasion."

With our victory in the Mexican War, the United States stretched from "sea to shining sea," but the war was not without its costs. Although 'only' 1,721 American soldiers were killed in combat, nearly 11,000 died of disease. The acquisition of all these new territories re-opened the argument about where slavery should be permitted. Slavery had become a seemingly permanent fixture on the national scene, not just in the South. The value of slaves rose dramatically with the growing world demand for cotton. Twelve American presidents had owned slaves; Chief Justice John Marshall was a slave owner as was his successor, Roger Taney. Most members of the House and Senate were slave-owners. The issue of slavery in the new western territories could no longer be ignored. The nation had to now decide whether this vast new territory would be slave or free.

CHAPTER FIVE

CIVIL WAR

> "I am not, nor ever have I ever been in favor of bringing about in any way the social and political equality of the white and black races. There must always be the position of superior and inferior, and I, as much as any man, am in favor of having the superior position assigned to the white race."
>
> Abraham Lincoln

> "Truth compels me to admit that Abraham Lincoln was preeminently the white man's president, entirely devoted to the welfare of the white people of this country."
>
> Frederick Douglass

The Civil War was America's second revolution. The worst war in our nation's history was not fought to end slavery. The conflict was between two economic systems – southern agriculture and northern capitalism. The prize was the newly developing western territories. When the smoke cleared, 1.1 million of our finest young men were either dead or wounded and they had no idea that it was all about economics.

Although the moral and economic aspects of slavery were often debated, it was never really an important political issue. After all, the Constitution guaranteed slavery's existence and legality. Politically, Congress was equally divided between northern and southern states – between 'slave' and 'free' states. This balance meant that most sectional issues or disputes were compromised. Slavery only became a 'hot' political issue when the new western territories were opened to expansion. The South in particular was worried that if slavery was forbidden in these new states, eventually the slave states would become a distinct minority in Congress, and that would lead to tampering with the constitutional mandate to maintain a slave-based economy.

Our Founding Fathers repeatedly spoke of slaves as property, and as property they could be moved anywhere – just like any other possession. The Constitution also explicitly guaranteed that the laws of one state had to be respected by all other states. As far as the South was concerned, they were willing to let each new state decide whether they wanted slavery or not. What could be fairer than that?

The northern part of the United States in the mid-1800s had realized Alexander Hamilton's dream of an industrialized commercial power led by a business elite of bankers, merchants, and entrepreneurs. The South was not envious of the North's financial success. They were happy with their own unique situation. The southern rich were a different kind of capitalist; they were not driven by the need to accumulate more and more wealth. They enjoyed their material comforts and the beauty of their southern landscape, and the thought of industrial development with its horizon of smokestacks spewing dark smoke into the atmosphere was abhorrent at any price.

Eli Whitney's cotton gin had increased cotton production fifty-fold and made growing cotton immensely profitable. In 1790, a thousand tons of cotton was produced in the south; by 1860 it was a million tons and over 60 percent of the world's cotton supply. Cotton did not only benefit the South. New England had 472 cotton mills with hundreds more scattered throughout the north. This boom created an insatiable need for more slave labor and the slave trade could hardly keep up with the demand. Harriet Beecher Stowe, author of the abolitionist novel, *Uncle Tom's Cabin*, astutely commented that slavery was just the way northerners liked it: all the benefits and none of the screams.

New York was the fulcrum of the cotton trade – merchants, shippers, auctioneers, bankers, brokers, and insurers were making fortunes in ventures directly or indirectly related to cotton. People like the Lehman brothers (later to become major investment bankers), J.P. Morgan Sr., John Jacob Astor, and Charles Tiffany – to name just a few – made millions from the cotton trade. The northern economy was so intertwined with southern cotton that when South Carolina became the first state to secede, Fernando Wood, the mayor of New York, made a stunning proposal: facing the loss of the cotton trade from the south, Wood proposed that New York secede along with the southern states!

Capitalism is never satisfied – that is both a positive and negative aspect of the system. Northern capitalists loved the profits that were rolling in from the slave South, but they also envisioned enormous profit possibilities if slavery was kept out of the new western territories. They had already invested huge sums of money in new technology; the steam engine, telegraph, and the railroads. They understood that the new western territories were filled with unparalleled natural resources – timber, coal, iron, lead and copper – but these rich resources could only be turned into profits if they were developed commercially. These capitalists were ready and willing to invest more money and borrow additional capital if necessary, but extending slavery into these territories would only hamper their efforts – it would perpetuate an agrarian economy that was in conflict with industrialization. They wanted slavery to remain intact in the South, but an expansion of slavery would only interfere with their plans in the west.

White laborers in the new territories agreed; slavery would keep their wages low if it spread westward. Most religious groups did not object to slavery; they pointed to passages in the Bible that permitted and even encouraged slavery. Abolitionists, on the other hand, considered slavery immoral and wanted it abolished, but for the most part the debates about slavery centered around economics, not morality.

By 1818, the Missouri territory gained sufficient population to warrant statehood. Its settlers had migrated largely from the south and it was expected that Missouri would permit slavery. Concerned that the South would now have a representational advantage in Congress, the North forced a compromise whereby the northern part of Massachusetts would become the State of Maine and be admitted into the Union as a free state. The compromise insured that the equal balance in Congress would remain unchanged: 12 slave states and 12 free states.

This 'Missouri Compromise' also called for an imaginary line to be drawn across the Louisiana territory – land north of this line would be free and anything below the line would be slave. In 1854, the Kansas-Nebraska Act replaced the Missouri Compromise. Congress now decided they should stay out of the slave issue entirely and leave the decision to the voters in each state. Until a state expressly outlawed slavery, southerners were free to take their slaves into the western territories and maintain them there as slaves. This appeared to open the new territories to a pro-slavery invasion. A storm of protest broke out by those against the extension of slavery. Scores of political leaders branded the Kansas-Nebraska Act a sinister southern plot to extend slavery and increase southern political power in Washington.

The Dred Scott decision in 1857 had an enormous impact on sectional feelings. Dred Scott (originally Sam Blow) was born to slave parents in Virginia in 1795 and became the immediate property of the Peter Blow family. Throughout his early life, Dred Scott knew no other home and was well treated. Peter Blow owned many acres in Virginia, but at the age of fifty-three he was ready for something new and the thought of going westward was exciting. In 1830, the family – his wife Elizabeth, their three daughters and four sons, along with their six slaves, including Dred Scott, moved to St. Louis where slavery was permitted. So far there was no problem. Dred Scott was and remained a slave in St. Louis.

When financial difficulties set in for Peter Blow, Dred Scott was sold to John Emerson, a doctor in the United States Army. Emerson was transferred from St. Louis to Fort Armstrong, Illinois, where slavery was prohibited. Like many other slave-owning army officers, Emerson did not believe his assignment in a 'free' state subjected him to the anti-slavery laws, so he brought Dred Scott with him. Two years later, Emerson was transferred again, this time to Fort Snelling, a part of the Wisconsin territory where slavery was also banned. Soon Emerson met and married Irene Sandford. Around the same time, Dred Scott married Harriet

Robinson, a teenage black slave who was also Emerson's property. The Emersons and the Scotts returned to St. Louis in 1842.

John Emerson died in 1843, leaving all his possessions to his wife. When Emerson's widow rented Dred Scott to another army captain, Scott refused to go. When Scott received a financial commitment from his previous owners, he offered to buy his family's freedom from Mrs. Emerson. The offer was refused. On April 6, 1846, Dred and Harriet Scott filed petitions in the Missouri Circuit Court claiming their freedom on the basis of their previous residency in Illinois and Wisconsin. Dred Scott appeared to have a strong case. For decades, Missouri courts had ruled that slaves taken by their masters to 'free' states were automatically emancipated.

Scott lost the first trial on a technicality. The following year, a St. Louis Circuit Court ruled that Dred Scott and his family were free. Two years later, the Missouri Supreme Court reversed the decision of the lower court – Scott was now officially a slave again. Scott then appealed to the United States Supreme Court. During all these litigation years, Dred and Harriet Scott remained slaves and worked as hired hands, rented out on behalf of Mrs. Emerson.

The United States Supreme Court at this time had nine justices - seven were southerners, including Chief Justice Roger Taney. All seven southern justices owned slaves or came from slave-owning families. The case remained on the docket for more than a year. The Court realized it had an explosive issue on its hands. Slave revolts in several states drew the nation's attention to this case. Dred Scott's name was now familiar to most Americans who followed the course of national affairs. Not wanting to affect the presidential election of 1856, the high court postponed its ruling until two days after President James Buchanan's inauguration. Buchanan's election by a decisive margin made it clear that a majority of the nation favored slavery and opposed anti-slavery agitation.

Chief Justice Roger Taney delivered the 7-2 majority opinion – as expected, it was an emphatically pro-southern, pro-slavery decision. Taney's opinion said that slaves were not citizens, could never be citizens, and therefore could not bring a lawsuit in any court. "Blacks," Taney held, "were so far inferior that they had no rights that any white man was bound to respect." Slaves had no claim to freedom - they were property - and as property their status never changed no matter where they resided - once a slave, always a slave.

Taney's opinion ventured into areas that were not germane; once he ruled that Dred Scott was not a citizen and could not bring a lawsuit, the case should have been dismissed on those grounds. Instead, Taney went out of his way to declare that Congress had no authority to keep slavery out of the new territories – any attempt to prohibit the spread of slavery was unconstitutional. Taney's decision meant that slavery could legally proceed westward.

After the ruling, Scott was returned to Mrs. Emerson. In 1857, she remarried. Her second husband opposed slavery, so Dred Scott and his family were returned to the Blow family, where he was granted his freedom. In 1858, less than a year-and-a-half later, Dred Scott died at the age of sixty-three.

The Dred Scott decision heightened sectional tensions. The South applauded the decision and hailed Justice Taney for upholding the Constitution and the legality of slavery. Anti-slavery proponents believed the Supreme Court had become a cog in a great conspiracy intent on nationalizing slavery. The Dred Scott decision was followed by a series of violent upheavals. Fighting erupted in Kansas as pro-slavery and free-soil advocates collided in bloody conflict - proof that slavery was far too volatile an issue to be left to the courts or local politics. Violence came to a boiling point when John Brown arrived on the scene.

John Brown was a white man who killed white people to free black people. He was a 'fire and brimstone' Puritan from Connecticut and he became the new focus of the nation's headlines. A hero to many, a madman to others, John Brown was one of the most controversial figures in pre-Civil War America. Like all abolitionists, his goal was to end slavery in the United States, but unlike other anti-slavery activists, he was not a pacifist willing to work through political and legal channels. Instead, he was a militant activist who believed that change could only be achieved through bloodshed.

Brown's hatred of slavery began early in life and increased steadily into adulthood. His father was profoundly religious and a committed abolitionist. When John Brown was a boy, the family moved to the free-state of northern Ohio. As a young man, he engaged in many peaceful abolitionist activities. His non-violence changed, however, when he moved to Kansas in 1856 to join the anti-slavery forces. At this time, Kansas was embroiled in a bloody civil war over whether it should join the Union as a 'slave' or 'free' state. When a band of pro-slavery extremists burned the free-state town of Lawrence, Kansas, killing dozens, Brown led his group of partisans, including four of his sons, in exacting revenge. They dragged five unarmed white people from their homes and hacked them to death.

In July 1859, John Brown led another uprising with 21 men (16 whites and 5 blacks) at Harper's Ferry, Virginia. This attack sent shock waves throughout the nation. Harper's Ferry contained a U.S. arsenal that had been assembling army weapons for the past sixty years. Brown's plan was to capture the arsenal and distribute 100,000 rifles to the local slaves as the first step in a national uprising. Brown asked black abolitionist Frederick Douglass to join him in this revolt, but Douglass declined.

Brown's plan failed when the slaves did not rally to his side. The U.S. Army sent in troops under the command of Lt. Col. Robert E. Lee. They battered down the doors of the armory and captured seven of the rebels, including the severely wounded Brown, but not before Brown's men had killed four and wounded nine others. Ten of Brown's men were killed, including two of his sons. In all sectors of the country, Americans breathed a sigh of relief that this insane plan had been squashed.

Brown was tried in Virginia for murder and treason. His defense was that he acted under the "higher law" of the New Testament. Brown was found guilty and sentenced to death along with his other followers. His interviews and prison letters circulated through northern newspapers and were published as best-selling pamphlets. As Brown was taken to the gallows, he handed a note to his guard. It read: "I, John Brown, am now quite certain that the crimes of this guilty land will never be purged away except with blood."

The impact of Harpers Ferry transformed the nation. Southern Democrats branded the Harper's Ferry raid a Republican conspiracy – a wild and vicious scheme to destroy the southern way of life. The Virginia General Assembly declared that the entire North was behind the Harpers Ferry raid: "All northerners are fanatics - they want to incite the slaves to rape and murder."

Even though no slaves joined John Brown's revolt, rumors of slave "stampedes" and abolitionist invasions swept across the South, plunging the region into convulsions of hysteria. Imagining revolts and attacks, southerners mobilized their militia and slave patrols, imprisoned unattended blacks and suspicious-looking strangers, and imposed severe discipline in the slave compounds. Such massive overreaction to Brown's abortive venture may seem difficult to comprehend. After all, nothing really happened. No slave rebellion occurred; Brown had been summarily hanged and most northerners thought he deserved it. But southerners were in no mood to treat Harpers Ferry as an isolated incident. For them, Brown's attack carried sinister implications about the future of 'their' America.

The Abraham Lincoln-Stephen Douglas senatorial contest of 1858 in Illinois was unprecedented in both form and substance. In many respects Douglas was Lincoln's opposite. At five-foot-four inches tall he was a foot shorter than Lincoln, walked with a strut as opposed to Lincoln's long loping strides, and had a pugnacious temperament that prompted friends to call him "the little Giant." While Lincoln lived frugally and abstained from alcohol and tobacco, Douglas loved expensive wines and fine cigars, drank too much, and liked to speculate in real estate.

Lincoln was a homely man, careless about his looks. He seemed awkward with his unusually long arms and legs, lanky frame, huge head, large ears, distinctive Adam's apple, thick eyebrows and his always unkempt hair. Douglas wore elegant suits; Lincoln's were inexpensive and fit badly. Douglas dined at the best hotel restaurants; Lincoln preferred local taverns. Douglas traveled in his own special train car with his exquisitely dressed wife, while Lincoln rode alone in the coach section with everyone else.

Lincoln always appeared composed and relied on carefully chosen words; Douglas acted like a wily fighter in a barroom brawl. While Lincoln was sympathetic towards the plight of the blacks, Douglas was a virulent racist; the word "nigger" rolled off his tongue like water. In essence, their differences could be reduced to this: Douglas championed the rights of the white majority, including the right of one man to enslave another, while Lincoln defended "minority rights" without advocating any change in the existing slave structure.

The seven face-to-face Lincoln-Douglas debates are rightly regarded as classics in the history of campaign oratory. Senators at the time were still chosen by their state legislatures, so both men were not really running against one another – it was a contest to determine which political party would control the Illinois legislature – that in turn would determine who would be the senator to represent Illinois. Douglas was the incumbent senator seeking a third term and he seemed destined to become the Democratic Party's choice for president in 1860, which is why these Illinois debates commanded such national attention.

In these debates, each candidate tried to portray the other as an extremist – Douglas portrayed Lincoln as an abolitionist and Lincoln portrayed Douglas as wanting to spread slavery everywhere. Making full use of the newly constructed railroads, the two candidates traveled nearly ten thousand miles crisscrossing the state; their tireless voices intermingling with the sound of bands, parades, fireworks, cannons, and cheering crowds. Each of their debates followed the same format. The first contestant spoke for an hour, followed by a one-and-a-half hour response, after which the man who had gone first would deliver a half-hour rebuttal. The debates focused almost exclusively on the Dred Scott decision: Douglas supported the Supreme Court decision; Lincoln believed it was a horrible mistake, but he "was not in favor of citizenship for Negroes."

"I believe this government," said Douglas, "was made by white men for the benefit of white men, and only white men are entitled to citizenship – not Negroes, Indians, or other inferior races." But, Douglas was careful not to antagonize voters who thought otherwise: "Some people think slavery is wrong, others think it is right. Let the people of each state or territory decide whether or not they want slavery."

Lincoln's views were not much different. He constantly voted in Congress to retain the slave trade. "I am not," he argued, "nor have I ever been in favor of bringing about in any way the social and political equality of the white and black races."

Lincoln assured the voters that he had no intention of tampering with the institution of slavery in the southern states – and that the federal government had no legal power to do so. He intended to uphold the Constitution – not change it. What he wanted was for the new territories in the west to decide for themselves. However, he believed that if the spread of slavery was not stopped, it would sweep into Illinois, Indiana, Ohio, Pennsylvania, New York, Massachusetts and all over the north until America became a nation of slaves exploited by a minority of white overseers. "As much as I hate slavery, I would consent to the extension of it in the west rather than see the Union dissolved, just as I would consent to any great evil to avoid a greater one." The Illinois election was extremely close. Lincoln lost, but the campaign elevated him to national prominence.

The Republican Presidential Convention of 1860 was held in Chicago; Lincoln was one of twenty-one possible candidates. His strategy was to be "available" should the convention deadlock over their primary choices – New York Senator William Seward, Ohio Governor Salmon P. Chase, and Missouri's distinguished Judge Edward Bates. Seward was the clear favorite.

On the Convention's first ballot, Seward gathered 173 votes; Lincoln received 102, Chase had 49, and 48 were cast for Bates. On the second ballot Lincoln pulled almost even with Seward, and then won a stunning victory on the third ballot. The news that Lincoln had been nominated came as a shock to much of the country. Most people viewed him as the accidental candidate of the consolidated anti-Seward forces. The southern delegates, led by Senator Jefferson Davis, walked out of the Convention when the northern delegates refused to support a southern proposal that federal legislation would protect slavery in all the western territories.

The Democratic Convention in Charleston, South Carolina, ended in chaos. The slavery issue could not be veiled any longer, especially after the Dred Scott decision and John Brown's raid on Harpers Ferry. Unable to secure a two-thirds vote for any nominee, the deadlocked convention was forced to reconvene in Baltimore. There Douglas finally received the nomination he had long pursued, but hard-line southerners refused to accept Douglas. They bolted from the Party and held a separate convention where they nominated John Breckinridge of Kentucky, a staunch believer that slavery must not be excluded from the new western territories. To complicate matters further, other Democrats formed a Constitutional Union Party and nominated John Bell of Tennessee on a platform rooted in the illusory hope that the dissolution of the Union could be avoided by ignoring the slavery question altogether.

Now it was a four-man race – three Democrats and the Republican Lincoln. The Republicans were united behind their single candidate while the opposition was divided. No one expected any of the candidates to receive the required 152 electoral votes. If that happened, the election would be decided by the House of Representatives, where anything could happen.

The election was really two separate contests - Douglas against Lincoln in the north and west - Brekinridge against Bell in the south. None of the candidates presented abolition of slavery as an issue to the voters. Lincoln continued his plea that slavery should not spread to the new territories, but emphatically pledged not to interfere with slavery in the southern states.

Lincoln prevailed with 40 percent of the popular vote, sweeping every 'free' state, except New Jersey. He captured 180 electoral votes compared to 123 electoral votes for the other three candidates combined. Douglas, with 12 electoral votes ran a distant last. Lincoln was now the sixteenth president of the United States – a man who had never been a vice-president, senator, governor, commander in the army, or a member of any presidential cabinet.

His sole experience was one term in Congress; other than that he never held any national elective office. Most important of all, he was a sectional president; in ten states he did not get a single popular vote. Indeed, he was not even on the ballot in some states.

News of Lincoln's victory spread quickly; the South's worst fears had finally been realized. The South had long ago lost its majority in the House of Representatives where representation was apportioned by population. If new states in the west were admitted as 'free' states, the South would lose its parity in the Senate as well. America at this time had 39 states; nineteen were considered 'free' states – sixteen in the north, plus Kansas, California, and Oregon in the west. This does not mean that all these states favored eliminating slavery – there was a huge difference between local preference and a national mandate.

Lincoln's reassurances regarding the constitutional protection of slavery did not mitigate the South's fears – they were convinced otherwise. What was driving southern secession was panic, not reason. The South feared that the balance of power was about to shift dramatically and if that happened, in time the slave system would be dismantled and the entire economy of the South would collapse. The thought of blacks roaming around free was a nightmare for southerners who were certain that a freed black would seek vengeance for past wrongs. The frenzy was so out of control that between 1830 and 1860, three hundred southern *whites* were lynched for expressing sympathetic sentiments about emancipation.

The South was divided into two sectors—each with divergent economic structures and different degrees of commitment to slavery. The seven lower southern states—South Carolina, Mississippi, Florida, Alabama, Georgia, Louisiana, and Texas—were highly dependent on cotton and nearly half its population were slaves. These lower southern states would all secede and form the Confederacy.

The upper southern states - Virginia, Tennessee, North Carolina, and Arkansas - had become more industrialized and contained large regions of non-slaveholding whites. These states had twice the number of white residents as the lower south and they were divided as to whether to remain bound to their fellow southerners or remain loyal to the Union. They loved the Union, mistrusted Lincoln, but accepted his election. All four of these states would eventually secede and join the Confederacy.

There was a third region – the Border States. They were slave states, but slavery seemed to be in decline in their region. These were the states of Maryland, Kentucky, Delaware, and Missouri. Maryland and Delaware would remain neutral during the Civil War although they were under constant pressure to join one side or the other. Kentucky and Missouri technically remained neutral, but large factions supported the Confederacy.

On December 20, 1860, little more than a month following Lincoln's election, the South Carolina legislature voted to leave the Union. In the early weeks of 1861, the other six lower southern states followed South Carolina. This action of secession was not as radical as it might seem. After all, the American Revolution had been an act of secession from Great Britain. We did not seek to remove King George from his throne or dissolve the Parliament in London. Colonists believed their interests were incompatible with Great Britain so they left the British Empire and formed their own government. England continued on its course without America. The South saw their action in a similar vein.

In February 1861, representatives from the seven secessionist states met in Montgomery, Alabama, and formed a new federation of their own, the Confederate States of America. They demanded that the United States government turn over all property, military as well as civil, that was now located on Confederate soil. The ceded states also set up a temporary Confederate Congress, adopted a provisional constitution, and elected fifty-two year old Jefferson Davis as their president.

Jefferson Davis lived a life that a romantic novelist might have invented. The handsome, elegantly dressed senator from Mississippi was a former West Pointer and a war hero in not one, but two wars - the Black Hawk Indian War and the Mexican War - and he even served as secretary of war under President Franklin Pierce. Owner of a successful cotton plantation with 106 slaves, he was a benevolent master. Other planters ridiculed Davis, referring to his slaves as "Jeff Davis's free Negroes." Davis even built a hospital for his slaves on the grounds of his plantation and employed a full-time nurse.

Upon becoming the South's president, Davis proclaimed that his goal was "peace not war. All we want is to be left alone." He argued that "slavery was in no way the cause of the conflict; it was only incidental. Africans were born the slaves of barbarian masters, untaught in all the useful arts and occupations, reared in darkness, and sold by their heathen masters. They were transferred to our enlightened shores by the rays of Christianity." Davis continued, "Blacks put into servitude in America were trained in the gentle arts of peace and order and civilization. They increased from a few unprofitable savages to millions of efficient Christian laborers. Their servile instincts rendered them contented with their lot, and their patient toil blessed the land of their abode with unmeasured riches. Now the North wants to put arms in their hands and train their humble but emotional natures to deeds of violence and bloodshed, and send them out to devastate their benefactors."

Lincoln was determined to keep the Union together. "The essence of secession is anarchy, which I will not permit." He warned that succession was illegal and unconstitutional and would not be tolerated. "The momentous issue of civil war is in your hands, not mine." For Lincoln, what was at stake was democracy. "When people vote, the majority rules, and the minority cannot be allowed to voice their disapproval by insurrection – that is not democracy."

Both sides stood poised, but no fighting erupted. Many believed that secession was nothing more than bluster meant to extort political concessions. The upper southern states held back from leaving the Union. If they remained with the Union, the Confederacy had to fail. If they joined the Confederacy, a bloody war was inevitable. The key was Virginia – the nation's founding colony was undecided about secession.

Virginia was the largest state in territory, population, influence, and slave holding. Virginians owned more than 40 percent of the nation's slaves. It was the Virginia slaves that grew the tobacco that helped buy America its independence. Virginians had always been the most eloquent spokesmen for freedom and equality. George Washington led America in battle against the British; Thomas Jefferson wrote the Declaration of Independence; and James Madison was one of the primary drafters of the Constitution. Virginians were elected to the presidency of the United States in thirty-two of the first thirty-six years of the country's existence and four of the country's first five presidents were slaveholders.

Virginia was important not only because of its prominent and distinguished role in early American history, but it was geographically sandwiched between the North and the South. Culturally and economically it was as much a part of the North as the South. Both sides realized that Virginia was the key to the fate of the Union and each side brought enormous pressure to bear to sway its decision. Virginia was the only state that possessed the moral authority to save the Union. Instead of rushing to secede, Virginia tried everything it could to effectuate a compromise that would keep the Union together. The one thing it wanted to avoid was making a choice and that meant there must not be any precipitous action by either side.

In January, Robert Hunter of Virginia presented the U. S. Senate with a list of conditions on behalf of the South, including a radical revision of the Constitution to permanently ensure equal southern representation in Congress. Lincoln now had to face his worst fears. Either a compromise had to be reached to save the Union or he would have to go to war to maintain it – letting the country dissolve into two separate nations was not an option he was willing to accept.

Lincoln again reassured the southern leaders that he had no intention or power to interfere with the legality of slavery in their states. On the day of his inauguration, he got the U.S. Senate to pass a resolution that would amend the Constitution to prevent any future Congress from interfering with slavery; this would guarantee slavery in the southern states forever. In his inaugural speech that day, Lincoln publicly announced his willingness to endorse this amendment, but the South did not trust his words.

All U.S. military garrisons in the ceded states retreated back to the North, leaving those forts and installations in Confederate hands. All that remained was Fort Sumter in Charleston Harbor, a fort that had symbolic rather than strategic value. The Fort Sumter garrison of Union soldiers was badly in need of food and reinforcements. Lincoln had to decide – reinforce the garrison or evacuate it. Withdrawing from Fort Sumter would avoid a crisis, but would be a sign of capitulation. Lincoln feared that would embolden and harden the South's position.

Arguments can be made on both sides as to who fired the first shots of the Civil War. Lincoln, on advice of his cabinet, decided not to abandon Fort Sumter; instead he sent supplies and non-military necessities. When the South learned that Union ships were headed for Fort Sumter, they attacked the fort. It was an unequal contest. The Confederate artillery pounded Fort Sumter until it capitulated. Jubilation reigned throughout the South; moral indignation fueled the North, but still the upper southern states remained uncommitted. Everyone continued to look to Virginia for a decision.

Just what Virginia tried to prevent had happened. It was hard to tell who to blame – Lincoln for provoking the confrontation or Jefferson Davis for ordering the assault. Virginians were either delirious with joy at a southern victory or depressed over the looming crisis. Virginia legislators met, but were still unable to decide on a course of action.

The day after the firing on Fort Sumter, the headline all across the country was: "War." Lincoln's Executive Order did not ask Congress for a declaration of war; instead, he called the conflict an insurrection. Lincoln's position was clear; no nation can declare war on itself. He never accepted secession as legally constitutional or appropriate. He called for 75,000 volunteers to enlist for three months of army service to "put down a domestic insurrection," and he gave the Confederacy twenty-five days to disband. The Constitution conferred no such executive power on the president. The raising of an army belonged to Congress, but Lincoln justified his actions by arguing that Congress was not in session and he had a duty as commander-in-chief to institute whatever measures were necessary to protect the safety of the Republic from rebellion.

An irate Virginia legislature considered Lincoln's military call-up a highly provocative act that was totally unnecessarily. They could no longer dodge the issue: the Virginia legislature voted 88 to 55 for succession. The other non-committed slave states were now compelled to choose sides. North Carolina, Arkansas, and Tennessee joined Virginia and seceded. Missouri, Maryland, Kentucky, and Delaware remained in the Union, but declared neutrality. Had Maryland sided with the Confederacy, the Lincoln White House would have been situated in a Confederate state. If all the non-committed slave states joined Virginia in secession, the Confederacy would have been too strong to be defeated. If none left, the Confederacy would have been too weak to commit to war. The tragedy for the country was that those states split roughly down the middle – half seceded and half stayed with the Union. It was the one outcome most likely to prolong the conflict.

Deciding whether to join or not join the Confederacy did not mean that all its citizens agreed or complied. Maryland was terribly divided. Approximately 30,000 men from Maryland ended up fighting for the Union, while 20,000 joined the Confederate side. In Kentucky, 50,000 fought for the Union and about 35,000 for the Confederacy. In Missouri, about 80,000 became Union soldiers, 30,000 fought for the Confederacy, and 3,000 became mercenaries looking for the best payday from either side.

The Union enjoyed several key advantages in the war with the South:

- The North had a five-to-two advantage in military manpower; twenty-two million against nine million, and one-third of those of military age in the South were slaves who the Confederacy feared to arm.

- The North could turn out 5,000 rifles a day compared to 300 in the South.

- The North had a seventeen-to-one advantage in the production of textile goods, a twenty-to-one edge in iron production, and an almost forty-to-one advantage in coal production.

- Although the South had vast wealth, its economy was built on an inedible cotton crop tended by a subjugated workforce; the North's wealth was more liquid and diversified.

- About 90 percent of the 50,000 miles of telegraph wire ran through Union states allowing their field generals to be in close communication with their headquarters.

- At the beginning of the war, the fledgling Confederate Treasury had to pay its army by first selling bonds to its own citizens; no such financial problem existed in the North.

The Confederacy possessed several important strengths:

- It did not have to conquer the North in order to win – all it had to do was not lose.

- Its armies would be defending home ground and three-quarters of a million square miles of southern terrain would pose a daunting obstacle to Union forces.

Certain factors favored neither side:
- Even though 900 of the 1,200 military officers remained with the Union, the quality of military leadership was approximately equal. The top generals from both sides trained at West Point and Robert E. Lee's military brilliance was unparalleled.

- Lincoln and Jefferson Davis were both effective commander-in-chiefs.

- Both sides hoped to gain the support of the neutral Border States.

Realistically, the South really had no chance of winning against the North's superiority. Twenty-three states in the North squared off against eleven in the South and the North simply had more of almost everything that mattered. Victory would not be achieved by the righteousness of any cause – history has shown that God is on the side that has the best artillery and the most battalions.

Beneath the apparent unity of the Confederacy there was conflict. Most southern whites did not own slaves. A few thousand families made up the plantation elite. Millions of other southerners were poor farmers cultivating unwanted land. For these poor whites no economic issue was at stake. But the rich and powerful convinced them that this war was about honor and independence, and that their future depended on the maintenance of slavery. Singing patriotic ditties, brave southern boys marched off to war in their spanking new gray uniforms, swords blazing and bands blaring, while the rich plantation owners stayed behind with their slaves hoping to produce the needed capital to finance the war.

In order to raise an army in the North, Lincoln offered volunteers a bonus of $24 and a federal bounty of 160 acres of land in the West. When this voluntary enlistment program proved insufficient, Lincoln instituted a draft lottery; names were to be drawn at random from enrollment lists of those between the ages of twenty and forty-five. However, anyone could be excused by paying the government $300 or arranging for a substitute to serve in his place. For the average worker this was a flagrant case of class discrimination, making the conflict a rich man's war and a poor man's fight - with the poor doing the dying. Among those who bought their way out of the war were J. P. Morgan, Andrew Carnegie, John D. Rockefeller, future presidents Chester Arthur and Grover Cleveland, and the fathers of Teddy and Franklin Roosevelt. The father of James Mellon advised his son to pay the $300: "A man may be a patriot without risking his own life or sacrificing his health. There are plenty of lives less valuable."

A crowd of 150 men gathered at the Ninth District draft office in New York on the first day of the draft lottery. Slips of paper were rolled tightly and bound with rubber bands, then placed in a cylindrical drum and rotated by a handle on the side to mix the names randomly. The *Daily News* dubbed it "the wheel of misfortune." The lottery proceeded peacefully that day. However, the apparent calm of the first day's lottery soon became unraveled when crowds began to form over the week-end to discuss the situation. What was this war really about, they asked? Was the government telling them the truth? Was the war about saving the Union, slavery, or economics? If the war was about freeing the blacks, they wanted no part of it. Why should poor whites in the north die to free black slaves in the south?

To the poor worker, the draft's $300 exemption was one more example of 'special privilege' conferred by the government on the wealthy privileged class and a confirmation of labor's declining status in the new industrial order. Unable to afford an exemption, thousands of draftees arrived Monday morning to protest. The day quickly turned violent and ugly. Needing to vent their hostilities, they turned their vengeance on New York's black population. The Colored Orphan Asylum with 233 children was burned to the ground with the mob shouting, "Burn the nigger's nest!" Only the calmness of the teachers saved the children. As these heroic teachers led the children down Seventh Avenue they were unsure what might happen to them next. When twenty of the children became separated from the group, they were surrounded by a mob and taunted with cries of, "Murder the damn monkeys," and "Wring the necks of the damned Lincolnites." Fortunately, the children were saved from harm by members of the local fire engine company.

Rioters grabbed blacks in the streets and beat their victims to death; then strung their bodies up on trees. Hundreds of stores were looted and dozens lost their lives. By dusk that night the city was essentially controlled by the rioters. The pillaging of entire black neighborhoods that began on Monday continued throughout Tuesday. On Sullivan and Roosevelt Streets, where many blacks lived, boardinghouses and stores were burned to the ground. Throughout the city, blacks were attacked, beaten, and hung from lampposts. Police stations were soon overflowing with those looking to escape the carnage.

After five days of unchecked rioting, Lincoln sent a regiment of federal soldiers from Pennsylvania to restore order, but the damage had been done. Eighteen blacks had been lynched; more than a thousand people were killed or wounded. The rioters had succeeded in scattering terrified free blacks to the edges of the city, a prelude to the formation of large black ghettos in New York and other major cities. Although some advised Lincoln to suspend the draft immediately, he insisted that it go forward - he was not going to give in to lawlessness.

Many in the country felt that Lincoln was amassing dictatorial powers and expanding the role of the central government beyond the powers enumerated in the Constitution. The draft, they said, was the ultimate expression of this arbitrary federal power and would be declared unconstitutional once the issue reached the Supreme Court. The governor of Maryland, very much aware of the delicate balance of opinion in his state, responded to Lincoln's call for troops by requesting a guarantee that his state's militia be used in Maryland or the District of Columbia and agreed to furnish troops only on that condition.

When the Sixth Massachusetts Volunteers attempted to march through Baltimore in order to reach the nation's capital, a mob of Confederate sympathizers attacked the soldiers, causing sixteen deaths and widespread rioting. Baltimore officials pleaded with Lincoln not to send any more federal troops through Maryland. To this Lincoln replied: "Our men are not moles who can tunnel under the ground." To prevent additional Union troops from entering Baltimore, the mayor ordered the destruction of all railroad bridges connecting the city with the North. Suddenly, the nation's capital was isolated and its citizens were gripped by fear. To restore order in Baltimore and enable Union forces to protect Washington, Lincoln declared martial law in Maryland.

In the course of arresting suspected secessionists, Union soldiers seized John Merryman and threw him into a military jail without a hearing or trial. Merryman immediately filed a petition for a writ of *habeas corpus*, seeking his release from military detention. The justice assigned to hear Merryman's petition was Supreme Court Chief Justice Roger B. Taney, the same justice who presided in the Dred Scott case. Taney ruled in *Ex parte Merryman* that only Congress was authorized to suspend the writ of *habeas corpus* and that Lincoln's executive order was unconstitutional. Moreover, because Merryman was not a member of the military forces of the United States, and since the civil courts in Maryland were open and functioning, ordinary judicial process in Maryland, rather than military authority, had jurisdiction over the matter. Taney ordered that Merryman had to be released. Taney's decision that Lincoln had acted unlawfully was celebrated throughout the Confederacy. Merryman was released, but never tried in Maryland. Lincoln realized that no Maryland jury would convict him.

Frederick Douglass and Abraham Lincoln are the two preeminent self-made men in American Civil War history. Lincoln was born dirt poor, had less than one year of formal schooling, and became one of our nation's greatest presidents. Frederick Douglass was born into slavery to a black female slave and an unknown white, perhaps her white master. Douglass looked like a man trapped between races. His skin was neither black nor white. He inherited light eyes and lean lips from his father and thick black curly hair from his mother. He spent the first twenty years of his life as a slave and had no formal schooling.

In the mid-1830s, Douglass successfully ran away and became the most famous black man in the western world. His memoir, *Life and Times*, is still one of the great American autobiographies. Published in 1845 for fifty cents, it soon became an international best-seller. Within three years, 11,000 copies were sold in the United States; by 1850 almost 30,000 copies had been sold. Douglass traveled all over the North preaching about the evils of slavery. He knew that the shame of slavery was not just in the South - the whole nation was complicit in it. On July 4, 1852, he gave the following Independence Day address:

> "Fellow Citizens: Pardon me, and allow me to ask, why am I called upon to speak here today? What have I or those I represent to do with your national independence? Are the great principles of political freedom and of natural justice embodied in the Declaration of Independence extended to us? Am I called to this national altar to express devout gratitude for the blessings resulting from your independence?

> To the American slave, what is your Fourth of July? I answer: it is a day that reveals to the slave, more than all other days of the year, the gross injustice and cruelty to which he is the constant victim. To him your celebration is a sham; your boasted liberty an unholy license; your national greatness, swelling vanity; your sounds of rejoicing are empty and heartless; your denunciation of tyrants, brass-fronted impudence; your shouts of liberty and equality, hollow mockery; your prayers and hymns, your sermons and thanksgivings, with all your religious parade and solemnity, are to him mere bombast, fraud, deception, impiety, and hypocrisy - a thin veil to cover up crimes which would disgrace a nation of savages. There is not a nation on earth guilty of practices more shocking and bloody than are the people of these United States at this very hour."

One journalist who heard the speech wrote, "Many persons in the audience could not believe that he was actually a slave. How could a man who spent his early life in bondage, and who had never gone to school a day in his life, speak with such eloquence and precision of language."

There was no practical way of ending slavery in the South without destroying the Union. The four million slaves represented a property value amounting to $3.5 billion in 1860 dollars and the entire economy of the South rested upon this servile labor. Freeing the slaves without compensation to their owners would only bring economic ruin to the South and to the country – the system was just too deeply entrenched. Even if emancipation came, what would be done with these four million slaves? What civil, economic, and political rights would they have? Practical men simply shuddered at the thought of such an enormous social revolution.

In March 1862, Lincoln drafted a proposal for "the gradual abolition of slavery" over the next thirty years. Lincoln's plan was not to have free blacks roaming across America – instead he made arrangements to ship them to Central America and Haiti. His plan was disguised as benevolence to blacks, but it really amounted to protectionism for whites. Emancipation would require the approval of the voters and an acceptable plan to compensate slave owners for the loss of their property. "In my judgment, gradual and not sudden emancipation is better for all," Lincoln said. His proposal also constituted sound military policy, for if the Border States accepted it, they would no longer be tempted to join the Confederacy.

Lincoln sent his proposal to Congress. According to Frederick Douglass, Lincoln's proposal was a sham. Slaveholders would never agree to free their slaves even with the inducement of monetary compensation because slavery generated far higher profits than stocks, bonds, or real estate. And it was hard to satisfy one's sexual lust on a stock certificate. As Douglass predicted, none of the Border States agreed to Lincoln's proposal.

In April, the Republican Congress, apparently inspired by Lincoln's gradual abolition plan, passed an emancipation act for the District of Columbia. Lincoln was not entirely satisfied with the bill, for it instantly (rather than gradually) liberated three thousand slaves and was forced upon the District of Columbia without the consent of its voters. But the act adhered to Lincoln's cherished "principles of compensation and colonization." It paid slaveholders $300 per slave and allocated $100,000 to ship them off to Central America.

To promote his scheme of sending blacks to the Republic of Columbia and Panama, Lincoln invited a group of Washington blacks to the White House to encourage them to leave the United States. "You and we are different races," Lincoln told them. "We have between us a broader difference than exists between almost any other two races. Your race is suffering, in my judgment, the greatest wrong inflicted on any people. But even when you cease to be slaves, you are far removed from being placed on an equality level with the white race. The very presence of blacks in this country," Lincoln added, "was the cause of the war. It is better for us both to be separated."

The speech was widely circulated, but most blacks scoffed at it. The harshest critique came from Frederick Douglass, who penned a public rebuttal: "In Central and South America, distinct races live peaceably together in the enjoyment of equal rights without civil wars," he noted. He sneered at the notion that blacks were the cause of the war. "A horse thief does not apologize for his theft by blaming the horse. No, Mr. President, it is not the innocent horse that makes the horse thief, but the cruel and brutal cupidity of those who wish to possess horses, or money and Negroes, by means of theft, robbery, and rebellion." He called Lincoln "a genuine representative of American prejudice" who had few principles of "justice and humanity."

Lincoln had to abandon the project after the neighboring countries of Honduras, Nicaragua, and Costa Rica protested and threatened to send in troops to prevent settlement of America's black slaves. Lincoln did not give up his plans for resettling the blacks. He soon latched on to another site: Cow Island, off the southern peninsula of Haiti. A group of New York financiers offered to ship five hundred blacks to Cow Island and "guarantee" them homes, schools, medical care, and good farmland in return for a fee of $50 per émigré, or $25,000. Although most of Lincoln's advisers opposed the plan, Lincoln agreed to it. In mid-April 1863, 453 former slaves set sail for Haiti.

Everything went wrong with the plan. Over the past month, smallpox had broken out on board the sailing ship, and when the blacks boarded the ship they were besieged with malarial fevers. When the ship arrived in Haiti, there were no homes, schools, or medical care on the island; the soil was poor; and no approval had been obtained from the Haitian government. Lincoln had been duped. After this fiasco, he abandoned the idea of colonization.

Robert E. Lee was a West Pointer who graduated second in his class. He had commanded U.S. troops in the war against Mexico and was considered by General Winfield Scott to be "the very best soldier I ever saw in the field." As soon as the Mexican War was over Lee went home to Virginia. When the slavery issue became a national debate, he freed his slaves and wrote, "Slavery is a moral and political evil in any society; a greater evil to the white man than the black." When the Civil War began he faced an acute moral conflict. Lincoln offered him complete command of the Union forces. He could have accepted on principle because he firmly believed that secession was wrong and unconstitutional, but five generations of Virginians in his family was too strong a heritage to break. Out of loyalty and affection he remained with the South.

The first major battle of the war was at Manassas, Virginia, where the Battle of Bull Run took place. Residents of Washington packed picnic lunches and took carriages out to the battlefield to watch. It wasn't long before they fled in horror, just steps ahead of the retreating Union army. At Fredericksburg, Virginia, in December 1862, men on both sides had to climb over the dead when charging the enemy. There were over 86,000 Union and Confederate casualties, and New York's Irish Sixty-Ninth Regiment of Volunteers was completely wiped out. The North was stunned – rumors began circulating that Lincoln was incompetent and had to be removed from office.

There were many famous battles during the Civil War, but none more important than the Seven Days Battle. The fighting started in April 1862, in the Chesapeake Bay area where Union General George McClellan routed the Confederates and marched towards Richmond. With the Confederate forces on the run, the war could have ended right there, but instead McClellan sent a steady stream of telegrams to Lincoln explaining why he was not quite ready to launch his final offensive. On June 1, Robert E. Lee took control of the Confederate forces. While McClellan procrastinated, Lee counter-attacked. McClellan's forces won, but again McClellan refused to follow-up his advantage. Conjuring up possibilities that did not exist, he refused to finish the job. Lee took advantage of McClellan's indecision and charged once again. McClellan panicked and the Union forces retreated in complete disarray.

Lee had McClellan on the run, but his forces were exhausted and depleted, and he recognized the futility of chasing the enemy. Nearly a quarter of his army had been killed or wounded during the previous week - twice the number of the Union casualties. The 30,000 casualties in the Seven Days Battle equaled the total in all the battles during the first half of 1862 – but greater destruction and loss of life was still to come. If Lee was unhappy that he let McClellan's army escape, the southern people did not share his discontent. Lee became the hero of the hour – southern tributes rang out, hailing "the brilliancy of his genius and the lasting gratitude of the South."

War is filled with ironies and the Seven Days Battle tops the list. Had McClellan attacked when he had the Confederate forces beaten, the war would have been over. The Union would have been restored with minimal destruction. Slavery would have survived as a legal institution and the nation would have moved on as it had before the war. Instead, Lee defeated McClellan; it was a great victory for the South, but the victory prolonged the war until it eventually destroyed slavery, the South, and nearly everything the Confederacy was fighting for.

Lee knew he did not have the manpower and resources to fight on indefinitely against a superior foe. He constantly looked for an opening to get the North to sue for peace so the war would end honorably without the horrible destruction he envisioned; the exact terms of the peace could be resolved later. At one point he sent Confederate Vice President Alexander Stephens on a mission to approach Lincoln – but Lincoln was too depressed to see him.

In May 1863, Lee's army defeated a Union force twice its size at Chancellorville. Seeking to capitalize on this victory, Lee thrust northward and invaded Pennsylvania hoping to crush northern morale and perhaps secure diplomatic recognition and support from England and France. His plan was not to get Lincoln to surrender; he knew that was impossible, but if the war could shift from the south to the north, Jefferson Davis would be in a strong position to call for a cease-fire and a negotiated peace.

Lee intended to march 70,000 Confederate troops from Virginia through Maryland and Pennsylvania, and then capture Washington. The Union learned of his plan and they sent 80,000 troops to stop him. Both sides converged at Gettysburg, a remote town in Pennsylvania that had no strategic significance. During the fighting that lasted four days, the North retained the vital high ground. Fighting uphill was a distinct disadvantage for Lee's forces, but he was stubbornly determined to succeed. It was a colossal blunder on his part.

On July 4, 1863, Lee ordered a retreat back to Virginia; otherwise his entire army would have been destroyed. In total, 53,000 men were killed – 23,000 Union soldiers and 30,000 Confederates. The number of wounded was staggering. Piles of amputated arms and legs were stacked up like small mountains – it was a horrifying sight.

As Lee's thoroughly beaten remnants retreated southward, he rode out to meet them. "It was all my fault," he confessed to anyone who had the strength to listen – and he was right – too many prior victories had made him think he was omnipotent and unbeatable. He tendered his resignation to Jefferson Davis, but it was refused. The war would continue for another two years, but Lee never ventured into the north again. He fought a purely defensive war, hoping that the North would tire of the fighting and offer a compromised peace. But he was wrong – there would be no compromise – only unconditional surrender.

However, the South was fighting to protect its homeland and way of life, and therefore fought tenaciously, giving no quarter. Many northerners feared that Lincoln's armies could not win the war. With blow after blow, Lincoln cried, "I cannot stand it." Things got worse when Confederate generals Jubal Early and John Breckinridge launched a surprise raid against Washington. Lincoln and his family had to flee their personal residence for the better protected White House. Eager to show he was not afraid, Lincoln, wearing frock coat and stovepipe hat, rode uphill to one of the city's northern defense outposts to give moral support to his troops. With bullets whizzing past his ears, a young Union captain – future Supreme Court Justice Oliver Wendell Holmes - called out to the unrecognized Lincoln, "Get down, you fool." In the end, thanks to belated Union reinforcements and Confederate tactical mistakes, the southern troops failed to seize the Capital. "We haven't taken Washington," cried General Early, "but we scared Abe Lincoln like hell."

Lincoln became severely depressed, a condition he suffered from all his life. He wished to know what God wanted: "In great contests each party claims to act in accordance with the will of God. One must be wrong. God cannot be for and against the same thing at the same time. In the present Civil War it is quite possible that God's purpose is something different from the purpose of either party." Lincoln walked the floor of his office moaning in anguish, "What has God put me in this place for?" He told members of his cabinet, "This war is eating my life out. We are now on the brink of destruction. It appears that the Almighty is against us and I can hardly see a ray of hope." He no longer slept and his eyes looked sunken and deathly. His political enemies ascribed the nation's troubles to this "fourth-rate man," and introduced a resolution in Congress calling for his resignation.

Out of desperation, Lincoln threatened to emancipate the slaves unless the rebellious states returned to the Union. Lincoln was certain the one thing the South feared more than Union troops shooting at them was former black slaves with rifles going after them. When South Carolina received the news that emancipation was coming, it predicted that once the blacks were free from their chains they would ravage the country – north and south alike. The reaction in the north to Lincoln's emancipation plan was divided. Abolitionists and 'free' blacks were ecstatic, but many northern merchants were bitter and thought the move would kill any chance of the profitable cotton economy recovering after the war.

Members of Lincoln's cabinet convinced him to delay his plans for emancipation until there was a major Union military victory, otherwise it might seem like an act of desperation and a "cry of distress." Lincoln agreed. In anticipating a public outcry after his Proclamation became public, he wrote an open letter to Horace Greeley, the editor of the *New York Tribune* explaining his position:

> "My paramount object in this struggle is to save the Union and is not either to save or destroy slavery. If I could save the Union without freeing any slave I would do it; and if I could save it by freeing all the slaves I would do it; and if I could save it by freeing

some and leaving others alone, I would also do that. What I do about slavery and the colored race, I do because I believe it helps save the Union."

But a Union military victory was not on the horizon. The Civil War seemed to be turning in favor of the Confederates. They had stopped the Union on the outskirts of Richmond, won a heady triumph at Second Manassas, and Robert E. Lee's forces were as resolute as ever. Lincoln badly needed a victory, any kind of victory. He finally got it on September 17 at Antietam when Lee's army was stopped and had to retreat. Lincoln now proceeded with his Emancipation Proclamation.

The Proclamation consisted of two executive orders. The first one, issued September 22, 1862, declared freedom for all slaves in any of the Confederate States that did not return to the Union by January 1, 1863. The second order, issued January 1, 1863, named the specific states where emancipation would apply. The document read in part: "All persons held as slaves within any state then in rebellion against the United States, shall be forever free." Emancipation applied *only* to those states in actual rebellion against the Union – slavery was untouched and remained legal everywhere else.

The Proclamation was very specific – it listed exactly which rebellious states were affected by emancipation:

> "To wit:: Arkansas, Texas, Louisiana, (except the Parishes of St. Bernard, Plaquemines, Jefferson, St. John, St. Charles, St. James Ascension, Assumption, Terrebonne, Lafourche, St. Mary, St. Martin, and Orleans, including the City of New Orleans) Mississippi, Alabama, Florida, Georgia, South Carolina, North Carolina, and Virginia, except the forty-eight counties designated as West Virginia, and also the counties of Berkley, Accomac, Northampton, Elizabeth City, York, Princess Ann, and Norfolk, including the cities of Norfolk and

Portsmouth; and which excepted parts, are for the present, left precisely as if this proclamation were not issued."

The Emancipation Proclamation is perhaps the most misunderstood document in American history. Lincoln undertook to abolish slavery where he had no power to do so, and protected it where he had the power to destroy it. And his action was illegal – slavery was specifically protected by the U.S. Constitution and only a constitutional amendment could change that. Lincoln knew this, but claimed he had the constitutional authority as commander-in-chief to effectuate "any necessary war measure for suppressing rebellion." Even if Lincoln was right, which is doubtful, his war powers certainly could not apply to the Confederacy, which was under the control of Jefferson Davis.

Lincoln privately admitted that his Proclamation would fail if it came before the Supreme Court, but he hoped the war would be over before any challenge reached the Court. Lincoln never stopped apologizing for the document that immortalized him. He told everyone who would listen that the Proclamation was not what he wanted and hoped that Congress would later find a way to soften the impact of emancipation and spread it over a long period of time. According to Secretary of the Navy Gideon Welles, Lincoln insisted that after the war a way had to be found to deport the emancipated blacks to another land, because 'they would never be recognized or admitted to be our equals." According to Lincoln, emancipation and deportation had to go together – you could not have one without the other.

Lincoln was a great writer and speech-maker, but the Emancipation Proclamation was not one of his great expressions. Its language was dry and technical, and lacked any moral claim. Despite its limitations, the creative force of the document came not from its words, but from its concept. What Lincoln's Proclamation did was ennoble what would otherwise have been a horrific and senseless Civil War.

When news of emancipation reached the South, thousands of blacks fled to the North and joined the Union military. At first these black soldiers were assigned the limited role of maintaining garrison forts, but by the spring of 1863 they were formed into segregated units under the command of white officers. They received less pay then their white counterparts, but Lincoln said this was a necessary concession to white prejudices.

The presidential election of 1864 was going to be the ultimate test of how this war would end. The Confederate president, Jefferson Davis, hoped that the northern voters would oust Lincoln in favor of General McClellan, the Democratic nominee. Lincoln had fired McClellan as commander-of-the-army in 1862. It was by no means certain that Lincoln would even win the Republican nomination since he was considered such a failure and his Emancipation Proclamation was very unpopular among many of the northern electorate. There was a widespread assumption that if McClellan were elected president he would quickly call a halt to the hostilities and restore the South to the Union with slavery.

Lincoln became the Republican nominee by default. He left the choosing of his vice-presidential running mate to the Convention delegates and they picked Andrew Johnson to 'balance' the ticket. Johnson was a Southern Democrat from Tennessee, an alcoholic slave owner, and the only senator from the South that remained loyal to the Union.

As the election of 1864 drew near, the scene became ominous and discouraging. The Emancipation Proclamation had not ended the war – on the contrary, Confederate forces fought harder than ever. The Democrats were outraged that Lincoln had made emancipation a war aim instead of focusing all attention on the restoration of the Union. During the election campaign, Democrats attacked Lincoln as "Abraham Africanus the First," and circulated "humorous" racist pamphlets featuring caricatured sketches of Lincoln with a black face. Campaign literature portrayed white women sitting on the laps of black men, white men with black women strolling through the park, and inter-married blacks exulting that they had reached the heaven of social and political equality.

In the election, Lincoln won 55 percent of the vote, carrying all but three states, and the Republican Party won dominating majorities in both Houses of Congress. The victory was not as overwhelming as it appears since none of the southern states participated in the voting and Lincoln would have been lucky to receive less than 10 percent of the votes in those states.

Lincoln's re-election was also saved by an unexpected military victory. In early September, General William Tecumseh Sherman's army won the Battle of Atlanta that opened the way for his devastating "March to the Sea." As he led his 60,000 men through Atlanta, he destroyed everything in sight. It was a systematic atrocity that haunted Sherman for the rest of his life. Fifteen years later, at the graduating class of the Michigan Military Academy, he spoke about those events: "I am tired and sick of war. It is only those who have neither fired a shot nor heard the shrieks and groans of the wounded who cry aloud for blood, more vengeance, and more desolation. War is hell."

"Forty acres and a mule" was a term of compensation awarded by Sherman to the slaves as he marched through the South. In his famous Special Field Order No. 15 issued on January 16, 1865, Sherman addressed the immediate problem of dealing with the tens of thousands of black refugees who joined Sherman's march in search of protection and sustenance. After meeting with U.S. Secretary of War Edwin M. Stanton, Sherman set aside a land grant of 400,000 farming acres for the blacks - 40 acres of land for each family to farm and a mule to drag a plow so the land could be cultivated.

Out of desperation, the Confederacy authorized the arming of black slaves and inducted them into the Confederate Army, promising them emancipation after the war. It was the final irony to this war of folly. On April 9, 1865, at Appomattox, Lee and his army surrendered. The two great generals, Lee and Grant, had fought side-by-side in the Mexican War and had been forced to be enemies these past bloody years. They were both exhausted and glad that the carnage was finally over. When Grant announced Lee's surrender to his troops, he cautioned them: "Do not cheer. The rebels are not just our prisoners – they are our countrymen once again."

In accordance with Lincoln's direct orders, the terms of the surrender were very lenient. The Union Army printed out about

30,000 parole slips for the Confederate soldiers who were allowed to keep their side arms and horses, but had to surrender their rifles. Lee and Grant met at the McLean House at Appomattox and Grant gave Lee the surrender terms. Lee was dressed in his finest starched uniform. He brought his sword because he fully expected this to be a traditional eighteenth or nineteenth century surrender. As Lee was about to ceremoniously hand over his sword, Grant said, "I don't want your sword; just go home." Lee nodded his appreciation and walked outside to address his thoroughly beaten and dejected troops. Lee told them: "I did the best I could for you. Go home now and God bless you all."

The war was now over. The South's agrarian society was just no military match against the North's industrial power. Both sides had fought in the name of freedom and God - now more than 620,000 Americans were dead; 360,000 northerners and 260,000 southerners. Over half a million others were wounded. Many survivors were without arms or legs; most were emotionally scarred for life. The southern cities were devastated; the northern ones were untouched. The Confederate economy was in ruins; its picturesque landscape all but destroyed. Billions of dollars of property lay in ruins. Except for those slaves that chose to remain on their former plantations, southerners, especially widows and war veterans without limbs, had nobody to help them start over. Their existence now depended on the charity of the federal government they hated so much.

Northern opportunists who spent the war in comfort back home now took advantage of the situation. Northern "carpetbaggers" rushed to the south looking to make advantageous deals with desperate widows and orphans. In the north, they bought up the land warrants from the returning Union soldiers, paying $50 for their 160 acres in the western territories. Huge fortunes were made from the miseries of both sides.

Slavery was now officially ended - but the freed blacks were not prepared to be admitted into society – and they certainly were not welcomed by whites with open arms. How much did liberty really mean if you were uneducated and had no trade other than what you knew as a slave? Emancipation deprived blacks of their security – they were no longer assured of food, clothing, and shelter. They were set adrift in the world, homeless and penniless, ill-equipped to enter the fierce competition for existence. For all practical purposes they were destitute.

Frederick Douglass captured the moment best when he said: "Our work does not end with the abolition of slavery; it only begins." His words were painfully true. Lincoln may have set in motion freedom for black slaves, but there was no plan as to what would happen next. When a young black man asked Douglass what he should do with his life now that he was free, Douglass answered: "Agitate, agitate, agitate!"

Lincoln realized that he had not controlled the events of the war; the events had controlled him. He thought about this a great deal, especially at night when he couldn't sleep, trying to understand the meaning of it all. He blamed himself that the dispute had grown into such a massive revolutionary struggle and had consumed so many lives. None of this had to turn out this way. Lincoln could have shown restraint over Fort Sumter. Jefferson Davis could have let reinforcements into the fort and not attacked. Lincoln did not have to provoke the situation by immediately calling for the enlistment of troops. Had Virginia not seceded, things would have undoubtedly been different. But, it was not to be. Secession was now a dead issue - so was slavery – but the sectional conflict remained. Politically, the Democratic Party would not recover until FDR's election in 1932. The Republican Party would go on to win twelve of the sixteen presidential elections between the Civil War and the Great Depression. They would control the U.S. Senate and hold a majority in the House for twenty-seven of the next thirty-two years.

Less than a week after the war ended, Abraham Lincoln was assassinated. He was attending a theatrical performance of *Our American Cousin* in Washington when he was shot by John Wilkes Booth, a southerner and one of America's leading actors. Booth had a deep hatred for Lincoln and the Republican Party. He could never bring himself to join the Confederate Army, but as the southern cause kept deteriorating he became obsessed with wanting to prove his manhood. A year earlier he had devised a plot to kidnap Lincoln, take him to Virginia as a hostage, and offer to exchange him for all the Confederate prisoners of war. The kidnap attempt was abandoned when Lincoln changed his plans at the last moment. Now such a plan was meaningless – the war was over and there were no prisoners to release.

Booth's plan now was more adventuresome; he planed to kill Lincoln, Vice President Andrew Johnson, and Secretary of State William Seward – all on the same day. Eight other conspirators were involved in the plot. On the night of the assassination, John Parker, the police officer assigned to the presidential box at the Ford Theater, left his post and went outside for a drink. At about 10:00 p.m., John Wilkes Booth quietly entered the presidential box, pointed his derringer pistol at the president's head from two feet away and pulled the trigger - one shot and Lincoln was dead.

Booth then jumped onto the stage from the low balcony, breaking his ankle. As he hobbled out the rear of the theater he shouted, "Sic simper tyrannis" ("Thus ever to tyrants!") - the Virginia state motto. Booth rode to Maryland where he met two of his accomplices and then headed for Virginia. Two weeks later, Union soldiers tracked him down. Booth locked himself in a barn and refused to come out. The soldiers set fire to the barn. What happened after that is unclear. It is known that a shot was fired and Booth was dead, but there is confusion as to whether a soldier shot him or whether Booth committed suicide.

On the same night as Lincoln's assassination, Secretary of State Seward was stabbed three times by two of the conspirators. Seward had been resting in his bed from an accident when the assassins conned their way into his home on the pretense of delivering medicine. The metal brace Seward was wearing deflected the knife from piercing his vital organs and saved his life. The plot to shoot Vice President Andrew Johnson never came off as the intended assassin became frightened at the last minute.

No one can pretend to know what reconstruction of the South would have been like had Lincoln lived since he died before any plan about the post-war could be formulated – that was left to Andrew Johnson – probably the worst man to be in charge of such a delicate and complicated mission. Northern capitalists, however, now saw new hope for confiscating property in the south as well as unimpeded expansion in the west. One northern capitalist put it this way: "While everyone is shocked by Lincoln's murder, the feeling is universal that the ascension of Johnson will prove a godsend."

Reconstruction after the Civil War was one long ten-year agonizing referendum on trying to knit the nation back together. Could two divergent views - black freedom and white supremacy ever be reconciled - and if they could not, what then? The challenge of reconstruction had to do with healing and justice. What truly constitutes the healing of a people and a nation that has suffered this scale of violence and destruction - and justice for whom?

Andrew Johnson was a virulent white supremacist who believed the United States should remain, "a white man's country forever." His first order of business was to deal harshly with the forces that had torn this country apart – there would be no leniency for these southern traitors. During the first six weeks of his presidency, Johnson instituted a reign of terror against all those who fought and sided with the South.

Within weeks of taking office, he ordered the conspirators involved in the Lincoln assassination to be tried before a military commission. All the prisoners were found guilty; four were hanged, including one woman. One of the conspirators fled to Canada, three others were sentenced to life imprisonment, and one received a six-year sentence.

Johnson then set out to prosecute Robert E. Lee and other southern leaders for conspiracy roles in Lincoln's assassination. "Treason must be made odious," the new president declared, "and traitors must be impoverished." A federal grand jury indicted General Lee and General Longstreet, along with several others from the Confederate high command for treason. Lee immediately wrote to Ulysses Grant and pleaded his case: how could this indictment be squared with the parole that Lee and his army had received at Appomattox? Grant agreed with Lee. He immediately telegraphed Secretary of War Stanton: "The officers and men paroled at Appomattox cannot be tried for treason as long as they observe the terms of their parole." President Johnson, however, disagreed; he was determined to exercise his new presidential powers and show the nation that he was a strong leader.

Grant traveled to Washington to press his case. What right, President Johnson angrily demanded, did a subordinate have to "protect an arch-traitor from the laws?" Grant was a man famous for control of his emotions, but not now. He was enraged. Grant told Johnson that Lee never would have surrendered if he thought he and his men would be subjected to criminal proceedings; and if they had not surrendered, the war would have dragged on indefinitely with far more loss of life to Union and Confederate forces. Then Grant leveled his verbal artillery at the stunned Johnson: "I will resign from the United States Army rather than execute any order to arrest Lee or any of his commanders so long as they obey the law!"

As arrogant and bigoted as Andrew Johnson was, he knew when he was outgunned; in any contest between himself and Grant, the country would back its beloved war hero. Johnson ordered the indictments dismissed. Grant's trust in Robert E. Lee was well-placed. Once Lee was free from the threat of federal prosecution he assumed the presidency of Washington College (now Washington and Lee) and dedicated the remaining five years of his life to education.

Johnson's next target was Jefferson Davis, the Confederacy's president. Davis was still at large and Johnson claimed that Lincoln's conspirators must have been procured by Davis. Johnson offered a huge reward for his capture. Five weeks later, he was captured and spent the next two years in prison. In December 1868, the prosecution dropped the case against him.

Shortly into his presidency, Johnson received a delegation of black leaders headed by Frederick Douglass. The black leaders were pleading for Johnson's support for Negro suffrage as part of the reconstruction in the South. Johnson remained civil and noncommittal. Afterward, he snarled to his secretary, "Those damned sons of bitches thought they had me in a trap. I know that damned Douglass; he is just like any nigger, and he would sooner cut a white man's throat as not." Douglass came away from his meeting with Johnson remarking, "Whatever this man may be, he is no friend of our race."

Forty-eight days after Lincoln's assassination, Johnson announced his plans for the reconstruction of the South. To be readmitted into the Union, a Confederate state had to abolish slavery and take a new oath of loyalty to the Union. Southern property, except for the slaves, was restored. Johnson revoked General Sherman's Order No. 15, and the land that had been awarded to the blacks was returned to its former white owners. For these former slaves, it meant the government could not be trusted to keep its word.

In Johnson's State of the Union address in December 1867, he openly declared, "In the progress of nations, Negroes have shown less capacity for government than any other race of people. No independent government of any form has ever been successful in their hands. Wherever they have been left to their own devices, they have shown a constant tendency to relapse into barbarism." Obviously, Johnson's racist positions could not lead to an orderly transition and unification that would heal the deep wounds of a torn country.

Between 1866 and 1868, fifteen different legislative bills developing a reconstruction plan were passed by Congress, vetoed by President Johnson, and overridden by Congress. The deadlock between Congress and the president was a constitutional crisis; a breakdown in federalism. Over President Johnson's veto, Congress passed the First Reconstruction Act, in which 700,000 blacks became registered voters. In five states - Alabama, Florida, Louisiana, Mississippi, and South Carolina - black voters now made up a majority. To prevent the president from obstructing this reconstruction program, Congress passed several laws restricting presidential powers. The Tenure of Office Act barred him from removing officeholders that had been appointed and approved with the 'advice and consent' of the Senate. In August 1867, Johnson tested the legality of this Act by removing Secretary of War Edwin Stanton. Johnson was convinced he had such power under the 'original intent' of the Constitution.

Amidst this political turmoil, impeachment proceeding were brought against Johnson. A nervous nation braced itself for civil war once again as the House voted to proceed with impeachment. The impeachment trial in the Senate lasted almost three months. The Senate voted three times: on all three occasions, thirty-five senators voted "guilty" and nineteen "not guilty." The Constitution required a two-thirds majority for conviction - thirty-six votes were needed to impeach, so the vote was one shy of the requirement. Had one senator changed his vote to guilty, Johnson would have been convicted and removed from office. The impeachment process proved cumbersome and exasperating, but ultimately achieved exactly the goal the Framers of the Constitution intended; the peaceful resolution to a grave national crisis.

CHAPTER SIX

CAPITALISM

"Capitalists have allegiance to no country; their only allegiance is to their pocketbook."

Thomas Jefferson

"Capitalism is the legitimate racket of the ruling class. It is the astounding belief that the wickedest of men will do the wickedest of things for the greatest good of everyone."

John Maynard Keynes

"If you steal $25, you're a thief.
If you steal $250,000, you're an embezzler.
If you steal $2,500,00 0, you're a financier."

Charles Mitchell
President of National City Bank

Why does capitalism have such a bad image, especially since it is the single most descriptive explanation for America's phenomenal success? President Calvin Coolidge once proclaimed, "The business of America is business." But, can you imagine a current-day President of the United States going on national television to commend capitalists on having an excellent year because they kept wages low and profit margins high; or telling the public that we need to go to war to expand corporate markets or to grab another country's oil? Our economic and foreign policies are so intertwined as to be virtually indistinguishable. Is there something wrong with telling the people this truth?

Capitalism is a paradox; it creates great wealth for a few, but is selfishly uncaring about the rest of its fellow citizens. It is economic Darwinism; survival of the fittest and strongest. To become 'king' of the jungle, the lion leaves behind lots of dead bodies; so it is in our capitalist jungle – the strong and powerful advance, but the winners may not be our finest moral examples.

Maybe the best description of capitalism was by Ayn Rand in *Atlas Shrugged*. Her main character, Nat Taggart, based on the real-life Cornelius Vanderbilt, expressed capitalist philosophy this way:

> "Capitalism demands the best of every man and rewards him accordingly. It leaves every man free to choose the work he likes, to specialize in it, to trade his product for the products of others, and to go as far on the road of achievement as his ability and ambition will carry him.
>
> I do not want my attitude to be misunderstood. I shall be glad to state it for the record. I work for nothing but my own profit - which I make by selling a product to people who are willing and able to buy it. I do not produce it for their benefit at the expense of mine, and they do not buy it for my benefit at the expense of theirs. I do not sacrifice my interests to them nor do they sacrifice theirs to me. We deal as equals by mutual consent to mutual advantage - and I am proud of every penny I earned in this manner. I am rich and I am proud of it. I have made my money by my own effort, in free exchange and through the voluntary consent of every man I dealt with - the voluntary consent of those who employed me when I started, the voluntary consent of those who work for me now, and the voluntary consent of those who buy my product.

I shall answer all the questions you are afraid to ask me openly. Do I wish to pay my workers more than their services are worth to me? I do not. Do I wish to sell my product for less than my customers are willing to pay me? I do not. Do I wish to sell it at a loss or give it away? I do not. If this is evil, do whatever you please with me, according to whatever standards you hold. These are mine. I am earning my own living as every honest man must."

Adam Smith, a Scottish professor, was a pioneering political economist and the author of two major treatises explaining how capitalism worked: *The Theory of Moral Sentiments* (1759), and *An Inquiry into the Nature and Causes of the Wealth of Nations* (1776). The latter was one of the earliest attempts to systematically explain the historical development of industry and commerce. His economic theories were predicated on the principle of *laissez-faire*: that life, liberty and the pursuit of property was best accomplished without government interference. Let 'free market' economics take its natural course without artificial guidance from tariffs, duties, quotas, subsidies, bailouts, and trade rules. In this way, world trade would grow exponentially as each country maximized its "comparative advantage." There will be highs and lows, but in the long run the natural supply and demand of the market will control events.

Smith explained that self-interest is an essential ingredient in economics. 'Supply and demand' governs the market. High prices lead to an increase in production and supply. But, with more goods now available, prices begin to fall. When prices start falling, consumers rush to purchase more goods. This new increase in demand forces prices back up and eventually leads to a shortage of goods, which in turn promotes increased production - and the cycle keeps repeating itself.

Adam Smith called his theory the "invisible hand" of the market. The "invisible hand" was a strange term to use, almost conjuring up an image of God guiding a capitalist world order – especially in America, where capitalism and Protestant fundamentalism would flourish hand in hand.

Smith's economic theories were soon applied to social reform. He advocated that government should leave people alone to work things out for themselves: "Let the poor lift themselves up by their own bootstraps." Real happiness, according to Smith, is the same for the rich or the poor; the peace of mind of the poor is no different from that of the rich. If government becomes responsible for the welfare of the needy, the funds can only come from taxing the rich. Government involvement is unnecessary, since the rich, out of self-interest, will benevolently administer to the needs of society.

Although some features of capitalism existed in the ancient world, its dominance began with the Industrial Revolution in England. During the last half of the eighteenth century, a series of inventions transformed manufacturing and created a new mode of production - the factory system substituted machines for human skill and effort. These improvements yielded an unprecedented increase in productivity and fundamentally altered economic life. For the first time, women and children found work outside the home.

Although many of the industrial ideas came from England, soon America became known as the nation of innovators. Geographic factors greatly helped America since our coastlines were ideal harbors for trade and our land was abundant with precious metals and raw materials. Cheap immigrant labor was available to produce America's vast array of goods and to lay the railroad tracks for our expansion westward. But, economic success bred greed and trumped humanitarian concerns. Harsh working conditions and low wages became a normal part of the system. Anything that increased profits was deemed acceptable.

Karl Marx was born in 1818 into a relatively affluent family. He studied philosophy in Berlin under the great German philosopher, Georg Wilhelm Friedrich Hegel. After receiving his PhD, Marx became involved in leftist politics. In 1843, he was exiled to Paris where he began a life-long collaboration with Frederich Engels. Marx spent his life studying and defining what he appropriately called capitalism. His two major works were the *Communist*

Manifesto published in 1848 and *Das Kapital* in 1867 (two other volumes of *Das Kapital* were published after his death).

According to Marx, history was all about class struggle. In capitalism, everything had a value – whether it was a commodity or a human worker. Marx divided the capitalist society into two classes, those who produced a profit by utilizing their capital (bourgeoisie), and the workers (proletariat) that had to sell their labor in order to exist. The bourgeoisie contracted for proletariat labor at the lowest possible wage in order to achieve the highest profit, while the worker bargained for the highest wage possible. 'Supply and demand' theories ruled the labor marketplace.

Marx believed that the bourgeoisie and the proletariat could not peaceably co-exist because capitalist greed for profit would always lead to the exploitation of the working class. It was hopeless to try to humanize the system – the only real hope for the proletariat was the complete destruction of capitalism. According to Marx, no system deserved to exist if its foundation and success was dependent on the exploitation of others. Once the working class recognized it was being exploited, they would revolt and replace capitalism with a more compassionate economic system. Marx believed that Christianity's mantra, "All men are brothers," kept the workers subjugated; more appropriately the slogan should be, "workers of the world unite."

According to Marx, controlling the means of production is what gave the capitalists their power. The workers were powerless in comparison. This inequality of wealth was an endless struggle: the power of the few seeking to hold on to their wealth, while the masses struggled for survival. Eventually, an ever-shrinking number of capitalists would control more and more of the total wealth. This increasing chasm between the wealthy and the poor would inevitably lead to a revolution in order to restore a more equitable semblance of parity. To Marx, this sequence of events was as clear as night following day; the few that benefited from the system were delusional if they thought they could forever maintain control over an impoverished majority.

However, Marx's revolution could only come about if the masses were united; therefore, the goal of capitalism was to keep the workers divided. Obviously, this meant no unions. The Christian Church aligned itself with capitalism. At first glance this seems like an unholy alliance, but the success of both capitalism and the Church were dependent on the same thing: the control of the masses. The Church preached that the poor should be content with their lives because everlasting joy awaited them in some afterlife fairy-tale heaven; this was music to capitalist ears. Religion, according to Marx, was the root cause of this class struggle – it was a drug that stifled improvement of the human condition; it was "the opium of the people."

Marx believed that capitalism was a contradiction – it had to keep growing bigger otherwise it would collapse, but once growth was no longer possible, collapse was inevitable; it would be destroyed by its own greed and corruption. Capitalism would begin innocently enough, but when local markets became saturated, capitalists would turn to global markets for customers and cheap resources. Since this drive for profit had no borders, it was imperialistic by its very nature. This quest for more and more markets dictated a country's foreign policy and eventually had to lead to war. All wars, according to Marx, were capitalist wars. Worst of all, the poor and the workers were duped into sacrificing their lives, while the rich capitalists stayed home and racked in the profits.

Although Marx's prediction about the collapse of capitalism has not happened, the debate continues over which type of society is best - one where a few live in splendor while the rest struggle, or a society where there is a more balanced distribution of wealth and all live moderately well. One thing that history has proven is that if the rich wish to maintain domestic peace, it is smart to give the poor a piece of the 'pie' before they gang up and take it all.

The period from 1860 to 1900 in America was like no other. American capitalism went through perhaps the greatest transformation in its history. It was during this period that the railroads were built and Wall Street emerged in order to finance the nation's growth. The era was filled with rags-to-riches stories that came to be known as the 'American Dream.'

****

When Cornelius Vanderbilt was born to a family of farmers in New York's Staten Island section, nobody could have foreseen that he would become the richest man in America. Cornelius was an outdoor type of youngster who never got much out of school. He could barely read or write, yet, he was visionary enough to see the future and smart enough to establish a financial dynasty.

Vanderbilt quit school at age eleven ("If I had learned education, I would not have had time to learn anything else.") and by sixteen he was operating his own business, ferrying freight and passengers between Staten Island and Manhattan. Charging a fee for transporting commercial goods was always an accepted business practice, but charging passengers for safe passage was akin to the medieval baron who charged a fee to pass through his castle grounds unmolested. Over time, the term 'robber baron' became synonymous with unscrupulous business practices. Whether this was an accurate depiction or not, the term stuck to those who built great industrial empires.

During the War of 1812, Vanderbilt received a government contract to ferry supplies to the military forts around New York City. In 1818, he turned his attention to steamships. By 1837, he was the largest ship-owner in the country and was dubbed with the honorary title, Commodore. His business philosophy was simplicity itself: run the most efficient low-cost organization possible and compete fiercely by means of price until the opposition is either broke or willing to sell out.

By the 1840s, Vanderbilt owned more than 100 steamboats and employed more people than any other company in America. He married his second cousin, Sophia Johnson, and had thirteen children. He built a huge estate on Staten Island, but as hard as he tried, the cigar-chewing, tobacco spitting gambler and womanizer could never get accepted into New York society. When he decided to move the family to Manhattan, Sophia resisted. His solution was to have her committed to an insane asylum until she agreed.

In the 1860s, nearing the age of 70, Vanderbilt decided that the wave of the future was in another direction and he set out to establish a railroad empire. Railroads were a big financial risk; they were capital-intensive and represented an economic unknown.

Vanderbilt, however, was intuitive enough to realize that the railroad solved the problem of overland transportation that steamboats could only partially alleviate. Steamship transportation, up and down narrow canals, was feasible in areas of good rainfall, but useless in winter in the northern areas. Railroads, on the other hand, could operate all year.

The railroad was not a single invention. It was a technologically complex array that took decades to reach full fruition. It began with James Watt's rotary steam engine in 1784. Engineers then began to think about attaching the engine to a carriage on rails. It was not until the turn of the nineteenth century that the railroad became a practical possibility.

It is difficult to overstate the importance of the railroad boom in American history. The railroad opened much of the agricultural West to settlement. Farmers were now able to ship their wheat crops and cattle to eastern markets and invest their profits in heavy equipment that converted the prairie into productive farmland. The railroad allowed the mineral wealth of the West to be transported from the mountains to the cities of Chicago and St. Louis, and allowed oil to be transported cheaply and quickly from remote Appalachian and Texas oil wells to the great urban centers. The railroad shifted much of the power from the eastern coastline cites to the newly emerging western cities that did not have to rely on seaports for economic growth. Unquestionably, the railroad changed the face of America.

Vanderbilt became known as the greatest nineteenth century railroad man never to have built a railroad. He was a wheeler-dealer – using capital, brains, and gumption to achieve his empire. He started by acquiring the Long Island Railroad, followed by the N.Y. Harlem Railroad, and then the Hudson River Railroad. He acquired the Central Railroad and merged it with his other railroads to form the N.Y. Central. He eventually owned and operated sixteen railroads, but the crown jewel in his empire was Western Union. Just as the railroad was linking the country together, so the telegraph was revolutionizing the speed of communications.

Cornelius Vanderbilt was ruthless in business and made many enemies. His public persona was that of a vulgar, mean-spirited man who made life miserable for everyone around him, including his family. His constant evasion of the law was legendary. He would say, "My God, you don't suppose you can run a railroad in accordance with the legal statutes of New York, do you?" Not modest about his success, he put his portrait on every stock certificate that was sold to the public.

In 1868, when his wife died, the seventy-four year old Vanderbilt married Francis Crawford, his thirty-three year old cousin. Under her guidance he soon began charitable undertakings, including a million dollar donation to a small southern university that became Vanderbilt University. At the time of his death at age 82, he had amassed over $100 million ($96 billion in present-day dollars), which was more money than the entire U.S. Treasury. In his will, he gave his son William $90 million; the remaining $10 million was split up among his other children.

The Vanderbilt heirs had no trouble spending their inheritance. By 1900, eight lavish Vanderbilt mansions could be found between 51st and 59th Streets in Manhattan, including one with 137 rooms. There were also ten major summer estates including an $11 million extravaganza in Newport, Rhode Island, and a 250-room chateau in Asheville, North Carolina. Vanderbilt's son, William, took over the business empire and became as ruthless as his father. His comment, "The public be damned," would become legendary capitalist folklore.

****

There were lots of new inventions at the beginning of America's economic revolution, but it was the discovery of oil that transformed this country into an industrial colossus. It all began in the Allegheny Mountains in western Pennsylvania. For a century or more, Pennsylvania farmers had found their streams muddied by a kind of black glue. First, the farmers cursed it, and then, on an old tip from the Indians, they bottled it and sold it as medicine.

In 1849, Samuel Kier put the 'black glue' in pocket-sized bottles with his own printed label: "Genuine petroleum." Kier's petroleum was touted far and wide as a cure for asthma, rheumatism, gout, tuberculosis, cancer, and fallen arches. It also made a pretty good, though smelly lighting fluid. Later, a distillation process produced an almost odorless liquid when burned – kerosene. In 1859, the bonanza came.

The owner of a tract of land that ran along Kier's Oil Creek decided that somewhere underground there had to be a primary source for this glob that was being bottled so profitably. The landowner hired a middle-aged railroad conductor, Edwin L Drake, who was similarly inquisitive, and together they began exploring for wells by pick and shovel. After they nearly drowned when an underground spring erupted, Drake concluded that oil lay deeper in the ground than water. He got a blacksmith to sink a seventy-foot shaft into the ground and on a sweltering afternoon in August 1859 the black glue burst to the surface. The blacksmith jumped on his mule and raced into the town of Titusville, crying: "Struck oil! Struck oil!" He had indeed hit the first oil gusher.

In 1860, Oil Creek shipped an estimated 200,000 barrels of crude oil. The following year it shipped two million barrels. Within thirty years, a sprawling mass of shanty towns along Oil Creek was producing 31 million barrels of oil a year. There was no central system of control or conservation in those days. It was every man for himself in the well-established American tradition: discover a new resource, work it to exhaustion, ravage the land, and move on. What the oil business needed was organization. The man who would provide that was John Davison Rockefeller, a prim, methodical twenty-one-year-old bookkeeper from Cleveland, Ohio.

The year after Drake's strike, a group of financial venture capitalists in Cleveland sent Rockefeller to Oil Creek to look the situation over and report back on the possibility of investment. Rockefeller was not well received by the oil wildcatters, one of whom called him, "that bloodless Baptist bookkeeper." After his first survey, Rockefeller learned all he needed to know. He went back to Cleveland and deliberately lied to his employers that oil had no commercial future. Although everyone knew the black glue could be used for lighting, Rockefeller recognized the potential oil had for heating, lubrication, and power – and he did not intend to share this information with anyone.

Rockefeller heard of a candle-maker who had successfully refined lard oil and was beginning to tinker with the refining of petroleum. He invested $4,000 in the candle-maker's venture and then convinced outside investors to finance the building of a refinery. When Rockefeller realized the enormous profit potential of the enterprise, he lied once again, telling his investors that the plan was useless and 'magnanimously' bought them out. When Rockefeller was thirty, he formed Standard Oil of Ohio - by then he owned twenty-five oil refineries.

Rockefeller built this monopoly with ruthless determination. It was open knowledge that he "owned" the best state legislatures and U. S. senators that money could buy. He pressured the railroads into secretly giving him low rates and special rebates that drove his competitors out of business. When this secret arrangement with the railroads leaked to the public, it provoked a national outcry, but Rockefeller rode out the scandal by the well-known expedient of sitting back and letting the lapse of time make everyone forget.

By the late nineteenth century, Rockefeller owned 90 percent of all the oil refineries in America, including all the main pipelines. Standard Oil controlled the entire oil process – from raw materials through production and distribution, and then on to wholesalers and retailers. Soon Rockefeller moved into iron, copper, coal, shipping, and banking. His annual profits were $81 million in an era when a construction foreman earned $1.25 a day and a common laborer could be hired for as little as two cents an hour.

Although Rockefeller became the first billionaire in history, he lived a simple life. All that mattered to him was his Christian religion and capitalism. His devotion to work, thriftiness, and savings, spoke eloquently to the piety instilled in him by his evangelical Baptist mother. In his New York mansion he always had the Bible close by, though its resting place was on top of his bedside safe. His creed was simple: "I believe the power to make money is a gift from God to be developed to the best of our ability for the good of mankind. Having been endowed with this gift, I believe it is my duty to make money and still more money, and to use the money I make for the good of my fellow man according to the dictates of my conscience."

In 1930, the Rockefeller family began work on a complex of 19 commercial buildings covering 22 acres between 48th and 51st Streets in New York City, which became known as Rockefeller Center. Since this was to be the largest private complex of its kind in the world, the entrance had to be dramatic and eye-opening. Rockefeller decided to commission a huge color fresco mural to adorn the 1,071 square-foot lobby wall, and he put his son Nelson in charge of the project. Nelson (later to become governor of New York) wanted the commission to go to Henri Matisse or Pablo Picasso, but neither artist was available. Instead, Diego Rivera, a well known and respected Mexican painter was commissioned to create the mural. He was given a theme: New Frontiers.

Diego Rivera was an outspoken socialist and critic of capitalism. He had previously painted a controversial mural in Detroit entitled *Detroit Industry*, which was commissioned by the Ford family. Thus, it should have come as no real surprise when Rivera's *Man at the Crossroads* created a storm of protest when it was unveiled. The mural contained scenes of 'May Day' parades, portraits of Russian revolutionaries Leon Trotsky and Vladimir Lenin, drunken Americans carousing with the opposite sex, and other scenes of a totally decayed capitalist society. Enhancing the socialist image were slogans like 'Down with Imperialist Wars!', 'Workers Unite!' and, most shocking of all, 'Free Money!' In the center of the mural stood a heroic industrial worker trying to choose between capitalism and socialism. For Rivera, the answer was easy: virtue lay on the side of socialism.

To place such a propaganda image in the headquarters of one of the great capitalist dynasties in America was to invite disaster. Nelson Rockefeller issued a written warning to Rivera to replace the offending figures. Rivera refused. When no compromise could be reached, Rivera was paid his fee in full and the mural was destroyed - smashed to bits and hauled away in wheelbarrows.

****

Andrew Carnegie emigrated from Scotland to the United States in 1848 at the age of 13. He was a poor boy with fierce ambitions and a driving devotion to hard work and self-improvement. One of his first jobs was as a messenger delivering telegrams for Western Union. During the course of his duties he met Tom Scott and opportunity struck.

Scott was the superintendent of the Pennsylvania Railroad. He took a liking to the young Carnegie and hired him at the unheard of salary of $35 a week. Carnegie saved his money and invested astutely, making huge profits on several stock purchases. During the Civil War, he was appointed superintendent of the Union's military railways and telegraph lines. His efficient organization significantly assisted the Union in its eventual victory.

It was during these Civil War years that Carnegie realized that the country's future was in iron and steel. One of his early successful ventures was a partnership with the inventor of a sleeper railway car, which Carnegie promoted for first-class travel. When Carnegie's company merged with George Pullman, Carnegie was then able to supply sleeping cars to all the railroads in the United States. At the age of 25, Carnegie was already a rich man, but he continued to look for new ways to increase his wealth.

In 1864, he invested $40,000 in Oil Creek in Pennsylvania. In one year, the investment yielded over $1 million in cash dividends. He then devoted his energies to the ironworks trade. His iron cables helped build the 1,100 foot Brooklyn Bridge – the greatest engineering feat of the century. From iron, he turned his sights to steel. Under his guidance and close supervision, Carnegie Steel became the largest manufacturer of steel railroad tracks in the world.

During this period of enormous economic growth in America, labor began to organize and demand better wages and working conditions. Capitalists equated unions with socialism and they feared that unless these unions were destroyed, power would shift to the workers and capitalism would die. By 1892, a handful of giant corporations controlled all the state governments and had enormous political influence in Washington. They bought and sold politicians freely and had the final say on major federal and state appointees, court decisions, and new legislation.

These titans of industry met secretly and decided to use their political power and vast resources to halt the advances of the growing labor movement. When Carnegie Steel's union contract was about to expire, the union began negotiating for a wage increase. Andrew Carnegie decided he would be the first capitalist crusader to crush the unions in America.

The Homestead Strike of 1892 became a bloody labor confrontation that lasted 143 days at Carnegie's main steel plant in Homestead, Pennsylvania. Carnegie met with his management team and planned the tactics and strategy; then he left the country for Scotland so as not to sully his image with the ugly violence that was sure to follow. Implementation of Carnegie's plan was left in the hands of his partner, Henry Clay Frick. Instead of a raise in wages, Frick inflamed the negotiations by proposing an 18 percent wage reduction, and individual worker contracts rather than one overall union agreement.

The union rejected Frick's outrageous offer and threatened to strike. Frick never expected the union to agree and he now put Carnegie's battle plan into action. He had a high wooden fence erected around the plant, cut loopholes in the fence for rifles, covered the top of the fence with barbed wire, and mounted searchlights on several towers inside the grounds.

Two days before the labor contract was to expire, Frick locked his workers out and hired cheap immigrant replacements. When the strikers blocked the 'scab' labor from entering the plant, the Pinkerton Agency private police force was waiting. After a pitched battle, forty union workers were shot and nine were killed. Twenty of Pinkerton's men were wounded and seven died. Nearly three hundred men were injured in the fracas.

Calm was finally restored only after Frick telegraphed Pennsylvania Governor Robert Pattison and 8,000 state militia men were immediately dispatched to the strike site. With the state militia now guarding the plant facilities, Carnegie Steel resumed operations with its non-union labor. The strike quickly disintegrated. The workers could only stay unemployed for so long.

They needed work and a reduced paycheck was better than none. Discouraged and humiliated, they admitted defeat and trudged back to work.

Once the strike was over, Andrew Carnegie returned to the United States, but his reputation was permanently tarnished by the incident. However, the violence at Homestead did not end. On July 23, Alexander Berkman, a union anarchist, gained entrance to Frick's office and shot him twice. Miraculously, Frick survived the attack. Berkman was sentenced to 22 years in prison.

In 1901, at the age of 66, Carnegie was considering retirement. At the time, John Pierpont Morgan was the leading banker and deal-maker in America. Morgan envisioned a vast integrated steel company that would control the world market. To accomplish this end, he wished to acquire Carnegie Steel along with several other major producers, and combine them into one company. During a round of golf, Morgan told Carnegie he wanted to buy his empire and he should name his price. Carnegie did not respond until they finished the eighteenth hole. Then Carnegie whispered to Morgan: $450 million. Morgan agreed on the spot and the deal was done.

Morgan combined Carnegie Steel with eleven other steel companies and called the combine U.S. Steel; it was the first corporation with a market capitalization in excess of $1 billion. Over drinks one night, Carnegie told Morgan that he sold out too cheaply. "I should have asked for $100 million more," he said. "I would have paid it," Morgan replied. No matter, Carnegie was now the second-richest person in the world, only behind John D. Rockefeller.

Carnegie spent his last years as a philanthropist, giving away most of his riches to fund libraries, schools, and universities. He summed up his new beliefs as follows:

> "Man does not live by bread alone. If man must have an idol, no idol is more debasing than the worship of money! To choose a life where the goal is to make as much money in the shortest period of time is degrading beyond hope of permanent recovery. It is the mind that makes the body rich. There is no class of people as pitiably wretched as

that which possesses money and nothing else. My aspirations take a higher flight - to contribute to the enlightenment and joys of the mind and to the things of the spirit. I hold this the noblest possible use of wealth."

These were noble sentiments and Carnegie did gave away his money to fund worthwhile causes, but the hundreds of thousands of workers who helped him earn his millions saw little reward for their efforts during their lifetime. The Carnegie steel towns were filled with shacks and horrible living conditions and there was much Carnegie could have done to better the lives of those in his employ. In these later years, he would often comment on the irony between his life of wealth and the lives of his workers and it was disturbing to him. "Maybe by giving away his money," commented biographer Joseph Wall, "he felt he could justify what he had done to amass all that money."

Carnegie died on August 11, 1919 in Lenox, Massachusetts. He had already given away over $350 million (approximately $5 billion in today's figures) and at his death, his last $30 million was given to foundations and charities. Carnegie believed that leaving wealth to family members would only create idleness that would rob them of the drive and joy of creating a life on their own terms, unencumbered by inherited wealth. "The parent who leaves his son enormous wealth generally deadens the talents and energies of the son, and tempts him to lead a less useful and less worthy life than he otherwise would."

****

The impact of radio, refrigerators, and the airplane pale in comparison with that of the automobile. The motor vehicle transformed societies, provided unprecedented individual mobility, and freed people from the constraints of existing transportation just as fundamentally as the railroad freed them from water transport. The history of the automobile is not only one of capitalism's great success stories, it also reflects America's love affair with a mechanical invention that shaped the public's concept of status and wealth.

Henry Ford was raised in rural Michigan and showed an early aptitude for mechanical devices. He served a three-year apprenticeship in Detroit where he learned how to build and repair steam engines. In 1891, he was hired by the Edison Illuminating Company (owned by inventor Thomas Edison) where he rose to the position of chief engineer. In 1896, he built one of his first cars, the Quadricycle, which linked an internal combustion engine with four bicycle-style wheels and was steered by a boat tiller.

When Henry Ford decided to start his own company he had no capital; all he had was his automobile invention and instinctive business ability. After being turned down for a loan by J.P. Morgan, he scraped together $28,000 and began building cars. His first automobile, the Model T was a two-cylinder, eight-horsepower car with a chain drive. These first motor cars were toys for the rich, but Ford's automobile came steadily down in price and soon became accessible to ordinary citizens. In 1909, Ford sold 1,700 cars; by 1915 one million cars were being produced, and by the 1930s, twenty-eight million cars rolled off the Ford assembly lines.

Ford's assembly line reduced the time necessary to make an automobile chassis from twelve hours to ninety minutes. He was assisted in this project by Frederick Winslow Taylor, an industrial engineer who viewed time and motion studies as an academic discipline. Taylor would break a job into its component parts and measure each function to the hundredth of a minute. He advocated that maximum production results could be achieved from a precise standardization of simple repetitive tasks that even the dumbest worker could perform. Ford agreed with this approach and was outspoken about this philosophy – he believed there were few operations in an ordinary plant that required intelligence. "A moron," he said, "is quite as useful in industry as a Socrates." Many liberal newspapers chastised him for these sentiments, claiming that he viewed his workers as slaves. What of it, responded Ford's supporters – are the slaves complaining? They have jobs don't they?

Ford refused to get into morality debates about business, claiming that he was only a modest manufacturer of cheap, durable, and infinitely hideous automobiles. Working men were made by the Lord God Jehovah, not by him, and if Jehovah made some of them content to just screw in nuts and bolts all day - they should continue doing what they were capable of. "The vast majority of men," Ford said, "want to be led, have everything done for them, and not have any responsibility."

During World War I, Ford began building an enormous integrated complex on the River Rouge near Detroit. The plant would ultimately have a workforce of 120,000 and redefine modern manufacturing. The Rouge covered 2,000 acres and boasted the longest assembly line in the world. The plant became the hub of Henry Ford's industrial empire as well as a monument to the man himself. Iron and coal arrived on Ford's private boats fresh from his mines, rubber was imported from his plantation in Brazil, and wood came from trees harvested on land that Ford owned.

The Ford plants were non-union and Henry Ford intended to keep them that way. There were no collective bargaining agreements – Henry Ford personally resolved all wage issues. No one was paid extra for overtime. If a man worked an extra hour he was entitled to take an hour off the next day, or he could accumulate his extra hours and take a day off, or use them towards a vacation.

But, by the beginning of 1914 the Ford Motor Company found itself in trouble. The monotony and dehumanization of the assembly line had made it increasingly difficult to retain workers. At one point it was necessary to hire nearly one thousand workers to keep one hundred on the payroll. More worrisome still was a campaign begun the year before by the nation's largest industrial union, the IWW, targeting the Ford plant for unionization.

Whether motivated by a genuine concern for the welfare of his workers, or the fear of unionization, or simply a stroke of advertising genius, Henry Ford announced a revolutionary policy that would permanently alter the worker-employer relationship. Henceforth, Ford announced, the minimum daily wage for Ford workers would be more than doubled, from $2.34 to $5.00, and the working day would be reduced from nine hours to eight. An elaborate system of incentive profit-sharing would be introduced. "Our workers are not sharing in our good fortune," declared

Henry Ford. "There are thousands out there in the shop who are not living as they should."

The effect was electrifying; it signaled nothing less than a new era in American industry. The next morning, every newspaper in the country announced Ford's new policy with blaring headlines. "It is the most generous stroke of policy between a captain of industry and his workers that the country has ever seen," wrote the *Michigan Manufacturer and Financial Record*. According to the *New York Globe*, Ford's new wage scheme had "all the advantages and none of the disadvantages of socialism." Overnight, Ford was hailed as a national hero. One newspaper called him "the new Messiah."

However, negative notes were sounded by his fellow industrialists. They regarded Ford a traitor to capitalism and were worried that their own workers would expect similar treatment. The *Wall Street Journal* – the voice of American big business - called the wage increase blatantly immoral; an "economic crime." Treating workers humanely could set a dangerous precedent that might threaten the entire capitalist system, the newspaper warned. What nobody realized was that Ford was speeding up the production lines and that made up for his higher labor costs; it also insured that his workers would not organize into a union.

To his detractors, Ford explained that the new policy was merely good business and would result in increased productivity and higher profits. Grateful American workers saw humanity in Ford's proposals and sent thousands of letters and telegrams thanking him for his generosity and promised to buy his automobiles. That week, police had to be summoned to quell a riot when more than 12,000 men lined up at the gates of the Ford plant in hope of a job. Ford workers, thrilled with their higher wages, became buyers of Ford cars – financed on the installment plan by the Ford Credit Company. Ford also pioneered the franchise dealer system, creating an efficient sales and distribution system throughout the nation.

Newspaper reporters descended on Ford's corporate headquarters to record the new hero's every utterance and Henry Ford was glad to oblige. His homilies on every conceivable topic blended folksy wisdom with a homespun philosophy on life. "A business that makes nothing but money is a poor kind of business," he said. On certain subjects he kept his thoughts confined to his close circle of business cronies: "It is good that the people of this nation do not understand our banking and monetary system, for if they did, I believe there would be a revolution before tomorrow morning."

Ford's wage hike created more than two million lines of favorable advertising publicity and thousands of editorial endorsements. As Ford predicted, his company enjoyed an immediate surge in production, sales, and profits, making him a billionaire and one of the world's richest men. Ford reveled in his new-found celebrity status. Countless newspapers called on him to run for president. A nationwide poll ranked him the third greatest man in history - behind only Napoleon and Jesus Christ. Socialists such as Vladimir Lenin admired him as one of the major contributors to the twentieth-century revolution and it was not unusual to see portraits of Ford and Lenin hanging side by side in Soviet factories.

Ford used the media to create an entirely new persona, portraying himself as a self-made man who began life as the son of a poor farmer. He enchanted the press with story after story about how he clawed his way out of the depths of poverty to learn a trade and build his first car. However, according to his sister Margaret, "there was no truth in any of his tales." Henry Ford's father was a prosperous landowner who owned a number of other enterprises. In addition, Ford cultivated the myth that he was a mechanical genius even though his cars were engineered and designed by others; his genius was in his ideas and business acumen.

In 1919, Ford quietly purchased a small weekly newspaper called the *Dearborn Independent*. For the first sixteen months of operation, the *Independent* was barely distinguishable from any other weekly newspaper. The paper supported Prohibition, prison reform, and printed innocuous articles about local issues. However, soon Ford's new obsession - the Jews - found its way into the newspaper.

On May 22, 1920, under a banner that announced the *Dearborn Independent* as *The Ford International Weekly*, a huge bold headline fired the opening salvo: THE INTERNATIONAL JEW: THE WORLD'S PROBLEM. For the next ninety-one weeks, each edition of the *Dearborn Independent* further embellished the picture of a Jewish conspiracy so vast and far-reaching that its tentacles touched every facet of American life. "In America alone," announced the paper, "most of big business, the trusts and the banks, the natural resources and the chief agricultural products, especially tobacco, cotton and sugar, are in the control of Jewish financiers and their agents - Jewish journalists are a large and powerful group - Jews are the largest and most numerous landlords - Jews control the circulations of publications in this country." No American institution, according to the *Independent*, was immune from the grasp of Jewish control.

This was not the ranting of some ordinary man without influence. What Henry Ford said, on any subject, influenced millions of people around the world. Each week readers were treated to what Ford's paper called "a lesson" in the insidious tricks Jews used to control the country. Ford introduced the American public to one of the biggest racial forgeries in history - an obscure document known as the *Protocols of the Learned Elders of Zion* that was circulated as proof that the Jews were plotting to take over the world by "creating wars and revolutions to destroy the Gentile race." The Jews, according to Ford, "will seize power during the resulting chaos and rule with their claimed superior intelligence over the remaining races of the world - as kings over slaves."

An oft-repeated claim was that the Jews plotted the recent Russian Revolution and were responsible for Bolshevism. Other newspapers and periodicals jumped on Ford's bandwagon of hate. The *Christian Science Monitor* published an editorial entitled "The Jewish Peril," highlighting Ford's revelations and warning its readers of the dangers represented by international Jews. An editorial entitled "World Mischief," appeared in the *Chicago Tribune* and argued that Bolshevism was merely a "tool" for the establishment of Jewish world control.

The American Jewish Congress issued an eighteen-page response refuting the charges and exposing the *Protocols* as hate-filled nonsense, but Ford was undeterred. He explained to a reporter that he was only trying to "awake the Gentile world to what is going on." Not only did Ford continue to pursue his campaign, but in October 1920, he published, *The International Jew*, a 200-page pamphlet reprinting the newspaper's articles about the "Jewish Question." The preface to the first edition explained that "the *Dearborn Independent* was fulfilling a duty to shed light on a matter crying for light." More than half-a-million copies of *The International Jew* were distributed free through Ford's vast nationwide network of dealerships; thousands more were sent to some of the country's most influential figures, including college presidents, politicians, bankers, and clergymen.

Around this time the *London Times* published definitive proof that the *Protocols* were a forgery. When a reporter from the *New York World* informed Ford of this, he replied, "The only statement I care to make about the *Protocols* is that they fit in with what is going on." Ford was convinced and nothing was going to deter him from his mission to expose the international Jewish menace. Moreover, the letters that poured into his office from average Americans convinced him that the people supported his efforts.

The *Independent* proved to be a runaway success. When Ford purchased the newspaper in 1919 its circulation was 72,000; by 1922 circulation had increased to 300,000 and eventually reached a peak of 700,000 two years later. Ford was tapping into a vein of racial hatred that ran deep in a large segment of the American psyche. Astonishingly, Ford appeared genuinely puzzled as to why his Jewish friends voiced such strong objections to his campaign.

For years, Ford lived next door to Rabbi Leo Franklin, one of the most respected members of Detroit's Jewish community. Ford regularly entertained Franklin at his home, and as a token of friendship each year sent the rabbi a brand new Model T automobile right off the assembly line. But in June 1920, a month after the *Independent* began its attack on the Jews, Franklin sent back his latest gift with a note explaining, "You claim that you do not intend to attack all Jews, but it stands to reason that those who read these articles will naturally infer that it is your purpose to include in your condemnation every person of the Jewish faith."

When he received the note, Ford immediately phoned the rabbi and asked, "What's wrong, Dr. Franklin? Has something come between us?" That Ford could be so oblivious to the effects of what he was propagating speaks volumes about his character. His bewilderment was genuine. The *Independent's* business manager, Fred Black, later recalled, "He was very much surprised that the Jews he considered 'good Jews' were opposed to what he was saying."

Henry Ford's anti-Semitism attracted those of similar ilk. On the afternoon of December 28, 1931, Adolf Hitler, a rising Nazi politician at the time, was interviewed in Germany by a reporter from the *Detroit News*, a newspaper with a very large German immigrant readership. After the interview, the reporter inquired about an oil painting of Henry Ford that hung directly behind Hitler's desk. "The reason is simple," explained the future Fuhrer, "I regard Henry Ford as my inspiration."

Hitler also praised Ford for his cash contributions to his cause. "I shall do my best to put Henry Ford's theories into practice in Germany," Hitler expressed on many occasions. It was no accident that Ford's brilliance in assembly line mass production became the prototype for the efficient processing of extermination at all of Hitler's death camps.

On the occasion of Henry Ford's 75th birthday, he became the first American recipient of the "Grand Cross of the Supreme Order of the German Eagle," created by Adolf Hitler as the highest honor Germany could give a distinguished foreigner. The formal citation read: "in recognition of Germany's admiration and for his humanitarian ideals and devotion to the Fuhrer's cause of peace." It was signed personally by Adolf Hitler on July 7, 1938 – the day that Austrian Jews were rounded up and sent to Mauthausen, a newly opened concentration camp where most eventually perished.

The cries of denunciation from Jewish-Americans arose almost immediately. Eddie Cantor, the world famous entertainer, fired off the first salvo, calling Ford a "damn fool" for accepting Hitler's medal. "Doesn't he realize that the German papers are reporting the citation as evidence that all Americans are behind Nazism? Whose side is Mr. Ford on? I question his Americanism and his Christianity. The more men we have like Ford the more we must organize and fight." Three days later, the Jewish War Veterans urged Ford to repudiate the award and Jewish groups called for a boycott of Ford automobiles. Ford was undaunted by the attacks. It confirmed his views about the attempted domination by Jews and he would not budge. He kept Hitler's medal throughout his lifetime and wore it regularly.

By December 1941, 250 American firms were operating in Germany and Ford was one of the largest. In the months following the declaration of war between Germany and the United States, the Nazis seized American companies as "enemy property" and incorporated their holdings into the Hermann Goring Werke, a giant industrial combine. An exception was made for Ford-Werke. All ongoing profits accumulated by Ford-Werke were simply placed in an escrow account for distribution to the American parent company at a later date.

Ford-Werke amassed huge profits during the war servicing the Nazi military effort. Of the 350,000 trucks that the German Army possessed in 1942, at least 120,000 were built by Ford. When a significant portion of the German male work force was called into the armed services, Ford-Werke was in desperate need of labor to maintain its extraordinary output. In August 1944, Nazi armaments minister Albert Speer transferred 12,000 inmates from the nearby Buchenwald concentration camp to Ford-Werke to ensure that the company kept producing at maximum capacity for the German war effort.

****

'Black gold' was not like oil, coal, or precious metals that had to be wrested from the ground with hard labor and expensive equipment. The 'black gold' of Asa Candler was cold and delicious – tart, yet sweet, and went down a parched throat on a hot summer's day like nothing else. This black liquid was Coca-Cola.

Asa Candler was born in Georgia in 1851. His father, a gold prospector, had struck it rich and became a well-to-do planter and merchant. Asa was the eighth of eleven children and even as a youth he was the quintessential capitalist. With the Civil War raging and all the southern schools closed, Asa became an apprentice pharmacy clerk. At the age of twenty-one he left for Atlanta with $1.75 in his pocket. In Atlanta, he married, opened a drug store, and dabbled in patent medicines.

Asa found his true business calling when he met John Pemberton, a fifty-four-year-old druggist with a morphine addiction. Pemberton had invented a formula for a drink that he sold in his drugstore and promoted as patent medicine. The drink contained two key ingredients - cocaine and caffeine - it also contained some alcohol as an added punch. Pemberton sold his drink as a coca winecalled Pemberton's French Wine Coca for five centsa glass. He claimed that his drink cured morphine addiction, dyspepsia, neurasthenia, headaches, indigestion, and impotence. Although drugstores were perfect locations to promote a drink embellished with such health claims, Pemberton had very little success.

In 1886, Atlanta passed the country's first prohibition legislation. The days of Pemberton's wine-based medicine appeared doomed, although it depended on how the law would define alcohol. Pemberton was not taking any chances – he altered his formula, making it essentially a carbonated non-alcoholic version. He left in the cocaine and caffeine, added sugar and mixed in citric acid. Only an inconsequential thousand gallons were sold during the next two-year period.

One might wonder what Asa Candler, a clear-eyed conservative businessman, saw in this little-known tonic. The answer lay not with the financial figures; Chandler felt the drink soothed his constant migraine headaches and melancholic depression. Pemberton's tonic pepped him up, made him feel good and energetic, alive and vigorous. Asa decided that he had to own the rights to this golden elixir. He met with the dying Pemberton and bought the formula for $2,300. The rest is Coca-Cola history.

Asa Candler was guided by three principles: religion, capitalism, and patriotism. A devout Christian and Sunday school teacher, he recognized the power of repeated messages to get people to accept

Jesus and he decided to apply those same principles in converting everyone to Coca-Cola. His salesmen covered the country like Christian missionaries, promoting Coke as a kind of secular communion drink. The key to his success was advertising. It was all about image and the seductive energetic qualities of Coca-Cola. His advertisements appealed to all classes: "the millionaire may drink champagne while the poor man drinks beer, but they both love to drink Coke-Cola soda-water." Candler was certainly right; today, annual sales top $30 billion and 900 million Cokes are consumed every day.

Coke was by no means the first of these carbonated soft drinks. Charles Hines, a Philadelphia Quaker, concocted a concentrate of sixteen wild roots and berries and called it Hines Root Beer. Charles Alderton created Dr. Pepper as a cherry soda fountain drink in 1885 with ads featuring a naked, robust young woman cavorting in the ocean, her crotch teasingly covered by a wave, and the advertisement asserting that Dr. Pepper "aids digestion and restores vim, vigor, and vitality."

But, nobody marketed their drink as extensively as Asa Candler. Soon, Coke sales spread from Atlanta to all across the South. Candler advertised Coke as both a "'brain tonic" that would cure headaches and exhaustion, and a "'nerve tonic" that would calm the most jangled nervous disorders. In 1889, 2,171 gallons of its syrup was sold. Five years later sales topped 64,000 gallons, and by 1895, Candler could truthfully claim that "Coca-Cola is now sold and consumed in every state and territory in the United States."

Originally all that Candler sold was syrup. People came into a drug store, sat at the soda fountain, ordered a glass of Coca-Cola, and watched the pharmacist mix an ounce of syrup with five and a half ounces of carbonated water. The local fountain in the 1890s was a social center where drinks were served from glasses set in silver-plated holders by a pharmacist who wore a white jacket and a black bow tie. These fountains provided a kind of refuge where men, women, and children could sit in curlicue iron chairs in front of marble counters, drink their Coke and make a social family event out of it. They could drink it fast or slow, but they always had to drink it inside the establishment. There was no way to take the drink home or outside the drugstore.

Candler soon realized that if he could put Coke in bottles it could be consumed anywhere. Soon, Coca-Cola bottling plants began appearing all over the country and by 1928 more Coke was sold in bottles than at soda fountains and the Coke bottle became instantly recognizable. The exact formula of Coca-Cola still remains a famous trade secret, guarded as securely as any nuclear weapon at the Pentagon. It is something of a paradox in this age of heightened consumer awareness that millions of Americans still drink a beverage filled with unidentified ingredients. When asked what is in the bottle, the Company simply answers: "It's a secret."

The rise to Coca-Cola's greatness was not a straight upward line - there were bumps along the way. Competitors wanted the 'secret' formula and spent millions trying to steal or duplicate it. Coca-Cola imitations showed up everywhere. Competitors lobbied Congress to outlaw Coke as a dangerous product. Doctors signed affidavits that their patients were dying from it and that Coke was addictive to children. The federal government conducted investigation after investigation, but Asa Candler never relented or gave in.

Like many successful capitalists of his day, Candler was a man of contradictions. He saw nothing wrong with women and children working sixty-hour-work-weeks in horrid conditions for 50 cents a day, yet, at the same time he gave millions to establish Emory University.

In 1916, after withdrawing from the active management of Coca-Cola, he was elected mayor of Atlanta. The following year he gave away all his stock in Coca-Cola to his children. Two years later, his family sold all their stock to a group of investors headed by Ernest Woodruff for $25 million. Asa Candler was never consulted and he was furious. True, the stock was theirs to sell, but he was shocked by his family's actions, especially since he always hated Woodruff. "Once everyone looked up to me; now I'm nobody," he would tell those who were willing to listen.

****

James Duke single-handily made the cigarette part of our modern culture. Following the Civil War, Duke's father built a facility that produced a bright leaf chewing tobacco. Cigarettes were deemed a curiosity, a cheap commodity for those who could not afford tobacco chew, snuff, pipes, and cigars. The problem with cigarette production was that it was labor intensive. There had been many attempts to replace laborers with automated cigarette-rolling machines, but bringing tobacco filler and paper together with speed and precision proved extremely difficult, and hand rolling remained the only process reliable enough for commercial cigarettes.

However, when James Duke took over his father's business, things changed. The breakthrough came when James Bonsack, a Virginia inventor, designed and introduced a cigarette rolling machine that produced 200 cigarettes every minute, almost as many as a skilled hand roller could produce in an hour. Duke signed a secret contract with Bonsack for machines at a twenty-five percent discount that competitors would not enjoy. The Bonsack machine marked a transformation in cigarette production from artisan-based production to one that emphasized standardization, control, and long production runs.

Duke understood that this new revolution in increased production required an equally significant increase in consumption; without consumer demand the benefits of this advanced machine technology would be for naught. Duke's marketing campaigns centered on premiums, coupons, and collecting cards, freely distributed with each pack of cigarettes. The cards illustrated themes such as sports and adventure, Civil War generals, fashion, flags, stamps of foreign countries, and most important of all, exotic actresses usually not fully clothed. To entice women to smoke cigarettes, advertisements emphasized the new free liberated modern woman. Soon, billboards throughout the country carried Duke's advertisements, studding urban and rural landscapes with towering promotions.

Duke began acquiring his competitors as early as 1887. In January 1890, Duke convinced the four major cigarette producers to join him in a consortium named the American Tobacco

Company. The "Tobacco Trust," as it quickly became known, aggressively acquired independent firms, closed up their plants, and consolidated machinery and inventory.

With James Duke at the helm, the American Tobacco Company quickly claimed 90 percent of all cigarette sales in the United States. Once he had absolute control over the industry, he took steps to establish a fully integrated operation. This brought to an end the famed competitive tobacco auctions as farmers had no option but to accept Duke's price. His next step was to create a national sales force, and when that was in place his thoughts turned global.

In 1924, Duke turned his attention to philanthropy. He established the Duke Endowment, a $40 million trust fund (about $500 million in today's dollars), and gave lavishly to Trinity College, later renamed Duke University. On his death, he left half his huge estate to support Davidson College, Furman University, Johnson C. Smith University, not-for-profit hospitals, and rural United Methodist churches. The remainder of his estate, estimated at over $1 billion in today's dollars, went to his twelve-year-old daughter Doris, making her literally "the richest girl in the world."

In 1964, Surgeon General Luther Terry announced that experiments had proven conclusively that cigarettes caused lung cancer. Instead of supporting research to remove the cancer-producing substance, the cigarette industry responded with a new and unprecedented public relations program. Its goal was to produce scientific controversy that would disrupt the emerging evidence about the harmful aspects of cigarette smoking. Throughout the 1960s, tobacco companies featured doctors and medical authorities in advertisements that reassured consumers about the safety in smoking cigarettes.

However, the cigarette industry knew from their own testing laboratories that there was a link between cigarettes and lung cancer. Rather than disclose these findings to the public, they introduced the filter tip cigarette, claiming that tar and nicotine was now filtered out from reaching the smoker's lungs. However, the filters were made from crocidolite asbestos, known to be the most nefarious of the asbestos varieties, resulting in high rates of mesothelioma, a cancer of the lungs and abdomen. Pack-a-day cigarette users were inhaling 131 million asbestos fibers each year; thousands of smokers died without knowing the truth.

As the tobacco companies continued to lose ground in the United States, they aggressively sought new consumers in the developing nations. More than 20 percent of Americans still smoke regularly and tobacco kills hundreds of thousands of our citizens each year, but the number of deaths in the United States is dwarfed by those now occurring around the world, especially in the poor Third World countries where tobacco is a growth industry. It is projected that in the course of the twenty-first century, one billion people across the globe will die of tobacco-related diseases.

****

Capitalism's genius is in turning something that appears to be nothing into something of immense value. The success stories of men like Vanderbilt, Rockefeller, Carnegie, Ford, Candler, and Duke, attracted new generations of the best and the brightest to capitalist pursuits. How should American history judge these men? Are they American icons to be revered alongside Washington, Jefferson, and Lincoln? Should our American youth study their lives and be taught to emulate their ways? Should special days celebrate their birth like Martin Luther King? Do these men represent the best or the worst of America's ideals?

CHAPTER SEVEN

SPANISH-AMERICAN WAR

"The day is not far distant when the whole hemisphere will be ours; in fact by virtue of our superiority of race, it already is ours morally."

President William Howard Taft

"This is a government of the people, by the people, and for the people no longer. It is a government of corporations, by corporations, and for corporations."

President Rutherford B. Hayes

The Thirteenth, Fourteenth and Fifteenth Amendments became known as the Civil War or Reconstruction Amendments and radically altered the very essence of our Constitution; one could almost say it was an entirely new document.

The Thirteenth Amendment abolished slavery in 1868. The Fourteenth Amendment reversed the Dred Scott decision. Negroes were now considered citizens and all citizens were guaranteed "equal protection of the laws," but what did that actually mean? Surely it did not mean that all citizens had a right to be treated identically. State laws could prohibit teenagers from driving a car or the right to vote, as well as mandating separate facilities for blacks and whites.

The Fifteenth Amendment gave blacks the right to vote. Ironically, now that blacks were counted as a full person instead of three-fifths, the southern states gained substantial increases in congressional representation, which made them a more powerful political force.

Elizabeth Cady Stanton and Frederick Douglass, two of the most famous progressive reformers of the 19th century, had been colleagues and friends through two decades of public service. Douglass, the former slave, had gained international fame as a writer, editor and activist; Stanton began her career by organizing the first women's rights convention in Seneca Falls in 1848. They had worked closely together on a variety of social reform issues, particularly abolition. The friendship and comradeship between Douglass and Stanton ended with the enactment of the Fifteenth Amendment; blacks got the right to vote, but women were still excluded.

During the Civil War, many women, including Stanton, had willingly put aside their fight for women's rights to campaign for the emancipation of the slaves. After the war, they even stood by patiently when Congress passed the Fourteenth Amendment defining citizens solely as "male." The politicians soothed the women's rights advocates by assuring them that their turn would come soon. But in 1869, when the Fifteenth Amendment proposed giving blacks the right to vote, outraged women demanded to know why they were not included. They were informed by their allies in Congress that public opinion left room for just one minority group to make it through the door of suffrage, and this was "the Negro's hour."

Stanton felt betrayed when Douglass supported the Fifteenth Amendment as written. She responded with a series of furious attacks, ridiculing the idea of giving the vote to the "lower order" of men including blacks, Irish, Germans and Chinese, while American white women were being denied. Her campaign to reject the Fifteenth Amendment created a bitter schism in the long alliance between abolitionists and suffragists.

There was a significant political reason why the Republican controlled Congress granted blacks the right to vote while denying women the same right. Republicans knew that black suffrage would create a whole new 'block' of Republican voters that would shore up their precarious majority in Congress. There was no doubt that black voters would support the Republican Party of Abraham Lincoln. However, giving the vote to white women ran the risk of creating as many new Democratic voters as Republicans – so women were deliberately excluded and would have to wait another five decades before the Nineteenth Amendment gave them the vote in 1920.

The Democrats in the South had no intention of losing their political majorities because of all these new black Republican voters. Before emancipation, southern whites could punish and control blacks indiscriminately as property; now with the passage of the Civil War Amendments things changed, but newly empowered southern legislatures began enacting a number of repressive laws, called Black Codes, aimed at controlling their former slaves. Their intent was to rebuild the South to its former glory by using black labor as a camouflaged form of slave labor. In the words of W.E.B. DuBois, "the slave went free; stood for a brief moment in the sun; then moved back again toward slavery."

Under these new laws, blacks were denied the right to serve on juries, testify against whites in court, buy or lease real estate, or refuse to sign yearly labor contracts. Blacks were excluded from public schools, black orphans were "apprenticed" to their former owners, and black "servants" were required to labor from sunup to sundown for their new "masters." Many were given two weeks to find work or else they had to leave the state. If they refused, they were randomly arrested for minor offenses, sentenced to unconscionable prison terms, and then 'rented' or 'sold' to corporations, where they slaved away in mines, steel mills, lumber camps, quarries, farms, and factories.

In a typical situation, a black was picked off the streets of Montgomery, Alabama, hauled before a judge and sentenced to "a year in prison or one hundred dollars." A corporate representative of U.S. Steel would step forward, pay the judge the $100 and leave with his new cost-free laborer. Repeatedly, surges in arrests coincided with seasonal corporate demand. These black laborers would spend every waking hour at back-breaking jobs and were whipped and tortured if their production 'quota' was not sufficient. At night they were chained up like wild dogs. They were slaves in all but name, and tens of thousands of them died from this ruthless corporate exploitation.

But, the political machinery slowly showed glimpses of sunshine for the newly empowered black. Blanche Bruce, a former slave, was elected by the Republican Mississippi state legislature to the U.S. Senate and Frances Cardozo served as South Carolina's secretary of state. When Louisiana governor Henry Warmouth stepped down as a result of impeachment proceedings, P.B.S. Pinchback, the lieutenant-governor at the time, became the first black governor in American history. Twenty-two blacks were elected to the House of Representatives from eight Southern states. Blacks also won numerous positions as mayors, state supreme court justices, superintendents of education, and state treasurers. Of the five hundred blacks elected to various federal and state offices in South Carolina between 1867 and 1876, more than half of them were black.

While the blacks in the South were struggling to enter white society, elsewhere, political corruption and illegal deal-making was rampant. Congressional legislation was bought and sold to the highest bidder. The history of this period is best exemplified by the presidential election of 1876, in what many refer to as the fraud of the century. The political situation was such that after sixteen successive years of Republican rule, the country was ready for a change. The South, now fully readmitted into the Union, was solidly Democratic. Blacks had the right to vote and supported the Republican Party, but they were easily intimidated into not voting or casting their ballot for the Democratic candidate.

The Republicans nominated Rutherford B. Hayes, a Civil War hero who had been wounded four times and was the three-term governor of Ohio. The Democrats countered with the intellectually aloof Samuel Tilden, the bachelor governor of New York.

This was more than a contest between two men and two political parties. Barely a decade had passed since the end of the Civil War. Men who had suffered and bled for the Union naturally resisted the notion of handing the federal government back to the Democratic Party, which rightly or wrongly, they still identified with slavery, treason, and disunion. Thousands of federal employees owed their livelihoods to Republican patronage and faced discharge if Tilden won. Both sides resorted to the vilest tactics of bribery and intimidation. That two essentially decent men were running did not prevent this from being the most corrupt election in American history.

When the ballots were counted, Tilden was the clear winner. Both candidates went to bed that night believing the election was over. The problem was that the Republicans were contesting Tilden's victory in three southern states - Louisiana, South Carolina, and Florida. Without those states, Tilden's 203 electoral votes would shrink to 184, and the total for Hayes would increase from 166 to 185. In each of these three states the incumbent Republican governor also appeared to lose to the Democratic challenger, but those results were also being contested. Each gubernatorial candidate claimed victory and control over the state's slate of electors; and each sent an electoral certificate to Congress – the newly elected Democratic governors sent one proclaiming victory for Tilden; the incumbent Republican governors sent one claiming that Hayes was the winner.

William Chandler, heading an investigatory contingent of Republican senators, arrived in Tallahassee, Florida, with a carpetbag stuffed with $10,000 in ready cash. Not surprisingly, he announced victory for Hayes. Democrats also investigated and they proclaimed Tilden the winner in those three states. Four months passed and the country was still without a political resolution or an official president.

The retiring incumbent president, Ulysses Grant, remained in the White House awaiting the nation's decision. Civil war loomed once again as both sides rushed to take up arms if their candidate was not inaugurated. Confederate generals reconstituted their militias. Thousands of heavily armed supporters on both sides began massing for war. Dark rumors spread that forces were about to march on Washington and install Tilden by force. "Tilden or Blood!" became a popular cry. Grant, however, was taking the necessary precautions. He ordered seven U.S. Army companies to Washington and had them take up positions around the federal arsenal.

The Constitution was maddeningly vague about a situation such as this. Who would determine the winner of those 19 electoral votes? If the contest was given over to the Republican Senate, Hayes would win. If it was given over to the Democratic House of Representatives, Tilden would win. The Senate immediately passed a resolution calling for a bipartisan committee of four Republicans and three Democrats. The House of Representatives approved a similar resolution, but it called for four Democrats and three Republicans.

In order to avert civil war, the contest was placed in the hands of an electoral commission comprised of 15 members. Five members came from the House, five from the Senate, and five from the U.S. Supreme Court. The majority party in each legislative chamber would get three seats on the commission and the minority party would get two. The Supreme Court would be represented by two Republicans, two Democrats, and Justice David Davis, arguably the most trusted independent in the nation.

However, before the commission could take up its business, the Illinois Legislature elected Justice Davis to the U.S. Senate, making him unable to serve on the electoral commission. President Grant appointed Republican Joseph Philo Bradley to replace Davis on the Supreme Court and he also became the fifth justice to serve on the commission. The commission was now comprised of eight Republicans and seven Democrats, and not surprisingly, the vote was 8-7 in favor of Hayes in all three contested states. Hayes was announced the presidential victor: 185 electoral votes to 184.

Hayes took the presidential oath of office secretly, afraid that he would be assassinated if it was administered in public. He pledged to serve only one term. Democrats were outraged – newspapers referred to Hayes as "His Fraudulency," and "Rutherfraud." Tilden took the entire affair in stride and refused to continue the fight: "everybody knows that the man who was elected was not elected by the people. If my voice could reach throughout the country and be heard in its remotest hamlets, I would say: Be of good cheer. The Republic will survive. The institutions of our fathers will not expire in shame. The sovereignty of the people shall be rescued from this peril and will be reestablished."

The infamous era of corporate 'robber barons' followed on the heels of the Hayes election. Men like Rockefeller, Morgan,

Carnegie, Mellon, Vanderbilt, and Gould, had as much power as the President of the United States. The great merger wave began and created corporate monopolies in industries from steel to tobacco. Massive corporate public relations campaigns were mounted to convince Americans that bigness was good for everyone – that it increased efficiency and lowered prices – despite the diminution in competition.

Although the growing American economy enriched a few; conditions for most ordinary people were steadily deteriorating. By 1893, every sixth American worker was unemployed. Child labor was widespread; eleven million families subsisted on an average of $380 a year. Plummeting agricultural prices killed off a whole generation of small farmers. These conditions gave impetus to a growing clamor for unionization and that provided fertile ground for the thriving socialist movement taking root in America. Strikes and labor riots broke out from New York to Chicago to California. Secretary of State Walter Gresham alarmingly said that he saw "symptoms of revolution" spreading across the country.

On Saturday, May 1, 1888, union rallies were held for an eight-hour work day. The largest rally was in Chicago, where an estimated 90,000 people participated. In the next few days, 350,000 workers nationwide went on strike at 1,200 factories. On May 3, a fight broke out as replacement workers attempted to cross the picket lines in Chicago. Chicago police intervened and attacked the strikers, killing four people. A rally to protest the killings was held at Haymarket Square, then a bustling commercial center. The rally began peacefully on the evening of May 4, but when the police ordered the rally to disperse, a bomb was thrown killing one of the police officers. The police immediately opened fire. Seven policemen and four workers were killed; hundreds were wounded or injured.

Eight men were brought to trial. There was no evidence that any of the defendants had any connection with the bombing. However, Judge Joseph Gary openly declared at the trial: "You are on trial because you are anarchists, not because you threw the Haymarket bomb." All eight defendants were convicted on the theory that their speeches had encouraged some unknown bomber to commit the act. Seven of the defendants received the death sentence; one defendant was sentenced to fifteen years imprisonment.

On appeal, two of the death sentences were commuted to life in prison. One defendant committed suicide on the day of his hanging. On November 11, 1887, the other four defendants were hanged before a public audience. The Haymarket trial is often referred to as one of the most serious miscarriages of justice in U.S. history. A later investigation proved that the police provoked the incident. On June 26, 1893, Illinois Governor John Peter Altgeld signed pardons for the three men still in prison and publicly announced that all eight defendants were innocent. Obviously, the reversal came too late for those already executed.

Grover Cleveland, the Democratic governor of New York, was elected president in 1884 in a close election. Four years later the Republicans regained the White House, as Benjamin Harrison of Indiana ousted Cleveland in another very close election. Cleveland ran again in 1892, and this time his margin of victory was substantial.

Immediately upon assuming office, Cleveland's presidency was beset with major problems, especially the 'Great Panic' and Depression of 1893. Financially over-extended railroads went bankrupt, stock prices on Wall Street plummeted, banks called in loans, credit disappeared, 15,000 businesses failed, and 600 nationally chartered banks locked their doors. Unemployment rose to 2.5 million workers or 20 percent of the labor force. Many once secure middle-class homeowners could no longer meet their mortgage obligations and were either dispossessed or had to walk away from recently built homes.

In the bitter winter months, unemployed "tramps" crisscrossed the countryside, hitchhiking or riding on freight trains. Many appeared at the back doors of houses pleading for work or food. Stories of despair and suicide appeared daily in most newspapers. Those unaffected by the Depression accused the unemployed of laziness. A series of bitter and violent labor conflicts captured the nation's attention and divided the country along class lines. The lower and middle-class sympathized with the plight of the underpaid and unemployed, while the wealthy upper-class blamed the violence on the strikers and feared that anarchy was about to take over the reins of government.

In 1896, William Jennings Bryan of Nebraska became the presidential nominee of both the Democratic Party and the insurgent People's Party. Bryan, the thirty-six-year-old former congressman and newspaper editor, was the greatest popular orator of the age; an evangelist as much as a politician. More than anyone else, he represented the moralist in politics. He accused the Republicans of advocating policies intended to keep the rich in control of the common people. His platform called for the elimination of business monopolies and a promise that government would not interfere with the worker's right to strike.

William McKinley of Ohio, a rising Republican star, intended to be capitalism's expansionist champion. He believed that the politics of wealth, if presented boldly and without apology, could be transformed into a broad-based movement, and that workers and farmers could be convinced that what was good for the industrialists would also be good for them.

Capitalists like J.P. Morgan and John D. Rockefeller were convinced that if Bryan was elected, he would dismantle the industrial economy and disperse their fortunes. Labor leaders like Eugene Debs and Samuel Gompers endorsed Bryan, but employers warned their workers that if Bryan was elected their factories would close. The final vote was 271 electoral votes for McKinley; 176 for Bryan.

As soon as McKinley became president, he sent Congress a proposal calling for the annexation of Hawaii despite petitions of protest from Hawaiians. When Japan protested this move, fearing that it was the first step in a dangerous encroachment of American military power in the Pacific, the U.S. Navy dispatched reinforcements to Pearl Harbor. Tensions lessened when McKinley's proposal fell short of the two-thirds majority needed in the Senate to ratify annexation. However, American capitalism pressed forward with its expansionist plans.

With a Republican now firmly entrenched in the White House, J.P. Morgan took command of the national economy. Morgan's plan was for the politicians to assuage the public, while he and his business colleagues managed the economy. In order for Morgan's expansionist plan to work, the public's focus had to be diverted away from their economic plight at home and center instead on the complicated issues of foreign policy. This was not as easy as it sounds. There was no national security threat from abroad, and America was protected from foreign intrusion by two great oceans.

Theodore Roosevelt now entered the scene. TR, as he was known, came from a wealthy family, graduated from Harvard, dropped out of Columbia Law, hobnobbed aimlessly with high society, and then after 'sowing his oats,' decided he wanted to do something 'important' with his life. In 1897, urged on by Congressman Henry Cabot Lodge, President McKinley appointed the delighted thirty-nine year old TR to the post of assistant secretary of the navy. War has always been an expedient way to get out of a depression and Teddy Roosevelt echoed the sentiments of the industrialists, "I welcome almost any war for I believe this country needs one. Otherwise, we shall lose our virility and sink into a nation of mere hucksters, and that can only lead to decay." Teddy Roosevelt saw life like a western movie film; "a showdown between good and evil."

Playing a major part in creating "war fever" was the newspaper media. The national newspaper scene in the 1890s was fiercely competitive; in New York City alone there were fifteen daily newspapers and thirty weeklies. New printing technology allowed for large press runs, but it was also very expensive. Newspaper survival depended on obtaining significant advertising revenues and that depended on large circulations won from competitors. The result was lurid headlines and sensationalist stories.

Joseph Pulitzer was a Jewish immigrant who served in the Union cavalry during the Civil War and then settled in St. Louis where he took up journalism. He learned the rudiments of the trade on a German-language newspaper before gaining control of the *St. Louis Post-Dispatch*. However, New York was the great political and media arena, and Pulitzer wanted to be part of it. In 1883, he bought the losing *New York World* from financier Jay

Gould and quickly turned losses into profits by delivering a paper that was more titillating than accurate.

By 1898, Pulitzer had built a fortune, but success had come at a tremendous cost; his health was destroyed by the physical and mental strain of overwork. Almost completely blind, he was also plagued by a hypersensitivity to noise that forced him to spend much of his life in soundproof rooms. Despite his severe ailments, he found it impossible to surrender the excitement of putting out a daily newspaper - especially since he was now faced with the greatest challenge to his newspaper empire.

Before being expelled from Harvard, William Randolph Hearst worked on the *Harvard Lampoon* university newspaper and he was hooked. His first paying job came as a junior reporter for Pulitzer's *World*. He went home to San Francisco with a plan. Hearst's father, a rough-and-ready miner had struck it rich and now owned the city's losing newspaper. The young Hearst assured his father that he could turn the newspaper into a money-maker by using Joseph Pulitzer's methods - and he quickly did. Hearst's success drew him back to New York. He bought the *New York Journal*, and was soon battling Pulitzer for readership.

Territorial expansion was nothing new to American capitalists, but now the United States was fully settled and our borders were fixed and permanent. Further expansion could only come from foreign markets and access to the natural resources of other countries. Indiana Senator Albert Beveridge echoed the sentiments of American capitalists: "American factories are making more than the American people can use. Fate has written our policy for us. The trade of the world must and shall be ours."

These new foreign markets could no longer be found in Europe because European governments protected their domestic industries behind high tariff walls. American capitalism had to look elsewhere. In order to accomplish this ambitious global plan the United States needed a network of military bases around the world and the protection of a strong navy to defend any faraway economic interests. But, before such a program of economic expansion could be undertaken, an extensive propaganda campaign was needed to convince the American public. What ensued was the quickest and most profound reversal of public opinion in the history of our country.

Spain, an intensely pious Catholic country, had been one of the wealthiest nations in Europe during the fifteenth and sixteenth centuries, but by the seventeenth century its power and political influence had weakened dramatically. Although Spain's overseas empire had fallen apart, her prize possession was still Cuba, a lush tropical island just ninety miles off the southeastern tip of Florida, whose most successful industry was the raising of sugar cane by tens of thousands of slave laborers. Capitalist elites urged annexation of the island, and if Spain refused a fair monetary offer, the plan was to simply seize it.

By the end of the nineteenth century, the United States already dominated Cuba economically. Exports to the United States increased from 42 percent in 1859 to 87 percent by 1897. United States investments in Cuba were $50 million; trade at $100 million. In any fight over this tiny island, it would be virtually impossible for Spain to successfully defend its interests. The situation was perfect for American imperialist expansion. All the United States needed was a convenient excuse.

For ten years, a rebel movement that had been fighting for Cuba's independence. When it appeared to be gaining support, Spain sent General Valeriano Weyler to squash the rebellion. Newspaper stories about events in Cuba could interest U.S. readers only so far. Facts were boring and they soon gave way to very questionable accounts of what was going on in Cuba. Atrocity stories filled the daily pages of Joseph Pulitzer's *New York World* only to be topped by those printed by William Randolph Hearst's *New York Journal*.

Hearst sent the great American artist and photographer Frederic Remington to Cuba during a lull in the fighting. "There is no trouble here," Remington cabled Hearst, "there will be no war. I wish to return." Hearst quickly responded by telegram. "Please remain. You furnish the pictures; I'll furnish the war." Pulitzer's *New York World* fanned anti-Spanish sentiment with front page depictions like: "Blood on the roadsides, blood in the fields, and blood on the doorsteps. Blood, blood, and more blood! The old, the young, the weak, and the crippled - all are butchered without mercy."

Hearst was closely aligned with America's corporate interests and he urged the United States to go to war. War would divert attention away from the bad economy at home and begin our quest for a global empire – war would resolve everything. What was needed was a villain on whom the American public could focus its outrage. The King of Spain would not do; he was only a fourteen-year-old boy. Hearst settled on Spain's General Weyler. Daily accounts in Hearst newspapers depicted a series of blood-curdling stories that made Weyler the personification of evil. Fueled by these reports of inhumanity, Americans were becoming convinced that maybe an "intervention" in Cuba was the Christian thing to do. Spain, in an effort to diffuse all this talk about war, recalled General Weyler.

President McKinley now had to decide what to do. He believed that once Spain left Cuba, control of the country would shift over to America's powerful business interests. But, Cuban rebel leaders had other ideas; they were promising their people sweeping social reforms, starting with land redistribution, and that struck fear into the hearts of American capitalists who had all this money invested on the island.

Early in 1898, McKinley decided to send both Spain and Cuba a strong message. He ordered the battleship *Maine* to leave its place in the Atlantic and head for Havana. Officially the *Maine* was simply making a "friendly visit," but everyone knew that the battleship was serving as a "gunboat calling card," a symbol of America's power and determination to control the course of events in the Caribbean. For three weeks the *Maine* lay quietly at anchor in Havana. Then, on the night of February 15, 1898, the ship was torn apart by a tremendous explosion. More than 250 American sailors perished. News of the disaster electrified America.

The moment Hearst heard about the sinking of the *Maine*, he recognized it as a great opportunity to sell newspapers. For weeks he filled page after page with "scoops" and fabricated interviews with unnamed government officials that the battleship had been "destroyed by Spanish treachery." The *Journal's* daily circulation doubled in four weeks. Other newspapers joined the frenzy with the slogan, "Remember the Maine! To hell with Spain!"

The newspaper's campaign brought Americans to near-hysteria. Spanish officials denied the deed, conducted its own inquiry, and found no evidence of an eternal explosion. The Spanish inquiry concluded that the explosion must have resulted from some combustion aboard the ship. Understanding that the United States would not likely accept this conclusion, Spain proposed that the two countries hold a joint investigation, and also offered to submit the question to binding arbitration. President McKinley never replied to Spain's proposal.

The mystery of the *Maine* was not officially solved until 1911 when the U.S. decided that the *Maine* should not remain at the bottom of the sea. When the ship was raised to the surface it was discovered that the disaster was caused by an internal boiler explosion – it had nothing to do with the Spanish. Of course, by that time the war was over. The accident aboard the *Maine* provided the perfect excuse for President McKinley to ask Congress for a declaration of war. "War is our only option," declared the Hearst newspaper headlines.

Spain made a last ditch effort to resolve the crisis. McKinley dismissed all overtures as insincere - the Cuban situation, he maintained, could only be resolved by a force of arms. McKinley knew that any negotiated settlement would lead to an independent Cuba – an outcome that American business interests did not want. What the U.S wanted could only be won by military conquest.

The United States threat of military intervention also alarmed the Cuban revolutionary leaders. They believed that it would be better for Cuba to rise or fall on its own rather than contract debts of gratitude from such a powerful neighbor as the United States. Cuba's legal counsel in New York warned that American intervention into Cuba would be taken as "nothing less than a declaration of war by the United States against the Cuban revolution," and vowed that rebel forces would resist any American attempt to take the island by force of arms. "The Cuban people," he said, "will fight as tenaciously against the United States as it has against the armies of Spain."

In spite of these threats from the Cuban rebels, President McKinley was committed to war. On April 11, he delivered his war message to Congress. It began with one of the more notable deceptions in the annals of presidential messages. Conveniently ignoring Spain's concessions, he lied to Congress about having "exhausted" all diplomatic means to secure peace. The larger dictates of humanity, he said, called for the forcible intervention of the United States. "I ask the Congress to authorize and empower the president to take whatever measures are necessary to secure a full and final termination of hostilities between the Government of Spain and the people of Cuba; to secure on the island a stable government, and to use the military and naval forces of the United States as may be necessary for these purposes."

On April 19, Congress passed a joint resolution calling for the United States to go to war. The American people were jubilant; their domestic woes were temporarily forgotten. Americans greeted the war in a tumultuous holiday spirit, for in truth it was a holiday – a vacation from the years of economic struggle and disillusion. McKinley called for 125,000 military volunteers - more than twice that number poured into recruiting stations.

William Randolph Hearst's *Journal* proposed that an army regiment be formed from our finest athletes; he was certain that they would rout Spain by their sheer physical presence. William "Buffalo Bill" Cody offered to form a regiment of Native American Indians and ride into Cuba on horseback to resolve the situation. Frank James, brother of the infamous outlaw Jesse James, volunteered to lead a company of cowboys.

"It was a war entered into without misgivings and in the noblest frame of mind," the historian Walter Mills wrote thirty years later. "Seldom has history recorded a plainer case of military aggression; yet seldom has a war been started in so profound a conviction of its righteousness."

Events moved quickly in the weeks that followed. Assistant Secretary of the Navy Teddy Roosevelt, without clearing his decision with his superior or the president, ordered Commodore George Dewey to proceed to Manila Bay in the Spanish-owned Philippines and be ready to attack. When McKinley found out what Roosevelt had done, it was too late to reverse the action – to back down now would show weakness, something no president wants to do.

Tampa, Florida, was to be the jumping off point for materials and our troops going to Cuba, but there was a problem. The War Department wanted the invasion postponed until after the summer, fearing Yellow Fever and other tropical diseases. When the president refused to postpone the invasion, the War Department picked 10,000 soldiers to be the first force into Cuba – half of these men were black Americans thought to be immune from such diseases because of their tropical African ancestry. These units were even called the "immunes." When four black regiments arrived in Tampa, there was consternation and anger by the local citizens at the sight of all these blacks in their pristine white city. Riots broke out, but they subsided as soon as the blacks were shuffled off to war.

Theodore Roosevelt quit his post as assistant secretary of the navy and formed the first volunteer cavalry unit, which the press labeled Roosevelt's "Rough Riders." Six weeks later, American soldiers landed on Cuba's southeastern coast. They fought three one-day battles, the most famous being the one in which Teddy Roosevelt, dressed in a special uniform that he ordered from Brooks Brothers in New York, led a charge up San Juan Hill. On July 3, American cruisers destroyed the few decrepit Spanish naval vessels anchored at Cuba's harbor and the Spanish forces ended their resistance.

On August 12, barely two months after the American landing in Cuba, diplomats representing Spain and the United States met at the White House and signed a "protocol of peace" that ended the war. Only 385 Americans had been killed in action, but about 2,000 died of wounds and disease. In the words of Secretary of State John Hay, this was "a splendid little war."

With victory won, the time had come for the United States to begin its withdrawal. Under a congressional mandate called the Teller Amendment, once victory was achieved, the United States had to "leave the government and control of the Cuban island to its people." Instead the United States did the opposite. President

McKinley proclaimed the "absolute necessity of controlling Cuba for our national defense," and rejected the Teller Amendment as "a self-denying ordinance that was passed only in a moment of national hysteria."

Cuban patriots were incensed. They had promised their people that independence would stabilize the country and promote social justice. American capitalism wanted something quite different. McKinley said our troops had to stay in Cuba because of the country's political and economic instability. When General Leonard Wood, the new American military governor in Cuba was asked what was meant by a stable Cuban government, he replied, "When money can be borrowed at six percent and American capitalists are willing to invest on the island, then a condition of stability will have been reached."

That autumn, Congress passed the Platt Amendment - a crucial document in the history of American foreign policy. The Amendment gave the United States a way to control Cuba by maintaining a submissive local regime that took orders only from Washington. The United States would apply this system in many parts of the Caribbean and Central America, where to this day it is known as *plattismo*.

Under provisions of the Platt Amendment, the United States agreed to end its occupation of Cuba as soon as the Cubans accepted a constitution that gave the United States the right to maintain a permanent military base in Cuba (Guantanamo); the right to veto any treaty between Cuba and any other country; the right to supervise the Cuban treasury; and the right to invade Cuba whenever the United States saw fit. In essence, the Platt Amendment gave Cubans permission to rule themselves as long as the United States could veto any decision they made. Cuban democratic independence became a farce; it could last only as long as it served America's economic interests.

With Spain gone from Cuba, American capitalists took over the railroads, mines, and sugar properties. Within a few years $30 million of additional American capital was invested. A major U.S. company, United Fruit, took over Cuba's sugar industry and bought 1.9 million acres of land for twenty cents an acre. The American

Tobacco Company grabbed all the tobacco rights. By 1901, at least 80 percent of the export of Cuba's minerals was in the hands of Bethlehem Steel.

A few weeks after disposing of the Spanish in Cuba, the United States occupied Puerto Rico without firing a shot. On May 1, the United States ended Spanish rule in the Philippines. Admiral Dewey destroyed the Spanish fleet with astonishing ease after giving his famous command, "You may fire when ready, Gridley."

When the final peace treaty with Spain was signed in Paris, the island of Guam was also ceded to the United States. To complete a successful year of expansion, legislators declared Hawaii a "naval and military necessity and the key to the Pacific," and finalized the annexation of Hawaii.

Corporate America was fascinated with the prospect of selling goods in China. The Philippines, with its close proximity to China, was a natural springboard for American traders on the way to the Orient. However, Japan saw the American move into the Asian market as imperialist; the United States professed self-determination and non-involvement in Asian affairs, but the U.S. had grabbed the Philippines and were building a powerful long-range navy. It did not take much insight for Japan to figure out that the United States was seeking a military as well as economic presence in Asia.

American expansionism was now in for a big shock. The Philippine rebels refused to lay down their arms. They did not want to become an American colony. They wanted the Philippines to be an independent nation and if they had to fight the Americans instead of the Spanish to get it, so be it. In America's early history our colonies had fought powerful England - now the process was being reversed – the United States became the powerful imperialist trying to deprive a small native population of its independence.

The American public had accepted McKinley's reasons for going to war over Cuba, but they could not fathom what this war with the Philippines was all about. The public rationalized that somehow it was indirectly part of the conflict with Spain. The truth about the importance of the Philippines as a gateway to trade in the Orient was too complicated and mundane for the American

Lies and Deceits

public. It was time for the U.S. to invent a more plausible excuse that ordinary Americans would accept.

President McKinley was a devout Christian living in an era of religious revivalism. He informed Congress that while wrestling with the Philippine question, he fell to his knees, "and prayed to Almighty God for light and guidance," and God, according to McKinley, answered him. God told McKinley that it was the duty of the United States "to civilize and Christianize" the Filipino people. "One late night God came to me," McKinley revealed. "There is nothing left for us to do but to educate the Filipinos, uplift them, Christianize them, and by God's grace do the very best we can for them as our fellow men for whom Christ also died."

It is estimated that at least half a million Filipinos died as a result of McKinley's 'chat' with God. It took the United States almost four years to crush the rebellion. We used 70,000 troops - four times as many as landed in Cuba. American firepower was overwhelmingly superior to anything the Filipino rebels could put together. As one American soldier recalled after shooting scores of Filipinos as they swam across a river in retreat: "It was more fun than a turkey shoot." In the very first battle, Admiral Dewey steamed up the Pasig River and fired 500-pound shells into the Filipino trenches. Dead Filipinos were piled up so high that a British witness said: "This is not war; it is simply massacre and murderous butchery." Reports of our atrocities were censored and never reached the American mainland.

While the United States Army was carrying out these atrocities, Secretary of War Elihu Root was insuring the American public about our humanitarian mission: "An American soldier is different from soldiers of all other countries. He is the advance guard of liberty and justice, of law and order, and of peace and happiness." American history books to this day refer to the war in the Philippines as an "insurrection," as if the Filipinos were rebelling against legitimate U.S. authorities. In reality, it was American conquest in one of the cruelest conflicts in the annals of Western imperialism.

On December 21, McKinley issued an "executive letter" proclaiming American sovereignty over the Philippines and condescendingly referring to the Filipinos as "my little brown brothers." He may well have convinced the American public that it was all God's doing, but American business elites knew it was really the economic gods of capitalism. In the Senate, Albert Beveridge spoke on behalf of America's mission:

"Mr. President, the times call for candor. The Philippines are ours forever - and just beyond the Philippines are China's unlimited markets. We will not retreat from either. We will not renounce our part in the mission of our race to be the trustee under God of the civilization of the world. The Pacific is our ocean. Where shall we turn for consumers of our surplus? Geography answers the question. China is our natural customer. The Philippines give us a base at the door of the entire East.

There are not 100 men among the Filipinos who comprehend what Anglo-Saxon self-government means, and there are over five million people there to be governed. It has been charged that our conduct of the war there has been cruel. Senators, it has been the reverse. We must remember that we are not dealing with Americans or Europeans; we are dealing with Orientals."

On September 6, 1901, while standing in a receiving line at the Pan-American Exposition in Buffalo, Leon Frank Czolgosz, a twenty-eight-year-old Russian-Polish immigrant reached the front of the line and shot President McKinley twice at point-blank range. Members of McKinley's security team, as well as citizens in the crowd, immediately subdued Czolgosz, beating him so severely it was initially thought he might not live to stand trial.

McKinley died from his wounds on September 14. A special grand jury quickly indicted the assassin. Czolgosz was assigned two lawyers who publicly declared they were sorry to have to plead the case of such a depraved criminal as the assassin of "our beloved" president. The new president, Teddy Roosevelt, proclaimed that "the anarchist is the enemy of all mankind." Czolgosz was convicted and sentenced to death. His last words before being electrocuted were: "I killed the president because he was the enemy of the good people - the good working people. I did it for the American people. I am not sorry for my crime."

Smedley Butler was a prominent major-general in the U.S. Marine Corps who joined the service in 1898 to fight in the Spanish-American War. After that he was involved in American military interventions in China, the Philippines, Nicaragua, Panama, Honduras, Mexico, and Haiti. On two occasions he was awarded the Congressional Medal of Honor. However, at the end of his brilliant military career, Butler came to see his actions in a new light. In 1935, he wrote,

> "I spent thirty-three years and four months in active military service as a member of this country's most agile military force, the Marine Corps. I served in all commissioned ranks from Second Lieutenant to Major-General. During that period, I spent most of my time being a high class muscle-man for big business, Wall Street, and for the bankers. In short, I was a racketeer, a gangster for capitalism.
>
> I helped make Mexico safe for American oil interests. I helped make Haiti and Cuba a decent place for the National City Bank boys to collect revenues. I helped in the raping of half a dozen Central American republics for the benefits of Wall Street. I helped purify Nicaragua for the international banking house of Brown Brothers. I brought light to the Dominican Republic for American sugar interests. In China, I helped Standard Oil go along its way unmolested. During those years, I had, as the boys in the back room would say, a swell racket. Looking back on it, I feel that I could have given Al Capone a few hints. The best he could do was to operate his racket in three districts; I operated on three continents."

CHAPTER EIGHT

WORLD WAR I

"The first casualty when war comes is the truth."
Senator Hiram Johnson

"War does not determine who is right - only who is left."
Bertrand Russell

World War I was a pivotal moment in history – it closed out the old era and ushered in the modern world. Everyone expected hostilities to break out in Europe, but nobody thought it would mushroom into a world war, or the kind of war that had never been experienced before. World War I represents the Industrial Revolution coming to warfare – killing machines were predominant for the first time – artillery, air power, tanks, poison gas, and machine guns mowed down wave after wave of onrushing infantry by the millions.

When the war was finally over, there would be 20 million dead and another 21 million wounded – and it solved nothing. A whole generation of young people disappeared from the earth in a war that was merely a prelude for the more destructive war to come.

How and why did the United States get involved in a territorial war in Europe? Regardless of the slogans and political rhetoric, whenever America goes to war, it is always about economics.

Early in 1906, banker Jacob Schiff told a group of colleagues that if the United States did not modernize its banking and currency systems, its economy would, in effect, fall off a cliff - that the country would "have such a panic as will make all previous panics look like child's play." Yet the country failed to reform its financial institutions, and conditions deteriorated steadily over the next twenty months. During that period, there was a worldwide credit shortage, the stock market crashed twice, and the newly established Dow Jones industrial average lost half its value.

In October 1907, terrified depositors lined up to get their money before the banks failed. The United States at the time had no Federal Reserve System, the U.S. Treasury lacked any real political authority, and President Theodore Roosevelt was too busy hunting in Louisiana to curtail his vacation plans.

J.P. Morgan, the 70-year-old iconic private banker, quietly took charge of the situation. In the absence of a central bank, Morgan had for decades been acting as the country's unofficial lender of last resort, gathering reserves and supplying capital to the markets in periods of crisis. For two harrowing weeks in 1907, with the whole world watching, he operated like a military general, bringing two other leading bankers, James Stillman of National City Bank and George Baker of the First National Bank, into a senior "trio" to make executive decisions.

The Morgan team figured out which companies were impossibly over-leveraged and should be allowed to fail, which were basically sound but merely crippled by the panic, and which were too big to be allowed to fail. Once they determined which companies should be saved, they supplied them with the needed cash to survive the crisis. When the New York Stock Exchange nearly closed because financial institutions were calling in loans and choking off the market's money supply, Morgan came up with $24 million to save the day. When New York City ran out of cash to meet its payroll and interest obligations, Morgan conjured up a $30 million loan that prevented default.

At the end of the first week's financial panic, Morgan called fifty bankers to his private library on East 36th Street, locked the doors, and did not let them out until they had signed on to a final $25 million 'stimulus' package. Though Morgan had a large sense of public duty, he was not acting out of pure altruism. His clients - many of them Europeans, had invested billions with Morgan who in turn pumped the money into the growing American economy.

Thomas Woodrow Wilson was born in Staunton, Virginia, and grew up in Augusta, Georgia. His parents, Presbyterian minister Dr. Joseph Ruggles Wilson and Janet "Jessie" Woodrow, both came from highly religious families. Thoroughly southern in sympathy, they bequeathed their loyalties to a son who never forgot hearing with dread the news of Lincoln's election and of later seeing a defeated Jefferson Davis paraded in handcuffs.

Dyslexic, the young Woodrow initially displayed little brilliance; but he persisted, taught himself shorthand, and attended North Carolina's Davidson College before graduating from Princeton in 1879. He studied law at the University of Virginia and obtained a doctorate in political science from Johns Hopkins University. He taught at Bryn Mawr and Wesleyan before returning to Princeton as a professor of jurisprudence and political science, establishing himself as the university's most popular and influential lecturer.

In June 1902, Princeton trustees unanimously elected him president; the first person to be so honored without formal theological training. In 1910, supported by what was then known as the Money Trust, Wilson ran as a Democrat for his first elective office; governor of New Jersey. After Wilson won the governorship, his backers immediately set their sights on the presidential election of 1912. Wilson campaigned hard and won more presidential primaries than any other Democratic candidate, but he came into the convention a decided underdog. When the convention failed to agree on a candidate, they turned to Wilson on the forty-seventh ballot.

At the Republican Convention, the incumbent President William Howard Taft secured the nomination, trouncing former President Teddy Roosevelt. A new third party, the Progressive Party or the "Bull Moose" Party was immediately formed and selected Roosevelt as their presidential candidate. It was hard not to like Teddy Roosevelt; he was bigger than life, a force of nature, maybe even bulletproof.

On the evening of October 14, 1912, as Roosevelt was getting into a car on his way to a campaign speech in Milwaukee, a thirty-six year old Bavarian immigrant, John Schrank drew a .38-caliber revolver from his coat and shot Teddy Roosevelt. The bullet tore through the fifty-page speech Roosevelt had nestled inside his jacket pocket, through his metal spectacle case, and ripped three inches into TR - just short of his vital organs. Roosevelt, being TR,

Lies and Deceits

didn't even realize he was hit until a bodyguard noticed the bullet hole in his jacket and the blood gushing out of his body.

Undaunted by the shooting, Roosevelt refused to go to a hospital. Instead, he continued on to the Coliseum where he told the wildly enthusiastic crowd: "I'm going to ask you to be very quiet, and please excuse me for making a short speech. I'll do the best I can, but you see there's a bullet in my body. But it's nothing. I'm not hurt badly." He unbuttoned his coat and vest, displaying to the horrified crowd his blood-soaked white shirt. He then spoke for ninety minutes.

After TR finished his speech, he was helped off the platform and rushed to the hospital. By the time he returned to the campaign, everyone knew the election was over. Said one Vermont Republican newspaper editor: "Vote for Taft, pray for Roosevelt, and bet on Wilson." The split between Taft and Roosevelt assured Wilson of victory; winning with only 41.8 percent of the popular vote.

Wilson took his victory calmly, believing it was predestined: "God has ordained that I should be the next President of the United States. No mortal can prevent it." Sigmund Freud would later offer his analysis of Wilson's comments and mental state: "A man who is capable of taking the illusions of religion so literally and is so sure of a special personal intimacy with the Almighty is unfit for relations with ordinary mortals."

Most of Europe at this time was made up of empires, not independent nation-states. The Hapsburg Empire contained Austria, the Czech Republic, Hungary, Slovakia and parts of what is now Bosnia, Croatia, Poland, and Romania. The Romanov Empire stretched into Asia, and included Russia, Poland, and the Ukraine. The Ottoman Empire covered modern Turkey and parts of today's Bulgaria, Greece, Romania and Serbia, and extended through much of the Middle East and North Africa. Throughout the 1890s, these European countries were taking sides, making alliances, and creating rivalries. All these machinations and secret intrigues made Europe a ticking bomb – all that was needed was a spark to ignite a major conflagration.

The events in Europe that led up to World War I are too complicated to go into depth here, but there were several key elements. The Crimean War of 1853-1856 was the prelude – Imperial Russia was on one side, and an alliance of France, Britain, the Kingdom of Sardina, and the Ottoman Empire on the other side. Peace, arranged in 1856, lasted until France was crushed by the German states in the Franco-Prussian War of 1870–1871. At the conclusion of these hostilities, Prussian Chief Minister Otto von Bismarck combined thirty-nine previously independent states into a unified German Empire. This powerful new Germany, right in the middle of Europe, was strong enough to scare France and England in the west and Russia in the east. Great Britain, especially, saw this new Germany as a threat to its dominance and control of Europe.

The Ottoman Empire at this time was on the verge of disintegration. This empire had endured for five centuries, and for half that time it was the biggest state in Europe, the Mediterranean, and the Middle East. The so-called 'Great Powers' had different aims about the Ottoman Empire. Russia wanted access to the Mediterranean and followed a pan-Slavic foreign policy in which they supported Bulgaria and Serbia. Britain wished to deny Russia access to the Mediterranean, so they supported the integrity of the Ottoman Empire, though it also supported a limited expansion of Greece as a backup plan. France also wanted to strengthen her position in the region. Austria-Hungary favored a continuation of the Ottoman Empire, since both were multinational entities ruled by small elites and the collapse of the one could affect the other. Serbian nationals wanted to unite all Serbian territories into one united Serbia. However, the Hapsburg Empire, with its large Serbian and Croatian populations, was strongly against any such unification. If this all sounds complicated - it was.

In 1912 and 1913, two successive military conflicts deprived the Ottoman Empire of almost all its remaining territory in Europe. Serbia and Bulgaria declared war on Turkey and threatened to bring in Austria and Russia, which would ignite a general European war. Almost half a million people left their traditional homelands, either voluntarily or by force. Muslims left regions under the control of Bulgarians, Greeks, and Serbs; Bulgarians abandoned Greek-controlled areas of Macedonia; Greeks fled from regions of Macedonia ceded to Bulgaria and Serbia. These Balkan Wars became the first phase of the greater and wider conflict that would result in the First World War.

The reaction of the world's financial markets was immediate and profound; all economic indicators declined abruptly. Nothing creates more economic uncertainty than war. Interest rates rose and gold began to flow out of the United States as European banks liquidated their American investments. The crisis passed when Russia backed down, but the world remained an unstable place. An international wave of assassination and terrorist acts stirred anxieties: the assassination of an Austrian empress; a Russian tsar; kings of Italy, Serbia, and Portugal; prime ministers of Spain and Russia; and the president of France.

Then, on June 28, 1914, Archduke Franz Ferdinand, heir to the throne of Austria, was assassinated at Sarajevo by Gavrilo Princip, a Serb nationalist. This led Austria-Hungary to declare war on Serbia. Austria did not want a major European war; it just wanted to punish Serbia for murdering the Archduke and to put an end to Serbia's plots to pull apart Austria's empire. But, the retaliation by Austria-Hungary activated a series of military alliances that set off a chain reaction of war declarations.

In defense of its ally Serbia, Russia started to mobilize its troops. Germany supported Austria-Hungary and prepared for war. France, forever hostile to Germany supported Russia, which meant that Germany had to prepare for a two-front war, with the French attacking in Alsace and Russia marching against Prussia. Great Britain decided that if Germany invaded Belgium, British "honor" demanded that she fight alongside France and against Germany. And so it came to pass: everyone was at war with one another.

Socialists saw the war as an opportunity to advance their cause. They urged the workers of each country to stop war production and refuse to serve in the army. To the dismay of Socialist leaders, the workers did no such thing. Instead, nationalism prevailed as each side to the conflict used propaganda and patriotic speeches to create mass support for the war. Sons and fathers rushed to enlist as marching bands blared while crowds cheered and praised God that "war had arrived at last."

America resolved not to get involved in this European mess. We favored Britain, France, Italy, Russia, and Spain against Germany, Austria-Hungary, and the Ottoman Empire, but it was their fight, not ours. Over one-third of the United States was made up of immigrants or were the children of immigrants. Few German-Americans wanted to fight against Germany and fewer Irish wanted to fight for England. Other immigrants had little desire to fight for or against Italy or Austria or Russia.

American capitalists, however, saw the war as a golden opportunity for making money. During the three year period 1914-1917, the United States sold as much armaments as it could produce to its friends in Europe. American exports more than doubled. The country's trade surplus was five times prewar levels. American munitions sales abroad, just $40 million in 1914, were $1.3 billion in 1916. United States exports of wheat went from 18 million bushels to 98 million. Net farm income more than doubled. Overall, the gross national product of the United States increased 21 percent while manufacturing increased 25 percent.

The wartime profits of DuPont rose from $6 million a year to $58 million as they supplied the European allies with 40 percent of their munitions. The war transformed DuPont from a large gunpowder company into a chemical industrial giant. DuPont's military contracts in the four years of war were 276 times what it was before the war. Up until 1914, the largest contract Bethlehem Steel ever signed was for $10 million, but in November of 1914 they signed a $135 million deal with England for guns, shells, and submarines. Bethlehem's profits went from $6 million a year to $49 million. U.S. Steel doubled its yearly earnings; Anaconda Copper went from $10 million a year in profits to $34 million; International Nickel from $4 million to $73 million. By 1918, more than 14,000 planes were being constructed in the United States – they were virtually 'flying' off the assembly line.

The United States watched the war in Europe from the safety of being far across the Atlantic Ocean. We had been in a recession in 1914, but thanks to the war in Europe, American industry was now prospering. With things going well, what made America get involved in this European madness?

At the time of the war, U.S. trade was ten times more with Britain and France than with Germany. Both Britain and France owed American bankers and Wall Street huge amounts of money. The United States may not have been at war, but our entire economy was at risk.

Our European allies paid for their purchases by liquidating what they could: goods, gold, and eventually foreign investments. The British treasury had to liquidate $2 billion in U.S. securities to pay for the armaments from America. They turned their securities over to J.P. Morgan, who managed to sell them quietly without adversely impacting stock values. Morgan's commission amounted to $30 million.

Even with this liquidation, there was not enough money for Britain to prosecute the war. They would have liked to borrow money directly from the United States, but the U.S. Congress declared that a loan to any nation at war was inconsistent with American neutrality. However, Wall Street has always been able to get around the dictates of Congress and the will of the people.

In September 1915, the Morgan Bank arranged a private loan of $500 million to the British government, far and away the largest bank loan in history up to that point; but this was only the beginning. A year later, Wilson lifted the ban on loans, arguing that loans to belligerents were not a violation of neutrality. Soon, Morgan arranged loans totaling $9.6 billion to Britain and France, a sum equal to eight times the entire American national debt. The result was that the United States was totally bound to the success of the Allies.

With the war in Europe going badly for our side, J.P. Morgan became alarmed, and made his concerns known to President Wilson on November 28, 1916. That day, the price of American war stocks plunged. Within a week, values in the securities market fell by $1 billion. Britain was now in a desperate financial crisis. German submarines were sinking her merchant ships faster than they could be built, and she only had a three week supply of wheat left to feed the country. She was desperate for U.S. food, munitions, and other supplies, but she had lost the means to pay for these goods. Her only hope was that the U.S. would enter the war on the side of England.

The situation in Russia is critical to understanding the war and its aftermath. Back in 1904, Russia and Japan went to war over imperial ambitions in Manchuria and Korea. To the consternation of the world – Russia lost! The thought that an Asian nation could defeat a major European power was incomprehensible. It was the first time it had happened in the modern era. European nations considered any imperialism on their part as morally justified - after all, Europe represented Christianity, commerce, and civilization, even as they pursued god, gold and glory.

One year after this humiliating defeat a revolution led by Vladimir Lenin rocked Russia, but was defeated by the Czarist government. Lenin went into exile, but his determination to change Russia did not abate. Things did not get better for Russia during World War I as they suffered defeat after defeat at the hands of the German-Austrian forces. Dissatisfaction in Russia with their government's conduct of the war grew.

In March 1917, demonstrations in St Petersburg culminated in the abdication of Tsar Nicholas II. This led to confusion and chaos both at the war front and at home and the Russian Army became increasingly ineffective. Discontent led to a rise in the popularity of the Bolshevik Party. Lenin's promise to pull Russia out of the war gained enormous popular support. The triumph of the Bolsheviks in November was quickly followed in December by an armistice with Germany. Russia ceded Finland, the Baltic provinces, parts of Poland and the Ukraine to Germany, and withdrew completely from the war. Russia's withdrawal was seen across the world as either a great step forward for the will of the people, or a dreadful catastrophe that would destabilize the world.

Lenin, however, was unconcerned about world opinion or the territory he just gave away. He accomplished what he wanted – he got Russia out of the war. He told his comrades that the peace treaty with Germany should not be seen as a defeat, "Sometimes you have to take a step back in order to take two steps forward." Lenin could now concentrate on solidifying his power, establish a new communist state in Russia, and export his revolution to the world.

With Russia out of the war and Germany no longer having to fight on two fronts, it was becoming clear that Wall Street's loans to Britain and France were in serious jeopardy. In addition to the loans, those two countries owed American business interests billions for unpaid goods. If our two Allies lost the war, it would create an insurmountable catastrophe for American banks and our major corporate interests. The losses, many believed, would be unsustainable. After a series of secret meetings in Washington, President Wilson became convinced that the only solution was for the United States to go to war to rescue American capitalism.

Going to war to save wealthy American investment bankers and U.S. companies that had made millions in war profits was "not going to fly" with labor or Middle America. Americans were not going to march off to be killed in faraway Europe because capitalists faced financial ruin by backing the wrong side. An Englishman who reported back to his government after a fact-finding tour of America wrote, "The great bulk of Americans simply do not believe that the present conflict, whatever its upshot, touches their national security or endangers their power to hold fast to their ideals of politics and society and ethics."

Wilson had been reelected in 1916 on the slogan, "He kept us out of war." The American people took for granted that the war in Europe had nothing to do with them. It was virtually unanimous that America would and should remain neutral. To most Americans the carnage in Europe was simply the inevitable outcome of Europe's ancient rivalries and their contemptible appetites for territory and power. Americans could see no special virtue in either side of the conflict. If a public opinion poll had been taken, Germany was probably slightly more detestable than Britain.

Wilson's problem was how to mobilize American public support and patriotic passions for war against Germany. It would be fatal if the electorate divined his real intentions or doubted his sincere determination to keep the peace. He realized that he could only bring America into the war if it appeared that Germany was forcing war on America.

Wilson began his campaign by being openly critical of foreign-born American citizens who opposed his pro-British foreign policy. In his message to Congress, he said, "The gravest threats against our national peace and safety have been uttered within our own borders. There are citizens of the United States, I blush to admit, born under other flags, but welcomed by our generous naturalization laws to the full freedom and opportunity of America, who have poured the poison of disloyalty into the very arteries of our national life."

A major concern during the European conflict was what was happening on the high seas. Passengers on trans-Atlantic ocean liners were under the jurisdiction of whatever ship they traveled on. However, they traveled at their own risk. When the British mined German waters and blew up German ships, German submarines retaliated by sinking British vessels. It became dangerous for American travelers to sail on either British or German ships. This risk could be avoided by the simple expedient of booking passage on a neutral ship.

Wilson, instead of insisting that Americans keep off ships of belligerent nations, sent a note to the German government that "if German submarines caused the death of American citizens on the high seas, the United States would view the act as an indefensible violation of its neutrality rights." The neutral United States was forbidding the German government, on pain of extreme consequences, to sink an enemy ship because Americans chose to be aboard. Quite deliberately, Wilson was pushing the United States into a collision course with Germany.

Sure enough, on the afternoon of May 7, a German submarine fired a torpedo into the *Lusitania*, a British Cunard liner carrying 1,257 passengers, including 159 Americans, 702 crew members, and 4,200 cases of rifle ammunition. In the remarkably brief span of eighteen minutes, the mighty vessel sank. Among the 1,195 lives that were lost, 124 were American. Our entire country was thrown into a state of shock. The European war that seemed so remote had suddenly reached out without warning and seized America by the throat.

However, the sinking of a British liner, as horrible as it was, simply did not seem to the American people a just cause for war. Instead, the American public began voicing sharp disapproval of Americans who had chosen to travel on it. No one had forced them to sail on the British liner. When the press reported that the *Lusitania* carried a cargo of munitions, American indignation found yet another venue: the audacity of the British trying to protect their shipment of war materials with a shield of American travelers – it was akin to putting women and children in front of an advancing army.

When Wilson realized that the country was not going to support a war to defend the rights of rich Americans traveling on luxury liners, he decided to establish the Committee on Public Information (CPI), a government-run propaganda agency to influence American public opinion. New York publicist George Creel was retained to design a public relations campaign that would swing American opinion to support Britain.

Wilson understood that it is more important to use propaganda to control the minds of the masses in a democracy than it is in a totalitarian state where political terror will do the trick. A new art developed in America; manufacturing consent through media propaganda. What George Creel set out to prove was that the mind can be trained to conform to whatever the state says. Within six months the CPI turned a pacifist population into a hysterical, war-mongering nation that wanted to destroy everything that was German.

In January 1917, President Wilson, broke off diplomatic relations with Germany. A month later came the so-called Zimmermann telegram incident. On January 16, the German foreign minister, Arthur Zimmermann, cabled the German ambassador in Mexico coded instructions for a counter-move against America *should* the United States declare war on Germany. British agents intercepted and deciphered the telegram. The famous cable read:

> "We intend to begin unrestricted submarine warfare on the first of February. We shall endeavor in spite of this to keep the United States neutral. In the event of this not succeeding, we make Mexico a proposal of alliance on the following basis: make war together, make peace together, generous financial support, and an understanding on our part that Mexico is to re-conquer the lost territory in Texas, New Mexico, and Arizona."

The cable was to be delivered when and if the United States entry into the war was a certainty. There was nothing villainous about Zimmermann's instructions. It was a war strategy aimed against America that was contingent on the United States waging war against Germany.

The Zimmermann telegram was just what Wilson needed. The CPI propaganda machinery went into action. It didn't take long for American public opinion to become manipulated and outraged. The Federation of Churches publicly announced its "intention to mobilize its Christian strength behind President Wilson." On Sunday March 11, churchmen in every American city urged their parishioners to join the president in the great forthcoming struggle.

The American historian, Charles Beard, called Wilson's reasons for going to war all lies. Morality and making the world safe for democracy was pure bunk, Beard said. Citing the plight of several million American blacks, Beard suggested that we as a nation could find extensive outlets for our moral outrages right here at home. "If we as a nation want to spread our moral values to the rest of the world let us start right here at home by setting an example, rather than imposing our values on others. How can a nation that has failed to get its own house in order have the effrontery to assume that we can solve the problems of Asia and Europe?"

But Beard's plea was in vain. With public opinion now on Wilson's side, he asked Congress for a declaration of war - less than a month after his "I kept our boys out of war" pledge that secured his second presidential term. Wilson declared that the

German imperial government had driven the United States into the position of a belligerent because of the Zimmermann telegram. The United States, according to Wilson, had no alternative except to reply by force. "The world," according to Wilson, "must be made safe for democracy. America is privileged to spend her blood and her might for the principles that gave her birth."

Wilson depicted Germany's "outlaw U-boats" as "warfare against mankind." This was America's opportunity to imprint its values on the Old World, he exhorted the Congress. "We created this nation not to serve ourselves, but to serve mankind." Wilson promised it would be a short war and afterwards there would be a just and lasting peace. It would be "a war to end all wars." When Wilson finished his brief address, everyone in the packed chamber of the House rose to their feet; clapping, shouting, and enthusiastically waving small American flags.

However, a small dissenting voice challenged the president. Senator Robert La Follette of Wisconsin took the floor to deliver one of the bravest speeches ever made in the U.S. Senate. With a cold and noble fury, La Follette proceeded to tear to shreds, pretense by pretense, distortion by distortion, the glib propaganda for war that the president foisted upon the American public. La Follette conceded that "in time of war the citizen must surrender some rights for the common good," but he argued that this did not include the "right of free speech." To the contrary, even "more than in times of peace it is necessary that the channels of free public discussion be open and unclogged so that citizens may freely discuss every important phase of the war, including its causes, the manner in which it is being conducted, and the terms upon which peace should be made."

La Follette continued: "If Germany's submarine warfare is against the commerce of all nations as President Wilson insists, why is the United States the only nation that finds it necessary to declare war on that account? It was not Germany who first sank neutral ships without warning – it was England that sowed the entire North Sea with submarine mines. Yet, the Wilson administration agreed to the lawless act of Great Britain and never uttered a word of protest. There can be no greater violation of our neutrality than the requirement that one of two belligerents shall adhere to a certain code, but not the other. Because of Wilson's false neutrality, America has lost the character of a neutral."

As La Follette spoke, senators one by one got up from their seats and left the senate chamber. It was not a pleasant speech for most of them to hear, but La Follette was not really speaking to his fellow senators. In a sense he was not even speaking to the American people. More than anything else, he was speaking for the record, for history.

"The power of the people," he concluded, "sometimes sleeps; sometimes it seems the sleep of death, but the sovereign power of the people never dies. It may be suppressed for a time; it may be misled, be fooled, and silenced. I think, Mr. President, that it is being denied expression now. I think there will come a day when it will have expression. The poor, sir, who are the ones called upon to rot in the trenches, have no organized power, have no press to voice their will on this question of war and peace, but at some time they will be heard. There will come an awakening, and on that day of awakening, hopefully they will remember not the glib, dishonest phrases of a hypocrite president, but the dense honest utterance of the valiant senator from Wisconsin."

When La Follette finished his speech, with tears of grief and unspent anger streaming down his face, one reporter in the press gallery turned to his friend and said: "This is the greatest speech either of us will ever hear. It will not be answered because it is unanswerable." A few hours later the Senate voted for war, 82 to 6. The next day the House voted with the Senate, 373 to 50. On April 6, 1917, Wilson at last had his war.

Not only did Congress give Wilson his war, they gave him lavish war powers. The president was authorized to requisition whatever supplies the army deemed necessary, to fix prices, take possession of mines, factories, railways, steamships, all means of communication, and license the importation, manufacture, storage, and distribution of all necessities. Wilson discontinued the eight-hour work day for federal employees and took over industries that he deemed hobbled by labor strife. In a series

Lies and Deceits

of cases decided after the war, the U.S. Supreme Court upheld virtually all the president's actions.

"In war," Chief Justice White would write, "the scope of governmental power becomes highly malleable." According to the Court, the exigencies of war justified an enormous expansion of the powers of the chief executive. The eminent Harvard law professor, Zechariah Chafee, disagreed with the Court: "The war served merely a pretext; of that there can be little doubt. In a war fought three thousand miles from our shores, Americans under Wilson lost every liberty they could possibly be deprived of."

Although Wilson remains enshrined in textbook mythology as the "great idealist," the historical record is quite different. Between 1914 and 1918, while Wilson was pontificating about the "rights of small nations to self determination" and that "no nation had the right to interfere in the affairs of another country," the United States landed troops in Mexico in 1914, Haiti in 1915, the Dominican Republic in 1916, Mexico again in 1916, Cuba in 1917, and Panama in 1918. The United States occupied the Dominican Republic for eight years and Haiti until 1934. In Mexico, Wilson sent in troops nine times during his presidency – all were acts of undeclared war to prevent Mexico from nationalizing land owned by U.S. investors, principally American oil companies.

For Wilson, the contradictions between the promotion of democratic ideals and the assertion of U.S. power through military intervention were resolved by his conviction that what was best for the United States was best for the world. Despite all his pronouncements about democracy and liberty, Wilson was the most ruthless presidential enemy of civil liberties and conscientious dissent in American history. The witch hunts and blacklists of the early Cold War years pale in comparison to the reign of terror unleashed by the his administration. On the day after our entry into World War I, he authorized supervisors at all government agencies to dismiss employees for any "disloyal talk." The postmaster general was given the authority to censor what he might consider "seditious" magazines and newspapers and to impound the mail of unpatriotic organizations. What began as a wartime measure to protect Americans on their soil evolved into a homeland war waged against anyone who did not agree with 'Wilson's war.'

Approximately 200,000 private citizens were enlisted by the U.S. attorney-general to be neighborhood watchdogs and amateur detectives and to collect information of every kind. Especially susceptible targets were suspected agitators like college professors and labor leaders. Any private citizen willing to play the role of informer became part of this network. In offices, factories, churches, homes, schools, restaurants, and stores, government watchers could be found listening to conversations and reporting their "findings" to Washington. Fear and repression worked its way into every nook and cranny of ordinary life. Free speech was a hazard everywhere. Dissent became disloyalty. Americans were arrested for remarks overheard by government spies. The repression drove millions of independent minded Americans into political solitude. It was safer to say nothing; better to be apathetic.

The CPI began churning out stories that depicted Germans as evil monsters. According to false press releases issued to our media, German soldiers were so busy raping Catholic nuns it was hard to see how they found time for war. Atrocity-of-the-minute stories were cranked out about babies being hacked up and nun's breasts being chopped off. None of the so-called atrocities could be verified. American propaganda promised that "if Germany wins the war its soldiers will be bayoneting American girls and women rather than take the trouble to shoot them."

Particular targets of the CPI were the eight million German-Americans living in this country. In April 1917, all males older than fourteen who were still "natives, citizens, or subjects" of the German Empire were declared enemy aliens; the next year, Congress extended this category to include women and girls over fourteen. Under regulations issued by Woodrow Wilson, enemy aliens could not own firearms, aircraft, or radio equipment. They could not "attack" United States government policy in print. New regulations issued in November prohibited enemy aliens from entering the District of Columbia, or approaching facilities including railroads, docks, and warehouses. Enemy aliens could not travel by air. The attorney-general was authorized to issue any restrictions on alien travel he saw fit, and to require aliens to register weekly with local authorities.

Riding the wave of intolerance, Attorney General Gregory's private armies of "snoopers and informers" were obsessed at rooting out a treacherous internal enemy they believed was conspiring to destroy America. They stopped every man of draft age and demanded to see his registration card. If he could not produce it, they called the local police to have him arrested; or flashing their badges, they demanded that some suspicious looking civilian come with them to be interrogated.

As often happens in wartime when blind patriotism reigns, World War I crushed all dissent and supplied lasting labels of un-Americanism on anyone who questioned our nation's policies. To reinforce what the government was doing, Congress passed the Espionage Act, laying heavy penalties on all persons who interfered in any way with the mobilization of the military and naval forces of the nation. Not content with the sweeping provisions of this law, President Wilson asked for and received from Congress a still more severe measure: the Sedition Act of 1918 made any criticism of the Wilson administration illegal.

The suppression of civil liberties was not a wartime aberration; it was an opportunity to create a new phenomenon on a frightened American public – the national security state. For the first time in American history, the federal government created machinery to punish unorthodox political opinion. And punish they did – 2,000 lawsuits were brought against U.S. citizens resulting in 900 prison terms.

President Wilson led the attack: "The authority to exercise censorship is absolutely necessary to the public safety." Under these newly enacted laws the government instituted widespread censorship of the press. Socialist newspapers were banned from the mails. Individual critics of Wilson's war program were rounded up, without warrants, and thrown in jail where they were held incommunicado without bail. They were then tried in courts where the atmosphere was heavily charged with passion, lectured by irate judges, and sent to prison for long terms.

A Vermont minister was sentenced to fifteen years in prison because he cited Jesus as an authority on pacifism. A New Hampshire newsman who wrote, "This is J.P. Morgan's war," was sentenced to three years imprisonment and told by the judge that he was fortunate not to be hanged. A woman who wrote to her newspaper that, "I am for the people and the government is for the profiteers," was tried, convicted, and sentenced to ten years in prison. In Montana, a man was sentenced to twenty years hard labor for refusing to kiss the flag. Another man received a twenty-year sentence and a fine of $10,000 for telling a Liberty Bond salesman that not only did he not want to buy any bonds, but he also hoped the "government would go to hell."

Peace rallies were attacked and protesters beaten unmercifully. One German-born socialist who gave a speech against the war was wrapped in an American flag and hanged by an angry mob. It didn't take long for dissent to crumble. Schools dropped German from their curriculum and some universities abolished their German departments. German-Americans lost their jobs and were publicly humiliated. Distinguished symphonic conductors of German heritage were dismissed. The great German violinist, Fritz Kreisler, had his concerts cancelled. The Boston Symphony Orchestra was banned from playing works by German composers.

Despite the rousing words about a war "to end all wars" and our duty "to make the world safe for democracy," Americans did not rush to enlist. A million men were needed, but in the first six weeks after the declaration of war only 73,000 volunteered. When it became obvious this would not suffice, Congress voted overwhelmingly to institute a military draft.

While the War Department maintained overall control over the draft, the actual work was done by local civilian draft boards that were given broad guidance and rules, but not much more. Local board members determined which draftees could be deferred. Opportunities for favoritism and corruption were rampant. By the end of the war, over 24 million men were registered, but only 2.8 million would be drafted. Notables who found ways to remain home were J. Edgar Hoover, Joseph Kennedy Sr., FDR, and of course, the 'captains' of industry.

Lies and Deceits

Emma Goldman was probably the most celebrated American anarchist. Emma was born into a Jewish family in czarist Russia on June 27, 1869. Her young sensibilities were steadily assaulted by the spectacle of wives and children being beaten, peasants whipped, pregnant girls ostracized, Jews outcast, and even the poorest peasant shaken down by an endless stream of corrupt petty officials.

Emma arrived in New York at the age of sixteen full of golden images and dreams. Like so many other immigrants from Eastern Europe, she hoped to find freedom and opportunity, and instead found repression, squalor, and hard times. Earning her living as a seamstress or in a factory, Goldman plunged into the work of the labor movement. She was the leading organizer of women in the 1890 cloak-maker's strike. In 1893, she was imprisoned for publicly urging unemployed workers, "Ask for work. If they do not give you work, ask for bread. If they do not give you work or bread, take bread." Convicted on "inciting a riot," she served a one-year-sentence. On February 11, 1916, she was arrested and imprisoned for distributing birth control literature. After serving that prison term, she went around the country organizing rallies against World War I. She preached that, "The greatest bulwark of capitalism was militarism."

On June 15, 1917, shortly after the military draft became law, the offices of Emma Goldman's *Mother Earth* labor publication were raided and ransacked by federal marshals - the contents were confiscated and Goldman and her co-editor, Alexander Berkman, were arrested. At their trial they were accused of conspiring "to induce persons not to register for the draft" and for advocating violence in their publications.

On the street below the courtroom, a recruiting station had been set up, assisted by a military band that periodically played The Star-Spangled Banner. Whenever the music drifted up through the window, everyone in the courtroom was ordered to stand. The defendants, however, resolutely remained seated.

Acting as her own attorney, Goldman read into the record portions of her essays, and called many celebrated witnesses. How could she and Berkman be secret revolutionaries and guilty of "conspiracy" when their political and social positions were known to "a hundred million people" through their publications? Logic did not prevail. After deliberating for thirty-nine minutes, the jury declared both defendants guilty. The judge sentenced each to two years in prison and imposed the maximum $10,000 fine. After serving her two-year prison sentence, Emma Goldman, along with 248 others were deported to Russia.

The 1.5 million American soldiers who were sent overseas in 1918 arrived at a time when influenza was ravaging Europe. Many of our soldiers caught the disease and brought it back to the United States. Over the next sixteen months, 25 million Americans came down with the illness and approximately 675,000 of them died from the flu. American propaganda blamed the epidemic on German espionage agents. The U.S. Health Department issued a warning that, "It would be easy for one of those German agents to turn loose influenza germs in a movie theater or some other place where large numbers of persons are assembled. The Germans have started epidemics in Europe, and there is no reason why they should be particularly gentle with America." The effect was to exacerbate the fear that already gripped the country and incite recriminations against American citizens of German origin.

The day after Congress declared war, the Socialist Party in the United States issued a declaration calling the war, "a crime against the American people." Charles Schenck, the general-secretary of the Socialist Party was arrested in Philadelphia for printing and distributing 15,000 leaflets denouncing the draft and the war. The leaflet recited the Thirteenth Amendment provision against involuntary servitude: "A conscript is little more than a convict. He is forced into involuntary servitude. He is deprived of all freedom of conscience in being forced to kill against his will. The Conscription Act is a monstrous wrong against humanity that serves only the interests of Wall Street's chosen few."

The leaflet concluded with these words: "Do not submit to intimidation." The other side of the leaflet read: Assert Your Rights! The body of the text explained that the draft law violated the Constitution. "Exercise your rights of free speech, and petition the government for a redress of grievances. Come to the headquarters of the Socialist Party and sign a petition to Congress for the repeal of the Conscription Act." The leaflet did not tell the readers to take any action other than voicing their objection to the draft law.

The 15,000 copies of Schenck's leaflet that he intended to mail to draftees, never made it to the mailboxes. Federal officials got wind of the leaflets, secured a search warrant and confiscated the material. Schenck and four executive committee members were arrested and charged under the Espionage Act for conspiring to "obstruct the recruiting and enlistment services of the United States."

After a four-day trial in December 1917, the federal judge who presided directed the jury to acquit three defendants for lack of evidence; however, Schenck was found guilty and given a six-month sentence. Schenck appealed, arguing that the Espionage Act violated the First Amendment's freedom of speech. Under rules allowing cases that challenged federal laws on constitutional grounds to bypass the circuit courts, Schenck's appeal went directly to the Supreme Court.

The U.S. Supreme Court upheld Schenck's conviction. The unanimous decision was written by Oliver Wendell Holmes, the Court's most famous liberal. He summarized the contents of the leaflet and said it was undoubtedly intended to "obstruct" the carrying out of the draft law. Holmes concluded that Schenck was not protected by the First Amendment. "When a nation is at war many things that might be said in times of peace are such a hindrance to its effort that their utterance would not endure so long as men fight, and no court could regard them as protected by any constitutional right."

Holmes concluded: "The character of every act depends upon the circumstances in which it is done. The most stringent protection of free speech would not protect a man in falsely shouting fire in a theater and causing a panic. The question in every case is whether the words are used in such circumstances and are of such a nature as to create a clear and present danger that they will bring about the substantive evils that Congress has a right to prevent."

Holmes's analogy was clever and attractive. Few people would think free speech should be conferred on someone shouting fire in a movie theater and causing a panic. But, did that example apply to a citizen's right to criticize the war? Holmes thought that it did.

American intelligence operatives were certain that Germany was behind the Russian Revolution. The new Bolshevik government had pulled Russia out of the war causing German troops to withdraw from the eastern front and strengthen their offensive against the Allies on the western front. A new American propaganda campaign now began against Russia. Claims were made that the three million Russian immigrants in this country were Bolshevik supporters and spies. Russia, we were warned, was now a country of free love; all boys and girls upon reaching the age of eighteen became the property of the state and all offspring from arranged matches became government property.

Newspaper reports accused East Side New York Jews of being Bolshevik supporters of the Russian Revolution. Russians were depicted as "madmen" and "beasts," and Bolshevism as the anti-Christ. American propaganda depicted bloody scenes of Bolsheviks roasting their enemies in furnaces and chopping them up with axes. The American public was told that all labor strikes throughout the United States were Communist inspired attempts to bring down the American form of government, were incitements to revolution, and a Bolshevist plot for world domination.

President Wilson convinced the country that in order to protect against this imminent revolution, stronger and more restrictive laws were needed to curb the actions of aliens and radicals. There were few voices in opposition, but there were some. Journalist William White wrote that President Wilson should leave the Russians alone: "If the Bolsheviks have got something worthwhile to develop in the form of government, they should have the opportunity to do it without interference from us. If what they have is nothing, they'll go on the rocks soon enough."

American blacks were also targeted. The U.S. government established a special section devoted to "Negro Subversion." During the war, unrest in black communities was blamed on German agitation; after the war the unrest in black neighborhoods was blamed on the Bolsheviks seeking to foment revolution in the

United States. In no case was our government willing to admit that the problem was a U.S. problem, not a foreign one.

Wilson was always a firm believer in segregation. He had come of age in the decades immediately after the Civil War, and though he was an educated northerner, he was in essence a southern white supremacist who looked favorably on the manner in which the South arranged to keep black Americans in their place. Throughout his life he was always condescending to people of color and his administration is forever marked by the continuance of segregation in government buildings and in the armed forces.

A minor incident occurred in a faraway remote city in Russia that provided the U.S. with a pretext for military action against the Bolshevik government. Once Russia declared itself a neutral in the war, its soldiers withdrew from the fighting and returned home. On May 17, 1918, a clash occurred between a legion of Czechoslovakian soldiers and Soviet authorities. The incident escalated rapidly over the next few weeks. Whoever was to blame, American officials seized upon the fracas as a perfect rationale for sending American troops to fight against the new Russian government.

In August, the first American troops landed in Siberia. The public was told that the action served a proper military purpose, but the reality was that it contradicted Wilson's own principle of self-determination and nonintervention. We were now fighting against a declared enemy in Germany and against a legitimate neutral nation in Russia.

U.S. Senator William Borah objected to our actions in Russia and said, "Congress has not declared war on Russia, yet we are carrying on war with the Russian people. We are engaged in a military intervention to put down a certain force in Russia and establish a government satisfactory to the allied powers. Every American boy who dies in Russia is a sacrifice to this unlawful and intolerable scheme. If the Russians see fit to have a Soviet government, it is their business."

Although President Wilson and the American "establishment" depicted Russia as the blackest symbol that could ever confront our nation, many considered the Russian Revolution as the only

Eugene Solomon

bright spot on the horizon. The most notorious case in America involving this conflict over Bolshevism involved Mollie Steimer, a twenty-one-year-old Russian immigrant girl, four-feet-nine-inches tall, and weighing barely ninety pounds.

In 1913, Mollie Steimer arrived at Ellis Island with her parents and her five brothers and sisters, part of the flood of immigrants fleeing poverty and anti-Semitism is czarist Russia. Two days after her arrival, the fifteen-year-old Mollie went to work in a garment factory. Faced with continuing hardship and bleak prospects for the future, she began to explore the radical literature of Michael Bakunin, Peter Kropotkin, and Emma Goldman. She soon became involved in trade union activities. By the age of nineteen, she was a committed anarchist. Steimer believed in a new social order in which no group would govern any other, private property would be abolished, and people would no longer divide themselves into warring nations. Her dedication to this ideal was so deep that she vowed to "devote all my energy, and, if necessary, render my life for it."

With the outbreak of the Russian Revolution in 1917, Steimer threw herself into political action. She joined a group of young anarchists who published a clandestine Yiddish journal, *The Storm*. A year later, the group launched a new publication, *Freedom*. Enlarging upon Thomas Jefferson's observation that "government is best which governs least," the group's standard became "government is best which governs not at all." Steimer's group included a dozen young workers, mostly men and women of Eastern European Jewish origin. They met regularly at 5 East 104th Street where they printed their publications on a hand press and distributed copies secretly at night. Because of the paper's strident antiwar, anti-capitalist stance, secrecy was essential.

When the United States sent its contingent of marines into Russia, the group saw this as a move to crush the Russian Revolution. They printed two leaflets opposing the U.S. intervention in Russia; one in Yiddish, the other in English. The leaflets called for a general strike to protest our government's action. After distributing these leaflets throughout the city, Steimer threw the remainder from a washroom window on an upper floor of the building in which she worked. As the leaflets floated to the street below, they were retrieved by passing workmen, one of whom summoned the authorities.

Two army sergeants entered the building and discovered an informant who implicated Steimer and the other members of the group. Steimer was arrested along with four of her comrades (Jacob Abrams, Samuel Lipman, Hyman Lachowsky, and Jacob Schwartz). All were charged under the Espionage Act of 1917 and the Sedition Act of 1918 with conspiracy to publish disloyal material intended to obstruct America's war effort and cause contempt for the government of the United States.

The trial opened on October 10, 1918, in the federal courthouse in New York. One of the defendants, Jacob Schwartz, died the night before the trial. The cause of death was reported as pneumonia, but inmates at the prison insist that he was a victim of police brutality. At his funeral procession, mourners wearing red sashes paraded with signs, "You can kill men. You cannot kill ideals."

The leaflets at the center of the controversy read in part:

> "Our President Wilson, with his beautiful phraseology, has hypnotized the people of America to such an extent that they do not see his hypocrisy. His shameful, cowardly silence about American intervention in Russia reveals the hypocrisy of the plutocratic gang in Washington. He is too much of a coward to come out openly and say: "We capitalistic nations cannot afford to have a proletarian republic in Russia.
>
> What have you to say about it? Will you allow the Russian Revolution to be crushed? YOU – yes we mean YOU – the people of America! The Russian Revolution calls for the workers of the world for help. Workers of the World! Awake! Rise! Put down your enemy and mine!"

At the trial, the spit-fire Mollie Steimer refused to stand when the judge entered the courtroom and she refused to take the oath when she testified. When the judge addressed her as Mollie she refused to answer until he referred to her as Miss Steimer. On the witness stand, she said that her intent in distributing the leaflets was "to call attention to the workers that international capitalism was seeking to crush the Russian Revolution and that the Allies were acting just as tyrannical as the Germans by invading a neutral country."

Disclaiming any sympathy for Germany, "for militarism anywhere is always evil," Steimer insisted that she only wanted to point out the hypocrisy of the United States government, which claims it supports the right of every nation to self-determination and yet "seeks to abolish the present Russian government that the Russian workers established."

The prosecution asked Steimer if she was an anarchist. Unwilling to give a simple yes or no answer, she was allowed to give a fuller explanation. "I understand anarchism to be a new social order, where no group of people shall be in power, or no group of people shall be governed by another group of people. Individual freedom shall prevail in the full sense of the word. Private ownership shall be abolished. Every person shall have an equal opportunity to develop both mentally and physically. We shall not have to struggle for our daily existence, as we do now. Every person shall produce as much as he can, and enjoy as much as he needs. Instead of striving to get money, we shall strive towards education, towards knowledge. The workers of Russia are trying to establish such a system. If America does not crush them, they will succeed."

The lawyer for the defense, Harry Weinberger, argued that to be pro-Russian was not to be pro-German. There was no criminal intent on the part of the defendants and there was no evidence that anyone who actually read the leaflets had tried to obstruct the war against Germany. After all, the sweatshops of the lower East side made clothing and buttons, not bullets and bayonets. Some of the defendants had even offered to join a regiment of Russian immigrants to fight against Germany. What his clients protested was U.S. military aggression against a nation with which the United States was not officially at war.

Weinberger claimed that the defendants had the right to question and protest actions by the United States government. "Whatever one thinks about the defendants and their cause, they only wished to bring their views to the American people. They believed that America's action in Russia was a wrongful act by the President of the United States, without the authority of Congress. They did not call for insurrection; they were merely appealing to the conscience of the American public to protest our government's unlawful actions." Weinberger argued, "How could pro-Russian leaflets fluttering onto Broadway profoundly damage the war effort against Germany? Sad is the day when America becomes afraid of mere words that are spoken or printed."

On July 24, 1918, the jury found four of the defendants guilty; one defendant was acquitted. The three convicted men were each fined $1,000 and sentenced to twenty years in prison; Mollie Steimer was fined $500 and sentenced to fifteen years in prison. The defendants were released on bail pending appeal to the Supreme Court. Steimer immediately resumed her political activities. She joined several other young anarchists in secretly publishing and urging workers to replace a society based on economic slavery with one based on individual freedom. By September 1919, J. Edgar Hoover had decided that the twenty-year-old firebrand was too dangerous to remain free. He ordered agents of the FBI to detain her for possible deportation.

Steimer was arrested, released, rearrested, imprisoned, threatened with deportation, held at Ellis Island (where she conducted a hunger strike), released once more, and then arrested and imprisoned again. Because she refused to acknowledge the authority of the prison officials, she was denied all privileges - no exercise, no visitors, no mail, and no books. When asked by the warden why she had been sent to prison, she replied, "Because I am fighting for freedom." When she persisted in advocating anarchism to her fellow prisoners, she was locked in a dark, isolated cell and placed on a ration of bread and water. On April 30, 1920, Steimer was transferred from the temporary penitentiary in Jefferson City, Missouri, to begin serving her fifteen-year sentence.

The war in Europe ended at the end of 1918, but the United States secretly continued fighting in Russia in an attempt to topple the Bolshevik government. However, the publicity regarding the Mollie Steimer trial 'woke up' America about the extent of our military involvement in Russia. Soldiers' families, shocked to learn that the end of the war in Europe did not end the fighting in Russia, were signing petitions and organizing protests.

Hiram Johnson, a senator from California was irate that U.S. troops were still fighting in Russia: "The first casualty when war comes is the truth." He submitted a resolution to the U.S. Senate calling for a recall of all American troops inside Russia. He asked: Was there a government policy that he had missed? Did America want to destroy a nation whose legal and economic principles were not the same as ours? Were we conspiring to annihilate the world's first workers' state before it spread to other nations? "The Russian situation is a disgrace; a lie to all our declarations about democracy."

With the government losing public support, our troops were finally pulled out of Russia. America tried to justify its actions with lots of double-talk, but it was all about the fear that Bolshevism might spread and threaten American capitalism. Unfortunately, it was not the end of America's fight to safeguard capitalism from communist ideology; it would be only the beginning.

Mollie Steimer and her associates appealed their convictions to the U.S. Supreme Court. In the famous case of *Abrams v. United States*, the Supreme Court affirmed the convictions by a vote of 7-2. However, in a surprise move that would have major long-term consequences, Justices Holmes and Brandeis dissented. Holmes, who wrote the opinion in the *Schenck* case, now altered his position on free speech. To his credit he had the courage to admit that he had not gotten it exactly right in his *Schenck* opinion. He now said that freedom of speech was a natural right that could not be taken away. If an unlawful act occurred as a consequence, the unlawful act should be punished – but speech could not be censored or punished.

The war was over, but President Wilson stubbornly refused to pardon Mollie Steimer and her fellow accomplices. Finally a deal was worked out – they could go free on condition that they return to Russia, but the United States would not pay for their deportation. In November 1921, private citizens provided the necessary funds allowing Mollie and her fellow accomplices to sail for Moscow.

Eugene Debs was the leader of the leader of the Pullman strikers in 1894. He was also one of the founders of the International Workers of the World in 1905, and the Socialist Party presidential candidate in 1904, 1908, and 1912. In 1912, Debs received 900,000 votes – almost seven percent of the popular vote. His vision for America was that one day the United States would become a classless society. "The great issue in America is socialism versus capitalism. I am for socialism because I am for humanity. Wealth and money constitutes no proper basis of civilization." He would ask rhetorically, "What is socialism?" and then respond; "Socialism is merely Christianity in action; it recognizes the equality in men."

In June 1918, Debs visited three socialists who were in prison for opposing the military draft. After the visit, he spoke for two hours to an enthralled audience that had gathered outside the prison. He spoke about the evils of war; where all the wartime powers were capitalist imperialists seeking to enlarge their profits at home and plunders abroad. Debs was arrested for violating the Espionage Act. The government argued that draft-age youths were in the audience and his words could "obstruct the recruiting of enlistment service." Debs refused to take the stand at his trial. He denied nothing, but before the jury began its deliberations, he was allowed to speak:

> "I have been accused of obstructing the war. I admit it. I abhor war. I would oppose war if I stood alone. I have sympathy with the suffering struggling people everywhere. It does not make any difference under what flag they were born or where they live. Five percent of Americans control two-thirds of our country's wealth. John D. Rockefeller has an income of $60 million a year, $5 million a month, and $200,000 a day – at a time when average American wages are only pennies an hour. I have no quarrel

with Mr. Rockefeller personally, or with any other capitalist. I am simply opposing a social order in which it is possible for one man to amass a fortune of hundreds of millions of dollars, while millions of men and women work all the days of their lives and secure barely enough for an existence."

The jury found Debs guilty. Debs addressed the judge before being sentenced: "Your honor, years ago I recognized my kinship with all living beings and I made up my mind that I was not one bit better than the meanest on earth. I said then, and I say now, that while there is a lower-class, I am in it; while there is a criminal element; I am of it; while there is a soul in prison, I am not free."

The judge denounced Debs and those "who would strike the sword from the hand of this nation while she is engaged in defending herself against a foreign and brutal power." He sentenced Debs to ten years in prison for speaking out against the war.

Debs appealed, but it was not decided by the U.S. Supreme Court until 1919. By that time the war was over. Oliver Wendell Holmes, speaking for a unanimous court, affirmed his guilt. Holmes said that when Debs made "the usual contrasts between capitalists and laboring men, the implication running through it was that the working man should not be involved in the war." Thus, Holmes said, the natural and intended effect of Debs' speech was to obstruct recruiting and that was a violation of the Espionage Act.

Debs spent thirty-two months in prison. In 1920, while he was still an inmate in prison, Debs once again became the Socialist Party nominee for president. He received nearly one million votes – more than twice the number he polled in 1916 when he was not incarcerated. On his last morning as president, the sick and crippled Wilson was asked to pardon Eugene Debs who was rotting his life away in a federal penitentiary. Unforgiving, Wilson refused. In 1921, at the age of sixty-six, Debs was finally pardoned by President Harding.

The question of what constitutes patriotism remains unanswered: Is an American hero someone who protests injustices, inequality, and prejudice? Or is it someone who protects the American public from the disruptions and confrontations of dissenters and protesters? Is it the worker who goes on strike to improve wages and conditions; or is it the manager who struggles to keep production moving during the strike? America's idealistic view about individualism and freedom sometimes confused the notions of villains and heroes. Often those Americans most vilified in their own time became the heroes of the future, while those lauded during their lifetime were later regarded as the most destructive people of their era.

It was supposed to be a short war, at most a few months. Instead, it dragged on as wars generally do. By the time it was over, an estimated 20 million people would die and twice that number would suffer wounds of varying degrees. The United States had military deaths amounting to 126,000 and 365,000 casualties. France lost 1.4 million men; virtually 50 percent of all its men between the ages of 20-32 and 25 percent of those not killed were maimed forever and would never be the same. Germany lost 1.8 million and suffered over 7 million casualties. Russia had close to 2 million military deaths and 9 million casualties. The British Empire lost 900,000 men and Austria 1,200,000.

One of the most striking results of the war was a large redrawing of the map of Europe. The German Empire lost its colonial possessions. The Austrian-Hungarian and Ottoman empires were completely dissolved. Independent nation-states replaced dynasties. In the new borders of Czechoslovakia, barely half the population was Czech and nearly a quarter was still German. The Kingdom of Serbs, Croats and Slovenes were merged into a new national entity that would become known as Yugoslavia. The Russian Empire, which had withdrawn from the war in 1917, now became the Soviet Union, but they lost much of their western frontier as the newly independent nations of Estonia, Finland, Latvia, Lithuania, and Poland were carved out of their previous territory.

The disintegrated Ottoman Empire and much of its territory was awarded as protectorates to various Allied powers; what remained of her empire became the Republic of Turkey. In 1919, the Greek government invaded Turkey, seeking to carve out a "greater

Greece." Meeting with initial success, the Greek forces looted and burned villages in an effort to drive out the region's ethnic Turks, but Turkish forces eventually regrouped and pushed the Greek army back, engaging in their own ethnic cleansing against local Greeks along the way. A process of population transfers was formalized in the 1923 Treaty of Lausanne: all ethnic Greeks were to go to Greece and all Greek Muslims to Turkey. To accomplish this, Turkey expelled 1.5 million people and Greece displaced almost 400,000. Elsewhere in Central and Eastern Europe, roughly 25 million people continued to be part of ethnic minorities in the countries in which they lived.

The war also ushered in communism and elevated the United States to a world power. Americans groped to understand why the war occurred and what it had been all about. Many reasons were offered, from blunder, arrogance, and stupidity, to the accumulated tensions of international rivalries, ambitions, national disputes, and ethnic hatreds. What the average American didn't understand was that we went to war to salvage the billions in loans owed to America's capitalists.

The Peace Armistice signed on November 11, 1918, was greeted with relief by most people. On December 4, 1918, President Wilson traveled to the Paris Peace Conference at Versailles, proclaiming to make the world "safe for small nations and sound for business."

For the next six months, Paris was the capital of the world and the peacemakers were its most powerful people. The proceedings would occupy the time of over a thousand delegates. They would meet day after day; argue, debate, quarrel, and then start all over again. High on their agenda was the formation of a League of Nations that would prevent a world war from ever happening again.

Rival factions came to Paris to argue their cause and slogans filled the air: "China belongs to the Chinese" - "Kurdistan must be free" – "Poland must live again." The delegates spoke in many languages. Some argued that the United States now had to be the world's policeman; others wanted America to go home. Slovaks argued about Czechs; Croats about Serbs; Arabs about Jews; Chinese about Japanese. Those in the East pondered the threat of Western materialism. Europeans wondered if they would ever recover from the war. Asians saw a bright new future, while Africans feared that the world had forgotten them.

The peace conference was filled with many illustrious figures. Besides the major victors represented by Woodrow Wilson, Lloyd George of England, and Georges Clemenceau of France, there was Lawrence of Arabia wrapped in his mysterious Arab robes, Ignace Paderewski the pianist turned Polish politician, the future prime minister of Japan, and the future president of Israel. None of the five defeated nations were invited to attend the conference; neither was Bolshevik Russia – they would have to wait to learn what the victors decided. In spite of Wilson's democratic slogans, the peace terms would be imposed dictatorially.

Rather than entrust the U.S. mission to trusted delegates, Wilson decided to head the delegation himself. He was the first American president to leave the western hemisphere while in office and he spent only two weeks in the United States between December 3, 1918 and July 8, 1919 – an absence unique in the history of the U.S. presidency.

Intoxicated with power, Wilson believed he personally could save the world – but he was sadly mistaken. For one thing, the midterm elections of November 1918 produced Republican majorities in both houses of Congress and Wilson would need the support of two-thirds of the Senate to ratify any peace treaty. In addition, the delegation he took to Paris included no prominent Republican politician, which was a giant political blunder.

Wilson and his staff were woefully ignorant about all the intense ethic rivalries and geographical divisions that were highly significant to the other members. There is a story that Wilson and his staff met in his hotel room, got down on the floor, and pored over the maps of Europe only to discover small enclaves they never knew existed – yet these men were entrusted with making the world safe from any future war.

A big unresolved problem was what to do about Russia, a country that fought with the Allies and then unilaterally pulled out of the war and signed a separate peace with Germany. Another problem was Vietnam. The young revolutionary, Ho Chi Minh, traveled to Paris to meet with Wilson and plead his cause for a Bill of Rights for his Vietnamese people. Wilson refused to see him. Japan put forth proposals that the peace treaty should include a declaration of racial equality among all peoples, not just whites. Wilson refused to consider Japan's motion. Italy, one of the victors of the war, walked out of the Conference because its vast territorial demands were not met.

Wilson was disillusioned to discover that his European counterparts had their own ideas about the postwar. Lloyd George of England and Clemenceau of France, were more interested in imposing blame and vindictive reparations on Germany than in restoring a lasting peace. They also needed money to pay back what they owed to American banks and financial lenders. What better way than to milk the Germans dry? To make matters worse, the leaders of the three major powers did not get along. Clemenceau's view was particularly condescending: "Talking to Wilson is like talking to Jesus Christ himself," and on another occasion he remarked: "God gave us the Ten Commandments and we broke all of them. Wilson brings forth his 'Fourteen Points' – we shall see how that fares."

France and Great Britain wanted Germany crippled so it could never be a world power again. Not only was the German Empire dismantled, it had to give up territory considered an intrinsic part of its historical domain. Ten percent of German territory was taken away along with 13 percent of its population. In addition, Germany was divested of all its colonial holdings, which were divided between France and Great Britain. Germany was ordered to disarm down to a minuscule police force of 100,000 men and its military staff was dissolved. Germany's fleet of ships was reduced by 90 percent; its great armaments factories were demobilized causing the unemployment of tens of thousands of workers. Adding to the swelled ranks of the unemployed were the returning soldiers that had no jobs and no prospects of getting one. In order to stifle any future German development, Great Britain and France demanded the staggering sum of 132 billion gold marks in reparations – a sum far in excess of Germany's ability to pay. In a final act of revengeful hubris, Germany had to admit that it alone was solely responsible for the war.

The Allies gave Germany another ultimatum: it had five days to sign the treaty. With the threat of invasion hanging over their heads, the German government and the military command had no choice. On June 28, 1919, exactly five years after the assassination of Archduke Franz Ferdinand, and in the Versailles Hall of Mirrors where the German Empire had been proclaimed in 1871, two members of the German government signed the peace treaty. Over the next fourteen years, Germany would fight and argue about every single issue they were forced to accept. On only one item could all Germans agree: Versailles was deeply unjust; a victors' peace that saddled Germany with enormous burdens to the benefit of foreign nations.

Wilson reluctantly signed the treaty, hopeful of rectifying its worst features through the creation of an international government body, the League of Nations, a global organization in which every country's participation would provide collective security for all. In an attempt to outlaw offensive war, each county pledged to protect all other members against external aggression. Any war or threat of war would become the concern of all - no country could remain neutral in any future conflict. Disputes among nations had to be arbitrated and hostilities suspended for three months. Any country disregarding these principles would be subject to economic sanctions and the possibility of military intervention by the other members.

The main thing wrong with the League of Nations was that the United States never became a member. For the United States to join the League, the Versailles Treaty first had to be ratified by the U.S. Senate and they did not want any part of it. When President Wilson returned home from Paris and put before the nation his postwar plan that included active participation in the League of Nations, it was flatly rejected. Congress was not interested in Wilson's lofty words about America's obligation to protect weak countries or foster someone else's independence. American boys had died for no reason during this war; now the United States turned inward, embracing isolationism.

Senator Henry Cabot Lodge, one of the staunchest opponents of the League of Nations, expressed the mood of the country on the floor of the Senate: "I never expected to hate anyone in politics with the hatred I feel towards President Wilson. It is easy to talk about a League of Nations and the beauty of peace, but the hard practical demand is, are we ready to put our soldiers and our sailors at the disposition of other nations. America is not willing to enter into a permanent and indissoluble alliance that could be summoned by the authority of some organization other than what is authorized by our Constitution. Our American people do not wish to go into an overseas war unless it is for a very great American cause or where the issue is absolutely plain."

Wilson's reacted with contempt: "I will crush anyone who opposes me." Lodge humored Wilson by issuing a list of "Fourteen Reservations" akin to Wilson's Fourteen Points. The Treaty of Versailles could be ratified only if Lodge's reservations, which were meant to protect America's sovereignty and freedom of action, were added to the treaty. Lodge calmly reassured his Republican senatorial allies, "The only people who have votes on the treaty are here in the Senate, not the president."

On July 10, 1919, Woodrow Wilson entered the Senate chamber with a copy of the treaty under his arm and presented it to those assembled. He waved the bulky copy at the senators and challenged them: "Dare we reject this treaty and break the heart of the world?" Hardly had the president finished and left the chamber when Senator Lodge rose to utter a single quiet sentence, "Let's send it to committee." That simple sentence had as much significance as all of Wilson's eloquence. Woodrow Wilson was now to be reminded of the power of the Senate.

Under the Senate's inviolable rules, a proposed treaty had to be considered by the Foreign Relations Committee before it could be voted on - and Lodge had a solid majority of Republican members on the committee that were allied against Wilson. The proposed treaty was 268 pages long. Lodge began the committee hearings by reading the treaty aloud - every page – to an empty room except for a single clerk who recorded what he said. The reading of the treaty took two weeks. Then the committee called scores of witnesses to testify against the treaty. While Lodge was playing for time, his allies were flooding the country with anti-League advertising and holding anti-League rallies in major cities.

In one speech, Lodge spoke for two hours, eloquently expressing his reasoning and objections: "You may call me selfish, conservative, or reactionary, or use any other harsh adjective you see fit to apply, but an American I was born, and an American I have remained all my life. I can never be anything else but an American, and I must think of the United States first in an arrangement like this. I have never had but one allegiance - I cannot divide it now. I have loved but one flag and I cannot share that devotion and give affection to the mongrel banner invented for a League of Nations."

The president tried to fight back, but his mind-numbing headaches seemed to grow steadily worse until finally he was struck by a massive stroke. Paralyzed and nearly blind, he hovered for weeks on the edge of death, but sympathy for his condition would not succeed in changing a single vote in the Senate. Wilson's proposed treaty was defeated. For decades, scholars have asked why Wilson allowed the treaty to go down in defeat, why he did not just swallow hard and compromise. Many have speculated that the reason was physical, that Wilson's judgment was clouded, but most of all it was his stubbornness. He believed there was, "Wilson's way and the wrong way." For a politician, the inability to compromise spells certain doom.

The League of Nations remained in force, but was completely ineffective without the United States. Wilson's fall from the heights of glory was swifter and steeper than any other president in our history. He was a broken man, crippled in mind and spirit, thoroughly discredited and publicly reviled, his deeds denounced as crimes. America's need to go to war was an illusion. Wilson had deceived and betrayed his countrymen; he had falsely maneuvered them into a war that robbed them of the lives of its finest young men. The 2.6 million Americans that returned home from Europe hated the war they had been forced to fight and it was President Wilson who conscripted them.

Wilson was now partially paralyzed, his mind was gone, and he was without speech or movement on his left side. His wife,

Edith, shielded him from the media to keep the seriousness of his condition a secret from the American public. The White House was turned into a hospital, as doctors, nurses, and equipment poured in. There were no details and no explanations beyond misleading bulletins that described Wilson's condition as "nervous exhaustion and fatigue."

For the next year-and-a-half, Edith Wilson took over the day-to-day running of the presidency. The Republican Congress went looking for Wilson's scalp. "We have a petticoat Government!" exclaimed New Mexico Senator Albert B. Fall. Throughout Washington the word was that, "Mrs. Wilson is president!" However, with a new election so near, no move was made to replace the incapacitated Wilson.

Wilson's "war to end all wars" was a cruel hoax; all the mass destruction of World War I was merely a prelude of worse things to come. The dreadful peace devised at Versailles in 1919 turned out not to be peace at all, but merely a twenty-year truce; an interlude between the worst war in human history and one that would be far worse in terms of lives lost and treasure squandered. The European victors, Britain and France, would never again be a major force in world affairs. Only the United States emerged from the struggle strengthened. It had already been the world's leading industrial power for three decades; now it replaced Britain as the world's leading financial power as well. Wall Street, rather than Lombard Street, became the new world financial center.

America's emergence from the war as a world power redefined her mission. The involvement of so many American soldiers in what was at root a European war represented a watershed in American history - a first crucial step on the road to 'globalism' that would come to characterize American foreign policy for most of the twentieth century.

CHAPTER NINE

THE NEW DEAL

> "Anyone who is not a socialist before he is thirty has no heart. Anyone who is still a socialist after he is thirty has no head."
>
> Popular saying in the 1930s

The year 1919 was a year of extreme violence. The end of the war in Europe did not bring 'normalcy' back home in America. The Russian Revolution of 1917 had shown that a tiny group of committed radicals could seize power, overthrow centuries of rule, and institute a reign of terror against the wealthy. Bolshevism spread to Germany and Hungary, with riots and bloodshed in the streets. Lenin was proclaiming that this was the start of a worldwide revolution. In 1919, the American Communist Party was formed in the United States. American capitalism went into catatonic shock: Could what happened in Russia also happen in America?

With lightening speed, all socialist minded 'leftists' were transformed from being "pro-German" to "pro-Red." Communism became the new scare tactic for conservatives, capitalists, and the Church. With the American press assisting, 'Red Hysteria' was born. Labor strikes were stamped Bolshevik agitation, "inspired by and overseen by Lenin personally." In increasing numbers, young American idealists turned from peaceful political reform to issuing calls for revolution and anarchy. However, the bulk of left-wing dissidents were peaceful; conflict came when demands for social change were met with armed brutality.

In late April 1919, in an audacious act of terrorism, 30 bombs were mailed disguised as free samples from New York's prestigious department stores. The recipients were prominent Americans, including John D. Rockefeller and J.P. Morgan. The plot failed - the bombers did not put enough postage on their packages - but shock waves rocked the country.

The anarchists quickly struck again. First, the Mayor of Seattle found a bomb in his mail that was powerful enough to blow up the entire building. The next day a bomb blew the hands off a colored maid in the home of a Georgia senator who was Chairman of the Immigration Committee considering restricting Russian immigration. On May 1, a traditional day of celebration for labor, sixteen more bombs were discovered in the central Manhattan Post Office and eight others were found scattered throughout the country. On June 2, eight bombs went off at the same hour in eight different cities, including Washington, D.C. Finally, as the year came to a close, a bomb blew up in front of the Washington residence of Attorney General Mitchell Palmer.

Palmer reacted quickly. He ordered raids in thirty-three major cities and placed 6,000 aliens behind bars and held them for possible deportation. These indiscriminate arrests were followed by intimidating interrogations; all the suspects were held on excessive bail and denied legal counsel. J. Edgar Hoover, then head of the Justice Department's General Intelligence Division, argued that to allow the detainees access to lawyers would "defeat the ends of justice," and that lacking proof of guilt they should nonetheless be held on the off-chance that evidence might be discovered at some future date. Hoover was certain they were all avowed revolutionaries. "Out of their sly and crafty eyes leap cupidity, cruelty, insanity, and crime; from their lopsided faces, sloping brows, and misshapen features may be recognized the unmistakable criminal type."

Distinguished lawyers and legal scholars, including future Supreme Court Justice Felix Frankfurter, Harvard Law School Dean Roscoe Pound, and leading constitutional scholar Zechariah Chafee, issued a report that federal agents used torture, illegal searches and arrests, "as had been familiar in old Russia and Spain." The Justice Department responded to these charges by searching intelligence files to see if Frankfurter and other critics had radical associations and beliefs.

The anarchists retaliated against Palmer's raids and Hoover's tactics. A huge bomb exploded at noon on New York's crowded Wall Street killing thirty people. The perpetrator was never found. The fanaticism worked both ways. In Hammond, Indiana, an immigrant yelled out, "To hell with the United States." He was shot dead by Frank Petroni, an Italian-born naturalized immigrant. Petroni pleaded not guilty by reason of patriotism. The jury deliberated for only a few minutes before setting Petroni free.

The trial and execution of Nicola Sacco and Bartolomeo Vanzetti remains one of the blackest pages in American justice; it is a cautionary tale of lethal passions fueled by political fear and ethnic prejudice. In 1921, Nicola Sacco, a shoemaker, and Bartolomeo Vanzetti, a fish peddler, both Italian immigrants and anarchists, were arrested and charged with murder and robbery in South Braintree, Massachusetts. Their trial took place before a jury contemptuous of foreigners and a judge who referred to them privately as "anarchist bastards." It was blatantly clear that the political climate and anti-immigration fervor made a fair trial impossible.

Sacco and Vanzetti were the perfect scapegoats for a nation intent on exacting vengeance on the influx of foreigners that complained about the conditions in America while they were at the same time taking away jobs from loyal patriotic Americans. During the course of the trial the defendants were wheeled into the courtroom in an iron cage where they remained during the proceedings. There was never any positive identification linking either man to the crime. Witnesses claimed the defendants "looked like" the robbers. That was enough evidence for the court, especially when the judge in the case, Webster Thayer, told the jury, referring to Vanzetti, "This man, although he may not have actually committed the crime attributed to him, is nevertheless culpable, because he is the enemy of our existing institutions." In a trial that lasted seven weeks, heard over 160 witnesses, and gained national attention, it took the jury just five hours to find Sacco and Vanzetti guilty and sentence them to death.

Intellectuals and artists around the world protested the proceedings and demanded a new trial. During the next six years, all appeals were turned down even after the governor received a clemency petition containing 500,000 signatures. The guilt of Sacco and Vanzetti was even affirmed by a special three-man panel consisting of the presidents of Harvard and MIT and a retired judge. Prominent journalist Heywood Broun wrote bitterly, "What more can the immigrants from Italy want? Not every person has the president of Harvard University throw the switch. If this is lynching, at least the fish-peddler and his friend may take solace that they will die at the hands of men in dinner jackets and academic gowns."

On August 23, 1927, as police broke up protests with arrests and beatings, and troops surrounded Charlestown Prison – Sacco and Vanzetti were electrocuted. Whether they were guilty or innocent is still debated to this day – but what is indisputable is that neither of them got a fair trial because they were foreigners.

Today, eugenics is a dirty word associated with racists and Nazis, but back in the early twentieth century it was applauded with vigor in the United States. Many pointed to Darwin as scientific proof to justify a process of "social selection" of the fittest. Christian theologians preached that eugenics was mandated in the bible; the poor and retarded were such because God had ordained their state in life. Wealthy capitalists agreed; eugenics explained why the strongest rose to the top. Margaret Sanger, the American birth control activist, was another early supporter. She believed that without eugenics all efforts to improve the human race would be in vain. Eugenics was divided into two branches: positive eugenics encouraged "superior" men and women to breed large families, while negative eugenics sought to limit the birth of "defectives" such as the feeble-minded, prostitutes, paupers, the insane and the illiterate.

In 1907, Indiana passed the first compulsory sterilization law, authorizing the sterilization of confirmed "criminals, idiots, rapists, and imbeciles." Thirty other states enacted similar statutes – eventually 60,000 individuals in the United States would be forcibly sterilized. The U.S. Supreme Court in *Buck v. Bell* upheld our government's practice of sterilization as perfectly legal. Oliver Wendell Holmes wrote the decision: "It is better for the entire world if instead of waiting to execute degenerate offspring for crime, or to let them starve for their imbecility, society can prevent those who are manifestly unfit from continuing their kind. Three generations of imbeciles are enough."

H.H. Goddard was one of the first 'experts' to use intelligence tests in America. He conducted a series of IQ tests on incoming immigrants at Ellis Island and concluded that 83 percent of Jews were feeble-minded, as well as 79 percent of Italians and 87 percent of Russians. These biased tests, all in English that few of the immigrants understood, were all the ammunition that racist America needed to enact strict immigration quotas. In 1924, the United States Congress limited the number of new foreigners by basing the quotas on the census of 1890. This insured the exclusion of as many foreign groups as possible, especially Jews from Eastern Europe. President Calvin Coolidge, upon signing the legislation said, "This will insure the purity of the white race in America." Over in Germany, Hitler watched with amusement. Racial superiority and eugenics was exactly what he had in mind.

During the early 1920s, the country experienced a period known as the "Roaring Twenties," highlighted by rising hemlines and wild parties, but the wildest party of all was on Wall Street. Gambling on stocks became a national sport as the air was filled with stories about fortunes being made overnight. "Buy, buy!" investors shouted over the phone to their brokers. Everyone spoke reassuringly of a new era of continual bullishness as the stock market far outpaced the economy. Credit, once the privilege of the rich, now attracted ordinary wage earners. It wasn't long before everyone was buying stocks and taking advantage of the low margin requirements. With a swiftly rising stock market and 90 percent financing, big profits were easy to come by and it was all done with credit. Many corporations were also buying stocks - making profits in the stock market was easier than selling merchandise. As long as the market kept going up everything was rosy.

In 1928, Herbert Hoover ran in the presidential primaries as both a Democrat and Republican, but astutely chose to run as a Republican. He was elected by a landslide over Al Smith, a

Catholic whose religion was distrusted by many. Hoover, a Quaker orphan from Iowa, graduated first in his class from Stanford and used his engineering education to make millions in the gold fields of California, Australia, and China; he then devoted his efforts to humanitarian causes. After World War I, he served as commerce secretary under Presidents Harding and Coolidge.

Hoover was optimistic that the nation's good times were first beginning. "We in America shall soon see, with the help of God, the day when poverty will be banished from this nation." As for the booming stock market, Hoover assured investors it would go even higher. But, bad things began happening immediately as greed overcame reason. Billions of dollars had been accumulated by organizing holding companies, investment trusts, and corporate pools, to trade in stocks rather than invest in machinery and plant expansion. Inside information was passed around the elite "clubs" resulting in millions being made before the general public had any awareness. Ordinary Americans only knew that stock prices were going up and up, and they merrily continued their buying spree unaware of the 'behind the scenes' manipulations. Speculation became a disease; there was no longer any relation between price and value.

As 1929 approached, the American economy appeared to be extraordinarily healthy. Employment was high and inflation was virtually non-existent. Industrial production had risen 30 percent between 1919 and 1929 and per capita income had climbed from $520 to $681. The United States accounted for nearly half the world's industrial output. However, all booms nurture the seeds of their own destruction. A downturn in the economy is not unusual; what was unusual about this one was its severity.

Had the prosperous Americans looked carefully they would have seen that for many groups of Americans this prosperity was a cruel illusion. Even during the most prosperous years of the 1920s, most families lived below what contemporaries defined as the poverty line. In 1929, economists considered $2,500 the income necessary to support a family. In that year, more than 60 percent of the nation's families earned less than $2,000 a year, the income necessary for basic necessities, and over 40 percent earned less than $1,500 annually. Although labor productivity soared during the 1920s because of electrification and more efficient management, wages stagnated or fell in mining, transportation, and manufacturing.

The word 'panic' is essentially a psychological term that reminds us that fundamentally economics is the study of human beings with all their unpredictable quirkiness in the marketplace. When panic sets in, people rush to convert their stocks into cash and gold. If they begin to fear the soundness of banking institutions, they withdraw their deposits and stash the cash elsewhere. In a sense, all banks are perpetually insolvent. If depositors make a "run" on a bank they can quickly drain that bank of cash, forcing it to close, at least temporarily. Naturally, this makes depositors in other banks nervous and the contagion of fear spreads.

With banks becoming more and more illiquid, thousands of small businesses failed because they could not secure loans. A heavy burden of consumer debt also weakened the economy. Consumers built up an unmanageable amount of consumer installment and mortgage debt, taking out loans to buy cars, appliances, and homes in the suburbs. To repay these loans, consumers cut back sharply on discretionary spending. Drops in consumer spending led inevitably to reductions in production and worker layoffs. Unemployed workers naturally spent less and the cycle repeated itself.

When the market tumbled in 1929, the Wall Street tycoons had to do something to protect their own holdings and the investments of their wealthy clients. At noon on the day that stocks were plummeting, Thomas Lamont, of J.P. Morgan, summoned representatives of four major banks to his office at Broad and Wall Street. At 1:15 that afternoon, Richard Whitney, the New York Stock Exchange floor operator for J.P. Morgan, started buying shares of stock, especially U.S. Steel. Upon seeing that the Morgan firm was buying, floor traders immediately stopped selling and began buying for their clients. The effect was electric and stocks suddenly rallied. A miracle had taken place; or so it appeared on that day. As the market steadied, the major banks had an opportunity to call in enough loans to avoid heavy losses. Then they slowly sold the stocks they had just bought, probably at a profit in the now rising market. Four days later, as stocks spiraled downward again, J.P. Morgan and his associates sat back and watched. Their loss positions had been resolved and they were no longer in jeopardy. The public was left holding the bag.

On October 24, 1929, no buyers could be found to buy stocks at any price. On October 29, sellers appeared in force and dumped thousands of shares into the bottomless pit. Bewildered, small investors now joined in the selling, too late to salvage anything but a mere pittance. Between September 1929 and January 1933, the Dow Jones value of the top thirty industrials fell from $427 to $62. The value of certain assets, especially real estate, went down sharply, directly jeopardizing bank loans. By the end of 1929, 5,000 banks with deposits of $1.5 billion had collapsed. The following year 640 more banks failed, and the next year another 1,553 banks closed its doors. Between 1929 and 1933, 11,000 out of 25,000 banks failed. If you had your money in a bank that went bust, you were wiped out. Millions of people hid their few remaining assets under their mattresses or where no one could steal them without a fight. The country was in a panic. If banks could fold like that, what disaster might come next?

Railroads were also in trouble. People were not traveling and goods were not being transported. Major bond firms went bankrupt. The value of farm property decreased by $20 billion and more than 450,000 farmers lost their farms. Anyone connected with farm liquidation auctions lived in fear of being lynched. A Kansas lawyer who handled a foreclosure was found dead in a field. An Iowa bankruptcy judge was dragged from the courtroom, stripped and beaten. Armed farmers gathered at foreclosure auctions to threaten the lives of bidders, ready to buy their neighbors' possessions for a dollar or two and then return the property to the original owners.

In April 1930, three million people were out of work. By October of that year the number was up to four million. A year later there were almost seven million unemployed and by the beginning of 1933 the number rose to twelve million. In Chicago, one out of every two workers was without a job. In Toledo, Ohio, unemployment reached 80 percent. Those lucky enough to have jobs were averaging $2.39 a week. Over 150,000 Americans a year were losing their homes in foreclosure actions and half of all home mortgages were in default. Thousands of dispossessed families pitched tents in the middle of Central Park. Right-wingers blamed the crisis on the foreigners that were taking away jobs from true-blue Americans.

Thousands of World War I veterans marched on Washington to demand they be paid their wartime bonuses that were not due until 1945. President Hoover opposed accelerating the payment date and threatened to veto any attempt to pass such a bill. The veterans, along with their families, camped out in front of the White House demanding some action. Hoover termed the entire affair a Communist plot and ordered the police to evacuate the area. When the police were unable to remove the demonstrators, Hoover called in the army. General Douglas MacArthur arrived with cavalry, tanks, machine gunners, and four infantry squads. Chaos ensued as tear gas was thrown into the crowd and the makeshift shacks were burned to the ground. Women and children, choking from the tear gas and flames, fled the scene in a panic.

Not everyone was suffering from the economic downturn. *Fortune* magazine belittled the crisis by declaring, "No one has starved to death yet." When asked about the nation's deterioration, J.P. Morgan shrugged his shoulders and told reporters, "What depression? I don't know anything about any depression." The Vanderbilts, Belmonts, Harrimans, and most of the rest of New York's "400 Club" still cavorted stylishly every summer in Newport, as they had done for decades, playing croquet or sipping cocktails on the lawns of their ornate Victorian mansions, competing on the grass covered tennis courts at the Casino, sailing their yachts down Narragansett Bay, oblivious to what was going on in the country. True, certain of their investments were in decline, but they had so much wealth that their way of life was not affected.

The biggest economic threat was coming from the collapsing banking system. In December 1930, the Bank of the United States, which despite its name was a private bank, went bankrupt in the largest single bank failure in U.S. history, freezing $200 million in depositor's funds. The Hoover administration, trying to head off a panic asked Henry Ford to help a large troubled Detroit bank. Two top administration officials came to Dearborn, Michigan, to make a personal appeal, telling Ford that the state's banks were on the verge of failing, endangering one million deposits that supported three million state residents. If Michigan's banks failed, they warned, other state banks would likely follow. "Let the crash come," Ford is said to have replied. "Everything will go down the chute. But I feel young. I can build again."

In the spring of 1932, the mood of the country turned ugly. In May, the railway unions met with President Hoover and presented him with the following proclamation: "Mr. President, we have come here to tell you that unless something is done to provide employment and relieve distress among the families of the unemployed, we cannot be responsible for the orderly operations of the railroads in this country, and we refuse to take responsibility for the disorder which is sure to arise if conditions continue. The unemployed citizens who we represent will not accept starvation while the two major political parties struggle for control of the government. There is a growing demand that the entire business and social structure in this country must be changed because of the general dissatisfaction with the present system. We are not socialists or communists and we are not anarchists – but we can no longer ignore this situation. Something must be done."

Economic management was Hoover's specialty. He appeared to be the best equipped man for the job of fighting the Depression, but he foolishly opposed direct action by the federal government, maintaining that the solutions belonged to the local governments and to private charity. Hoover was following the capitalist tradition; let the people and the states fend for themselves. He insisted that "it is not the function of the federal government to relieve individuals of their responsibilities to their neighbors, or to relieve private institutions of their responsibilities to the public, or the local governments to the states, or state governments to the federal government. These are the fundamental principles of our social and economic system."

Hoover believed the country's economic problems would correct themselves if everyone would just be patient: "Congress cannot pass legislation that would get the country out of this Depression just as they cannot exorcise a Caribbean hurricane by statutory law." He called on big business to continue maintaining its payrolls in spite of curtailed production and for labor unions to refrain from demanding wage increases. His vision of an American society based on voluntary cooperation was delusional; it went against the interests of each segment of the marketplace.

Historian Charles Beard argued against Hoover's approach. Beard believed that *laissez-faire* was a myth; government had to be involved: "The cold truth is that the individualist creed of everybody for himself and the devil take the hindmost is principally responsible for the distress in which Western civilization finds itself."

When Hoover finally acted, everything he did was wrong. High tariffs were placed on foreign imports, insuring that the price of domestic goods remained high. When foreign countries retaliated by imposing their own high tariffs, world trade collapsed. The United States had exported $5.2 billion worth of products in 1929; by 1932 it was down to $1.6 billion. Contributing to the debacle, the Federal Reserve did nothing about interest rates. By 1932, with the economy in virtual free-fall, Hoover pushed Congress to enact the greatest percentage tax increase in American history – probably the worst thing he could have done.

The human toll of the Great Depression is almost impossible to fathom. Fifteen million people – a quarter of the nation's workers – had no job and no hope of getting one. Factoring in their families, this meant that in a nation of 130 million, perhaps 60 million literally had no money for rent, food, or clothing. Factories lay idle and business investment was down 90 percent. People stood on breadlines or they waited their turn in soup kitchens. Millions of Americans who had never known poverty were faced with the threat of starvation. When two hundred men and women stormed into an A&P food market in Van Dyke, Michigan, and stole every item in the store, a large, round-faced woman who had stuffed a bologna, five loaves of bread, and half a dozen cans of soup into a big sack, said: "Do you expect us to starve when there's food on the shelf?" No better story exemplified the Great Depression in America, and worst of all, nobody knew where the bottom was.

Was it any wonder that many Americans began exploring communism as a better alternative to capitalism? People looked at Russia and saw a new form of government that was acting directly on behalf of the public and not for the protection of private interests. No doubt there was repression in Russia, but there was no unemployment.

Leading industrialists in this country, fearing that American labor would emulate the Bolshevik success, staged their own campaign to quiet the tempers. Charles Schwab, the steel manufacturer, told the nation that business was "a lot healthier today than it had been six months earlier, and all indications were that next year will prove to be a year of normal business progress. Just grin and bear it and keep on working. Stop worrying about the future." James Farrell of U.S. Steel made a public announcement that "the peak of the Depression passed thirty days ago." A poll of bankers concluded that "there is nothing very unnatural about present conditions. Depression is inherent in the system and so is recovery. Let nature take its course." Henry Ford told his workers, "Things are better today than they were yesterday," and he cautioned the government "to leave business alone. Unemployment insurance will only insure that we always have unemployment."

However, Henry Ford's reassuring statements did not stop him from setting up an elaborate spy system in his factories that monitored everything from production performance to bathroom breaks, with an especially close watch for anything that hinted at union agitation. Troublemakers were summarily fired and if they objected too strenuously, they were escorted out by Ford's strong-armed security thugs.

On March 7, 1932, workers in Dearborn, Michigan, marched in protest against Henry Ford's tactics. They were met with tear gas by the police and Ford's personal security force. At the end of the day, four men were killed, including a sixteen-year-old boy; more than sixty other marchers were wounded. Dearborn police rounded up hundreds of protesters and threw them in jail. Five days later there was another march, this one included 15,000 mourners for the slain auto workers. After this demonstration, Ford stockpiled tear gas in every one of his plants and had machine guns installed at his home estate.

For the first time since the Civil War, armed men patrolled the entrances to federal buildings while machine gunners perched on rooftops. Newspapers debated whether the president should assume wartime authority. A headline in the *New York Herald Tribune* read: "Dictatorship If Necessary." After all, the Italian Fascist Benito Mussolini was in power for a decade and was very popular. Not only was the clash between labor and business, but race relations between black and white was also reaching the breaking point.

Every year, more and more blacks were being lynched in the South and Midwest. It was not just outright murder; it was a social event in which people packed picnic baskets as if attending an outdoor barbecue party. Abel Meeropol, a Jewish high-school teacher from the Bronx, wrote a poem entitled "Strange Fruit" about the lynching of two black men. Transcribed to music, the song became a regular part of Billie Holiday's live performances. Reaction to the song was so emotional that it was banned from the recording studios and from most live performances outside of New York.

> Southern trees bear a strange fruit,
> Blood on the leaves and blood at the root,
> Black body swinging in the Southern breeze,
> Strange fruit hanging from the poplar trees.
>
> Here is a fruit for the crows to pluck,
> For the rain to gather, for the wind to suck,
> For the sun to rot, for a tree to drop,
> Here is a strange and bitter crop.

The 1931-37 trials of the 'Scottsboro Boys' epitomized every ugly aspect of poverty, racism, and injustice in this country. In March 1931, a group of nine black youths, ages 12 to 20, were riding the freight train in Alabama, traveling around looking for odd jobs. They met up with a group of tough white boys also on the freight cars and a fight ensued. The white youths were pushed off the train and they reported the incident to the local police. A posse of fifty white men armed with shotguns stopped the train and arrested all the black boys. The police also discovered two white women on the freighter who were dressed as 'hobo' men. The frightened women told the police they had been "gang raped" by the black youths.

Twelve days later the nine blacks were tried for rape, a capital offense subject to the death penalty. They were assigned two incompetent attorneys with no trial experience and the jury was all-white. Both accusers, Ruby Bates and Victoria Price, testified that they had been raped, although Bates could not be sure whether the defendants were the perpetrators; Victoria Price, however, made positive identifications. The prosecution argued that "if we don't give these men death sentences for this heinous crime, the electric chair might as well be abolished." The defense made no closing argument and did not argue against the death penalty. All nine "Scottsboro Boys" were found guilty; eight were sentenced to death; the twelve-year-old youth was sentenced to a long prison term.

From this point on, the case assumed political dimensions. The lawyer at the center of the case was a New York Jewish attorney named Samuel Leibowitz, regarded as a worthy successor to Clarence Darrow as the nation's leading criminal lawyer.

Leibowitz managed to secure a new trial for the defendants, and at the retrial he proved that the two alleged rape victims were both prostitutes and had engaged in voluntary sex with certain men just before boarding the train. Tests confirmed there was no rape. Ruby Bates then confessed that there had been no rape; Victoria Price stuck to her story. During the prosecution's summation, the jury was told, "Show the world that Alabama justice cannot be bought by Jew money from New York." The all-white jury once again returned a verdict of guilty and sentences of death.

The case aroused outrage around the world and symbolized the lack of justice for black Americans in the U.S. legal system. The American Communist Party became a leading force in demanding justice for the nine blacks. With protests continuing, the case came before the U.S. Supreme Court. In a landmark decision that still has many far reaching applications, the Court reversed the convictions on the ground that the due process clause of the Constitution guaranteed not only the assistance of counsel at a criminal trial, but that such assistance be competent and effective. The original attorneys clearly had not provided the defendants with such competency. In addition, the defendants could not get a fair trial due to the mob atmosphere that prevailed at the time, and the systematic exclusion of blacks from the jury was contrary to the "equal protection of law" guaranteed by the Fourteenth Amendment.

There was no doubt that Herbert Hoover would not win re-election in 1932, especially since he kept maintaining that "the overshadowing problem in our country is not the Depression; it is crime." The only question was who would be able to stem the tide. In some quarters, the election of 1932 was considered the nation's last chance to salvage its system of capitalism and democracy by peaceful means.

In order to understand the New Deal and our entry into World War II, we must first turn to what was happening in Germany at this time. Across the Atlantic, Germany was also mired in the worst economic depression in its history, and like America, it was about to make a momentous decision.

The Nazi Party started with seven members in 1919. By 1928, they represented 2.6 percent of the vote, 18.3 percent in 1930, and 37.4 percent by July 1932. Adolf Hitler would complete his ascension to power with his election on March 5, 1933. The forty-four-year-old Hitler could not believe his good fortune. He was now in complete control of Germany and it was all achieved legally through democratic elections.

After the First World War, Germany was in shambles; only the indulgence of its creditors saved the country from bankruptcy. Nine million Germans, almost 15 percent of the population was unemployed. Families were starving as fear gripped the nation. Nobody had an answer; only Hitler and his Nazi Party offered the German people a semblance of hope. His program was to create a kind of socialism that was not really socialism, but it was also not *laissez-faire* capitalism.

Hitler's program of National Socialism combined socialism with nationalism - the German nation rather than the individual would be paramount. Unlike traditional systems where the nation served the people, in Hitler's fascist state the individual would serve the nation. Class distinctions were obliterated – a new classless community was created where loyalty to the nation came first, even before allegiance to the Church. The public good transcended personal interests. Hitler promised "the creation of a socially just state, a model society that would continue to eradicate all social barriers. Germany will be at its greatest when its poorest citizens are also its most loyal."

No one in Germany expected the subsequent events to turn out the way they did. For most Germans, National Socialism did not mean mass murder; it meant the restoration of national pride and a return to normalcy. All of Germany was still protesting a lost war, the dictates of the Versailles peace treaty, the injustice of reparations, the ban on rearmament, the seizure of German territories, the Communists, the conspiracies of the Jews, and the Great Depression. Germans now looked forward to economic recovery and a return to world prominence under their new inspirational leader.

What Hitler did was adopt the economic ideas of British economist John Maynard Keynes, arguably history's most acclaimed economist. Keynes wrote extensively on how to overcome downturns in economic cycles. To remedy vast unemployment, Keynes advocated public works. He believed that the state, not the private sector, had to drive economic policy. Government, according to Keynes needed to spend itself out of a depression and create jobs – debt and deficits would get resolved at a later time.

Hitler acted swiftly to avert a complete economic collapse. He smashed the labor unions, thereby enticing German businesses and banks to buy his new government bonds, promising to repay them in five years out of future tax revenue. With money in hand, he started his vast public works program, rebuilding roads, towns and cities. National production rose 103 percent from 1933 to 1937 and national income doubled. Tax burdens were shifted to benefit low-income wage earners, while taxes were increased on single people, married couples without children, and those in the high income brackets. Germans were encouraged to invest their new earnings in government bonds, which allowed Hitler to further accelerate his economic plans.

Creating jobs not only meant employment, it created loyalties and lifted morale. By 1937, Germany had full employment. Wages remained low, but the people were working and the government no longer had to make welfare payments. Rearmament followed; Hitler's emphasis shifted from building roads and bridges, to bullets, tanks, and fighter planes. Profits soared, strikes were forbidden, imports were reduced to a bare minimum, severe wage and price controls were introduced, dividend payouts were restricted, and small businesses were replaced by larger more efficient business cartels.

Today, Adolf Hitler and Franklin Delano Roosevelt are seen as antipodes; indeed, it is hard to imagine a more dramatic study in human contrasts. Hitler is remembered as the plebeian hysterical dictator, the incarnation of barbarism, evil, and totalitarianism. Roosevelt is fondly recalled for his patrician manner, innate personal charm, and liberal-democratic humanism. But back in the 1930s, contemporaries viewed them both as charismatic leaders who held their country's masses in their sway. Without their personal magnetism, neither National Socialism nor the New Deal would have been possible.

Little more than a month after Adolf Hitler became chancellor of Germany, Franklin Roosevelt, on his fifty-first birthday, took the oath of office as the thirty-second President of the United States. Both men came to power because of their country's severe economic crisis and both used the same means to bring their respective countries to recovery. Hitler succeeded first, but Roosevelt was watching and learning from Hitler's success. As Hitler's economic miracles unfolded, FDR geared America's policies along those same lines. Roosevelt also recognized the harsh reality behind Hitler's policies – public works and spending could provide stimulus and growth, but could not solve all the problems – only a war economy could do that.

FDR is one of America's great stories. It is hard to believe that a man who was paralyzed from the waist down could be nominated and elected President of the United States four times, and enact a program of landmark liberal legislation that continues to be the bedrock of America today.

FDR grew up as part of our nation's power elite. He had what many would call "old money." His grandfather, Warren Delanos, made a fortune trading opium and other commodities with China. Delanos was a rock-solid Republican who liked to say that while not all Democrats were horse thieves, it was his experience that all horse thieves were Democrats. His twenty-six-year-old headstrong daughter Sara married James Roosevelt, a fifty-two-year-old widower. James Roosevelt was a successful businessman, and a well-connected Democrat whose family arrived in the New World from Holland in 1650. The family made its fortune importing sugar from the West Indies to make rum, which they then invested in New York real estate.

Franklin was an only child. He grew up with lots of private tutors and motherly love, but very few friends. The Roosevelt family lived practically next door to the far wealthier Vanderbilts, but considered them socially undesirable and refused every one of their dinner invitations for fear of having to reciprocate the gesture.

FDR would remain a social elitist all his life. As a youth, he attended dinners with President Grover Cleveland and traveled to Europe eight times by the time he was twelve. After attending Groton, an elite boys' boarding school in Massachusetts, he entered Harvard where his big scoop for the college newspaper was an interview with his cousin, Vice President Theodore Roosevelt. Columbia Law School followed after his graduation from Harvard.

Franklin met Eleanor at a Madison Square Garden horse show when he was seventeen and she was fourteen. She was a distant cousin and Theodore Roosevelt's favorite niece, which served as an aphrodisiac for the ambitious Franklin. They were married in

1905; President Teddy Roosevelt gave away the bride. The Roosevelt marriage was an unhappy one from the start. FDR loved the social life; parties, elite country and social clubs, and the attention of powerful men and beautiful women. Eleanor remained at home most of the time, fulfilling her wifely duties by having six children in rapid succession.

In 1913, Eleanor Roosevelt hired Lucy Mercer as her social secretary. FDR had recently been installed as assistant secretary of the navy and Eleanor, in the early stage of pregnancy, was overwhelmed with the demands of Washington society. Attractive, personable, and seven years younger than Eleanor, Lucy quickly became an ancillary member of the Roosevelt family. She and Franklin probably became intimate in 1916. In September 1918, while unpacking for her husband who had just returned from England, she accidentally discovered a bundle of incriminating letters.

Eleanor offered Franklin a divorce, but Franklin's formidable mother stepped in. She told her son that if he left Eleanor he would be cut off without a cent. That would mean the end of his political career and young Franklin would have to go out and work for a living – something he had no wish to do. Instead, he did the only sensible thing: he agreed to stay in the marriage. However, Eleanor insisted on two conditions: he had to immediately terminate his relationship with Lucy Mercer, and he could never again share his wife's bed. Franklin agreed. Their marriage in conjugal terms ended, but a political partnership was born.

Franklin's lifelong goal was to become President of the United States. In order to get there, he forsook the practice of law and concentrated solely on politics. He climbed rapidly, winning a state senate seat, gaining an appointment as assistant secretary of the navy, and then running as vice-president in James Cox's unsuccessful presidential campaign against Warren Harding in 1920. The following November, Roosevelt was elected governor of New York.

In the summer of 1921, Roosevelt contracted polio, a major blow that would have ended the aspirations of most men, but not FDR. Prior to his crippling disease, he rode, swam, played golf and tennis, and sailed. "He did every damn thing under the sun a man could think of doing," remarked his close friend Louis Howe. All of a sudden Roosevelt was flat on his back with nothing to do but think. He began to read and gather people around him who could expand his political awareness.

His battle with polio didn't stop him from continuing his extramarital affairs. Blue-eyed and twenty, Marguerite "Missy" LeHand, began working for him during his vice-presidential campaign in 1920; she would stay at his side through most of the years of his presidency. Roosevelt would eventually rewrite his will and leave half his estate to her, something his children did not appreciate.

To compensate for his withered legs, FDR lifted weights to build his upper body, which became so strong that the skinny young man now appeared barrel-chested and manly in photographs. At the 1928 Democratic Convention in Houston, he was chosen to nominate Alfred Smith for president. FDR was determined to reach the podium without a crutch. He developed a slow painful way of propelling himself forward that entailed gripping one of his sons with his left arm and a small cane with his right hand. He would pretend to "walk" by rotating one heavily braced leg, then the other, in a semicircle in front of him.

Franklin had two cardinal rules as he neared his own nomination for president in 1932: he must never be carried in public or photographed as a cripple. Of the 35,000 photographic images in the Roosevelt library, only two pictures, taken by his trusted cousin for private use, show him in a wheelchair. He was the first major world leader in history who could not walk on his own, but he never wanted America or his enemies to perceive him as weak. With the press actively cooperating in this deception (which is unimaginable today), no close-up pictures of him being handicapped were ever printed.

"The country needs, and unless I mistake its temper, the country demands bold experimentation," he said in a speech just prior to his nomination. "It is common sense to take a new method and try it: If it fails, admit it frankly and try another. But above all, try something." He won the nomination, but not everyone was impressed. Walter Lippmann, the premier journalist of the day, dismissed Roosevelt as "a pleasant man whose only important qualifications for the office is that he would very much like to be president."

With the 1932 Democratic nomination in hand, FDR decided to enter the convention hall with a dramatic flourish. By long standing tradition, candidates did not accept their nominations on the convention floor, even if they were present at the convention. Acceptance speeches usually occurred in the hometown of the nominee, often seven or eight weeks after the convention ended. But FDR, taking his cue from the hypnotic public appearances of Adolf Hitler, notified the Chicago convention that if it remained in session, he would fly in from New York and accept the nomination in person. The galleries went wild with excitement. This was only five years after Charles Lindbergh had first flown across the Atlantic Ocean. Only a small fraction in attendance had ever been in an airplane, and no American president or presidential candidate had ever before flown in one. It was a brilliant and bold gesture, demonstrating that he was not bound by his apparent physical infirmity.

As the throng at the convention mingled about waiting, they were given constant updates on FDR's journey. With stops for refueling in Buffalo and Cleveland, the plane, facing stiff headwinds, arrived three hours late. When the delegates were informed that FDR had landed and was on his way from the airport, the buzzing on the convention floor grew in intensity. When it was announced that he was entering the hall, everyone stood and began yelling with excitement. Suddenly, the lights went out, the band struck up "Happy Days Are Here Again," and a spotlight illuminated the entrance behind the rostrum. The frenzied crowd was so electrified that they would have gone wild even if Adolf Hitler appeared!

In his acceptance speech FDR promised that if elected, his administration would take active steps to put people back to work and that *laissez-faire* would be replaced with a managed form of capitalism that would benefit the poor as well as the rich. "I pledge you, I pledge myself," FDR promised the delegates, "to a new deal for the American people."

FDR picked Texas Democrat John Nance Garner as his running mate. Garner once described the office of the vice-presidency as "not worth a bucket of warm piss." The election was a landslide victory for Roosevelt; he carried forty-two of the forty-eight states. The Republicans lost 12 seats and their majority in the Senate plus a staggering 101 seats in the House. Voters paid scant attention to the candidates of the far left; Socialist Norman Thomas failed to receive 900,000 votes and Communist Party candidate William Foster had a feeble showing of 102,221. Blacks, who traditionally voted Republican, switched heavily to the Democrats where their economic interests were now better represented.

The transition from Hoover to Roosevelt, from Wall Street to Washington, and from a business dominated government to one that was concerned about the welfare of the 'common folks' was indeed a social revolution of major proportions. FDR understood that his first job was to restore confidence, to give people a sense that something was going to be done to get the country moving again. He immediately instituted major banking regulations that removed the incentive for people to pull out their money from the banks.

In FDR's first radio speech as president, he told the American people: "Confidence and courage are the essentials of success in carrying out our plan. You must have faith; you must not be stampeded by rumors. Let us unite in banishing fear. We have provided the machinery to restore our financial system and it is up to you to make it work. It is your problem, my friends, your problem no less than it is mine. Together we cannot fail."

Probably never before had so many bright people descended on Washington to work for the national government. Frances Perkins was especially emphatic about her goals before she accepted the position as secretary of labor. She met with FDR and ticked off the items she intended to change during the course of her administration: a forty-hour work-week, minimum wages, worker's compensation, a federal law banning child labor, direct federal aid for unemployment relief, Social Security, a revitalized public employment service, and health insurance. The scope of her list was breathtaking.

Lies and Deceits

In the first three months of Roosevelt's administration, the country was subjected to a presidential barrage of new programs unlike anything known in American history. By June 15, 1933, the exhausted 73rd Congress left the following record:
- Emergency Banking Act.
- Economy Act.
- Civilian Conservation Corps.
- Abandonment of the gold standard.
- Federal Emergency Relief Act.
- Agricultural Adjustment Act.
- Emergency Farm Mortgage Act.
- Tennessee Valley Authority Act.
- Truth-in-Securities Act.
- Home Owners' Loan Act.
- National Industrial Recovery Act.
- Glass-Steagall Banking Act.
- Farm Credit Act.
- Railroad Coordination Act.

The Unemployment Relief Act became the Works Progress Administration (WPA). The WPA lasted eight years, spent $11 billion, employed eight-and-a half million men and women, and gave the country not only a renewed spirit, but a fresh face. WPA projects included the Triborough Bridge, Lincoln Tunnel, LaGuardia Airport, Central Park Zoo, Grand Coulee Dam, and the Tennessee Valley Authority. From 1935 until the end of the decade, the WPA built or repaired 600,000 miles of highways, streets, and roads, and laid 24,000 miles of sidewalks. It constructed or restored more than 110,000 public libraries, schools, auditoriums, stadiums, and other public buildings. It constructed 5,898 playgrounds and athletic fields and 1,667 parks. It built 256 new airports and fixed 385 more, built 880 sewage treatment plants and repaired 395 others, spanned rivers and creeks with 75,266 bridges and viaducts, laid 22,790 miles of sewage lines, and dug 770 municipal swimming pools. There was not a city or county in America that was not touched by the WPA in one way or another.

FDR's most far-reaching domestic program was Social Security. The United States was late in adopting this concept - the first modern Social Security program was enacted in Germany in 1883, while the United States clung to the idea that the elderly should be forced to fend for themselves or rely on private charity. However, in a capitalist society such as ours, how were the elderly supposed to support themselves once they were too old to work? In 1937, FDR proposed the Social Security Act, but the money would come from the workers salaries rather than a government handout. To appease the private sector, FDR sold the concept as 'insurance' which resonated more with private business than 'social benefits.'

To help finance all his programs, FDR increased the deficit, called for a graduated tax on corporate incomes, and a hike in the maximum income tax rate from 59 to 75 percent. New tax sources were developed, notably manufacturer's excise taxes, liquor taxes, and higher estate and gift taxes. The Hearst newspaper chain denounced the measures as communism. When FDR was asked, "Are you a communist, socialist, or fascist," he replied: "None of those. I'm merely a Christian and a Democrat." That was a glib answer, but not entirely true: every corner of the economic market was now under the supervision, control, and regulation of the federal government. An increasing number of Americans became directly or indirectly dependent upon Washington for their employment and income. The era of big government had arrived in the United States. It was socialism – American style.

During these first 'Hundred Days,' FDR sent fifteen messages to Congress, delivered ten speeches, held press conferences and cabinet meetings twice a week, conducted talks with foreign heads of state, sponsored an international conference, made all the major decisions in domestic and foreign policy. His mastery of the issues was astonishing.

Roosevelt's 'New Deal' policies seemed revolutionary; not because it introduced fundamental changes, but because it was carried through with such breathless speed. The New Deal was a full array of programs rather than a coherent scheme, but all the programs shared the idea that government could help an ailing economy and help people suffering its adverse effects. Probably the smartest initial move FDR made was to repeal Prohibition. Suddenly beer parties sprung up all over the country and people were happy for the first time in a long time; a sign that things might finally get better.

The American Communist Party was able to take advantage of FDR's New Deal legislation. Under the new National Labor Relations Act, employers were prohibited from interfering with the right of workers to form unions and bargain collectively. Tens of thousands of laborers joined unions as activists; an activist like Mary Elizabeth Lease made provocative speeches that proclaimed:

> "This is a nation of inconsistencies. The Puritans fleeing from oppression became oppressors. We fought England for our liberty and put chains on four million blacks. We wiped out slavery and began a system of white wage slavery. Wall Street owns the country. It is no longer a government of the people, by the people, and for the people, but a government of Wall Street, by Wall Street, and for Wall Street. The great common people of this country are slaves, and monopoly is the master. Money rules."

In November 1933, FDR, without getting approval from Congress, recognized the government in the Soviet Union and instituted diplomatic relations. A big banquet was held at the Waldorf-Astoria in New York to honor this historic moment. The titans of American capitalism attended hoping to get an early footing into this vast new consumer market. Among those present were, Alfred Sloan of GM, Gerald Swope of GE, and Thomas Watson of IBM. In the background the American flag hung next to the 'Hammer and Sickle,' and capitalism's giants rose and sang *The Internationale*, the anthem of international socialism. The lure of capitalist profits creates strange bedfellows!

FDR and Hitler both used the new communications of radio and cinema to further their causes. FDR utilized his *Fireside Chats* and motion picture newsreels to invoke confidence in America's new direction. Hitler used cinema as an even more effective tool. He personally supervised spectacular torchlight rallies with thousands of red and black swastika flags and banners, hundreds of blazing searchlights, and Richard Wagner's *Twilight of the Gods* blaring from loudspeakers.

Despite all of FDR's legislative accomplishments, most Americans in 1933 had good reason to believe the economy could still go lower. At the beginning of the year, thirty-six of forty key economic indicators hit their lowest point; meanwhile, communism in Russia was forging ahead. Many conservatives in America feared that the balance of power was shifting to the working class and the unions, and they predicted that the Communist flag would fly over some state capital by the end of the year.

When FDR proclaimed, "The only thing we have to fear is fear itself," he was trying to calm not just the general public, but the rich as well. However, the business community was not listening or buying into his program. They brought legal action against the New Deal legislation calling it unconstitutional, and the conservative majority on the Supreme Court agreed that Roosevelt had gone too far. The Court struck down much of the New Deal legislation and sent it back to Congress for revision.

FDR was furious that the Supreme Court could block the programs that were needed to deal with the current crisis, but with the presidential election of 1936 against Kansas governor Alf Landon so near, he avoided any confrontation with the Court. After FDR won a sweeping victory, taking every state but two in the election, he announced his 'court-packing' plan. FDR's solution was to expand the number of justices on the Court in order to shift the Court's decisions from the 'right' to the 'left.' With 'tongue in cheek,' he argued that the workload of the Court was too great and many of the justices were too old to think clearly. For every judge that failed to retire by the age of seventy-and-a-half, the president would name an extra justice to the Court. The number of justices would increase, but not higher than fifteen. The prospect of six more seats on the Supreme Court just happened to match the number of justices who were then older than seventy.

Everyone recognized what FDR was up to and they did not like it. Chief Justice Hughes told the Senate that the Court had no need for additional justices and was "fully abreast" of its workload. FDR responded by making a national radio speech calling the Court a "super-legislature" that frustrated the will of the people and Congress. The Senate voted down Roosevelt's plan; the number of justices would remain at nine, but the political pressure of Roosevelt's plan persuaded the conservative justices to abandon their partisan objections to the New Deal. The Court switched from a posture of judicial activism to one of judicial restraint, giving the president broad deference to regulate the economy.

Despite a doubling of federal expenditures and the creation of dozens of new federal programs, the economy was only slightly better in 1938 than it had been in 1933. Things did improve, but not to the extent that FDR had hoped for. Unemployment that was 24.9 percent in 1933 was still very high at 14.3 percent, and the federal debt had increased from $19.5 billion to $33.8 billion. Roosevelt recognized that despite his best efforts, the New Deal had not ended the Depression, but Congress would allow Roosevelt's socialism to go only so far – and no further.

Meanwhile, Germany was enjoying full employment. FDR knew that Hitler's rearmament program had restored its national economy to full health. Roosevelt wanted to establish a similar war economy, but in order to justify such a move America needed an enemy and a threat to its national security. Roosevelt had his chance to go war on July 17, 1936 when fascist forces led by General Francisco Franco, with substantial assistance from Germany and Italy, tried to overthrow the democratically elected leftist government in Spain. However, the American public wanted nothing to do with war. Italy sent troops and tanks to Franco; Nazi Germany sent its air force. During the course of the war, German planes systematically bombed civilian populations for the first time in any war.

The United States remained neutral during fascism's war with Spain; instead the U.S. imposed an embargo on all military material to either side. It was the first time in U.S. history that we refused to sell arms to a legally elected government. The Catholic Church, obsessed with 'godless' communism, supported the fascists. FDR decided that Catholic support for his domestic program was more important than alienating either the Church or America's Catholic voters. By doing nothing, FDR and the allies lost the opportunity to stop Hitler before the conflagration spread throughout Europe. Although the United States remained neutral, this did not stop General Motors, Ford, and Texaco, from supplying trucks and oil to fascist Franco – after all, 'a buck is a buck.'

The Soviet Union was the only nation to come to the aid of Spain; it sent tanks and planes and an international brigade of 40,000 volunteers, but it was not enough. In America, 3,600 volunteers formed the *Abraham Lincoln Brigade*, and sailed to Spain to fight the fascists. Their cause was supported by people like Paul Robeson, Ernest Hemingway, Lillian Hellman, Langston Hughes, Albert Einstein, Carl Sandburg, A. Philip Randolph and Helen Keller.

When the Spanish government ran out of weapons and ammunition, it capitulated. On April 1, 1939, the war was over; fascism had tested the resolve of democracy – and democracy had failed. The war, with all its brutality, was merely a 'dress rehearsal' for what was to come. Five months later, Adolf Hitler invaded Poland and World War II in Europe began.

Half of the brave members of the *Lincoln Brigade* were killed in action. Those lucky enough to return home were viewed suspiciously as communist sympathizers. When America entered World War II in 1941, J. Edgar Hoover persuaded President Roosevelt not to award officer commissions to any of the former *Lincoln Brigade* members. After the war, these same men would be hounded and persecuted by a new enemy - Senator Eugene McCarthy and his Red Scare.

CHAPTER TEN

WORLD WAR II

"I have said this before, but I shall say it again and again and again: Your boys are not going to be sent into any foreign wars."

President Franklin Delano Roosevelt
October 30, 1940

Since George Washington rejected a third term in 1796, no president dared to violate this unwritten law. Thus, Roosevelt felt that his best strategy for a third term in 1940 would be to feign extreme reluctance and have a grass-roots popular movement demand that he stay in office to guide them through the world emergency. There was as yet no constitutional limit on the number of times an American president could seek reelection, but the very idea of a third term was anathema to most conservatives and raised a cry of fascism. Republicans, however, knowing that Roosevelt could not be defeated; offered not to oppose a third term if he would accept a Republican as vice-president – a government of national consensus. FDR would not agree.

John Garner of Texas had been FDR's vice-president since 1933, but he opposed FDR's third-term nomination at the 1940 convention. Instead, FDR chose Henry Wallace as his running mate. Henry Agard Wallace - geneticist, agronomist, editor, economist, and businessman - was the best secretary of agriculture the United States ever had. He was a fervent New Dealer, and a scientist whose own research led to a global agricultural revolution. He also instituted programs for land-use planning, soil conservation, and erosion control. With these successes, it was hardly surprising that FDR picked him as his running mate.

On Tuesday, July 16, 1940, FDR was nominated again. He told the Democratic Convention and a nationwide radio audience that "his conscience would not let him refuse a third term." To assuage the nation's fear that he wanted to join the European war (he had already instituted the nation's first peacetime draft), the Democratic Party's platform included a pledge to stay out of "foreign wars." However, FDR coyly added the phrase "except in case of attack." Privately, Roosevelt said with sarcastic humor: "If someone attacks us, it isn't a foreign war, is it?"

There is a fine line between democracy and totalitarianism. In a totalitarian state, extreme nationalism prevails under a supreme leader who decides what is best for the people. In a democracy, power emanates from the people to its elected representatives, but the system does not prevent the people from electing leaders that are potential tyrants. Such was the case in Democratic Germany where the economic crisis combined with the fear of communism brought a duly elected Adolf Hitler to power.

Who was this man who believed he was on a divine mission to save Germany and the world, but will always be remembered as the "madman" responsible for the genocide of six million Jews and countless millions of other innocent victims? To write him off as a mere madman ignores the enthusiastic devotion that captured the German imagination and mesmerized an entire nation with unquestioning loyalty, pride, admiration, love, and reverence. For sixty-five million Germans, he became the new messiah. His rise to power is one of the most unbelievable and terrifying stories of our modern era. Most important of all, what happened in Germany was not an aberration. It can happen whenever widespread fear panics an intelligent public into believing that extraordinary times demands extraordinary measures.

What was the fatal attraction of a civilized nation to this evil man? Did a whole nation go mad or were their actions all too human?

Adolf Hitler was a man whose private life and thoughts were obsessively secret. He was Austrian, not German; baptized and raised as a good Catholic. He was uneducated and unemployed most of his life. Physically, he was short, squat, kind of dumpy looking and had that funny little mustache. His ill-fitting suits only made his appearance worse. He was bashful, shy, and introverted in private. He never smoked or drank alcohol, and was a vegetarian who thought that the killing of animals was barbaric. His favorite diversions were Wagner's heroic music and Hollywood movies. His favorite actress was Shirley Temple.

Hitler was born with only one testicle, which must have had severe psychological implications for him throughout his lifetime. He was never seen naked, even by his personal valet. He never married (except as a gesture just prior to his suicide) and the stories about his impotency and sexual inadequacies are legendary. Six of the seven women reputed to be physically involved with him died under mysterious circumstances. His film library of pornography was extensive. We probably will never know all the intimate details of his private life, but nothing in it could ever match the intensity of cosmic emotion and outpouring of love that the crowds displayed during his highly charged political speeches. Certainly, no other major public figure ever had such a powerful grip on every segment of the population.

American business interests, paranoid that the spread of communism would destroy American capitalism, enthusiastically supported Hitler's regime and his programs. The upper echelon in America believed you could do business with Hitler. The Germans were, after all, very much like 'good' Americans – Protestant, white, cultured, learned, and business oriented. The Russians, on the other hand, were backward and primitive – a nation of mixed races and mongrels.

Between 1926 and 1936, Father Charles Coughlin rose from obscurity as a Roman Catholic parish priest to prominence as a national figure. The secret of Father Coughlin's influence was his inimitable radio voice; a rich, mellow, musical brogue that charmed and inspired. He began his radio career by turning his energies against communism, which he linked to divorce, birth control, and free love. He connected so effectively with the despair and discontent of the Depression that by the mid-1930s his weekly radio audience ran into the tens of millions. He characterized Roosevelt as the "Great Betrayer" and adopted the battle cry

"Roosevelt and Ruin!" By 1936, Coughlin's journal, *Social Justice*, had a circulation of more than a million, and by 1938, he was sounding more and more like a European fascist as he praised the "social justice" of the Third Reich, and proclaimed that it was time for the American people to halt the international Jewish conspiracy's spread of communism. Germany celebrated him as one of the few Americans who had the courage to withstand Jewish intimidation. Railing against "the problem of the American Jews," Coughlin frequently lifted entire passages of his sermons from Nazi propaganda. He would tell his millions of listeners every week, "Think Christian, act Christian, and beware of world Jewry."

In the years leading up to America's entry into the war, fascism in the United States was becoming increasingly popular. Part of its appeal was Germany's economic success. America's capitalistic economy was still stuck in the Great Depression. By contrast, Germany's unemployment fell from 30 percent to two percent, while America's hovered at 20 percent. A typical letter to FDR, from a woman in New York, reflected the attitude of a growing number of Americans. "On all sides is heard the cry that you have sold out the country to the Jews and that they are responsible for the continued Depression, as they are determined to starve the Christians into submission and slavery. You have two hundred Jews, they say, in executive offices in Washington, and Jew bankers run the government." During these uncertain times, one thing was certain: America was not going to war because of what Hitler was doing to Jews in Europe.

On March 12, 1938, German troops marched into Austria to the delight of the Austrian population. Hitler, a native of Austria, was viewed as the returning hero, especially by the 6.5 million ethic Germans living in Austria. Austria represented an ambiguous situation; it shared with Germany a common culture and language, thus, demands to unite Germany and Austria had a historical plausibility. The following month the Austrian electorate voted to confirm its union with Germany. The *Anschluss* was approved by 99.73 percent and Austria was officially incorporated into the Third Reich. No fighting ever took place. Within weeks, the massive concentration camp at Mauthausen was completed and began to receive its first consignment of Jews. None of these actions provoked notable public outcries in the West.

The next step in the expansion of Germany was its demand to annex the Sudetenland, the German area of Czechoslovakia. This area contained 3.3 million ethnic Germans along with millions of non-Germans. Hitler made what was a troubling, but essentially logical claim. If Germany could annex Austria, why should it not be able to annex the Sudetenland, since that too was part of the German racial homeland? The proposed annexation contained some new dimensions however. First, it meant the dismemberment of a country; Austria had at least been taken over whole. Second, it meant the absorption into Germany of large numbers of people who were not ethnic Germans. The lines, then, were not as clear-cut as they had been in Austria. Yet there were enough similarities to force the Western powers to finally agree to Germany's demands.

In two meetings in southern Germany with Hitler in mid-September 1938, Britain's Prime Minister Neville Chamberlain agreed to a gradual, orderly transfer of the Sudetenland to German control. But Hitler refused this concession; he wanted an immediate transfer of the entire territory. With each passing day, war seemed imminent. France called up half-a-million reservists and the British began digging air-raid shelters in London parks. Then, in a last fateful concession, Chamberlain agreed to attend a third conference on September 29 in Munich, where the fate of the Sudetenland was infamously sealed and was turned over to Germany.

In the streets of London, huge crowds cheered Chamberlain's announcement that the Munich agreement meant "peace in our time." FDR sent Chamberlain a telegram: "Good man. I am not a bit upset over the final result." But Neville Chamberlain's capitulation was a disaster for the Czechs and a catastrophe for all those hoping to stem the German war drive.

On April 15, 1939, Roosevelt in a widely publicized message, offered to sit down with Hitler and Mussolini to settle disarmament and trade issues if they would guarantee not to attack thirty specified countries during the next ten years. Mussolini saw no reason to respond and attributed Roosevelt's absurd message to his "infantile paralysis." Nazi Air Marshal Hermann Goering sneered that "Roosevelt was suffering from an incipient mental disease."

Journalist William Shirer later described Hitler's response to Roosevelt as the most brilliant oration Hitler ever gave. For sheer eloquence, craftiness, irony, sarcasm and hypocrisy, it reached a level that Hitler was never to approach again. For more than two hours Hitler took up the points of Roosevelt's telegram.

> "Mr. Roosevelt, I took over a country that was faced with complete ruin. I have conquered chaos in Germany, re-established order and enormously increased production [the implied contrast with America's continuing Depression], developed traffic, caused mighty roads to be built and canals to be dug, and called into being gigantic new factories. I have succeeded in finding useful work once more for the whole of our seven million unemployed. You, Mr. Roosevelt, have a much easier task in comparison. You became President of the United States in 1933 when I became Chancellor of the Reich. From the very outset you stepped to the head of one of the largest and wealthiest countries in the world. Conditions prevailing in your country are on such a large scale that you can find time and leisure to give your attention to universal problems. My world, Mr. Roosevelt, is unfortunately much smaller.
>
> Herr Roosevelt, I fully understand that the vastness of your nation and the immense wealth of your country allow you to feel responsible for the history of the whole world and for the history of all nations. I, sir, am placed in a much more modest sphere. My concerns are much smaller, although for me it is more precious than anything else, for it is limited to my people! You declare that all international problems can be solved at the council table. The

freedom of North America was not achieved at the conference table any more than the American Civil War between your North and the South was decided there. My answer to you is that I would be very happy if these problems could really find their solution at the council table. My skepticism, however, is based on the fact that it was America herself who gave sharpest expression to her mistrust in the effectiveness of conferences. For the greatest conference of all time was the League of Nations – created in accordance with the will of an American president. The first state, however, that shrank from the endeavor was the United States.

I should not like to let this opportunity pass without giving the President of the United States the following assurances - I hereby solemnly declare that any assertions which have been circulated concerning an intended attack or invasion on or in American territory are rank frauds and gross untruths."

For sheer gall, guile, and hoodwinking, the speech was a masterpiece. American isolationists crowed that this was Roosevelt's reward for his gratuitous meddling.

Hitler's plan called for establishing an alliance with Poland and then going after Russia. He never planned a war against Britain and there seemed no reason to start a war with Poland – after all, Poland had joined Germany in the dismemberment of Czechoslovakia after Munich. German Foreign Minister Ribbentrop offered the Poles a Berlin-Warsaw alliance against Russia, which seemed like a natural arrangement since the Poles were fiercely anti-Bolshevik and anti-Russian, and as Catholics they seemed natural allies in a crusade to eradicate communism. To Hitler's astonishment, Poland refused. The Poles considered themselves a great world power, which was a fairy tale they would soon regret. On January 5, 1939, Hitler invited the Polish powers to

Germany for negotiations. Hitler's demands were quite moderate, but again Hitler was rebuffed.

On March 31, 1939, England informed the world that "in the event of any action which clearly threatened Polish independence and which the Polish Government accordingly considered vital to resist with their national forces, His Majesty's Government would feel themselves bound at once to lend the Polish Government all support in their power." The British government of Neville Chamberlain, supported by Winston Churchill, was now committed to fight for Poland. Former Prime Minister Lloyd George thought those who made this decision "ought to be confined to a lunatic asylum." The decision, according to him was "madness" and "demented."

Hitler believed Britain was bluffing. Hadn't Neville Chamberlain succumbed to all of Hitler's demands at Munich? Would Britain now, defend and protect Poland, a country that was clear across Europe and wedged between Nazi Germany and Bolshevik Russia? Didn't Britain understand that its war guarantee to Poland could only lead to the slaughter of tens of millions of people? Hitler knew that England at the time had no military draft and only two divisions ready for combat. Not only was England unprepared, but their war guarantee was emboldening Poland, allowing them to think they could take on Germany instead of negotiating some sort of peaceful settlement.

Why did Britain do it? Many believe that England, having already been deceived and betrayed by Hitler at Munich, acted out of shame and humiliation. After all, this was the great British Empire. They had been made to look foolish in the eyes of their own people. Now Hitler had to be taught a lesson. However, rather than commit to a war she could not win, England could have adopted a policy of containment and let the world's two great dictatorships, Germany and Russia, fight each other to a frazzle. Such a struggle would have weakened both Communism and Nazism and placed the democracies in the supreme power position.

Suddenly, Germany and Britain, neither of which wanted war with the other, were on a collision course that would engulf all of Europe. Within hours of Britain's declared war guarantee on behalf of Poland, Hitler ordered invasion plans to be drawn up. September 1 was the target date.

Hitler understood that once Poland was attacked, England was honor bound to enter the war, which would derail his plan to attack Russia in the East. What Hitler did not want was to fight a war on two fronts at the same time. Hitler decided that if he made a pact with Stalin it would allow him to achieve his goals one at a time. Stalin was trying to avoid a war his country was not prepared for. He preferred a pact with England and France, but when negotiations with those two countries dragged on without any resolution, he welcomed Hitler's overture. Just as Lenin had made peace with Germany to remove itself from World War I, Stalin now followed the same course of action. However, Stalin should have known that if there was one man in the entire world that could not to be trusted it was Adolf Hitler.

On August 24, 1939, in an unbelievable turn of events, the world was stunned to learn that Hitler and Stalin, arch enemies representing two divergent economic systems, signed a nonaggression pact and pledged not to go to war with one another. They also mapped out a secret plan to divide Poland and Eastern Europe between them. Hitler was now free to move on Poland.

On September 1, 1939, with Russia neutralized on the Eastern Front, Germany fabricated a pretext for military action against Poland. On the night of August 31, he staged a Polish attack on the German-Polish border. A dozen Jewish concentration camp inmates, dressed in German and Polish uniforms were shot and their bodies strewn about as if a fierce gunfight had taken place. The next morning, Hitler proclaimed that the attack was an unprovoked Polish incursion into German territory and the Nazi blitzkrieg of planes and tanks rolled into Poland. The mechanized German military was met by Polish forces riding on horseback. It was a massacre.

Great Britain and France stood by their pledge to come to Poland's aid and declared war. In Washington, Roosevelt's first public pronouncement was a plea to all belligerents to refrain from "bombardment from the air of civilian populations or of unfortified cities" – an ironic request considering America's nuclear bombing of Hiroshima and Nagasaki six years later. On the evening of September 3, Roosevelt took to the radio to deliver another of his famous *Fireside Chats*. "I had hoped that some miracle would prevent a devastating war in Europe, but now that war has irreversibly come, this nation will remain neutral. The United States will keep out of this war. Let no man or woman thoughtlessly or falsely talk of America sending its armies to European fields. We need only think of defending this hemisphere."

Congress passed the Neutrality Act forbidding the United States from providing assistance to any of the nations at war. Britain and France urgently pleaded that the Neutrality Act be amended, otherwise they faced certain defeat. Roosevelt called for a special session of Congress to consider a revision. The president's announcement instantly galvanized the champions of isolation; they warned FDR that tampering with the Neutrality Act would surely lead to eventual American entrapment in the war.

On the following day, the celebrated aviator Charles Lindbergh (an avid admirer of Hitler) made the first of several impassioned radio addresses against any neutrality revision. "The destiny of this country does not call for our involvement in European wars," Lindbergh said. "One need only glance at a map to see where our true frontiers lie. What more could we ask than the Atlantic Ocean on the east and the Pacific on the west? An ocean is a formidable barrier, even for modem aircraft." Lindbergh and other isolationists filled the airwaves with denunciations of Roosevelt's request to amend the neutrality provisions.

However, after six weeks of contentious debate, Congress granted Roosevelt's request. A revised Neutrality Act lifted the arms embargo – England and France could place orders with the United States for war material, including combat aircraft, but only on a cash-and-carry basis. Credit to belligerents was absolutely prohibited; purchasers of arms and ammunition had to make full cash payment and take title before the goods left American docks. This offered the allure of peace without sacrificing American profits and prosperity. With assistance on the way from the United States, it was assumed that the French army could take care of

Lies and Deceits

Hitler with the help of British sea power. That was a very wrong assumption.

On May 10, Germany invaded France. On June 13, Paris was evacuated by French forces in the face of the advancing German army. On the 23rd of June, France surrendered; it was a humiliating defeat. What Germany had failed to accomplish in the Franco-Prussian War of 1914-1918, it now succeeded to do in just six weeks. Terms of the surrender included the disarmament of French forces and the occupation of two-thirds of France by the Germans.

Hitler was overjoyed by the swiftness of his victory in France. He selected Compiegne as the site for the formal surrender. Compiegne was where the 1918 armistice ending the First World War with a defeated Germany was signed. Hitler joyfully relished in using this same location for Germany's supreme moment of revenge. He even transported to Compiegne the very same railway carriage in which the 1918 Armistice was signed, and he personally arrived to dictate the terms of surrender. After listening to the reading of the surrender preamble, Hitler, in a calculated gesture of disdain, left the carriage, leaving the negotiations to his underlings, and rode triumphantly into Paris.

Meanwhile, Germany's new ally, the Soviet Union, was easily overcoming Finland, Lithuania, Latvia and Estonia. In 1940, Germany marched into Denmark, Norway, Belgium, Luxembourg, the Netherlands, Romania, and Hungary. The following year the German 'Afrika Korps' arrived in North Africa and a pro-axis regime was set up in Iraq and Iran. When Yugoslavia and Greece capitulated, the Germans were the masters of the European continent. All that remained was England.

In London, the War Cabinet gathered to consider a peace feeler from Germany: if Britain agreed to stop fighting, Hitler would allow the British to keep most of her empire. The notion seemed tempting, especially under the dire circumstances. However, Prime Minister Winston Churchill refused to be bullied into a secret deal. He told members of Parliament: "If this long island story of ours is to end at last, let it end only when each one of us lies choking in his own blood on the ground." After four days of debate, England decided to fight on. When Churchill announced the decision to the British people on June 4, he spoke magnificently: "We shall fight them fight on the beaches - we shall fight them in the fields - we shall never surrender."

Germany continued bombing England day and night as America watched safely from across the ocean. Roosevelt knew that Germany would never declare war on the United States. To the contrary, Hitler strove in every way to avoid any incident that might bring the United States into the European conflict. When Hitler would not furnish Roosevelt with a pretext for war, Roosevelt turned his attention to the Far East and increased his pressure on Japan.

On September 16, 1940, Congress approved the first peacetime military draft in American history (it passed the House by a single vote, 203-202), and 16.4 million men between the ages of twenty and thirty-five registered. The new law specified that none of the draftees were to serve outside the Western Hemisphere and their term of service would not exceed twelve months.

Oil was the key to any successful war effort. The United States was the world's leading oil producer at the time, possessing half of the world reserves. Britain quickly turned to America for help. The United States, always mindful of its self-interest, took advantage of Britain's desperate need and dictated a deal whereby the United States would take Saudi Arabia's oil at the conclusion of the war, leaving the British with Iran. Britain and the United States also agreed to share the oil in Iraq and Kuwait.

Germany was not as fortunate as Britain – Hitler did not have America's economic power or oil resources. On June 22, 1941, a day that would change history, Hitler surprised the world by invading Russia in order to gain control of their vast oil reserves in the Caucasus region. Hitler assured his troops that "the Master Race will prevail against the inferior breed."

History says that Hitler committed the biggest blunder of the war by reneging on its pact with Russia and invading the Soviet Union. But, Hitler was no fool. By 1941, he had most of Western Europe under his control and everything was going according to plan, except he was running out of oil. Though Hitler had access to oil in Romania, he knew those supplies would be insufficient to win the war. What Hitler wanted was the Soviet Union's extensive oil fields and he was willing to risk everything in order to get it. He knew that without oil his master plan would fail.

The Germans took great care not to give any public sign of displeasure to their Russian friend, and, indeed, went out of their way to engage in an elaborate charade of deception and disinformation to lull Stalin into a false sense of security. In the early morning hours of June 22, 1941, the German Army, three million strong, with 600,000 motor vehicles and 625,000 horses, struck along a wide front. The German onslaught caught Russia completely off guard. The hard-nosed Stalin could not believe he had been so easily duped and he went into a nervous collapse that lasted several days.

Hitler's boast about the Russian campaign, that "we'll kick the door in and the house will fall down," seemed amply borne out in the first weeks of the campaign. Initially, the Germans moved even faster than expected, driving back the disorganized Soviet forces. Victory appeared almost at hand, except for some mopping up. However, there were soon some preliminary signs that the Germans were stretching themselves too thin. They had seriously miscalculated their supply needs, including the need for fuel. On the antiquated Russian roads and difficult terrain, vehicles burned considerably more fuel than anticipated, sometimes twice as much. The larger vehicles, which sank into the unpaved roads and could not move, had to be replaced with small Russian wagons drawn by horses. But warnings about looming shortages were ignored in the initial euphoria of early victories.

In August, German generals sought Hitler's permission to make Moscow the prime target. Hitler refused. "The most important aim to be achieved before the onset of winter is not to capture Moscow, but to seize the Crimea and the industrial coal region on the Donets, and to cut off the Russian oil supply from the Caucasus area." To the arguments of his generals, Hitler responded with what would become one of his favorite maxims - "My generals know nothing about the economic aspects of war."

Later, Hitler changed his mind and put Moscow at the top of his objectives, but critical time had been lost. As a result, while the Germans did manage to reach the outskirts of Moscow, they did not do so until the end of autumn 1941. There they bogged down in the mud and snow of a fast-approaching winter. The shortages of oil and other essential supplies had finally caught up with them.

On December 5, Russian General Yuri Zhukhov launched the first successful Soviet counterattack, thus preventing the Germans from moving any further and keeping them tied down for the winter. German troops never reached the Caucasus. They had vastly underestimated the reserves of Soviet manpower and the capacity of Soviet soldiers and citizens alike to tolerate hardship and deprivation.

The city of Stalingrad, to the northwest of the Caucasus, was meant to be a sideshow to the main campaign, a secondary objective. But, from the very beginning, its name made its fate pregnant with symbolism for both sides. It became the scene of a titanic, decisive struggle fought in the winter of 1942-43. After more than eighteen months of unrelenting effort and extraordinary costs in human and material resources, the tide of battle turned and the Germans were routed.

In a midnight phone call, Field Marshal Erich von Manstein begged Hitler to redeploy German forces from the Caucasus to Stalingrad. Hitler refused. "It is a question of oil, Field Marshal," Hitler said. "Unless we get the oil, the war is lost. Without oil you will be unable to do anything." But it was too late; the German army was surrounded and trapped. German tanks were out of oil, and its troops were frozen and hungry. At the beginning of February 1943, the German forces at Stalingrad surrendered.

With Germany's surprise invasion of Russia, the Soviet Union was suddenly transformed from an enemy into an American ally. Russia was now our comrade in arms! FDR was in a quandary; he wanted Russia to assist our British ally, but that would align the U.S. with capitalism's bitter communist enemy. However, the saying, "the enemy of my enemy is my friend" was never more appropriate. When Winston Churchill was asked how he could embrace Russia and Joseph Stalin after his previous harsh indictments about communism and the Russian regime, Churchill responded: "If I learned that Hitler invaded Hell, I would have something good to say about the devil."

On August 9, 1941, off the coast of Newfoundland, FDR and Winston Churchill met for the first time to discuss how the United States could be provoked into this war. Their discussions and plans remain secret to this day. What came out of the three-day meeting was the Atlantic Charter, a broad statement of friendship. At the conclusion of the meeting, the two great aristocratic statesmen were serenaded by the combined naval crews of both countries. They sang, appropriately enough, *Onward Christian Soldiers.*

When Churchill returned to London he told the war cabinet that "Roosevelt would wage war, but not declare it. He would become more and more provocative in the hopes of forcing an incident. The president made it clear that a way would be found to justify bringing America into the hostilities."

That moment almost arrived on September 4, 1941. An American destroyer, the *U.S.S. Greer*, was on a mail run to Iceland when a British patrol plane signaled the American ship that a German submarine was about to attack. The British plane and the American ship preempted and destroyed the submarine. It was the first time that the U.S. Navy fired on a German vessel. Before going down, the submarine fired its torpedoes at the American ship, but they missed.

Hitler called the sinking of the submarine a deliberate provocation by the United States, but he took no action. On September 11, FDR addressed the nation. "In spite of what Hitler's propaganda bureau has invented; despite what American obstructionist organizations may prefer to believe, I tell you that the German submarine fired first upon the *U.S.S. Greer*. When you see a rattlesnake poised and ready to strike, you do not wait until he has struck before you crush him. These submarines are the rattlesnakes of the Atlantic."

We now know that FDR was lying to the American people and to Congress. He deliberately distorted the facts, trying to find a justification for going to war. The public was outraged by the incident with the German submarine, but not enough to go to war, especially since no Americans had been killed. It would take something bigger and deadlier before Americans would be ready to go to war. That would come in three months with Pearl Harbor.

To understand how Japan became part of this war "axis" we have to go back to 1853. Prior to that year, Japan had repelled all invaders and shunned contact with the outside world. But, in July 1853, an American naval officer, Commodore Matthew Perry, arrived with a flotilla of warships in Edo Bay, what is today the city of Tokyo. The Americans did not mince words: they told the Japanese that if they did not start trading with American capitalists, U.S. military forces would attack Japan. Japan had been a feudal society, stable and isolated on its islands, and closed off from the rest of the world. They suddenly realized, to their profound shock and dismay, that they were basically naked before the superior military technology of the Western world.

In 1858, the Japanese government was compelled to sign a treaty with the United States, followed quickly by a series of similar treaties with the other Western powers. These came to be known as the Unequal Treaties, because they clearly reflected the lopsided power relations between Japan and the white foreigners from Europe and the United States. The treaties set tariff levels for imports and exports, stipulating that the Japanese government could not alter these rates. If a foreigner committed a crime on Japanese territory, the laws and courts of Japan had no jurisdiction over the case: all such trials would be conducted by foreign judges, applying the laws of the accused person's home nation. In these and other ways, the treaties brazenly infringed Japan's sovereignty, imposing unfair terms to which the Japanese had no choice but to submit. In effect, these 'unequal treaties' imposed a semi-colonial status on Japan.

Politically and economically, Japan was now legally subordinate to foreign governments. This very humiliating process set modern Japanese nationalism in motion. Out of this brush with colonial subjugation was born a determination among the Japanese to never allow this kind of inferior status to be imposed on them again: they would do whatever it took to become strong, to control their future, and to defend their national independence.

In the name of 'progress' Japan turned its back on its ancient ways that had hindered their development into the modern world. What followed was an absolutely breathtaking crusade for economic and social modernization, arguably the most rapid and successful industrialization of any economy in the world's history. In less than four decades, Japan transformed itself from a largely agricultural society into an industrial powerhouse, far and away the most modern and dynamic economy in Asia. They organized an army and navy equipped with the most modern weapons, and when they were strong enough militarily, they marched into Formosa, Korea, Manchuria and China. They did to the rest of Asia what America had done to them!

The tragedy of Japanese history between 1900 and 1945 is the story of these nationalistic sentiments running gradually out of control and ultimately delivering the nation's polity into the hands of brutal militarist leaders hell-bent on foreign conquest. The Japanese, having narrowly escaped being colonized themselves, argued that the creation of their new empire constituted nothing less than an act of self-defense. In this dog-eat-dog world of imperialism, only the strong could remain independent – and that meant having a large imperial territory outside their borders. The logic of this expansion was rooted in the general model of capitalist development in which the search for markets was pursued at least partly through colonialism and imperialism. Unlike Great Britain or the United States, Japan had few of the natural resources necessary for industrial production; therefore the acquisition of foreign markets became one of the cornerstones of Japan's new foreign policy.

In 1895, Japan forced China out of Taiwan and in 1910, Korea was annexed. In each case the pretext was that Japan was protecting its economic interests. By the 1920s, Japan faced two choices. It could appease the West by remaining a 'secondary' world power, or it could establish a kind of "Asian Monroe Doctrine," asserting its rights to be the dominate power in the Asiatic region. It chose the latter course.

In 1931, Japan invaded Manchuria, a large province on the outskirts of northern China. Japan claimed it was a "humanitarian mission to restore order," but coal and oil made Manchuria the richest province in Asia. China decided not to contest the Japanese invasion because they were too busy trying to contain Mao Zedong and his communist rebel forces. The League of Nations condemned Japan's action, but could do nothing more. Japan's reply was to withdraw from the League.

Full-scale war started in earnest in 1937, when Japan invaded the Chinese mainland. For ten years, American business firms had made huge profits supplying the Japanese with the necessary war materials, but a declared war between Japan and China changed things, especially when stories of atrocities and the bombing of civilians began filtering back to the United States. Horrified Americans wanted no part of any Asian war.

China was no match for the determined and dedicated Japanese. In October 1939, President Roosevelt ordered our Pacific Fleet to shift its home base from San Diego to Hawaii in the mid-Pacific. This aggressive body language was to show the Japanese that the United States disapproved of Japan's aggression in China. Roosevelt loudly condemned Japan, but he did little more than that. America's token aid to China consisted of secretly sending 182 American airmen, each accompanied by two mechanics, to fly warplanes for Premier Chiang Kai-Shek. Chiang, however, still seemed undecided whether his principal foe was the Japanese invaders or his Chinese communist opponents.

The war in China settled into a stalemate, while the situation in Europe dramatically worsened. On September 27, 1940, Japan signed a Tripartite Pact with Germany and Italy: a firm military alliance that if any of the three signatories were attacked by an outside party, the other two would leap to the defense. This was just what Roosevelt wanted. If Japan could be provoked into war, Germany and Italy would have to follow and we would have the war Roosevelt believed the country needed to get out of the Depression.

Economically, Japan was not self-sufficient. It relied on imports for the resources it could not produce on its own, and its number one trading source was the United States. This left Japan in a very precarious position. By 1940, Japan depended on the United States for a long list of indispensable materials, including oil - eighty percent of Japan's fuel supplies came from America. Knowing how dependent Japan was on American trade and resources, FDR chose to slowly tighten its stranglehold; "We'll put a noose around their neck and jerk it from time to time."

Our ambassador to Japan, Joseph Grew, warned Roosevelt that he was pushing Japan too far: "If we cut off Japanese supplies of oil she will out of necessity have to attack the Dutch East Indies for its oil." The United States and Japan were never in any territorial conflict: Japan's priority was Asia – America's prime interest was Europe, but escalating the confrontation with Japan was the only way for Roosevelt to get America into the European conflict.

In December 1940, Roosevelt began embargoing iron ore and pig iron; the following month, copper and brass – but still not oil. Roosevelt then tightened the screws further by declaring an immediate freeze on all Japanese assets in the United States. Japan could still buy from the United States, but their purchases would have to be cleared through a government committee. On January 24, 1941, Joseph Grew sent a wire from Japan to Washington: "There is a lot of talk around town to the effect that the Japanese, in case of a break with the United States, is planning to go all out in a surprise mass attack at Pearl Harbor."

By November 1941, there was a total embargo on exports to Japan. The Japanese now watched with envy and anger as American tankers loaded with oil headed for Russia while Japanese tankers were turned away from America's West Coast. By putting Japan in this untenable position we left Japan with no viable options – Pearl Harbor was inevitable.

Japanese Prime Minister Tojo Hideki told his advisory cabinet, "Two years from now we will have no petroleum for military use. Ships will stop moving. When I think about the strengthening of American defenses in the southwest Pacific and the expansion of the American fleet at Pearl Harbor, I see no end to difficulties. We can talk about austerity and suffering, but can our people endure such a life for a long time?"

When Japan bombed Pearl Harbor on December 7, 1941, it was as President Roosevelt aptly described, "a day that will live in infamy." Over 2,400 American soldiers were killed; almost 1,200 more wounded; 149 planes were destroyed on the ground; six of the eight battleships were shattered; all at a cost of fewer than thirty Japanese planes. Later that day, the Japanese attacked Formosa and Guam and wiped out all the American military bases there. Without a doubt, the attack constituted one of Japan's worst strategic blunders; Japan fell right into FDR's trap.

In America's pride and psyche, Pearl Harbor was a disaster. In military terms, Pearl Harbor was not a catastrophe. The fleet's vital aircraft carriers were 'surprisingly' out on patrol. All the battleships that were sunk were World War I vintage and their useful days were numbered. But, to millions of Americans the news about Pearl Harbor came as something incredibly unreal. Most Americans thought of Japan as a remote Asiatic nuisance that had issues with China, but what did that have to do with the United States?

As the awful details of Pearl Harbor poured in, incredulity turned to anger and an implacable determination to avenge these unprovoked and dastardly attacks. The next day, Congress declared a state of war with Japan. Jeanette Rankin of Montana, the first woman ever to be elected to the U.S. House of Representatives, cast the lone dissenting vote. She was hissed and booed. Rankin, a lifelong pacifist, had also voted against U.S. entry into World War I.

Roosevelt considered asking Congress for a declaration of war against Germany, but he realized it would be unnecessary; Germany's pact with Japan would accomplish that. Hitler was furious about Japan's surprise attack. The one thing he never wanted was for the United States to be provoked into this war, but what was done was done. Against the advice of his most intimate advisers, Hitler felt he had no choice. On December 11, Germany and Italy honored their treaty commitments to Japan and declared war on the United States. Roosevelt now had the war he wanted.

It is almost impossible to imagine that FDR, an icon in American history, would engineer a conspiracy to get America

Lies and Deceits

into war. We accept that evil foreign rulers might do such a thing, but deny it in our own leaders. Our leaders and their actions are 'always' considered Christian and righteous; and those who label them otherwise are unpatriotic, or worse, traitors. However, recent declassified documents, kept secret for over fifty years, confirm that the Japanese attack was allowed to happen in order to unite American public opinion to support our entry into the war.

By 1941, the Untied States had already broken all the Japanese codes and we knew their every move. At noon on Tuesday, November 25, a week before Pearl Harbor, a major policy meeting was convened at the White House. According to the diary of Secretary of War Henry Stimson, the president said, "We were likely to be attacked perhaps next Monday and the question is how to maneuver Japan into firing the first shot without allowing too much danger to ourselves."

Robert Stinnett, in his book, *Day of Deceit*, provides overwhelming evidence that FDR and his top advisers knew that Japanese warships were streaming towards Pearl Harbor. FDR, foreseeing America's public reaction to such an attack, approved a plan to allow Japan to commit an overt act of war against the United States. When FDR was certain the Japanese were about to attack, he issued orders to his military commanders at Pearl Harbor on November 27 and 28: "The United States desires that Japan commit the first overt act."

U.S. top brass in Hawaii - Admiral Husband Kimmel and Lt. General Walter Short - were deliberately made the scapegoats for allegedly failing to anticipate the Japanese attack (in May 1999, the U.S. Senate finally cleared their names). As the Japanese fleet made its way towards Pearl Harbor, Army intelligence was tracking the enemy fleet all the way. Roosevelt knew his gamble would cost lives. How many, he could not have known.

Three months earlier, a Japanese Imperial Conference concluded that if a reversal of the American embargo policy was not achieved through diplomatic means by early October, Japan would have to launch what it called *Southern Operation*; the objective would be the oil in the Dutch East Indies. For that operation to be successful, Japan needed to knock out the huge

British naval facility at Singapore, deny the Americans the use of the Philippines as a forward basing area, and cripple the main elements of the American pacific fleet at Pearl Harbor.

The plan was very ambitious, but not insane. Its slender logic resided largely in the hope that the Americans did not want to fight a protracted war and would instead accept a negotiated settlement guaranteeing Japan a free hand in Asia. The Japanese planners understood that a conventional victory ending in the complete defeat of the United States was impossible. Japan was well aware that they were a small Asian power with limited resources and could never succeed in an all-out war against the size and strength of the United States. However, when diplomatic efforts failed to resolve the embargo crisis, the Pearl Harbor plan became Japan's only remaining option.

By December 4, Roosevelt and a small group of advisers, including Stimson, Knox and Marshall, were faced with several options. They could publicly announce word of the approaching Japanese fleet, which would certainly force the Japanese to turn back. Second, they could inform their commanders at Pearl Harbor that Japanese carriers were northwest of Hawaii and order them to engage the Japanese fleet. Once discovered, the Japanese fleet could easily claim they were merely on maneuvers and had no intention of committing a belligerent attack. A third option was to allow Japan to proceed with its attack. This was the option that Roosevelt took.

Charles Beard, the great American historian had much to say about Roosevelt and this era. Beard realized that the Great Depression threatened the entire fabric of American society and that the New Deal, which Beard had supported, was not succeeding. He met often with FDR and urged him to expand the New Deal polices even further. But, Roosevelt had gone as far as he could with socialist-type reform – a solid wall of Republican opposition would block any new measures. Beard realized that Roosevelt's only remaining option was to submerge the domestic problem in a foreign crisis and go to war.

In a masterful, if controversial study, entitled *President Roosevelt and the Coming of the War,* Beard bitterly accused

Roosevelt of lying to the American public, assuring them that he was for peace and neutrality, while all the time he was actually engaging in a surreptitious campaign to lead the nation into war. Beard concluded by saying: "The practice of protecting the people from the truth in order to save them from themselves damages the fiber of a society. No society can survive its own hypocrisy." Once war was declared, Beard stopped his criticism and supported America's war effort, "I am in favor of pushing the war against Germany, Japan, and Italy to a successful conclusion. Whether it is righteous in the sight of God, I leave to the theologians."

As soon as America entered the war, FDR signed Executive Order 9066 calling for the arrest, without warrants or indictments or hearings, of every Japanese-American person in the United States – almost 160,000 men, women, and children – sixty-two percent of whom were United States citizens. These Japanese-Americans lost their property and liberty, and were transported to ten 'relocation centers' in desert and mountain areas where they were kept in concentration-like camps for over three years. Millions of German-Americans and Italian-Americans were untouched by the Executive Order – only the Japanese-Americans were singled out for internment – and there were no protests from the American public. On the contrary, "Japs must go" signs appeared all over the West Coast.

Three young Japanese-Americans decided to resist. Fred Korematsu was a shipyard worker in the San Francisco Bay area. He had volunteered for military service, but was turned down on medical grounds. He wanted to remain with his Caucasian girlfriend and changed his identity to avoid evacuation to the relocation camps. Gordon Hirabayashi was a university student in Seattle, Washington. He was a Quaker pacifist who objected to serving in the military on religious grounds. He turned himself in to FBI agents, but was still charged with violating the evacuation orders. Minoru Yasui was a lawyer in Portland, Oregon. He was an Army reserve officer and was turned away when he reported for duty after the Pearl Harbor attack. All three men were tried and convicted in proceedings that took less than a day.

In December 1944, the U.S. Supreme Court decided the *Korematsu* case. Justice Hugo Black wrote the majority opinion upholding the internment all Japanese-Americans. Justice Black stated that "military urgency" required the mass evacuation. Justice Frank Murphy originally drafted a dissenting opinion, but Justice Frankfurter persuaded him that any disagreement within the Court would be disastrous for the nation. Murphy therefore reluctantly recast his draft as a concurring opinion, although it reads like a dissent. Justice Owen Roberts, however, did dissent, calling the relocation centers "a euphemism for concentration camps."

Not until after the war did the story of the Japanese-Americans become known to the general public. The month after the war ended, an article by Yale Law Professor Eugene Rostow, called the Japanese evacuation "our worst wartime mistake." In the 1970s, Japanese-Americans began a campaign for "redress and reparations." Congress set up a blue-ribbon commission that found the internment was based on "race prejudice, war hysteria, and a failure of political leadership." Congress approved compensation of $20,000 to internment survivors and a national apology. The convictions of Korematsu, Hirabayashi, and Yasui were all reversed. In 1998, President Clinton awarded the Presidential Medal of Freedom to Fred Korematsu at a White House ceremony.

Everyone knows that the Holocaust was a horrible crime, visited by the wicked on the innocent, while 'good' citizens stood by and watched or came up with reasons to justify inaction. The United States was not blameless: we restricted immigration that trapped the Jews inside Europe; sold armaments to the Nazi regime to enhance our corporate profits; allowed anti-Semitism to flourish in this country, which affected our nation's political policies and decisions; and our cold indifference encouraged the Nazis to murder Jews without restraint.

America's role was subtle; certainly not the direct murderous involvement of those who instituted the Nazi policies and carried out the exterminations. But, the more we smugly place the blame on 'them' and pat ourselves on the back for winning the war, the more we lie about our nation's complicity. When we make the

Holocaust the ultimate evil of others, an aberration that was the work of a few mad, utterly perverse Germans that shares no commonalty with our American society, then there is nothing to be learned from those tragic years – and that would be a very big mistake.

In the summer of 1938, delegates from thirty-two countries met at Evian in France to deal with the Jewish refugee crisis. The initiative for convening the conference was President Roosevelt. He wanted to do "something" for the people being persecuted by the Nazis, without spending money or changing the immigration quotas in the United States. FDR thought that by putting the prestige of the United States at the head of an alliance of nations, he would score political points with the liberals in America, satisfy his Jewish constituents, present a united front against Nazi Germany on a sensitive issue, and have most of the Jewish refugees absorbed in other countries, thereby satisfying the conservative opposition to immigration at home.

When Roosevelt announced the formation of the Evian Conference, Hitler was overjoyed and he issued the following statement, "I can only hope that the world, which has such deep sympathy for these Jews, will convert this sympathy into practical aid. We on our part are ready to put them all at the disposal of other countries. We will even put them on luxury ships."

For nine days, the delegates met along with representatives of thirty-nine private relief organizations. One by one, they gave excuses why they could do nothing. The Australian delegation was most candid: "We don't have a racial problem in Australia and we don't want to import one." For Canada, "none was too many." Venezuela was reluctant to disturb the "demographic equilibrium" of its country. Holland and Denmark were ready to extend temporary asylum for a "few" refugees. The conference ended leaving the Jews without any avenue of escape. Evian marked a bitter moment in Western history. Its message was loud and clear - if Germany was bent on making the Third Reich *Judenrein* – free of Jews – emigration was no longer a feasible option. No country, including the United States, was willing to receive them.

Hitler laughingly responded when the conference ended: "Since many countries recently regarded it as wholly incomprehensible that Germany did not wish to preserve its Jews, it now appears astounding that all the countries at the Evian Conference seem in no way anxious to make use of these Jews now that the opportunity is available."

A new eruption of Nazi ferocity soon riveted the world's attention. On November 7, 1938, a seventeen-year-old German-Jewish refugee shot and killed a German diplomat in Paris. Reprisals swiftly followed throughout Germany. It was an officially sanctioned orgy of pillage, arson, and murder. The police were instructed not to interfere. In a single night, in what has become infamously known as *Kristallnacht* (Night of the Broken Glass), more than a thousand synagogues were destroyed; tens of thousands of Jewish businesses and homes were ransacked; ninety-one Jews were killed and thousands were sent to concentration camps. All this took place under the gleeful eyes and cheers of ordinary Germans who rushed into the streets to watch the carnage of their Jewish neighbors.

Two days later, with lunatic cruelty, the German government announced that the property damage during *Kristallnacht* would be repaired by levying a fine of one billion Reichsmarks on the Jews. All insurance claims for the burned or confiscated properties were deemed null and void. *Kristallnacht* served as the prelude for what was to follow. The world did not respond. Catholic and Protestant churches refused to condemn the Nazi actions. Pope Pius XI made no response. Speaking to reporters five days after *Kristallnacht,* President Roosevelt pointedly declared that he "could scarcely believe that such things could occur in a twentieth-century civilization." Yet, when a reporter asked FDR, "Would you recommend a relaxation of our immigration restrictions so that Jewish refugees could be received in this country," Roosevelt shot back, "That is not in contemplation; we have a quota system."

Some people in this country tried to help the trapped Jews. Congressman Samuel Dickstein sponsored legislation that would "mortgage" future quotas, accelerating Jewish immigration by allowing refugees to anticipate the quotas for 1940 and 1941. New

York's Senator Robert Wagner and Representative Edith Rogers of Massachusetts introduced a bill to allow 20,000 German Jewish children under the age of fourteen, to enter the United States. This was to be a one-time exemption, not a permanent change in the immigration quotas. The legislation received no support from the Roosevelt administration, and it even failed to reach the floor of Congress. New York Congressman Emmanuel Celler pleaded that America should save these doomed children on humanitarian grounds. His pleas were in vain. When Americans were polled, two-thirds opposed any legislation that would admit Jewish refugee children. None of the children survived.

As Hitler's death camps began operating around the clock, Rabbi Stephen Wise, a major leader in America's Jewish community, met with FDR on December 8, 1942. Rabbi Wise presented FDR with a twenty-page document entitled, "Blue Print for Extermination." It was a country-by-country analysis of annihilation. The president said that he was profoundly shocked to learn that two million Jews had already perished. He assured Rabbi Wise that the United States and its Allies would take every step to end the crimes "and save those who may yet be saved." But no such action was taken. FDR was ambivalent on the Jewish question; he believed that the Jewish issue was a political liability. He wanted to avoid making World War II a war to save Jews. That would not go over big with America's predominantly Protestant and Catholic electorate.

The man handling the Jewish refugee 'problem' in the State Department was Assistant Secretary of State Brekinridge Long, a man who belonged to the "old school" elite crowd – money, Princeton, and Protestant. Brekinridge Long was typical of those bureaucrats in the State Department who were anti-Semitic and resented the intrusion of Jews into the upper echelons of their "club." The attitude of the State Department was known to all: Jews were not welcome. Their preference was for those of their own kind, not "pushy" Jews from the city colleges.

Long's responsibilities extended over twenty-three of the department's forty-two divisions, including the granting of visas to foreigners seeking admission into the United States. Everything connected with the Jews of Europe passed through his department and was under his supervision. Long felt it was his personal responsibility to protect the nation against an invasion by radicals and foreign agents. He viewed this fight against the refugees as primarily a battle against Jewish communist agitators. He did not openly profess his anti-Semitic sentiments; instead he deliberately delayed and postponed requests for admission of Jews into the United States, and even tried to conceal news of the 'Final Solution.'

On November 30, 1942, the Romanian government sent word that it would agree to 'liberate' and send 70,000 Jews to other countries, including Palestine, for the sum of $1,250 per head, or $87.5 million in total. Chaim Weizmann, later to become the first President of Israel, wrote to the United States urging that "consideration of humanity should prevail." The U.S. State Department dismissed the proposal. "To allow this would mean serious prejudice to the successful prosecution of the war and we are concerned with the difficulties of relocating 70,000 Jewish refugees whose rescue is envisaged by the plan. For this reason we are reluctant to agree to any element of the plan."

The situation of Henry Morgenthau Jr. during the FDR regime has a very special irony. In 1929, Roosevelt, as Governor of New York, appointed Morgenthau to the Agricultural Advisory Committee and the Conservation Commission. In 1933, after Roosevelt became president, Morgenthau was appointed to the Federal Farm Board. In 1934, Morgenthau became secretary of the treasury, an act that enraged conservatives. Many people believed that Morgenthau was FDR's closest friend. Whether that was true or not, he certainly was FDR's liaison to the Jewish community.

On January 13, 1944, Morgenthau's office in the Treasury Department prepared a secret report on the State Department's blocking role regarding the Jews. The report was entitled, "A Report to the Secretary of the Treasury on the Acquiescence of the Government in the Murder of the Jews." Its detailed contents concluded that the State Department had deliberately and consistently sabotaged efforts to rescue Jews. It was a devastating document. It read in part:

"State Department officials have not only failed to use the Government machinery at their disposal to rescue Jews from Hitler, but have even gone so far as to use this Governmental machinery to prevent the rescue of these Jews. They have not only failed to cooperate with private organizations to work out individual programs of their own, but have taken steps designed to prevent these programs from being put into effect. They not only have failed to facilitate the obtaining of information concerning Hitler's plans to exterminate the Jews of Europe, but in their official capacity have gone so far as to surreptitiously attempt to stop the obtaining of information concerning the murder of the Jewish population of Europe."

Morgenthau presented the report to President Roosevelt on Sunday, January 16, 1944. Roosevelt read the report in Morgenthau's presence and immediately understood that the report was political dynamite, especially since 1944 was an election year. If the report was made public, the damage to the prestige and good faith of his Administration would be incalculable, and although Jews in America only totaled 3.6 percent of the population, they were a very involved and influential political minority.

Roosevelt, being the brilliant politician that he was, immediately established a War Refugee Board to set in motion an effort to save the Jews, but it was too little and too late. The four years that it had taken to remove the Jewish rescue operation from the State Department was crucial. The time lost could not be regained, nor could the dead be brought back to life.

A new business sprung up in Germany - the sale of false visas. Hundreds of desperate refugees clutching visas of dubious legality crammed aboard ships seeking safe haven from the oncoming Holocaust. One such ship, the Hamburg-American *SS St. Louis*, with 930 Jewish refugees aboard, arrived safely in New York harbor, but was not allowed to discharge its passengers. Urgent appeals were made to the U.S. State Department, which decided not to intervene. The passengers sent telegrams to President

Roosevelt, but their pleas went unanswered. The *New York Times* ran an editorial, "We can only hope that some hearts will soften and some refuge will be found." But there was no response to the pleas. The ship was forced to return to Germany with its doomed human cargo.

Henry Ford's close association with Adolf Hitler is usually cited as the prime example of American business involvement with the German Reich, but Ford was only one of many American business interests that profited from Hitler's rise to power. There is the stunning story of IBM's strategic alliance with Nazi Germany beginning in 1933, the first weeks after Hitler came to power, and continuing well into World War II. As the Third Reich embarked upon its plan of conquest and genocide, IBM technology identified and cataloged the Jewish populations in Germany and throughout Europe so the Jews could be targeted for efficient asset confiscation, ghettoization, deportation, enslaved labor, and ultimate annihilation.

What Hitler needed for such a monumental project was a computer, but in the 1930s no such system existed. However, IBM's Hollerith punch card technology did exist. IBM organized nearly everything for Germany. They did not merely sell the machines to Germany and walk away. Instead, IBM earned high fees, leasing, training, and operating these machines, and became the sole source of the billions of punch card data that Hitler needed to exterminate European Jewry. As Hitler's troops marched into every town and village, they had precise details about the Jews to be eliminated.

All that mattered to American corporations doing business with Hitler was profits. In addition to Ford and IBM, the list is shocking: DuPont, Boeing, Sperry, Hearst, GM, Union Carbide, Westinghouse, General Electric, Gillette, Goodrich, Singer, Eastman Kodak, Standard Oil, and ITT. Following right behind these corporate giants were renowned Wall Street law firms such as of Sullivan & Cromwell, and the banking houses of J.P. Morgan and Dillon, Read and Company, as well as the Union Bank of New York, owned by Brown Brothers & Harriman and managed by Prescott Bush, an ardent supporter of Adolf Hitler.

The considerable profits Prescott Bush made launched his son and grandson into the Bush presidencies.

American business leaders found to their immense satisfaction that the Führer's brand of fascism was extremely useful to American capitalism. With the labor unions dissolved and the communists and militant socialists thrown into concentration camps, American firms eagerly took advantage of these new opportunities. Ford-Werke reduced its labor costs from 15 percent to 11 percent. Coca-Cola's workers at the bottling plant in Essen were forbidden to strike or change jobs. Since wages remained fixed by German law, American profits in Germany soared.

Capitalists such as William Knudsen, chairman of General Motors, and ITT boss Sosthenes Behn, openly expressed their admiration for Hitler and his policies. In August 1938, James Mooney, a senior executive at General Motors, received the Grand Cross of the German Eagle for his distinguished service to the Reich. Hitler also personally showed his appreciation by awarding prestigious decorations to Henry Ford and IBM's Thomas Watson.

American capitalists loved the idea that Hitler would attack and destroy the Soviet Union – the arch enemy of American capitalism. In order to further Hitler's ambitions, American companies provided him with whatever he needed. At one point, GM and Ford accounted for half of Germany's entire production of tanks. ITT helped Germany construct fighter planes supplied with advanced communication systems. Texaco and Standard Oil helped the Nazis stockpile fuel and other petroleum products that were desperately needed for their *blitzkrieg* offensives. Ford-Werke created a "cloak company" to produce war equipment, specifically machine parts for German airplanes. This factory was deeply involved in the top-secret development of turbines for the infamous V-2 rockets that wreaked havoc and devastation on London.

Roosevelt knew what was going on, but he turned a blind eye because of Corporate America's vast influence in Washington. Token legal action was taken in 1942 against Standard Oil, the best-known violator of "trading with the enemy," but Standard Oil pointed out that it "was also fueling a high percentage of America's Army, Navy, and Air Force, thus making it possible for the United States to win the war." The Rockefeller family, owners of Standard Oil, agreed to pay a minor fine. A tentative investigation into IBM's treasonous activities with the Nazi enemy was aborted because the United States needed IBM technology as much as the Germans. Most other major American corporations that did business with Hitler were never bothered.

In July 1943, Jan Karski, a leader of the Polish underground, met with President Roosevelt in the White House along with Secretary of State Cordell Hull, Secretary of War Henry Stimson, Attorney General Francis Biddle, OSS Chief William Donovan, and Supreme Court Justice Felix Frankfurter. Karski informed them of the exterminations that were taking place. No action was taken.

Walter Rosenberg and Alfred Wetzler escaped from Auschwitz in early 1944 and provided the first eyewitness account of the magnitude that was taking place inside that death camp. With remarkable specificity gained from being registrars within Auschwitz, they diagrammed the exact locations of the gas chambers and crematories. Their 32-page report was sent to the British and United States governments, the Vatican, and the International Red Cross. The report became known as the *Auschwitz Protocol*. On April 4, 1944, an Allied plane confirmed the report when it photographed Auschwitz. The question now became whether the U.S. should bomb the Auschwitz death facilities in order to save Jewish lives?

U.S. State Department files reflect the following memo: "The War Department is of the opinion that the suggested Auschwitz air operation is impracticable for the reason that it could only be executed by diversion of considerable air support essential to the success of our forces now engaged in decisive operations. It is considered that the most effective relief to victims of enemy persecution is the early defeat of the Axis, an undertaking to which we must devote every resource at our disposal."

The State Department's position would be understandable if it were true; however, it was a lie. Between early July and August

29, 1944, the United States continually bombed the Auschwitz industries, but the gas chambers and crematoriums were never touched. Over 1.7 million Jews were gassed at Auschwitz; at least 500,000 could have been saved.

In the United States, the country was united in its war effort against the enemy, but that did not mean that black Americans were treated as comrades-in-arms. Even though racial discrimination in the armed services was technically illegal, 95 percent of African-Americans serving in the navy were restricted to mess hall duties or menial jobs. Secretary of War Henry Stimson stoutly upheld these policies, claiming that blacks were "less capable of handling modern weapons." In the army, black GIs slept in segregated barracks, ate in 'Jim Crow' mess halls, and were forced to spend their leisure time in 'colored only' recreational buildings. When they were sent overseas to the combat theaters, they were mostly restricted to support and logistical assignments. Late in the war a few segregated black combat units were finally created, but always with the ironclad rule that they would be led by white officers.

World War II was a catastrophic disaster. The material damage to homes, livestock, railways, and industrial plants was terrible enough, but was insignificant when set against the human losses. No other conflict in recorded history killed so many people in so short a time. The Soviet Union had 13.6 million military deaths and 7.7 million civilian deaths - 3.3 million Russians died from starvation and mistreatment in German concentration camps. In comparison, Germany had 3.2 million military deaths and almost 4 million civilians were killed. The United States suffered 295,000 military deaths.

Did the United States really need to provoke its way into the war? What would have happened had we maintained our neutral isolationist policy? Would Germany have prevailed against Russia and England without U.S. involvement? It is highly questionable whether Hitler would have ever succeeded in Europe. Certainly, Hitler would never have declared war on the United States. As we have seen, Hitler's desperate lunge into Russia ended in catastrophic defeat at Stalingrad. It was then that he knew "the war was lost." Even without America's entry into the war, Germany was doomed.

Had America remained neutral and let the European belligerents fight it out, the war probably would have ended in some negotiated settlement. In all likelihood, atomic bombs would never have come into existence, which would make everyone breathe easier today. Hundreds of thousands of Americans died heroically and patriotically during the war – but it is a lie to say that they died defending the liberties of Americans back home or for the Jews in Europe. They died because FDR believed it was the only way to get the country out of the Depression.

CHAPTER ELEVEN

HIROSHIMA

"The world will note that the first atomic bomb was dropped on Hiroshima, a military base. That was because we wished in this first attack to avoid, insofar as possible, the killing of civilians."

Harry S. Truman

"I'll tell you what war is about. You've got to kill people, and when you've killed enough people they stop fighting."

General Curtis LeMay

There were four major conferences among the Allied powers during World War II: Casablanca, Teheran, Yalta, and Potsdam.

On January 15, 1943, FDR flew to Casablanca for an eight-day meeting with Prime Minister Winston Churchill, General Henri Giraud of French North Africa, and General Charles de Gaulle of the "Fighting French" in exile. Joseph Stalin was not present because Soviet armies at the time were throwing back the Germans at Leningrad and were about to complete the destruction of the German army at Stalingrad. The war in the Pacific had turned around as well. After the American conquest of Guadalcanal, one island after another fell as the Japanese began a steady retreat. By January, there was no longer any prospect of a Japanese victory.

On the last day of the Casablanca Conference, Roosevelt, overriding the objections of Churchill, insisted on defining the Allied war aim for the first time as "unconditional surrender" of the Axis powers. Peace could come to the world only by "the total elimination of German and Japanese war power." Sounding this note of unprecedented and even brutal determination, Roosevelt's declaration carried grave implications. Unconditional surrender promised the destruction of not just the enemy army, but its whole society.

The Nazi war propaganda machine would tell Germans that this demand for unconditional surrender meant that the Allies were set on "making slaves of our entire nation. Children would be stolen, women turned into sex slaves, men cut to pieces, and livestock left to rot." To put such dread in the hearts and minds of an enemy population was to make inevitable a fight to the death. Roosevelt would have been better advised to follow the teachings of Sun Tzu, the ancient Chinese theorist of war, who wrote, "When you surround an army, leave an outlet free. Do not press a desperate foe too hard."

Churchill understood Roosevelt's reasoning for using the phrase 'unconditional surrender' - it was a political slogan to show that Americans had toughness and resolve, but Churchill never thought the Allies should enforce it rigidly. Fighting to the end would only inflict a tremendous cost in lives on both sides. The surrender terms, according to Churchill, might be "expressed in some other way," so the Allies would be able to secure all of "the essentials for future peace and security and yet allow the enemy some way of saving their honor."

Unconditional surrender meant the enemy would have no reason to mitigate the ferocity of its resistance. It was an invitation to the Germans and Japanese, as their likely defeat came closer, to fight back without restraint, preferring to take their chances with the brutally immoral tactics of a last stand rather than accept defeat at the hands of an enemy that refused to offer any terms whatsoever. Roosevelt's declaration also doomed the fate of the Jews in Europe; it delayed the end of the war and enabled the Nazi death machine to do its worst. Without the demand for unconditional surrender there is no telling how much earlier the war would have ended and how many lives would have been saved.

The next conference took place at Teheran from November 29 through December 1, 1943, with Roosevelt, Churchill, and Stalin in attendance. When Stalin met Roosevelt for the first time, FDR remained seated. They shook hands and as Stalin sat down he looked with amazement at FDR's legs and ankles. At dinner, later that evening, Stalin told FDR, "Now I understand how difficult an effort it was for you to come on such a long journey – next time I will go to you."

At the time of the Teheran Conference the conclusion of the war was still in doubt, but the Allies, with their superior industrialization and oil resources were definitely winning and extremely confident. Of the three leaders, Stalin was already envisioning his position in a postwar world. He recognized that Soviet power would stand supreme in Eastern Europe and he meant to keep all the territories now being overrun by his Red Army. Stalin's major abuse was reserved for the French: "The entire French ruling class is rotten to the core. Having handed their country over to Hitler, the French now were actively helping the common enemy, and deserve no consideration in the postwar arrangements. It would be unjust and positively dangerous to leave them in possession of their former empire."

The Soviet Union, the only country of the three Allied powers to be invaded, would lose over 21 million people during the war, three times what Germany would experience. Stalin saw the acquisition of Eastern Europe as a buffer zone to insure that would never happen again to his country. If the Western Allies can be said to have forfeited Eastern Europe to Russia, it was because of their strategy to delay an American invasion until 1944, thereby letting the Russians bear the brunt of the casualties while they pushed through Eastern Europe to Berlin.

A deal was struck as the Big Three sat around and mapped out the future. Postwar Eastern Europe would become a Soviet zone of influence. Stalin would get eastern Poland, but Poland would get a slice of eastern Germany as compensation. Russia would get 90 percent of Romania; Great Britain and the U.S would get 90 percent of Greece – Yugoslavia would be split 50-50, but 75 percent of Bulgaria would go to Russia.

Stalin made it clear that he intended to deal harshly, even cruelly, with his Nazi foes. He spoke bitterly about the political docility and submissiveness of the German people. Roosevelt, mindful of his country's reluctance to international involvement, stopped well short of accepting Stalin's suggestion that American ground forces participate in the long-term occupation of a splintered Germany. By way of explaining to Churchill and Stalin the persistent strength of American isolationism, Roosevelt observed that "if the Japanese had not attacked the United States, he doubted very much if it would have been possible to send any American forces to Europe."

Roosevelt's repeated references to the tenuousness of American internationalism cannot have failed to make a deep impression on Stalin's calculations about the shape of the postwar international order. The Americans, Stalin had every reason to conclude, would in all likelihood retire from the international scene after the end of the war just as they had done after World War I. Stalin, on the other hand, wanted to regain Russian territories lost in World War I, including the Baltic states, and to expand into traditional czarist areas of influence, particularly around the Black Sea. The concept of territorial security was fundamental to Russia's future. When Stalin raised the subject of postwar Eastern Europe, especially Poland, FDR sarcastically joked, "I don't care two hoots about Poland. Wake me up when we talk about Germany."

All three leaders then formally approved a plan that called for a massive attack across the English Channel in May 1944, supported by landings in the south of France and coordinated with a Russian offensive in the east. They further agreed to implement a "cover plan" to mystify and deceive the enemy as to the site and timing of the invasion. "The truth," said Churchill, in one of his inimitable flourishes, "deserves a bodyguard of lies."

At the farewell dinner, there were lots of cocktails and toasts. Stalin rose to give the last toast. "Let me tell you, from the Russian point of view, what the President of the United States has done to win the war," Stalin said. "The most important things in this war are machines. The United States has proven that it can turn out from 8,000 to 10,000 airplanes per month. Russia can only turn out, at most, 3,000 airplanes a month. England turns out 3,000 to 3,500, which are principally heavy bombers. The United States, therefore, is a country of machines. Without the use of those machines, through Lend Lease, we would lose this war."

Upon arriving back in the United States, FDR told the nation about the meeting. "The war is now reaching the stage where we shall all have to look forward to large casualty lists – dead, wounded, and missing. War entails just that. There is no easy road to victory, and the end is not yet in sight." As for his first meeting with Joseph Stalin, FDR said: "I got along fine with Stalin. He is a man who combines a tremendous, relentless determination with a stalwart good humor. I believe he is truly representative of the heart and soul of Russia, and I believe we are going to get along very well with him and the Russian people – very well indeed.'

The third conference was held at Yalta in February 1945. By the time the 'Big Three' met at the former tsarist retreat in the Black Sea resort town, the Red Army had "liberated" much of Eastern and Central Europe and was poised to drive toward Berlin. Meanwhile, Germany's last-ditch December 1944 counteroffensive slowed the U.S. advance. The end of the European war was in view, but much hard fighting lay ahead.

Uncertain whether the atomic bomb would be available in time or indeed would work, U.S. military leaders agreed "with FDR that Soviet entry into the war against Japan was essential to secure victory at an acceptable cost. Although the Allies differed significantly on crucial postwar issues, Roosevelt still hoped for the great powers to cooperate. The trip for an already ill FDR was exhausting. The classic photographs of a drawn and haggard president adorned in that loose-fitting black cape graphically manifest the illness that would soon kill him.

Four issues dominated the agenda: the voting procedures and membership rules for the new United Nations Organization; the fate of Eastern Europe, Poland in particular; the treatment of defeated Germany; and Soviet participation in the war against Japan. At Teheran, the discussions had been mostly about military matters. At Yalta, with the exception of Soviet entry into the Asian war, the discussions were about political issues. Yalta set the stage for the dawning international intrigue that came to be known as the Cold War.

Franklin Roosevelt had his own thoughts about the state of the world after the war was concluded. "When this war is over and the postwar world is divided up among the victorious powers, there will be more than a billion 'brown people' ruled by a handful of whites. They will resent it," the president mused aloud. "America's goal," he said, "must be to help them achieve independence – having over a billion enemies is dangerous."

Stalin set the tone for the week's discussions. He was self-confident, assertive, demanding, and sarcastic. Sometimes he paced impatiently behind his chair as he talked. As for Roosevelt, those at the conference found him "vague and loose and ineffective." Militarily, Stalin held all the high cards. In an amazing turn of events, just as Russia was on the brink of defeat, the Red Army turned back the German onslaught and was now just miles from Berlin; along the way it had overrun Romania, Bulgaria, Hungary, Poland, and East Prussia. The Western Allies, meanwhile, had not yet crossed the Rhine.

The subject of the United Nations was the least difficult of the topics at Yalta, though not without its vexations. Stalin held out for a single-power veto in the Security Council, a reasonable demand, and for two extra Soviet votes in the General Assembly for the Soviet Republics of Ukraine and White Russia; a transparently unreasonable attempt to pack the Assembly in favor of the USSR. Eager to please, Roosevelt acceded readily to the first Soviet request, though only grudgingly to the second.

Stalin was adamant about Poland; no subject was discussed at such length as Poland. The Polish question came up at every conference hour. It was discussed in the private talks that Churchill, Stalin, and Roosevelt had with one another, in the group meetings of the Foreign Ministers, and at all the secondary sessions. It became the testing ground between the West and Russia.

Poland had always played a crucial role as a buffer and intermediary between Germany in the West and Russia in the East. Whenever there was a war in Europe, one of those two great powers always grabbed Poland and annexed huge chunks of land. At Teheran, Roosevelt had indicated that he had no objection to ceding much of eastern Poland to Russia. But now Stalin wanted more - not more territory, but more iron-fisted political control over the postwar Polish government. "For the Russians," Stalin said, "Poland is a question of both honor and security, even one of life and death." Roosevelt and Churchill agreed – Poland would pass from German hands to Russia after the war.

The 'Big Three' next turned to the question of Germany. Stalin wanted to dismember Germany and exact heavy reparations from the conquered Reich. He proposed to strip Germany of at least $10 billion worth of industrial equipment for shipment to the Soviet Union. Churchill called the Soviet demands unrealistic. Roosevelt "thought the division of Germany into five or seven states was a good idea," but tried to deflect the conversation to the topic of zones of occupation, a matter well short of permanent partition. As for reparations, though the Americans agreed in principle to the Soviet proposal for $10 billion in industrial transfers, the fact remained that it would be the British and the Americans who would control the industrial heartland of western Germany and could later grant or withhold reparations as they pleased.

The most controversial agreement at Yalta concerned Soviet entry into the war against Japan. Roosevelt told Stalin that he "hoped that it would not be necessary to actually invade the Japanese islands," but to avoid that bloody business he needed Soviet help. A Soviet declaration of war against Japan would shock the Japanese into recognizing the hopelessness of their cause. Roosevelt calculated that bringing Russia into the war in the Pacific would enable the Red Army to tie down the large Japanese force in Manchuria, make Siberian military bases available to the United States for bombing Japan, and keep the Russians occupied from working more mischief in Europe. America's Joint Chiefs estimated that a Soviet declaration of war might shorten the fighting by a year or more and thereby preclude the dreaded invasion of Japan itself. The atomic bomb, still untested, and its possible effects unknown, did not figure into any of these calculations.

Stalin replied that "it would be difficult for him at the present time to explain to the Soviet people why Russia was entering the war against Japan." But, he added rather smugly that if certain "political conditions were met, it would be much easier to explain such a decision." Specifically, he wanted to restore Russia's losses from the Russo-Japanese War of 1904; in particular, the Sakhalin

Islands, the ports of Dairen and Port Arthur, and control over the Chinese-Eastern and South Manchurian railroads. These considerable demands came largely at China's expense. Roosevelt agreed to all Stain's conditions without bothering to consult with Chiang Kai-Shek, revealing how little FDR had come to regard China as America's client state.

Did Yalta fail or succeed? Many statesmen feel we gave away too much to Stalin and then lied to the American people about our accomplishments. That may be true, but the location of the Red armies in Europe at the time did not give the Americans much leverage or negotiating power.

Controversy over Yalta reverberated well into the postwar years. It has been alleged that Roosevelt, sick and mentally enfeebled, had foolishly trusted Stalin, cut backroom deals, betrayed Poland, delivered Eastern Europe into Soviet hands, and sold out Chiang Kai-Shek, which led to the eventual communist takeover in China. If Yalta represented an American diplomatic failure, Roosevelt believed he had few options. "I didn't say the result was good," Roosevelt privately conceded to an associate, "I said it was the best I could do."

After concluding the Yalta Conference, Roosevelt met with Saudi Arabia's King Ibn Saud aboard the *USS Quincy*, an American cruiser anchored in the southern portal of the Suez Canal. The king was transported to the meeting by a U.S. destroyer with a huge tent pitched on deck that contained his entire entourage of forty-eight persons, including Bedouin bodyguards, household slaves, and the royal astrologer.

Saudi Arabia was not under attack and had no prior ties with the United States, but Roosevelt's aides convinced the president that Saudi oil was crucial to America's future security. Those who witnessed this meeting remembered it as nothing short of extraordinary: on one side, the acknowledged leader of the Allied powers and a passionate defender of democratic ideals; on the other, an absolute monarch who had never traveled farther from home than neighboring Kuwait and adhered to an extremely strict form of Islam.

The president hoped to persuade the king to acquiesce in a Jewish homeland. What he got was adamant opposition to further Jewish settlement – even to the planting of trees in Palestine. "Amends should be made by the criminal, not by the innocent bystander," he told FDR, proposing instead a Jewish homeland in Germany. Taken aback, Roosevelt pledged that he would "do nothing to assist Jews against the Arabs and would make no move hostile to the Arab people."

Most historians and government officials believe that the two leaders forged a tacit alliance - one which obliged the United States to protect Saudi sovereignty and independence in return for a Saudi pledge to uphold American dominance of the Saudi oil fields. A partnership was formed: Saudi oil in exchange for American military security. The relationship that Roosevelt and Saud initiated has evolved considerably since 1945, but its basis was fully established at this meeting.

On March 1, 1945, Roosevelt appeared before a joint session of Congress to report on the Yalta parley. He delivered a patchy incoherent speech laced with ad-lib remarks that one close associate described as "wholly irrelevant and bordering on the ridiculous." He occasionally slurred his words and his hands trembled. He touted the agreements on the United Nations, which was scheduled to convene for the first time in San Francisco on April 25. He made no reference to his acquiescence to Stalin's demand for two extra Soviet votes in the U.N. General Assembly. Word of that odd concession nevertheless quickly leaked, lending credibility to the soon rampant suspicion that Roosevelt had brought back from Yalta a box full of "secrets" that compromised the interests of the United States.

When FDR was nominated in 1944 for an unprecedented fourth term, his re-election was assured; the country was never going to change administrations while the war was still raging. The Democratic Party 'bosses' however were concerned that whoever became vice-president would very soon be president. It was obvious to those close to FDR that he would never make it through another four years.

Henry Wallace, the current vice-president, was the logical choice, but his highly opinionated left-wing views doomed him with the political establishment. His fate was sealed on April 9, 1944, when he gave this interview to the *New York Times*:

> "The American fascist is one who wants to achieve what Hitler achieved, but would prefer not to use violence. His method is to poison the channels of public information. He never presents the truth to the public, but wants instead to use the media to deceive the public into giving him and his group more power. They claim to be super-patriots, but they would destroy every liberty guaranteed by the Constitution. They demand free enterprise, but they are the spokesmen for monopoly and vested interest. Their final objective in all this deceit is directed to capturing more political power, and using the power of the state and the power of the market simultaneously, so that they can keep the common man in eternal subjugation"

The power elites in our country wanted no part of a Wallace presidency. They wanted someone they could control, not some idealist socialist. Roosevelt, in physical decline and his mental faculties rapidly deteriorating, was pressured to leave the choice of the vice-president up to the convention; the Party bosses did the rest. They decided to promote the little known Harry Truman, senator from Missouri, someone who owed his career to the corrupt political machinery back in his home state.

Harry Truman was a World War I veteran who never finished college. A month before getting married, he opened a haberdashery store in downtown Kansas City. After a few successful years, the store went bankrupt. He then tried his hand at oil drilling. When his wife convinced him to chuck in this foolish venture, he sold his shares. Shortly afterward, oil was discovered. With no business prospects in sight, he became part of the Missouri political machine of Tom Pendergast and was elected a county judge and eventually to the U.S. Senate.

After Roosevelt was nominated by acclamation, seventeen names were placed in nomination for vice-president. The vote at the end of the first ballot was 429 for Wallace and 319 for Truman; 589 were needed to gain the nomination. On the second ballot it was 489 for Wallace, still 100 short of the nomination. Then the Democratic bosses rolled up their sleeves and went to work - ambassadorships were offered, postmaster positions were handed out, and cold cash exchanged hands. When the smoke cleared, Harry Truman was selected to replace Henry Wallace as Roosevelt's running mate. Wallace felt betrayed, but he campaigned across the country for the Roosevelt-Truman ticket. Roosevelt rewarded him after the election by naming him secretary of commerce.

On April 12, 1945, FDR died of a heart attack in Warm Springs, Georgia. It was one of those days that Americans who were alive always remember. It was the passing of an era unlike any other in American history; closing an unprecedented thirteen years in the Oval office that ran the gambit from the Great Depression to World War II.

There is much to applaud during Roosevelt's tenure. Certainly mistakes and misjudgments were made, but the country had confidence in his leadership and maybe that's the most important quality that determines the success of a leader. Roosevelt's major fault was that U.S. foreign policy depended too much on Roosevelt and he never provided for an orderly transition of power. Truman had been selected out of political utility, not because of ability. Worst of all, he had no experience in foreign affairs.

Once Roosevelt was re-elected, Truman was assigned peripheral and routine tasks, and was kept out of the "loop." Truman's succession to the presidency was potentially catastrophic for the country. The war was still on, decisions about the use of the atomic bomb had to be made, and there were signs of a postwar power struggle developing between the United States and the Soviet Union – and the fate of America was dumped into the lap of someone completely unprepared for the task. After seventy-three days as vice-president, Harry S. Truman was President of the United States.

One of Truman's first acts upon becoming president was to fire Henry Wallace as secretary of commerce. Roosevelt's advisers, notably Harry Hopkins, were replaced with anti-Soviet hardliners such as Averill Harriman, Joseph Grew, James Forrestal, and James Byrnes. His new team became completely responsible for foreign policy. When Truman gave his first address as president to Congress on April 16, the packed chamber rose thunderously to its feet when he uttered the words "unconditional surrender." Truman was advised that he would appear weak if he backed off from Roosevelt's declaration. With all America watching to see who this unknown new president was, abandoning unconditional surrender at this climactic moment would be branded with that vilest of epithets, "appeasement."

After Germany surrendered, Japan was left without its major ally and no strategic resources to speak of. Japanese tankers became sitting ducks for U.S. warships and Japan's air force was virtually out of fuel. The end of the war was plainly in sight. America would win because it had the oil; Germany and Japan did not.

With the combat concluded in Europe, the three major powers agreed to meet in Potsdam, just outside war-torn Berlin, to finalize postwar issues and begin the transition from wartime to peace. By far the most pressing question was that of Germany: should Germany be rebuilt in order to stabilize Europe, or keep it weak and repeat the mistakes that occurred after World War I.

On July 17, 1945, after only two months as president, Truman met Joseph Stalin for the first time. The diminutive president was delighted to discover that the legendary Stalin was just "a little bit of a squirt." On July 26, a Potsdam Proclamation was issued that once again called for "the unconditional surrender of all Japanese armed forces." For the next several days, discussions among the 'Big Three' rambled tediously, at times bitterly. Issues that had been intractable at Yalta proved no easier now. It was Truman's diplomatic baptism. He was understandably edgy, unsure of himself, and overawed by the power politics at this level. He wanted to appear resolute, in command, a worthy and credible successor to the fallen Roosevelt, but he paled in comparison to Stalin and Churchill.

Churchill would not complete his stay at Potsdam. In the midst of the conference, he received word that the British elections had turned him out of office. The British system elects members to Parliament and the majority party chooses the prime minister. The people of England at this time wanted more socialism and the Labor Party was voted in; Churchill was out of power and Clement Atlee took over the British prime minister's seat for the remainder of the conference.

Truman was a novice among giants and unfortunately everybody knew it. He was uncertain about everything and his bumbling attempts at humor were not well received. Knowing that things were not going well for him, he decided to impress Stalin by revealing that the United States was testing an atomic bomb.

After a contentious session late in the afternoon of July 24, Truman nonchalantly walked up to Stalin and whispered, "We have a new weapon of unusual destructive force." The Russian premier showed no special interest. All he said was that he was glad to hear it and hoped the United States would make good use of it against the Japanese. It was a singularly undramatic moment. Neither man gave any sign that he appreciated the potential of the "new weapon" to alter the course of history. Truman's revelation came as no surprise to Stalin; he already knew about the American bomb from his spies. Truman first learned about the bomb when he became president – Stalin knew about it long before that.

America's effort to build the atomic bomb began late in 1941. It was named the Manhattan Project for the ten sites in Manhattan in which uranium laboratories worked feverishly to learn how to harness atomic power into a weapon of immense destruction. At least 125,000 people were involved in this super-secret project, most of them only knowing enough to get their particular job done. Eventually, thousands of experts were gathered in the mountains of New Mexico to make the world's first atom bomb. The project was so secret that the bomb was never referred to as such; instead it was only spoken of as the "gadget."

The two main centers were Oak Ridge, Tennessee, and Los Alamos, New Mexico. The goal of the Manhattan Project activities in Oak Ridge, was to separate and produce uranium and plutonium for use in developing a nuclear weapon. Working under assumed names, Enrico Fermi and his colleagues developed the world's first nuclear reactor. The facilities in Los Alamos hosted thousands of employees under the directorship of J. Robert Oppenheimer. It was here that all the scientific research was coordinated. On July 16, 1945, in the desert north of Alamogordo, New Mexico, the first nuclear test took place.

Secretary of War Stimson and General Leslie Groves gave Truman his first extensive briefing about the Manhattan Project on April 25, 1945 – just a dozen weeks before Potsdam. "Within four months we shall in all probability have completed the most terrifying weapon ever known in human history. One bomb will be able to destroy an entire city." The conversation lasted forty-five minutes.

In the weeks that followed, various groups of Washington policymakers and atomic scientists discussed the implications of the Manhattan Project's imminent success. Given the potential destructibility involved, and in light of all the subsequent controversy about its use, it is striking that virtually nobody in Truman's inner circle seriously contemplated not dropping the bomb.

Back on September 19, 1944, Roosevelt and Churchill, amidst the brilliant foliage of a Hyde Park autumn afternoon, had agreed that the new atomic weapon, if available in time, "might perhaps, after mature consideration, be used against the Japanese, who should be warned about this bombardment beforehand to encourage their surrender." But the deliberate mood of that now distant day had long since given way to the chaotic circumstances of Truman's sudden ascension to the presidency – mature consideration proved to be a fantasy.

On July 17, 1945, a petition to the President of the United States was signed by 155 Manhattan Project scientists, headed by Leo Szilard, one of the leading physicists that developed the bomb. The petition read:

> "Discoveries of which the people of the United States are not aware may affect the welfare of this nation in the near future. The liberation of the

atomic power which has been achieved places in your hands as Commander-in-Chief the fateful decision whether or not to sanction the use of such bombs in the present phase of the war against Japan.

We, the undersigned scientists, have been working in the field of atomic power. Until recently we have had to fear that the United States might be attacked by atomic bombs during this war and that her only defense might lie in a counterattack by the same means. Today, with the defeat of Germany, this danger is averted and we feel impelled to say what follows.

The war has to be brought speedily to a successful conclusion and attacks by atomic bombs may very well be an effective method of warfare. We feel, however, that such attacks on Japan could not be justified, at least not until the terms which will be imposed after the war on Japan were made public in detail and Japan were given an opportunity to surrender.

If such public announcement gave assurance to the Japanese that they could look forward to a life devoted to peaceful pursuit in their homeland and if Japan still refused to surrender, our nation might then, in certain circumstances, find itself forced to resort to the use of atomic bombs. Such a step, however, ought not to be made at any time without seriously considering the moral responsibilities which are involved.

The development of atomic power will provide nations with new means of destruction. The atomic bombs at our disposal represent only the first step in this direction, and there is almost no limit to the destructive power which will become available in the course of their future development. Thus a nation which sets the precedent of using these newly liberated forces of nature for purposes of destruction may have to bear the responsibility of opening the door to an era of devastation on an unimaginable scale.

If after the war a situation is allowed to develop in the world which permits rival powers to be in uncontrolled possession of these new means of destruction, the cities of the United States as well as the cities of other nations will be in continuous danger of sudden annihilation. All the resources of the United States, moral and material, may have to be mobilized to prevent the advent of such a world situation. Its prevention is at present the solemn responsibility of the United States - singled out by virtue of her lead in the field of atomic power.

The added material strength which this lead gives to the United States brings with it the obligation of restraint and if we were to violate this obligation our moral position would be weakened in the eyes of the world and in our own eyes. It would then be more difficult for us to live up to our responsibility of bringing the unloosened forces of destruction under control.

In view of the foregoing, we, the undersigned, respectfully petition: first, that you exercise your power as Commander-in-Chief, to rule that the United States shall not resort to the use of atomic bombs in this war unless the terms which will be imposed upon Japan have been made public in detail and Japan knowing these terms has refused to surrender; second, that in such an event the question whether or not to use atomic bombs be decided by you in the light of the consideration presented in this petition as well as all the other moral responsibilities which are involved."

Truman and his advisers ignored the Szilard petition.

On July 21, Truman received the news of the first successful atomic test from General Leslie Groves: "The test was successful beyond the most optimistic expectations of anyone." According to Secretary of War Henry Stimson, Truman was so elated that he went skipping to his next meeting "like a little boy with a big red apple."

The United States accepted Japan's surrender after it dropped atomic bombs on Hiroshima on August 6, 1945 and another on Nagasaki three days later. Both bombs were detonated high above the cities and swooped down to destroy everything in sight. In Hiroshima, 70,000 were killed instantly; another 60,000 by November and another 70,000 by 1950. In Nagasaki, 70,000 were killed by the explosion and another 70,000 died from radiation within five years. In total, the decision to drop these two bombs killed 340,000 people. Those two blasts placed the human race on the endangered specie list.

Americans back home never blinked at the horror and consequences of our decision – we were just glad to get our loved ones back safe and sound. However, according to Admiral Nimitz, who was in the Pacific at the time, the dropping of the atomic bomb was completely unnecessary; the Japanese had been trying to surrender ever since Germany's defeat in Europe three months earlier. Truman lied to the nation when he justified the horrific destruction as necessary to end the war and save hundreds of thousands of American lives. Why did Truman lie?

The subject of Hiroshima and Nagasaki is highly charged with emotion. Sixty years have passed since we dropped "the bomb." Many Americans continue to experience pain and confusion over its use. Other Americans believe that the decision to use the bomb was justified and absolutely necessary. But it has never been easy to reconcile what we did with a sense of ourselves as a decent people. To this day it remains a raw nerve in our history. However, if Americans knew the truth about our terrible abuse of power at Hiroshima and Nagasaki, they would be ashamed.

By mid-June 1945, Japan was collapsing. Six weeks earlier, Adolf Hitler blew his brains out and a week later the Germans surrendered. The Japanese knew there was no hope. Sixty-five of Japan's largest cities had been blasted from the air in a crescendo of attacks that killed 300,000 persons and left about eight million homeless. This was total warfare, aimed at the destruction of a nation, not just its military targets. Japan's access to foodstuffs, oil, and raw materials, was sealed off by the U.S. Navy. High ranking navy officials assured Washington that Japan would collapse within a few months.

Japan's Supreme War Council convened and conceded that continuing to fight was useless. The emperor ordered the Council to "immediately work out specific measures to end the war and implement them quickly." Japan's foreign minister cabled Moscow that "unconditional surrender is the only obstacle to peace. Japan will immediately surrender if Hirohito and the emperor system can be preserved in name only." Japan asked for no other concession; all other terms of surrender would be 'unconditional.' Russia relayed the message to the United States.

According to declassified papers made available in 1980, Allen Dulles, on July 20, 1945, under instructions from Washington, went to Potsdam and reported to Secretary of War Stimson that Japan had requested to surrender and end the war. "Tokyo desires to surrender if they can retain the emperor as a basis for maintaining discipline and order in Japan after the Japanese people receive the devastating news of surrender." Secretary Stimson then wrote a draft accepting Japan's surrender that included language guaranteeing the continuance of the imperial dynasty. He summed up his thinking in a detailed memorandum to Truman.

"Contrary to much popular misconception, I believe Japan is susceptible to reason. Japan is not a nation composed wholly of mad fanatics of an entirely different mentality from ours."

Stimson recommended that Japan be allowed to continue its constitutional monarchy under her present dynasty. Such a guarantee would end the war immediately.

Stimson was not alone in this opinion. Former ambassador to Japan, Joseph Grew, was also urging Truman to offer the Japanese assurances about the future of the emperor. Presidential advisor, John McCloy, issued a formal proposal to the White House recommending a political rather than a military solution to the war. His memo read in part, "In connection with such surrender, we should not insist on treating the emperor as a war criminal, but should be prepared to preserve the institution of the emperor as the leader of a democratic constitutional monarchy."

Winston Churchill urged Truman to allow the Japanese "to save their honor and some assurance of their national existence. Sticking to the letter of unconditional surrender, whatever that meant, is the only obstacle to peace."

Truman bluntly dismissed Churchill's argument; under no circumstances was he going to show any signs of weakness. Truman was determined to show Stalin, Churchill, and the American public, that he was as strong a leader as FDR had been. He would not bend from Roosevelt's declaration of unconditional surrender – a term that had never been explicitly defined.

The significance of the emperor in Japanese society was no secret to American leaders. The Japanese regarded the emperor as a deity - more like Jesus or the incarnate Buddha than an ordinary human being. The emperor tradition could be traced all the way back to 660 B.C. The first Japanese emperor, Jimmu, was according to legend, a descendant of the sun goddess Amaterasu, making him and all of his successors' divine beings. The reigning Emperor Hirohito was by Japanese reckoning the 124th in a direct line of descent.

To the Japanese it was unthinkable that the emperor be harmed or humiliated; for them it was a "point of honor." They would fight to the last man to uphold this principle. To the Americans, the wrangling about the emperor was completely inconsequential – he was merely a symbolic figure – nothing that really mattered. The irony was that there would have been no way to get most Japanese soldiers to quit the fight except by the emperor's order; by then they were fighting for him, pure and simple. Thus the Allies needed Hirohito in place to end the war.

The surrender terms concerning the emperor were always irrelevant - the U.S. intended to replace Japanese military authoritarianism with a civilian democracy. The emperor would have no authority and Japan understood all this. The single promise they wanted was to leave the emperor on his throne as a figurehead, which in no way altered any of the terms of surrender. Had the United States not stubbornly held to some meaningless declaration, the war would have ended without the terrible consequences that followed.

When Secretary of War Stimson, briefed General Dwight Eisenhower at his headquarters in Germany, laying out the plan to use the atomic bomb against Japan, Eisenhower expressed, "my grave misgivings, first on the basis of my belief that Japan was already defeated and that dropping the bomb was completely unnecessary, and secondly because I thought that our nation should avoid shocking world opinion by use of a weapon whose employment was no longer mandatory to save American lives." Eisenhower reports that Secretary Stimson was annoyed by his statement.

While Japan was pleading to surrender with honor, back in the United States the Manhattan Project was proceeding with accelerated speed. Secretary Stimson formed an 'Interim Committee' of eight civilian officials, supplemented by a four-member scientific panel, to advise Truman about the bomb. Though Stimson later described the Interim Committee as having "carefully considered such alternatives as a detailed advance warning or a demonstration of the destructive power of the bomb in some uninhabited area," in fact, the committee did no such thing. Although it was well known that Japan was desperately looking for an honorable way to surrender, the Interim Committee made its formal recommendation: "the bomb should be used against Japan as soon as possible and without prior warning."

A 'Target Committee' was formed to choose the unlucky cities. According to files that became declassified in the 1970s, they rejected the use of the weapon against some remote military base. The objective was no longer military - the Japanese were already finished militarily – the goal was to kill as many civilians as possible.

The psychological effect of vast devastation was of great importance to the committee members. The committee agreed that "the targets should provide spectacular effects for our publicity, so the world would not regard it as just another weapon." The target, therefore, had to be a large urban city that would sustain substantial loss of human life. Targets that had not been previously bombed were preferred so the damage from the blast could be accurately measured.

Hiroshima was such an urban city – it had not been bombed previously because it was judged to be a low priority target. It was chosen now because its large civilian population insured that the bomb would cause great destruction. The Target Committee said: "the hills around Hiroshima were likely to produce a focusing effect which would considerably increase the blast damage." The center of the city contained several reinforced concrete buildings, but the area around the center was congested with small wooden houses, making the city highly flammable.

Nagasaki was another city on the target list. It was one of the largest sea ports in southern Japan and like Hiroshima had not been bombed during the war. In contrast to many modern aspects of Hiroshima, Nagasaki's residences were of old-fashioned wood-frame construction and not designed to withstand explosions.

Secretary Stimson was able to get the ancient capital of Kyoto, a shrine of Japanese art and culture, removed from the roster of proposed atomic targets because "the bitterness which would be caused by such a wanton act might make it impossible during the long postwar period for the Japanese to favor us rather than the Russians."

The list of targeted cities was finally reduced to four - Kokura, Niigata, Hiroshima, and Nagasaki. Word was sent out to all American command centers – under no circumstances were any of these cities to be bombed.

By July 31, 'Little Boy' as the first bomb was called, was ready, but a typhoon in Japan delayed the operation. Meanwhile, plans were being made for the flights. Seven planes were to take part in the mission: three B-29s acting as weather observers were to fly to Hiroshima, Kokura, and Nagasaki; two planes would escort the bombing plane to the target, one with scientists, one with photographers, and one other plane would be held in reserve at Iwo Jima in case of emergency.

On August 4, Colonel Paul Tibbets, the pilot designated to fly the mission, held a briefing with his crew, revealing for the first time that they would be dropping an atomic bomb. Capt. William S. Parsons, the navy officer assigned to assemble the first atomic bomb, showed the flight crews a motion picture of the atomic bomb test. One of the crew members, Abe Spitzer, who secretly kept notes of the briefing, recorded his impressions: "It is like some weird dream, conceived by one with too vivid an imagination."

On the following day, August 5, weather forecasters predicted improved conditions. At 2 PM, General Curtis LeMay, Chief of Staff of the 21st Bomber Command in Guam, officially confirmed that the mission would take place on August 6. That afternoon, 'Little Boy' was loaded into the B-29 that Tibbets named *Enola Gay* after his mother.

By dinnertime, all preparations were completed. At midnight, Tibbets called his men together for a final briefing. A Protestant chaplain read a prayer hastily written on the back of an envelope, asking the Almighty Father "to be with those who brave the heights of Thy Heaven and who carry the battle to our enemies." After a preflight breakfast and a group picture, the crew boarded the plane. At 2:45 AM the *Enola Gay* took off, followed by two B-29 observation planes at two-minute intervals. At 8:15 AM Hiroshima time, 'Little Boy' was dropped on Hiroshima.

Tibbets announced on the intercom: "Fellows, you have just dropped the first atomic bomb in history." The copilot, Robert

Lewis, peering down at the devastation he was party to, wrote in his log, "My God, what have we done?"

The bomb exploded 1,900 feet above the courtyard of Shima Hospital, 550 feet off its target; it had a yield equivalent to 12,500 tons of TNT. The temperature at ground zero reached 5,400°F immediately creating a fireball within half-a-mile, roasting people "to bundles of smoking black char in a fraction of a second as their internal organs boiled away."

Thousands of charred rotting bodies were strewn in the streets. A man sitting on the steps of a local bank waiting for it to open vaporized, leaving only his shadow on the granite steps. Children died of thirst, many sucking the pus from their blistered wounds before they expired. Fires broke out all over the city, devouring everything in its path. People walked aimlessly in eerie silence, their skin black with burns, the skin peeling from their bodies. Others frantically ran to look for their missing loved ones. Thousands of dead bodies floated in the river. Everywhere there was unprecedented pain, suffering, and horror. Then the black rain fell, soaking everyone with radiation. Those who survived the initial shock began dying from the intense radiation.

President Truman was having lunch aboard the battleship *Augusta* on its return from Potsdam when Captain Frank Graham of the White House Map Room handed him a report with the message, "Big bomb dropped on Hiroshima. First reports indicate complete success - visible effects greater than in any earlier test." Truman was exultant and beamed with joy. He jumped to his feet and shook hands with Graham. "Captain," he said, "this is the greatest thing in history." Then he went from person to person on the ship, officers and crew alike, telling them the great news that they had just killed hundreds of thousands of Japanese.

Truman made the following statement to the country: "We have just dropped a new bomb on Japan that has more power than twenty thousand tons of TNT. It has been an overwhelming success. The world will note that the first atomic bomb was dropped on Hiroshima, a military base. That was because we wished in this first attack to avoid, insofar as possible, the killing of civilians." The statement was a complete lie. Truman went on to say that the

Japanese had begun the war by attacking Pearl Harbor and that the bombing of Hiroshima was justifiable retribution for that act. The truth would not come to light for many years.

The Russians were not expected to declare war on Japan until August 15. Hiroshima changed their minds. On August 8, two days after the Hiroshima blast, Russia, knowing that Japan was finished, declared war on Japan and looked to add to its possessions in the Pacific before the official surrender. This was exactly one of the prime reasons for our nuclear attack – the United States, now that the atomic bomb project was completed, no longer needed Russia's involvement to end the war against Japan and we did not want them to get a foothold in East Asia.

Japan was stunned by the attack on Hiroshima – communications were completely disrupted by the atomic blast. Japan would have readily agreed to any terms to prevent another such nuclear attack, but they were never given the chance. When Emperor Hirohito learned of the destruction at Hiroshima, he quickly told his cabinet to forget about saving face: "No matter what happens to my safety, we must put an end to this war as speedily as possible so that this tragedy will not be repeated." His plea came too late.

On August 9, the United States dropped the second atomic bomb on Nagasaki. This one was even more powerful than the first one. It was called 'Fat Man,' named after Winston Churchill. The blast would kill 140,000 people; 65,000 houses were burned or damaged. The devastation of the city was mitigated because the bomb fell off target and exploded behind a mountain that sheltered much of the city from the blast.

On the morning of August 10, the day after the bombing of Nagasaki, the Japanese government again offered to surrender, and again retained the provision regarding the emperor. It was the same offer that had been made before the dropping of the two atomic bombs. Truman convened his war cabinet upon receiving the message. The question was should the United States accept the surrender offer. Secretary of State James Byrnes was adamant in wanting to reject the Japanese offer because acceptance would, as he put it, open the United States "to criticism and questions as to why those surrender terms had not been accepted by Washington months before."

This time the United States could not find an excuse, or a believable lie, for not accepting Japan's surrender offer – we had delayed long enough to explode our two bombs – there was nothing more for us to do. To accommodate Secretary Byrnes, we added a sentence that the Emperor would be under the authority of the new American Supreme Commander, but that had always been the case. Everyone knew the extra sentence was a farce to make it appear that now the surrender was unconditional. The added sentence confused the Japanese - it was sufficiently ambiguous that some Japanese officials hesitated to accept it. In a highly unorthodox display of imperial command, Hirohito made the decision. At noon on August 15, the Emperor's unfamiliar voice, speaking over the radio in a courtly archaic Japanese dialect that most of his listeners could scarcely understand, declared Japan's war at an end.

On August 14, President Truman announced: "I have received this afternoon a message from the Japanese Government – I deem this reply a full acceptance of the Potsdam Proclamation that specifies the unconditional surrender of Japan. There is no qualification." That too was a lie, but nobody really cared. The final result was greeted with wild enthusiasm throughout the United States. Our boys were coming home. Everyone was told that the 'bomb' saved their lives, but that was not true. There was virtually no criticism from important political figures or the mainstream press when they learned that the emperor had retained his position. To say that this was not our finest hour is a gross understatement. Worse yet, is America's refusal to recognize that we committed one of the most grievous war crimes in history; killing 340,000 innocent civilians for no legitimate military reason. Our reasons for this genocide were political – they were never to save American lives.

Why were the bombs dropped? There were two main reasons for Truman's decision: economics and power politics. The immense nuclear project was a bureaucratic industrial colossus that had grown to over 120,000 employees with facilities all over the country. Federal expenditures approached $2 billion with no definite assurance that it was worth either the cost or effort. After all the testing was completed, we had two bombs ready to go. Many people in the upper echelons of government believed, "what's the point of it all if we don't use the damn things."

The two bombs had different technologies. The uranium bomb dropped on Hiroshima utilized a fairly simple "gun-type" design; the plutonium Nagasaki bomb employed a complex "implosion" mechanism. In order to find out which worked best on a 'live' population, our military establishment wanted both bombs tested on the Japanese. Besides the economic justification, three years of intensive research and development was a strong motivating factor. The destruction of human life did not factor into our decision.

The second reason for dropping the bombs had to do with power politics and the Soviet Union - it established the rules of the game for the Cold War era. The bombs were dropped as a sign of our power – to warn the Soviet Union against attempting to gain influence in a world that we intended to dominate. The people of Hiroshima and Nagasaki were sacrificed to ensure that "the Soviets would be more accommodating to the American point of view." The message to Stalin was clear – the United States has the ability and the will to wantonly destroy hundreds of thousands of human beings – not just once, but twice – so beware. The dropping of the atomic bomb was not so much the last military act of the Second World War as the first major operation of the Cold War with Russia.

While no one will openly admit it, there was a racial element involved in the decision to destroy Hiroshima and Nagasaki. For certain, no atomic bomb would have ever been dropped on Berlin. For all of Germany's horrors, its people were Caucasian - white, Christian, cultured and well-bred. Even our wartime propaganda films portrayed the Germans as tall, blond, and good-looking. In the Pacific, however, our anger was directed against the infamous "Japs" - a monkey race of savages and beasts. We were conditioned to wipe out "these little yellow creatures that smiled when they bombed our boys."

Whatever distorted reasoning justified the first bomb against Hiroshima; the second one against Nagasaki was pure madness; an unparalleled war crime. Those who participated in that decision should have been punished as severely as the criminals at the Nuremberg and Tokyo war trials. Unfortunately, only the losers get charged with war crimes; the winners justify their actions under a mountain of lies.

Declassified documents from the Joint War Plans Committee, the body that was responsible for providing the Joint Chiefs of Staff with information for all planning, estimated that if an invasion of the Japanese homeland was necessary, it would result in 40,000 U.S. deaths. Generals Marshall and MacArthur both agreed with that estimate. Truman, however, kept justifying his use of the bombs by building estimated American deaths to gargantuan proportions and they kept growing with his every utterance.

In 1945, just months after Hiroshima, Truman wrote: "It occurred to me at the time that a quarter of a million of the flower of our young manhood were worth a couple of Japanese cities, and I still think they were and are." Years later, in his memoirs, Truman claimed that his decision saved a million American lives.

To be sure, 40,000 U.S. dead in a land invasion of Japan would be a horrendous number, representing family tragedies many times that, but it is far short of the figure Americans were led to believe. It was all a lie anyway – there was never going to be any invasion of Japan.

On September 20, 1945, several weeks after the Japanese surrender, General Curtis LeMay held a press conference in which he said: "The war would have been over in two weeks without the atomic bomb. The atomic bomb had nothing to do with the end of the war at all."

The decision by Truman to use the atomic bomb carried the United States across a forbidding threshold, one that marked the opening of a new chapter in the history of warfare and diplomacy. When news articles appeared in the United States describing the horrors of Hiroshima, Secretary of State James Byrnes immediately released a report of more than two hundred atrocities committed by the Japanese during the war. The timing was the government's attempt to blame the Japanese for the destruction we caused.

A few years after Hiroshima and Nagasaki, Admiral William D. Leahy, a five-star admiral who presided over the U.S. Joint Chiefs of Staff, made the following public statement:

"It is my opinion that the use of this barbarous weapon at Hiroshima and Nagasaki was of no material assistance in our war against Japan. The Japanese were already defeated and ready to surrender. My own feeling was that in being the first to use it, we adopted an ethical standard common to the barbarians of the Dark Ages. I was not taught to make war in that fashion and wars cannot be won by destroying women and children."

The decision of the United States revealed that we could brutality destroy 340,000 people by the decision of ordinary men as easily as Germany liquidated European Jewry. The mass murder at Hiroshima and Nagasaki was a perfect example of dispersed responsibility so characteristic of modern bureaucracy, where an infinite chain of policy-makers, committees, advisers, and administrators make it impossible to determine who is accountable.

It is certainly the case that America was badly served by its leaders in connection with the promulgation of Hiroshima myths and that President Truman systematically lied about the basic facts. Furthermore, an entire generation of American soldiers still clings to the belief that the atomic bombs dropped on Hiroshima and Nagasaki saved their lives. Their understandable relief based on this lie has added to the strength of the deceit. What is equally disturbing is that future generations of Americans continue to accept these lies, refusing to question our moral responsibility or acknowledge the horror we inflicted. How will we ever prevent a future Hiroshima if our children never learn the truth?

CHAPTER TWELVE

THE COLD WAR

"Never before has there been such utter confusion in the public mind with respect to U.S. foreign policy. The president doesn't understand it; the Congress doesn't understand it; nor does the public or the press. They all wander around in a labyrinth of ignorance and error and conjecture, in which truth is intermingled with fiction at a hundred points. Only the diplomatic historian, working from the leisure and detachment of a later day, will be able to unravel this incredible tangle and to reveal the true aspect of the various factors and issues involved."

George Kennan
U.S. Ambassador to the Soviet Union

The war now was over – it had been won by a Russian-American alliance – success resulted from the pursuit of compatible military objectives by incompatible economic systems. Even before the fighting officially ended and victory achieved, the Cold War began – a tense, ideological stand-off that would last for nearly a half-century. Instead of enjoying the fruits of victory, this tense struggle turned into a very dangerous chess game. For the Soviets, it was about security; for America it was about new markets and profits. People were pawns or consumers in this dangerous ideological struggle.

The origins of the Cold War go back to Marx and Lenin – to the Russian Revolution of 1917 – to the fear that communism was going to become a world revolution eventually overthrowing the American capitalist system. During World War II the United States and Russia set aside their differences and became allies in a common struggle against Hitler.

With the war over, General Eisenhower flew to Moscow as the guest of Marshal Georgi Zhukov, the top Soviet general, to celebrate the victory over Germany. Eisenhower was received warmly, met with Joseph Stalin, and stood atop Lenin's Tomb in Red Square alongside Stalin as thousands of Russians paraded across the cobblestone plaza, passing below the towering walls of the Kremlin and the ornate domes of St. Basil's Cathedral. Spirits were high, the personal chemistry between Eisenhower and Zhukov was good, and the future looked promising. As he prepared to depart, Eisenhower declared, "I see nothing in the future that would prevent Russia and the United States from being the closest of friends."

Eisenhower was wrong. He did not fully understand Russia's loss and their fears. He also did not understand that Corporate America and our State Department were already planning a new kind of war; a global economic invasion. It seems the world was not big enough to accommodate two different economic systems.

The end of World War II changed the face of the world like never before. France's pitiful performance eliminated her as a world power. Great Britain, once the master of the universe, was bankrupt and in ruins; her empire was gone. The rest of Western Europe was in turmoil. The war left 11 million refugees, bureaucratically labeled "displaced persons." Some 15 million ethnic Germans had fled or were expelled from countries they occupied.

The statistics for Russia in this war were staggering: an incomprehensible 21 million Russians were killed, 1,700 Soviet towns and 70,000 villages were destroyed; all its factories were leveled, and millions of Russians were left without homes. Stalin vowed this would never happen again to his homeland. At the end of the war, Russia was in possession of the eastern half of Europe and Stalin intended to keep it as a barrier against any future invasion.

Our history books do injustice to the claim that the United States was the conquering hero that won World War II. The war was really decided between July 17, 1942 and February 2, 1943 at the Battle of Stalingrad, when the Soviet Union routed the German army and pushed them all the way back to Berlin. By the time the United States landed in Europe in 1944, the war was all but officially over.

America lost 295,000 men during the war; a significant but minuscule number in comparison to Russia's 21 million. America's homeland was untouched and its industrial might was never stronger. The war served America's purpose; we were no longer in a Depression, and we were economically and industrially stronger than ever. And maybe most important of all, we had the "bomb" and had shown a willingness to use it. That was enough to frighten anyone.

If blame for the Cold War could be assessed, the majority of the blame would fall on the United States. While it is true that the breakdown in relations was not all Washington's doing, what is true is that America was strong and Russia was weak, and thus the United States had more options and greater room for flexibility. Diplomacy is also difficult when one side has this awesome atomic destructive technology that the other side does not yet possess. Had the United States made a huge effort to establish a non-threatening relationship with the Soviet Union maybe that would have assuaged Soviet fears, but we did no such thing because it was not the economic worldview that we wanted to pursue.

Despite all its destruction and loss of life, the Soviet Union emerged from World War II as Europe's leading military power. It was the sole power with experienced leadership. Roosevelt's death had catapulted the inexperienced and ill-informed Harry Truman into the White House, and three months later, Churchill's unexpected defeat in the British general election made the far less formidable Clement Attlee prime minister. The Soviet Union, in contrast, had Stalin, its unchallenged ruler since 1929, the man who led Russia to victory in World War II.

Stalin was no communist ideologue. He was devious yet cautious, opportunistic yet prudent, a "battle scarred tiger" who was most of all pragmatic. Crafty, formidable, and to all appearances calmly purposeful, the Kremlin dictator knew what he wanted in the postwar era – a buffer zone of countries to protect Russia from the West. Soviet armies now occupied Poland, Czechoslovakia, Hungary, Bulgaria, and a third of Germany, including the eastern half of Berlin. In Asia, it added a military presence in Manchuria, the northern islands of Japan, and the northern part of Korea. However, the Soviet Union realized that territory alone was no longer sufficient security - an American president could now cripple the USSR with one push of a 'button.'

Most Americans found it difficult to believe that "Uncle Joe" Stalin was another Hitler bent on world domination. They just wanted to settle back down and enjoy the good life. The last thing the American public wanted was a new global struggle. However, our capitalist elite saw the end of the war as a 'once-in-a-lifetime' opportunity. With growth within our borders saturated and our consumer population limited, growth could only take place in the context of a U.S. controlled global economy that opened new markets and catered to billions of new consumers. This constant capitalist necessity to expand brought great masses of human beings into conflict. This does not mean that American business leaders dictated U.S. foreign policy, but the close connection between our foreign policy and corporate business interests became so closely intertwined as to be indistinguishable.

Charles Edward Wilson, the president of General Electric, exemplified this new determination. He saw the United States in a position of power that it had never been in before, and he and his cronies intended to seize the opportunity. For an economic system that thrives on growth, returning to a peacetime economy just did not make sense. Instead, a continuing war economy was essential - even though no state of war or threat to our national security existed. Maintaining tensions became an excuse to spend billions of dollars on a vast military-industrial complex at the expense of America's social programs. But, in order to "sell" this program to the American public we needed an enemy – any enemy would do – but the Soviet Union and its communist ideology was perfect.

The Soviet Union was not stupid about our intentions. They feared that the United States wanted capitalism to dominate country after country until the Soviet Union was completely surrounded. To combat this economic aggression, the Soviet Union set out on its own communist expansion, not so much for world domination, but as protection from a perceived capitalist imperialist threat.

And the Soviets were not really paranoid. Their analysis and suspicions were quite correct. Americans like to pretend that we have no imperialistic past, but that is not true. One just has to look at America's history to see that our wars and excursions into foreign lands were all related to American capitalism.

Not surprisingly, the first major issue in the growing Soviet-American postwar antagonism was over Germany. Russia had been invaded by Germany in both World Wars and the Soviets were determined that only a weak and divided Germany could insure future Soviet security. America, on the other hand, wanted a strong Germany for two reasons: economic stability in Europe was essential to capitalism, and a strong pro-U.S. Western Europe, with Germany at the center, would be a bulwark against any communist encroachment. Once it became apparent that the United States and the USSR had reached a deadlock over Germany, the division of the world into American and Soviet spheres of influence logically followed.

America's first test of its new power came seven short months after the end of the war. The Russian army was prolonging a wartime occupation in northern Iran, seeking oil leases like those of the British in the south. Truman summoned Soviet Ambassador Andrei Gromyko to the White House and demanded that the Russian troops evacuate Iran within forty-eight hours or the United States would use the atomic weapon that only it possessed. "We're going to drop it on you," he told Gromyko. The Russian troops moved out – but Stalin would not forget America's use of the atomic threat. It was a signal to the Kremlin that power, not peace, was the key to survival.

In March 1946, President Truman arranged for Winston Churchill to deliver a major speech on foreign affairs at Westminster College in Missouri. With Truman sitting at his side, Churchill declared that an "iron curtain" had descended across Europe, beyond which the forces of communist totalitarianism ruled and would sweep across Europe if the United States did not intervene. To view the Soviet Union in this light was ludicrous. Russia could not even control its 'puppet' regimes in Eastern Europe, and America had enough atomic bombs to reduce the Soviet Union to ashes. Truman even fantasized in his diary: "Got plenty of atomic bombs – might drop one on Stalin."

In January 1947, Truman replaced James Byrnes as secretary of state with General George C. Marshall and picked George Kennan, a career diplomat, to head a newly formed policy planning department. Kennan published an article in *Foreign Affairs* magazine that was nothing short of a call to arms. He called Russia's postwar advances in Europe another chapter in the never-ending story of the effort by barbaric peoples of the Asiatic heartland to overrun Western civilization. It was up to America to act, Kennan said. The best approach would be containment, a policy just short of war itself, but opposing force with force – drawing a line and establishing a defensive perimeter, and telling the Russians, "This far you can go and no further." Kennan argued that we didn't have to actually defeat the Soviet Union, only outlast it. This policy also included encircling the Soviet Union with U.S. bases.

Secretary of State George C. Marshall revealed his plan for the reconstruction of postwar Europe in a commencement address at Harvard University on June 5, 1947. "Our policy is directed not against any country or doctrine, but against hunger, poverty, desperation, and chaos. Political passion and prejudice have no part."

On its surface the Marshall Plan appeared to be a humanitarian effort to bring devastated Europe back to normalcy, but it was all a camouflaged pretext to further American economic ambitions; the Marshall Plan initiated the age of American globalism. Its underlying purpose was to make the world safe for capitalism and to deter a possible communist threat in Europe.

The U.S. was convinced that with Europe in such a devastated postwar condition, communism would take over Europe and capitalism would become stifled. However, if the United States was able to do away with leftist governments in Europe that would allow the U.S. to trade freely with that continent. Marshall explained his plan to Congress in these terms: "The paramount question before us can be stated in business terms. The consequences of failing to carry through on this plan would be to confront America with a trade barrier to the detriment of ordinary business, commerce, and trade."

The Marshall Plan, or European Recovery Program (to give it its formal title), proposed to grant or loan some $13 billion over four years to sixteen European countries to enable them to reignite their economies with American industrial and agricultural goods. The Marshall Plan, therefore, became a defining episode in the Cold War in which the European continent was split along geopolitical lines; it was a classic example of the overt use of economic power in foreign policy.

The plan had two basic aims – to halt a feared communist advance into Western Europe and to build an international economic environment that would be a strong outlet for U.S. exports. The Marshall Plan was about putting American dollars in the hands of Europeans so they could buy back the tools of recovery from America. The United States would get back its dollars; Europe would recover, but would be straddled with debt. If some nation did not want to play this game of ours and was willing to refuse our billions – so be it – but who would have the nerve to do that without being lynched by its citizens? The whole thing was contrived economic blackmail. Sixteen European nations signed up for the Marshall Plan – we now had 16 new global outlets for our goods.

The Marshall Plan was never intended to help the USSR or any of its satellites recover from the war. On the contrary, it divided Europe into two hostile camps – our side and the Soviets. When a country from our side misbehaved, we stopped the flow of funds until they corrected their behavior. When labor unrest broke out in France, the U.S. halted its aid program there until the situation was resolved to our satisfaction. When the labor strikes collapsed, our aid was resumed.

When Italy faced a crucial election, the CIA flew in with bags of money to insure that the communists would not gain control. When the election was still in doubt, Pope Pius XII publicly excommunicated members of the communist party on the eve of the election. It is no wonder that the communists lost half their support overnight. The message was clear – behave and enjoy the benefits – or suffer the consequences.

The Marshall Plan also contained an espionage element. The mechanics were surprisingly simple. Congress would appropriate $13.7 billion over five years, but five percent of those funds - $685 million – went secretly to CIA offices overseas. It was a global money laundering scheme that remained secret until well after the Cold War. In each country where the Marshall Plan provided funds, the CIA set up a spy network with a continuing source of untraceable cash for its secret operations. Within a few short years, the CIA would become a worldwide network with 15,000 people, half-a-billion dollars in secret funds, and more than fifty overseas stations.

Secretary of State Dean Acheson privately admitted: "The measures behind the Marshall Plan are only partly humanitarian; they are also a matter of national self-interest." The Russians saw the Marshall Plan as an imperialist declaration of war for control of Europe. They viewed America's actions as an attempt to isolate Russia economically in order to contain her. Not unreasonably, given Soviet history, Stalin saw U.S. intentions in a restored Europe, and especially a rebuilt Germany, as a threat to Soviet security.

What is sadly ironic about the situation is that Stalin never had a master plan for world domination, nor the means to pursue it. He was afraid of us more than we were of him. His country had just lost 21 million people and billions in property damage; the one thing he did not want was another war. He was pathological only about two things: turning Eastern Europe into an enormous shield as protection against any possible future invasion of his country, and murdering anyone inside Russia who he perceived as a personal threat to his power.

The United States, on the other hand, put every nation on notice – you were either with us or against us – and if you were against us, you could forget about U.S. economic aid. Control of the non-aligned countries evolved into a contest between the two superpowers where both sides probed and tested. Each would advance to the precipice and then, after peering into the abyss, shudder and pull back. Neither side was willing to pull back or pull the trigger. The policy of containment was born.

The atomic bomb intensified Soviet-American distrust. The Americans secretly developed the weapon as part of the Manhattan Project, but it was not secret enough. Soviet intelligence discovered what it needed to know through espionage. The fact that Stalin mounted a major operation to spy on his allies during the middle of World War II is a strong indication of his lack of trust, although it has to be acknowledged that the United States did not choose to tell Stalin about the bomb until after its first successful test in the New Mexico desert.

We now know that Stalin had all our atomic bomb secrets long before Truman even knew there was such a thing. However, Stalin reacted strongly when the United States actually used the weapon against the Japanese. An atomic test in the desert was one thing - actually using it against human beings was something else again. "War is barbaric, but using the A-bomb is super-barbarity," fumed Stalin. "Hiroshima has shaken the whole world." Stalin authorized a crash Soviet program to catch up. "The balance of power has been destroyed. That cannot be. The A-bomb is an American policy of blackmail."

America expected their atomic bomb monopoly to last for at least six to eight years: therefore, the Red Army's disproportionate conventional ground force advantage in Europe did not greatly worry them. "As long as we can out-produce the world, control the sea, and strike inland with the atomic bomb," Secretary of Defense James Forrestal observed late in 1947, "we can assume certain risks otherwise unacceptable." That philosophy would come crashing down on August 29, 1949, when the Soviet Union got its own atomic bomb.

Stalin authorized no public announcement of their first successful test in the Kazakhstan desert. Within days, America detected the radioactive fallout - an unmistakable indicator that an atomic bomb had exploded in Soviet territory. Surprised that this had happened so soon, but fearing leaks if he tried to suppress the evidence, Truman revealed the existence of the first Soviet nuclear weapon. The Kremlin then confirmed it.

With Russia now having nuclear capability, it became a wholly different world for the United States. America was no longer protected by two oceans from the ravages of war. A quiet sense of dread spread through the country. Without its monopoly on the bomb, the U.S. could no longer feel complacent about military superiority. Our Defense and State Departments immediately began to explore the ramifications on our national security in light of the Soviet bomb. In effect, we began planning for doomsday.

Paul Nitze, a high ranking U.S. government official, was the principal author in 1950 of a highly influential secret National Security Council document (NSC 68), which provided the strategic basis for a sweeping reorientation of U.S. policy.

NSC 68 was occasioned by two events. The first was the Soviet detonation of its nuclear device. The Soviet test did not diminish overall U.S. nuclear superiority, nor did it mean that the Kremlin yet possessed a deliverable weapon. Its immediate impact was largely psychological. The sudden disappearance of our absolute nuclear monopoly took the United States by surprise, ratcheting up the fear that cities like New York and San Francisco could one day suffer the fate of Hiroshima and Nagasaki.

The second disturbing event was the loss of China to the communists. A week after the announcement about the Soviet atomic bomb - a victorious Mao Zedong emerged in China proclaiming a new Peoples Republic of China. The celebration Mao staged in Beijing's Tiananmen Square marked the end of a civil war that had been going on for almost a quarter of a century. Mao's triumph surprised both Truman and Stalin: neither anticipated the possibility that within four years of Japan's surrender the nationalists would be fleeing to the island of Taiwan and that the communists would be governing the most populous nation in the world.

Mao had no intention of being a Soviet satellite, but he was committed to being a communist ally. The new Chinese leader was a dedicated Marxist-Leninist who built his movement with very little help from Moscow. He was more than willing to defer to Stalin as the head of the international communist movement as long as Stalin did not interfere in Mao's Asian peninsula. "The Soviet Union cannot have the same influence in Asia as Communist China. By the same token, China cannot have the same influence as the Soviet Union has in Europe. Stalin should take more responsibility in Europe, while we do the same in Asia; that is our unshakable duty."

China under Mao remained a backward and impoverished nation incapable of threatening the United States. The Communists may have gained power in China, but that fact alone did not make China a power.

Regardless of these two disturbing events, the United States stood at the very zenith of power and influence. However, according to NSC 68, it now found itself in "deepest peril" with "the destruction our Republic and all of civilization suddenly looming as a real possibility." Indeed, the American system, according to Nitze, was "in greater jeopardy than ever before in our history."

Nitze's argument began with the claim that the world faced a battle between freedom and slavery, with the enslavers plotting to destroy the United States. We might have the upper hand now, but that would not last without a change in policies. As soon as the enslavers gained the atomic lead, they would be tempted to strike. Thus, America's survival depended on a rapid buildup of the armed forces. This was our only hope to "check and to roll back the Kremlin's drive for world domination."

According to Nitze's analysis, the Soviet Union - a country leveled by World War II and barely in the recovery phase - already enjoyed a clear preponderance of power. Day by day, the Soviet Union was "widening the gap between its preparedness for war and the unpreparedness of the free world for war."

To respond to this unprecedented threat, Nitze could only divine three options: isolationism, preventive war (which implied a nuclear first strike against a country incapable of responding in kind), or a rapid build-up of American military power. NSC 68 rejected the first option as tantamount to capitulation. It dismissed the second as "repugnant" and "morally corrosive." That left only option number three.

Nitze's proposed military build-up called for massively increased defense spending, with particular emphasis on accelerating the development of a hydrogen bomb; increased security assistance to train and equip the armies of friendly nations; efforts to enhance internal security and intelligence capabilities; and an intensification of covert operations aimed at "fomenting and supporting unrest and revolt" inside the Soviet bloc. Since national security had to rank first among the nation's priorities, NSC 68 called for curbing domestic expenditures.

Were this document merely an artifact of historical interest, it would not merit much attention, but NSC 68 was much more than that. It was a blueprint for a militarized America that dominated U.S. policy from administration to administration. The implications of NSC 68 were daunting. Without an atomic monopoly, it suddenly became imperative for the U.S. to upgrade its conventional forces, possibly even station American troops permanently in Europe, and build more atomic bombs if we were to maintain a quantitative and qualitative lead over Russia. According to Nitze, the United States had to consider an even more draconian option - attempting to build a "super-bomb" - a thermonuclear hydrogen bomb that would be a hundred times more powerful than the bombs that devastated Hiroshima and Nagasaki.

Fear now gripped America. In July 1948, the government charged twelve Communist leaders, including Eugene Dennis, the party's leader, with violating the Smith Act. The Smith Act had been passed in 1940 making it a crime to advocate the violent overthrow of the U.S. government. The charges against the current 12 communists were largely based on the party's distribution of writings by Marx, Lenin, and Stalin. During the trial the defendants testified that their purpose was disseminating information and education, not revolution. The defendants were convicted and sentenced to five-year prison terms.

****

The creation of the State of Israel became a major Cold War issue in 1948. Survivors of the Holocaust were pouring into their biblical homeland and Britain was rapidly pulling out of Palestine. The problem of what to do about Palestine was tossed into the lap of the U.N. Meanwhile, the fighting between Jewish settlers and Palestinian Arabs was escalating and threatening to engulf the entire region.

It is hard to discern Truman's real reasons for supporting the creation of the State of Israel, but Truman was first and foremost a politician. Throughout his adulthood, Truman privately used anti-Semitic slurs that were all too common in that era. He described New York City as "Kike town" and the "U.S. Capital of Israel." He referred to some of his political cronies as "greedy Jewish merchants." His personal diary is filled with hundreds of such derogatory statements. However, in May 1947, Soviet Minister Andrei Gromyko announced at the United Nations that the Soviet Union supported the creation of a Jewish state. Now everyone looked to see what the United States would do.

As the 1948 U.S. presidential election approached, the popular Republican governor of New York, Thomas Dewey, was the clear favorite. Polls showed Truman running well behind Dewey, with Henry Wallace and Strom Thurmond siphoning normally Democratic votes from the left and the right. A Gallup poll in June 1948 showed that almost three times as many Americans "sympathized with the Jews as sympathized with the Arabs." In 1948, Jews constituted an estimated 3.8 percent of the population (now 1.8 percent), but their influence was greater than their numbers. Whoever endorsed the creation of the State of Israel would surely get the Jewish vote and Dewey had already come out in favor of a Jewish homeland.

In a close election like this every vote was critical. Truman's most trusted foreign policy advisers were dead set against the birth of Israel. To those in the anti-Semitic State Department, Israel was one ally too many. Lovett, Forrestal, Kennan, Bohlen, and Acheson all formed a united front against a Jewish homeland. Secretary of State George Marshall told Truman he would vote against him in the upcoming election if that was to be his policy. However humanitarian a Jewish homeland might seem, the State Department argued it posed a real risk to U.S. national security; it was absolutely vital that the U. S. maintain its pipeline to Mideast oil. Supporting the Zionist cause would only antagonize the Arabs; worse, it might drive them and the oil into the arms of the Soviets. The State Department also argued that if we supported the creation of Israel, the U.S. would inevitably be drawn into a vicious war. All the top officials believed - wrongly as it turned out - that the Jews would not be able to go it alone; that they would need U. S. soldiers fighting alongside in order to survive the Arab onslaught.

Secretary of Defense James Forrestal bluntly told President Truman, "You just don't understand. There are four hundred thousand Jews in Palestine surrounded by forty million Arabs. Those forty million Arabs are going to push four hundred thousand Jews into the sea. That's all there is to it. Oil – that is the side we ought to be on." Truman was not unmindful of the problem, but in order to win the election he needed the Jewish votes. When the British mandate expired, Truman recognized the new State of Israel. Truman was right – the election was so close that the Jewish vote elected Truman.

In December 1949, Mao made the long trip to Moscow – his first ever outside China – to work out a common strategy with his communist ally. The visit lasted two months and produced a Nino-Soviet Treaty in which the two communist states pledged to come to the assistance of the other in case of attack. Upon his return to China, Mao told his people, "Now if the imperialists invade us, we have a friend to help us."

By the fall of 1950, many of our nation's young men were once again headed off to war while our politicians made patriotic speeches and remained comfortably out of harms way. The Korean War is sometimes called the forgotten war. This national amnesia does not do our nation credit. It was a war in the fullest sense – one that lasted from June 1950 to July 1953. It has not gotten the attention or the recognition for our fighting troops because it seems inconsequential compared to the two World Wars and our ten-year battle in Vietnam – but at the time it was being fought it loomed large both at home and abroad.

Korea had been part of the Japanese empire since 1910. When World War II was nearing its end, we encouraged the Soviet Union to undertake the task of seizing Korea from Japan. But as Soviet troops entered Korea, we became skittish about a Soviet occupation and offered to take the southern part ourselves, proposing the 38th parallel as a dividing line. The Soviet government agreed, suggesting that they had no plans to control Korea.

Soon separate administrations were established above and below the 38th parallel, each viewing Korea as a single country that would eventually be reunited. In the late 1940s, the U.N. tried unsuccessfully to reunify Korea, but confronted a difference in political persuasion between the southern and northern administrations.

During 1948-49, American troop withdrawals started to take place, but there was still no agreement on who would run the country. Instead, Korea remained divided, with the American-supported republic in the south, while the Soviet-supported regime ruled the north. Each side claimed to be the legitimate government of Korea and threatened to invade the other. Neither could do so, however, without superpower support.

The South Korean president, Syngman Rhee, repeatedly sought support in Washington for his ambitions to liberate the north, but he never got it. The Americans decided instead to concentrate on the defense of strong-points like Japan, Okinawa, and the Philippines. Rhee's North Korean counterpart, Kim Il-sung, had similar designs on the south, but he also was repeatedly turned down by his Russian superpower sponsor.

In January 1950, Kim Il-sung got a more encouraging response. What made the difference, it appears, was Stalin's conviction that the Americans would not respond to an invasion of South Korea. America had done nothing, after all, to save the Chinese nationalists, and Secretary of State Acheson had recently announced that the American "defensive perimeter" did not extend to South Korea.

After conferring with Mao Zedong, Stalin informed Kim Il-sung that "according to information coming from the United States, the prevailing mood is they will not interfere." Kim in turn assured Stalin that "the attack will be swift and the war will be won in three days."

Stalin's "green light" to Kim Il-sung was part of the larger strategy for seizing opportunities in East Asia. Shortly after endorsing the invasion of South Korea, Stalin also encouraged Ho Chi Minh to intensify the Viet Minh offensive against the French in Indochina (Vietnam). Victories in both locations would maintain the momentum generated by Mao's victory in China. This would counter American efforts to bring Japan within a U.S. postwar military alliance. Most importantly, Stalin's strategy would not require direct Soviet involvement: the North Koreans would do all the fighting.

On June 25, 1950, some 135,000 North Korean troops, equipped with Soviet tanks, crossed the 38th parallel and swept into South Korea. Washington was surprisingly unprepared; our Intelligence failed totally. Four days before the attack, the State Department's Dean Rusk told a congressional hearing, "We see no present indication that North Korea has any intention to cross the border or start a major war in that region." South Korea, in and of itself was of little importance, but the blatant invasion across the 38th parallel appeared to challenge the entire structure of the postwar balance of power in Asia.

The early reports out of Korea were grim. Clearly the invasion could not be stopped without the intervention of American military forces. Truman did not involve Congress in the decision. The United States, he decided, would have to fight. He later explained, "I just had to act as commander-in-chief, and I did." Some might argue this was a plausible argument, but according to the U.S. Constitution only Congress could declare war. For the first time in American history, a U.S. president asserted that the title commander-in-chief brought with it an unwritten power to take the country into a major overseas war on his word alone.

Truman's action was unprecedented. No president had ever before launched anything on this scale without permission from Congress. Members of Congress, eager to appear tough against Communism, did nothing to block Truman's action. When Truman's decision to send in troops was announced, members of both houses of Congress stood and cheered. When Truman asked Congress for an emergency defense appropriation of $10 billion, they stood and cheered once again, and approved the request almost unanimously. They also authorized Truman to call up the army reserves, extend the draft, and gave him war powers similar to those exercised by Roosevelt during World War II.

The American public was never told how bloody a conflict this might be, but the State Department knew. According to Dean Acheson, "If the best minds in the world had set out to find the worst possible location for us to fight a war, the unanimous choice would have been Korea." Without knowing the facts, the American people supported going to war. Polls indicated that nearly three-quarters of the public approved Truman's actions. Americans were already conditioned that the 'red menace' had to be stopped before it was too late. That Korea had nothing to do with our national security was irrelevant.

A recent declassified document reveals that J. Edgar Hoover of the FBI had a plan to imprison some 12,000 Americans he suspected of disloyalty. Hoover sent his plan to the White House twelve days after the Korean War began. Hoover's plan envisioned putting suspect Americans in military prisons and mass arrests to "protect the country against treason, espionage and sabotage." The arrests would be carried out under "a master warrant attached to a list of names that Hoover had been compiling for years. Ninety-seven per cent of Hoover's suspects were citizens of the United States. Truman refused Hoover's request as premature.

The Reverend Billy Graham championed our war mission in Korea. He accused the communists of trying to undermine the very foundation of Western civilization and dammed any effort at appeasement or compromise. He assured his audiences that those who trusted in the great truths of Christianity should be confident that God was on our side in this "just" war. "Communism is anti-God, anti-Christ, and anti-American. The struggle between Communism and Christianity is a battle between Christ and the Anti-Christ. It will be a battle to the death - either Communism must die or Christianity must die." Truman's top aide John

Steelman warned television viewers that "if communism were not stopped, they would rob Americans of their cars and TVs."

When Truman held a press conference on June 29, a reporter asked if this was a war or would it be accurate to call the fighting a police action. "Yes," Truman replied, delighted to have a phrase that didn't call it a war. "That is exactly what it amounts to." While the U.N. was useful, their help was irrelevant. America was going to lead the fight in Korea. Truman was going to show history and the Soviets that he had as much 'moral courage' and toughness as FDR. American troops were told not to worry – they would be home in six weeks. How could these little Koreans stand up to the Americans that had defeated Adolf Hitler?

Truman was able to act quickly for two reasons. The first was that an American army was conveniently stationed nearby; we were still occupying Japan. The second was an oversight on Stalin's part. There was no Soviet representative present in the U.N. Security Council when the matter was presented for a vote. The Soviet delegate had been withdrawn as a protest against the U.N refusal to seat the Chinese Communists as the new legitimate representative of China. With the Russians not present to veto, the U.N. approved a resolution for the international community to mobilize and counter this new threat to world security.

General Douglas MacArthur, at the age of seventy, was in charge of all operations in Korea. MacArthur was a larger-than-life commander ideally suited to command America's military. Born in 1880, the son of a career army general and Medal of Honor winner, MacArthur lived and breathed army life right from the beginning. He attended West Point where he excelled as an athlete and graduated first in the class of 1903 with the best record in more than 25 years. He was a man with a tremendous ego who truly believed he was infallible.

MacArthur's first combat experience was in the Philippines during World War I. He returned to West Point as its superintendent in 1919, but in 1930, President Hoover appointed him chief-of-staff of the army; Dwight D. Eisenhower was his deputy. During World War II, MacArthur was in charge of U.S. operations in Asia against Japan. After the war, he presided over the rebuilding of

Japan, transforming that nation into an industrial democracy. The Korean War once again brought him to the forefront.

However, things in Korea immediately went from bad to worse. Our inexperienced troops were forced to retreat to the southeastern tip of the Korean peninsula and might have had to evacuate Korea altogether had it not been for a brilliant military maneuver by MacArthur who surprised the North Koreans with a daring amphibious landing at Inchon, near Seoul. He trapped the North Korean army and his forces were advancing almost unopposed through North Korea. Shocked by this sequence of events, Stalin was on the verge of accepting a humiliating defeat.

North Korea borders China and the Soviet Union. There was concern in Washington about the possibility of Chinese intervention and for that reason Truman ordered MacArthur not to advance all the way to the Sino-Korean border. Meanwhile, the State Department, through various intermediaries, was seeking to deter China by raising the prospect of nuclear strikes that would result in horrendous Chinese casualties.

Russia tried to head off a widening of the war. The Soviets placed a resolution before the U.N. that called for a cease-fire, the withdrawal of all foreign forces from the peninsula, and a general election under U.N. supervision to produce a united Korea. The United States rejected the offer. U.S. forces were on the offensive in Korea and MacArthur was headed straight for the Chinese border. Truman was dazzled by the prospect of outright victory and personal vindication. He figured this was no time for a cease-fire. He was assured by the CIA that the Chinese were not going to enter the war. Inside China, Mao was also assessing the situation. He feared that a U.S. invasion would attempt to re-establish the old Chiang Kai-Shek regime. He was not going to let that happen.

The Chinese assault into Korea began on October 25, 1950 when 270,000 Chinese soldiers stormed down in human waves with bugles blowing. The front was three hundred miles wide. American troops had never fought in any war more frightening than this one, facing as they did wave after wave of Chinese soldiers seemingly impervious to U.S. firepower. This was no longer the "police action" that Truman called it. "We face an entirely new war," MacArthur cabled Washington. The Americans were overwhelmed by the Chinese onslaught and they ran. The Pentagon rushed to plan for an evacuation of all American forces. Dean Acheson described what was happening as the worst defeat of U.S. forces since the Battle of Bull Run in the American Civil War.

MacArthur was relatively unmoved by the Chinese attack. He was simply too egotistical to think he could ever be defeated, and he refused to believe that the Chinese could prevail. However, Mao's tough battle-seasoned men knew the climate and terrain better than we did. They wore warm padded jackets to fend off the bitter cold, and carried only eight pounds of equipment as opposed to sixty pounds for most American soldiers. They were skilled at holding still when U.S. planes were buzzing overhead. After the planes left, the Chinese swarmed as close as possible to the American enemy, blasting away with automatic fire and engaging in terrifying hand-to-hand combat. Often fighting at night, they overran American soldiers huddled on the frozen ground and bayoneted them to death through their sleeping bags.

On November 30, at a Washington press conference, with the mortifying rout still under way, Truman declared that the Korean conflict was the result of Russian aggression and the source of a new world crisis. Moscow was the real enemy; Korea was only Moscow's forward line and Truman was determined to hold that line. He promised to take "whatever steps are necessary."

"Did that include the atomic bomb?" a reporter asked. "That includes every weapon we have," Truman answered, and then added, "Using the bomb has always been under active consideration." When a reporter pressed for further amplification, Truman cut him off, saying, "It's a matter for the military people to decide. I'm not a military authority that passes on those things. The military commander in the field is in charge of the use of our weapons."

There it was. The atomic bomb was now just another weapon in the U.S. arsenal – and the decision was in the hands of MacArthur, not the president. That afternoon, headlines screamed that the bomb was being readied for use against the Chinese. A headline in *Times of India* read: "No, No, No!" Reports came to Washington that half a million Soviet soldiers were mobilizing in Siberia and that Russian bombers had been moved to within range of Korea. Stalin, as post-Cold War Soviet archives reveal, was sure that MacArthur wanted to bring the war to China in order to trigger a global war; it was something Stalin did not want.

Stalin was right. MacArthur was prepared to invade China. To him complete victory was everything. The idea of a limited war – fighting to a draw – was not in his mindset. MacArthur openly demanded a nuclear attack. China appealed to Russia to do likewise if the Americans unleashed its atomic arsenal. Both sides appeared ready, but neither wanted to take that fatal first step as the world held its breath.

Truman had been the only man to ever order the use of atomic bombs, and beneath the veneer of his permanent insistence on its necessity against Japan, he remained haunted by what he had done. Truman now stepped back from the brink – there would be no wider war, he decided. There would be no atomic bombs for MacArthur. Just as Truman changed the course of history by deciding to use the atomic bomb in 1945, he changed the course of history again by deciding not to use it in 1951. Truman established the precedent of limited war. Some things were just not worth the cost of victory.

Truman hastily flew to Wake Island in the Pacific to meet with MacArthur. In his memoirs, Truman described MacArthur as arrogant and condescending when he heard that the atomic bomb was no longer an option. MacArthur continued to give interviews to journalists in Tokyo, repeating his main theme: "limited" war was unthinkable. His complaints angered Truman and other top advisers, but they were afraid to remove so legendary a war figure as MacArthur, or even seriously reprimand him. When General Matthew Ridgway asked General Hoyt Vandenberg, the air force chief, why the Joint Chiefs didn't tell MacArthur what to do, Vandenberg shook his head. "What good would that do? He wouldn't obey the orders. What can we do?"

When Truman told MacArthur that he secretly planned to seek a negotiated settlement with the Chinese, MacArthur sabotaged this idea by issuing a public statement in which he offered to meet with the Chinese. If the Chinese refused his offer, MacArthur said his troops might invade China. When Truman heard of this, he was enraged. Truman's advisers wanted MacArthur fired, but Truman's ratings in the polls were at an all-time low of 26 percent, and he feared the firestorm that would erupt if he got rid of MacArthur. Instead, he sent a mild reprimand to MacArthur and awaited a more flagrant act of insubordination that would justify removal.

Sure enough, MacArthur obliged. He conducted unauthorized press conferences, made contacts with Chinese Nationalist leaders in Taiwan, and mobilized a following among conservative members of Congress. When he sent a letter to Joseph Martin, the House Republican leader, in response to a speech that Martin had given in February, MacArthur sealed his fate.

The United States, Martin proclaimed in that speech, must be in Korea to win! If not, "this administration should be indicted for the murder of American boys." MacArthur's reply heartily endorsed Martin's sentiments. In writing such a letter to a political foe of the president, and in placing no restrictions on its publication, MacArthur crossed the line of no return. When Martin read MacAthur's letter on the floor of the House, Truman knew he had to act. He removed MacArthur from command on April 11, 1951.

Truman fired MacArthur in order to preserve the important constitutional principle of civilian control over the military. MacArthur had repeatedly disobeyed orders. He had been insubordinate, directly challenging the president's constitutional standing as commander-in-chief. Although the firing required a certain amount of political courage, Truman later explained to a reporter that "courage had nothing to do with it. He was insubordinate and I fired him."

Because of a communications snafu, MacArthur got news of his removal during a radio broadcast while he was at a luncheon in Tokyo. He turned to his wife and said, "Jeannie, we're going home at last." Within forty-eight hours, Republican conservatives in this country went berserk. "This country is in the hands of a secret inner coterie which is directed by agents of the Soviet Union.

Our only choice is to impeach President Truman," said Senator William Jenner of Indiana. "Truman's decision to fire MacArthur must have been made while he was drunk. This is perhaps the greatest victory the Communists have ever won," snarled Senator Joe McCarthy. Around the country, flags flew upside down at half-staff. The president was denounced as "a pig." Both Truman and Acheson were hung in effigy in Denver.

A few days later MacArthur flew home to the United States. He received a hero's welcome in Hawaii and San Francisco before arriving in Washington on April 19. Around noon that day he went to Capitol Hill to give an address to a joint session of Congress. It was a scene of high drama and MacArthur did not disappoint. He strode confidently down the aisle, whereupon members of Congress gave him a standing ovation. All his life he had been holding audiences spellbound and now he had his largest audience as 30 million watched on television.

He spoke for thirty-four minutes, during which time he was interrupted by applause thirty times. Those present were struck by his control as he outlined his now familiar differences with American policies. "Once war is forced upon us, there is no alternative than to apply every available means to bring it to a swift end. Why surrender military advantage to the enemy? The very object of war is victory – not prolonged indecision. In war there can be no substitute for victory."

MacArthur ended his speech in dramatic fashion.

> "I am closing my fifty-two years of military service," he said. "The world has turned over many times since I took the oath at West Point - but I still remember the refrain of one of the most popular barracks ballads of that day which proclaimed most proudly that, 'Old soldiers never die; they just fade away.' And like the old soldier of that ballad, I now close my military career and just fade away - an old soldier who tried to do his duty as God gave him the light to see. Good-bye."

President Truman, watching on television, pronounced MacArthur's speech, "one hundred percent bullshit." However, those in attendance thought differently. Dewey Short, a conservative Republican from Missouri, said, "We heard God speak here today, God in the flesh, the voice of God." Members of Congress erupted into pandemonium; many were sobbing and struggling to touch his sleeve. MacArthur then left the Capital for the Washington Monument where he was to give another speech. He rode triumphantly down Pennsylvania Avenue, where an estimated 300,000 people cheered him. Jet bombers and fighters flew in formation overhead. It was high-drama.

In New York the next day, MacArthur received a ticker-tape parade the likes of which the city had never seen before. Office workers and residents clustered on balconies, rooftops, and fire escapes, and threw down blizzards of confetti. Men shouted, "God bless you, Mac!" On the river, tugs and ocean-going boats tooted, adding to the din of the occasion. MacArthur, his cap white with paper, climbed onto the folded top of the open car and acknowledged the adoration. At City Hall, he accepted a gold medal and exclaimed, "We shall never forget this tremendous reception." Harry Truman, watched the parade on television and shook his head in disbelief, "I think this is the only son-of-a-bitch who got a ticker tape parade for getting fired from his job."

While the homecoming orgy was taking place, Americans throughout the country were letting Truman and Congress know what they thought about the issue. Within twelve days of the firing, the White House received more than 27,000 letters and telegrams, which ran twenty to one against the president. Many of these were so hostile and abusive that they were given over to the Secret Service for investigation. Members of Congress got another 100,000 messages during the first week; most demanded Truman's impeachment. Although tempers cooled in May and June 1951, they revealed a sobering fact: Americans had small patience for lingering "limited" war.

Reports kept filtering back to the United States that captured U.S. Air Force officers confessed to dropping biological germ bombs on the North Koreans. Each airman confessed that the aim of the attacks was to create a contamination belt across central North Korea so as to stop the movement of soldiers and supplies south. When the United States emphatically denied the charges, the North Koreans produced physical evidence: several of the bombs had failed to explode.

At the end of the war in 1953, the fliers were repatriated and flown to U.S. bases for debriefing. When they emerged, they retracted their confessions. The U.S. government claimed the airmen had been brainwashed. The reports were marked: "Highly classified - not to be released."

The American public elected Dwight David Eisenhower as president in 1952 on his pledge to end the Korean War. His Democratic opponent, Governor Adlai Stevenson of Illinois had no chance against the popular World War II hero. During the campaign, a woman is reputed to have come up to Stevenson and exclaimed, "Governor Stevenson, all the thinking people of America are for you," to which Stevenson responded, "I know, Madame, but we need a majority."

As soon as Eisenhower was elected, he personally went to Korea to find out what could be done to end the conflict. An armistice was finally agreed to in July 1953. All the parties, except South Korea, signed the peace treaty. South Korea believed the deal amounted to a sellout, while the U.S. claimed it had successfully resisted communist aggression. The Korean War was certainly not a victory for the United States, especially since it was fought against such an inferior foe. After three years of fighting and millions dead, the North remained a Communist bulwark and the South turned into a nasty dictatorship – and the forces of international communism seemed greater than ever. With the war over, the Chinese left Korea, but now began pouring men and weapons into Vietnam.

It is true that Eisenhower managed to end the fighting in Korea, but his success owed as much to circumstance as to diplomatic proficiency. The decisive event in the Korean settlement seems to have been Stalin's death. Problems of succession and rising unrest in Eastern Europe compelled the new Soviet leaders to seek a breathing space through the relaxation of tensions. Eisenhower insisted that peace in Korea was an essential first step. Mao Zedong seems grudgingly to have concluded that any possible gain from continuing the war would not be worth the cost.

The Korean War ended up being a political disaster for the Soviet Union as well as the United States. Russia's central objective, the unification of the Korean peninsula under North Korean leadership was not achieved. Furthermore, Soviet relations with Communist China were seriously affected. China felt the Soviets had used them as a surrogate fighting force while Russia committed no manpower to the war.

According to official statistics, 36,568 Americans died in combat with over 100,000 wounded. In all, 54,000 Americans did not come home. No such specificity is possible in calculating other losses, but it is likely that some 600,000 Chinese troops and well over three million Koreans perished during the three years of fighting; another five million were homeless. The dividing line between North and South Korea remained exactly where it was before the invasion. Communism had been challenged and stalled. Neither side could claim victory and the ideological battle moved on to new locales. The only decisive outcome of the war was the precedent it set: there could be a bloody and protracted conflict involving nations armed with nuclear weapons - and they chose not to use them. For the United States, it was a sobering experience. It proved that limited wars offer notable opportunities to belligerents of limited means. We would learn this lesson again in Vietnam.

In the years that followed, the Soviet Union tried to keep pace with the United States both economically and militarily, but eventually the arms race bankrupted the Russian economy. It was the classic story of an agrarian economy not being able to compete with an industrialized nation. But, it took almost fifty years for this to become apparent. During the interim these two mighty nuclear powers squared off and almost brought about a worldwide holocaust. Millions of innocent people died in some swamp or rice field; millions more were traumatized by the fear of what might happen next. Both superpowers aimed its nuclear arsenal at each other, but nobody fired. When the tension of the Cold War was over, nobody was sure what it had been all about.

During these Cold War years the United States perfected the great lie, instilling fear in Americans that the 'red menace' and godless monster wanted to destroy American democracy and Christianity. Americans became convinced they were going to be "nuked" and our only salvation was to spend whatever was necessary in order to retaliate in kind. School children practiced diving under desks for shelter in case of a nuclear attack; families built fallout shelters in their basements and stocked them with survival necessities – none of these things would have done any good in case of a nuclear attack – but it did traumatize school children, parents, and the general population. In addition, the nation was convinced that communist agents were infiltrating our government, media, movies, and educational system. America's fear and paranoia became the perfect setting for the McCarthy era that followed.

CHAPTER THIRTEEN

JOSEPH McCARTHY

"I have here in my hand a list of 205 known communists in our State Department."

                                        Senator Joseph McCarthy

"Have you no sense of decency, sir?"

                                        Joseph Welch, attorney

"I can't believe what is happening to me."

                                        J. Robert Oppenheimer

McCarthyism existed long before Senator Joseph McCarthy arrived on the scene. The seeds began taking root in 1917 with the Bolshevik Revolution, but in America the "Red Scare" really began in the 1930s during the depths of our Great Depression. In 1925, there were only 16,000 communists in this country; a minuscule number that had no power. However, once unemployment reached 25 percent in this country, concerned Americans began to look beyond capitalism for a solution – not out of disloyalty, but out of desperation.

    The communist movement began to peter out when FDR implemented his wide array of social programs and disappeared completely when we entered World War II, especially since Russia was aligned with Germany. Many former U.S. communists and liberal left-wingers rejoined the Communist Party when Russia became our staunchest ally. However, once the war was over and the Cold War started, America became paranoid about communism; especially about those who had been communist sympathizers back in the 1930s and now occupied positions of influence in the United States.

Fear of a communist conspiracy in the United States made headlines on August 3, 1948 when Whittaker Chambers, a writer and editor at *Time* magazine walked into a hearing room in Washington and told the House Un-American Activities Committee (HUAC), that during the 1930s he had been a member of a secret communist cell whose members included high officials in the current American government. One of those he named was Alger Hiss. Chambers not only accused Hiss of being a communist, but also of being an espionage agent for the Soviet Union.

Alger Hiss was born in Baltimore, Maryland. His early life was repeatedly marred by tragedy. His father committed suicide when he was two years old, his elder brother died of Bright's disease when Alger was 22, and he lost his sister to suicide when he was 25. His mother relied largely on family members for financial support in raising her five children.

Hiss was educated at Johns Hopkins University, where he graduated Phi Beta Kappa and was voted "most popular student" by his classmates. In 1929, he received his law degree from Harvard, where he was a protégé of future U.S. Supreme Court Justice Felix Frankfurter. Before joining a Boston law firm, Hiss served for one year as clerk to Supreme Court Justice Oliver Wendell Holmes Jr.

In 1933, Hiss entered government service, working in several areas as an attorney in President Roosevelt's New Deal, and in 1936, he began working for the State Department. In 1944, he became a special assistant to the Director of the Office of Special Political Affairs, a policy-making office that concentrated on finalizing plans for the United Nations. In 1945, Hiss became a member of the U.S. delegation at the Yalta Conference, where the 'Big Three' of FDR, Stalin, and Churchill met to coordinate postwar strategy. Hiss left government service in 1946 to become president of the highly prestigious Carnegie Foundation. As one can surmise from his background and accomplishments, Alger Hiss was a widely respected public servant with an unblemished record of service. In addition, he looked the part; confident, tall, slim, and immaculately dressed.

The life and career of Whittaker Chambers was quite different. Chambers had left home clandestinely as a teenager and bummed around the country until he ran out of money. He dropped out of Columbia University, joined the Communist Party, lived a bohemian life in and around New York City, edited a Communist journal, did some translation work, and then settled into the life of a full-time Communist spy. He married, had a child, and then, in 1938, broke with the Communist Party and landed a job as book reviewer for *Time* magazine. Eventually promoted to foreign affairs editor, he earned the admiration of the publisher, Henry Luce, but also the enmity of some of magazine's reporters, who accused him of editing their copy to make it fit his now anti-liberal obsessions.

At the HUAC committee hearings to ascertain the veracity of his accusation, the forty-seven year-old, extremely overweight and slovenly Chambers, wore an ill-fitting suit and a shirt with a collar that kept popping up. He read his testimony in a monotone voice, rarely looking up. After Chambers was finished, Hiss took the stand and reacted to the charges with indignation. Visibly restraining his anger, he slowly and emphatically read a statement saying he was not and never had been a member of the Communist Party, had never adhered to the tenets of the Communist Party, was not a communist sympathizer, and never had any friends he suspected of being communists.

Questioned by the committee, Hiss responded patiently, coolly, and sometimes with flashes of wit. As the hearing drew to a close, one of its members apologized to Hiss for the damage done to someone whom "many Americans, including members of this committee, hold in high repute." Several members of the committee went up to him afterward to shake his hand. Meeting in closed session later, almost all of the members of HUAC wanted to drop the whole matter and move on to something else. They had been bamboozled by Chambers, who was obviously some kind of nut. But, one member of the committee dissented. Freshman congressman Richard Nixon of California thought the committee should not give up so easily. He offered to chair a subcommittee to continue the investigation. Reluctantly, the committee agreed.

Nixon was relentless; this was just the kind of media opportunity he was looking for to further his career. Eventually, a grand jury was convened and Hiss was charged with lying about his Communist affiliations. Chambers, who was granted immunity because he was the prosecution's star witness, claimed that Hiss took State Department documents home, typed copies (or had his wife type them), and gave the copies to Chambers who forwarded them to the Soviet Union.

At the first trial, many notables testified to Hiss's character, including Secretary of State Dean Acheson, President Isaiah Bowman of Johns Hopkins University, Governor Adlai Stevenson of Illinois, and Supreme Court Justices Felix Frankfurter and Stanley M. Reed. On the witness stand, Alger's wife Pricilla admitted she was a socialist. The prosecution tried to show that "socialism is nothing more than communism with the claws retracted." Alger Hiss claimed he was nothing more than a "New Dealer." The trial ended in a hung jury and Hiss went free.

That would normally have ended the affair, but bizarre evidence kept turning up involving microfilm in pumpkins and letters written on a beat-up Woodstock typewriter. In addition, the American mood altered dramatically as the Cold War heated up - the Soviet Union exploded an atomic bomb and Mao's Red Army took over China's mainland. At the same time, HUAC began its probe of alleged Russian espionage in our atomic-energy program.

In this charged setting the second trial of Alger Hiss began on November 17, 1949. The espionage charge against Hiss was dropped because the statute of limitations had run out, so the only accusation against him was perjury. At the conclusion of the second trial, the jury took less than twenty-four hours to reach a guilty verdict. Hiss was sentenced to five years imprisonment; he served forty-four months in Lewisburg Federal Prison.

Hiss devoted the rest of his life in a quest for vindication. His efforts culminated in the publication of his memoir, *In the Court of Public Opinion*, arguably the dullest book ever written about the case. He died in 1996 at the age of 92. Whittaker Chambers died in 1961 at the age of 60. In 1984, President Ronald Reagan posthumously awarded him the Presidential Medal of Freedom.

Richard Nixon's prestige in the Alger Hiss probe soared; it gave him the reputation of a successful spy-hunter, helped him gain a U.S. Senate seat in 1950, the vice-presidential nomination two years later, and the presidency in 1968. Right-wingers turned Hiss into a symbol of supposed treason that lay behind New Deal policies, particularly in the State Department.

Subsequent disclosures revealed that during the government's prosecution against Hiss, vital evidence was withheld from the defense team, and that the government conducted illegal surveillance before and during the trials, including phone taps and mail openings. All of these illegal activities would have resulted in a mistrial had they been known at the time. On the other hand, recent disclosures from the Soviet archives reveal decoded transcripts of cables sent to the USSR from the Soviet Embassy in Washington from 1943 to 1946 that implicates Hiss as one of their spies. Scholars have concluded that it may take another generation or more before historians have free access to the full range of Soviet, American, and other Cold War files pertaining to Alger Hiss. Whatever the truth may turn out to be, the Alger Hiss controversy provided a perfect launching for the McCarthy era.

Senator Joseph R. McCarthy's anti-communist crusade, during which 10,000 Americans lost their jobs, began less than three weeks after Alger Hiss's conviction in 1950. McCarthy seized the issue: if someone like Hiss could be a communist, who else was lurking in the shadows looking to undermine the foundations of our country's ideals?

HUAC immediately convened public hearings on "communist infiltration in the motion-picture industry." Headlines were full of accounts of the "Hollywood Ten," a group of screenwriters and directors including Ring Lardner, Jr., Dalton Trumbo, and Albert Maltz, who were summoned before the committee and asked to testify about their prior activities and ties to the Communist Party. All members of the "Hollywood Ten" had been communists and some still were, but they refused to testify or identify others in the film industry who might have been communists at one time. Cited for contempt of Congress, all of them served jail sentences ranging from six months to a year, and afterward all were blacklisted and could not find work.

The national anxiety during the Cold War was further heightened when it was revealed that individuals in the United States had provided Russia with our A-bomb secrets. J. Edgar Hoover informed Truman that in light of these events the FBI would "intensify its investigation and take steps to list all members of the Communist Party and others who would be dangerous in the event of a 'serious crisis' with the Soviet Union." Truman agreed and directed Hoover to give top priority to investigating possible communist espionage, especially within the federal government.

J. Robert Oppenheimer was a Jewish-American physicist and professor at the University of California in Berkeley. He was an outspoken left-winger at the time of his appointment as the scientific director of the Manhattan Project. Oppenheimer was never a member of the Communist Party, but many of his friends were members or active supporters of communist causes. With full knowledge, the U.S. picked Oppenheimer to lead America's most secret mission. As scientific director, Oppenheimer's power over the project was virtually absolute. He recruited scientists and assembled all the equipment necessary to solve the 'mystery' of the atom and bring this ultimate weapon of mass destruction from theory to actual fruition.

Many eminent scientists involved in the project had qualms about the moral aspects of the bomb. The medical team at Los Alamos determined that the after-affects of a nuclear explosion would leave those alive with enough toxic materials in the human body to eat away at vital tissues, disintegrating human kidneys and causing fatal bone cancer. None of this mattered to Oppenheimer – ego was his driving force. He was obsessed with success and paranoid about failure; the perfection of the 'job' overrode all other considerations.

After the war, Oppenheimer became a chief adviser to the newly created United States Atomic Energy Commission. He used his position to lobby for international control of atomic energy and to avert a nuclear arms race with the Soviet Union. His opinion about not building hydrogen and other 'super' bombs was well known throughout our government circles. He believed that the extreme pressures and temperatures released from a hydrogen bomb might set fire to the atmosphere and destroy the world.

J. Edgar Hoover and the FBI had been monitoring Oppenheimer's activities since the time he was a radical professor openly expressing communist sympathies. In his present role as political adviser and sometimes critic of administration policies, the man known as the 'father of the atomic bomb' made many political enemies. J. Edgar Hoover, in particular, considered any form of dissent as communist inspired. When Hoover furnished the White House with the FBI's incriminating file on Oppenheimer's early communist ties, President Eisenhower asked Oppenheimer to resign. Oppenheimer refused. Thus began a series of events that would destroy Oppenheimer's career and reputation.

FBI agents broke into Oppenheimer's files and seized control of all his classified papers. That same day, Oppenheimer received a letter of formal charges informing him that he had to testify before the House Un-American Activities Committee, to determine "whether your continued employment on Atomic Energy Commission work will endanger the common defense and national security of the country."

During the weeks before his testimony, Oppenheimer's phones and those of his family were secretly tapped, and hidden microphones recorded all his private meetings and conversations with his attorneys. In addition, his attorneys were not allowed to examine the 'classified' evidence that would be used against him at his hearing. Depressed and disconsolate, Oppenheimer lamented to those closest to him, "I can't believe what is happening to me."

In his testimony before a specially selected three-member panel, Oppenheimer admitted that during the 1930s he knew people who were members of the Communist Party and even attended 'discussion groups,' but he refused to name who they were. When Oppenheimer's testimony was completed, he went home to await the panel's judgment. When the formal verdict came down, Oppenheimer's security clearance was revoked and he was publicly humiliated. The decision did not accuse Oppenheimer of violating any laws or security regulations. Instead, the verdict claimed that "being loyal to one's friends above reasonable obligations to the country was not consistent with the interests of national security." Oppenheimer was not guilty of disloyalty; his only crime was excessive friendship. A brilliant and loyal American, who served his country more than most, he was now destroyed.

The implications of Oppenheimer's dismissal were enormous. All U.S. scientists were now on notice that there could be serious consequences for those who challenged our government policies. Wernher von Braun, a colleague and supporter of Oppenheimer, summed up the matter with a quip to a congressional committee: "In England, Oppenheimer would have been knighted." Oppenheimer died in 1967 at the age of 62. At his eulogy, a fellow physicist spoke about the travesty that had been committed: "Such a wrong can never be righted; such a blot on our history never erased. We regret that his great work for his country was repaid so shabbily."

Joseph McCarthy, Republican Senator from Wisconsin from 1947 until 1957, epitomized America's hysteria about communism. The country was gripped with a fear that Russia might do to us what we did to Hiroshima and Nagasaki - and McCarthy took advantage of that fear to escalate himself into the upper echelon of American politics. During his ten years in the U.S. Senate he notoriously branded anyone with leftist sympathies as communists – often ruining careers, marriages, and driving innocent people to suicide.

McCarthy stood out immediately because he was so young; at thirty-eight, he was the youngest member of the U.S. Senate. Nationwide concern about communist spies active in government intensified in early 1950 when McCarthy gave a speech in Wheeling, West Virginia. He waved a sheet of paper and told his audience that he was privy to damning information about spy infiltration: "While I cannot take the time to name all the men in the State Department who have been active members of the Communist Party, I have here in my hand a list of 205 names that were known to the secretary of state and who, nevertheless, are still working and shaping the policy of our country." The paper

McCarthy had in his hand was actually his laundry list - it was all bluff and bravado – but nobody knew he was lying.

In the U.S. Senate, Democratic majority leader, Scott Lucas, demanded that McCarthy prove his accusations. McCarthy, however, refused to reveal the names, explaining that it would be inappropriate for him to make the names public. Still bluffing, he pulled stacks of papers from his bulging briefcase, suggesting he had the proof. He rambled on for some five hours, rattling off fabricated statements about the allegedly subversive activities and associations of unnamed State Department employees. Senators were stunned at what they were hearing.

Over the next few months, McCarthy, aided by his assistant, Roy Cohn, produced some names, and several individuals were hauled in to testify before congressional committees. The public was transfixed: McCarthy had hit a raw nerve with many Americans. Suddenly, suspected communists were everywhere. As with many movements of mass hysteria, the charges contained a kernel of truth – many individuals had communist sympathies back in the 1930s.

In speeches across America, McCarthy stormed that there was a "plot" at the highest reaches of the government "to reduce security and intelligence protection to a nullity." He roared that "no one can be for the Democratic Party and at the same time be against communism," and he charged the Democrats with shielding "traitors" and undermining the very "foundations of our Republic." Audiences were enthralled; swept away by his absolute certitude and impassioned patriotism. Fellow Republicans came to see McCarthy as "their ticket to political power" and he was in demand to speak all over the country.

Although some critics denounced McCarthy's "campaign of indiscriminate character-assassination," most Americans believed he had uncovered the truth about Soviet spies in our government. McCarthy's lies were believable because he possessed a truly unique character. He had the "gift" of unparalleled audacity, unyielding stubbornness, an instinct for the jugular, and a natural talent for self-promotion.

The Korean War instantly magnified McCarthy's appeal. He linked the ineffectiveness of the war with secrets being leaked by American communists within our State Department. On July 2, 1950, McCarthy charged that "American boys are dying in Korea because a group of untouchables in the State Department sabotaged the aid program for Asia." McCarthy roared that in this Cold War the enemy was not only a soldier on a battlefield, but also, a neighbor, co-worker, teacher, reporter, union member, or passing acquaintance. "Americans should be fearful not only about their military security, but also about the security of their religious, moral, and national values, their free enterprise system, their labor movement, their media, and their educational system." The enemy was not just the Russians and the Chinese; the enemy was "un-Americanism."

McCarthy had the unwavering support of all those who were remotely anti-communist, including the Church and its religious leaders. Cardinal Spellman of New York, Cardinal Richard Cushing of Boston, and Fulton Lewis Jr. were particularly ardent supporters who helped finance McCarthy's efforts. McCarthy also had the protection of a powerful cadre of right-wing journalists, publishers, businessmen, and politicians; including Joseph P. Kennedy, William Randolph Hearst Jr., and influential columnists and broadcasters like Westbrook Pegler. Finally, McCarthy was embraced by the vast majority of the Republican Party, including most moderate Republicans who saw him as the instrument through which they could finally unravel the New Deal and regain control of the national government.

Nothing best illustrates the "Red" hysteria than the incident concerning the *Scientific American* magazine. After the Soviet Union exploded its first atomic bomb, the Truman administration debated whether to develop a hydrogen bomb. The *Scientific American* published a series of articles on the bomb. An April 1950 article by the noted physicist Hans Bethe contained only declassified information, but government agents descended on the magazine's offices and seized all 3,000 copies of the magazine. The magazines were burned and the original printing plates destroyed.

Almost as remarkable as the government's action was the virtual absence of any public or congressional outcry.

The year 1950 also saw passage of the McCarran Act, which required communist and "communist-action" organizations to register with the government. In addition, their mail had to carry the label "Communist." Individual members were ineligible for passports, barred from government employment, and were required to register with the government. The U.S. Attorney General was empowered with the right to detain any individual in a concentration camp if "there was reasonable ground to believe that such person probably will engage in, or will probably conspire with others, to engage in acts of espionage or sabotage."

President Truman vetoed the McCarran Act as a product of public hysteria that would lead to "Gestapo witch hunts," but Congress passed the McCarran Act over Truman's veto. The bill was endorsed by most liberal Democratic senators who were anxious to establish their anti-communist credentials. Attorney General Tom Clark supported the bill stating that "those who do not believe in the ideology of the United States should not be allowed to stay in the United States." Under the McCarran Act, the United States was allowed to deport aliens and members of the Communist Party, and immigrants were threatened with deportation if they did not end their pro-labor activities or refused to turn in Communist Party relatives. Throughout the nation, dissent had terrible personal consequences.

Red-baiting reached unprecedented levels in the 1950 elections. Republican John Foster Dulles, challenged liberal New York Democrat Herbert Lehman for the U.S. Senate, and said of Lehman, "I know he is no communist, but I know also that the communists are in his corner." In California, Congressman Richard Nixon secured election to the U.S, Senate by circulating a 'pink' sheet accusing his Democratic opponent, Helen Gahagan Douglas, of voting the communist line. And in Florida, Republican Congressman George Smathers defeated Claude Pepper by describing him as "Red Pepper" and tarring him as an "apologist for Stalin."

Milo Radulovich, an Air Force reserve officer, became a searing symbol of the excesses of anti-communism in the 1950s when he was discharged because his father and sister were accused of being Communist sympathizers. Radulovich was summarily judged to be risky by association. His father was suspect because he read a Slavic newspaper that some considered pro-Communist, and his sister was suspect because she picketed a Detroit hotel that refused to lodge the renowned Negro singer Paul Robeson.

Television newscaster Edward R. Murrow wanted to bring the story to the public's attention, but CBS executives refused because the corporate sponsor, Alcoa Aluminum, relied heavily on military contracts and was against the story being broadcast. Murrow put up $1,500 of his own money for an advertisement in the *New York Times* to promote the program. Viewers responded by sending over 8,000 letters and telegrams to CBS and Alcoa in support of Mr. Radulovich, who was soon reinstated in the Air Force Reserves.

On June 14, 1951, as public fear and frustration intensified over the Korean War and the possibility of Chinese intervention, Joseph McCarthy addressed the U.S. Senate. In a three-hour harangue, he attacked General George C. Marshall, former chief of staff of the American military and former secretary of state, as a tool of the communists. McCarthy asked, how can Americans "account for our present situation in Korea unless we believe that men high in this Government are concerting to deliver us to disaster?" McCarthy charged Marshall with being the central figure in this "conspiracy of infamy and strategy of defeat."

McCarthy's speech was his apex in irresponsibility. It was an outrageous rant, in which Marshall was made the villain for everything from Pearl Harbor, the loss of China to the communists, and the Korean War. McCarthy was arguing that there was "a conspiracy on a scale so immense as to dwarf any previous venture in the history of America."

Marshall refused to comment. He told friends that if he had to explain that he was not a traitor at this point in his life, it was not worth the trouble. He retired that September at the age of seventy-one, perhaps disgusted with the political climate. In 1953,

Marshall won the Nobel Peace Prize. Governor Adlai Stevenson of Illinois called the attack against Marshall "hysterical" while Senator William Benton of Connecticut characterized McCarthy's performance as the product of an "unsound mind."

President Eisenhower, who personally owed much to Marshall, was furious, but said nothing. Eisenhower detested McCarthy and his methods, but refused to challenge him head-on. His refusal to speak out against McCarthy represented a major moral blot on his presidency. During the 1952 presidential campaign, Eisenhower and McCarthy finally came face to face in Wisconsin in early October. Sharing the same podium with McCarthy, Eisenhower planned to say:

> "I know that charges of disloyalty have been leveled against General George C. Marshall. I have been privileged for thirty-five years to know General Marshall personally. I know him as a man and as a soldier. He has always been dedicated with the profoundest patriotism to the service of America. This current episode is a sobering lesson in the way freedom must not defend itself."

But, the day before Eisenhower's scheduled address, McCarthy and Eisenhower met in private. Eisenhower scolded McCarthy for his "un-American methods in combating communism," and told him, "I'm going to say that I disagree with you." McCarthy warned Eisenhower, "If you say that, you'll be booed." Eisenhower replied that he had been booed before and that it did not bother him – but moments before the speech, Eisenhower capitulated and deleted his defense of Marshall. It was not Eisenhower's finest moment.

At the 1952 Republican National Convention, McCarthy was invited to deliver a major speech. He roused the convention, thundering to a cheering audience, "My good friends, I say one communist in a defense plant is one communist too many. One communist on the faculty of one university is one communist too many. One communist among the American advisers at Yalta was one communist too many. And even if there is only one communist in the State Department, that would still be one communist too many." In keeping with McCarthy's theme, Eisenhower selected Richard Nixon as his running mate, one of the nation's most infamous Red-baiters.

During the 1952 campaign, Eisenhower invoked the issue of communist infiltration on more than thirty occasions. Joseph McCarthy campaigned for the Republican ticket and charged that the Democratic nominee, Adlai Stevenson, had "given aid to the communist cause." Nixon, true to form, labeled the Democrats the "party of communism" and referred to Truman and Stevenson as "traitors."

Republicans swept the 1952 elections, winning the House, Senate, and the White House. Joe McCarthy was reelected to the U.S. Senate and seemed to be invincible. As William S. White wrote in the *New York Times*, Senator McCarthy "is now in a position of extraordinary power. He is a very bad man to cross politically." With the U.S. Senate now firmly in Republican hands, McCarthy became chairman of the 'Permanent Subcommittee on Investigations.' With this impregnable political base, McCarthy planned to investigate communist infiltration in the State Department, the Federal Communications Commission, and in America's colleges and universities. Both *Newsweek* and the *New York Times Magazine* were speculating that McCarthy was aiming for the presidency in 1956.

Republicans finally began to worry that McCarthy was a 'loose cannon.' Eisenhower's brother publicly described McCarthy as "the most dangerous menace to America." However, President Eisenhower steered clear of any confrontation with McCarthy. He confided to friends that the whole McCarthy business "is a sorry mess, and at times I feel like hanging my head in shame when I read some of his unreasoned, vicious outbursts of demagoguery." However, Eisenhower refused to act, saying that he would not "get into the gutter with that guy."

In spite of Eisenhower's personal feelings, his administration was intensifying the government's anti-communist campaign. By 1953, the federal government was investigating 10,000 citizens for possible denaturalization and 12,000 aliens for deportation. Attorney General Herbert Brownell directed twelve more organizations to register under the McCarran Act as "communist fronts." In December 1953, Americans regarded communists in government as the nation's number one problem. The following year, Eisenhower signed the Communist Control Act, which outlawed the Communist Party and declared that it was "not entitled to any rights, privileges and immunities."

In 1953, Julius and Ethel Rosenberg were convicted of passing secrets to the Soviets and were condemned to die in the electric chair – a punishment far in excess of any purported wrongdoing. A plea was made to the United States Court of Appeals to stay the execution. Liberal Judge Jerome Frank addressed Rosenberg's young idealistic lawyers: "If I were as young as you are, I would be sitting there saying the same things you are saying, making the same points you are arguing, that the planned executions are invalid, but when you are as old as I am, you will understand why I cannot do it." Frank then stood up and walked out of the courtroom. The lawyers were stunned that someone like Jerome Frank had succumbed to the communist paranoia. Julius and Ethel Rosenberg were executed on June 19, 1953.

The consensus now is that Ethel Rosenberg, while aware of her husband's espionage, did not actively participate and was innocent of all charges. Richard Nixon, in an unpublished 1983 interview, said that Ethel Rosenberg should have been spared the death penalty because the evidence against her was tainted. Prosecutors hoped that pushing for conviction against her and the imposition of the death sentence, would persuade either Ethel or her husband to openly confess and implicate others. That strategy failed; Ethel Rosenberg did not talk, but it was too late to prevent her execution. In September 2008, previously classified transcripts were released confirming that the trial testimony of several witnesses was in conflict with what they had previously told the grand jury. The most important aspect of the Rosenberg case is not whether they were guilty; rather it was impossible for them to get a fair trial in the atmosphere of Cold War hysteria.

The long shadow of the House Un-American Activities Committee fell across virtually every aspect of American culture. Committee chairman, Francis Walter, estimated that there were "200,000 Communists in the United States, equivalent to twenty combat divisions of enemy troops engaged in propaganda, espionage, subversion, and loyalty only to the Soviet Union." Loyalty programs, undercover surveillance, legislative investigations, and criminal prosecutions of alleged communists swept the nation. Teachers were intimidated and frightened that they might lose their job if they misspoke or ventured the wrong slant on history or current events, and they had to sign "loyalty oaths" or they were fired. Few had the courage or economic means to resist. At one university in Buffalo, New York, 895 teachers out of 900 signed the oath. The five who refused to sign, eventually won their legal case before the U.S. Supreme Court, but it took years and lots of personal funds before justice prevailed.

Loyalty hearings before committees often took on the character of a medieval inquisition. The charges tended to be vague and almost impossible to rebut: "You are known to have sympathetically associated with members of organizations known to be subversive." But, the accused was not told who he associated with or what organization he supposedly belonged to – or when or where this might have happened. The accused could only guess.

Individuals accused of disloyalty were fiercely interrogated and asked:

- How many times did you vote for Henry Wallace?

- Have you provided any sort of religious training for your children?

- Do you think workers in the capitalist system get a relatively fair deal?

- What are your feelings concerning racial equality?

- Have you read "suspicious" books, seen "foreign films," or listened to the records of Paul Robeson.

In less than ten percent of the cases was membership in the Communist Party actually proven. None of the hearings involved current members in the Communist Party; rather, they focused on charges of past membership in other "listed" organizations, or, most often, more remote forms of "guilt by association." A signature on a petition, a small donation, a name on a mailing list, presence at a public meeting, a conversation with a passing acquaintance - all could generate suspicion of "sympathetic" association. Two-thirds of the cases that reached the hearing stage included a charge that the individual had in some way associated with others who might be subversive. It was safer not to join any organization; one never knew who else might be a member.

The loyalty program created a pervasive sense of being "watched." It was as if a noxious cloud had engulfed the nation. Almost every federal agency employed its own "security officers," whose job it was to unearth information about its employees. These officers scrutinized and recorded the conduct, sentiments, associations, relationships, conversations, and personal lives of every employee. They compiled secret dossiers on "suspect" individuals and shared the information with the FBI. They rewarded "tips" and encouraged employees to report on one another. To keep things simple, they often proposed "deals" to employees against whom they harbored "suspicions"- if the employee would resign, the security officer would suspend the inquiry. The pressure on loyal, law-abiding employees to yield to the whims, prejudices, and abuse of security officers was often insurmountable.

The FBI's insistence on shielding the identity of informers exacerbated the danger. In only six percent of the loyalty hearings did the accused learn the identity of his or her accuser. The anonymity of informers left every federal employee open to the vagaries of crackpots, schemers, scandalmongers, and personal enemies. In those few cases in which the informer's identity came to light, the stupidity or venality of the accusation was often shocking, adding to the sense of vulnerability. In one case, the informer testified that she had reported the accused because he had a mustache and never wore his tie home at the end of the day. The informer explained that she had "heard people say that those are indications that he is not a capitalist." In another case, the informer revealed that he accused the employee of disloyalty because the employee "thought colored people should be entitled to as much as anybody else," a view the informer associated with communism.

The cost of being ensnared in a loyalty investigation was fearsome. Those dismissed from government employment could not find jobs and were constantly hounded by the FBI. In addition, their social standing in the community was ruined; they received crank mail and their friends deserted them. It was dangerous to be seen speaking with the wrong person or reading the wrong journal. One federal employee discovered a collection of the communist *New Masses* when he moved into a new house. To avoid the risk that someone might think he read such material, he quickly burned the magazines rather than dump them in the garbage.

In May 1953, President Eisenhower announced a new and even more expansive standard of disloyalty. Executive Order 10450 stated that "any behavior, activities or associations which tend to show that the individual is not reliable or trustworthy" would henceforth be sufficient cause for dismissal. In October, Eisenhower added another basis for automatic dismissal - invocation of the Constitution's Fifth Amendment privilege against self-incrimination before a congressional committee in an inquiry involving alleged disloyalty. The Fifth Amendment, when written, was one of the greatest protections to individual rights. Under Eisenhower's edict, it became indissolubly linked with the image of a guilty person parroting words in order to avoid punishment.

"Are you now or have you ever been a member of the Communist Party" was the culminating question of congressional hearings, and being forced to answer that question could be devastating. Most refused to answer and invoked their Fifth Amendment rights: "I refuse to answer on the grounds that it might tend to incriminate me." But, by invoking their Fifth Amendment right against self-incrimination they were 'blacklisted' from their jobs. The real evil was the very idea that Congress had a right to interrogate people about their political views. Often, just getting your name mentioned in a newspaper gossip column was enough to get fired from your job. Employers did not want the possible stigma of having a 'commie' on their payroll. Vice President Nixon boasted that 7,000 federal employees had been dismissed or resigned as a result of the Eisenhower program and that the administration was "kicking the communists and fellow travelers out of government by the thousands."

A right-wing journal, *Counterattack*, published *Red Channels*, a pamphlet-style book containing 151 names of actors, writers, musicians, broadcast journalists, and other purported communists in the entertainment industry. The list included many well-known artists, such as Burgess Meredith, Edward G. Robinson, Orson Welles, Pete Seeger and Leonard Bernstein. Most of these established figures were able to survive the smear against them, but many lesser-known artists crumbled as they saw their life's work destroyed. Dashell Hammett, writer of the *Thin Man* and *Sam Spade* mysteries, received a six-month prison sentence. He was released after five months, a man broken physically as well as professionally.

"The Goldbergs" was one of America's most popular radio and television programs, conceived and starring Gertrude Berg. Philip Loeb, who played Molly Goldberg's husband on the show, was a tireless worker on behalf of Actors Equity, the union that championed the rights of actors. When Loeb was labeled a Communist sympathizer, the sponsor, General Foods, delivered an ultimatum that Loeb be fired within two days. Berg stood by Loeb and threatened to persuade the public to boycott all General Foods products. Although General Foods backed down, the show was canceled several months later. Berg appealed to Cardinal Francis Spellman for help. Spellman agreed to help, but only on condition that Gertrude Berg convert to Roman Catholicism, which she refused to do. A broken man, Philip Loeb committed suicide in 1955.

Actors like Zero Mostel came forth and said they would gladly discuss their own past conduct, but would not name others. Many others, however, gladly co-operated with the committee, either out of misguided patriotism or fear. These "friendly" witnesses included Gary Cooper, Robert Taylor, Adolphe Menjou, Ronald Reagan, and George Murphy, as well as the writer Ayn Rand and

Hollywood studio executives Louis Mayer, Jack Warner and Walt Disney. Their "patriotism" destroyed a number of careers even though most of them did not know the difference between Karl Marx and Groucho Marx.

When Elia Kazan, a prize winning Hollywood director, was called before the committee, he also named names. He told the committee, "It is my obligation as a citizen to tell everything I know." Kazan said that he had been a party member for nineteen months in a group that included Morris Carnovsky, Clifford Odets, J. Edward Bromberg, and three or four others. Kazan insists in his autobiography that he did nothing wrong in being a "friendly" witness even though he writes movingly about the traumatic effect the testimony had on his life.

Kazan and Pulitzer Prize author Arthur Miller had been life-long friends. Miller also appeared before the committee where some of his works were criticized as anti-capitalistic. The committee pointed to his play *Death of a Salesman*, written in 1949, as depicting its principal character, Willy Loman, as someone whose harsh feelings about the dog-eat-dog business world was un-American. In later years, Miller would write *The Crucible* about the Salem witch trials, which was really an analogy about the House Un-American committee hearings.

Arthur Miller was never a Communist Party member, but he counted many former communists among his friends. He agreed to answer questions about his own political past and opinions, but refused to name others. The Committee told Miller that "any real American would be proud to give us names." Miller responded, "The meetings you speak of happened nearly ten years ago. At that time the Communist Party had not been declared a conspiracy; it was legally recognized and accorded the privileges of a political party. I could comply with your request, but if I did, I would hate myself in the morning." Miller, who refused to invoke the protection of the Fifth Amendment, was convicted of contempt of Congress. His conviction was overturned on appeal. Miller was so incensed at his friend Elia Kazan for naming names and ruining the lives of others that he never spoke to Kazan again.

Arthur Miller became the moral hero of all those who were being persecuted. His impact can only be understood in the context of those times. A nation had been brought to its knees by the anti-communist juggernaut. Arthur Miller certainly was not alone in standing up to it. Others were even bolder and suffered for it, but Arthur Miller was in a position to get headlines with it. During these awful times, a besieged community needs heroes, and Arthur Miller, like a hero from one of his plays, stepped forth and refused to disavow his principles.

Whatever one's convictions, there was little room for maneuvering once you were called before the committee. A few, like Lucille Ball, were allowed to pass with garbled and meaningless testimony, but most were pinned down. Fame was no protection. A lifelong non-communist progressive like Sam Jaffe was blacklisted for refusing to cooperate. Jaffe, who had been nominated for an Oscar for *The Asphalt Jungle* (1950) and was famous for roles in *Lost Horizon* (1937) and *Gunga Din* (1939), was reduced to teaching high school math. Lee Grant, nominated for an Oscar for her role in *Detective Story* (1951), was blacklisted for refusing to testify against her first husband, screenwriter Arnold Manoff.

Over the next several years, some 250 writers, directors, and actors were blacklisted; 90 percent would never be able to resume their careers in Hollywood. Even the biggest names were vulnerable. Larry Parks, fresh from triumphs in two films about Al Jolson, was banned. Charles Chaplin, the most famous face in the world, was a British citizen and a firm believer in socialist causes. Although he had never been in the Communist Party, Chaplin was not allowed to reenter the United States following a trip to Europe. Jose Ferrer took out paid advertisements in a desperate attempt to rehabilitate his career. When Edward J. Robinson sent a check to the family of a blacklisted writer, he was harassed and denied work.

Clifford Odets, Jerome Robbins, Lee J. Cobb, and Sterling Hayden, all stood firm, but then "repented their sins" under pressure. While all this was going on, Ronald Reagan, who was the head of the Screen Actors Guild, kept in constant touch with the FBI about "disloyal" actors. Reagan could thank his lucky stars that the Communist Party turned him down when he wanted to join in 1938. Now he was an eager informant, telling all he knew about leftist colleagues.

What finally brought McCarthy down was the Army-McCarthy hearings. These hearings lasted thirty-six days and were televised – which gave all the participants an important stage on which to perform. It was "live" television drama – often sensational – with an estimated 20 million viewers glued to their television sets every day.

To assist McCarthy in these hearings, he hired Roy Cohn, Robert Kennedy, and David Shine. The twenty-five-year-old Cohn became McCarthy's chief counsel. Brilliant, ambitious, and ruthless, Cohn graduated from Columbia Law School at the age of nineteen and quickly developed an interest in subversive activities. As an assistant U.S. Attorney, he helped prosecute Julius and Ethel Rosenberg. Robert Kennedy was twenty-seven at the time and a recent graduate from Virginia Law School. He was an ardent admirer and supporter of McCarthy, but would eventually resign from the committee – he and Roy Cohn could never get along – they were both hot-tempered and vindictive, and their personalities clashed. David Schine was the committee's unpaid chief consultant.

With his staff in place, McCarthy's investigations grew increasingly extreme. He held a series of closed-door hearings to investigate communist infiltration in the U.S. Army and then informed the press that he had uncovered a dangerous spy ring in the upper echelon of the Army. As a result of his accusations, thirty-three civilian employees were suspended pending further investigation. Secretary of the Army Robert Stevens completed a full investigation of all the suspended individuals and found no evidence of disloyalty.

Over the next four months, McCarthy continued his hearings in an effort to embarrass the Army. He accused another fifty civilian employees of disloyalty, slandered witnesses, ridiculed, debased, and humiliated dozens of innocent individuals, many of whom had to litigate for years to regain their positions. Some never recovered their reputations.

During these hearings, McCarthy interrogated General Ralph W. Zwicker about a former Army dentist who had ties to the Communist Party. McCarthy accused Zwicker, a battlefield hero of World War II, of being unfit "to wear that uniform." He told Zwicker he did not have "the brains of a five-year-old child."

The *New York Times* described McCarthy's treatment of Zwicker as "arrogant, narrow-minded and reckless." Edward R. Murrow devoted his entire *See It Now* television show to a "chillingly effective" attack on McCarthy. Murrow let the film clips of McCarthy's demeanor and tactics speak for themselves. Murrow concluded his telecast with these words:

"This is no time for men who oppose Senator McCarthy's methods to keep silent. No one can terrorize a whole nation unless we are all his accomplices. We are not descended from fearful men - who feared to defend causes which were unpopular. The actions of the junior senator from Wisconsin have caused alarm and dismay - and whose fault is that? Not really his; he didn't create this situation of fear; he merely exploited it, and rather successfully. Cassius was right, the fault, dear Brutus, is not in our stars, but in us."

A few days later, Secretary of the Army Stevens issued an order forbidding any Army officer from appearing before McCarthy's committee. Stevens explained that he would not "permit the loyal officers of our armed services to be subjected to such unwarranted treatment." Enraged, McCarthy threatened Stevens in a telephone call: "Just go ahead and try it. I am going to kick the brains out of anyone who protects communism. You just go ahead and do it. I guarantee you will live to regret it."

The Eisenhower administration, concerned about possible divisions within the Republican Party, instructed Stevens to bow to McCarthy's demands and allow Army personnel to testify before the committee. Reluctantly, Stevens gave in. McCarthy gloated that Stevens could not have surrendered "more abjectly if he had got down on his knees." The Eisenhower administration's capitulation triggered a firestorm in the nation's press and the momentum seemed to shift.

Sitting across from McCarthy during these Army hearings was Joseph Welch, a sixty-three-year-old lawyer from the prestigious Boston law firm of Hale & Dorr. Welch had been retained to represent the Army. Short, paunchy, and balding, Welch had a folksy manner, a keen mind, and incisive instincts. He had originally intended to bring two young associates with him, James St. Clair and Frederick G. Fisher, but Fisher informed Welch that as a law student at Harvard he had belonged to the National Lawyers Guild, a left-wing legal organization. Welch sent him back to Boston because he did not want anything to divert attention from the task at hand.

The most dramatic moment of the hearings occurred on June 9. During Welch's cross-examination of Roy Cohn, McCarthy interrupted and in a malevolent tone of voice announced to the world that Welch "has in his law firm a young man named Fisher - who has been for a number of years a member of an organization that is part of the legal bulwark of the Communist Party."

Welch's response, seen live by millions of television viewers, was withering:

> "Until this moment, Senator, I think I never really gauged your cruelty. Little did I dream you could be so reckless and so cruel as to do an injury to that lad. If it were in my power to forgive you for your reckless cruelty, I would do so. I like to think I am a gentleman, but your forgiveness will have to come from someone other than me. Let us not assassinate this lad further, Senator. You have done enough. Have you no sense of decency, sir? Have you no sense of decency left?"

Welch then rose and walked out of the hearing room. There was a moment of silence and then the room burst into applause. It was the moment that indelibly exposed McCarthy as the ruthless demagogue that he was. That was the end of Joe McCarthy. He had destroyed himself on national television.

The U.S. Senate now brought McCarthy up on charges of censure, which is the way they handle misconduct by one of their own. This presented a particular problem for Senator John F. Kennedy. McCarthy was strongly admired by many of Kennedy's Massachusetts Catholic constituents and by JFK's family. Bobby Kennedy had worked for McCarthy and his wife Ethel Kennedy was close to McCarthy's family. JFK's sister Eunice and her husband Sarge Shriver were also good friends of McCarthy.

Most of Democratic senators, however, lined up against McCarthy. They disliked his methods and regarded him as an embarrassment to the U.S. Senate. When the first roll was called in July 1954, JFK knew that if he voted with his fellow Democrats he would be defying his family and many in his home state, but if he voted against censure he would be denounced by the leading members of his Party. Whichever way he voted, he faced trouble.

On December 22, 1954, the U.S. Senate voted to "condemn" McCarthy by a vote of 67 to 22. JFK was the only member of the senate whose position went unrecorded. He checked himself into the hospital before the vote, claiming back pain. He could have forwarded his vote to senate, but he chose not to. For a man who received a Pulitzer Prize for his book, *Profiles in Courage*, it was not a very courageous example.

Two years later, McCarthy sat slumped in a chair, staring vacantly ahead. Snubbed by his colleagues in the U.S. Senate and ignored by the press, he bemoaned his fate. "I can't take it," he sighed. "They're after me. They're out to destroy me. I'm trying. I'm trying. I'm doing everything I can to ferret out these rats, these people who want to destroy our country. No matter where I go, they look at me with contempt. I can't take it any more." A chronic alcoholic, McCarthy died of cirrhosis of the liver on May 2, 1957. He was only forty-eight-years-old and still a United States Senator.

CHAPTER FOURTEEN

WHY THEY HATE US

"When I give food to the poor, they call me a saint. When I ask why the poor have no food, they call me a communist."

Brazilian Archbishop Dom Helder Camara

"We will not allow any leftist leaders in our backyard."

Henry Kissinger

On January 22, 1946, President Truman issued an executive order establishing the Central Intelligence Agency. On the face of the law the CIA simply appeared to have the task of correlating, evaluating and coordinating the collection of intelligence. On June 18, 1948, Truman's National Security Council took a further step and approved top-secret directive NSC 10/2, which sanctioned the CIA (known as the Agency) to carry out a broad range of covert operations including, "propaganda, economic warfare, sabotage, and subversion against hostile states, including assistance to underground resistance movements, guerrillas, and refugee liberation groups." If caught violating international law, the CIA was instructed to lie, lie, lie.

From its inception, the CIA engaged in secret covert activities authorized by the President of the United States. 'Covert action' is a term of art in intelligence operations, referring to those operations that are intended to influence the politics and policies of a target state without the hand of the acting state being disclosed. Once you engage in covert actions, lies and deceits are inevitable. Covert cannot be covert if the government has to tell the truth, which is why our Constitution never wanted the executive branch to have such enormous power.

The new law exempted the CIA from all federal laws that required disclosure of "functions, names, official titles, salaries, or the number of personnel employed by the Agency." It gave the Director of Central Intelligence the staggering and unprecedented power to spend money "without regard to the provisions of law and regulations relating to the expenditure of government funds." The Director was granted the unique right to spend hundreds of millions of dollars from a secret annual budget simply by signing his name. The law allowed "such expenditures to be accounted for solely on the certificate of the Director." That and that alone, the law said, "shall be deemed a sufficient voucher." In effect, the CIA became the president's secret army.

On January 29, 2002, President George W. Bush described Iran as part of an "axis of evil" that put it in a class with Hitler's Germany. Bush gave notice that the United States was going make a regime change in Iran. In response to this implied threat, Iran forged ahead with its nuclear bomb program, putting the two countries on a nuclear collision course that has yet to be resolved.

The seeds of Iran-U.S. hostility not surprisingly was all about oil. World War I changed the way wars were fought. The tank and airplane brought a new mobility to warfare - and everything was now dependent on oil. At the time, the United States with sixty-five percent of the total world output was king of the oil universe. However, after the war ended, the hunt was on all over the world for more oil. For the first time, oil became a key component in America's foreign policy.

The rivalry between the U.S. and other world powers for control of Middle East oil quickly became intense. The U.S. demanded an "Open Door" to Middle East oil. America's rising global power made it too dangerous for Britain to resist, especially since Exxon supplied half of the United Kingdom's oil. The result was the 1928 "Red Line Agreement" that divided Middle East oil between American, British, Dutch, and French companies. The Agreement provided that no single power would develop the region's oil without the participation of the others. The U.S. firms of Exxon and Mobil would share 23.75 percent, while British Petroleum, Royal Dutch Shell, and Compagnie Francaise would receive equal shares.

Iran was at the center of this oil boom. Bordering Iraq, Pakistan, Afghanistan, Turkey, and Central Asia; it was also a stone's throw away from Saudi Arabia, Kuwait, and Russia. When World War II broke out, Iran allied itself with Germany. Great Britain and the Soviet Union invaded Iran on August 25, 1941, and replaced the shah with his twenty-one-year-old son, Mohammad Reza Pahlavi. As a British protectorate, it was allowed to have a representative government and a parliament.

Mohammed Mosaddeq, a European-educated aristocrat, was sixty-nine years old when he was elevated from the Iranian Parliament in 1951 to prime minister by a vote of 79-12. Modern Iran has produced few figures of Mosaddeq's stature. On his mother's side he was descended from Persian royalty. His father came from a distinguished clan and was Iran's finance minister for more than twenty years. Mosaddeq studied in France and Switzerland, and became the first Iranian to earn a doctorate in law from a European university.

Mosaddeq was a true eccentric: he held cabinet meetings and received foreign dignitaries while in bed or dressed in his pajamas. He was a hypochondriac and frequently canceled public events or played for sympathy by claiming to be at death's door. He had a flair for melodrama and employed rather hackneyed theatrics - crying during his speeches, hobbling on a cane one minute and then breaking into a trot the next - but his countrymen loved him. Indeed, many foreigners underestimated Mosaddeq because they assumed his outward idiosyncrasies indicated a weak man underneath, but he wasn't weak; he was shrewd and calculating.

Mosaddeq believed passionately in two causes: Iranian nationalism and democracy. Nationalism meant taking control of his country's oil resources and expelling the foreigners. Democracy meant concentrating political power in the elected parliament and prime minister, rather than in the monarch Mohammad Reza. With his call for nationalism, Mosaddeq turned Britain into an enemy; with his demand for democracy he alienated the young shah.

In the spring of 1951, the Iranian parliament voted unanimously to nationalize the oil industry. The British were furious. By the end of June, British warships were already stationed off the coast of Iran. British commanders drew up plans for 70,000 troops to seize Iran's oil fields. Before taking precipitous action on its own, Britain consulted the United States.

President Truman, however, was not sympathetic to Britain's problem especially since the United States was still king of the world's oil. Instead, Truman felt the British should cut a fair deal with Iran, as American interests had done with Saudi Arabia. Truman and Secretary of State Dean Acheson believed that Mosaddeq was part of a nationalist revolution sweeping the Middle East and that the eloquent and colorful prime minister was in fact a bulwark against communism. Truman was worried that the use of Western force against Iran might trigger Soviet intervention and could set off World War III. "There will be no U.S. support for a coup," Truman told the British, adding that a mishandling of the Iran crisis could produce "a disaster to the free world."

Great Britain took its case to the U.N. Security Council. Mosaddeq rushed to the United Nations to defend the Iranian cause in person. Arriving in New York on October 8, 1951, he couched the struggle in terms of the wretched of the earth versus the rich and powerful. He related tales of how a "cruel and imperialistic British oil company" had stolen the resources of a "needy and naked people." Iran needed money and to get money it had to nationalize its oil industry. When questioned as to how nationalization would bring in revenue if it simply triggered an oil boycott, he responded: "Rather than come to terms with the British, I will seal the oil wells with mud."

Mosaddeq's performance at the U.N. was dazzling. He twice addressed the Security Council, but, claiming illness, he spoke at times through his son. Sometimes, he seemed meek and helpless; at other times he roared and electrified his audience. He embarrassed the British by producing a number of documents that demonstrated widespread illegal interference in Iran's political affairs. In the end, he triumphed and prevailed. The Security Council agreed that Iran's nationalization was an internal matter and therefore did not fall under U.N. jurisdiction.

After his victory at the United Nations, Mosaddeq spent several weeks in Washington at the invitation of President Truman, who hoped to work out a compromise between the Iranians and British. Assistant Secretary of State George C. McGhee spent many hours with Mosaddeq struggling to craft an agreement. Although he could not get the prime minister to budge on the issue of nationalization, he did work out a compromise position, but the British would not accept it.

Mosaddeq returned to Iran in mid-November without a settlement. He also failed to get any economic assistance from the United States or to have American oil companies buy more Iranian oil in order to break the British embargo. Truman felt bound by America's ties to Great Britain. The American position became even more complicated when Winston Churchill returned as prime minister and quickly indicated that the whole matter should be cleared up with what he termed "a bit of gunboat diplomacy." In addition, 1951 was the height of the Korean War and Churchill bluntly told Truman that British support in Korea would come at the price of American support for Britain in Iran.

In January 1952, Mosaddeq was named 'Man of the Year' by *Time* magazine - choosing him over Winston Churchill, Douglas MacArthur, Harry Truman, and Dwight Eisenhower. *Time* called him "the Iranian George Washington" and "the most world-renown man his ancient race had produced for centuries."

That year, after a dispute with the shah, Mosaddeq resigned. When the shah announced that he planned to reverse many of Mosaddeq's policies, the Iranian people revolted. Things spiraled out of control as the military and demonstrators clashed; 69 people were killed and about 750 were wounded. Four days later the shah asked Mosaddeq to return as prime minister. Mosaddeq replied that he would, but only if the shah remained on his throne as a figurehead with no power. The shah reluctantly agreed and went into luxurious exile in Europe. Mohammed Mosaddeq, the lifelong constitutional democrat, had effectively made himself ruler of Iran without an election.

Mosaddeq's rise to power thrilled Iranians, but outraged British leaders. The idea that a backward country like Iran could deal Britain such a blow was incomprehensible. They vowed to resist. "Persian oil is of vital importance to our economy," Foreign Secretary Herbert Morrison declared. "We regard it as essential to prevent the Persians from getting away with a breach of their contractual obligations."

Over the next year, the British considered bribing Mosaddeq, assassinating him, or launching a military invasion of Iran. The British sabotaged their own oil installations at Abadan in the hopes of convincing Mosaddeq that he could not possibly run the oil industry without England. They blockaded Iranian ports so tankers could not enter or leave, and they appealed unsuccessfully to the International Court of Justice. Finally, they concluded that their only remaining option was to organize a coup and oust Mosaddeq.

Officials in London ordered their agents in Tehran to set such a plot in motion. Before the British could strike, Mosaddeq discovered what they were planning. On October 16, 1952, he ordered the British Embassy shut and sent all its employees out of the country, including the intelligence agents who were organizing the coup. This left the British disarmed. Their covert agents had been expelled from Iran, President Truman's opposition made an invasion impossible, and the U.N. refused to intervene. The British government faced the disorienting prospect of losing its most valuable foreign asset to a peasant country led by a man they considered, "wild, fanatical, absurd, gangster-like, completely unscrupulous, and clearly unbalanced."

In 1953, when Eisenhower became president, he turned the CIA into the secret army of the executive branch. During his administration, the CIA would undertake 170 major covert actions in 48 nations in order to install pro-western governments, overthrow regimes unfavorable to the U.S., or assassinate unfriendly world leaders. The first year of his presidency, the CIA budget rose to $800 million; ten times what it was the previous year. Eisenhower saw every social reform movement or struggle for national liberation as a communist plot. Where Truman had seen Mosaddeq as an honest nationalist who was a nuisance, Eisenhower saw him as a tool of Moscow.

The chief of CIA operations in the Middle East, Kermit Roosevelt (Theodore Roosevelt's grandson) happened to be passing through London on his way home after a visit to Iran. He met with several of his British counterparts and they presented him with an extraordinary proposal. They wanted the CIA to carry out the coup in Iran that they could no longer execute.

Under the plan called *Operation Ajax*, the Americans would bribe Iranian journalists and other opinion leaders to create distrust, hostility and fear of Mosaddeq and his government. Then the CIA would hire thugs to carry out "staged attacks" on religious figures and other respected Iranians, making it seem that the orders came from Mosaddeq. The plan also called for bribes to members of the Iranian parliament to demand Mosaddeq's resignation. On "coup day" thousands of paid demonstrators would converge on parliament demanding that Mosaddeq be dismissed. Parliament would then vote to do just that; if Mosaddeq refused to resign he would be arrested.

Kermit Roosevelt presented the plan to Eisenhower. CIA Director Allen Dulles was enthusiastic. "If Iran becomes communist, all the other countries in the Middle East will follow. Sixty percent of the free world's oil will then be in Moscow's hands. This disastrous loss would seriously deplete our reserves for war and lead to gasoline rationing in the United States." Eisenhower agreed to support the CIA operation in Iran, but he established the doctrine of "plausible denial." Any CIA covert action or assassination attempt had to be so thoroughly disguised that the truth about U.S. involvement could be plausibly denied by the president, and any later investigation would lead nowhere. Lies and deceits now became official U.S. policy as long as the president in his sole discretion believed the ends justified the means.

After a deal "to share the wealth" in Iran between the U.S. and Britain was agreed upon, Allen Dulles approved $1 million to Kermit Roosevelt to be used "in any way that would bring about the fall of Mosaddeq." Roosevelt slipped into Iran at a remote border crossing on July 19, 1953, and immediately set about his subversive work. Spending lavish amounts of money, his first step was to control Iran's media. News stories bombarded Iran's public proclaiming that Mosaddeq favored the USSR and was leading the country into economic collapse. Additional reports claimed he had been corrupted by power and that he was a homosexual and an enemy of Islam.

Organized street mobs began demanding the return of the shah. The capital of Tehran was paralyzed with violent demonstrations. Soon all of Iran was aflame. Bribed religious leaders began giving sermons calling Mosaddeq an atheist, a Jew, and an infidel. Mosaddeq could have cracked down, but he had such an exaggerated faith in democracy that he did nothing to repress what was happening.

Kermit Roosevelt chose August 19 as the climatic day. He mobilized thousands of demonstrators shouting "Long live the shah," as they rampaged through the streets, demanding Mosaddeq's resignation. The demonstrations appeared spontaneous - an important ingredient for any covert success. Military and police units were bribed, and with Roosevelt directing the activities, they seized control of Mosaddeq's house. The coup had succeeded.

No one was more surprised at the turn of events then the shah. He was dining in Rome with the empress when he heard the news. He is reported to have jumped up and shouted, "I knew it! I knew it! They love me!"

The shah returned immediately to Iran. Roosevelt paid a farewell call on the shah before leaving Tehran. Over vodka, the shah offered Roosevelt a toast, "I owe my throne to God, my people, my army – and to you." With that Roosevelt left knowing he had changed the course of Iranian history. The shah would be grateful to America for the rest of his life.

Kermit Roosevelt was awarded the National Security Medal by Eisenhower, who called the coup "the CIA's greatest single triumph. We have changed the whole course of a country here." America now had a new foreign policy vehicle to shape the world to U.S. interests.

Lies and Deceits

After the 1953 coup, the triumphant shah imposed three years of martial law and tightened his control over the country. He ordered the execution of several dozen military officers and also Hussein Fatemi, Mosaddeq's foreign minister. It was too risky for the shah to have Mosaddeq executed. Instead, he arranged for the old man to be tried for treason and found guilty. Mosaddeq was sentenced to three years in prison and spent the rest of his life under house arrest in his home. He died in 1967 at the age of eighty-five.

Upon taking power, the shah called upon the CIA to help him create a new intelligence service and secret police, which became known as SAVAK. This new Gestapo-like force, murdered and tortured with impunity, and enforced the shah's royal dictatorship for more than twenty years. The people of Iran knew that SAVAK was an extension of America's lies about it being a 'beacon of democracy.' Our role in overthrowing Mosaddeq and our embrace of the dictatorial shah eventually led to the rise of anti-Americanism in Iran. In 1978, the people of Iran revolted and forced the shah to flee. Not even the CIA could stop the flow and venom of anti-Americanism.

On March 17, 2000, Secretary of State Madeleine Albright admitted that, "In 1953, the United States played a significant role in orchestrating the overthrow of Iran's popular Prime Minister Mohammad Mosaddeq. The Eisenhower administration believed its actions were justified for strategic reasons; but it is now easy to see why many Iranians continue to resent American intervention in their internal affairs."

What was Iran's response to Madeleine Albright's speech? Ayatollah Khamenei, Iran's supreme leader gave Tehran's answer to the assembled masses at Mashhad:

> "Just a few days ago an American minister delivered a speech. After half a century, the Americans have now confessed that they staged the August 19, 1953 coup. They confessed that they supported the suppressive, dictatorial, and corrupt shah for twenty-five years. Please pay attention. More than forty years have elapsed since that infamous coup

d'etat. It is only now that they are admitting that they were behind it. They finally admit that they supported and backed the dictatorial, oppressive, corrupt and subservient regime of the shah for twenty-five years. What do you think the Iranian nation, faced with this situation and these admissions, feels?"

When we ask, "why do they hate us?" - Iran is one reason.

****

While Eisenhower was covertly changing regimes in Iran, he was also overturning FDR's *Good Neighbor Policy* in Latin America. The election in Guatemala of Jacobo Arbenz in 1950 was the first Latin American challenge to the United States of the post-World War II period. Arbenz's election occurred in the same year that Mohammed Mosaddeq became prime minister in Iran. Each assumed leadership of a wretchedly poor nation that was beginning to achieve democratic status. Each challenged the power of U.S. corporate interests.

Plans for a coup against Arbenz had been kicking around the CIA for almost three years. Eisenhower's brother, Milton, returned from a fact-finding mission of Latin America and informed the president that "the Arbenz government has succumbed to communist infiltration." President Eisenhower was alarmed. Suppose Guatemala went under? What then for its neighbors? "My God," Eisenhower exclaimed during a cabinet meeting, "just think what it would mean to us if Mexico went Communist! It's like a row of dominoes; you knock over the first one, and what will happen to the last one is that it will go over very quickly." With American corporate interests at risk throughout the region, the CIA was given the 'green light' to overthrow the democratically elected regime in Guatemala and install a 'friendly' new leader.

Few private companies have ever been as closely interwoven with the United States government as United Fruit was during the mid-1950s. Secretary of State John Foster Dulles had for decades been its principal legal counselor. His brother Allen Dulles, the CIA Director, had also done legal work for United Fruit and owned a substantial block of its stock. John Moors Cabot, the assistant secretary of state for inter-American affairs, was a large shareholder. His brother, Thomas Dudley Cabot, the director of international security affairs in our State Department, had been United Fruit's president. General Robert Cutler, head of the National Security Council, was United Fruit's former Chairman of the Board. John J. McCloy, the president of the International Bank for Reconstruction and Development, was a former United Fruit board member. Undersecretary of State Walter Bedell Smith and Robert Hill, the American ambassador to Costa Rica, would join the United Fruit board after leaving government service.

During the first half of the twentieth century, United Fruit made great profits in Guatemala because it was able to operate without interference from the Guatemalan government. It simply claimed good farm land, arranged for legal title through one-sided deals with the government, and then operated plantations on its own terms, free of such annoyances as taxes or labor regulations. As long as that system prevailed, the United States considered Guatemala a 'friendly and stable' country.

Jacobo Arbenz was not anti-American. He was a democratically elected left-leaning nationalist. His plan was to expropriate vacant and inactive lands owned by United Fruit and distribute it to landless peasants. He modeled his program after the U.S. Homestead Act. United Fruit was not going to let this happen.

When Eisenhower came into office, he and Secretary of State Dulles were determined to get rid of the troublesome regime in Guatemala, but they did not have a clear idea of how to do it. Kermit Roosevelt's CIA triumph in Iran showed them the way. They decided to design a Guatemalan version of the successful Iranian coup and code-named it *Operation Success*. They offered Kermit Roosevelt the top command post, but he turned it down, preferring more sophisticated operations in Arabia and Egypt. The CIA, however, believed that their success in Iran could be duplicated in Guatemala even without Kermit Roosevelt.

On December 3, 1953, the CIA authorized an initial $3 million to set the plot in motion. It would start with a propaganda campaign, proceed through a wave of destabilizing violence, and culminate in an attack staged to look like a domestic uprising. This operation though would be much larger in scale than the one in Iran.

The CIA started by planting stories designed to generate anxiety and uncertainty. They spread rumors that the Guatemalan government was going to ban Holy Week, exile the archbishop, confiscate bank accounts, expropriate all private property, and force children into reeducation centers. They transmitted radio shows taped in Florida and beamed in from Nicaragua that made it seem as if a widespread underground resistance movement was gaining strength.

The United States Information Service (USIS), working with the CIA, began placing articles in Latin American newspapers "labeling certain Guatemalan officials as communists and labeling certain actions of the Guatemalan government as communist-inspired." The press in America followed the administration's lead, depicting Arbenz as a communist threat.

If the Arbenz government was in the Soviet camp, it did not act the part. It had no diplomatic relations with the Soviet Union, and at the United Nations it generally supported our views. Arbenz, while he himself had no affiliation with Guatemala's Communist Party, had appointed communists to posts in his bureaucracy, especially in his land reform agency, but of the fifty-two members in the Guatemalan Congress only four were communists and none served in Arbenz's cabinet.

When Arbenz refused to change his stand on the United Fruit land, President Eisenhower instructed the CIA to overthrow him. The CIA plan was to find a suitable leader among Guatemalan exiles, equip him with a militia that could pose as a full-scale rebel army, hire American non-military pilots to bomb Guatemala City, and then with the country in chaos, have the American ambassador inform the Guatemalan military commanders that peace would return only if they deposed Arbenz.

In January 1954, a hitch developed in the plan when one plot supporter gave Arbenz incriminating letters written by two conspirators. Arbenz published the letters and charged that the United States was colluding with the plotters. Our State

Department denied any role, calling Arbenz's charge "ridiculous and untrue," and affirming, "it is the policy of the United States not to intervene in the internal affairs of other nations."

Secretary of State Dulles chose John Peurifoy, a West Point dropout from South Carolina, to be ambassador to Guatemala. On the evening of December 16, Peurifoy had his first and only meeting with Arbenz. It lasted for six hours over an extended dinner at Arbenz's official residence. When Arbenz began to discourse on United Fruit's abuses, Peurifoy interrupted to say that the real problem in Guatemala was "commie influence."

The next day Peurifoy sent Dulles a curt assessment of the man they targeted: "If he is not a communist, he will certainly do until one comes along." Peurifoy added ominously, "Normal approaches will not work in Guatemala. The candle is burning slowly and surely, and it is only a matter of time before the large American interests will be forced out entirely."

These were the words Dulles wanted to hear. He brought the cable to Eisenhower, who read it gravely. By the time he finished reading, according to his own account, Eisenhower gave *Operation Success* his final approval. His order set the CIA covert operation in motion. "Go to it, my boy," Dulles said as he notified the CIA chief in charge. "You've got the green light." *Operation Success* was now fully approved and funded with more money than the CIA had ever spent on a covert operation. It lacked only one essential element: a Guatemalan to play the role of rebel leader.

Colonel Carlos Castillo Armas had led an abortive uprising in 1950 and had become a familiar figure in Guatemalan exile circles. CIA agents found him in Honduras, flew him to Opa-Locka in Florida, told him they were working with United Fruit on an anti-Arbenz project, and proposed that he become its alleged leader. He accepted immediately.

During the spring of 1954, Castillo Armas waited in Honduras while the CIA hired fighters, requisitioned planes, prepared bases, and secured the cooperation of Honduran and Nicaraguan officials. The CIA station on the fourth floor of the American Embassy in Guatemala City buzzed with activity. So did the operational base at Opa-Locka, Florida.

One of the agents assigned to *Operation Success*, Howard Hunt, who later became notorious for his role in the Watergate burglary, came up with the idea of using the Roman Catholic clergy to turn Guatemalans against Arbenz. Catholic priests and bishops in all Latin American countries, were closely aligned with the rich ruling class, and they loathed left-wing reformers like Arbenz.

Hunt met secretly with the most powerful Catholic prelate in the United States, Cardinal Spellman of New York, and asked him if he could bring his Guatemalan priesthood into the coup plot. Spellman assured him that would be no problem. Soon, CIA agents were writing scripts and leaflets for the Guatemalan clergy that went out in pastoral letters warning the faithful that a demonic force called communism was trying to destroy their homeland and called on them to "rise as a single man against this enemy of God and country."

The CIA operation was now in full swing. They recruited 500 Guatemalan exiles, American soldiers of fortune, assorted Central American mercenaries, and sent them to training camps in Nicaragua, Honduras, and Florida. A CIA clandestine "Voice of Liberation" radio station, supposedly transmitting from somewhere in Guatemala, but actually based in Florida, was broadcasting a stream of false reports about popular unrest and military rebellions. It was now time to send the CIA's handpicked "liberator," Colonel Castillo Armas, into action.

Soon after dawn on June 18, Castillo Armas packed his men into jeeps and trucks, and led them northward in his command car, a battered old station wagon. They crossed the Honduran border into Guatemala without incident. Then, following the orders of his CIA handlers, Armas led his motorcade six miles into Guatemalan territory. There he stopped; this was the extent of the invasion.

Meanwhile, the CIA's radio station was broadcasting breathless reports of Armas's supposed swift progress through the countryside. CIA planes buzzed low over the main military barracks in Guatemala City, firing machine-gun rounds and dropping a fragmentation bomb that set off a series of loud explosions. Ambassador Peurifoy, one of the few people in the country who knew what was happening, heard the bombs from his

Lies and Deceits

embassy office. He looked out his window, saw smoke billowing up from the barracks, and dashed off a gleeful cable to CIA Director Allen Dulles.

The air raids continued for several days. One plane shot up the airport in Guatemala City; others hit fuel tanks and military posts across the country. This led to several injuries and some property damage, but the purpose was not military. Like the bogus radio broadcasts, they were aimed at creating the impression that a war was under way. Each time a plane strafed another town, Guatemalans became more insecure, confused, and fearful. Their only option was to believe the propaganda lies from the "Voice of Liberation."

On the afternoon of June 19, the U.S. State Department issued a false statement saying it had news of "serious uprisings" and "outbreaks of violence" in Guatemala. "The United States has no evidence that indicates this is anything other than a revolt of the Guatemalan people against their government." Arbenz knew the statements out of Washington were untrue and that the United States was behind the rebellion, which meant that he could not defeat what was going on with armed force. This realization drove him to address his country by radio; he declared that "the arch-traitor Castillo Armas was leading a United Fruit Company expeditionary force against his government."

In the days after that speech, things began looking better for Arbenz. The army remained loyal to him and his popularity among ordinary Guatemalans remained solid. At a meeting of the U.N. Security Council in New York, France introduced a resolution calling for an end to "any action likely to cause bloodshed" in Guatemala and directed all countries to refrain from "rendering assistance to any such action." A resolution was introduced for the U.N. to investigate what was going on in Guatemala. The United States ambassador to the United Nations, Henry Cabot Lodge, worked feverishly to defeat this motion. He assured the U.N. Assembly that "what was going on in Guatemala was a revolt of Guatemalans against Guatemalans." On June 25, the Security Council voted not to investigate what was happening in Guatemala.

The CIA air raids over Guatemala began tapering off when one of our P-47 Thunderbolts was shot down and a second plane crashed. The command post at Opa-Locka, Florida, was in a panic. An urgent cable was sent to CIA Director Allen Dulles stating that *Operation Success* was on the verge of collapse and would probably fail without more air support. Dulles immediately received President Eisenhower's permission to dispatch more planes. Eisenhower could see no realistic alternative. "If at any time you take the route of violence or support violence, then you commit yourself to carrying it through, and it is too late to have second thoughts."

As the bombing campaign intensified, Arbenz began to lose his grip. At one point he considered calling the peasantry to armed resistance, but his military commanders would not hear of it. He was out of options. At midday on Sunday, June 27, he notified the American Embassy to arrange the terms of his surrender.

Castillo Armas was given a hero's welcome in Washington. Vice President Richard Nixon hosted a gala dinner in his honor and offered the following toast: "We in the United States have watched the people of Guatemala record an episode in their history deeply significant to all peoples. Led by our guest of honor this evening, Castillo Armas and the Guatemalan people revolted against the corruption of communist rule." Armas thanked Nixon for his kind words and told him: "Tell me what you want me to do and I will do it."

The coup in Guatemala produced a stable government friendly to U.S. interests, but for Guatemala it brought disaster. The overthrow of Arbenz shattered the political center and initiated a cycle of violence that would last for more than four decades.

Castillo Armas was not an especially honest man and it did not take long for him to become enmeshed in webs of corruption and intrigue. On the evening of July 27, 1957 he was shot and killed at his official residence. Seconds later someone killed the assassin. There was no serious investigation. Many people believe the whole thing was staged and orchestrated by the CIA.

The events in Guatemala had an unexpected effect that did not become clear until years later. During the Arbenz years, scores of

Lies and Deceits

curious Latin American leftists gravitated to Guatemala. One of them was a young Argentine doctor named Che Guevara. After the CIA coup toppled Arbenz, Guevara fled to Mexico where he met the Cuban revolutionary Fidel Castro. They discussed the events in Guatemala at great length and from them drew a lesson that has reverberated through all of subsequent Latin America history.

"Cuba is not Guatemala!" Castro liked to shout when he taunted the United States for its inability to overthrow him during the 1960s.

When we ask, "why do they hate us?" – Guatemala is one reason.

****

One of the best examples of how the combined forces of U.S. business interests and our government work together is the story of Chile, a Latin American country with a history of democratic elections. Yet, the United States, under President Lyndon Johnson and then Richard Nixon, secretly crushed the democratically elected government of Salvador Allende without any awareness on the part of the American public.

Chile would seem an odd place for the United States to launch a risky and violent covert operation. It is a small country, far from American shores, and has never posed the slightest military threat to the United States. But, Chile was a world leader in copper and 80 percent of its production was controlled by U.S. firms, most prominently Anaconda and Kennecott Copper. Profits for the American firms were enormous. Kennecott's operations in Chile earned the Company a profit of $20 million per year; Anaconda's annual profits were $30 million. Companies like Pepsi-Cola and International Telephone and Telegraph also had virtual monopolies in Chile.

Salvador Allende was the classic bourgeois revolutionary. Although born into privilege, he was a passionate advocate of radical social change. Horn-rimmed eyeglasses, tweedy jackets, and a slightly raffish mustache gave Allende the air of a college professor or Harvard intellectual. His political philosophy emerged out of Marxism and the realities of life he saw around him. Despite Chile's relatively prosperous position among South American nations, millions of its people lived in desperate poverty while the top two percent received 45.9 percent of the country's income. This inequality genuinely disturbed Allende; equally outrageous to him was the fact that foreign companies controlled his country's wealth. Allende had unsuccessfully run for president in 1958 as a member of the Socialist Party. In 1964, he tried again; campaigning to nationalize the American owned companies and to balance the income inequality among Chile's citizens.

The CIA spent at least $20 million to defeat Allende in 1964. Additional support came from a group of American corporations known as the *Business Group for Latin America*, which was led by David Rockefeller, the chairman of Chase Manhattan Bank. The group's purpose was to use its power, money, and political clout "to fight the spread of communism in Latin America." The threat of communism was a scare tactic meant for public consumption – what really mattered was the threat of nationalization of profitable American corporate interests.

With all this financial clout massed against Allende it was not surprising that he was defeated. Secretary of State Dean Rusk told President Lyndon Johnson that Allende's defeat was "the result of the good work of the CIA." After the election, the CIA continued to operate at will throughout Chile, primarily seeking to repress radicals and leftists. Most of these operations were designed to support moderate and conservative candidates in Chilean congressional elections.

While U.S. officials believed that the United States had purchased the right to guide the course of Chilean politics, they did not realize that change was sweeping across Latin America. In Cuba, guerrillas overthrew the Batista dictatorship and imposed a radical social and political program; other dictators fell in Peru, Colombia, Venezuela, and Argentina. In 1965, the U.S. had to send 22,000 Marines into the Dominican Republic to protect the corrupt military junta we had installed.

In 1970, it was time for a new election in Chile. President Frei's six-year term had expired and he could not run again. Allende ran for president again; this time at the head of a leftist coalition called Popular Unity. The challenge of keeping him out of power obsessed American business interests. Early in 1970, with President Nixon's insistence, our Chilean Ambassador Edward Korry and his CIA station chief Henry Hecksher, embarked on a covert campaign to block Allende. They coordinated their efforts with the *40 Committee,* named after the presidential directive that created it, which was composed of the country's top national security officials and private business executives. Henry Kissinger was in charge of the committee.

On March 25, 1970, the CIA launched its campaign to prevent Allende from winning the election. CIA agents dusted off their files and used many of the same tactics from their successful operation against him in 1964. As the campaign against Allende intensified, ITT Chairman Harold Geneen decided to personally intervene. He met with the CIA's chief of covert operations in the ITT suite at the Sheraton Carlton Hotel in Washington and Geneen said that his company wanted to use the CIA as a conduit to covertly pass money to the campaign of Jorge Alessandri – Allende's opponent. The CIA agreed. ITT gave $350,000 to the CIA and arranged for other American firms to donate another $350,000.

This time all our money and false propaganda did not work. On September 4, 1970, Chilean voters went to the polls and gave Allende his victory. However, there was a glitch. Since Allende did not win a majority – he received 36.3 percent in a three-way race - his victory had to be confirmed by the Chilean Congress. In past cases like this, the Congress always chose the first-place finisher and it seemed certain to do so again – but the CIA and the United States had other ideas. The CIA had plenty of experience fixing an election before the balloting started; now it had seven weeks to reverse the outcome of one that had already taken place – and President Nixon demanded that it be done.

Agustin Edwards was one of Chile's richest and most powerful men. He owned most of the nation's copper mines, the country's largest newspaper, and Chile's Pepsi-Cola bottling plant. If Allende nationalized the economy, Edwards would suffer huge financial losses. Obviously, he did not want Allende confirmed. President

Nixon's corporate supporters also had huge financial interests at stake in Chile. They certainly did not want Allende confirmed. Nixon knew his friends would soon be knocking on his door looking for help.

When Nixon asked to see the classified CIA report on Chile he was surprised and annoyed. The report concluded that, "Allende posed no national security threat to the United States, and the world military balance of power would not be significantly altered by an Allende government." This was not what Nixon wanted to hear.

On September 9, the directors of ITT held their monthly meeting in New York. ITT's prize asset, the Chilean telephone system, was high on Allende's list for nationalization. During that ITT board meeting, Harold Geneen took one of the board members aside to make an audacious proposition. "What he told me," the board member later testified, "was that he was prepared to put as much as a million dollars in support of any plan that would eliminate Allende." That board member was none other than former CIA Director John McCone. McCone had joined ITT less than a year after leaving the CIA, but remained a paid consultant to the CIA, which meant that he was simultaneously on both payrolls. This unique arrangement made him the ideal link between ITT and the top levels of the United States government. McCone went to Henry Kissinger, the president's national security advisor, and conveyed Geneen's million-dollar offer. McCone also presented Geneen's offer to his successor at the CIA, Richard Helms.

Meanwhile, Agustin Edwards arrived in Washington to meet with his old friend and business partner Donald Kendall, who was now chairman and chief executive officer of Pepsi-Cola. On September 14, Kendall, one of Nixon's biggest campaign contributors, went to the White House. He told Nixon what Edwards said about Chile: if Allende was allowed to take office, he would nationalize the Chilean economy, force American business out, and steer Chile into the Soviet-Cuban orbit. Nixon listened attentively and agreed that Allende had to go – by any means.

That afternoon, Kissinger, Attorney-General John Mitchell, and CIA Director Richard Helms came to the Oval Office at Nixon's request. Their meeting lasted only thirteen minutes. Nixon was so explicit that no more time was needed. Nixon wanted Allende's election stopped. As Nixon spoke, Helms scribbled a page of notes that has become a classic document in the history of covert action. Helms wrote that Nixon authorized $10 million, more if necessary, to bring Allende down. "The president was adamant that he wanted something done and he did not care how, and he was prepared to make available as much money as was necessary." Helms later testified, "This was a pretty all-inclusive order."

Nixon ordered Helms to produce an anti-Allende plan within forty-eight hours. Early the next morning, Helms met with his covert action specialists. He told them, "President Nixon has decided that an Allende regime in Chile is unacceptable, and he wants the Agency to prevent him from coming to power or to unseat him, and the Agency is to carry out this mission without coordination with the State Department or the Department of Defense."

The anti-Allende operation had two parts. The first was aimed at blocking Allende by "legal" means. This approach failed. The second approach was to foment a military coup. Plotters at CIA headquarters in Langley, Virginia, directed their agents in Santiago to begin "probing for military possibilities to thwart Allende," and to look for ways of "strengthening the resolve of the Chilean military to act against him."

To create that climate, the U.S. needed to push Chile toward chaos. Kissinger set out to do so, using all of the considerable resources at his command. He justified this effort with what became one of his most-quoted maxims: "I don't see why we need to stand by and watch a country go communist due to the irresponsibility of its own people." Advocating a complete disdain for democracy, he said, "The issues are much too important for the Chilean voters to decide for themselves."

As this project was taking shape, several diplomats and CIA officers expressed serious doubts. Henry Hecksher, chief of the CIA station in Santiago, reported that with the election now over, he would "not consider any kind of intervention in the constitutional process desirable." Another CIA officer wrote in a memo that Allende was not likely to take orders from Moscow or Havana and that plotting against him would be "repeating the errors we made when we drove Fidel Castro into the Soviet camp." Assistant Secretary of State Charles Meyer predicted that covert action against Allende would "further tarnish America's image in Latin America."

These doubters did not realize how fiercely determined Nixon was to block Allende. David Atlee Phillips who ran the highly successful "Voice of Liberation" radio campaign during the 1954 coup against Jacobo Arbenz of Guatemala now became co-director of the CIA's newly formed Chile Task Force. Phillips' instructions were to create a "coup climate," and a "pretext for action." CIA agents contacted and bribed nearly two dozen Chilean military officers to lead the coup and gave them assurances of strong support at the highest levels of the U.S. government.

The first blows struck by the United States were economic. Two principal American foreign aid agencies, the Export-Import Bank and the Agency for International Development, acting under classified instructions from the National Security Council, announced that they would no longer approve "any new commitments of U.S. assistance to Chile." The United States representative at the Inter-American Development Bank was instructed to block all proposals for loans to Chile. Chile's credit rating was reduced from grade B to grade D.

The Export-Import Bank, citing the credit rating reduction, canceled a scheduled $21 million loan. At the World Bank, the American representative arranged for the suspension of a multi-million dollar livestock improvement loan to Chile and then announced that the United States would oppose all new World Bank lending to that country. This cutting of aid, loans, and credits to Chile became known as an "invisible blockade," but it was relatively straightforward.

The CIA passed the word to the highest levels of the Chilean military that "the United States government was willing to support any military move to deny Allende the presidency." A principal impediment to a successful coup was Rene Schneider, Chile's commander-in-chief, who opposed any interference with the country's constitutional process. To get him out of the way, the CIA arranged for Schneider to be eliminated. After two failed attempts, Schneider's car was rammed as he was driving to military headquarters. His rear window was smashed and he was shot three times. He died after unsuccessful surgery. His murderers were never apprehended.

Schneider's death deepened the determination of the Chilean Congress. They would not be intimidated. They voted to give the election to Allende and they unanimously approved a constitutional amendment authorizing the nationalization of Kennecott, Anaconda, ITT, and other foreign ownerships. Allende proclaimed that day would henceforth be "National Dignity Day." He informed Kennecott and Anaconda, "We will pay for any appropriation if it is just, but we will not pay what is not just." He did not encourage the companies to hope for much in the way of compensation.

These actions merely infuriated Nixon further and intensified his resolve to eliminate Allende. After Allende's inauguration, leading American corporations secretly formed a Chile Ad Hoc Committee dedicated to working with U.S. government officials in Washington to "handle the Chile problem." Over the next few months, its members set out on a quiet destabilization campaign in Chile that included office closings, delayed payments, slow deliveries, and credit denial. It was so effective that within two years, one-third of Chile's buses and 20 percent of its taxis were out of service due to a lack of spare parts.

Between 1970 and 1973, the CIA carried out a wide-ranging series of covert operations in Chile, including millions of dollars of anti-Allende propaganda. Millions more was funneled to business, labor, and civic organizations in order to organize protests, demonstrations, and violent actions against Allende's administration.

The anti-Allende project was under way for more than a year when the secrecy surrounding it was spectacularly breached. Washington newspaper columnist, Jack Anderson, obtained twenty-four internal ITT memos that detailed the company's "plot to stop the 1970 election of Allende." The memos told of ITT's offer of $1 million; its regular contacts with the CIA, the National Security Council, and the State Department; and its many efforts to push Chile to "economic collapse" in order to bring about "an internal crisis requiring military intervention." Many Americans were outraged. A *Washington Post* editorial asked, "How could an American president consider the possibility of acting to prevent a democratically elected president of a friendly country from taking office?"

Twenty-one years earlier, Prime Minister Mohammed Mosaddeq of Iran had come to the United Nations to present his case against a foreign corporation that controlled his country's basic resources. Allende was in a similar position. His country was a victim of the resource curse, just as Iran had been. The riches that lay beneath their soil came under the control of foreign corporations, and when they tried to reclaim those riches, the might of the U.S. was marshaled against them.

At eleven o'clock on the morning of December 4, 1972, Allende strode to the U.N. General Assembly podium to proclaim "his battle in defense of national resources." He accused ITT of trying to provoke a civil war in his country. "They propose economic strangulation, diplomatic sabotage, and social disorder to promote panic among the people, allowing the army to overthrow a democracy and put in a dictatorship controlled by the United States." His speech eerily echoed Mosaddeq, showing how little the relationship between Corporate America and weak foreign countries had changed over the course of two decades.

In Washington, a furious Nixon overhauled his Chile team and replaced CIA Director Richard Helms. To smooth Helms' fall, Nixon named him ambassador to Iran. At his confirmation hearing, Helms blithely replied, "'No, sir" when asked if the CIA had tried to block the election of Allende in 1970. That two-word statement would later lead a federal court to convict him of perjury.

On September 11, an ironic date in history, the CIA finally toppled Allende. When it was all over, Allende was dead. He was sixty-five years old and had been president of Chile for 1,042 days. With General Augusto Pinochet now in charge, more than 3,200 people disappeared or were executed, at least 80,000 were imprisoned, and 200,000 fled the country for political reasons – 80 percent of these political prisoners were union workers and peasants.

The war of the rich against the poor and middle-class became the real story of Chile's new economy. By 1988, 45 percent of the population had fallen below the poverty line. The richest 10 percent in the country saw their incomes increase by 83 percent. By 2007, Chile had become one of the most unequal societies in the world - out of 123 countries in which the United Nations tracks inequality, Chile was the 8th most unequal country on the list.

Between 1985 and 2002 Pinochet would personally pocket $16 million. He would eventually flee to London where the aging ruler was kept under house arrest as he faced charges of genocide, torture and terrorism.

When we ask: "why do they hate us?" – Chile is one reason.

****

Whatever one may think about Fidel Castro and the Cuba he symbolizes, he has long been an object of fascination. Praised or damned, he has outlasted nine U.S. presidents and what he says and does is remarked on around the world. The stories surrounding him are legend, and the tales of America's attempts to assassinate him, reveal an obsession so nefarious that it is hard to believe that he has not succumbed to our country's covert schemes to kill him.

Fidel Castro Ruz was born on a farm in Biran, on August 13, 1926. Biran was not a town or a village; it was just a few isolated houses. His father, Angel Castro, was a Spaniard who came to Cuba to fight against the United States in the Spanish-American War. After Spain's defeat, Angel remained on the island and made a very good living growing sugar cane for United Fruit.

Fidel attended elite Catholic private schools in Santiago and Havana. He was movie star handsome and an outstanding athlete. During his college days he starred in basketball and track, and was offered a bonus to sign with the N.Y. Giants baseball club. He turned it down because he was politically committed by that time.

While at the university, he joined a student group against political corruption. He was a member of the Cuban People's Party and in 1947 became a leader of its left-wing. That same year he volunteered for an armed expedition against the Trujillo dictatorship in the Dominican Republic, but was not allowed to leave Cuba. As a student leader, he went to Venezuela, Panama and Colombia to help organize a Latin American anti-imperialist student congress. While in Colombia, he participated in the April 1948 popular uprising in Bogota.

In 1948, Castro married the daughter of a lawyer for the United Fruit Company and settled down in an exclusive and prosperous community where high-level United Fruit employees lived and played separate and apart from the Cuban people. Access to the town beach was controlled by a gate that barred the non-elitists. Each time Castro crossed that gate, he became enraged. He hated a system where one class of people lived better than another. In 1950, Castro graduated law school from the University of Havana. In 1955, he and his wife divorced; they had one son.

Fulgencio Batista was born on January 16, 1901, only miles away from the Castro family. His father worked for United Fruit cutting sugarcane. Batista had a smooth amber complexion, perfect teeth and hair, and exotic facial features – a type of handsomeness that was the envy of both men and women. In 1932, he joined the army, and was immediately elevated in rank. As a young sergeant, in alliance with students and labor leaders, he led non-commissioned officers in a rebellion against Dictator Gerardo Machado. Later, he conspired with U.S. Ambassador Sumner Welles to force the resignation of provisional president Ramón Grau San Martín. By the age of thirty-two, Batista was a colonel and the strongman behind a succession of U.S. puppet presidents in Cuba.

The real power in Cuba during these days was American Mafia gangster, Meyer Lansky. In the long history of the American underworld, there had never been anyone like little Maier Suchowljansky; a Jew surrounded by Italians. Born in 1902, at a time when Poland was occupied by czarist Russia, he was ten-years-old when his family fled the pogroms directed at Jews. His family headed for New York City and the Brownsville section of Brooklyn. Meyer was an exemplary student and he loved school, but the poverty of his family drove his ambitions in other directions.

It did not take long for the brash hustling Lansky to find a home with the local mobsters, and he soon became known throughout the mob circles as the smart Jew; the one with a global vision. With the permission of his "boss" Lucky Luciano, Lansky set his sights on Cuba as a mecca for vice and gambling.

Lansky and Batista established a very profitable relationship. Batista controlled the army and Lansky guaranteed him between $3 to $5 million a year as long as the mob had a monopoly on the casinos and illegal activities on the island.

In 1940, the U.S. government promoted and supported Batista's election as president. Batista was guaranteed U.S. financial support as long as he continued to help American corporations such as United Fruit garner huge profits on the island.

Batista ruled with an iron fist. Leaders of rival political parties were assassinated and editors of dissenting newspapers were kidnapped, never to be seen again. Censorship was crudely enforced and civil liberties were dispensed according to Batista's whims. Student demonstrations and labor agitation were dealt with harshly, often resulting in mass arrests and imprisonment. Meanwhile, Batista was pocketing millions through kickbacks, graft, and fraudulent government contracts.

In 1944, with World War II winding down and the Cold War looming, the U.S informed Batista that he was too "pink" and had to step aside as the island's ruler. The U.S. feared that the communists would gain too much influence in the Cuban government if Batista won a second term. Batista obeyed "orders" and settled into comfortable exile in a Daytona Beach mansion up the coast from Meyer Lansky's Florida turf in Broward County.

For the next eight years, Batista's successors presided over corruption and irresponsibility in Cuba. As new elections approached in 1952, Batista was given the "green light" to run again for the presidency. As election day approached the indications were that Batista would come in a distant third. Instead of waiting for defeat, Batista, with Lansky's help, seized the government on March 10, 1952 in a coup d'etat - taking by force what Cuban voters were about to deny him.

With Batista back in power, Havana began to fulfill Lansky's dream of a Las Vegas in the Caribbean; casinos, mob-organized junkets, prostitution, narcotics, and wholesale abortions. Batista helped Lansky finance this new empire by having the Cuban government match, dollar for dollar, any hotel investment over $1 million. Within a few years, hotels and casinos were everywhere. Havana in the fifties became the capital of organized crime; an anything-goes 'Disneyland' run by the mob.

Washington's attitude toward such corruption and crime just ninety miles from the Florida mainland ranged from a curious unconcern to boys-will-be-boys approval. John F. Kennedy, then a senator from Massachusetts, was a frequent visitor to Havana. Meyer Lansky saw to it that the young Kennedy had all the women he could handle.

By 1958, American investments on the island approached the $1 billion mark. Cuba ranked third among nations of the world in U.S. investments. The signs of American business were everywhere: United Fruit, Anaconda, Chase Manhattan Bank, Proctor and Gamble, Colgate, Texaco, Goodyear, Remington, Bordens, Sears, Ford, U.S. Rubber, Standard Oil, Coke, Pepsi – all had substantial holdings on the island – and Batista was getting a kickback on everything. To insure his absolute control, he suspended the constitution, called off elections, dissolved all political parties, outlawed the Communist Party, and prohibited strikes by labor unions.

However, not everyone was happy with what was going on in Cuba. Fidel Castro was a candidate running for congress and stood a good chance of winning when Batista called off all elections. Castro's anger at having his political aspirations shattered was a manifestation of the frustration and helplessness that many Cubans felt at the time. It was at this point that Castro began to organize a revolutionary organization to overthrow Batista.

Lies and Deceits

On July 26, 1953, Castro and two dozen others were captured and imprisoned. While in prison, Castro wrote the pamphlet *History Will Absolve Me*, which became his revolutionary treatise and guide. Originally sentenced to 15 years, he and his comrades were released after twenty-two months as a result of growing public protests. The amnesty would prove to be the biggest mistake of Batista's life.

Castro was not going to hang around Havana and wait to be assassinated by Batista. On July 7, 1955, he left for Mexico, where he organized a guerrilla expedition to return to Cuba. In order to raise money to support his movement he spent seven weeks in the United States giving speeches and soliciting funds from the large Cuban communities in New York, Tampa, and Miami. He returned to Mexico City with enough money to purchase the weapons he needed. On December 2, 1956, along with 81 other fighters, including his new revolutionary friend Che Guevara, the rebel army reached the Cuban coast.

The Cuban Revolution was not plotted or manufactured in the Soviet Union. Russian troops and arms played no role in deposing of the Batista regime or in establishing Castro's authority in Cuba. It was in every respect a revolution by the Cuban people. President Eisenhower, faced with Batista's military ineptness and growing unpopularity, informed Batista that the United States could no longer support his regime. Batista understood; he wanted to go back to his mansion in Daytona Beach, but the United States was embarrassed to have him living luxuriously in America. On New Year's Eve 1958, the night before Castro victoriously entered Havana, Batista left Cuba with 180 of his closest associates, having amassed a fortune of $300 million. He lived the rest of his life in splendor in Spain and Portugal.

When Castro rode triumphantly into Havana he unquestionably had the overwhelming support of the lower-class Cuban population. Doubts about Castro began to arise when some 600 "war criminals" were executed within the first three months of his rule. Some of those executed were certainly guilty of heinous crimes under Batista's regime, but the spectacle of these executions was unnerving to many. Batista supporters and wealthy Cubans fled. By 1963, an estimated 215,000 had left Cuba. Most settled in Miami and awaited Cuba's liberation by the United States so they could return to the wealth they left behind.

One of Castro's first acts in office was to go to the United States to seek economic aid and support for his new government. President Eisenhower refused to see him and banned all Cuban sugar imports from coming into the United States. Castro left the United States disappointed and angry. His next stop was the Soviet Union. The Soviets were happy to have an affiliate so close to the United States. They contracted for all of Cuba's sugar and arranged to provide Cuba with economic and military assistance. For Washington, Castro's move toward Moscow was the last straw. Labeling the Cuban a "madman," Eisenhower decided that Castro had to be eliminated and instructed the CIA to begin preparations for a covert-type operation.

Acts of aggression against Cuba began virtually immediately. U.S. military aircraft violated Cuban airspace at will, almost daring a confrontation. The United States deprived Cuba of the fuel it needed to operate its industries, transportation, and power stations. We prohibited the shipment of a large number of products to Cuba, including vital medical supplies. Eventually, a complete embargo was placed on Cuba.

The United States froze all Cuban assets in the United States and prohibited the transfer of dollars to or from Cuba, together with any transaction carried out through third countries. In addition, the CIA attempted to kill Castro on nine different occasions. All of this was done because a tiny inconsequential island wanted to govern its own affairs and refused to be dictated to by the United States.

Fidel Castro was a man of many words; often long-winded, undiplomatic, and truthful to the point of provocation. On September 26, 1960 he came to New York to address the U.N. General Assembly. His words, now viewed from the distance of historical perspective, are chilling and still provocative. At the time Castro spoke, few people in this country knew what to make of this bearded rebel in his army fatigues. Whether one admires or hates Castro, nobody believed he would remain in power for forty-nine years. Here is what he told the world back then:

> "Let us speak of the problem of Cuba. Some of you may be well informed, others not - it all depends on your sources of information. As far as the world is concerned, the problem of Cuba that has arisen in the last two years is a new one. Previously there were few reasons for the world to know that Cuba existed. For many, Cuba was something like an appendage of the United States. Even for many U.S. citizens, Cuba was seen as a colony of the United States. As far as the map was concerned, that was not so; but in reality that was the case.
>
> How did our country become a colony of the United States? It was not so by origin. Cuba was the last country of the Americas to free itself from Spanish colonial rule, to cast off the Spanish colonial yoke, and because it was the last, Cuba had to struggle the hardest. Spain had one last foothold in the Americas and defended it tooth and nail. Our people, small in numbers, had to stand alone confronting an army that was considered one of the strongest in Europe. For thirty years Cubans fought alone for their independence.
>
> A joint resolution of the U.S. Congress on April 20, 1898, declared that "Cuba is, and by right ought to be, free and independent." The people of the United States sympathized with the Cuban struggle. This joint declaration adopted by the U.S. Congress was the law by which the United States declared war on Spain. But, that illusion was ended by a cruel deception. After two years of military occupation of our country, the unexpected happened. At the very moment when the people of Cuba were drafting

their own constitution, a new law was passed by the U.S. Congress; a law proposed by Senator Platt, which is an unhappy memory for Cuba.

That law stated that Cuba's constitution must contain a stipulation granting the U.S. government the right to intervene in Cuba's political affairs, and to lease certain parts of Cuba for naval bases. In other words, according to a law passed by the legislative body of a foreign country, Cuba's constitution had to contain a stipulation with those provisions. The drafters of our constitution were told that without that amendment, the U.S. occupation forces would not be withdrawn.

At this point a new colonization of our country began. This included the acquisition of the best agricultural land by U.S. firms, concessions of Cuban natural resources and mines, concessions of public services for purposes of exploitation, and commercial concessions of all types. All these things, together with the constitutional right to intervene in our country, transformed our country from a Spanish colony into a U.S. colony. Cuba became a colony where orders were given by the ambassador of the United States to Cuba.

Fulgencio Batista's government was the type most suited to the U.S. monopolies in Cuba, but it was obviously not the type most suited to the Cuban people. Therefore, the Cuban people, at a great cost in lives, threw that government out. When the revolution came to power, what did we find?

First of all, we found that 600,000 Cubans, able and ready to work, were unemployed. Three million out of a population of a little more than six million had no electricity. Three-and-a-half million Cubans lived in huts, in shacks, in slums, and without the most minimal sanitary facilities. Some 37.5 percent of our population was illiterate; 70 percent of the rural children lacked teachers; 100,000 persons suffered from tuberculosis; 95 percent of the children in rural areas suffered from parasites. Infant mortality was astronomical; life expectancy was very low. One-and-a-half percent of the landowners controlled forty-six percent of the total area of the country. Public services, the electricity and telephone companies, all belonged to U.S. monopolies. The majority of sugar production, the best land, and the most important industries in all fields in Cuba, all belonged to U.S. companies.

This is what the revolutionary government inherited. Until that moment when Batista was overthrown, the country's destiny was determined by these American corporate monopolies and the rulers who served the interests of the monopolies. Did anyone object? No, no one objected. Did this bother anyone? No, this did not bother anyone. The monopolies went about their business, and these were the results. This was the situation that confronted us. Yet, it should not surprise many of the countries represented here in this Assembly; for what we have said about Cuba is but an x-ray view that could be applied to many of the countries sitting here before me.

What alternative was there for the revolutionary government? Should we betray the people? According to the President of the United States, what we have done is a betrayal of our people. He surely would not have considered it a betrayal if, rather than being true to its people, the revolutionary government had instead been true to the American monopolies that were exploiting Cuba. What crime has the revolutionary government done to warrant the treatment we have been given here by the United States? Why do we have such powerful enemies?

When we arrived in Havana we captured American foreign officers (CIA) fighting alongside the Batista government forces. We could easily have considered them to be prisoners of war. Yet, this was not our approach. We merely asked them to go home. When the revolutionary government reduced rents by 50 percent, those who owned the buildings and apartment houses were upset. But, the people rushed into the streets rejoicing, as they would in any country - even here in New York - if rents were reduced by 50 percent for all families.

Then we passed another law; a law canceling the concessions that had been granted by the Batista dictatorship to the telephone company, which was a U.S. monopoly. The revolutionary government reestablished the prices for telephone services that had existed previously. Our next measure was the reduction of electricity rates, which had been among the highest in the world. After this came the agrarian reform laws. Nobody except an ignoramus would dare to deny that agrarian reform in the underdeveloped countries of the world is one of the essential conditions for economic development. In Cuba, more than 200,000 peasant families lived in the countryside without land to plant essential foodstuffs. We divided up the land so they would no longer starve.

Then the question of payments and indemnities for what we nationalized came up. The United States never asked about our problems, not even to express sympathy, or to admit responsibility in creating these problems. They never asked us how many died of starvation in our country, how many were suffering from tuberculosis, how many were unemployed. No. Never. In every conversation we had with the representatives of the U.S. government, all they asked was how are we were going to pay the U.S. for the nationalization. Naturally, the first thing they should have asked was not "How?" but "With what?" This was a poor, underdeveloped country - where would we find the means to pay the prices they wanted? We proposed to pay for it the only way we could - by bonds that would mature in twenty years at 4.5 percent interest amortized annually. How else could we have paid for it?

Land was not the only thing in the hands of the U.S. monopolies; they also controlled the principal mines. For example, Cuba produces large amounts of nickel and all the nickel was controlled by U.S. interests. Under the Batista dictatorship, a U.S. company called Moa Bay had obtained a juicy concession that in a mere five years was able to amortize its entire investment of $120 million, and the Company never had to pay taxes to Cuba for any of its profits. What was this enterprise going to leave for the Cubans - the empty used-up mines, the impoverished land - all without having contributed in the slightest to the economic development of our country? So the revolutionary government passed a mining law that obliged these monopolies to pay a 25 percent tax on the export of minerals.

This was more than the U.S. government and monopolies could tolerate. They eliminated our sugar quota on which our entire tiny island depends. What could Cuba do when confronted with this reality? On our honor we swear that up to that time we had not had the opportunity to even exchange letters with the distinguished prime minister of the Soviet Union, Nikita Khrushchev. When the U.S. press, that supplies information to the world, was saying that Cuba was a "red menace" with a government dominated by communists, the revolutionary government had not even had the opportunity of establishing diplomatic or commercial relations with the Soviet Union.

We asked the United States to remove its naval and military forces from Cuba. How can the U.S. justify to the world that it maintains a military base in Cuba against Cuba's wishes? How can it stand before the world and justify something so arbitrary. They are hoping that we provoke them by forcing them out of our country so it will be an excuse to attack us. But, we will not do that. We ask that they be removed within the framework of international law.

The problem of Cuba is merely an example of the conditions of Latin America. Who will help us? It certainly will not be the United States monopolies. The problems of Latin America are like the problems of the rest of the underdeveloped world in Africa and Asia. The world is divided up among these monopolies. The same monopolies we see in Latin

America are also seen in the Middle East. There the oil is in the hands of monopoly companies that are controlled by the financial interests of the United States, Britain, the Netherlands, and France. This is the case in Iran, Iraq, Saudi Arabia, and all corners of the world. The same thing happens in the Philippines. The same thing happens in Africa. The world has been divided up among the U.S. monopolistic interests. Who would dare deny this historic truth? And the monopolistic interests do not want to see these nations develop. What they want is to exploit their natural resources and to exploit their people.

The problems that the Cuban people have with the imperialist government of the United States are the same problems that Saudi Arabia would have if it decided to nationalize its oil fields, or if Iran or Iraq decided to do so. These are the same problems that Egypt had when it nationalized the Suez Canal; these are the same problems that Indonesia had when it wanted to become independent.

Have the colonialists or the imperialists ever lacked pretexts to invade a country? Never! They have always managed to find some pretext. Colonization and economic expansion is the crux of the question of war and peace. Since the beginning of humanity, wars have arisen for one reason and one reason alone: the desire of some to plunder the wealth of others. End the philosophy of plunder and the philosophy of war will be ended as well. End the existence of colonies and the exploitation of countries by monopolies, and humanity will have achieved a true era of progress.

Some of the delegates here have come up to me and asked: what exactly are the aims of the revolutionary government of Cuba. Let me answer. We believe in the following principles: The right of peasants to the land; the right of workers to the fruit of their labor; the right of children to education; the right of the sick to medical and hospital care; the right of young people to a job; the right of students to free education that is both practical and scientific; the right of blacks and Indians to the full dignity of man; the right of women to civil, social, and political equality; the right of the elderly to a secure old age; the right of intellectuals, artists, and scientists to use their work to fight for a better world; the right of nations to nationalize the imperialist monopolies thereby recovering their national wealth and resources; the right of countries to engage freely in trade with all the peoples of the world; and the right of nations to their full independent sovereignty."

In 1985, Fidel Castro gave an extensive interview to U.S. House Representative Mervyn Dymally. Castro's comments are further insights into the United States-Cuban impasse:

"To be America's friend requires that we must close our eyes and remain silent to injustice. We cannot condone U.S. intervention in Grenada, Santo Domingo, and Nicaragua; or to the overthrow of the Arbenz government in Guatemala and the Allende government in Chile, or to the overthrow Goulart in Brazil.

The anti-communist indoctrination has been drilled into the minds of Americans for over 100 years. It is a prejudice by American capitalist forces against socialism. The American people are really some of the worst informed people in the world, despite their huge technological resources and mass media. And I say this with sorrow: they are one of the least politically educated and worst-informed peoples on the realities of the Third World, Asia, Africa, and Latin America. All this is actually at the root of the anti-Cuba, anti-Castro feelings.

I want to remind you of something. Years ago terrible things were said about China, about Mao Tse-tung, about Chinese communism, about the 'Red' threat, about the 'Yellow' threat, and all the threats that China posed. However, that's no longer the case. Today, there are excellent diplomatic relations, investments, and increasing trade with China. There never was any threat to the United States."

On February 24, 2008, at the age of eighty-one, Castro stepped down from office after forty-nine years. If we want to know why so many countries hate us – we have to study the actions of the United States against Castro and the tiny island of Cuba. All our actions stemmed from Fidel Castro's belief that socialism was better for his country than American capitalism. Was that not Cuba's right?

Chalmers Johnson in his provocative book, *Blowback: The Costs and Consequences of American Empire,* argues that it is typical for an imperial power to have a short memory for unpleasant imperial acts, but those on the receiving end have long, unforgiving memories. In the United States, the "short memory" of the American public is complicated by our democratic electoral cycle. Mistakes are blamed on past administrations; each incoming administration promises that theirs will be different, but it never is.

On October 11, 2001, President George W. Bush was asked at a press conference, why do all these countries hate us? Bush was mystified: "I'm amazed that people hate us because I know how good we are."

CHAPTER FIFTEEN

CUBA

"I want to say that there will not be, under any conditions, an intervention in Cuba by the United States Armed Forces. The basic issue in Cuba is not one between the United States and Cuba. It is between the Cubans themselves."

John F. Kennedy

"During all my years on the U.S. Intelligence Board, never once did I hear anybody raise the question: Is this course of action legal; is it moral and ethical?"

William C. Sullivan
FBI Assistant Director

On March 17, 1960, President Eisenhower approved a CIA plan entitled *A Program of Covert Action against the Castro Regime*. The plan to overthrow Castro was to be all sleight of hand. The CIA would create "an appealing and unified Cuban opposition," led by recruited agents. A clandestine radio station would beam propaganda into Havana to spark an uprising. Cuban exiles would be trained to infiltrate the island from Panama; then the CIA would drop arms and ammunition to them. Training camps were set up in Guatemala and Florida. Richard Bissell of the CIA assured Eisenhower that Fidel Castro would fall in six to eight months. An initial budget of $4.4 million was approved; the actual invasion would cost $46 million. But, Eisenhower decided that any invasion would have to wait until after the presidential election between John F. Kennedy and Richard Nixon.

John F. Kennedy was born to wealth and indulgence, had stunning good looks, an inquisitive mind, and a biting sense of humor. He thrived on adoration and surrounded himself with star-struck friends and colleagues. Women swooned; men stood in awe. He wrote a Pulitzer Prize winning book, *Profiles in Courage*. His father, Joe Kennedy, was the driving force behind his son's ambitions. Papa Joe's plan from the beginning was for Jack to be president. "It's either the White House or the shit-house," he would tease his son, but there was much truth behind the sarcastic humor.

Jack Kennedy's attitude toward marriage followed the pattern his father set: get married, stay married, have lots of children, and sleep with as many women as you can. When his wife Jacqueline had enough of his overt philandering, she gave notice that the marriage was over. Papa Joe came to the rescue by agreeing to give her a fortune if she stayed so as not to ruin Jack's chances for the presidency. Jacqueline agreed; money was her aphrodisiac.

The shadow of Joe Kennedy hovered over the entire Kennedy clan. During the Depression years, he made his fortune in bootleg liquor, a business dominated by organized crime. In order to survive with the mob, he became 'partners' with New York mobster Frank Costello, Newark's Abner "Longy" Zwillman, and Chicago's Al Capone. When Prohibition ended, he parlayed his bootleg fortune into legitimate businesses and set his sights on politics. He was a major contributor and fund-raiser for Franklin D. Roosevelt's first successful campaign for the presidency. Roosevelt astonished Washington and Wall Street in mid-1934 by naming Kennedy as the chairman of the Securities and Exchange Commission, a New Deal agency set up to regulate and reform the financial markets. FDR explained his perplexing choice with a laugh, citing an old adage, "It takes a thief to catch a thief."

Early in 1938, Joe Kennedy became America's ambassador to London, another curious appointment by FDR since Kennedy was an isolationist and a Hitler sympathizer. Kennedy would remain ambassador for three years; replaced only after America entered the war against Germany.

Salvatore (Sam) Giancana had an even more sensational career than Joe Kennedy. He started out as a bodyguard to 'hit' man Jack "Machine Gun" McGurn, one of the prime suspects in the

'St. Valentine's Day' massacre in which Al Capone wiped out the rival Bugs Moran gang. From there Giancana rose to the top of Chicago's Mafia.

When Joe Kennedy needed his son John F. Kennedy's first marriage annulled and removed from all legal documents, he went to see Sam Giancana. When a misunderstanding occurred between Joe Kennedy and the New York mob, it was Giancana who straightened everything out. When John F. Kennedy ran for president, Joe Kennedy and Giancana made several deals to ensure a Kennedy victory. Giancana took care of the very important West Virginia primary, and then when John F. Kennedy became the presidential candidate, he delivered the Illinois vote on a platter. Just what Joe Kennedy promised Giancana besides money is not known, but Giancana told his family, "If I cannot be president, at least I can own one."

John F. Kennedy was only forty-two years old in 1960 and he had lots of competition for the presidential nomination: senate leader Lyndon Johnson, the liberal Herbert Humphrey, and previous Democratic nominee Adlai Stevenson. Ex-President Harry Truman opposed Kennedy's nomination, disliking his Catholic religion, his family, and his wealth. Farmers and labor were for Humphrey; the South was for Johnson; Jewish voters, liberals and intellectuals were for Stevenson. The opposition of Eleanor Roosevelt particularly hurt Kennedy; her favorite was Stevenson. She distrusted Kennedy's father and thought he was trying to buy the White House for his son. In the end, she supported Kennedy, but only after Stevenson withdrew.

People kidded JFK that his father was seen running from state to state with "A little black bag and a checkbook." At a family Kennedy gathering, the matter of financing this very expensive election was raised. Papa Kennedy replied: "We have come this far, we are not going to let money stand in our way; whatever it takes, even if it requires every dime I have." Bobby Kennedy jokingly piped up: "Wait a minute now – there are others in the family." During his campaign swing around the country JFK liked to joke to his cronies, "I just got a telegram from my father. It said, 'don't buy one more vote than is necessary. I'll be damned if I'll pay for a landslide.'"

The chief obstacle to Kennedy's nomination and election was not doubts about his age or experience, or his controversial family, or his voting record in the U.S. Senate, or even his health (he was secretly on steroids for Addison's disease); it was his Roman Catholic faith. Bigots, mostly but not exclusively in southern and rural America, believed all the vicious lies about the Catholic Church. Many others opposed the Catholic Church's position on public funds for parochial schools and its attempts to influence public policy on subjects from contraception to divorce. Kennedy used to joke to his staff: "The nuns and the priests will all vote for me. Only the bishops and cardinals will support Nixon."

Kennedy's first major decision after securing the nomination was choosing Lyndon Johnson as his vice-presidential running mate. Johnson's experience counter-balanced Kennedy's relative inexperience. Kennedy regarded LBJ as a bridge to the southerners and conservatives whose support he needed and might otherwise have difficulty obtaining. The most important element in the JFK-LBJ alliance was to defeat Richard Nixon.

This was the first presidential race to feature televised debates. Kennedy's victory in the initial debate was based more on appearance than his words or policies. The pasty-faced Nixon, with his dark five o'clock shadow, projected an image not unlike that of Joe McCarthy, while the tanned good-looking Kennedy seemed the essence of youth, energy, and virility. Later polls showed that those who listened to the debate on radio thought Nixon had won the debate, while those who saw it on television judged Kennedy the winner.

Looming in the background as a major issue during the debates was Cuba and Fidel Castro. Nixon, in his 1994 book *Six Crises*, acknowledges the key role he played in instituting the plot to overthrow Castro. Nixon writes that "early in 1960, the position I had been advocating for nine months finally prevailed, and the CIA was given instructions to provide arms, ammunition, and training for Cubans who had fled the Castro regime and were now in exile in the United States and various Latin American countries."

Nixon laments that this program to overthrow Castro "had been in operation for six months before the 1960 presidential campaign got under way." However, when Kennedy in their October 21, 1960 debate, strongly advocated military aid to the exiles to overthrow Castro, Nixon could not say a word about the existing program because the operation was covert and secret.

CIA Director Allen Dulles had briefed Kennedy (since he was a presidential candidate) on "the Cuban operation and invasion of the Cuban mainland," and Nixon felt that Kennedy was going beyond the expected "hard-hitting" tactics of a campaign by advocating a policy he already knew was in existence and that Nixon could not talk about. Nixon said he actually had to oppose, during the debate, the position Kennedy was taking, a position Nixon knew was popular with the American people and one that he had "fought for within the administration."

The election was one of the closest in history. It was not until the next morning that Kennedy was declared the winner. The margin of victory in the popular vote was one-tenth of one percent; 112,881 votes out of 68 million cast. In Illinois, Sam Giancana delivered the state to Kennedy by a mere 8,858 votes. The Democratic lead in the Electoral College was more comfortable: 303 to 219. Nixon knew the election had been bought, but as political reporter Theodore White later revealed, when it came to stealing votes there were 'shenanigans' on both sides – Papa Joe was just better at it.

In his farewell address to the nation as president, Eisenhower warned the American public about the disturbing growth and power of the military-industrial complex.

> "Every gun that is made, every warship launched, every rocket fired, signifies in the final sense a theft from those who hunger and are not fed, those who are cold and are not clothed. The cost of one heavy bomber could instead provide a modern brick school in more than 30 cities; it could provide two electric power plants, each serving a town of 60,000; it is two fully equipped hospitals; it is fifty

miles of concrete pavement. We pay for a single destroyer with new homes that could house more than 8,000 people.

Our immense military establishment and arms industry is new in the American experience. The total influence – economic, political, and spiritual – is felt in every city, every statehouse, and in every office of the Federal government. We recognize the imperative need for this development, yet we must not fail to comprehend its grave implications. In the councils of government, we must guard against the acquisition of unwarranted influence, whether sought or unsought, by the military-industrial complex. The potential for the disastrous rise of misplaced power exists and will persist. We must never let the weight of this combination endanger our civil liberties or democratic processes."

Eisenhower's words were a warning, but need never have been spoken since he was in charge for the past eight years and could have put a halt to the nuclear arms race and the power of the military-industrial complex. In 1960, when Eisenhower was informed at a National Security Council meeting that the United States could produce almost 400 Minutemen nuclear missiles a year, he said with obvious disgust. "Why don't we go completely crazy and plan for a force of 10,000? The whole thing is crazy and unconscionable." But, he did nothing to stop the Pentagon. There were approximately 1,000 nuclear warheads when Eisenhower entered the White House – there were 18,000 when he left. For all his concern about nuclear war, for all his skepticism about the Pentagon, for all his unique military knowledge, he never seized control of the military-industrial complex. "Being only one person," he lamely explained, he had not felt he could oppose the "combined opinion of all his associates."

JFK's Inauguration on January 21, 1961 was a special changing of the guard. The forty-three-year-old president, bareheaded and without an overcoat despite the biting cold, announced that the "torch has been passed to a new generation of Americans – born in this century." Millions watched the event on television, captivated by the image of the youthful, vigorous, and eloquent Kennedy, who proclaimed, "Ask not what your country can do for you; ask what you can do for your country. Ask not what America will do for you, but what together we can do for the freedom of man."

Sam Giancana watched the inauguration with evident good humor; he was convinced he had scored the ultimate coup by delivering the election to Papa Joe's son. The heat would now be off the Chicago Mafia syndicate. Giancana thought the new president's decision to make his brother Robert the attorney-general was a stroke of genius. It covered up all the dirty tricks that the Kennedy's had played during the election campaign. But, it still made Giancana nervous that this "young punk" was in charge of organized crime.

Robert Kennedy at the age of thirty-five had never tried a case in his life, but he was now in charge of the huge Justice Department – 1,700 lawyers and 30,000 civil servants. Giancana was right about Robert Kennedy; he didn't understand the new rules, but he would learn. When a member of the Mafia was brought to the Justice Department for questioning, he defiantly told Bobby Kennedy, "You can't touch me. I've got immunity." When Bobby asked him, "Who gave you immunity?" the gangster replied, "The CIA. I'm working for them, but I can't talk about it. Top secret." When Kennedy checked out the gangster's story, he was shocked to learn it was true.

Besides having Bobby at his immediate side, JFK surrounded himself with an illustrious and erudite group, which many in this country labeled "the best and the brightest." Many of them were academic people from Harvard and other elite institutions. Dean Rusk, the new secretary of state was a Rhodes Scholar; Robert McNamara, McGeorge Bundy, and Douglas Dillon were Republicans appointed to important cabinet positions. For America, it was a time of hope and optimism. Most Americans felt proud. It was like the fairy-tale story of "Camelot" with JFK and his beautiful wife Jackie reigning as the handsome king and queen, worshiped by all.

But there was trouble in Camelot. The Kennedy brothers were brash and arrogant. They both loved women and exercised their new power to philander even more than before. On top of that, there were some major problems inherited from the Eisenhower administration. Heading the list was Vietnam and Cuba. In both cases, JFK's youth, lack of experience and imperial hubris, would doom him.

Immediately upon taking office, President Kennedy was advised that the CIA operation to invade Cuba was ready. Kennedy and his advisers were euphoric about all this new power. Right from the start the brash energetic administration suffered from a bad case of overconfidence; virtually no one stopped to think about possible failure. Even if they had, it is not simple to stop a project, overt or covert, once it is under way. There was no turning back. Politically, Kennedy could never have halted the invasion plan; the criticism for abandoning a project started and authorized by President Eisenhower would have been too great.

Kennedy summoned CIA Director Allen Dulles and his chief deputy, Richard Bissell, to Palm Beach and received a detailed briefing on the Cuban operation. But, reports of secret training camps in Florida and Guatemala were already seeping into public print. A front-page story in the *New York Times* told of guerrilla training that was going on under the tutelage of the CIA. Hasty denials were issued by Washington, but the secrecy in which the CIA had wrapped the Cuban invasion was beginning to unwind. Kennedy, however, was assured that the covert operation would quickly suppress Castro and his forces. After all, Castro was nothing but an irritating gnat to be swatted into oblivion!

Meanwhile, the Kennedy administration was lining up diplomatic support for the invasion. Generally, countries in the Western Hemisphere do what they are told by the United States or they are punished in several subtle ways, but Mexico refused to go along with the campaign against Cuba. The Mexican ambassador to the United States said, "If we publicly declare that Cuba is a threat to our security or the security of the United States, forty million Mexicans will die laughing."

The plan from the beginning was seriously flawed. The CIA success rate with past covert actions blinded them to reality. Cuba was not Iran, Guatemala, or Chile - and Castro was not Mosaddeq. The largest covert operation in CIA history was too large to remain covert and too small to be successful.

The original plan called for a daytime landing at Trinidad, a city on the southern coast of Cuba near the Escambray Mountains, but Kennedy and his advisers thought the plan exposed the role of the United States too openly. They favored a night-time landing at the Bay of Pigs. U.S. bombing raids would destroy Castro's fledgling air force prior to the invasion and that would allow our CIA-led Cuban forces to land without interference. Our attacking planes would be disguised to look like Cuban planes flown by defecting Cuban pilots. Once the exiles were safely ashore, the U.S. would recognize the rebels as the legitimate Cuban government and immediately send military reinforcements.

Richard Bissell of the CIA stated at the time, "It is hard to believe that the president and his advisers felt the plans for a large-scale complicated military operation that had been ongoing for more than a year could be reworked in four days and still offer a high likelihood of success. It is equally amazing that we in the Agency (CIA) agreed so readily." A night-time amphibious landing, which had only been accomplished successfully once in World War II, diminished the possibility of a popular Cuban uprising and the new location made it practically impossible to retreat into the Escambray Mountains. The plan, however, seemed to breed an infectious optimism.

On March 29, U.S. Senator Fulbright, who was privy to the invasion plan, sent Kennedy a memo which stated, "To give this activity even covert support is the same hypocrisy and cynicism for which the United States is constantly denouncing the Soviet Union in the United Nations and elsewhere. This point will not be lost on the rest of the world - or on our own consciences." At a meeting on April 4 at the State Department, Senator Fulbright verbally opposed the plan. The operation, he said, was wildly out of proportion to the threat. It would compromise our moral position in the world and make it impossible for us to protest treaty violations by the Soviet Union. "The Castro regime," according to Fulbright, "might be a thorn in the flesh, but it was not a dagger in the heart."

Five days before the invasion, Kennedy was asked at a press conference how far the U.S. would go to help an uprising against Castro. He answered: "First, I want to say that there will not be, under any conditions, an intervention in Cuba by the United States Armed Forces. The basic issue in Cuba is not one between the United States and Cuba. It is between the Cubans themselves."

Castro analyzed all the signs and figured out what was going to happen. When U.S. disguised aircraft began attacking four Cuban airfields on April 15, Castro was prepared. He left some obsolete unusable planes on the ground to fool the attackers and draw the bombs. The other planes belonging to the Cuban Air Force were dispersed and camouflaged and waiting.

Shortly after the bombing, U.N. Ambassador Adlai Stevenson flatly rejected Cuba's assertion that the United States was behind the attack, saying that the planes were from the Cuban Air Force and presented a copy of a photograph proving his case. Stevenson was extremely embarrassed a few hours later when the truth was revealed and he learned that Kennedy had referred to him as "my official liar."

The CIA-Cuban invading force of 1,500 men began landing shortly before midnight on Sunday, April 16. A team of U.S. frogmen had gone ashore and set up landing lights to guide the operation. Castro would later equate our sneak attack with Pearl Harbor, but unlike the Pearl Harbor attack, this operation did not go as expected.

On April 17, with the invasion well under way, U.S. Secretary of State Dean Rusk gave a press conference. "The American people are entitled to know whether we are intervening in Cuba or intend to do so in the future," he said. "The answer to that question is no. What happens in Cuba is for the Cuban people to decide."

That day, Kennedy received a letter from Khrushchev in which the Soviet leader declared: "It is no secret that the armed bands invading Cuba were trained and equipped in the United States. The planes that are bombing Cuban cities belong to the United States of America; the bombs are supplied by the American government. It is still not too late for the United States to avoid the irreparable. The government of the United States has the ability to stop this invasion from growing into an incomparable conflagration. As far as the Soviet Union is concerned, there should be no mistake about our position: we will render to the Cuban people all necessary help to repel any armed attack on Cuba."

In a political environment full of posturing, threats and confusion, Secretary of State Dean Rusk advised Kennedy to back off, concluding that additional strikes would tilt international opinion too far against the United States. A second bombing attack was sure to focus attention on American involvement. The administration decided not to follow through with the CIA plan; the death and capture of hundreds of Cuban patriots was preferable to acknowledging an American preemptive attack. The CIA and the Joint Chiefs were stunned by Kennedy's refusal to order further military assistance. Richard Bissell of the CIA could not believe what was happening. "It was inconceivable that the president would deliberately let the operation fail when he had all that immense fire-power at his disposal."

There were many tragedies that day. The death of the twenty-nine-year-old exile commander, Jose "Pepe" San Roman, was a metaphor for the entire invasion. San Roman watched in horror as his troops were slaughtered while waiting in vain for promised air support from the United States. San Roman's radio pleas for help remain chilling to this day.

At dawn he sent the following message: "Do you people realize how desperate the situation is? Do you back us or quit? All we want is low jet air cover - we need it badly or we cannot survive." An hour later he radioed: "Blue Beach under attack. Where is the promised air cover?" Shortly thereafter, "Enemy on trucks coming from Red Beach." An hour later: "Situation critical - urgently need air support." At 9:14 that morning: "Where the hell is jet cover?" At 9:55: "Can you throw something into this vital point in battle? Anything. Just let the jet pilots loose." Just before the end: "Out of ammo. Enemy closing in. Send all available aircraft now." Five hours later, the invasion brigade commander transmitted a final message from inside Cuba: "We have nothing left to fight with. How could you do this to us?" When a final call for U.S. aid was denied, San Roman replied, "And you sir, are a son of a bitch. Over and out." Without supplies or air cover, the invading forces fell; it was an unbelievable betrayal by the United States; 200 rebel soldiers were killed and 1,197 others were captured.

On April 20, Fidel Castro announced over Havana radio that, "we have destroyed in less than 72 hours the army the U.S. imperialist government had organized for many months. We have always been in danger of direct aggression. We have been warning about this in the United Nations: that the United States would find a pretext to organize some act of aggression. The United States has no right to meddle in our domestic affairs. We do not speak English and we do not chew gum. We have a different tradition, a different culture, our own way of thinking. We have no borders with anybody. Our frontier is the sea, very clearly defined. How can the crooked politicians in the U.S. and their corporate exploiters have more rights than the Cuban people? What right does a rich country have to impose its yoke on our people? It is because the United States has might and no scruples; they do not respect international rules. They should be ashamed to engage in this battle of Goliath against David - and to lose it besides."

On that same day, President Kennedy discussed Cuba before the American Society of Newspaper Editors and continued to deny U.S. involvement. "This was a struggle of Cuban patriots against a Cuban dictator. While we could not be expected to hide our sympathies, we made it repeatedly clear that the armed forces of this country would not intervene in any way. But let the record show that our restraint is not inexhaustible - if the nations of this hemisphere should fail to meet their commitments against outside communist penetration - then I want it clearly understood that this government will not hesitate in meeting its primary obligations which are to the security of our nation."

At the massive celebrations in Havana less than two weeks after the attack, Castro spoke again about the invasion: "Humble, honest blood was shed in the struggle against the mercenaries of imperialism. We can tell the people right here that at the very instant that our airports were being bombed; the Yankee government was telling the world that these attacks were from our own air force. The United States cold-bloodily bombed our nation and told the world that the bombing was done by Cuban pilots with Cuban planes. This was done with planes on which they painted our insignia. If nothing else, this deed should be enough to demonstrate how miserable the actions of the United States are."

Fidel Castro did not continue to gloat about America's failure. Instead, he put the captured soldiers on television for all to hear their pitiful confessions. For the first time in history the United States had been humiliated in Latin America. Mass trials were held for the 1,197 captured men and each was sentenced to 30 years in prison. After twenty months of negotiation, most were released in exchange for $53 million in food and medicine.

After the failure of the invasion and the embarrassment of America's covert involvement, a Gallop poll showed an unprecedented 83 percent approval rating for the president. Kennedy tossed aside the report and laughed: "It's just like Eisenhower. The worse I do, the more popular I get."

As a result of the Bay of Pigs disaster, President Kennedy fired long-time CIA Director Allen Dulles, Deputy Director Charles Cabell, and Deputy Director Richard Bissell. Kennedy assumed full responsibility for the failure, although he secretly blamed the CIA and ordered a full investigation of the operation.

On November 21, 1961, the 150-page internal CIA report turned out to be a scorching indictment of the Agency's performance. The controversial report concluded that ignorance, incompetence, and arrogance on the part of the CIA were responsible for the fiasco. It criticized nearly every aspect of the CIA's handling of the invasion: misinforming the Kennedy administration, planning poorly, using faulty intelligence and conducting an overt military operation "beyond CIA capability."

Among the report's conclusions was that the operation was predicated on the belief that "the invasion would produce a shock-wave inside Cuba" that would trigger an uprising against Castro, but "the Agency had no evidence that there was any kind of leadership for such an uprising in support of the invasion." No names were mentioned in the report, but senior CIA officials were outraged by the report. Copies of the report were retrieved and destroyed; however, a few were locked away in the Director's office. The report was not declassified and released until February 19, 1998.

CIA Deputy Director Richard Bissell wrote about his dismissal from the CIA and the postmortem consequences of the Bay of Pigs failed operation. "To understand the Kennedy administration's obsession with Cuba, it is important to understand the mindset of the Kennedy boys. From their perspective, Castro won the first round at the Bay of Pigs, but they were ready to avenge their personal embarrassment by overthrowing Castro at any cost." Plans to assassinate Castro, which began in the Eisenhower administration, now accelerated. On August 10, 1962, a meeting at the White House with all the major Kennedy staff members discussed how to get rid of Castro. Robert McNamara emphatically expressed the prevailing mood: "The only way to take care of Castro is to kill him."

The CIA met with Norman Rothman, Meyer Lansky's ex-partner in Havana's gambling casinos. The CIA told Rothman they wanted Castro eliminated. The Mafia seemed a reasonable partner; they had controlled the gambling casinos that thrived in Cuba under Batista and were now out of business. The Mafia wanted to get back its hotels and casinos, and they had plenty of contacts inside Cuba to carry out an assassination. Once Castro was gone, they were assured they would be back in business.

Rothman told the CIA, "If you need somebody to carry out a murder like this, Johnny Rosselli is your man." Rosselli was the Mafia's "Mr. Smooth," assigned to run operations in Los Angeles in the 1930s and later in Las Vegas. When Rosselli was contacted by the CIA, he was astonished that the United States government wanted him for a "hit job."

"Me? You want me to get involved with Uncle Sam?" he responded when he met with the CIA. "The FBI is trailing me wherever I go. Are you sure you are talking to the right guy?" The

CIA eventually succeeded in convincing Rosselli that they did indeed want him to assassinate Castro.

The idea of using the Mafia to carry out a "national security" project was nothing new – it could be traced back to Lucky Luciano's work for the government during World War II. The CIA and the Mafia subsequently became tight fraternity brothers. "To understand how it works," said retired Air Force Colonel Fletcher Prouty, the former liaison officer between the Pentagon and the CIA, "you have to think of the CIA and organized crime as two huge concentric circles spread all over the world. Inevitably, in some places, the circles overlap."

The first meeting between the CIA and Rosselli took place at the *Brown Derby* restaurant in Beverly Hills in early September 1960. The next meeting was at the Plaza Hotel in New York. That set the stage for a third meeting at Miami's Fontainebleau Hotel. It was at this meeting that the mechanics on how to kill Castro were first discussed.

Rosselli brought along his boss, Salvatore Giancana, and his Miami counterpart, Santos Trafficante. In 1957, in Havana, Trafficante had arranged for Senator John Kennedy to stay in a special suite at his Commadora Hotel with three prostitutes. Trafficante would later say, "The biggest mistake of my life was not taking pictures of him when he was rolling around in bed with those broads. That was a big mistake."

At the Fontainebleau Hotel meeting, the CIA brought along a briefcase crammed with $150,000 in cash and dumped it on the table. They told those present they could use the money any way they wished. None of the Mafia chiefs ever looked at the money or reacted – the conversation continued and the money remained untouched on the table during the entire meeting. The "Castro job" was not about money anyway – it was about federal protection and free reign once the Mafia was back in business in Cuba.

The CIA assumed that the Mafia would simply gun Castro down, but Rosselli wanted something less noisy; something "nice and clean." He suggested a poison that was both lethal and slow acting, which would give the assassin a chance to get away. The CIA loved the idea and their Technical Services Division perfected a batch of pills containing botulin toxin, a deadly poison. There were three attempts in 1962 using these pills, but they all failed. Other assassination plots surfaced in early 1963; these fell into the "James Bond" category. One involved presenting Castro with a skin-diving suit dusted with a fungus that would produce a disabling and chronic skin disease. Another plot involved a ballpoint pen rigged with a hypodermic needle designed so the victim would not notice its insertion. Other plots included poison-laced cigars, LSD sprays, toiletries spiked with a drug that would induce a massive heart attack, and even an exploding seashell.

No two men could have emerged from more different backgrounds than John F. Kennedy and Sam Giancana, but both men had two things in common; power and an obsession with women. However, there was a difference - Kennedy got emotionally attached with all his women paramours, whereas Giancana equated them to "the best pair of shoes you can buy; wear them out and then throw them away."

Giancana's relationship with Frank Sinatra spanned thirty years. They were 'pals' and Giancana partied with all of Sinatra's cronies, including Joey Bishop, Dean Martin, Sammy Davis, Jr., and Angie Dickinson. JFK was also a common fixture with the Sinatra group. His brother-in-law, Peter Lawford, was a full-fledged member of the "rat pack." Kennedy loved the gaiety and the glamorous people, especially the beautiful women. If you wanted sex, Sinatra could get it for you at any time of the day just by snapping his fingers.

Judith Campbell Exner was no different from all the other beautiful women who hung around Sinatra and his buddies. She was in search of stardom, trinkets, excitement, and a good time. She was 'drop dead' beautiful; a Jacqueline Kennedy face with an Elizabeth Taylor body – irresistible, willing to please, and with a carefree unassuming demeanor.

During the election campaign of 1960, John Kennedy stopped off in Las Vegas for a week-end respite. Sinatra was appearing at the Sands Hotel and he introduced Kennedy to Judy Exner. It was instant chemistry. Four weeks later, Exner was Kennedy's mistress. The relationship would span the next eighteen months and place her in the middle of one the most covert operations in U.S. history.

When Sam Giancana learned that JFK was bedding someone on a regular basis, he was curious about Kennedy's taste in women. He called Sinatra and arranged to meet Kennedy's infatuation. When he met Judy Exner, he understood; Giancana was also smitten. He immediately showered her with flowers and expensive gifts and it did not take long before Judy Exner had two boyfriends – the future president of the United States and the current Chicago 'Godfather.' Each knew of the others involvement with Exner, but neither cared. On the night of the election, Giancana watched the election results with Judy Exner at his side and he was in great humor. He teased her, "Listen honey, if it wasn't for me your boyfriend wouldn't be in the White House."

Although JFK had many mistresses, Exner was undoubtedly his favorite. Once Kennedy settled into the White House, Judy Exner was a frequent overnight guest when Jacqueline Kennedy was away. Once, when Jacqueline supposedly found pink panties in her pillow case - she turned to her husband in bed and said, "Would you find out who these belong to because they are not my size?"

According to Exner, after she and the president had sex, they usually had dinner in a private room in the White House. "Bobby would come in and hand a manila envelope to Jack. They would discuss the contents and Jack would ask me to deliver it to Giancana. Bobby often would put his hand on my shoulder and ask me if I was comfortable acting as a courier. I never gave it a second thought. I did it because John Kennedy asked me to and he was the President of the United States."

Exner made ten or more trips to Sam Giancana and Johnny Rosselli with envelopes from Jack Kennedy. "I remember one trip," Exner continued. "I left the White House and went to Chicago and just stayed at the airport for one hour. Sam looked at the documents, and then put them back in the envelope. I then flew to Las Vegas and gave them to Johnny Rosselli. I left them there and returned to Washington. Very often that is the way it went." Twice Kennedy gave Exner large packages of money to deliver to

Giancana. According to individuals in the Giancana family, each package contained $250,000. Exner kept an extensive personal diary and recounted two meetings in 1961 in which John Kennedy and Giancana met. Both times she was asked to leave the room until they finished their discussions. She later learned the meeting was about Castro.

J. Edgar Hoover had Giancana under constant surveillance for years because of his underworld activities. Giancana once petitioned the federal court in Chicago for relief. He told the court, "How would you like it if you were on the eighteenth hole trying to line up a putt and there were six FBI agents watching you?" Giancana claimed that his golf score had soared to 115, some twenty-odd strokes above his normal handicap. Federal Judge Richard Austin sympathized with Giancana and granted an injunction stipulating that a disinterested foursome had to play between Giancana and the FBI agents whenever he was on the golf course.

From FBI wiretaps, Hoover learned that Exner was calling JFK in the White House from Giancana's phone. He quickly put Exner under surveillance. It did not take long before he had a six-hundred page file on what was going on. When columnist Drew Pearson predicted that Hoover was going to be fired by Attorney General Robert Kennedy, Hoover met with Bobby and showed him the file. Bobby became flustered and stuttered that Hoover should meet privately with his brother. On March 22, 1962, Hoover had a private luncheon with President Kennedy that lasted four hours. After the meeting, Kennedy stopped all communications with Giancana and ended his relationship with Exner. Hoover was immediately reconfirmed as head of the FBI. When JFK was asked by his close associates why he didn't get rid of Hoover, Kennedy glibly told them, "You don't fire God."

Judy Exner eventually got married, had a child, and lived a quiet unassuming life in California. She never spoke about her relationship with JFK or Giancana. She burst onto the national scene when the Frank Church Senate Committee called her to testify in 1975 about CIA assassinations. Her testimony was never released to the public, nor did it appear in any of the committee's documents, but when parts of her testimony leaked to the public, Exner published a memoir, *My Story*, that listed the times and places of her many rendezvous with Kennedy.

Ending JFK's affair with Judy Exner did not stop his sexual liaisons in the White House. Actress Angie Dickenson wondered what it would be like to have sex with the President of the United States inside the White House. Sinatra arranged it. Afterward, she flippantly reported, "It was the most exciting forty seconds of my life."

Cord Meyer, was the son of a wealthy senior diplomat. He graduated from Yale in 1942, joined the U.S. Marines and fought in the South Pacific. On July 21, 1944, a Japanese grenade was thrown into his foxhole. He was so badly injured that his commanding officer sent a telegram to his parents announcing he was dead. He lost his left eye, but was eventually well enough to be sent home. While recovering in New York City, Meyer met journalist Mary Pinchot. The couple married on April 19, 1945.

Around 1949, Cord Meyer started working for the CIA and became part of *Operation Mockingbird*, a CIA program to influence the American media. In 1953, Joseph McCarthy began accusing members of the Washington 'Georgetown Crowd' as being security risks. McCarthy claimed that the CIA was a "sinkhole of communists" and he intended to root them out. In August, 1953, CIA Director Richard Helms told Meyer that McCarthy had accused him of being a communist. Apparently, Meyer was a member of several liberal groups, but he was eventually cleared of all charges and allowed to keep his job.

In the summer of 1954, the Meyers got new neighbors in Georgetown. Senator John F. Kennedy and his wife purchased a house several hundred yards from where the Meyers lived. Mary became good friends with Jacqueline and they often went walking together. In 1958, Mary filed for and was granted a divorce. Meanwhile, Cord Meyer's career continued to prosper and he was now high enough in the CIA hierarchy to be involved in covert operations. As chief of the CIA's International Organizations Division, Meyer would meet periodically with President Kennedy and his staff. Many of the discussions revolved around plans to assassinate Fidel Castro.

In 1962, the divorced Mary Meyer entered into a CIA experimental hallucinogen drug program with Timothy Leary at Harvard University. Over thirty universities and institutions were involved in this extensive testing and experimentation program that included the administration of LSD to 'unwitting subjects in social situations.' Research centers were maintained at Boston Psychiatric, the University of Illinois Medical School, Mount Sinai and Columbia University in New York, the University of Oklahoma, the Addiction Research Center in Kentucky, the University of Chicago and the University of Rochester - all were secretly funded by the CIA.

That year Mary Meyer met JFK at a Washington social function. Since they were already well acquainted with each other from their days as neighbors in Georgetown, they immediately struck up a conversation. Within a few short weeks she became the president's new favorite mistress. Their frequent sexual liaisons included heavy doses of LSD, which JFK found relaxing and stimulating. Fortunately, he did not have to make any nuclear decisions while 'tripping out.'

On the night of October 12, 1964, Mary Meyer, age 43, was murdered while casually walking home in the Georgetown section of Washington. She was not molested and nothing was stolen. Her personal diary, which she always kept in her apartment, was never found. The murder remains unsolved to this day.

Marilyn Monroe was connected to the Mafia from the beginning of her career. Her first real break came when Sam Giancana introduced her to Joe Schenck, a Hollywood producer. By 1953, her two-bit movie days were over. She was now America's ultimate glamor girl, every man's dream sexual partner. Although Giancana said she'd been a good investment, he sadly commented to others that she was more comfortable with her clothes off than on.

Marilyn readily traded her body for success and fame. She was the quintessential victim. Her desire to achieve stardom, coupled with her childlike desire to please, was exploited by all. Her sexual charms were enjoyed by the Mafia, Sinatra and his pals, and anyone else of importance. She was occasionally employed by the CIA to frame world leaders from Asia to the Middle East. Marilyn reveled in the attention and the gifts from the world's most powerful men; she was a willing participant in the intrigue.

When JFK arrived in the White House, so did Marilyn. Throughout 1962, Hoover's wiretaps revealed that both Kennedy brothers were sexually involved with Marilyn. By July of 1962, her affair with the Kennedy's began appearing in Hollywood gossip columns. Her telephones were tapped by everyone: the FBI, CIA, and even the Mafia. Oblivious or reckless, her recorded conversations were candid and she professed a deep love for Bobby Kennedy who she pathetically believed was going to leave his wife for her.

One week before her death, a distraught Marilyn Monroe was 'invited' to Lake Tahoe. At dinner that evening with Giancana, Sinatra, and Peter Lawford, they watched as Marilyn drank herself into near oblivion, pouring out her heart that Bobby Kennedy was now refusing her phone calls (he had recently been voted "Family Man of the Year"). She ranted on and on that she was "nothing but a piece of meat" to the two Kennedy brothers and threatened "to blow the lid off the whole damn thing." Her emotional and mental instability posed a serious threat to the presidency. Within the week she was dead, an apparent suicide caused by a combination of alcohol and drugs.

The CIA and the Mafia could never kill Fidel Castro – but Marilyn Monroe was a more accommodating victim. She was killed by the same poison slated for Fidel Castro; it left no trace as to the cause of death. Marilyn's explosive red diary disappeared before her body was found. The records of her telephone calls to Bobby Kennedy were removed from the attorney-general's logs by J. Edgar Hoover. It was like she never existed.

While the Kennedy brothers were indulging in their sexual romps in the White House, the CIA and the Mafia were still busy trying to kill Castro. Fidel was dodging one assassination attempt after another – like a cat with nine lives. Then in the spring of 1962, forty thousand U.S. Marines launched a mock invasion of a Caribbean island as part of a military exercise that looked to everyone as a prelude to an invasion of Cuba. Castro got the message – he turned to the Soviet Union for help. Maybe Castro was always headed in that direction, but the openly hostile activities of the United States certainly precipitated that event.

American pressure on Cuba had risen steadily since the collapse of the Bay of Pigs invasion. In January 1962, Cuba was expelled from the Organization of American States and the U.S. imposed a trade blockade. Numerous American warships patrolled the Cuban coast and the island's air space was invaded around the clock by U.S. military planes. The CIA and the Pentagon prepared a secret plan known as *Mangusta* to undermine and overthrow Castro's regime. President Kennedy personally approved the plan. At the same time, the U.S. warned the Soviet Union of the risks of giving military and economic aid to Cuba.

Soviet Premier Khrushchev, however, saw Cuba as an opportunity. From Khrushchev's perspective, the United States had the ability to deliver a first-strike knockout blow against the Soviet Union with its missiles stationed in Turkey. Russia did not have that capability in the Western Hemisphere, but if Cuba had missiles aimed at the United States that would provide a counter deterrent. What followed was Khrushchev's decision to move Soviet nuclear missiles into Cuba. Castro gladly accepted the offer. He saw it as his only chance to save Cuba from continued American harassment and another U.S. invasion.

The crisis began on October 15, 1962 when U.S. reconnaissance photographs revealed Soviet missile sites under construction in Cuba. Early the next day, President Kennedy was informed of the installations. Kennedy immediately organized a group of his most important advisers to handle the crisis. Early in the debate, it became clear that the president had two main options. An air strike could take out the Soviet weapons and set up an invasion to remove Castro. Alternatively, a naval blockade could turn back the remaining Soviet ships and signal how seriously America took the crisis.

The group was split as to which alternative was best. Early on, Robert Kennedy announced that his brother would launch no

"Pearl Harbor," but later his hawkish side emerged. "It would be better for our children and grandchildren if we decided to face the Soviet threat, stand up to it, and eliminate it now," he said.

After seven days of guarded and intense debate, Kennedy imposed a naval quarantine around Cuba to prevent the arrival of more Soviet offensive weapons to the island. On October 22, he announced the discovery of the missile installations to the public and proclaimed that any nuclear missile launched from Cuba would be regarded as an attack on the United States by the Soviet Union and they would suffer the consequences.

A naval blockade was not what the Joint Chief of Staff wanted. They strongly recommended prompt military action and the invasion of Cuba. General Curtis LeMay kept constantly taunting the president, "I think that a blockade and political talk would be considered by a lot of our friends as being a pretty weak response, and I'm sure a lot of our own citizens would feel that way too." LeMay argued for a surprise attack on the Russian missiles as soon as possible. Kennedy asked: "what do you think the Russians reprisal would be? Will they do nothing?" LeMay guaranteed there would be no reprisals from the Russians. Kennedy listened, but resisted the mounting pressure for direct action.

After the meeting, Kennedy told his aide Dave Powers, "Can you imagine LeMay saying a thing like that? These brass hats have one great advantage in their favor. If we listen to them and do what they want us to do, none of us will be alive later to tell them that they were wrong." Kennedy told Arthur Schlesinger, "The military are mad."

As Soviet ships carrying the missiles to Cuba sped on course to Cuba, the world held its breath. Then the miracle occurred – Nikita Khrushchev decided not to risk war by challenging the U.S. quarantine. He ordered the Soviet ships to stop dead in the water. After much agonizing, both world leaders were now determined to find a way out that would not involve armed conflict. The problem was that it was practically impossible for them to communicate frankly with one another. Each knew very little about the intentions and motivations of the other side, and tended to assume the worst. The question was no longer whether the leaders of the two superpowers wanted war — but whether they had the power to prevent it.

October 27th was the darkest day of the crisis. On that day the U.S. foolishly sent reconnaissance U-2 surveillance flights into Cuba without thinking about the consequences. One plane flew directly over an anti-aircraft site and was shot down, killing its pilot. The Joint Chiefs of Staff recommended immediate military retaliation. Castro sent Khrushchev a wildly emotional letter saying that he was facing an imminent American invasion. Khrushchev sent Kennedy a very tough letter. That night Kennedy's cabinet went to sleep not knowing if they would awake in the morning, and their wives debated whether to stay in Washington with their husbands or go to safer rural hideaways.

Kennedy and Khrushchev recognized the magnitude of the crisis. They searched for a peaceful, face-saving way out, while their military chiefs kept preparing for war. In a dramatic confrontation at the Pentagon, the chief of naval operations told Secretary of Defense Robert McNamara that the navy would handle any engagement with the Soviets and needed no supervision from civilians. Furious, McNamara put new procedures into place that gave him and the president greater direct operational control.

The crisis was the closest the world ever came to nuclear war. The United States armed forces were at their highest state of readiness and Soviet field commanders in Cuba were prepared to use nuclear weapons to defend the island. We stood poised and ready to strike in the mistaken belief that they might strike us first, and they stood ready to strike us for the same reason. Fortunately, a secret deal was brokered between Robert Kennedy and Russian Ambassador Dobrynin. Russia publicly announced that it would withdraw its missiles from Cuba, and the United States secretly agreed to withdraw its nuclear warheads from Turkey and to never invade Cuba again. The American public was only told about the first part of the deal; the part about our concessions was kept secret. What was presented to the American public was a complete Russian capitulation; it was a lie to preserve the Kennedy image.

Years later, Soviet declassified documents explained Russia's decision. Khrushchev told his Foreign Minister Gromyko, "We have to help Kennedy find a way out of this mess before the military push him into war." What especially moved Khrushchev was Dobrynin's description of his meeting with Robert Kennedy. The president's brother was exhausted. Dobrynin could see from Robert Kennedy's eyes that he had not slept for days. RFK told Dobrynin, the president "didn't know how to resolve the situation. The military is putting great pressure on him, insisting on military actions against Cuba and the president is in a very difficult position. Even if he does not want or desire a war, something irreversible could occur against his will. That is why the president is asking for help to solve this problem."

The Cuban Missile Crisis may have been the most dangerous moment in human history. Humanity survived the crisis because of two things: Kennedy's refusal to listen to his military advisers, and Nikita Khrushchev's willingness to retreat from the brink. The crisis had a profound effect on JFK. He gained a new respect for Khrushchev. JFK realized that when the chips were down, Khrushchev did not want a nuclear war.

A few days after the end of the missile crisis, the president summoned the Joint Chiefs to the Oval Office to thank them for their role in the crisis, a particularly gracious gesture considering the friction between him and his generals who were constantly advising that war was the only solution. However, General Curtis LeMay was in no mood to celebrate. "It is the greatest defeat in our history," he thundered at Kennedy. "We should invade today!" Later, a disgusted LeMay fumed, "We had a chance to throw the communists out of Cuba, but the administration was scared to death the Russians might shoot a missile at us."

Castro was furious that Russia was pulling out of Cuba. When asked whether he would have launched nuclear weapons on the United States if he was attacked, he replied. "Yes, I would have because we took it for granted that it would become a nuclear war and before being totally destroyed we were ready to die in defense of our country."

Though the Soviets had extracted a pledge from the Kennedy administration not to invade Cuba, Castro did not trust America's word. He was proven right. The United States continued covert operations against Cuba, with all manner of schemes to assassinate Castro, destroy Cuban crops, and otherwise damage Cuba's economy. Without the Soviet Union as a partner, Castro now actively aligned Cuba with the other Latin American regimes.

CHAPTER SIXTEEN

JFK ASSASSINATION

> "I can't believe that!" said Alice.
> "Can't you?" The Queen said in a pitying tone.
> "Try again: draw a long breath, and shut your eyes."
> Alice laughed. "There's no use trying," she said.
> "One can't believe impossible things."
> "I daresay you haven't had much practice," said the Queen.
> "When I was your age, I always did it for half an-hour a day.
> Why, sometimes I've believed as many as six impossible things
> before breakfast."
>
> Lewis Carroll
> *Through the Looking-Glass*

Anyone who thinks that the assassinations of John and Robert Kennedy were haphazard unrelated events unconnected to the Mafia and CIA is not living in the real world.

After the Cuban missile crisis, Kennedy and Soviet Premier Khrushchev established a telephone hot line and exchanged twenty-three letters that were not declassified and released until 1993. Khrushchev's first private letter to Kennedy was twenty-six pages long. Kennedy thanked Khrushchev for initiating the correspondence and agreed with him that their discussions should remain private: "This will give us an opportunity to address the other in frank, realistic and fundamental terms. Neither of us is going to convert the other to a new social, economic, or political point of view. Neither of us is going to be induced by a letter to desert or subvert his country's cause. So these letters can be free from the polemics of the 'Cold War' debate."

Kennedy became convinced over the course of this correspondence that he and Khrushchev could negotiate a peaceful settlement to this nuclear madness. Both men agreed that a ban on nuclear testing was a critical first step. This would be followed by arms reductions and more open dialogue. Each was intent on pursing a peace based on a security that did not have to be enforced by nuclear stockpiles and a weapons industry.

On June 10, 1963, President Kennedy publicly made his intentions known to end the Cold War in a speech to the graduating class at American University. It was the beginning of a whole new look at the world. He said that "the most important topic on earth was world peace. A peace not enforced on the world by American weapons of war. I am talking about genuine peace, the kind of peace that makes life on earth worth living – not merely peace for Americans, but peace for all men and women – not merely peace in our time, but peace for all time."

Kennedy recognized the irony that our Pentagon and the Soviet Defense Ministry prospered symbiotically. Each military establishment claimed that the other side was ahead militarily in order to get bigger budgets for themselves. Kennedy intended to bring this arms race to a halt. He remarked to Norman Cousins, the editor of *Saturday Review*, "Mr. Khrushchev and I occupy approximately the same political positions inside our governments. He would like to prevent a nuclear war, but is under severe pressure from his hard-line crowd, which interprets every move in that direction as appeasement. I've got similar problems. The hard-liners in the Soviet Union and the United States feed on one another."

In October 1963, Kennedy and Khrushchev signed the Limited Nuclear Test Ban Treaty that banned nuclear tests in the air and in the water. Kennedy had also made up his mind about Vietnam: he was going to begin withdrawing U.S. troops. He issued National Security Action Memorandum (NSAM) 263 to that effect (the memorandum remained classified for the next three decades). Copies of NSAM were sent to the Secretary of State, Secretary of Defense, and Chairman of the Joint Chiefs of Staff.

One month later, on Friday, November 22, 1963, at 12:30 in the afternoon, John F. Kennedy was assassinated in Dallas. Kennedy knew the atmosphere in Dallas was hostile, but he refused to heed warnings that his enemies on the far right were out to get him. In fact, he planned to use his trip to Dallas, in the heartland of the militant right-wing, to denounce the threat of extremism in American life. He learned a lot during his three years in the White House and he now believed the Cold War was an illusion. Russia was not this evil empire intent on attacking the United States. It had too many of its own problems.

Kennedy planned to tell his audience that day that America must stop thinking that "peace was a sign of weakness." The most effective way to demonstrate America's strength was not to brandish its awesome weapons and threaten its enemies; it was to live up to the country's democratic ideals, "practicing what it preaches about equal rights and social justice," and pursuing peace instead of "aggressive ambitions." Kennedy had been warned not to inflame the city's right-wing passions, but he was undeterred. Now he was dead and the speech was never given.

When the shots rang out, John F. Kennedy slumped forward. The first lady, sitting at his side, filled the air with her frantic screams: "Jack, Jack!" And then: "They've killed my husband! I have his brains in my hands!"

Texas Governor John Connally was sitting directly in front of the president. Connally was seriously injured, but he survived. The president was rushed to Parkland Memorial Hospital where he died. An autopsy revealed that Kennedy had been shot from above and behind. Dave Powers and Kenneth O'Donnell, both close aides to JFK, were riding in the car directly behind Kennedy. They clearly saw shots coming from the right front of Kennedy's limo. "What the hell is going on?" they asked.

When Robert Kennedy received the news from a somewhat gleeful J. Edgar Hoover, his first thoughts were, "I knew they would get one of us." He never revealed who "they" were, but there were lots of candidates.

JFK had angered the CIA by refusing to support the Bay of Pigs invasion. He infuriated hard-core anti-Castro émigrés for the same reason. He invited the contempt of the military by his cautious response to the Cuban missile crisis and he alarmed much of the intelligence, military and foreign policy establishments with his desire to end the Vietnam War. John Kennedy was about to challenge virtually all the premises that were at the heart of the Cold War - that an unremitting conflict with communism was inevitable as long as the Soviet Union survived. He was in the process of formalizing an alternative path, one that rejected military action and called for peaceful cooperation with the Soviet Union – an unheard of change in policy. Many hard-liners considered that approach as tantamount to surrender and treason.

John Kennedy told his close aide, Kenneth O'Donnell, "In 1965, I am going to become one of the most unpopular presidents in history. I'll be damned everywhere as a communist appeaser, but I don't care. If I tried to pull out completely from Vietnam now, we would have another Joe McCarthy 'red scare' on our hands, but I can do it after I'm reelected. So we had better make sure that I am reelected." What Kennedy didn't know was that the word was out: "Kennedy is not going to make it to the election. He is going to be hit."

Bobby Kennedy quickly recovered from the shock of his brother's death and immediately went into action. He and Vice President Lyndon Johnson hated one another – the warfare between the two men was intense and personal. He knew that within days he would be barred from the White House and LBJ would have access to all the incriminating documents left behind. The Secret Service log of John Kennedy's personal visitors to his second floor quarters contained all the names and dates of his sexual liaisons and partners. That could not remain in LBJ's hands. Bobby had to act fast to eliminate the evidence that could forever destroy his brother's reputation. Mourning and grief would have to wait for a more propitious time.

Jack Kennedy's embarrassing files were not the only materials removed from the White House that day. The tape recording system in the Oval Office, Cabinet Room, and the president's living quarters on the second floor of the White House had to be dismantled and carted away.

Lyndon Johnson telephoned Bobby and offered words of condolence. He then moved closer to the point of his call, "A lot of people down here think I should be sworn in right away. Do you have any objections to that?" Kennedy was stunned by the question. It had only been an hour since his brother was shot and he didn't see what the rush was. He preferred that his brother's body be returned to Washington before Johnson was sworn in as the new president, but Johnson pressed the issue. Kennedy decided that his anger was personal and agreed to Johnson's request. Like it or not, LBJ was now in charge.

When Robert Kennedy was certain that all the arrangements for the removal of the incriminating evidence had been completed, he settled back in his easy chair, a drink in his hand, and pondered who could be responsible for his brother's death. His first suspect was Sam Giancana. He had repeatedly heard from FBI wiretaps that Giancana believed the Kennedy brothers would double-cross him on this Castro assassination business. Bobby knew that Giancana had no love for either he or his brother. Another target of Robert Kennedy's animosity was Teamster mobster Jimmy Hoffa. Could Hoffa have set up the killing? Was the CIA or Pentagon so fearful of a military-industrial cutback based on JFK's intended withdrawal from Vietnam? Bobby Kennedy was sure of one thing – the killer was not some sole deranged malcontent.

Lee Harvey Oswald was born in Slidell, Louisiana, on October 18, 1939. By the age of eighteen he had lived in twenty-two different residences and attended twelve different schools, mostly around New Orleans and Dallas. At age seventeen, he joined the Marines and was considered a very good, but not exceptional marksman. He was given an early discharge in 1959, ostensibly to return home to help his mother, but instead, he traveled to Russia where he presented himself at the American Embassy in Moscow to Consul Richard Snyder. Oswald said his purpose in coming to Russia was to renounce his U.S. citizenship. He handed Snyder a note that stated: "My allegiance is to the Union of Soviet Socialist Republics."

According to the Warren Commission Report, Oswald confided to Snyder that he told Soviet officials he would give them information concerning the Marine Corps and his radar specialty. Oswald had a "Crypto" security clearance, which was higher than "Top Secret," and his work immersed him in information about radio frequencies and the CIA's super-secret U-2 flights. If true, Oswald would have been the first U.S. Marine to ever defect to another country.

On June 13, 1962, Oswald, along with his wife and baby daughter, returned to Dallas. He was not met at the airport with arrest or prosecution, nor was he confronted in any way by the U.S. government. Nobody bothered him and nobody seemed to care. He just entered the country like any other loyal American citizen. How was this possible? Many believe that Oswald's "defection" was nothing but a cover; a U.S. intelligence ploy and that he was really on an assignment.

Upon his return to the United States, Oswald became a vocal pro-Castro advocate. He set up an organization called the Fair Play for Cuba Committee, but he was the only member. Oswald held several jobs in the Dallas area before moving to New Orleans, where his uncle was one of mobster Carlos Marcello's lieutenants. In late September, Oswald traveled to Mexico City in a failed attempt to get to Cuba. It is hard to discern what this was all about.

Oswald then returned to Dallas and took a temporary job at the Texas School Book Depository, a private company that acted as a processing center for a number of book publishers. Oswald filled stock orders for $1.25 an hour. Whoever assassinated Kennedy knew the exact route that JFK would take that day. As the Kennedy motorcade passed the Book Depository and turned up Elm Street, several shots were fired. Pigeons fluttered from the top of the Book Depository building directing attention to a sixth floor open window. As chaos took over in the area, with people running, falling, or just watching in amazement, police officers hurried to the building.

Police Officer Marrion Baker entered the building with supervisor Roy Truly. The two men rushed up the stairs. On the second floor, they found Oswald casually drinking a Coke by the vending machine. When Oswald's status was verified as an employee of the Company, they moved on with their search. Oswald then left the building, assuming there would be no further work that day because of all the commotion.

On the sixth floor, three empty cartridge shells were found under the open window where the Kennedy motorcade had passed. Three cartons of books were stacked under the window, providing an apparent resting place for aiming a rifle. A rifle was found behind boxes stacked near the stairwell on the far side of the sixth floor. It has never been explained why an expert assassin would amateurishly try to hide a rifle on the opposite side of the sixth floor knowing that it would be found, and also leave three incriminating bullet shells on the floor in full view.

In a 1968 interview with Dallas deputy sheriff Roger Craig, the sheriff told the *Los Angeles Free Press* that the shells found on the floor were neatly planted to frame Oswald. "The shells were all facing the same direction – not one of them was more than three-quarters of an inch apart, a feat very difficult to achieve with a bolt action rifle – or any rifle for that matter. I've fired many a bolt action rifle and in all my years I had never had two shells land in the same place. These three rifle cartridges looked as though they had been carefully and deliberately placed there."

The 6.6 mm Italian Mannlicher-Carcano rifle that was found was not even a high-powered rifle. It is hard to envision a worse weapon for what took place. In testimony before the Warren Commission – conveniently left out of the report – FBI firearm experts called the rifle "a cheap old weapon with a faulty scope that could easily be knocked out of adjustment." In searching Oswald's lodgings, no ammunition, gun-cleaning oil, or other related gun materials were found among his belongings. But, sixteen hours after the assassination the FBI announced that the $12.78 rifle and the $7.71 cheap Japanese telescopic sight were ordered from Klein's Sporting Goods in Chicago on March 12, 1963, by A. Hidell (an alias of Oswald) and shipped to a Post Office box in Dallas.

When Oswald left the Book Depository building after the assassination, he boarded a bus, but because the traffic was so heavy, he got off and took a taxi to his boardinghouse. He arrived there about one o'clock, stayed only a few minutes and then left.

About a mile away, Police Officer J.D. Tippit stopped a suspect. Tippit casually got out of his car and walked over to the suspect when suddenly the suspect pulled out a revolver and fired a number of shots, hitting Tippit four times and killing him. Witnesses never positively identified Oswald as the killer. The main witness was a 47-year-old waitress who was standing about half-a-block away waiting to catch a bus. She originally described the killer to the police as "a white male, about 25 years old, 5 feet 8 inches, brown hair, medium build and wearing a white jacket." When interviewed later that day by the FBI, she said the killer was, "a white male, about 18, had black hair and a red complexion, wore black shoes, a tan jacket and dark trousers."

There were now two separate manhunts going on in Dallas and most of the city was in panic-mode. When the police received a report that a suspicious looking man had entered the library, they raced to the scene with sirens blaring. Several blocks from the library, Johnny Brewer, manager of Hardy's Shoe Store, spotted a strange looking man outside his store. About a half minute later, curiosity got the better of Brewer and he stepped outside to see where this character was going. The suspect, already fifty yards away, walking at a good clip, neared a movie house showing a double feature.

Julia Postel, the forty-seven-year-old ticket-taker at the movie theater, had just stepped outside her booth to watch the police cars zooming past on the way to the nearby library. Meanwhile, Brewer saw the man slip into the theater without buying a 90-cent ticket. Brewer rushed over and told the cashier; she calls the police. Within minutes, police officers, plainclothesmen, and deputy sheriffs arrive at the movie theater armed to the teeth. They enter the theater and when the house lights go up, Brewer points out Oswald from among the twenty-four movie patrons. The police grab Oswald and after a tussle he shouts: "Don't hit me anymore. I am not resisting arrest. You're violating my civil rights."

As the police hustle Oswald out the front entrance, a television cameraman hears Oswald berating the police, "I want my lawyer. I know my rights. This is typical police brutality. Why are you doing this to me?" Outside the movie house, an angry crowd of about a hundred people begin shouting at Oswald: "That's him. Murderer! Kill the son of a bitch! Hang him! Give him to us, we'll kill him!"

Once Oswald is safely inside the police vehicle, he asks: "What is this all about? I know my rights. I don't know why you are treating me like this. Why am I being arrested? The only thing I've done is carry a pistol into a movie." One of the cops tells Oswald, "Sir, you've done a lot more. You have killed a policeman." Oswald denies the accusation. When they reach police headquarters they offer to cover his face from the television crews. "Why should I hide my face?" Oswald responds. "I haven't done anything to be ashamed of." Reporters ask Oswald: "Did you shoot the president?" Oswald answers without hesitation, "I didn't shoot anybody. They're taking me in because I lived in the Soviet Union. I'm just a patsy. I like the presidential family. They are interesting people."

Inside police headquarters, Oswald is searched; he has $13.87 and a pay stub for James A. Jackson from American Bakeries dated August 22, 1960 for $66.17. The FBI later located Jackson; he confirmed it was his paycheck stub, but said he never met Oswald and had no idea how Oswald got his three-year-old payroll stub.

Oswald was booked for both murders and interrogated for twelve hours without a lawyer being present. He never refused to answer any question that was put to him. No notes survive of the questions or answers other than that Oswald denied any guilt. The Dallas police chief told reporters that Oswald committed both murders. The police never sent out a manhunt for any other suspect. When Oswald was brought before reporters, he was asked about two bloody cuts on either side of his forehead; he replied: "A policeman hit me."

The pistol that was found on Oswald was a .38 Smith & Wesson that he owned. FBI firearms expert, Cortlandt Cunningham, test-fired Oswald's revolver and then tried to match up the markings and individual characteristics with the bullets that killed Tippit – he was unable to determine whether the bullets removed from Tippit's body were fired from Oswald's revolver.

Two persons filmed the Kennedy motorcade procession and recorded the assassination. Nineteen-year-old Beverly Oliver worked at the Colony Club, a strip club located next door to Jack

Ruby's Carousal Club. She filmed the entire assassination with her brand new Super-8 Yashica movie camera. After the shooting she was approached by two men and her camera and film were confiscated. She never saw her film again and there is no mention of either her or her film in the Warren Commission Report.

Perhaps the biggest debate is over the authenticity of a 27-second movie of the assassination, known as "the Zapruder film." This footage has been described as "the most significant amateur recording of a news event in history." The film was shot by Abraham Zapruder, a ladies' dress manufacturer with offices right near Jack Ruby's nightclub. The filming was done with a new Bell & Howell 8mm camera with a telephoto lens. On Monday, November 25, the print rights to the film were sold to *Life* magazine for $50,000, with Zapruder retaining any motion picture rights. A few days later, *Life* renegotiated the deal and bought the film outright for $150,000.

With the film now safely tucked away in *Time-Life* vaults, the only thing the public saw were still photographs in the Warren Commission Report. With the bootleg release of the Zapruder film in 1975, conspiracy fever reached zenith proportions. Of the 486 consecutive frames - frames 155, 156, 208, 209, 210, 211, 341, 350, and 486 were missing, leading many to believe that the film had been tampered with. Today, more than forty years after the event, a close viewing of the high-tech digital restoration clearly reveals that the second shot that blew Kennedy's head apart came from the right front.

According to the Warren Commission Report, Oswald's identity as the assassin was based on a description given by Howard Brennan, who looked up from the street and saw a figure at the sixth floor window. This identification of a momentary figure through a window six flights up supposedly enabled the police to positively identify Oswald.

During Oswald's interrogation that night, one of the police officers got a phone call from Jack Ruby, a Dallas nightclub owner with links to the mob, offering to bring them some sandwiches. The officer declined. At 11:30 that night, Ruby showed up at the police station where he was seen among the throng of reporters.

It was obvious that Ruby was quite friendly with the entire police crowd.

Police Chief Curry and District Attorney Henry Wade announced that Oswald would be shown to newsmen at a press conference in the basement to counter stories that he had been beaten. Ruby attended the chaotic press conference. Police Chief Curry said, "We don't have any proof that Oswald fired the rifle and no one has been able to put him in the building with a gun in his hand." When District Attorney Wade said that Oswald belonged to the "Free Cuba Committee," Ruby, standing on a table in the back of the room corrected him, saying that it was the "Fair Play for Cuba Committee."

The next morning, the Dallas police announced they were moving Oswald to a more secure location. As Oswald was being escorted to a waiting police cruiser, Jack Ruby was waiting with a crowd of reporters. At 11:21, with national television cameras filming the scene, Ruby emerged from between a newsman and a policeman and fired one bullet into Oswald's abdomen. Ruby was immediately grabbed by shocked officers and thrown to the floor. Oswald, lying on the floor, was asked whether he wanted to make a statement, but he shook his head no.

Dallas police rushed the stricken Oswald into an office, laid him on a desk and gave him artificial respiration - a procedure that was sure to kill anyone with an abdominal wound. Oswald died on his arrival at Parkland Memorial Hospital, the same hospital where John F. Kennedy expired. Jack Ruby's only comment to reporters as he was dragged away was, "I did it for the people of America. That man killed the president. I guess I had to show the world that a Jew has guts." During his police interrogation, Ruby claimed that he was acting alone and that killing Oswald was an impulsive act. Nobody could explain how the police let Ruby get so close to Oswald.

Ruby hired famed San Francisco lawyer Melvin Belli to represent him. Ruby told Belli that he shot Oswald because he wanted to save the president's widow the trauma of appearing in the Oswald trial. Marvin Belli never accepted that explanation:

Lies and Deceits

"The story was false because it didn't square with everything else we knew."

Jack Ruby, age fifty-six, was a Dallas nightclub owner, with ties to Cuba's pre-Castro gambling interests, including mobsters Meyer Lansky, Carlos Marcello and Santos Trafficante. Weeks before JFK's assassination, Ruby met with Johnny Rosselli, and just prior to that, he had a meeting with Santos Trafficante. Back in the late 1950s, Ruby was involved with smuggling guns from Florida and Texas to Fidel Castro and his band of rebels. At the time, the Mafia was hedging its bets by supporting both Batista and the insurrectionist Castro.

On the day of JFK's assassination, Fidel Castro was having lunch in Havana with French journalist Jean Daniel. They were discussing JFK's proposal for new talks between the two countries. When Castro was informed of Kennedy's death, he was horrified and became severely distraught. Three times Castro said, "This is very bad." When asked whether he was involved in any way, he said, "Why would I want to have anything to do with killing Kennedy? That would only give America a reason for invading my small country."

When Castro learned the details about Oswald, he remarked, "Thank goodness we didn't give this guy permission to visit Cuba. That would have been a tremendous provocation to implicate Cuba." Castro never believed the official assassination story. "I am a sharpshooter. I cannot imagine that with the rifle he had that you can fire, load, and fire again in a matter of seconds, because when you shoot with a telescopic sight, if the weapon moves a fraction of an inch you lose your target. Finding a target in motion in a fraction of a second and firing three times in a row so accurately is very difficult." When Castro was informed that Jack Ruby killed Oswald, he called the killing "incredible and inconceivable. That does not happen even in the most mediocre of Hollywood movies." Castro asked, "How in the world could this Jack Ruby get into the police station and kill Oswald? I have no evidence, but the whole thing sounds like a conspiracy to me."

In the Soviet Union, Khrushchev broke down and sobbed when he heard the news of Kennedy's assassination. He took the news as "a personal blow," said one aide. For several days afterward, Khrushchev was unable to perform his duties. When he and JFK originally met in Vienna in 1961, Khrushchev had little respect for the president who was twenty-three years his junior, an inveterate womanizer, and had amateurishly mangled the "Bay of Pigs."

Khrushchev remembered the private bantering that took place during that summit meeting where the Soviet leader argued that communism would triumph not by force of arms, but as a law of historical development. When Kennedy smiled and replied that "people should have free choice," Khrushchev countered with U.S. interference in Cuba, Iran, Vietnam, the Congo, Angola, and Algeria. But, he and Kennedy had drawn closer to each other during the thirteen-day Cuban missile crisis, exchanging private letters and confidential messages. Khrushchev later said that he had developed a "deep respect" for Kennedy because Kennedy did not allow right-wing forces to goad him into taking military action against Cuba. Khrushchev was convinced that Kennedy was killed by those very same forces that were bent on sabotaging the two leaders' efforts to reach détente. Khrushchev was now left without a partner in his hopes to end the Cold War.

Seven days after the assassination, the Warren Commission was established to investigate the murder. The commission was headed by Earl Warren, the Chief Justice of the Supreme Court. Other members included Representative Hale Boggs, Senator John Cooper, former CIA Director Allen Dulles, Representative Gerald Ford, diplomat John McCloy, and Senator Richard Russell Jr. The commission was created to resolve a political problem – dispelling the growing notion that the president might have been assassinated by some conspiracy that involved Russia, Cuba, or as part of a coup d'etat to get Lyndon Johnson into the White House.

Allen Dulles was a surprise choice – the very man whose career was terminated by President Kennedy in 1962 because of the failed Bay of Pigs invasion was now leading the inquiry into his murder. The former CIA chief never missed a meeting and lost no time in establishing himself as the dominant player, expertly deflecting the investigation away from the CIA and herding his fellow panelists toward the lone gunman theory. Many insiders believed the Warren Commission should have been named "the Allen Dulles Commission."

The other members of the commission were all busy men. Most of them were present only a small fraction of the time and their participation was minimal. Supporting the commissioners was a staff of fifteen lawyers who were also busy with their own private law practices; almost all the work was done by seven assistants. The commission heard testimony over the next ten months from 552 witnesses and received reports from ten federal agencies. However, there were several very odd omissions. The president's physician was never called to testify. The death certificate that refuted the claim that JFK's throat wound was caused by a shot from behind was never admitted into the official records. Robert Kennedy never testified before the commission, therefore, he did not have to reveal his opinions about the assassination under oath.

The Warren Commission report concluded that Oswald was a lone gunman, although this conflicted with reports that other shots were heard and seen coming from a grassy knoll to the president's right-front. Of the 90 persons who were asked this important question, 58 said the shots came from the direction of the grassy knoll and not the Book Depository – the other 32 people disagreed.

The Warren Commission could find no motive for the killing. They concluded that although Oswald was a mediocre marksman, he fired three shots within eight seconds from a cheap faulty rifle and hit the president twice in a moving car that was more than 200 yards away. Oswald then wiped off all the prints from the weapon, threw the rifle behind some boxes, left three cartridge shells lying by the open window, calmly walked out of the building, shot Officer Tippet four times, and then entered a movie theater without buying a 90-cent ticket. All these events took place within one hour: between 12:30–1:30 in the afternoon. The truth about the Kennedy assassination ended with Oswald's sudden death at the hands of Jack Ruby.

During the course of the Warren Commission investigation, Chief Justice Earl Warren and members of the commission privately visited Ruby in his prison cell. Ruby asked Warren on several occasions to take him to Washington, stating that he had important things to reveal. "I am being used as a scapegoat. I am willing to tell the truth to President Johnson. I am the only one who that can bring out the truth." Warren refused Ruby's request, citing security restrictions.

In a taped interview while in the Dallas jail, Ruby said, "The world will never know my motive and they will never know the true facts." Within four months of Oswald's killing, Ruby was tried for murder, found guilty and sentenced to death. Ruby appealed the conviction and it was reversed on the grounds that he could not receive a fair trial in Dallas under the prevailing hostile circumstances. His new trial was ordered moved from Dallas to Wichita Falls, a small Texas city near the Oklahoma border.

On December 9, 1966, two days after his new trial site had been announced; Ruby was moved from the Dallas County Jail to Parkland Memorial Hospital after complaining of persistent coughing and nausea. Doctors initially diagnosed his problem as pneumonia, but the next day the diagnosis was changed to lung cancer. Within a few days, it was announced that Ruby's cancer was too far advanced to be treated by surgery or radiation. Ruby claimed he had been deliberately infected with a poison by the CIA. Shortly before his death on January 3, 1967, a friend pleaded with Ruby to tell the truth before he died. Ruby replied, "Listen, you know me well, and you know I'm a reasonable businessman. I wouldn't have killed Oswald if I did not have to do it."

One of the only reporters to get a private interview with Ruby was nationally syndicated columnist, Dorothy Kilgallen. What transpired between the two is not known, but in 1965 Kilgallen made it known that she planned to break the case and that there was a conspiracy. "The Warren Commission is laughable," she said. "I'm going to break the real story and have the biggest scoop of the century." On November 8, 1965 she was found dead in her home. It was initially reported that she died of a heart attack, but this was quickly changed to an overdose of alcohol and pills. Her biographer, Lee Israel, claims that she did not die accidentally. Her notes and writings about Ruby were never found.

Lies and Deceits

The Warren Commission's 888-page report was issued on September 24, 1964, but the report never contained anything about Castro assassination plots or the involvement of the Mafia with the CIA and JFK. There was nothing about John Kennedy's sexual liaisons with Judith Exner and her role as courier between JFK and Sam Giancana. The Warren Commission report found no linkage between Jack Ruby and the assassinations of Kennedy and Oswald. All the files of the commission were sealed from public view for 75 years (until 2039) by executive order of President Lyndon Johnson.

All these new facts came to light in 1975 when Senator Frank Church began an investigation into CIA covert activities. The Church Committee record comprised over 8,000 pages of sworn testimony taken from 75 witnesses over 60 days. As the committee dug deeply into the facts and circumstances surrounding assassination plots; the relationship between the CIA and the Mafia exploded to the surface. Members of the committee began asking: If the CIA was capable of working hand-in-hand with Mafia assassins, what else were they capable of?

Sam Giancana was ordered to appear before the committee and to give information on the CIA-Mafia relationship and the plots to assassinate Fidel Castro. Before he could appear, someone gained entrance to his Chicago home and shot him point-blank in the back of the head. He was then shot six times in a circle around the mouth. For Mafia analysts, the method of execution imparted a clear message: that the victim was expected to "talk" and that he would never "talk" again. The murder was never solved.

Chuck Giancana, Sam Giancana's brother, reveals in his 1992 book *Double Cross* that his brother told him that he and the CIA "took care of Kennedy together." Sam Giancana said that a great many other people were involved; Jack Ruby was Giancana's representative in Dallas, and "Richard Nixon and Lyndon Johnson knew about the whole damn thing." According to Giancana, a "half-dozen fanatical right-wing Texans" were also involved in the assassination. Top-notch marksmen were hired for the kill: Charles Harrelson and Jack Lawrence came from Carlos Marcello's New Orleans organization and two from Tampa Mafioso Santo

Trafficante. Giancana sent three of his Chicago killers: Richard Cain, Chuckie Nicoletti, and Felix Anthony Alderisio. Seven assassins in all were sent to Dallas, but the actual killers, were Cain and Nicoletti.

The CIA, according to this account, arranged for Dallas police officers J.D. Tippit and Roscoe White to murder Oswald immediately after the assassination, but when Tippit wavered, White was forced to murder Tippit. Oswald's survival, according to Chuck Giancana, was "probably the only real screw-up in the whole god-damned deal," but it was a big one.

Ruby had been assigned to make sure everything went according to plan; once it didn't, it was Ruby's obligation to silence Oswald. According to Antoinette Giancana, Sam Giancana's daughter, the mob killed JFK and the CIA killed her father. "There is nothing my father could have said to the Church Committee that would upset the Mafia; only the CIA would have been embarrassed and severely compromised by his testimony."

At the same time, Jimmy Hoffa, another man the committee wanted to interview, disappeared before he could be called to testify. Hoffa's body was never found. In May 1976, Johnny Rosselli was subpoenaed to appear before the committee for closed-door questioning. On August 7, Rosselli's legless body was found stuffed into a weighted oil drum in North Miami. Rosselli's murder remains unsolved.

Jack Anderson, of the *Washington Post*, interviewed Rosselli just before he was killed. Anderson reported that Rosselli said: "When Oswald was picked up, the underworld conspirators feared he would crack and disclose information that might lead to them. This almost certainly would have brought a massive U.S. crackdown on the Mafia. So Jack Ruby was ordered to eliminate Oswald."

On March 29, 1977, Charles Nicoletti, a Mafia enforcer for Giancana was killed in Chicago immediately after the committee determined they wanted him to testify. His death was never solved. George DeMohrenschild, an adviser to the CIA and the mob, and a friend of Oswald, was also scheduled to testify, but he died on the day he was to be questioned. His death was ruled a suicide.

Lies and Deceits

According to Mafia insiders – none of these deaths were ordered by the mob. An insider may have been hired to pull the trigger, but the orders came from elsewhere because of what would have been disclosed.

Only Santos Trafficante remained alive to testify before the committee. Trafficante portrayed himself as an insignificant bit-player in the CIA attempt to murder Castro. CIA money? Poison pills? His memory was a total blank. Concerning Kennedy's slaying, Trafficante was equally evasive. The panel had evidence that Jack Ruby had worked for the mob in Cuba and that Trafficante knew him well. Trafficante's response was, "I don't remember." When asked to verify that he told a prominent Cuban exile that President Kennedy was "going to be hit," Trafficante answered, "I don't recall."

The committee decided not to publicize the Kennedy-Exner-Giancana mess. Many felt, or were persuaded, that the reputation of the presidency was at stake. Instead, the report concentrated on issues relating to national policy. The report accused the CIA of assassinating foreign leaders and documented nine attempts on Fidel Castro's life. They concluded that the FBI had deliberately withheld information from the Warren Commission, especially about the linkage of the Mafia to the CIA and to the president. Nobody believed that two bullets could cause a total of eight wounds.

The committee's report, released in 1979, concluded that there "probably had been a conspiracy in the JFK assassination," and blamed the FBI and CIA for depriving the Warren Commission of information that would have allowed it to reach the same conclusion. The committee noted that individuals such as Santos Trafficante and Carlos Marcello possessed the motive, means, and opportunity and might have acted together. It stated that "for organized crime to have been involved in the assassination, it must have had access to Oswald or Ruby or both." The evidence showed that "Oswald and Ruby did, in fact, have organized crime associations." When the committee's chief counsel, Robert Blakey, was asked by newsmen who he thought was responsible for John F. Kennedy's death, he replied, "I think the mob did it."

Howard Hunt served in the Office of Strategic Services during the Second World War. After the war he joined the Central Intelligence Agency. He was involved in many of the CIA's most nefarious operations, including the assassinations of Che Guevara, the coup in Chile against Salvador Allende, the plot against Jacobo Arbenz in Guatemala, the orchestration of the Bay of Pigs, and the plots to assassinate Fidel Castro. After Hunt retired from the CIA on May 1, 1970, he joined the President's Special Investigations Unit, informally known as "the Plumbers." Following the Watergate debacle, Hunt served 33 months in Federal prison.

In his near-death confession in 2006, Hunt gave his son handwritten notes and a voice recording that implicated LBJ and CIA operative Cord Meyer as the key players in the assassination of JFK. Included in the notes was a chain-of-command memo indicating the names of the CIA agents involved and placing Vice President Lyndon Johnson at the head. Others included David Atlee Phillips and William Harvey, as well as future Watergate burglar Frank Sturgis. Hunt revealed that LBJ and the military-industrial complex were both behind the plot and recruited the CIA men to carry it out.

New Orleans District Attorney Jim Garrison conducted an exhaustive investigation and concluded that the real masterminds behind the conspiracy were the CIA and Pentagon. "President Kennedy was killed for one reason," Garrison told the press, "because he was working towards reconciliation with the Soviet Union and Castro's Cuba. President Kennedy died because he wanted peace."

According to Garrison, JFK planned to withdraw American troops from Vietnam. This threatened the power of the newly emerging neoconservative war-hawk establishment and the profits of the military-industrial complex that relied on the continuance of huge military expenditures. The CIA and the Joint Chiefs of Staff wanted America kept on a constant war alert with billions going to defense and new weapons. The only way to stop this planned pull-back was to replace Kennedy with LBJ. Their reasons ranged from patriotism to self-interest.

Lyndon Johnson, according to Garrison, was quite willing to co-operate. Strong rumors were circulating that Kennedy was going to drop LBJ from the ticket in 1964. Even if LBJ remained Kennedy's running mate, Johnson was getting older and Kennedy was young and unlikely to die in office from natural causes. This was LBJ's only chance to become president and achieve greatness in American history. He had plans of his own and they could only be achieved if Kennedy was dead. Johnson believed that under his regime we would defeat Vietnam and topple Cuba. Johnson promised the war hawks: "I am not going to lose Vietnam."

Garrison argues that the JFK assassination was orchestrated by elements in the U.S. government that were in agreement with LBJ's aims. He asks, "Who benefited from Kennedy's assassination?" He answers, "In a very real and terrifying sense our government is the CIA and Pentagon; Congress has been reduced to a debating society. I've learned enough about the machinations of the CIA to know that this is no longer the dream-world America I once believed in. I have come to realize that in Washington, deceiving and manipulating the public are viewed by some as the natural prerogatives of office."

Robert Kennedy never bought into the sole gunman theory – he knew better. But, what was his alternative. To disclose what he believed to be the truth would only start a disastrous chain of events for the country and his brother's reputation. To avert such a catastrophe, it was prudent to pretend utter ignorance. He confided to an old friend, "If the American people knew the truth about Dallas, there would be blood in the streets."

Perhaps the country's solace is that John Fitzgerald Kennedy died in time to be remembered as he would like to be remembered; ever-young and handsome, his image untarnished, and still the shining light from Camelot. Once Lyndon Johnson assumed the presidency, everything changed. Castro and Khrushchev returned to their evil image in the media, the Cold War was back on, nuclear proliferation accelerated, and the war in Vietnam was expanded. The military-industrial complex was back in charge of America.

In 1964, Bobby Kennedy set out on his quest to reach the presidency; only there would he be able to find the true answers about his brother's assassination. Of course, a Robert Kennedy presidency would not sit well with either his enemies or those who might have been involved in Jack Kennedy's death.

Bobby Kennedy's first step was successful; he was elected to the U.S. Senate. When he entered the presidential race during the chaotic year of 1968, America was coming to grips with an unwinnable war in Vietnam and unacceptable social policies at home. RFK knew there were those who wanted to settle old scores. He often trembled at the podium and scanned crowds for an assassin's glare, living with a deep fear that his life would be cut short by violence. "I'm afraid there are guns between me and the White House," he told his close aides.

Shortly after midnight on June 5, 1968, while he and his staff were celebrating his win in the California presidential primary, he was assassinated in the hotel basement hallway as he was going to the main ballroom. The scene was a virtual re-enactment of Ruby killing Oswald. Once again history proved that the thread between power and nothingness can change in a second – all it takes is a bullet.

If anyone was destined to die by the hand of an assassin, it was Robert Kennedy. By 1968, he had made many powerful enemies. Among those who hated him were: Teamster boss Jimmy Hoffa, Louisiana Mafia czar Carlos Marcello, FBI Director J. Edgar Hoover, CIA agent William Harvey (who was banished by an angry Robert Kennedy after the Cuban missile crisis), and Republican presidential candidate Richard M. Nixon who regarded Robert Kennedy as the only Democratic candidate that could defeat him in the upcoming election.

Each of these individuals considered Robert Kennedy a spoiled rich kid who needed to be taught a lesson. One story out of many tells it all. On May 18, 1962, Jimmy Hoffa was indicted for receiving a million dollars in illegal payments. His trial ended in a hung jury, but Hoffa was indicted once again, this time for jury tampering. In July 1963, Hoffa and his lawyers came to Washington to inspect government records dealing with the prosecution's case. They were told they had to see Attorney General Robert Kennedy first. Hoffa was enraged when he was kept waiting for forty-five minutes in

Kennedy's outer office. Kennedy finally strolled in the front door with his dog on a leash and explained that he took his dog for a walk. Hoffa exploded.

"Where the hell do you get off keeping me waiting while you're walking your fucking dog!" When Kennedy smirked and made no reply, Hoffa lunged at him and knocked him against the wall. As he was choking Kennedy, he screamed into RFK's face, "You son-of-a-bitch. I'll break your fucking neck! I'll kill you!" Three of Hoffa's lawyers had to pull Hoffa off Kennedy. They are certain Hoffa would have killed Kennedy right there if they had not forcibly intervened.

Later, Hoffa told his lawyer, Frank Ragano, to pass along a message about Robert Kennedy to Trafficante and Marcello, "I want him dead. No more fucking around. We're running out of time – something has to be done." Marcello decided at the time that killing Bobby Kennedy was a bad idea. If Bobby was killed, JFK would unleash all the forces of government against the Mafia. But, if JFK were killed, Lyndon Johnson's first act would be to fire Robert Kennedy. It made more sense to kill JFK. This is the way that Marcello put it: "If you want to kill a dog, you don't cut off its tail, you cut off its head. The dog will keep biting if you only cut off its tail." John F. Kennedy was the head; Robert Kennedy was the tail.

After JFK was killed, Hoffa told Frank Ragano, "I told you they could do it. I'll never forget what Carlos and Santos did for me." He added, "This means Bobby is out as attorney-general." Marcello later told Ragano, "When you see Jimmy Hoffa, you tell him he owes me and he owes me big."

The mob was right – LBJ immediately replaced Robert Kennedy as attorney-general – but now the "snot-nosed kid" was making a run for the presidency. The mob was not going to allow that to happen. A Robert Kennedy presidency would seriously threaten their operations. For Jimmy Hoffa, it probably would mean serving out his entire thirteen-year prison sentence. (Hoffa received a presidential pardon after Nixon's election in 1971; he then mysteriously disappeared and was never found). For organized-crime boss, Carlos Marcello, a Robert Kennedy victory would mean certain deportation. For J. Edgar Hoover, it would mean the dreaded immediate retirement.

Jimmy Hoffa guaranteed to those close to him that Bobby Kennedy was a dead man. "He has so many enemies now they wouldn't know who did it." Of all the powerful array of enemies that Robert Kennedy had, who turned out to be the alleged assassin? Sirhan Sirhan was an Arab whose family had been forced out of West Jerusalem during the fighting in Palestine back in 1948. After working at many odd jobs, he became a horse groomer at the Santa Anita racetrack stables. He was a compulsive gambler and was well-known to many minor racketeers. His fellow exercise boys at the racetrack insist that Sirhan was apolitical and contemptuous of Arabs. With the range and power of Bobby Kennedy's known enemies there was something bizarre about Sirhan being the killer.

From the beginning, the investigation into RFK's murder was botched. Witnesses said that Sirhan approached Kennedy from the front and sprayed bullets into the throng, wounding five other people. However, the autopsy report stated that the three shots that actually hit Kennedy came from below and behind. Follow-up studies concluded that as many as twelve bullets were fired, four more than Sirhan could have discharged from his eight-shot pistol. For those who are experts in this sort of thing, this was a professional execution.

Sirhan was defended at his trial by Grant Cooper and Russell Parsons, lawyers that represented the Los Angeles mob syndicate headed by Mickey Cohen. His attorneys never brought up the coroner's finding that Sirhan was in the wrong position to have killed Robert Kennedy. Throughout the trial, Sirhan maintained that he had no memory of the event. He had blanked out, could not remember anything, and was not sure where the extra money he was carrying had come from. "Everything happened so fast," he said.

There are many who claim that Sirhan had been subjected to mind control. Sirhan was so disoriented following his arrest that he did not even know he had been arraigned. During pre-trial psychiatric examinations, Sirhan proved to be the ideal hypnotic subject, climbing the bars without knowing that he was carrying out post-hypnotic commands. Expert trial testimony established that his notebook passages containing repetitions of the phrase "RFK Must Die" were written in a hypnotic trance, and Sirhan spontaneously reproduced this phrase under hypnosis when asked in his cell for a description of Robert Kennedy.

Sirhan was convicted and sentenced to death. His sentence was commuted to life when California invalidated the death penalty. He has been routinely eligible for parole, but, as of 2006, parole has been denied thirteen consecutive times. The mystery of Robert Kennedy's death has never been solved to any one's satisfaction, but knowing what we now know about political killings and assassinations, it is highly unlikely that it was this 'patsy.'

The legacy of the Kennedy saga cannot be fully explained by the glamor, wealth, women, and the tragedies. Whatever their personal and even tragic failings, the Kennedy message that resonated so powerfully with America's young people back in the 1960s was that we could step beyond our narrow personal concerns to achieve great things; that we could do better, be better, and we must get on with the important work of making this planet a better place to live. The Kennedy brothers helped bolster our capacity to believe. They were inspirational – something that the politicians who followed afterward were unable to do; something this country has sorely missed.

CHAPTER SEVENTEEN

MARTIN LUTHER KING JR.

"I have a dream."

Martin Luther King Jr.

"He's nothing but a goddamn nigger preacher."

Lyndon Baines Johnson

Paul Robeson was born in Princeton, New Jersey, in 1898. His father, William Drew Robeson, was a slave, but escaped from a North Carolina plantation, graduated from Lincoln University, and became a church minister. Robeson's mother, Maria Louisa Bustill, came from an abolitionist Quaker family. Nearly blind, she died in a tragic fire in 1904 when Paul Robeson was six years old.

Robeson won an academic scholarship to Rutgers University, an almost unheard of event at the time. He was the only black student on campus. He dominated the debating and glee clubs, was Phi Beta Kappa and class valedictorian at graduation. During his stay at Rutgers, he earned fifteen varsity letters in football, baseball, basketball, and track and field. For his accomplishments in football, he was twice named to the first-team All-American team. However, when the United States government later considered him a communist subversive, his name was retroactively struck from the roster of the 1917 and 1918 college All-America football teams.

After graduating from Rutgers, Robeson earned a law degree from Columbia University. He helped pay his way through law school by playing professional football in the American Professional Football Association, later known as the National Football League. He graduated from law school in 1923 and was hired at the law firm of Stotesbury and Miner in New York City, but he quit after a white secretary refused to take dictation from him because he was black.

In 1921, he married Eslanda Goode, a remarkable woman who was educated in science and medicine. She fueled his ambitions to be an actor and singer, and he became one of the few truly great bass virtuoso voices in American music. On the theatrical stage he was the first black actor to portray Shakespeare's *Othello*. His 1943-1944 Broadway run of *Othello* still holds the record for the longest running Shakespeare play. In concert, his voice was like no other. His renditions of old spirituals were acclaimed. Between 1925 and 1942, Robeson appeared in eleven films. The 1936 film *Show Boat* was a box office hit, especially Robeson's highly acclaimed rendition of "Ol' Man River." However, because of the political controversy surrounding him, all his recordings and films were withdrawn from circulation.

In 1949, a benefit concert was held in Peekskill, New York, for a left-wing civil rights organization. Paul Robeson was to be featured singer, but before he arrived on stage, a mob of locals attacked concert-goers with baseball bats and rocks. The rioters shouted" "Commies, Niggers, Jews – You got in alive but you're not getting out alive. Go back to Russia. Hitler did not finish the job, but we will." Thirteen people were seriously injured before the police intervened.

On Robeson's frequent trips to Western Europe and the Soviet Union he was highly critical of the conditions experienced by black Americans in the United States. Robeson became captivated with the new Soviet society and its leadership, declaring "that Russia was entirely free of racial prejudice. Here in Russia, for the first time in my life, I can walk with full human dignity." He was convinced that American blacks, descended from slaves, had a common culture with Russian workers who were descended from serfs. Robeson's frequent trips to the Soviet Union led J. Edgar Hoover to keep Robeson under close FBI surveillance from 1941 to 1974.

In 1950, the State Department denied Robeson a passport and issued a "stop notice" at all ports, effectively confining him to the United States. When he and his lawyers met with officials at the State Department on August 23, 1950, and asked why it was "detrimental to the interests of the United States Government" for him to travel abroad, they were told that "his frequent criticism of the treatment of blacks in the United States was a 'family affair' that should not be aired in foreign countries." When Robeson inquired about being re-issued a passport, the State Department declined, citing Robeson's refusal to sign a statement that he would not give any speeches while outside the United States.

In 1956, Robeson was targeted by Senator Joseph McCarthy's House Un-American Activities Committee and grilled about his Communist sympathies. Robeson responded: "Whether I am a Communist, a Democrat, or a Republican, is my business. You are the non-patriots and the un-Americans, and you ought to be ashamed of yourselves. I am fighting for the rights of my people, who are still second-class citizens in this United States of America. In Russia I felt for the first time like a full human being. There was no color prejudice. It is here before this Committee today that I feel the pressure of color."

When Robeson was asked: "Why don't you stay in Russia?" he replied:

"My mother was born a Quaker in Pennsylvania and my father was a slave. My ancestors baked bread for George Washington's troops when they crossed the Delaware. I am going to stay here and be a part in building this country just like you, and no Fascist-minded people will drive me away. Is that clear? I am for peace with the Soviet Union; I am for peace with China; and I am for peace with decent people. I stand here struggling for the rights of my people to be full citizens in this country. And they are not. They are not in Mississippi. And they are not in Alabama. And they are not in Washington. They are nowhere to be found in these United States of America. You want to shut up every Negro who has the courage to stand up and fight for the rights of his people and for the rights of workers. That is why you are afraid of me and that is why I am here today."

In the spring of 1961, while Robeson was concertizing in Russia, he decided to visit Cuba and meet with Fidel Castro and

Lies and Deceits

Che Guevara. The timing of Robeson's trip was disastrous for the CIA since it would have occurred just before the U.S. planned Bay of Pigs invasion. It is impossible to underestimate the seriousness of Robeson's embrace of Castro at a time when our government intended to covertly overthrow the new Cuban regime.

Before leaving for Cuba, a surprise party was thrown for Robeson at his Moscow hotel. The party was secretly funded by the CIA. At the party, Robeson was slipped a synthetic hallucinogen drug called BZ. Unconscious, he was whisked away from Moscow and secretly admitted into London's Priory Hospital. There he was forced to endure fifty-four electroshock treatments at a time when electroshock in combination with psycho-active drugs was a favored technique of CIA behavior modification.

When his treatments were completed, Robeson's son was notified of his whereabouts and he flew to London to be with his father. When he arrived at the hospital, he could not believe his father's extreme paranoia and suicidal ranting. His father had always been an extremely healthy specimen; he was now a severe manic depressive. Paul Robeson never mentally recovered from the trauma and he died in 1977. In 1978, the United Nations honored Robeson. In 1995, he was re-inducted into the College Football Hall of Fame.

Robeson was the victim of a CIA secret mind-altering program called MK-ULTRA that began immediately after the Second World War. U.S. intelligence poured millions of dollars into probing alternative methods of influencing and controlling the mind. The letters MK identified the program as a current project; ULTRA was chosen as a reminder that it was one of America's most secret projects. Over thirty universities and institutions were involved in this extensive testing and experimentation that included various drugs and the administration of LSD on unsuspecting subjects.

Paul Robeson was only one of hundreds of MK-ULTRA casualties. On November 28, 1953, Frank Olson, a CIA biochemist and biological weapons researcher working on MK-ULTRA was found dead in his underwear on the sidewalk of New York City. The CIA claimed that Olson was severely depressed and committed suicide by jumping through the thirteenth floor plate glass window of the Statler Hotel. The New York police department made a meek investigation and ruled his death a suicide. It took fifty years for the truth to come out. Frank Olson was murdered by the CIA and those in the highest levels of the U.S. government participated in one of the great cover-ups in our country's history.

Frank Olson was one of the major pioneers in the MK-ULTRA program and was instrumental in the development of our country's large biochemical toxic arsenal that included anthrax, bacteria viruses, and lethal toxins – all outlawed under the Geneva Protocol. Olson also played a key role in the development of mind-altering drugs and brainwashing techniques, and directed MK-ULTRA experiments using human subjects as medical guinea pigs.

In 1953, Frank Olson had a change of heart about his work and told his CIA superiors that he had enough. He could no longer justify all the secret and illegal experiments on human beings; he found them morally indefensible. The top echelon of the CIA became concerned that Olson was about to go public with what he knew and they concluded that he was too dangerous to remain alive. Olson agreed to attend a last conference in New York. During his stay, he was drugged and thrown through his hotel room window to his death. The window was thick and sealed and later reports confirmed that it was impossible for Olson to charge through the window unassisted.

Frank Olson's son Eric was nine-years old at the time of his father's death and he grew up with no idea of the details. However, in 1975, during the course of a Senate committee investigating political assassinations by the CIA, documents going back to the 1950s were subpoenaed. Most of the MK-ULTRA records had been deliberately destroyed in 1973 by order of CIA Director Richard Helms, however, a sufficient number survived to paint a disturbing picture of the more than 150 MK-ULTRA programs. To the dismay of CIA hard-liners, William Colby, director of the CIA, complied with the subpoena request. The documents revealed the CIA's nefarious activities, including the MK-ULTRA program.

On the afternoon of June 12, 1975, Eric Olson sat completely stunned as he read the front page *Washington Post* story citing his father's involvement in the MK-ULTRA project. On July 21, 1975, President Ford publicly apologized to the Olson family. At this time, Donald Rumsfeld was White House Chief of Staff and Dick Cheney was a senior White House Assistant. Both men became involved in a cover-up to keep the details of Frank Olson's murder a secret. A bill was rushed through Congress to provide the Olson family with $1.5 million compensation – hush money to stifle any further investigation.

But, Eric Olson would not let the matter rest. He interviewed several of his father's retired colleagues and was told that they always suspected that Frank Olson had been murdered. After examining thousands of documents in the Gerald Ford Library, Eric eventually uncovered the truth. He got permission from the court to have his father's body exhumed. Surprisingly, the body was still in reasonable condition. The pathology conclusion was that Frank Olson had been knocked unconscious by a blow of tremendous force before exiting the window and that his death "was highly suggestive of homicide."

Based on these new findings, Manhattan District Attorney Robert Morgenthau re-opened the homicide investigation, but by this time most the participants were either dead or claimed "memory lapses." No charges were ever brought. There was nothing more Eric Olson could do. He forwarded copies of all documents to a British author, Gordon Thomas, who was working on a related CIA expose. The result was the publication of *Secrets & Lies* – a full account of Frank Olson's murder.

While the CIA was perfecting MK-ULTRA and playing all its secret covert 'games,' civil rights in this country was awakening from its sleep. Since 1896, the Supreme Court decision in *Plessy v. Ferguson* had upheld the constitutionality of racial segregation under the doctrine of "separate but equal." As long as blacks had relatively "equal" facilities, there was no discrimination.

Plessy continued to be the law until the *Brown v. Education* desegregation case in 1954. *Brown* was the lead case along with four other 'Jim Crow' school cases that were brought before the Supreme Court. In the *Brown* case, Kansas law allowed segregation in the grade schools in Topeka and Wichita. Linda Brown attended a segregated grade school and the NAACP convinced her parents to challenge the law. Lower courts ruled that they were bound by the *Plessy* case and the decision was appealed to the U.S. Supreme Court.

The preliminary vote in the *Brown* case was 5-4 to uphold *Plessy* and the doctrine of "separate but equal" - not because the judges felt it was necessarily right, but because public education issues and laws were always the obligation of the state and local communities. When Chief Justice Vinson died before the final vote was taken, everything changed. President Eisenhower was politically indebted to Republican California Governor Earl Warren and had promised him the first vacancy on the Supreme Court. No one figured that appointment would be as Chief Justice or that the "Warren Court" for the next fifty years would completely overhaul civil rights in this country.

Warren's first order of business as chief justice was to finalize the vote in the *Brown* case. Warren was convinced that *Plessy* had to be overturned. Being the political professional that he was, Warren argued, debated, cajoled, and twisted arms until the vote was turned around to 8-1, with Justice Stanley Reed the sole dissenter. Then Warren went to work on Reed. Finally, Reed capitulated and Warren announced on behalf of a unanimous Court: "We conclude unanimously that in the field of public education, the doctrine of 'separate but equal' has no place. Separate educational facilities are inherently unequal." He then ordered all school districts to proceed to integrate "with all deliberate speed." Unfortunately, 'all deliberate speed,' had different meanings to different school districts. In the South, it meant the least amount of integration over the longest period of time, and opened the gates for violence against black school children and years of litigation.

Justice Hugo Black, the Supreme Court's liberal stalwart, told guests at a dinner party, "There is going to be trouble and people are going to die," adding that "before the tree of liberalism can be renewed in the South, a few candidates must water it with their blood." Hugo Black had been a Ku Klux Klan member in 1923, marched in parades in his white robe, and spoke at nearly 150 Klan meetings. It was, he explained later, "the only way to get elected in Alabama." Now he was the Supreme Court's staunch champion of civil rights. Southern conservatives denounced him and the other Supreme Court liberals as communist sympathizers. It pained Hugo Black greatly that his home state of Alabama now shunned him, passed a resolution declaring that he could not be buried in Alabama, and that his son had to abandon a planned run for Congress. Hugo Black could not visit Alabama for more than a decade without wearing a bulletproof vest provided by the Secret Service.

President Eisenhower was not happy with the *Brown* decision. "The Supreme Court has spoken and I am sworn to uphold the constitutional process in this country," he said. But, the president refused to associate himself or his prestige in any way with *Brown*. "I think it makes no difference whether or not I endorse it," he said at one press conference. Eisenhower's refusal to publicly support the Court's decision did make a difference because in his confusing and ambiguous statements, white southerners heard sympathy for their position and a deep reluctance on the part of the federal government to interfere. Eisenhower's position gave southerners license to defy the Supreme Court.

"Separate but equal" was not the evil; it was only the symptom. The evil was white supremacy. Rather than adhering to the *Brown* decision, most southern public schools closed their doors and white kids were sent to private schools. Blacks who attempted to attend the few remaining open schools were taunted, beaten, and brutalized as never before. Federal troops had to be sent in to protect frightened black school children passing through a jeering, spitting mob. Southerners claimed this violence was the fault of the Negroes who were "too pushy" along with the Jews and liberal whites from the north. However, scenes of federal troops having to escort little black children to school while white foes hurled ugly epithets, made the United States lectures on democracy and liberty laughable throughout the communist world.

Emmett Till, a fourteen-year-old black boy from Chicago did not understand the unwritten laws of "Jim Crow." When he jokingly whistled at a white woman, he was doomed. That night he was dragged from his bed, brutally beaten and shot in the head.

Although his killers were arrested and charged with murder, they were quickly acquitted by an all-white male jury. Shortly afterward, the defendants sold their story to *Look* magazine, which included a detailed account of how they murdered Till. Despite the confession in a reputable national magazine, neither President Eisenhower nor FBI Director J. Edgar Hoover ever ordered the trial reopened.

Segregated education was not the only issue. Trying to vote took courage for black people in the South. Those who tried often lost their job the next day or were turned down for their annual "crop loan" and lost their farm. And of course there was the humiliation of the registration process. Many county Board of Registrars required black applicants to pass an oral test before they could be eligible to vote and the questions were flagrantly unanswerable. In Alabama, where 516,336 blacks were eligible to vote, only 52,336 managed to register. In the eleven southern states, only 1.2 million out of six million blacks were registered. Even those blacks that had registered often did not dare go to the polls for fear of violence or economic retaliation. There were scores of counties in the South that had tens of thousands of black residents, but not a single vote was ever cast by a black person. When civil rights workers tried to get the blacks registered they were met with violence by white segregationists. Peaceful marchers were bloodied by mobs; vicious dogs ripped them to shreds, all under the watchful eyes of the local police. No arrests were ever made.

Martin Luther King, Jr. was born on January 15, 1929. His grandfather and father were both pastors at the Ebenezer Baptist Church in Atlanta. Martin attended segregated public schools in Georgia, graduated from high school at the age of fifteen, and received a B.A. degree in 1948 from Morehouse College, a distinguished Negro institution from which both his father and grandfather had graduated. After completing three years of theological study at Crozer Theological Seminary in Pennsylvania, where he was elected president of a predominantly white senior class, he enrolled in graduate studies at Boston University and completed his doctorate in 1953. In Boston, he met and married Coretta Scott, a young woman of uncommon intellectual and artistic beauty. Two sons and two daughters were born into the family.

In 1954, King became the pastor at the Dexter Avenue Baptist Church in Montgomery, Alabama. In December 1955, a quiet dignified black seamstress named Rosa Parks refused to move to the back of a bus to make room for a white passenger. She was arrested for violating the Alabama bus segregation laws. Martin Luther King called for a boycott of the buses on the following Monday morning. But, many of Montgomery's blacks had no alternate means of getting to their jobs unless they walked for miles. No one was really sure whether King's boycott would work.

On Monday morning, the Reverend King's wife, Coretta King, was looking anxiously out her window to see the first morning bus that was usually jammed with Negro maids on their way to work. When the bus passed, she saw it was empty; bus after bus was empty. In spite of the bitter cold, fear of reprisals and violence, and their desperate need for wages, Montgomery's Negroes were staying off the buses. That morning, there was another startling development. At the courthouse where Rosa Parks was being tried, five hundred black Americans showed up to support her cause. She was fined $14 and released.

That evening, King told a cheering audience: "You know my friends, there comes a time when people get tired of being trampled over by the iron heel of oppression. If we are wrong, the Supreme Court of this nation is wrong. If we are wrong, God almighty is wrong. If we are wrong, justice is a lie." A mighty leader was born that day and the Montgomery blacks had found a new weapon – nonviolence.

King organized car pools so Montgomery's blacks could get to work without using the buses. On November 13, 1956, an Alabama court banned car pooling as an unlicensed transportation system. With another winter approaching, King confessed that without the car pool, "I'm afraid our people will go back on the buses. It's just too much to ask of them if we cannot provide other transportation." King's prayers were answered when the U.S. Supreme Court declared segregation on buses unconstitutional.

On the morning after the Supreme Court decision, a bus pulled up near Martin Luther King's home and he boarded it. The driver, a white man, smiled at him. "I believe you are Reverend King," he said. "Yes, I am," King said. "We are glad to have you with us this morning," the driver said. Martin Luther King sat down in the front row.

Southern whites reacted to this development with heightened fury. A shotgun blast was fired into King's home; snipers fired on the now integrated buses, one volley wounded a pregnant Negro woman; a car pulled up to a bus stop where a fifteen-year-old Negro girl was standing alone and five men jumped out and beat her; Ku Klux Klan caravans honked through Negro sections of Montgomery, and Klansmen marched through the streets in full regalia as fiery crosses burned in the night.

Praying for guidance at a mass meeting the next day, King looked up to the heavens, "Lord, I hope no one will have to die as a result of our struggle for freedom in Montgomery. Certainly I don't want to die. But if anyone has to die, let it be me."

In 1957, King was elected president of the Southern Christian Leadership Conference, an organization formed to provide leadership for the now flourishing civil rights movement. The ideals for this organization King took from Christianity and its operational techniques from Mahatma Gandhi. For the next eleven years, King traveled over six million miles and spoke over twenty-five hundred times, appearing wherever there was injustice, protest, and action. During that period he wrote five books and numerous articles. He was arrested twenty times and assaulted on at least four occasions. He was also awarded five honorary degrees and was named Man of the Year by *Time* magazine in 1963. In 1964, at the age of thirty-five, he became the youngest man to receive the Nobel Peace Prize. When notified of his selection, he announced that he would turn over the prize money of $54,123 to the furtherance of the civil rights movement.

Birmingham, Alabama, was one of the most segregated racist cities in the 1960s. In 1963, Dr. King, along with the Reverend Abernathy and the Reverend Shuttlesworth, led peaceful sit-in demonstrations at segregated lunch counters where they were refused food service, and "kneel-ins" on church steps where they were denied entrance because of color. Police arrested 45 protesters marching from the Sixteenth Street Baptist Church to City Hall. The next day, Palm Sunday, more people were arrested and two police dogs attacked nineteen-year-old protester Leroy Allen as a large crowd looked on. J. Edgar Hoover called the sit-ins a Communist plot to encourage racial paranoia in this country. Negro pastor Fred Shuttlesworth responded to Hoover's allegations: "I'm too American black to be a commie Red!"

On April 16, 1963, Martin Luther King, while sitting in a Birmingham jail cell, wrote the following letter to his fellow clergymen:

> "I am in Birmingham because injustice is here. I cannot sit idly by and not be concerned about what happens in Birmingham. Injustice anywhere is a threat to justice everywhere. We are caught in an inescapable network of mutuality, tied in a single garment of destiny. Whatever affects one directly, affects all indirectly. Never again can we afford to live with the narrow, provincial "outside agitator" idea. Anyone who lives inside the United States can never be considered an outsider anywhere within its bounds.
>
> We know through painful experience that freedom is never voluntarily given by the oppressor; it must be demanded by the oppressed. For years now I have heard the word 'Wait!' It rings in the ear of every Negro with piercing familiarity. This 'Wait' has almost always meant 'Never.'
>
> Perhaps it is easy for those who have never felt the stinging dark of segregation to say, 'Wait.' But when you have seen vicious mobs lynch your mothers and fathers at will and drown your sisters and brothers at whim; when you have seen hate-filled policemen

curse, kick and even kill your black brothers and sisters; when you see the vast majority of your twenty million Negro brothers smothering in an airtight cage of poverty in the midst of an affluent society; when you suddenly find your tongue twisted and your speech stammering as you seek to explain to your six-year-old daughter why she can't go to the public amusement park that has just been advertised on television, and see tears welling up in her eyes when she is told that 'Funtown' is closed to colored children, and see ominous clouds of inferiority beginning to form in her little mental sky, and see her beginning to distort her personality by developing an unconscious bitterness toward white people; when you have to concoct an answer for a five-year-old son who is asking: 'Daddy, why do white people treat colored people so mean?'; when you take a cross-county drive and find it necessary to sleep night after night in the uncomfortable corners of your automobile because no motel will accept you; when you are humiliated day in and day out by nagging signs reading 'white' and 'colored'; when your first name becomes 'nigger,' and your middle name becomes 'boy'and your wife and mother are never given the respected title 'Mrs.' - then you will understand why we find it difficult to wait. There comes a time when the cup of endurance runs over and men are no longer willing to be plunged into the abyss of despair."

In August 1963, King organized his first march on Washington. More than 250,000 men and women, white and black, marched peacefully to the nation's capital to demand equal rights. In a speech that still echoes today, Dr. King stood on the steps of the Lincoln Memorial and told the country that he had a dream:

"I say to you today, my friends, even though we face the difficulties of today and tomorrow, I still have a dream. It is a dream deeply rooted in the American dream.

I have a dream that one day this nation will rise up and live out the true meaning of its creed: We hold these truths to be self-evident: that all men are created equal.

I have a dream that one day on the red hills of Georgia the sons of former slaves and the sons of former slave owners will be able to sit down together at the table of brotherhood.

I have a dream that one day even the state of Mississippi, a state sweltering with the heat of injustice, sweltering with the heat of oppression, will be transformed into an oasis of freedom and justice.

I have a dream that my four little children will one day live in a nation where they will not be judged by the color of their skin, but by the content of their character.

I have a dream that one day all of God's children will be able to sing with a new meaning, 'My country 'tis of thee, sweet land of liberty, of thee I sing. Land where my fathers died, land of the pilgrim's pride, from every mountainside, let freedom ring.'"

The Lincoln Memorial was an ironic choice for King's "dream" speech. At the dedication ceremony back in 1922, blacks were seated in a segregated section. The black speaker at the dedication, Robert Russa Moton, president of the Tuskegee Institute, spoke from a text censored by the sponsors of the event before he delivered it. Among the deleted passages was a statement that the Lincoln Memorial was "but a hollow mockery, a symbol of hypocrisy, unless we can make real in every state and every section, the things for which he died."

In 1963, a shotgun blast killed the NAACP's Medgar Evers as he walked from his car to his front door in Mississippi. The killing was dismissed as "the inevitable result of agitation by do-gooders under the false flag of liberalism." Thirty-one years later, Bryon De La Beckwith was convicted of the murder. It turns out that the FBI knew who the murderer was all along. An informant had revealed that Beckwith bragged about every detail of the murder, but J. Edgar Hoover sat on the air-tight case, claiming he had to protect his informant's identity. That same year, a bomb ripped through a Birmingham church one Sunday morning killing four little black girls. Hoover again refused to co-operate with the Justice Department, claiming that to do otherwise would have compromised his Klan informants.

The story of Carl Hansberry, a prominent black real-estate developer, reflects one of the countless unsung struggles by individual African-Americans. It also points out the frustrations of fighting for equality through our legal system. In the 1930s, Hansberry wanted to move his family from one of Chicago's poor black neighborhoods to a nicer house in a community populated exclusively by whites. The white neighborhood's ethnic makeup was no accident; the homeowners had all signed an agreement pledging not to sell to blacks, a common arrangement at the time. The Hansberry family moved in anyway, and the neighbors sued to block them. The case went all the way to the U.S. Supreme Court, which in 1940 found in favor of Hansberry, but only on a technicality.

Carl Hansberry's daughter, Lorraine, became a celebrated playwright, fictionalizing her family's experience in one of the most important plays of the twentieth century. *A Raisin in the Sun* opened on Broadway in 1959. The play tells the story of a black family trying to decide what to do with an insurance check they received from the death of their father. The son wants to use the money to start a business; the daughter wants the money to fund her medical education; and the mother wants to move the family to a nicer house in a part of town reserved for whites. The family clashes over their differing dreams, but in the end they decide to move into the nicer house, over the white community's objections. Though their future remains uncertain, the play ends on a hopeful note.

Five years after the play opened to rave reviews, Lorraine Hansberry wrote an article describing the price a black person has to pay for peaceful non-violence.

> "My father was typical of a generation of Negroes who believed in the 'American way.' He undertook a battle to fight housing segregation in Chicago, a struggle that cost him a small personal fortune, his considerable talents, and many years of his life. That fight also required that our family occupy the disputed property in a hellishly hostile white neighborhood in which, literally, howling mobs surrounded our house. I remember my desperate and courageous mother, patrolling our house all night with a loaded pistol, doggedly guarding her four children, while my father fought the respectable part of the battle all the way up to the U.S. Supreme Court.
>
> The fact that my father 'won' a Supreme Court decision in a now famous case that bears his name, is ironically the sort of 'progress' our satisfied white friends allude to when they deride the more radical means of the black struggle. The cost, in emotional turmoil, time and money, which led to my father's early death, does not seem to figure in their calculations. And, after all his peaceful and sacrificial efforts, the Negroes of Chicago are as ghetto-locked as ever.

> That is the reality I am faced with when I now read that some Negroes say we must continue to act peacefully; we must lie down in the streets and tie up traffic in order to effectuate change. But, I know from personal experience that peaceful protests do not work. I am reminded of the final lines a Langston Hughes poem: 'What happens to a dream deferred? Does it explode?'"

J. Edgar Hoover, Director of the FBI since 1924, was an avowed white supremacist who thought the 1954 Supreme Court decision outlawing racial segregation in *Brown v. Board of Education* was a terrible error. In August 1963, he initiated a campaign to destroy Martin Luther King Jr., along with the civil rights movement. He tapped the telephones of King and his associates, bugged King's hotel rooms, and made tape recordings of King's conversations with and about women. The FBI then passed on the lurid details, including photographs, transcripts, and tapes, to Senator Strom Thurmond and other white supremacists. At FBI headquarters in Washington, King was classified as a "subversive" and purported communist.

In December 1963, less than a month after the assassination of John F. Kennedy, FBI officials met in Washington to explore ways of "neutralizing" King. The conference focused on how to "produce the best results without embarrassment to the Bureau." The result was that the FBI engaged in at least twenty clandestine burglaries to uncover incriminating material. FBI memos during this period reeked with racist language and a determination to "get" King.

The FBI campaign against King hit a new low in November 1964. The FBI, on instructions from J. Edgar Hoover, mailed King a cassette tape of recordings from fifteen illegal "bugs" placed in hotel rooms that he stayed in. The tapes contained intimate dialogues during sexual encounters with someone obviously not his wife. Included with the tape was an anonymous letter calling for King to commit suicide, otherwise the tape would be made public. Years later, the author of the letter was revealed to be William Sullivan, second in command at the FBI.

While the campaign to destroy Martin Luther King was picking up speed, other black leaders were discarding non-violence for a more militant activism. On February 21, 1965, Black Nationalist leader Malcolm X was assassinated while speaking in Harlem. Just before his assassination, he had come out against the Vietnam War. Malcolm's words had an incendiary bite to them: "Here lays the Vietnamese yellow man, killed by a black man, fighting for the white man, who killed all the red men."

Samuel Younge became active in the civil rights movement while a student at the Tuskegee Institute. In the winter of 1966, Younge was working as a voter registration volunteer. On January 3rd, he stopped at a service station to buy some cigarettes and use the toilet. When Younge discovered that blacks could not use the same facilities as whites, he complained to the owner, Marvin Segrest. During the argument that followed, Segrest picked up his gun and shot Younge dead. Younge was the fifth civil rights worker killed in Alabama within 12 months. After a protest march was organized by the students at the Tuskegee Institute, Segrest was arrested and charged with murder. An all-white jury found Segrest not guilty.

The day after Younge's funeral, SNCC's chairman, John Lewis, read the following statement at a press conference: "The murder of Samuel Younge is no different than the murder of peasants in Vietnam, for both are seeking the rights guaranteed them by law. We are in sympathy with, and support, the men in this country who are unwilling to respond to a military draft that would compel them to contribute their lives to United States aggression in Vietnam in the name of the 'freedom' we find so false in this country." Mainstream black leaders quickly distanced themselves from the Lewis speech, while white America was horrified by his condemnation of our government. Julian Bond, a black activist who had won election to the Georgia legislature with 82 percent of his district's votes, was asked if he supported Lewis's statement, "Sure I support it," he said. Bond's fellow legislators labeled him a traitor and barred him from being sworn in.

Black activists no longer used the word Negro or African-American – "Black" was in and "Black Power" was what they wanted. The peaceful demonstrations of Martin Luther King were not working fast enough for them and the country was doing nothing to prevent the killing of their best men. Activists like Stokely Carmichael decided to take matters into their own hands. "Black Power means arming black people and bringing this country to its knees. We are determined to gain our freedom by any means necessary."

Bobby Seale, co-founder of the Black Panther Party equated its actions to those of the panther in the jungle: "It is not in the panther's nature to attack anyone first, but when he is backed into a corner he will respond viciously and wipe out the aggressor." Seale advocated, "no more praying and boot-licking. No more singing 'We shall overcome.' The only way to 'overcome' is to apply righteous power." Seale quoted China's Mao Tse-tung: "Political power grows out of the barrel of a gun." By the end of 1969, thirty members of the Black Panther Party were facing capital punishment, forty others life in prison, fifty-five were serving terms of up to 30 years, and another 155 were being sought.

Fred Hampton established the Chicago chapter of the Black Panther Party when he was a twenty-year-old college student in 1964. He set-up community service programs that included free breakfasts for schoolchildren and a medical clinic that did not charge for treatment. One of his greatest achievements was to persuade Chicago's most powerful street gangs to stop fighting against each other. The FBI opened a file on Fred Hampton in 1967. Over the next two years the file expanded to twelve volumes and over 4,000 pages. Wiretaps were placed on the telephones of every member of his family. In May 1968, Hampton's name was on the FBI's "Agitator Index" and he was designated a "key militant leader."

Just before dawn on December 4, 1969, a fourteen-man police team led by the FBI stormed Hampton's apartment. When the shooting was over, two Black Panthers were dead, including Fred Hampton and Mark Clark. Witnesses claim that Hampton was wounded in the shoulder and then executed by a shot to the head. The Panthers that survived the raid, including Hampton's pregnant girlfriend, were arrested and charged with attempting to murder the police.

At a press conference the next day, the police announced that the arrest team had been attacked by the "violent and extremely vicious" Black Panthers and had defended themselves accordingly. In a second press conference on December 8, the assault team was praised for their "remarkable restraint, bravery, and professional discipline" in not killing all the Panthers. An internal investigation was undertaken and the assault team was exonerated of any wrongdoing. Afterward, ballistic evidence revealed that only one bullet had been fired by the Panthers; nearly a hundred came from police guns.

By 1967, black militancy had spread to the major inner cities. American ghettos had become war zones; seventy-five separate urban riots wracked the nation, resulting in 88 deaths, 1,397 injuries, 16,389 arrests, 2,157 convictions, and economic damage estimated at $664.5 million. Forty-three people were killed in Detroit, and twenty-six in Newark. Rage filled the streets of all the major cities. Black Panther leader Bobby Seale inflamed the situation more by telling blacks that when they saw a cop, "shoot him down – boom, boom, boom."

An 11-member commission called the Kerner Commission was established in July 1967 to investigate the causes of the race riots. Its mission was to answer the following questions: "What happened? Why did it happen? What can be done to prevent it from happening again and again?" The Commission's final report was released on February 29, 1968. The Kerner Commission placed the blame for the plight of blacks as a group on a single source: white racism. "What white Americans have never fully understood - but what the Negro can never forget - is that white society is deeply implicated in the ghetto. White institutions created it, white institutions maintain it, and white society condones it. White racism is essentially responsible for the explosive mixture which has been accumulating in our cities."

The Kerner Commission called upon the government to "close the gap between promise and performance" by creating new jobs, constructing new housing, and putting a stop to de-facto segregation. Its best-known quote was: "Our nation is moving toward two societies, one black and one white - separate and unequal."

President Johnson had his own ideas about the cause of the race riot; he called a cabinet meeting, demanding to know whether the Communists were behind all the riots. LBJ believed in the right to dissent, but "he did not believe that it should be exercised." When the safety of the nation was at stake, the people and their elected representatives should support the president and not publicly question or criticize his decisions. He was also concerned that white Democratic voters were switching their liberal political allegiances over to the conservative "law and order" Republican Party. Referring to Martin Luther King, he told his close confidants, "I'm not going to let that goddamn nigger preacher and his communist friends take over this government." Governor Ronald Reagan of California echoed the sentiments of white conservative America: "We must reject the idea that every time the law is broken, society is guilty rather than the lawbreakers. It is time to move against these dissidents; it is time to say, obey the rules or get out."

When more troops were needed for Vietnam, Lyndon Johnson approved *Project 100,000*, which he claimed was part of his 'Great Society' economic program. Instead of calling up the Army Reserves or the National Guard or abolishing student deferments – all of which would further inflame war protesters and 'white' America – LBJ conceived a plan that would draft the poor into the war and at the same time remove young black agitators from the streets. *Project 100,000* recruiters swept through urban ghettos and southern rural back roads. In all, 354,000 men were enrolled and given a one-way ticket to Vietnam. Inside our government, *Project 100,000* was laughingly known as the call-up of our 'moron' troops.

Heavyweight champion Muhammad Ali refused army induction claiming that the Vietnam War was wrong: "No Vietcong ever called me a nigger." Ali became a hero to the anti-war movement, but the white establishment lifted his title, convicted him of draft evasion, and sentenced him to five years in prison. Free on bail pending appeals, the defrocked champion could not fight in a boxing ring for three years.

A number of civil rights leaders urged Martin Luther King to keep quiet about the growing U.S. military intervention in Vietnam, but he could no longer separate the issues of economic injustice, racism, war, and militarism. In a speech to 3,000 congregants at the Riverside Church in New York, exactly one year before his assassination, he spoke out.

> "A few years ago there was a real promise of hope for the poor, both black and white, through the poverty program. There were experiments, hopes, and new beginnings. Then came the buildup in Vietnam, and I realized that America would never invest the necessary funds or energies in rehabilitation of its poor so long as adventures like Vietnam continued to draw men and skills and money like some demonic, destructive suction tube.
>
> Perhaps a more tragic recognition of reality took place when it became clear to me that the war was doing far more than devastating the hopes of the poor at home. It was sending the poor to fight and to die in extraordinarily high proportions relative to the rest of the population. We were taking the black young men who had been crippled by our society and sending them eight thousand miles away to guarantee liberties in Southeast Asia which they had not found in southwest Georgia and East Harlem. We faced the cruel irony of watching Negro and white boys on TV screens as they kill and die together for a nation that has been unable to seat them together in the same schools. We watch them in brutal solidarity burning the huts of a poor village, but we realize that they could not live on the same block in Chicago. I could not be silent in the face of such cruel manipulation of the poor.

> Over the last three years as I walked among the desperate, rejected, and angry young men of America, I have told them that violence would not solve their problems. But they asked, and rightly so, "What about Vietnam? Wasn't our nation using massive doses of violence to solve its problems, to bring about the changes it wanted?" Their questions hit home, and I knew that I could never again raise my voice against the violence of the oppressed in the ghettos without having first spoken clearly to the greatest purveyor of violence in the world today: my own government. For the sake of those boys, for the sake of this government, for the sake of the hundreds of thousands trembling under our violence, I cannot be silent. Somehow this madness must cease."

The historic Riverside Church speech ignited a firestorm of criticism throughout the black community, the media, and the federal government. Prominent black leaders rushed to distance themselves from King's ringing denunciation of our Vietnam policy. The NAACP and the Urban League rejected King's dissent on the war. Senator Edward Brooke of Massachusetts, the only black senator in the country, registered shock and disapproval, as did other eminent blacks, including Ralph Bunche, Undersecretary-General of the United Nations. They criticized King for the grave tactical error of linking racial reform with the peace movement.

The FBI used the Riverside Church speech to draw renewed momentum for its ongoing campaign to destroy King. Six days after the speech, Hoover sent a highly secretive classified file on King to the White House and to highly placed Washington officials, including the secretary of state, secretary of defense, and the attorney-general. The document included allegations about communist influence. The report claimed that King's anti-war views paralleled those of the Communist Party. According to the FBI, King's speech could have been drafted in Hanoi. The FBI concluded that King "was an instrument in the hands of subversive forces seeking to undermine our nation."

Lies and Deceits

The FBI set up a highly controversial counterintelligence program called COINTELPRO, which included infiltration, wiretapping, and burglaries into left-wing civil rights organizations. The purpose of this program was to thwart the efforts of any organization the FBI considered a threat to our government. The FBI recruited more than 3,000 contacts or "listening posts." Spies infiltrated the anti-war and civil rights movements, especially the Black Panther Party and the Student Nonviolent Coordinating Committee (SNCC). In Atlanta, the site of the Southern Christian Leadership Conference (SCLC), the FBI was able to turn members of its executive staff into paid FBI informers. Surveillance targeted educators, union leaders, writers, entertainers, scientists, and organizations as diverse as the ACLU, NAACP, and the Nation of Islam. A secret list contained 26,000 names of citizens to be rounded up and detained in a "national emergency." An unknowing public dismissed charges of illegal FBI activities as "crackpot" exaggerations.

In 1968, Martin Luther King organized the *Poor People's Campaign* to address issues of economic injustice. It was this new direction that made King a major threat to the elite establishment. Economic equality threatened the very essence of capitalism and the powers that ran the system. According to King, what good was it to sit at an integrated lunch counter if you didn't have the money to buy a meal! Billions of U.S. tax dollars were being spent in Vietnam while poor people at home were living in shacks.

King's campaign culminated in his second massive march on Washington, this one aimed at obtaining economic aid to the poorest communities in the United States. King's plan was to bring thousands of poor people and supporters to the nation's capital to pressure Congress into passing an *Economic Bill of Rights*. King's call for a redistribution of the wealth in America was a much greater threat to the establishment than civil rights. It was one thing to give some black in Mississippi the right to drink water from a non-segregated water fountain; it was a completely different and totally unacceptable concept for the white establishment to eliminate poverty in this country at the expense of the rich.

The first *Poor People's* march originated in Marks, Mississippi - from there Dr. King criss-crossed the country, gathering "a multiracial army of the poor." King's program called for a massive federal government jobs program to rebuild America's cities. He saw a crying need to confront a Congress that was appropriating "military funds with alacrity and generosity," but providing "poverty funds with miserliness." He asked Congress for a $30 billion antipoverty package that included an increase in housing for the poor and a guaranteed annual income for poor people across the nation. The *Poor People's Campaign* did not focus on just blacks, but addressed the poor of every minority. King labeled the campaign the "second phase" of the civil rights struggle. The "first phase" focused on racial equality; this phase had to do with economic equality.

An editorial in the influential *Reader's Digest* magazine warned the nation that King's campaign would lead to "insurrection." It was bad enough that Middle America was protesting the war in Vietnam, but inciting them about economic injustice could turn 'peaceful' demonstrations into an armed revolution. The United States government was not waiting around for any revolution. Everyone connected with the *Poor People's Campaign* was placed under surveillance and FBI agents secretly infiltrated King's organization.

Martin Luther King was assassinated in Memphis, Tennessee, on April 4, 1968. He came to Memphis to support the city's 1,100 striking sanitation workers, 90 percent of whom were black. The workers staged a peaceful march on March 28 and the police responded with mace and clubs. Looting and rioting began almost immediately. Hundreds were bloodied; one person was killed. When the violence could not be stopped by the local authorities, the National Guard was sent in.

The night before his assassination, King delivered a prophetic speech to a crowd of 2,000 gathered in a local church.

> "I don't know what will happen to me now, but it really doesn't matter because I have been to the mountaintop. Longevity has its place, but I am not concerned about that now. God has allowed me to

see the Promised Land. So I am happy tonight. I am not worried about anything. I do not fear any man."

When King's assassination was announced, FBI agents in the Atlanta office cheered. With King dead, the *Poor People's Campaign* quickly lost its focus and came to an end. The powerful elite establishment had won; the poor and powerless lost once again.

King's purported killer was James Earl Ray, a high school dropout and two-bit criminal. Ray began his life of crime by stealing a typewriter in Los Angeles in 1949, holding up a Chicago cab in 1952, stealing money orders in 1955, and robbing a supermarket of $120 in 1959.

After King's assassination, James Earl Ray remained a fugitive from the law until he was arrested in London on June 8, 1968. His court appointed lawyer informed Ray that the FBI knew the whereabouts of his father, an escaped convict, and they would send his father back to prison if Ray did not confess to the King murder. Ray was guaranteed that if he cooperated he would be pardoned within two years. Ray confessed to the murder on March 10, 1969.

James Earl Ray, a small-time thief and burglar, had never before committed a violent crime and never fired a rifle since his discharge from the Army in the late 1940s. The case against him never came to trial. He was sentenced to 99 years in the state penitentiary. Two days after his sentencing, Ray withdrew his confession and claimed he never shot King. He asked for a public hearing, but his request was denied. Instead, the FBI investigated and concluded that James Earl Ray was a loner motivated by race hatred. Ray, however, kept contending that he was innocent.

The King family met with Ray several times in prison and did their own independent investigation. King's widow, Coretta King, publicly stated that she did not believe Ray had anything to do with her husband's murder. She told those who were willing to listen, "You have to understand that when you take a stand against the establishment, every attempt will be made to discredit you. When that fails, it will ultimately result in your physical termination or assassination." In 1997, King's son, Dexter King, proclaimed James Earl Ray innocent of his father's murder and accused the federal government of being responsible. Ray died in prison on April 23, 1998 from complications related to a kidney disease, supposedly caused by hepatitis contracted from a blood transfusion given at the prison.

Before James Earl Ray died, he wrote a book entitled, *Who Killed Martin Luther King Jr.?* The Reverend Jesse Jackson, who was with King at the time of his death, wrote the Forward:

> "No thoughtful person, after reviewing the evidence, can believe that this one man, James Earl Ray – who bungled everything he ever tried, including criminal activity – acted alone, killed Martin Luther King, escaped during the evening traffic rush, traveled to Canada and England with international passports, avoided an international network in search of him, and was only caught sometime later. Such a scenario strains the imagination, not to mention the reasoning process.
>
> I have never accepted the 'one crazy man' theory of political assassinations. I always believed there was a conspiracy in Dr. King's assassination. I always believed that the government was part of this conspiracy, either directly or indirectly, to assassinate him because of their deep emotional hatred and fear of Dr. King, who they perceived as a threat to our national security. Dr. King threatened the interests of the military-industrial complex and the ideology and mentality of the Cold War warriors. Thus, he had to die."

John F. Kennedy, Robert Kennedy, and Martin Luther King were all assassinated within four years. The question is not who pulled the trigger, but why were these men killed? Were they isolated coincidences or conspiracies? Was it an FBI-CIA-Mafia connection, or was each assassin an unrelated lone malcontent?

Have we been told the truth or deceived once again? The official explanations seem too incredulous – so do the conspiracy theories. Americans should keep asking – why were these men killed – who was threatened by their presence? Therein lays the answer.

CHAPTER EIGHTEEN

VIETNAM

"We are not about to send American boys 9,000 or 10,000 miles away from home to do what Asian boys ought to be doing for themselves. There will not be a mindless escalation of the war in Vietnam."

President Lyndon Johnson

"Hey, hey, LBJ; how many kids did you kill today?"

Popular anti-war slogan on college campuses.

"What the hell is going on? I thought we were winning this war."

Walter Cronkite
CBS Newscaster

Vietnam did not simply happen. Men of power and responsibility, sitting behind their desks in Washington caused this disastrous war. Our 'best and brightest,' shielded by a body of lies and deceits and the words 'top secret,' maneuvered and manipulated our country down the road to war and bitter defeat.

Vietnam, a country of no strategic importance, became a defining moment in American political history. We fought this war because of a misguided policy that we had to contain communism wherever it erupted, even if it was the people's choice. The United States was willing to destroy a country and its inhabitants in order to save it from themselves – and four U.S. presidents; Eisenhower, Kennedy, Johnson, and Nixon, Democrats and Republicans, all lied to the American people and went along for the ride.

Ironically, when the conflict in Vietnam ended in a communist victory, the rest of Southeast Asia remained intact. The so-called "domino" theory to justify the war was bogus. Countries did not topple one after another into the communist camp. The American public had been hoodwinked once again.

The indisputable facts about the war are these: the longest war in U.S. history lasted 11 years, but there was never an official declaration of war by the U.S. Congress; 70,000 Americans fled to Canada to avoid the draft; we dropped over 7 million tons of bombs on Vietnam compared to 2 million tons during all of World War II; an estimated 3 million people were killed and over 1 million were wounded; 58,168 Americans were killed and another 211,471 were casualties.

On January 23, 1973, the U.S. signed an agreement "to end the war and bring peace with honor in Vietnam and Southeast Asia." We sent all our troops home, but the fighting in Vietnam continued. By 1975, all of South Vietnam was in communist hands and no one in the United States cared any more. There are those who are ashamed that we lost the war and there are those who are ashamed that we fought it - but shame is the common denominator.

The war in Vietnam was really two wars. The first involved the French from 1946-1954. Vietnam had been a French colony since the ninetieth century. Generations of French families built lives there, carving rubber plantations out of the jungle, and turning the capital city of Saigon into an exotic colonial outpost.

During World War II, when Japan invaded Vietnam, the French fled. An army of communist partisans led by Ho Chi Minh, waged guerrilla war against the Japanese occupiers, using weapons dropped to them by the Americans. Ho's forces called themselves the Viet-American Army. After the Japanese surrender, Ho Chi Minh, declared his country's independence.

On September 2, 1945, before a large crowd in the northern city of Hanoi, Ho Chi Minh read Vietnam's new Declaration of Independence. The document is noteworthy because of the aims and ideals it espoused. Its first sentence read: "All men are created equal. They are endowed by their Creator with certain inalienable rights; among these are Life, Liberty, and the pursuit of Happiness."

Ho Chi Minh was an ardent admirer of America's fight for independence against the British and he wanted his country's ideals to be based on the righteousness of that struggle. Just as America's Declaration of Independence listed our grievances against England; Ho Chi Minh's document incorporated Vietnam's grievances against the French:

> "For more than eighty years, the French imperialists, abusing the standard of Liberty, Equality, and Fraternity, have violated our Fatherland and oppressed our fellow citizens. They have acted contrary to the ideals of humanity and justice. In the field of politics, they have deprived our people of every democratic liberty. They have enforced inhuman laws; they have set up three distinct political regimes; in the North, the Center, and in the South of Vietnam, in order to wreck our national unity and prevent our people from being united. They have built more prisons than schools. They have mercilessly slain our patriots and drowned our uprisings in rivers of blood.
>
> In the fields of economics, they have fleeced us to the backbone, impoverished our people, and devastated our land. They have robbed us of our rice fields, our mines, our forests, and our raw materials. They have invented numerous unjustifiable taxes and reduced our people, especially our peasantry, to a state of extreme poverty, mercilessly exploiting our workers.
>
> In the autumn of 1940, when the Japanese invaded our territory to establish new bases in their fight against the Allies, the French colonialists either fled or surrendered, showing that they were

incapable of "protecting" us. From that date, our country ceased being a French colony and became a Japanese possession.

After the Japanese surrendered to the Allies, our people established the Democratic Republic of Vietnam. The truth is that we wrested our independence from the Japanese and not from the French. Our people have finally broken the chains and won independence. We have overthrown the monarchic regime that reigned supreme over us for dozens of centuries.

For these reasons, we, members of the Provisional Government, representing the whole Vietnamese people, declare that from now on we break off all relations of a colonial character with France; we repeal all the international obligations that France has so far subscribed to on behalf of Vietnam and we abolish all the special rights the French have unlawfully acquired in our Fatherland. We are determined to fight to the bitter end against any attempt by the French colonialists to re-conquer our country.

For these reasons, we solemnly declare to the world that Vietnam has the right to be a free and independent country, and we will sacrifice our lives and property in order to safeguard this new independence and liberty."

Between October 1945 and February 1946, Ho Chi Minh wrote eight letters to President Truman reminding him of the self-determination promises of the Atlantic Charter. Truman never replied.

In October 1946, the French bombarded Haiphong, a port in northern Vietnam, and there began the eight-year war between

Ho Chi Minh's Vietminh movement and the French over who would rule Vietnam. France's war in Vietnam had nothing to do with communism. France's great fear was that if an insurgency wrested Vietnam away, it would encourage a similar revolt in Algeria, which had a population of more than a million Algerian born French citizens. However, fighting a war is expensive and France after World War II was broke.

The U.S. State Department wanted a strong France to prop up a war-torn and devastated postwar Europe. If the price of a strong France was supporting her crumbling empire in Southeast Asia, America was ready to provide that support. The issue for America was France, not Vietnam. Vietnam was merely a minor irritant, one more in a long list of such trouble spots. On May 7, 1950, a deal was struck. France agreed to share coal and steel with Germany – an essential step in rebuilding Europe – and the United States began the flow of military supplies to France for use in Indochina. In the next four years, the United States would spend $2.5 billion to finance France's losing war in Southeast Asia, more than it spent through the Marshall Plan to rebuild France itself. And that was just the beginning.

France's war in Vietnam was reaching its climax when Dwight Eisenhower assumed the presidency in 1953. By that time China had fallen to the Communists; the Korean War was still being fought, and the United States was supplying the French with $1 billion annually for its war effort in Vietnam.

America's war 'hawks' within the Eisenhower administration considered the doctrine of massive retaliation "an easy way to conduct diplomacy." U.S. nuclear weapons, or perhaps simply the threat of nuclear weapons, would determine the global balance. The Pentagon developed such a plan for aiding the French in Vietnam. Aptly-named *Operation Vulture*, the plan called for massive bombing of Vietminh positions, followed by three atomic bombs.

The Joint Chiefs of Staff, Secretary of State John Foster Dulles, Vice President Richard Nixon, and Atomic Energy Commission Chairman Lewis Strauss all enthusiastically supported *Operation Vulture*. The use of nuclear weapons was rationalized because "we just cannot fight any other kind of war against a fanatically committed bunch of guys who don't need anything except a bag of rice."

Eisenhower's caveat was that France and Britain had to first endorse the nuclear attacks. To prepare the political and diplomatic ground, Senate Majority Leader Lyndon Johnson was consulted and his support was secured. The president then explained the situation to Congress. If Vietnam fell, the rest of Asia, including, possibly, Taiwan and Japan, would soon follow. This "domino theory" of what might happen – was never proven, nor did it ever happen. It was a fear tactic to get the American public and Congress to support the administration's war aims.

Britain's Winston Churchill, however, did not believe British public opinion would support the use of atomic bombs and he challenged the assumption that the loss of Vietnam would lead to the collapse of Western influence in Asia. The French were no more receptive. French Foreign Minister Bidault declined the U.S. offer, thinking it impossible to predict China's response, and "if those nuclear bombs are dropped on Vietnam, our side will suffer as much as the enemy."

On May 7, 1954, the French government had enough and sued for peace. The Geneva Accords provided for a general election within two years to reunify the country. The Accords were endorsed and signed by all but one of its participants - only the United States did not join in the agreement. France officially ended its rule over Vietnam on October 9, 1954. Under a rainy sky, a small group of soldiers assembled around a flagpole at the Mangin Athletic Stadium in Hanoi and lowered the Tricolor flag. There were no songs or speeches. In its misbegotten eight-year war, France lost a staggering 44,967 dead and another 79,560 wounded.

Ho Chi Minh had inflicted a stunning defeat on a far richer and seemingly more powerful enemy. He was the country's most popular figure. His victory was not complete because Vietnam had to remain divided for two years, but two years is not long for most Vietnamese; then Ho Chi Minh would reunify their country.

Secretary of State Dulles, however, was not going to sit idly by for two years and watch Vietnamese voters elect a Communist to lead a unified Vietnam. Instead, he set out to undermine the Geneva agreement by making the country's division permanent.

To direct this ambitious project, Dulles chose Colonel Edward Lansdale, the most accomplished American counterinsurgency expert of that era. Lansdale had won a great victory by crushing guerrillas in the Philippines, working in partnership with an English-speaking Filipino leader, Ramon Magsaysay, who was installed as America's puppet president. Lansdale needed the same kind of partner for his Vietnam project. One was waiting.

Ngo Dinh Diem was a devout Catholic who came from a long line of Vietnamese mandarins. He had studied public administration and while still in his thirties served as interior minister in Vietnam's pro-French cabinets. In 1950, he traveled to the United States where he spent two years living an ascetic life at Maryknoll seminaries in New Jersey and upstate New York. He also made valuable political contacts, including New York's Cardinal Spellman, who made a special point of introducing him to Catholic politicians, among them Senator John F. Kennedy of Massachusetts.

When the Americans had to find a Vietnamese to be their puppet ruler in Saigon, Diem was one of the few anyone knew. Neither Dulles nor Lansdale had ever met him, but Lansdale vouched for his anti-Communist credentials and that was all Dulles needed to hear. Diem was duly anointed.

Diem's government was anything but democratic. It was based on a Catholic minority in a predominantly Buddhist country. With Diem now firmly in control, Lansdale and the CIA began their anti-Communist campaign. Lansdale's tactics ranged from sabotaging city buses in Hanoi to paying soothsayers to predict doom under the Communists. One of his biggest projects was helping to set off an exodus of hundreds of thousands of Catholics from North to South, urging them to flee with a campaign that included radio messages proclaiming, "Christ has gone to the South" and "the Virgin Mary has departed from the North." None of this provoked the rebellion Lansdale expected. By 1961, Eisenhower had funneled more than $2 billion into Vietnam and the government in the South was more unpopular than ever as the nationwide elections drew closer.

Everyone realized that the elections would carry Ho Chi Minh to the presidency of a united Vietnam. Our intelligence sources estimated that "possibly 80 percent of the population" would vote for him. This presented the Americans with a serious dilemma. When an aide brought Secretary of State Dulles a cable from Diem, he immediately saw the way out. Dulles turned to those present at that meeting and said, "Diem does not want to hold elections and I believe we should support him in this." Democratic elections were cancelled since "our" man would have lost.

With no election, there could be no reunification. Instead, two new nations emerged: North Vietnam and South Vietnam. Ho ruled North Vietnam in traditional Communist fashion through a politburo made up of trusted comrades. In South Vietnam, Diem shaped a government made up of close relatives. Diem's eldest brother, Ngo Dinh Can, held no official post, but ruled central Vietnam like a feudal warlord. Another brother, Ngo Dinh Thuc, was a Catholic archbishop and also an avaricious investor who made a fortune in rubber, timber, and real estate. A third brother, Ngo Dinh Luyen, became ambassador to Britain. Most important of all was the president's fourth brother, Ngo Dinh Nhu, and his flamboyant wife, Madame Nhu, sometimes called the "Vietnamese Rasputin." She became President Diem's closest adviser and alter ego.

America's determination to defend an independent South Vietnam led Ho and his comrades to launch their third anti-colonial war. In 1960, they proclaimed a military campaign aimed at "the elimination of the U.S. imperialists and the Diem regime." A few months later, leaders of a dozen dissident political and religious groups announced the formation of a new coalition, the National Liberation Front; they would confront Diem politically while guerrillas called Viet Cong, waged war on the battlefield.

Secretary of State Dulles fell ill, retired, and died in 1958. After that, President Eisenhower seemed to lose interest in Vietnam. On January 19, 1961, the day before he left office, Eisenhower briefed President-elect Kennedy on world trouble spots. There was plenty to talk about. The pro-American regime in Laos was collapsing; an anti-colonial rebellion was raging in Algeria, and another seemed about to break out in the Congo. The CIA was training a secret army to invade Cuba in the hope of deposing Fidel Castro's new regime. Tensions were rising in Berlin. It took several months, though, for Kennedy to realize the oddest aspect of that meeting. "You know," JFK marveled to an aide, "Eisenhower never mentioned a word about Vietnam."

John F. Kennedy assumed the U.S. presidency and supported the prior administration's objectives in Vietnam. While he may have developed doubts about the U S. role in Indochina late in his administration, all his early public statements emphasized the importance of taking a stand in Vietnam. In May 1961, he secretly dispatched four hundred Special Forces (Green Berets) and another one hundred "advisers" to the anti-communist insurgency. Simultaneously, and with equal secrecy, the CIA began a covert war against North Vietnam - training, assisting, and infiltrating South Vietnamese sabotage teams into North Vietnam.

The U.S. military commitment in Vietnam was supposed to be limited to helping the South Vietnamese help themselves. Instead, the number of American soldiers in Vietnam rose from 675 to 16,500 during Kennedy's administration. We were no longer "advisers" – we were in active combat. Kennedy sent jet fighters, helicopters, heavy artillery, and all manner of other weaponry, none of which turned the tide of battle.

One of the first special envoys Kennedy sent to Vietnam was Vice President Lyndon Johnson. LBJ came back convinced that if the Communists were allowed to take South Vietnam they would soon push their war all the way to Hawaii. He went on to praise Diem as "the Churchill of Southeast Asia." When asked afterward about this appraisal, Johnson said, "Shit, Diem's the only boy we got out there," meaning that no one else fit American requirements.

As with so many of our other foreign adventures, the United States believed it could hand-pick a leader who appeared on the surface to be a crowd-pleasing nationalist, but would secretly govern according to Washington's wishes. Meanwhile, American troops kept pouring into Vietnam. Between 1961 and 1963, U.S.

Special Forces engaged in hundreds of firefights and American planes flew thousands of bombing sorties against Viet Cong positions. During that same period, 108 Americans were killed and the United States lost twenty-three aircraft.

When our U.N. Ambassador Nolting told Diem that the United States wished to "share in his decision making process,' Diem replied, "Vietnam does not want to be a protectorate." The CIA started calling him a reluctant protégé, a client who refused to behave like a client; a puppet who pulled his own strings. The worst news for America came when Diem's brother and chief adviser, Ngo Dinh Nhu, suggested that perhaps the time had come to negotiate with the Viet Cong. Nhu told a television interviewer, "I consider the communists as brothers; as lost sheep. I am not for an assault against the communists. We are a small country and we only want to live in peace."

The final act in the drama of Diem's rule began to unfolded when Buddhists gathered in the city of Hue to mark the 2,527th birthday of the Buddha. The local strongman, Ngo Dinh Can - the president's brother - decided to enforce an old decree prohibiting the celebrants from flying the traditional blue-red-saffron Buddhist flag, even though a few days earlier the sky had been aflutter with Catholic banners to mark the 25th anniversary of Archbishop Ngo Dinh Thuc's ordination. Buddhists began a series of protests. Police fired on them, killing a woman and eight children.

Buddhist leaders in Vietnam reacted by launching a nationwide campaign against Diem. They distributed leaflets, met with foreign journalists, and staged hunger strikes. People flocked to their cause, often for reasons that had little to do with religion. They were the 'have-nots' rebelling against the rich; ordinary people defying authoritarian power. When Diem did not respond to this campaign, Buddhist leaders announced that monks might commit suicide as a way of showing the depth of their anger. Diem dismissed the threat; so did the Americans in Washington.

On the morning of June 11, a monk named Thich Quang Duc burned himself to death. He was sixty-seven years old, had been a monk for nearly half-a-century, and was revered as a *bodhisattva*, a being on the path to enlightenment who chooses to forgo his own enlightenment in order to help others become enlightened. In a statement that his comrades distributed after his death, he made a "respectful" plea to Diem to show "charity and compassion" to all religions.

The ruling family's most outspoken member, Madame Nhu, ridiculed the burning spectacle, calling it a "barbecue." "Let them burn; we shall clap our hands," she said gleefully. Diem's response further shocked international opinion. He said he would "gladly supply the gasoline for other Buddhists." Thousands of monks were arrested; some were killed and many were brutally beaten. Diem's foreign minister resigned after shaving his head in symbolic solidarity with the Buddhist leadership.

By now the Viet Cong guerrillas had established control over 20 percent of South Vietnam and moved freely in an area twice that large. The South Vietnamese army was proving reluctant to fight and Diem was losing popularity. To keep order, he ruled with increasing repression. As the situation deteriorated, Kennedy decided to replace U.S. Ambassador Nolting. He considered naming Lansdale, but there was an unwritten rule against appointing CIA officers as ambassadors. Instead, he chose one of his oldest political rivals, Henry Cabot Lodge, an aristocratic pillar of the Republican establishment.

Lodge had represented Massachusetts in the U.S. Senate until 1952, when he lost his seat to JFK. After his defeat, Secretary of State Dulles arranged for him to be named Ambassador to the United Nations, where he played a supporting role in the overthrow of Jacobo Arbenz in Guatemala. In 1960, Lodge was Richard Nixon's running mate on the Republican ticket that lost to Kennedy. Cabot's prominence, his diplomatic experience, his strong political base in Washington, and his mastery of the French language made him a logical choice for the Vietnam post. Kennedy and his aides knew that the Saigon post was full of risks and he liked the idea of having a Republican to blame if things went wrong.

Lodge found South Vietnam in turmoil when he arrived on Friday evening, August 23, 1963. Growing unrest, including the self-immolation of four more Buddhist monks had led President Diem to place the country under martial law.

That weekend in Washington, in an appalling display of confusion, the Kennedy administration stumbled into a "regime change" operation destined to end in blood. It was the culmination of weeks of debate over how to deal with Diem. Some in the administration believed that he was still the best hope for South Vietnam; others had given up on him and called for his demise. On Saturday, August 24, all three of Diem's most powerful supporters in Washington were out of town. Secretary of State Dean Rusk was attending a Yankee baseball game in New York, Secretary of Defense Robert McNamara was vacationing in Wyoming, and President Kennedy was at his home on Cape Cod. That left the American foreign policy apparatus in the hands of three lower-ranking officials, all of whom wanted Diem overthrown.

The most eager of these was Assistant Secretary of State Roger Hilsman, the administration's chief East Asia specialist. Hilsman considered himself an expert on both counterinsurgency and the politics of Indochina. That Saturday, he drafted a fateful cable to Lodge. It directed Lodge to tell Diem directly that the United States "cannot tolerate a situation in which power lies in Nhu's hands, and to demand that Diem sever all political ties to his brother." If Diem refuses, the cable said, "We must face the possibility that Diem himself cannot be preserved." The cable needed a chain-of-command approval before it could be sent.

That afternoon, Hilsman and one of his chief allies, Undersecretary of State Averell Harriman, sought out George Ball who was acting head of the State Department in Rusk's absence. They found him on the ninth green of the Falls Road Golf Course in Maryland. Ball was the third member of the State Department's anti-Diem troika. He liked Hilsman's cable and agreed to telephone Kennedy and recommend that it be sent. For reasons that remain unclear, Kennedy did not focus on the seriousness of this cable. He may have been distracted by his weekend 'pursuits.' Ball phrased his appeal in terms that he knew would reassure the president. Kennedy made only one minor change in the message and then approved it. "If Rusk and Gilpatrick agree, then go ahead," Kennedy said.

Neither Dean Rusk nor Deputy Secretary of Defense Roswell Gilpatrick had yet been consulted, but Ball did not mention that. After hanging up, Ball called Rusk in New York and told him he was preparing to send a cable to Saigon that President Kennedy had already approved. Rusk, as was his habit, replied that anything the president approved was fine with him.

According to State Department protocol, a cable of this importance had to be approved not simply by the president and secretary of state but also by the secretary of defense, the director of the CIA, and the chairman of the Joint Chiefs of Staff. All were out of reach on that Saturday evening, so Ball checked with their deputies instead. Officials at that level do not have the courage to veto presidential directives and none tried to do so.

Once the anti-Diem group had secured these approvals, they needed only Kennedy's final go-ahead. Michael Forrestal, a member of the National Security Council, called Kennedy to obtain his approval. To his surprise, he found the president suddenly hesitant. He had been having second thoughts. "Are you sure about this?" Kennedy asked. Forrestal managed to reassure him, and that was that. At 9:43 that evening, a clerk at the State Department dispatched the cable.

The debate that should have taken place beforehand broke out on Monday morning. An angry Kennedy summoned his foreign policy advisers to the White House and began by sternly reprimanding Hilsman, Harriman, Ball, and Forrestal for what he called their "impulsiveness." General Maxwell Taylor, chairman of the Joint Chiefs, was just as upset. He said he would never have approved the cable, and accused those who drafted it of staging "an aggressive end run" that could only have been possible on a weekend. Vice President Johnson, Secretary of Defense McNamara, and CIA director John McCone, all warned that overthrowing Diem would create more problems than it would solve. The argument stretched out over four days of meetings, leaving Kennedy angry and frustrated.

The Kennedy administration now had to choose between awful alternatives: supporting a corrupt and unpopular government that was losing the war, or endorsing a coup to overthrow the government it had installed. From the vantage point of history, it is reasonable to ask why no one suggested the obvious third option. The United States could simply have washed its hands of the crisis and left it for the Vietnamese to resolve. That would probably have led to the establishment of Communist or pro-Communist rule over the entire country, but that is what ultimately happened anyway. A withdrawal at this point would have saved hundreds of thousands of lives, avoided the devastation of Vietnam, and spared the United States its greatest national trauma since the Civil War. Why did no one suggest it?

In fact, the idea did surface several times. Paul Kattenburg, chairman of the administration's Vietnam Interdepartmental Working Group, told the National Security Council on August 31 that the Vietnamese would never accept a foreign-backed regime in Saigon. He suggested that the time had come "for us to make the decision to get out honorably." Members of the National Security Council promptly slapped him down. "We will not pull out until the war is won," Rusk told him curtly to general approval.

On September 29, Nhu and his wife were reelected to the rubber-stamp parliament with identical winning percentages of 99 percent. A week later, another Buddhist monk burned himself to death, the first such suicide since the summer. On October 29, Kennedy gathered fifteen of his senior advisers for a final meeting about the imminent coup. Years later, a tape of that meeting surfaced. The transcript is deeply disturbing; a textbook example of how not to shape policy.

Kennedy's advisers presented differing views, as would be expected. What was remarkable about this meeting though was that so many of the participants expressed serious doubts about the coup. Even more bizarre, no one suggested that if there was so much dissent, maybe the coup should be suspended or canceled. There was no call for a vote, or even any discussion of what repercussions a coup might have.

Even the president expressed doubts. "If we miscalculate, we might lose our position in Southeast Asia," he mused at one point. Then, speaking of Lodge, he said, "Looks to be his ass. He's for a coup. He thinks there are good reasons for it. I say he's much stronger for it than we are here. Let's put the whole decision on him." With that cryptic, perhaps flippant comment, the coup was finally approved even though Kennedy and his advisers did not support it.

Some days later, the president was at a meeting in the Cabinet Room of the White House when Michael Forrestal rushed in with the report that Diem and Nhu were dead. JFK was stunned. Apparently he never considered the possibility that the coup might end this way. A set of photos were forwarded to Washington showing the mangled bodies of Diem and his brother with their hands still tied behind their backs.

At a White House staff meeting on the morning of November 4, the president's national security adviser, McGeorge Bundy, warned that the pictures would undoubtedly be in all the newspapers within a day or two. People would draw the obvious conclusion. "This is not the preferred way to commit suicide," Bundy dryly observed.

Kennedy was disconsolate. The killings in Saigon shook his confidence in the kind of advice he was getting. He also realized that the first Catholic ever to become a Vietnamese chief of state was dead, assassinated as a direct result of a policy authorized by the first American Catholic president.

The 1963 coup in South Vietnam had a profound effect in Washington. It led many policy makers to believe that the United States had assumed a new level of responsibility for South Vietnam. If the idea of pulling American troops out had seemed crazy before the coup, it was even more so afterward. "No one," Undersecretary of Defense William Bundy said, "could now consider withdrawing with the task unfinished."

Several of the men involved in planning the coup later came to consider it tragically misbegotten. General Maxwell Taylor wrote in his memoir that from the perspective of history, it could only be seen as "a disaster." Edward Lansdale said it was "a terribly stupid thing." William Colby, chief of CIA covert actions in East Asia and later director of the Agency, called it the "worst mistake of the Vietnam War."

The Kennedy administration never publicly admitted that it supported the coup. On June 30, 1964, when Henry Cabot Lodge returned to the United States, he gave a long interview to the *New York Times* in which he said: "The overthrow of the Diem regime was a purely Vietnamese affair. We never participated in the planning. We never gave any advice. We had nothing to do with it." That of course was a lie.

General Duong Van Minh, who carried out the coup, succeeded Diem as president. After holding power for just three months, he was overthrown in another coup. After that, a succession of military strongmen ruled South Vietnam. President Kennedy told several of his close associates that if he was reelected in 1964, he would pull American troops out of Vietnam. Whether he would have remains unknown. On November 22, just twenty days after Diem was assassinated, Kennedy suffered the same fate. Lyndon Baines Johnson was now president.

Lyndon Johnson of Texas was first and foremost a southerner. Despite his state's infamous long record of corruption, LBJ was reputed to be the biggest stealer of votes and elections in Texas political history. His voting record in the U.S. Senate for twenty years was consistent; he never supported any civil rights legislation. He not only could lie with the best, he was a master at invention. He often talked of his great-great-grandfather having died at the Alamo. When challenged, he said, "No, it was actually the battle of San Jacinto," but as biographer Doris Kearns Goodwin noted, that was not right either. Johnson's ancestor was a real estate trader who died at home in bed.

Lyndon Johnson agreed to become JFK's vice-president because he knew no southerner could ever become president on his own. Texas would always be considered a confederate state, and the eight most populous states in the country were all in the north or the west. This was his only chance to rise to the ultimate top.

LBJ had a complex about John F. Kennedy. Kennedy was young, rich, good looking, and well polished – the complete opposite of LBJ – except maybe for the womanizing. Upon assuming the presidency, he said to the nation, "I will do my best. That is all I can do. I ask for your help and God's." Privately, he told those who were close to him, "I don't believe I'll ever get credit for anything I do in foreign affairs - no matter how successful I may be. I didn't go to Harvard."

The United States might have won the war in Vietnam had it been willing to unleash its vast military arsenal, expand the military draft, and muzzle the press and dissension. But, Eisenhower and Kennedy were not willing to take such radical steps. Instead, we fought a war of containment; essentially fighting under the same constraints as during the Korean War. Neither Eisenhower nor Kennedy wished to risk a world war by using all the military means at our disposal to destroy the enemy.

General Curtis LeMay's solution was "to bomb North Vietnam back to the Stone Age." LBJ agreed; the only way to win in Vietnam was to increase the number of ground troops and escalate the bombings. The problem was how to get the American public to "buy into" an expansion of the war. Johnson had spent his entire life in the U.S. Senate manipulating people and "working out" difficult situations. This problem was no different – he just needed an opening. He was committed that the war in Vietnam would not be lost on "his shift."

In 1964, LBJ won a landslide election against Republican Senator Barry Goldwater of Arizona. Johnson portrayed Goldwater as a dangerous right-winger who wanted to expand the war in Vietnam and plunge the country into a nuclear confrontation with the Soviet Union. During the campaign, Johnson kept assuring the American public, "we are not about to send American boys 9,000 or 10,000 miles away from home to do what Asian boys ought to be doing for themselves."

LBJ's lies became apparent the following spring when he ordered a drastic escalation of the war. Draft calls rose rapidly. Between 1964 and 1965, the U.S. troop levels in South Vietnam went from 23,000 to 185,000. The escalation continued until more than half-a-million American soldiers were on duty in Vietnam.

In order to justify escalation, Johnson went on national television and lied once again to the American public. Lying came easy to LBJ and this was a classic performance. "The North Vietnamese regime has today deliberately launched an unprovoked attack against a U.S. destroyer that was on a routine patrol in the Gulf of Tonkin." According to Johnson, this "unprovoked attack" was followed by a "deliberate attack" on a pair of U.S. ships two days later. But, the truth was very different. Rather than being on a routine patrol, the U.S. destroyer *Maddox* was actually engaged in aggressive intelligence gathering maneuvers that was coordinated with offensive U.S. attacks.

Years later, White House tapes revealed President Johnson telling Secretary of Defense Robert McNamara that the attack on U.S. ships in the Gulf of Tonkin was pure fiction. No attack ever took place. In November 2005, the National Security Agency released documents that admitted, "The intelligence was deliberately skewed to support the notion that there had been an attack." Lyndon Johnson was preparing to bomb North Vietnam for two months. All he needed was fake intelligence that would fit perfectly into his preconceived policy. He got what he wanted.

Johnson's speech to the nation justifying the acceleration of the war won accolades from editorial writers. The *New York Times* proclaimed that the president "went to the American people last night with the somber facts," while the *Los Angeles Times* urged Americans to "face the fact that the Communists, by their attack on American vessels in international waters, have themselves escalated the hostilities." The *Washington Post* recited the White House line: "The United States turned loose its military might on North Vietnam last night to prevent the Communist leaders in Hanoi and Peking from making the mistaken decision that they could attack American ships with impunity."

American war propaganda was rived up, portraying Ho Chi Minh as a "devil" – the new Hitler that had to be eliminated. On August 7, 1964, Johnson went before Congress and asked for a war resolution that empowered him as commander-in-chief to do whatever he thought necessary to "repel an armed attack against the forces of the United States and to prevent further aggression."

The resolution passed the Senate by a vote of 88-2 and the House by a unanimous vote of 416-0. Two courageous senators, Wayne Morse of Oregon and Ernest Gruening of Alaska, provided the only "no" votes. Suddenly, the war in Vietnam became Johnson's war.

A declaration of war was thought not to be necessary because no one envisioned an 11-year war, or the massive build-up of American ground troops, or the ground swell of American opposition at home. It was hoped that our show of force would cause the North Vietnamese to halt their aggression. By the spring of 1965 it was obvious that was not going to happen, but the president did not want to go back to Congress and ask for a formal declaration of war. That might trigger a far wider war with both China and the Soviet Union.

Vietnam became the longest and ultimately the most unpopular war in United States history. While it lasted, the war directed vast financial resources to the military-industrial complex and diverted attention away from education, health care, America's infrastructure, and other needed social programs. The American public watched the war on television from the comfort of their living room, and then went about their business unconcerned, except for those who had loved ones in Vietnam.

When American deaths began mounting in Vietnam, the U.S. military high command inflated the number of Viet Cong deaths to make U.S. deaths seem insignificant in comparison. It is now known that the United States military systematically over-reported the number of enemy 'kills.' It is also clear that the press corps, with few exceptions, accepted these official numbers and reported them dutifully to the American public. We thought we were winning, but we were actually losing. According to our nation's leaders, the American public was being lied to "for its own good," like a child that does not have the mental capacity to comprehend the complexities of the situation.

When our brave young men began returning home without arms and legs, and told the American public of the horrors they experienced in Vietnam, the nation woke up. The war was no longer like some Monday night football game. Americans began to protest, and the protest grew into a crescendo that polarized American society.

There were those who demanded we fight to the bitter end, for admitting defeat was not the American way. Others vocally demanded that we pull out and go home; there was no communist menace and no domino theory - Vietnam was a civil war. Americans began asking: was the real enemy Hanoi, China, Russia; or was America seeking wider spheres of influence?

President Johnson feared that the American anti-war movement would drive him out of the White House. In 1967, he became convinced that the dissension was controlled and financed by communist influence inside the United States and he ordered the CIA to produce the evidence.

CIA Director Richard Helms reminded him that the Agency was barred from spying on Americans. LBJ told Helms: "I'm quite aware of that. What I want for you is to pursue this matter and to do what is necessary to track down the communists who are behind this intolerable interference in our domestic affairs." Helms obeyed the president's orders. In a blatant violation of his powers, the director of the CIA became a part-time secret police chief.

The CIA undertook a domestic surveillance operation codenamed *Chaos* that went on for almost seven years. Helms created a Special Operations Group to conduct the spying. They began working in secret with police departments all over the United States. CIA officers grew their hair long and infiltrated peace groups. Radical college students were especially targeted as were unfriendly journalists. In all, the CIA compiled a computer index of 300,000 names of American people and organizations, and extensive files on 7,200 American citizens.

Senator William Fulbright, chairman of the influential Senate Foreign Relations Committee, had supported the Gulf of Tonkin Resolution in August 1964, but by the summer of 1966 he realized that the president had lied to the American public. Fulbright now decided that our policy in Vietnam was misguided, doomed to fail, and part of a larger pattern of errors that if not changed would bring disastrous consequences for America and the world.

Fulbright published his views on Vietnam and his general critique of American foreign policy in his famous book, *The Arrogance of Power*. Fulbright's essential argument was that great nations get into trouble and go into long-term decline when they are "arrogant" in the use of their power, doing things they should not do and in places they should not be. He was suspicious of any foreign policy rooted in missionary zeal. He also thought that when we bring our power to bear in the service of an abstract concept, like anti-communism, without understanding local history, culture, and politics, we do more harm than good.

Dissent over the war in Vietnam now accelerated. SDS (Students For a Democratic Society) became the largest and most powerful 'New Left' organization in the 1960s. Started at the University of Michigan, its agenda was to make America aware of the injustices of poverty, racism, and the war in Vietnam. J. Edgar Hoover was convinced that the SDS was a creature of the American Communist Party, funded and controlled by secret agents of the Soviet KGB. He hired and trained provocateurs to infiltrate the movement and lure the protesters into felonies and public disgrace.

Other movements grew out of SDS. The Weathermen broke with SDS because they wanted a more violent and radical approach to change in America. The name 'Weatherman' was derived from Bob Dylan lyrics: "You don't need a weatherman to know which way the wind blows."

In order to avoid FBI infiltration and surveillance, the Weathermen split into small four or five-person "cells" and prepared to strike. In the first week of March 1970, the New York cell plotted to bomb Columbia University. One of the Weathermen, twenty-eight-year-old Diana Oughton, had been running a preschool in Ann Arbor, Michigan, less than two years earlier with her boyfriend Bill Ayers. They were trying to change the world through education, but nothing was happening. Now their tactics changed. However, they were inexperienced at this kind of warfare and the bombs they assembled exploded in their Greenwich Village town house. Weathermen Terry Robbins and Ted Gold, as well as Diana Oughton were instantly killed. After the tragedy, an extensive FBI hunt began. The Weathermen fanned out across the country, assumed false identities and contacted each other from pay phone at designated times. They would keep bombing government targets – often, with a prior warning to avoid killing any people.

Various groups, less militant than the Weathermen, protested recruitment on college campuses by the military-industrial complex and the CIA, the military draft, the financing of apartheid in South Africa by American banks, napalm production by Dow Chemical, and CIA involvement in Latin America. They tried to raise the consciousness of Americans by asking: what is the difference between throwing 500 babies into a fire and throwing fire from airplanes on 500 babies? Most of the demonstrations were peaceful, but depending on the organization and the level of frustration, violence did break out. When that happened, the FBI and the police brutally put an end to it.

President Johnson lashed out against those Americans who voiced opposition to the war in Vietnam. He accused the dissenters of betraying our nation's fighting men who were dying so Americans at home could enjoy the fruits of freedom. "We seek no wider war," LBJ assured the public. "Our bombing targets are only against military targets and they have been chosen with the greatest of care." Of course that was another lie. Napalm was incinerating thousands of innocent women and children in non-military areas. Johnson's lies that "we seek no wider war," were backed up by Secretary of Defense Robert McNamara, and at least a hundred officials within the administration became accomplices by their silence.

In the beginning, American public opinion was strongly against the student anti-war demonstrations. The Veterans of Foreign Wars held parades throughout the country, carrying signs that read: "Love America or leave it." High ranking government officials told the public that the anti-war advocates "just don't understand the Asiatic mind or the importance of stopping communism over there before it spreads to all free nations." Vice President Hubert Humphrey told students, "the alternative is just to leave Vietnam and admit defeat and we will not do that." Senator Ted Kennedy told angry students, "We know what you are against, but what are you for?" When asked what his position was, Ted Kennedy replied, "I am opposed to unilateral withdrawal."

Blaming dissent at home for problems on the battlefield became a standard tactic as the war went from bad to worse. It was the oldest alibi of frustrated generals and political leaders who claim, "We could have won the war if it had not been for those unpatriotic civilians back home." General William Westmoreland asserted that despite "repeated military defeats, the enemy is able to continue the struggle because he is encouraged by what he believes to be popular opposition in the United States."

To this kind of argument, the dissenters had a ready rebuttal. Although the United States enjoyed advantages over North Vietnam that included incalculably superior technological military power; the inherent long-term commitments of the two sides were tilted in opposite directions. For us the war was a nuisance that we wanted ended as soon as possible. The North Vietnamese, however, were fighting a life-and-death struggle for their national identity and homeland. They were prepared to fight and die until they won. Our young men and women were not willing to die for Vietnam. Vietnam was not our country. Johnson kept insisting that American forces were in Vietnam to repel aggression and that "if they will go home tomorrow, we will go home." The only problem was – the Vietnamese were home.

The CIA issued a top secret report to the president that the war had been a terrible mistake. There were not going to be any dominoes falling and the Red Army was not going to land on the beaches of California. Life would go on much as it had before the Vietnam War. But, nobody in power wanted to admit defeat.

By late 1966, the United States was spending $20 billion annually on the war. Millions of people around the world equated the United States with the picture of the naked little girl running down the road in Vietnam, fleeing a napalm attack. Defenseless cities in Vietnam were bombarded from the air, the inhabitants butchered like cattle. Back home, our public relations people told the American public that these attacks were part of a 'pacification' program.

Lies and Deceits

Harrison Salisbury of the *New York Times* visited North Vietnam and wrote a series of twenty-two articles beginning in December 1966. He reported eighty-nine civilian deaths in one town, forty in a second, twenty-four in a third, and that we were dropping more bombs in this "brush-fire war" than had been dropped on Japan during World War II. In Nam Dinh, North Vietnam's third largest city, he wrote of "block after block of utter desolation." He said the targeting of civilians was going on "deliberately" in order to get the North Vietnamese to end the war.

The Pentagon attacked Salisbury viciously. They assured the American public that Salisbury's reports were blown out of proportion. Maybe, they reluctantly admitted, a few hundred North Vietnamese civilians were accidentally killed. War hawks like Senator Bourke Kickenlooper of Iowa said it was hardly surprising that Hanoi would "let a *New York Times* reporter in rather than objective reporters." House Armed Services Committee chairman Mendel Rivers said we should "flatten Hanoi and tell the world to go fly a kite." Senator Sam Erwin endorsed that view, "We ought to bomb the North Vietnamese out of existence."

By 1967, lying about Vietnam had become a Washington way of life, and the biggest lie was that we were winning the war. When Defense Secretary McNamara was returning from a "fact-finding" mission in Vietnam, he asked his consultant Daniel Ellsberg, "Are we winning?"

Ellsberg replied that over the course of the last year things were pretty much the same. "We've put a hundred thousand more troops into Vietnam during the past year," McNamara said to Ellsberg. "That means the situation is really worse." When their plane landed in Washington, McNamara lied to the waiting reporters. "Gentlemen, I have just come back from Vietnam, and I am glad to report that we are showing great progress in every dimension of our effort."

In 1969, U.S. journalist Seymour Hersh exposed the My Lai massacre and the subsequent cover-up by the U.S. Army. Hersh received the Pulitzer Prize for International Reporting for his expose. Over 500 Vietnamese, mostly women and children, were massacred in cold blood by American soldiers. The only U.S. casualty was one self-inflicted gunshot wound in the foot.

Although the Army covered up the incident, a discharged helicopter gunner named Ron Ridenhour challenged the Army version by writing to several members of Congress. An Army investigation led to Lt. William Calley's arrest in September 1969 and he was charged with several counts of premeditated murder.

Calley defended himself at his military trial on these grounds: "In all my years in the army I was never taught that communists were human beings. We were there to kill ideology carried out by pawns, blobs, and pieces of flesh. I was there to destroy communism. We never conceived of communists as old people, men, women, children, or babies." His testimony was jarringly reminiscent of the Germans who testified at Nuremberg about the Holocaust.

In March 1971, Calley was found guilty of twenty-two murders and given a life sentence. Of the twenty-five other U.S. soldiers initially charged, none were convicted. President Nixon confined Calley to his barracks while he appealed his sentence. Other than the three-and-a-half years of house arrest pending the outcome of his trials, Calley never served any time in prison. In April 1974, Calley's sentence was reduced to ten years; that November he was paroled by the Secretary of the Army.

The atrocities at My Lai outraged the American public and added to the growing public dissent against the war. Unfortunately, incidents like My Lai happen in every war by both sides. Scared and frightened, battle-fatigued, lack of sleep and living in swamp infested jungles, young men who have seen the horrors of war over-react to real or perceived dangers. Often times they cannot tell friend from foe. All they know is that someone is trying to kill them. This is not to excuse the actions of Lt. Calley and his men, but they are helpless victims of the people who put them in 'harms way' in the first place. The real war criminals are those political leaders who are responsible for the deaths of hundreds of thousands and are never punished. At Nuremberg, we did not hang the soldiers in the field who followed orders – we hung the higher-ups who were responsible for the atrocities.

Lies and Deceits

In the latter months of 1967, many Americans believed that the war had degenerated into a bloody stalemate. General William Westmoreland, the senior commander in Vietnam, did not see it that way; by his primary metric - the body count - American forces were making significant headway. Under criticism by the growing anti-war movement at home, President Johnson decided to make General Westmoreland's optimism the focal point of an information campaign to convince the American people that we were winning the war.

In mid-November 1967, he brought General Westmoreland home to make the case. Upon arriving at Andrews Air Force Base, Westmoreland told waiting reporters that he was "very, very encouraged" by recent events. Appearing on *Meet the Press* two days later, he said American troops would be able to begin withdrawing "within two years or less." During an address at the National Press Club, he claimed that "we have reached an important point where the end begins to come into view." He consistently gave an upbeat account of how things were going in the war and that a corner had been turned.

While General Westmoreland was speaking in the United States, the Viet Cong were preparing a major offensive that was set to begin at the start of Tet, the Vietnamese New Year. In the early morning hours of January 31, 1968, North Vietnamese forces struck suddenly and with a fury breathtaking in scope. More than 80,000 soldiers from the North, combined with Viet Cong guerrilla forces, launched simultaneous attacks against major cities, towns and military installations. They seized and occupied Hue, the ancient imperial capital, and sent eleven battalions into Saigon to strike six targets, including the United States Embassy.

The American public and our military experts were shocked. Until Tet, the Viet Cong and the North Vietnamese army had fought in the jungles and paddies. Now, for the first time, they attacked in the cities. By the end of February, more than 1,100 Americans and 2,300 South Vietnamese soldiers had been killed, along with some 12,000 South Vietnamese civilians. The ferocity of the attack undermined the credibility of LBJ's claims that U.S. forces were in control of the country, and that the North

Vietnamese and the Viet Cong no longer had the capacity to wage anything but a hit-and-run war.

With a few notable exceptions - at Hue, Khe Sanh and Cholon - most of the Tet offensive was over in a few days as the American and South Vietnamese forces overcame the initial surprise and responded with superior firepower. The Americans won a tactical victory, but the sheer scope and ferocity of the Tet offensive and the vivid images of the fighting on the nightly television news convinced many Americans that the Johnson administration had lied to them, and the president's credibility plummeted. Walter Cronkite, America's most respected newscaster asked the nation, "What the hell is going on? I thought we were winning the war."

Democratic Mayor Richard Daley of Chicago told Lyndon Johnson that it was time to pull the troops out of Vietnam once and for all. "How am I to do this?" Johnson asked pleadingly. To which Daley is said to have replied: "You put the fucking troops on the fucking planes and you get them out of there!"

The Vietnam War destroyed Johnson's presidency. Depressed and dejected, he decided not to run for re-election. "I'm tired," he told his wife. "I'm tired of feeling rejected by the American people. I'm tired of waking up in the middle of the night worrying about the war." On March 31, 1968, Johnson went on national television to announce a partial suspension of the bombing campaign against North Vietnam and called for negotiations. He then stunned the audience by announcing that he would not run for re-election.

The Democratic Convention, held in Chicago in August 1968, stands as an important event in our nation's political and cultural history. Vice President Hubert Humphrey, a staunch supporter of LBJ's Vietnam policies, came to the convention with the presidential nomination sewn up.

Outside the convention center there was chaos – civil rights demonstrators, gay rights demonstrators, feminist demonstrators, and most of all, anti-war demonstrators. It did not take long for things to get out of control. Demonstrators, many fueled by drugs, clashed with 11,900 Chicago police, 7,500 Army troops, 7,500 Illinois National Guardsmen and 1,000 Secret Service agents over five days. The violence began when anti-war leaders tried to get permits from the city to sleep in Lincoln Park and to demonstrate outside the convention center. The permit requests were denied, but the protesters were undeterred. When they refused to leave the park, Chicago police bombed them with tear gas and moved in with clubs to forcibly remove them. Many innocent bystanders, reporters, and doctors offering medical help were severely beaten.

At the Republican Convention that year, Richard Nixon easily became the nominee. He promised the American people that he had "a secret plan to end the war." When asked whether he would use atomic weapons in Vietnam, he replied: "I will never consider using nuclear weapons in Vietnam, and I will never invade North Vietnam or any of the other countries bordering Vietnam." With the election of Richard M. Nixon the art of presidential lies and deceits was about to reach the apex in American history.

CHAPTER NINETEEN

WATERGATE

> "Watergate is nothing but a third-rate burglary.
> Why is everyone so upset?"
>
> Richard M. Nixon

In 1952, the Democrats nominated Adlai Stevenson for president. The Republican nomination was hotly contested between General Dwight Eisenhower and Ohio Senator Robert Taft. Eisenhower, at the age of sixty-two, was an international hero who had organized the Allied victory over the Nazis and briefly served as president of Columbia University. He had a kind face and a smile that beamed confidence and optimism, and he promised to go to Korea and end the war. Taft was a seasoned politician who was known as "Mr. Republican." The race for the nomination was 'nip and tuck' all the way to the convention.

California's delegates were pledged to its favorite son, Governor Earl Warren, and Eisenhower needed those votes to win the nomination. Senator Richard Nixon was offered the vice presidency by Eisenhower's top managers if he could get the California delegation to swing its votes from Warren to Eisenhower after the first ballot.

The voting at the convention was extremely close, but Eisenhower was nominated after a last-minute deal assured Earl Warren that he would be appointed to the first vacancy on the Supreme Court. Richard Nixon, as agreed, became the vice-presidential nominee.

All hell broke loose during the campaign when the *New York Post* disclosed a "secret Nixon slush fund" from potentially "illegal" contributions. Eisenhower, who was running on a campaign pledge of incorruptibility, was willing to cut Nixon adrift, but kicking someone off the presidential ticket halfway through the campaign had dangerous consequences. Eisenhower left the decision up to Nixon who decided to go on national television to explain his actions. If the public response was not positive, he agreed to step down.

Nixon asked for a prime-time television slot in order to reach the maximum audience. Not even Eisenhower knew what Nixon was going to say. "My fellow Americans," Richard Nixon began. "I come before you tonight as a candidate for vice-president and as a man whose honesty and integrity has been questioned." And off he went; "I am sure that you have read and heard the charges, that I illegally received $18,000 from a group of my supporters." He then shifted gears and told the public about his background.

"I worked my way through college (untrue) and I earned a couple of battle stars in the war (untrue). I own a 1950 Oldsmobile car, some furniture, and we have no stocks and bonds of any type. Now that is what we have. What do we owe? Well, in addition to two mortgages, the $20,000 mortgage on the house in Washington and the $10,000 one on the house in California, I owe $4,500 to the Riggs bank in Washington, with interest at four-and-a-half percent. I also owe $3,500 to my parents. I should also say that my wife Pat does not have a mink coat, but she does have a respectable Republican cloth coat, and I always tell her that she would look good in anything."

Then he closed his speech with what everyone who was listening will always remember. "One other thing I probably should tell you; we did get one gift. A man down in Texas heard Pat on the radio mention the fact that our two youngsters would like to have a dog. And, believe it or not, the day before we left on this campaign trip we got a message from Union Station in Baltimore saying they had a package for us. We went down to get it. You know what it was? It was a little cocker spaniel dog in a crate that this man sent all the way from Texas - black-and-white-spotted - and our six-year-old little girl Tricia named it Checkers. And the kids love that dog, and I just want to say this right now, regardless of what happens we are going to keep Checkers."

That line about the cocker spaniel went down in history as the *Checkers Speech*. And it worked. Over two million telegrams poured in and less than one percent was negative. Eisenhower had no choice – he welcomed Richard Nixon back with open arms. The Republicans won a landslide victory in the election and Richard Nixon was Vice President of the United States at the age of thirty-nine.

Eisenhower and Nixon won re-election easily in 1956. In 1960, Nixon ran for president and lost to JFK in a very close election. Two years later, he lost again when he ran for governor of California. Nixon then moved to New York City, where he became a senior partner in the law firm of Mudge, Rose, Guthrie & Alexander. During the 1966 congressional elections, he stumped the country in support of Republican candidates, rebuilding his base within the Party.

The presidential campaign of 1968 appeared to be between Richard Nixon and President Lyndon Johnson, but developments took a bizarre turn when LBJ stunned the nation by announcing that he would not seek re-election, and Robert Kennedy's candidacy ended with his assassination. Vice President Humphrey ended up with the nomination and became the Democratic nominee with Senator Edmund Muskie of Maine as his running mate.

Although Richard Nixon had mild challenges from Nelson Rockefeller and Ronald Reagan, he swept the Republican nomination. Spiro Agnew, governor of Maryland, was Nixon's vice-presidential choice. Nixon was elected, but the U.S. Senate and the House remained overwhelmingly Democratic.

Nixon was ecstatic when the election results rolled in. When victory was assured at 3 a.m. the next morning he went out celebrating with a couple of his close associates. "We won! We won!" he said, slapping his companions' shoulders. "We're going to kill them in '72." After many rounds of drinks, he slurred to Leonard Garment, his former law partner, "You'll never make it in politics, Len. You just don't know how to lie."

It is somewhat scary that someone as emotionally unstable as Richard Nixon could be elected to the highest office in this county and become our nation's commander-in-chief. When

Nixon sought the Republican presidential nomination in 1968, Henry Kissinger described him as, "a disaster who was unfit to be president." In spite of such a damning statement, Nixon and Kissinger formed a marriage of convenience spiced with mutual suspicion and resentment – it was a partnership like no other in presidential history.

Henry "Heinz" Kissinger grew up in a solidly middle-class Orthodox Jewish family in Bavaria, the southeastern part of Germany. Henry was fifteen when his family fled to America in August 1938. He attended New York's City College where he majored in accounting. He was drafted into World War II and served as a lecturer to our troops on German culture and history. After the war, his exceptionally high IQ got him into Harvard where he graduated at the top of his class.

After Harvard, he became a "think tank" specialist and wrote a book entitled, *Nuclear Weapons and Foreign Policy*. The volume was a dense treatise, but it became an overnight best seller. Nelson Rockefeller was preparing to run for president at the time and he added Kissinger to his staff, making him his foreign policy 'expert.' When Nixon emerged the victor and the Republican nominee, Kissinger, ever the opportunist, switched allegiances. Kissinger would quip: "I cannot be president because of this goddamn constitution provision forbidding a foreigner from being president, but there is nothing in the constitution against my being emperor."

Nixon appointed his old law partner William Rogers as secretary of state, but this was purely a front. Nixon's all-important adviser and collaborator was Kissinger. On inauguration day the president issued a memorandum, drafted by Kissinger, asserting that the Soviet Union bypass the State Department on important issues and deal directly and secretly with Kissinger. This 'back channel' diplomacy excluded the State Department and the Pentagon from the most important discussions about key issues of which there were many - especially Vietnam, the Middle East, and China.

The first fifteen months of the Nixon presidency centered largely on Vietnam – how to continue fighting the war, hold domestic opponents at bay, and pressure Hanoi into a settlement that did not saddle the United States with a military defeat that would diminish its international credibility. Always mindful that Vietnam had forced Lyndon Johnson out of office, Nixon sought to achieve an "honorable" end to the Vietnam War. The emphasis was on "honorable" - Nixon would settle for nothing less. However, Ho Chi Minh knew that time was on his side and he was not letting Nixon off with some meaningless face-saving settlement.

Despite growing anti-war sentiment and warnings from his field commanders that "the war had become a bottomless pit," Nixon clung to the conviction that he could use military pressure to force the North Vietnamese into an agreement that would deliver peace with honor. In June 1969, he started what looked like a withdrawal of U.S. troops from Vietnam, making it appear to the American public that he was fulfilling his campaign promise of winding down the war, but it was all a lie. In fact, he was already secretly increasing the air bombings and had plans for escalating the ground war.

By April 20, 1970, he completed the withdrawal of 115,000 troops and told the nation he planned to bring home 150,000 additional troops by the next spring. Ten days later, he spoke to the nation on television to report that he had ordered a short-term American invasion of Cambodia designed "to clean out major enemy sanctuaries on the Cambodian-Vietnam border." This invasion, he asserted, was "indispensable" for his withdrawal of troops program.

In explaining his actions Nixon stated, "For five years, neither the United States nor South Vietnam has moved against these enemy sanctuaries because we did not wish to violate the territory of a neutral nation." Actually, American B-52s had already carried out 3,600 bombing missions against Cambodian targets. Nixon had given explicit orders to Kissinger, "I want our planes to hit everything inside Cambodia – anything that moves should be destroyed."

The highest officials in the Pentagon falsified records so that our bombing of Cambodia appeared as routine missions over South Vietnam. Our pilots and navigators knew the bombs were being dropped on Cambodia, but the rest of the B-52 crews were

Lies and Deceits

told the targets were inside Vietnam. U.S. military teams also carried out more than 600 ground missions inside Cambodia.

When word began to leak out, Nixon went of national television and lied once again: "There are no American advisers in Cambodia and there will be no American combat troops or advisers in Cambodia." Senator John Kerry recalls his time in Cambodia: "I remember sitting on a gunboat and being shot at by the Khmer Rouge and Cambodians, and all the while listening on the radio to the President of the United States tell the American people that I was not there. It was absurd to almost be killed in a country in which Nixon was claiming there were no Americans troops."

When the Cambodian invasion was exposed, it spurred a new peak in the anti-war movement. At our nation's colleges and universities, students went berserk. Whether motivated by altruistic patriotism or the fear of being drafted, students occupied school buildings, blocked streets, boycotted classes, and vandalized property. Student reaction spread across our nation's campuses, nowhere more so than at Kent State University in Ohio. Two days after the country learned about our role in Cambodia, angry students torched the ROTC building on campus. When the National Guard was summoned to restore order, Guardsmen fired sixty-seven shots into a group of two hundred students, murdering Allison Krause, Sandra Scheuer, Jeffrey Miller, and William Schroeder. Nine others were wounded and one was paralyzed. The Guardsmen claimed they fired in self-defense.

Sixty percent of Americans believed that the students deserved what they got. A respected Akron lawyer said, "Frankly, if I'd been faced with the same situation and had a sub-machine gun, there probably would have been 140 of them dead." People expressed disappointment that the rabble-rousing professors had escaped: "The only mistake they made was not to shoot all the students and then start on the faculty." California Governor Ronald Reagan, when asked about campus militants, responded, "If it takes a bloodbath, let's get it over with."

Ten days after the Kent State murders, two students were killed and twelve wounded at Jackson State College in Mississippi when police fired into a group of demonstrators. In the weeks after the

Kent State and Jackson State murders, more than four million students clashed with police or the National Guard, or in some other way disrupted campus life. There was violence at seventy-three schools. Students went on strike at 350 schools, including all of the elite universities. Classes were suspended at 1,350 schools. More than 500 schools were forced to cancel classes and 51 closed for the balance of the semester. Thirty ROTC buildings were burned or bombed. Heavily armed National Guardsmen were called onto twenty-one campuses.

The most dramatic dissent against the war in Vietnam came from Daniel Ellsberg. Ellsberg had a Ph.D. in economics from Harvard, had served in the U.S. Marines for two years, and held important posts in the defense department, the state department, and at the American Embassy in Saigon. He had been a special assistant to Henry Kissinger and worked for the Rand Corporation, a private "think tank" contracted to do top-secret research for the U.S. government.

While Ellsberg was at Rand, he was asked to assemble a history of the Vietnam War from classified and secret documents. Ellsberg was already feeling pangs of conscience about the war in Vietnam. He had been in the field with the military and none of our reasons for being there made any sense to him. As he was reading all the secret documents, he realized he was right. He was appalled by the lies upon lies that had been told to the American public.

Ellsberg concluded that every U.S. administration since Truman had acted in a consistent way against Communist-nationalist movements. While we professed support for an independent and unified Vietnam, we were against anything that remotely smelled of a communist regime. Instead of encouraging elections to unify the country, we helped to create a separate regime in South Vietnam and took an increasing military role in support of that regime, which finally escalated into an enormous war. The mass of detail that Ellsberg was examining threw light on such things as presidential manipulation of Congress, the role of deception in forming public opinion, and the inaccuracy of military reports pertaining to Vietnam.

Lies and Deceits

Ellsberg was faced with a dilemma. He was not a constitutional lawyer; he was a patriotic American. Since he had a "top-secret" security classification, there were few people, if any, that he could discuss this matter with. Did the public have a right to know that the government was lying to them and that American boys were being killed in great numbers under false pretenses? How can 'lies and deceits' be exposed if it is labeled 'national security'? What is the duty and responsibility of a person with a classified clearance? Should he expose the truth or is he duty-bound to perpetuate the lies? Is a "leak" the act of a traitor or hero? Who decides whether exposure of the truth can cause irreparable harm to our troops, or is that just a sham device to keep the lies hidden?

Ellsberg would later write, "It became clear to me that journalists had no idea, no clue, not even the best of them, just how often and how egregiously they were lied to, and how easily and pervasively Congress and the public were fooled and misled, and how ignorant they were about the real issues that were occupying our policy makers."

Ellsberg grappled with these issues and decided to act regardless of the consequences. He retained one of the fifteen copies of his report. The other copies were distributed to the secretary of state, secretary of defense, and other high government officials. Ellsberg then secretly photocopied his entire 47 volume, 7,000 page history of America's involvement in the Vietnam War - the *Pentagon Papers* as they came to be called - and distributed copies to certain members of Congress as well as to the *New York Times*.

Early in 1971, the *New York Times* began printing this "top-secret" document. The revelations were a sensation and added to the growing public opposition to the war. The *Pentagon Papers* revealed that the U.S. government had deliberately lied to the American public about our expanded military role in Vietnam.

Nixon was incensed by the disclosure of the *Pentagon Papers*. He ordered Attorney General John Mitchell to obtain a court injunction stopping the *New York Times* from further publication. Mitchell sent a telegram to Arthur Sulzberger, publisher of the *Times*, stating that the articles contained information bearing "a top-secret classification." Mitchell added that "publication of this information was directly prohibited" by the Espionage Act of 1917 and that further publication would "cause irreparable injury to the defense and interests of the United States." He therefore requested that the *Times* "publish no further information of this character" and advised him that it had "made arrangements for the return of these documents to the Defense Department."

Two hours later, the *New York Times* transmitted a response, which it released publicly: "The *Times* must respectfully decline the request of the attorney-general, believing that it is in the interest of the people of this country to be informed of the material contained in this series of articles." The *Times* added that if the government sought to enjoin any further publication of the material, it would contest the government's position, but would abide by the final decision of the court.

That evening it was reported that Ellsberg had been the source of the leak. It was a bombshell. These startling revelations and staggering new insights had come from an insider. Where was his loyalty? Ellsberg was denounced as a traitor by those who believe that the primary loyalty of a government official is not to the people, but to the president. Nixon was furious; destroying Ellsberg became his new crusade.

All presidents are exasperated by leaks. They are really not, however, against leaks in principle. The selective leak is a familiar tool of government. What enrages presidents are the leaks they do not order themselves – leaks that embarrass, expose or undermine their policies, which is to say leaks that stimulate and fortify national debate. Presidents like to claim that such leaks do ineffable harm to national security. What they mostly mean is that leaks do harm to the political interests of their administration. The harm to national security through leaks is always exaggerated. No one has ever demonstrated that the publication of the *Pentagon Papers* harmed our national security.

Nixon was crazed. He wanted Ellsberg not just punished, but destroyed. He ordered Howard Hunt and his White House private CIA-type organization - the "plumbers" - named for those who stop leaks - to use any and all methods to uncover incriminating documents against Ellsberg. On May 3, 1972, Ellsberg learned

Lies and Deceits

that the CIA and FBI had received orders to find and totally 'incapacitate' him. Ellsberg immediately went into hiding. For almost two weeks, he was subject to what the press described as "the largest FBI manhunt since the Lindbergh kidnapping." During his days as a fugitive, Ellsberg was interviewed from secret places by a variety of journalists. In one instance, Walter Cronkite asked him what he considered "the most important revelations to date from the Pentagon documents." Ellsberg replied:

> "I think the lesson is that the people of this country can't afford to let the president run the country by himself without the help of the Congress and without the help of the public. What these studies tell me is we must remember this is a self-governing country. The people are the government. We cannot let the officials of the executive branch determine for us what it is that the public needs to know about how well they are discharging their functions."

On June 28, Ellsberg voluntarily surrendered to the U.S. Attorney in Boston. During his trial, the judge learned that Nixon's "plumbers" broke into Ellsberg's psychiatrist's office to photograph any confidential doctor-patient material that could be used against him, and that the FBI made fifteen illegal wiretaps that were ordered by President Nixon. Judge Byrne declared the case against Ellsberg tainted and dismissed the trial.

The government continued its efforts to obtain an injunction against the *New York Times* to prevent the publication of the *Pentagon Papers*. The legal issue was whether publication would endanger our national security and complicate our nation's efforts to end the Vietnam War. Government lawyers relied on *Near v. Minnesota*, a 1931 case that held that the government could restrain the publication of "the sailing dates of our transports or the number and location of our troops during wartime."

The *New York Times* contended that the *Pentagon Papers* dealt with past events, not current war plans, and that only "immediate and irreparable" harm to our national security could justify restraint. The document divulged no secret invasion plans; only diplomatic and political decisions reached by U.S. administrations no longer in office. Although the revelations were certainly profoundly embarrassing, the *New York Times* argued that they did not pose a "clear and present danger" to vital national security interests.

The U.S. Supreme Court ruled for the *New York Times* by a 6-3 margin. The opinion in the case was very brief because all the Court did was to concur with the decisions of two lower courts that rejected the government's request for an injunction. Justice Hugo Black wrote, "The guarding of military and diplomatic secrets at the expense of an informed representative government provides no real security for our Republic. Only a free and unrestrained press can effectively expose deception in government." President Nixon's response to the Court's decision was, "that son-of-a-bitch thief was made a national hero and the *New York Times* gets a Pulitzer for stealing documents. What in the name of God have we come to?"

Every day for a month the story dominated the nation's headlines. *New York Times* Pulitzer Prize reporter, Neil Sheehan, came to the sobering conclusion that the *Pentagon Papers* disclosed a secret government operating within our visible government, "far more powerful than anything else that had survived and perpetuated itself, using the issue of anti-communism as a weapon against the other branches of government and the press." This inner government "did not function necessarily for the benefit of the Republic, but rather for its own ends, using secrecy as a way of protecting itself, not so much from threats by foreign governments, but from detection from its own population."

Daniel Ellsberg was not the only top government official who knew the government was lying. Much later, high-ranking Robert McNamara and Clark Clifford both acknowledged they knew the truth, but refused to be martyrs. They each saw the 'true' daily tallies of Americans being killed and maimed, but they continued signing the bombing orders. They knew they were parties to an unprecedented deception, but they knowingly chose loyalty to their president over morality to our nation.

Lies and Deceits

The *Pentagon Papers* revealed that during 1969 Nixon could probably have ended the war in exchange for an American withdrawal according to a publicly announced schedule. This would have required admitting that the war was a lost cause. Nixon was determined that he would "not be the first president to lose a war." Instead, he threatened North Vietnam with savage assaults and the possibility of nuclear attacks. When those threats and his escalation of the war failed to break the Vietnamese, he widened the war to Cambodia.

Nixon's called his secret plan to end the war, his "Madman Theory." Nixon told his aide H.R. (Bob) Haldeman, "I want the North Vietnamese to believe that I've reached the point that I might do anything to stop the war. We'll just slip the word to them that for God's sake, you know Nixon is obsessed about communism. We can't restrain him when he's angry - and he has his hand on the nuclear button." According to Nixon, Ho Chi Minh would be in Paris in two days begging for peace.

During the month of October 1969, our U.S. military was ordered to full global war readiness alert with no explanation given to our commanders regarding the purpose. Nuclear armed fighter planes were sent to civilian airports, missile countdown procedures were initiated, missile-bearing submarines were dispersed, and long-range bombers were launched.

On October 27, in an action designed to make it seem that the "madman" was loose, the Strategic Air Command was ordered to dispatch B-52's loaded with thermonuclear weapons toward the Soviet Union. Eighteen of the bombers took off from bases in the United States in an operation named *Giant Lance*. The bombers crossed Alaska, were refueled in mid-air, and then flew in oval patterns toward the Soviet Union and back on eighteen-hour vigils.

The ominous flight of these H-bombers to the edge of Soviet territory continued for three days. Nixon was moving the world toward global Armageddon. This was all done in total secrecy from the American public. Of course, Nixon made sure the Russians knew what was happening – after all that was what this dangerous game was all about. Nixon's purpose was to intimidate the Soviet

Union into persuading the North Vietnamese to accept an end to the war on Nixon's terms.

The military commanders who were implementing Nixon's madman ploy may not have known what was behind it, but Secretary of Defense Laird knew and he vigorously opposed the alert as wildly dangerous. Nevertheless, it was carried out, mainly because Nixon's key adviser, Henry Kissinger, thought it might work. Kissinger praised Nixon in the midst of this adventure for having "the guts of a riverboat gambler." The transcripts of private conversations between Kissinger and Nixon reveal their cavalier attitude about nuclear weapons. At one point Nixon laughingly said to Kissinger, "Does using the nuclear bomb bother you, Henry? I want you to think big, Henry, for Christ's sake."

The war ended on April 30, 1975 with an embarrassing defeat for the United States. Not only was there 211,471 American casualties and 58,168 U.S. soldiers killed, but the Vietnamese people had 5,561,719 casualties. In addition, *Agent Orange*, a highly toxic chemical defoliant used by the United States, caused the death of hundreds of thousands of Vietnamese, and resulted in lingering cancers and birth defects. Tens of thousands of American soldiers were also exposed to *Agent Orange* and suffered similar horrific consequences.

One of the most frustrating aspects of the war was that the United States had been able to move almost a million soldiers in and out of Vietnam; feed, clothe, house, supply them with arms and ammunition, and generally sustain them better than any army in history. To maintain an army of this size halfway around the world was a logistics and management task of enormous magnitude, and the U.S. military was more than equal to the task. On the battlefield itself, our army was unbeatable. In engagement after engagement, the North Vietnamese Army was thrown back with terrible losses. We dropped 25 million bombs on Vietnam, yet, in the end it was North Vietnam, not the United States that emerged victorious.

During the signing of the peace treaty in Paris, the following conversation took place between two leading military antagonists; one from the United States and the other from North Vietnam:

"You know you never defeated us on the battlefield," bragged the American colonel.

His North Vietnamese military counterpart pondered this remark for a moment.

"That may be so," he replied, "but it is also irrelevant."

There is a saying that power corrupts and absolute power corrupts absolutely. Nothing better describes the presidency of Richard Nixon. Nixon was a presidential enigma; brilliant, but psychotically paranoid and a closet alcoholic. He self-destructed over a meaningless burglary in order to insure a re-election that he could not possibly lose.

As Nixon's first term in office was coming to a close, all his efforts became focused on re-election. Nixon drew up an 'enemies' list of those who opposed his administration. The concept was to harass them with tax audits and the threat of federal prosecution for crimes unnamed. Those on Nixon's list included Democratic fund raisers; powerful labor leaders; left-leaning newscasters, and Hollywood personalities such as Paul Newman, Jane Fonda, Barbara Streisand, and Bill Cosby.

Nixon's opponent for the presidency appeared to be Senator Edmund Muskie of Maine, Senator Eugene McCarthy of Minnesota, or Senator George McGovern of South Dakota. Nixon and his aides feared a close election because the war was not going well and public dissent was rising. Although no American president had ever been turned out of office during wartime, Nixon was paranoid that he might not get re-elected, and the thought of losing made him more delusional than usual. In addition, there was the unknown 'Wallace' element.

George Wallace was elected governor of Alabama as a Democrat four times: 1962, 1970, 1974 and 1982. He also ran for president four times: as a Democrat in 1964, 1972, and 1976, and as the American Independent Party candidate in 1968.

Back in 1958, Wallace was defeated by John Patterson in Alabama's Democratic gubernatorial primary. The Democratic primary was the decisive contest; the general election in highly Democratic Alabama was always a mere formality. Wallace's defeat in this primary was a political awakening. His opponent was supported by the Ku Klux Klan; Wallace was endorsed by the NAACP. After his defeat, Wallace said, "You know why I lost that governor's race? I was outniggered by John Patterson. And I'll tell you here and now, I will never be outniggered again." From that moment, Wallace became a hard-line segregationist and a symbol of racial bigotry.

In 1962, Wallace was elected governor in a landslide victory. He took the oath of office standing on the very spot where 102 years before, Jefferson Davis was sworn in as President of the Confederate States. In his inaugural speech, Wallace used the line for which he is best known:

> "In the name of the greatest people that have ever trod this earth, I draw the line in the dust and toss the gauntlet down before the feet of tyranny, and I say segregation now, segregation tomorrow, segregation forever."

When Wallace ran for president in 1968, he knew he could never win, but he hoped to receive enough electoral votes to force the outcome into the House of Representatives, presumably giving him the role of a power-broker to end federal efforts at desegregation. Nixon was worried that Wallace might steal enough votes away from him to give the election to the Democratic Hubert Humphrey. Wallace carried five Southern states, finished second in three, and received almost ten million popular votes; Nixon won the election by 31 electoral votes.

In early 1972, a Gallup Poll showed that Wallace was the seventh most admired man in America, just ahead of Pope Paul VI. That year, Wallace again declared himself a candidate for president, this time entering the Democratic primaries along with George McGovern, Hubert Humphrey, and nine other Democrats. In Florida's primary, Wallace carried every county to win 42 percent of the vote. Although Nixon's re-election seemed safe, if Wallace was able to split the conservative vote, a Democratic candidate might have a chance of winning.

On May 15, 1972, Wallace was shot five times by twenty-two-year-old Arthur Bremer while campaigning in Laurel, Maryland.

The shooting left Wallace paralyzed. The story of Arthur Bremer was familiar. Another crazy gunman, portrayed as a withdrawn loner, had taken down a leading political figure in our country.

But, there was something eerie about Bremer's comatose zombie behavior that was oddly reminiscent of James Earl Ray and Sirhan Sirhan. None of the purported assassins could remember anything afterward. According to one Federal officer at the scene of the Wallace shooting, Bremer "seemed incredibly indifferent to what was going on around him, even the things that affected him. He was blasé, almost oblivious. He seemed like a shallow, mixed-up man." Some witnesses commented about Bremer's "spine-tingling" smirk, or "silly grin." The same thing had been said about Sirhan Sirhan. Were the brainwashing drugs of MK-ULTRA at work once again or was it mere coincidence?

At the time of the shooting, Bremer was an unemployed dishwasher. His total finances were $1.73. His 1971 income tax return revealed that he earned $1,611 for the entire year. He spent at least two months traveling between Milwaukee, New York and Maryland before the Laurel incident. Yet, Bremer never had any source of income to pay for these trips. His last two jobs were as a busboy and a janitor. Nobody was able to explain how was he able to support himself, or how he was able to buy a tape recorder, a police band portable radio, binoculars, a car for $795 in cash, fly to and from New York City, stay at the exclusive Waldorf-Astoria Hotel, drive to and from Ottawa, Canada, and stay at an exclusive hotel there, buy three guns, take a helicopter ride in New York City, ride around in a chauffeured limousine, or tip a girl $30 at a massage parlor - to mention just a few oddities in Bremer's life. As with the cases of Lee Harvey Oswald and James Earl Ray, this "loner" clearly had financial support from some outside source.

Wallace was wounded in nine different places. Three other people were wounded. That makes twelve wounds. The gun found at the scene, presumed to be the only weapon used, could only hold five bullets. Doctors who treated Wallace said he was hit by a minimum of four bullets, possibly five. Yet three other victims were wounded and bullets were recovered from two of them. The *New York Times* reported that there was "broad speculation on how four persons had suffered at least seven separate wounds from a maximum of five shots," adding that although various law enforcement agencies had personnel on the scene, these agencies claimed that "none of their officers or agents had discharged their weapons."

According to the FBI, Bremer was a lone assassin. At his trial, the FBI admitted that Bremer's fingerprints were not found on the gun recovered at the scene even though Bremer was not wearing gloves. In addition, the gun could not be matched to the bullets that paralyzed Wallace. The FBI admitted that Bremer had tested negative for nitrates, which is found in gunpowder substances. The gun was not wrested from Bremer's hand, but was found on the pavement by Secret Service agent Robert A. Innamorati. He picked the gun up from the pavement and "kept it secure until 9:00 p.m. that evening," at which point he turned it over to the FBI. The gun was traced to Bremer.

The shooting of George Wallace came at a critical moment of upheaval within the FBI organization. J. Edgar Hoover, its longtime chief, had been dead for less than two weeks. In his place, Nixon appointed one of his faithful political operatives, L. Patrick Gray as acting director. Gray was 'out of the loop' during the first critical hours after the shooting. Instead, Mark Felt (later to become famous as "Deep Throat"), the assistant FBI director and ranking career officer in the Bureau, took charge of the case. Between five and eleven o'clock that day, Nixon's top aide, Charles Colson, conferred with Felt on at least a half-dozen times; twice President Nixon personally spoke on the phone with Felt.

The FBI entered Bremer's apartment in Milwaukee soon after the shooting, but for unexplained reasons they left and returned ninety minutes later, and it was then that they first sealed the apartment to all visitors. Unless they had instructions from very high up, the FBI would never have left the apartment open for ninety minutes knowing that anyone could have walked in and taken or planted incriminating evidence.

Some of the answers came later from secret White House tapes. President Nixon had Charles Colson order ex-CIA agent Howard Hunt to break into Bremer's apartment. When the FBI returned after that ninety-minute interval, they found McGovern campaign literature scattered all over the apartment. Colson then phoned journalists at the *Washington Post* and *Detroit News* saying the government has evidence that Bremer was a left-winger connected with the campaign of George McGovern. The reporters were also told that Bremer was a "dues-paying member of the Young Democrats of Milwaukee." None of this was true. A diary supposedly belonging to Bremer was found in the apartment, stating that he wanted to assassinate either Wallace or Nixon in order to become famous. Gore Vidal, wrote a long essay in the *New York Review of Books* in which he postulates that Howard Hunt actually penned Bremer's infamous diary.

At Bremer's five-day trial, his defense was insanity. His lawyer told the jury, "I am not trying to kid you. I do not know whether Bremer shot Wallace or not. I think some doctors will tell you that even Arthur Bremer does not know if shot Wallace." During the trial, Bremer was placed in the audience portion of the courtroom. Several witnesses could not identify him as having been the gunman they claimed to have seen or tackled.

The jury took an hour-and-a half to convict him. When asked if he had anything to say, Bremer replied, "Well, the prosecutor mentioned that he would like society to be protected from someone like me. Looking back on my life I would have liked it if society had protected me from myself. That's all I have to say at this time." Bremer was sentenced to fifty-three years in prison. He served thirty-five years and was released on parole in 2007.

George Wallace always maintained that Nixon ordered his assassination. In May 1974, Martha Mitchell, wife of the attorney-general, visited George Wallace in Montgomery, Alabama. She told Wallace that her husband, John Mitchell, confessed to her that Charles Colson had met with Bremer four days before the assassination attempt. In December 1992, Wallace's son gave an interview saying that he received information from several sources that someone who worked directly for Richard Nixon was behind the shooting of his father.

With Wallace out of the 1972 campaign, Nixon believed that knowing the Democratic Party's strategy was the key to victory.

In order to get this information, he authorized his "plumbers" to break into the Democratic headquarters in the Watergate Hotel complex and photograph their plans. Howard Hunt was in charge of the operation.

Actually, there were two Watergate break-ins. The first went off without a hitch. Three weeks later, the burglars returned intending to fix certain wiretaps that were not working. This second break-in did not fare well. Through a fluke, the operation was discovered. Five men – Bernard Barker, Virgilio Gonzalez, Eugenio Martinez, James McCord, and Frank Sturgis were arrested.

Who could imagine that people with connections to the highest levels of the White House would burglarize the offices of the Democratic National Committee or that the president would be involved in such an insane scheme? In the beginning there was no link between the burglary and the White House. Nixon's statements reassured the public and the media, especially since Attorney General Richard Kleindienst was conducting "the most extensive investigation since the assassination of President Kennedy." But, there was a leak. Mark Felt had been associate director of the FBI. He secretly revealed the White House involvement in the break-in to Carl Bernstein and Bob Woodward of the *Washington Post*. Their articles stunned the nation.

George McGovern won the Democratic nomination that year and selected Missouri Senator Thomas Eagleton as his running mate. A couple of weeks after the nomination, Nixon strategists let it be known that Eagleton had earlier in his life undergone psychiatric electroshock therapy for depression. McGovern was surprised by the disclosure, but initially claimed he would back Eagleton "one-thousand percent." Three days later, he asked Eagleton to withdraw. After a week in which six prominent Democrats refused the vice-presidential nomination, Sargent Shriver, brother-in-law to the Kennedy family and former ambassador to France, finally accepted. By this time, McGovern's poll ratings had plunged from 41 percent to 24 percent. Nixon was a landslide winner in the election. The Watergate burglary was never an important issue in the campaign.

Lies and Deceits

The trial of the Watergate burglars opened on January 10, 1973. During the course of the trial, one of the burglars, James McCord, a longtime CIA security officer, claimed that "there was political pressure applied to the defendants to plead guilty and remain silent." Later, it was revealed that Nixon secretly pledged to give each of the defendants executive clemency and up to $1 million each if they kept quiet. On February 7, the U.S. Senate, by a vote of 77-0 established a committee of four Democrats and three Republicans, with broad subpoena powers, to investigate what this whole Watergate mess was about. The Senate also decided that these hearings should be televised to the general public.

An estimated 85 percent of Americans tuned in to some portion of the hearings that were broadcast from May 17 through August 7. White House Counsel John Dean was the star witness along with many other former key administration officials. During the course of the hearings, the committee learned of the existence of presidential tape recordings that would prove or disprove White House culpability in the Watergate break-in. The tapes immediately became the focal point of the hearings. Republican Senator Howard Baker of Tennessee asked the memorable question: "What did the president know and when did he know it?" For the first time, the country was focused on Nixon's role in the scandal.

The same day that the public learned of the White House tapes, Secretary of Defense James Schlesinger admitted that the United States secretly bombed Cambodia during 1969 and 1970 and that senior civilian and military officials had falsified reports and withheld information from Congress to prevent public disclosure. During the next ten days Americans learned that President Nixon personally authorized the secret bombings of Cambodia and that Secretary of State William P. Rogers repeatedly lied about the bombings in classified testimony before the Senate Foreign Relations Committee.

Watergate had started a series of disclosures that was now spiraling out of Nixon's control. A troubled Nixon spent the weekend of April 28 and 29 at the presidential Camp David retreat. The next day he announced the resignations of his two top staff members, H.R. Haldeman and John Ehrlichman, along with

Attorney General Kleindienst. Elliott Richardson moved over from his position as secretary of defense to take over for Kleindienst. It was quite a shake-up, but now everyone wanted to know what was in those White House tapes. The committee subpoenaed the tapes. Nixon refused to turn them over, citing presidential privilege and national security.

As if Nixon didn't have enough to deal with, a Baltimore grand jury found that Vice President Spiro Agnew was the recipient of huge payoffs going back a decade and continuing after he became vice-president. On October 10, Agnew resigned after making a deal to escape prosecution. Gerald Ford, Republican leader of the House, replaced Agnew as vice-president, but the press was not happy about the Agnew arrangement. *Time* magazine criticized the Nixon deal with Agnew as "no shining example of equality under the law."

These rapid-fire developments led the U.S. Senate to investigate the enormity of what was going on. Archibald Cox, a distinguished Harvard law professor, was appointed special independent prosecutor with complete autonomy. Cox was determined to find any wrongdoing by the president or his staff. He dug deeply, to the point of precipitating an IRS investigation of Nixon's close friend, Bebe Redozo, and even into Nixon's own finances. Cox also probed illegal secret contributions from multi-millionaire Howard Hughes to Nixon after the 1968 election. Nixon was furious – claiming that Cox's investigation into these matters was beyond his authority.

But, Cox plugged along. He next requested Nixon's White House tapes. Nixon refused. On Saturday, October 20, Nixon ordered Attorney General Richardson to fire Cox. Richardson refused and resigned. Nixon told Deputy Attorney General William Rukelhaus to fire Cox. Rukelhaus refused and resigned. Next, he ordered Solicitor General Robert Bork to fire Cox – Bork fired Cox (in 1987, President Ronald Reagan would nominate Bork to the Supreme Court, but he would not be confirmed).

Forty minutes after Bork fired Cox, FBI agents arrived at Cox's office, and placed it under guard. Nixon then abolished the office of the Watergate Special Prosecutor, and returned the

Watergate case to the Justice Department where he could control it. Nixon maintained that he had "a constitutional responsibility to defend the office of the presidency from any encroachment on confidentiality." The press immediately labeled this series of events the "Saturday Night Massacre," and the president's approval rating fell to an unprecedented 17 percent.

Fifty-three senators then co-sponsored a resolution authorizing Federal Judge John Sirica to appoint another special prosecutor independent of the executive branch of government. Leon Jaworski, a wealthy corporate lawyer from Houston became the new special prosecutor. Jaworski proposed a deal. If the president would release eighteen specific tapes, Jaworski would drop his request for any additional tapes. Nixon decided to listen to the eighteen tapes before deciding.

After several hours in his hideaway office hunched over a tape recorder with earphones, Nixon decided not to release the tapes. He understood that these eighteen tapes would doom him by demonstrating his central part in the cover-up of the Watergate crimes. Instead, Nixon decided to release transcripts of the tapes. This proved to be an unqualified disaster. The transcripts were filled with foul language, threats, and ravings. It displayed the workings of an unstable mind and a president whose main concern was the maintenance of personal power at any cost. In addition, the transcripts omitted segments without offering any adequate explanation. Jaworski now subpoenaed all the tapes. Nixon again refused. It appeared that only the U.S. Supreme Court could resolve the issue.

Meanwhile, the press was having a field day. The *Wall Street Journal* characterized the president as "a pitiful, helpless giant who has no one to blame but himself." *Time* magazine described the transcripts as "showing a president creating an environment of deceit and dishonesty; of evasion and cover-up." The situation, according to *Time*, was one of the nation's "gravest constitutional crises." The *Kansas City Times* editorial summed it up best, "Does anyone believe anything anymore?"

John Mitchell practiced law in New York City from 1938 until 1968 and earned a reputation as the nation's preeminent municipal bond lawyer. He met Richard Nixon when Mitchell's law firm merged with Nixon's firm in 1967. The two men rapidly became friends, and in 1968, Mitchell agreed to become Nixon's presidential campaign manager. After Nixon became president, Mitchell was appointed attorney-general. Mitchell resigned in 1972 to manage Nixon's re-election campaign.

Tape recordings made by President Nixon and the testimony of others confirmed that Mitchell had participated in meetings to plan the break-in of the Democratic Party's national headquarters in the Watergate Hotel. In addition, he had met, on at least three occasions, with Nixon in an effort to cover-up White House involvement after the burglars were discovered and arrested. In 1972, he warned *Washington Post* reporter Carl Bernstein: "Katie Graham's gonna get her tit caught in a big fat wringer if that Watergate article is published." This implied threat against the *Washington Post* publisher is considered the most famous threat in the history of American journalism.

On July 10, 1973, the now former Attorney General John Mitchell testified before the Senate Committee and explained why he withheld information about the Watergate break-in from the police and the FBI. "The most important thing to this country was the re-election of Richard Nixon and I was not about to countenance anything that would stand in the way of that."

Mitchell's wife, Martha, an outspoken woman to say the least, contacted reporters and told them about her husband's role in the Watergate scandal. On February 21, 1975, John Mitchell was found guilty of conspiracy, obstruction of justice and perjury, and sentenced to two-and-a-half to eight years in prison for his role in Watergate. At his sentencing, Mitchell said, "It could have been worse. They could have sentenced me to spend the rest of my life with Martha Mitchell." John Mitchell served only 19 months of his sentence before being released on parole for medical reasons.

Nixon knew that the tape of June 23, 1972 was indeed the "smoking gun" and he had no intention of releasing it. On that tape, Nixon and his chief of staff discussed having CIA Director Richard Helms tell FBI Director Patrick Gray to stay away from investigating the Watergate break-in. Nixon asked with sincere innocence: "Watergate is nothing but a third-rate burglary. Why is everyone so upset?"

Nixon underestimated the public reaction to the steadily increasing disclosures. His arrogance of power caused him not to appreciate the meaning of Watergate and its potential for disaster. Nixon had one last chance to resolve the Watergate affair and remain in office. He might have survived had he burned the tapes, blamed the destruction on administrative laxity, feigned some ignorance, and pointed out that he fired the close aides involved. Without the tapes, there would have been no missing conversations, no eighteen-minute erasure, and no smoking gun. But, Nixon believed he would not be required to surrender the tapes - no other president had ever been forced to disclose White House communications. Presidential records were always considered the personal property of the president.

On July 24, 1974, the Supreme Court announced its 8-0 decision - President Nixon had to turn over the sixty-four tapes the special prosecutor had subpoenaed. On July 27, the Judiciary Committee voted 27-11 to impeach Nixon. The articles of impeachment charged President Nixon with obstruction of justice, abuse of power, and contempt of Congress. On August 5, Nixon admitted he lied and that he obstructed justice by attempting to misuse the CIA, but he believed those actions did not justify "impeachment and removal." In answer to a reporter's loaded question, he burst out in frustration, "I am not a crook." No president had ever before felt the need to make such a statement.

When Nixon canvassed Republican congressional leaders he realized he was doomed and that resignation was far better than impeachment. In his resignation speech on August 9, he explained that some of his judgments had been "wrong," but he "believed they were in the best interests of the nation at the time." Nixon never admitted any guilt. He was resigning because he no longer had a "strong enough political base in the Congress to effectively carry out the duties of the office." The bulk of the speech was more an act of self-justification than contrition.

The nation sat transfixed as they watched Nixon's humiliation. Not only had he been a participant and orchestrated the cover-up, but the stupidity of the President of the United States bugging his own office, saving the incriminating tapes, and then turning them over to a prosecutor was incomprehensible. The American public asked itself: how could we have elected this man twice to the highest office in our land? What does that say about our ability to choose a leader?

Gerald Ford, who had taken over the duties of the vice-presidency when Spiro Agnew was forced to resign in disgrace, was now President of the United States. Upon assuming office he proclaimed, "Our long national nightmare is over." On September 8, he pardoned Nixon for all crimes he "committed or may have committed," freeing Nixon from any criminal or civil liability in the Watergate affair. Ford's pardon and Nixon's failure to admit guilt troubled the nation. Three days later, the U.S. Senate adopted a resolution opposing any future pardon to a Watergate participant until after a trial and the completion of all appeals. Twenty of Nixon's chief lieutenants were eventually indicted, convicted, and sentenced.

Nixon perhaps expressed his most penetrating self-analysis of his role in Watergate during the spring of 1977, when David Frost, a British television program host, interviewed the former president for almost twenty-nine hours. When Frost pressed him about his decision "to do something illegal," Nixon replied, "Well, when the president does it, that means it is not illegal."

One of Watergate's immediate casualties was Vietnam; the two were negatively linked. When North Vietnam began a major assault on the South, President Ford, knowing the gravity of the situation, asked the Congress for emergency funding. In a hastily called session of the House of Representatives, they voted overwhelmingly against any additional military aid. Lacking American air support, the South Vietnamese army began crumbling before the North Vietnamese onslaught. Ford made a last-ditch request for $722 million in emergency military aid, but his proposal never made it out of committee. Finally, a Senate proposal that would have provided funds for the orderly evacuation of South Vietnamese personnel was rejected by the House. The Vietnam War thus ended with frantic screaming Vietnamese trying to cram into departing American helicopters.

In the aftermath of North Vietnam's victory, between 65,000 and 100,000 South Vietnamese were executed. An estimated one million people were imprisoned without formal charges or trials. Thousands were abused or tortured and hundreds of thousands of Vietnamese fled the country – becoming known as "boat people" in search of a safe haven. In Cambodia, the situation was even worse. The communist Khmer Rouge regime took over and began a monstrous social experiment that included the infamous "killing fields" in which approximately two million people were exterminated. People in the United States were no longer interested and the horrible events in Southeast Asia received scant news coverage. Americans just wanted to forget the whole nightmare.

CHAPTER TWENTY

IRAN

"America is the great Satan."

Ayatollah Khomeini

On January 29, 2002, President George W. Bush labeled Iran a danger to the world; a part of an "axis of evil." America was not going to tolerate a nuclear Iran that could potentially destabilize an already volatile area. The U.S. stood ready to take whatever military action was necessary to prevent that from happening. Iran replied that they were not a nuclear threat nor did they intend to become one. The whole thing was another U.S. lie - like Iraq's "weapons of mass destruction" – a pretext to justify U.S. dominance of Middle East and Persian Gulf oil. Harsh words do not lead to peaceful solutions.

Iran's hostility to the U.S. comes with lots of historical baggage. There was the 1953 CIA coup that ousted Iran's democratic leader Mohammed Mosaddeq and reinstated the shah and the police state. America's covert interference into Iran's internal affairs will never be forgiven. Iranians have also not forgotten our duplicitous actions in the Iran-Iraq War and the infamous Iran-Contra affair. The problem with having a history of lies and deceits is that current words and intentions are highly suspect. History lingers, it does not disappear with the past.

Back in 1963, Mosaddeq was an old man and still under house arrest. The shah had been back in power for 10 years, and from an American standpoint everything was fine. The shah was America's "puppet" in the oil rich Persian Gulf and Middle East. It was a workable arrangement - he was dependent on us and we were dependent on him. He got his military toys to play with and we got the oil. The only ones who did not benefit from the arrangement were the Iranian people.

Ayatollah Ruhollah Khomeini was the most visible leader of the Islamic resistance movement at the time. An outstanding student of Islam, he had trained in a seminary in the holy city of Qom and at the remarkably early age of thirty-two was deemed by his teachers to be a *mojtahed*, a clergyman capable of interpreting Islamic law in all areas of human life. He became known as an ayatollah al-ozma ("grand sign of God"), an honorific title that became widely used in the 1920s in Iran to designate especially learned religious leaders. Unusual for a Shiite Islamic leader, the Ayatollah Khomeini combined his steely and learned interpretations of the Koran with a love of traditional Persian poetry and a fervent mysticism that demanded not just knowledge of Islam, but an emotional experience of God's being.

Khomeini had what the phrase charismatic leadership means in the United States. With his burning eyes, clenched fists, and long white beard, the Ayatollah exuded a captivating moral urgency and prophetic power that pulled at the hearts of a great many Iranians who were spiritually torn by political strife, economic corruption, and the powerful allure of Western culture.

Khomeini believed that only in Islam could the Iranian people find their destiny and the Iranian state its political legitimacy. The attempts of the shah to use secular Western methods to advance Iran's development infuriated Khomeini, but he carefully hid his scorn, avoiding the shah's security forces and waited for a time when the people would have the courage to stop the forces of secularization. But, by 1963, the Ayatollah's scorn could no longer be contained. Openly and uncompromisingly, he attacked the shah's regime as an anti-Islamic sacrilege aimed at destroying the role of the clergy in Iran. Inspired by Khomeini and other mullah religious leaders, tens of thousands of people took to the streets, rioting and protesting. The shah and his men were caught completely off guard by the demonstrations.

SAVAK, the shah's military police thugs, were sent into action. They attacked the crowds and arrested Khomeini. Khomeini's followers, fearing that the Ayatollah would be singled out for retribution, amassed huge throngs of demonstrators. "Khomeini or death!" they defiantly chanted. Throughout Iran, bazaars shut down in protest. Hundreds of protesters were killed as martial law was declared. However, the time for an Islamic revolution had not arrived. The fury of SAVAK and the loyalty of the army repressed the dissenters. The Ayatollah was imprisoned for ten months until the streets quieted. The shah had weathered the first great storm of his rule.

The Ayatollah was not cowed by his imprisonment. When released from jail in early 1964 he began to think more strategically. Within a year he was arrested again. This time SAVAK agents took him to the Tehran airport and informed him that he was no longer welcome in Iran. He was shipped off to Turkey. In October 1965, Khomeini was allowed to continue his exile in the Shi'i city of Najaf in Iraq. He stayed there for the next thirteen years, expanding his contacts among anti-shah groups both inside and outside Iran, lecturing on Islamic theology, the moral degeneration of society, and the need for an Islamic state. Patiently, he waited for events to bring him home.

The shah seemingly had triumphed over his internal enemies. During the 1960s and early 1970s his hold on power grew more secure as his wealth skyrocketed. In October 1971, he celebrated his thirtieth year as shah and the 2,500th anniversary of the founding of the Persian Empire with one of the most expensive parties the world had ever seen. Kings, emperors, princes, presidents, sheiks, sultans, and hundreds of immensely wealthy jet-setters came to a tent city the shah had built for the occasion on the ruins of Persepolis. Everyone drank Dom Perignon Rose 1959 and Chateau Lafite Rothschild served in specially designed Baccarat crystal goblets, and supped on poached quail eggs stuffed with caviar, crayfish mousse, roast peacock stuffed with foie gras, and other delicacies prepared by *Maxim's of Paris*. The shah's shindig cost the Iranian people, a majority of whom lived in poverty, some $200 million.

By May 1972, the United States was navigating troubled international waters. American military involvement in the Vietnam War was in its last desperate months. The United States

Lies and Deceits

was going to be forced to accept defeat - no matter how the terms were dressed up by Nixon and his men. The American people were fed up with military intervention and wanted no part of any new foreign entanglements. But, Washington and American capitalism were too committed to growth and control, and entrenchment was not part of that plan, especially when it came to Middle East oil.

Whatever else can be said about Richard Nixon, he was an innovative practitioner of global hardball. In 1972, accompanied by national security adviser Henry Kissinger, Nixon pulled off a series of world-changing diplomatic coups. In February, he journeyed to Beijing, met with Mao and began the process of mutually beneficial cooperation. In late May, he and Kissinger flew to Moscow where the nervous Soviets, fearful of whatever devilry Nixon had devised with the Chinese, agreed to an arms control treaty and promised to pursue a more friendly set of relations with America. Nixon and Kissinger, eager to pull off one more master stroke, then flew directly from Moscow to Tehran to court the shah.

In Tehran, Nixon's meaning was clear: the shah was to be the protector of all American interests in the Persian Gulf. The shah enthusiastically agreed; it made him the most powerful figure in the region. As the regional-power designate of the United States, he went on a monumental military shopping spree. He studied military weapons catalogs and defense trade journals like some men flip through *Playboy* magazine. He wanted all the good stuff and he got it: F-14 Tom Cats, F-16 and F-18 fighter planes, C-130 transport planes, helicopters, rockets, and on and on.

American weapons manufacturers loved the new arrangement; they not only sold the equipment and the spare parts, but also contracted for technical training and maintenance. Bribery in Iran was a way of life and American corporations parceled out millions to high-ranking military officers and government officials to secure deals. Tens of thousands of American technicians, mechanics, and weapons trainers flocked to Iran where they quickly learned to live like rich men, surrounded by servants in guarded expatriate enclaves well removed from the grinding poverty that made up everyday life for most Iranians. Meanwhile, religious Iranians watched these hard-drinking, fun-loving Americans with scorn and hatred.

The shah paid for his weapons with oil revenues. The OPEC cartel forced the oil-guzzling world to accept price hike after price hike. Few people, at least in the short run, saw any alternative. During this era of "oil shock," the shah showed his new muscle, but he also demonstrated an allegiance to his American ally. Throughout the oil embargo that followed the October 1973 Arab-Israeli 'Yom Kippur' War, the shah continued to sell oil to the United States - and to Israel - which had been an unwavering, longtime supporter of the shah.

As is often the case, "puppet" rulers like to flex their own muscles from time to time. Such was the case with the shah and oil as he pushed harder for higher oil prices. In private correspondence, President Nixon tried to convince him to slow down his price demands, but the shah stood firm: "We are conscious of the importance of this source of energy to the prosperity and stability of the international economy, but we also know that for us this source of wealth might be finished in thirty years."

The shah was in the driver's seat, but there was big trouble brewing in Iran. The country's sudden, massive flood of oil revenues only served to exacerbate the resentment of the Iranian people. Many Iranians thought the expenditures on weaponry were unnecessary, especially since Iran did not face a real threat to its national security and the military was frequently used as an arm of state repression. The middle and lower-class Iranians felt a growing resentment that there was no "trickle down" from the oil wealth; there was only "trickle up" to the shah's super-rich comrades. They blamed the shah for this condition, but behind the shah was the power and support from seven different U.S presidents!

In 1977, Governor Jimmy Carter of Georgia entered the White House. He was the first southerner to be elected president since before the Civil War. His campaign promise was, "I will not lie to the American people." This was refreshing news after all the lies about Watergate, Vietnam, and our CIA covert activities. After being sworn in at the Capitol, he strolled, rather than taking a motorcade, down Pennsylvania Avenue to the White House. His wife Rosalynn, their three sons and daughters-in-law, and nine-year-old daughter Amy walked with him as enthusiastic crowds roared their approval.

That first day as president may have been his best. Seeming to spurn the trappings of office, he announced that he was selling the presidential yacht. Not long after taking office, Carter donned a cardigan sweater to give a televised fireside chat to the nation. He delivered what was probably the last fully honest message by a president to the American people:

> "In a nation that was proud of hard work, strong families, close-knit communities, and faith in God, too many of us now tend to worship self-indulgence and consumption. Human identity is no longer defined by what one does, but by what one owns. But, we've discovered that owning things and consuming things does not satisfy our longing for meaning. We've learned that piling up material goods cannot fill the emptiness of lives which have no confidence or purpose."

Carter urged Americans that night to sacrifice, and for the nation to tackle the real problems of energy and global warming. It was a speech Americans did not want to hear. Corporate America and their lobbyists went berserk. It was the last time a president would ask Americans to endure sacrifice for the greater good.

Though relatively untested, President Carter was a man of many gifts. He could never have advanced to the presidency so fast without them. His modesty veiled a sharp intelligence. His decency was as deep as his Baptist faith. Though fiercely ambitious, he was incorruptible and incontestably dedicated to serving the people of the United States. If integrity, tenacity, discipline, and IQ are measures of presidential greatness - then Jimmy Carter would have been one of America's most extraordinary leaders. Alas, in the game of presidential leadership, brainpower and character usually count for less than political skill. And in the latter category,

Carter was a complete failure. From start to finish the Carter administration was an unmitigated disaster.

In the early days of his administration Carter reiterated the mantra of his campaign. He promised to bring fresh approaches to government and keep his distance from Washington lobbyists and corporate influence peddlers. He would move quickly to tackle big, unresolved issues, including energy, welfare, health care, and urban problems. He indicated that he would advance a tax rebate plan and increase public works employment in order to invigorate the economy. In an effort to bring harmony to the nation, he pardoned all those young Americans that had evaded military service in the Vietnam War. By March, Carter's popular approval rating was at 75 percent. However, many who came into contact with him were developing doubts about his manner, especially in dealing with Congress. By mid-1977, his glow had dimmed, and many grew disenchanted with his "blissful ignorance" about how to get things done.

President Carter was not the architect of our strategic relationship with Iran. Rather, he inherited a peculiar array of policies that left the United States strategically dependent on the shah's regime for oil, and Carter's discomfort with that position was apparent. Carter realized he had lied; not to America, but to himself. The morality issue of human rights in Iran conflicted with political expediency. Carter abhorred the abuses of the shah and his secret police, but Iran, with its abundant oil reserves and strategic location was too great a prize to risk over human rights. Despite misgivings, Carter had no plans to challenge that policy – he knew the United States needed the shah. Carter intended to maintain a strong, enduring, and vital friendship with the shah. Hopefully, over time, maybe the shah would become more receptive to the issue of human rights.

However, the Iranian people were not waiting for some change of heart by the shah. Anti-shah demonstrations began in earnest in 1978. As Khomeini loyalists gained support, President Carter sent riot-control equipment to the Iranian army. When troops fired on demonstrators, the crowd chanted: "Carter gives the guns; the shah kills the people." To President Carter, the catastrophic nature of the Iran crisis appeared to have erupted almost overnight. The CIA, overly dependent on the intelligence it received from SAVAK, was also taken by surprise.

National Security Advisor Zbigniew Brzezinski believed that the United States could not allow Persian Gulf oil to be jeopardized by a hostile takeover of Iran. The Soviets, he believed, would feast on the instability an Iranian revolution would produce and would see the Carter administration's inability to back up a key ally as a powerful indicator of American weakness. If the shah fell, the Soviets would push hard throughout the region, jeopardizing the West's access to oil and investment opportunities. Brzezinski believed that the United States must take firm measures to restore the shah's authority. "Firm measures" is a political euphemism for "bloodbath."

The United States told the shah that they favored a military solution to the crisis in Iran, but the shah could not give the orders that would result in the deaths of so many of his people and turn him into an object of global horror. He had never, even during the years of SAVAK torture and mayhem, seen himself as the destroyer of the Iranian people.

Battling bouts of depression and illness, he went before the people, speaking over the radio and on television. He promised open elections and social justice. Breaking precedent, he offered a halfway apology for "past mistakes, unlawful actions, oppression and corruption." He pleaded with religious leaders to calm the situation by preaching peace and order. It was too late; nobody was listening. By the end of December, the streets were alive with protest and the country was paralyzed by strikes.

Until almost the end, the United States was convinced that the shah could hold on to his power, but the CIA misread all the signals. They were caught off guard by the revolution that was taking place inside Iran because they had never seen anything like it before. As a political force, Islam was thought to be waning, not rising. Everyone in the region was presumed to be preoccupied with the practical problems of economics and modernization. Our experts failed to grasp either the depth of hostility toward the shah or the loyal following that the Muslim clerics could muster. The Iranian uprising was not a coup, a call for regime change, or even a civil war; it was a true political earthquake. What was happening had nothing to do with either communism or democracy; it was based instead on a narrow and inflexible interpretation of divine will.

The 79-year-old Ayatollah Khomeini returned from his fourteen years in exile on February 1, 1979 and proclaimed a holy revolution to the joyous pandemonium on the streets of Tehran. He listed his three main enemies: "the shah, the American Satan, and Saddam Hussein."

Khomeini had a burning desire to oust Saddam Hussein. When Khomeini was in exile in Iraq, Hussein expelled him at the shah's request. Hussein and his Ba'th regime were secular and Sunni, but the majority of Iraq's population was Shiite like Iran. The Shiites in Iraq were treated as second-class citizens, but Khomeini intended to change all that. After correcting the situation in Iraq, he intended to export his form of Islamic fundamentalism to the other Middle East countries.

Khomeini's intention of establishing himself as a religious philosopher-king and controlling the government according to religious law was completely alien to existing political traditions. The notion of a popular revolution leading to the establishment of a theocratic state seemed absurd to Washington insiders, including those in the Carter White House. No one really imagined that Iran could be ruled by a fundamentalist Islamic theocracy. The mullahs, it was argued, could not run a complex government; they would have to turn to secular leadership. American observers were confident that the religious dimension was only superficial, and attempted to fit the Iranian events into more familiar models of revolutionary experience. Almost everyone in the U.S. misjudged the power, organizational capacity, and popular appeal of the revolutionary movement. And our government simply did not understand the hostility so many Iranians felt toward the United States. For the CIA, whose job it is to know these things, it was an embarrassment.

The United States decided against direct military intervention after the shah fled the country. We were not certain that the Iranian generals would be any better than the unknown Khomeini, and it would have put the United States in a direct confrontation with Islam. Moreover, even after the truly unthinkable had happened, and Khomeini's exotic vision of the ideal state was well on its way to realization, policy judgment continued to be impaired by an unspoken but intrinsic conviction that any regime so wildly contrary to all the rules of accepted political behavior would inevitably destroy itself through its own excesses.

As with all revolutions, Iran's upheaval was initially awkward and bloody. The new Iranian definition of justice was, "human rights means that unsuitable individuals should be liquidated so that others can live free." During the revolution's first nine months, almost 600 Iranians faced the firing squad. The revolutionary courts maintained that "there is no need for defense lawyers because they keep quoting laws to play for time and this tries the patience of the people." Within the next eighteen months there would be 3,000 executions.

The month that Khomeini returned to Iran, there was an attack on the American Embassy in Tehran and the ambassador and his staff were taken captive. Miraculously, no American was seriously injured. On that occasion, members of Khomeini's government intervened and the hostages were set free within the hour. Washington was upset, but happy that events had not gotten out of control. It was reassuring that Khomeini had acted rationally in the crisis by immediately freeing the hostages.

In September 1979, the shah sought refuge in the United States after spending time in Egypt and Morocco. President Carter decided that allowing the shah into the United States would jeopardize the lives of Americans still in Iran. Brzezinski, who was intensely uncomfortable about denying asylum to a man who had been an ally of the United States for many years, suggested that the decision be reconsidered. President Carter reacted angrily, commenting that he did not want the shah in the United States playing tennis while Americans in Tehran could be kidnapped or killed. That ended any further discussion of the matter.

The shah was actually dying of cancer at the time, but he kept it a secret from everyone. Having been refused admittance to the United States, he flew to Mexico. On October 8, 1979 he got violently ill and a team of U.S. doctors were flown to Mexico. They confirmed that the shah had an advanced case of lymphoma combined with a fatal form of cancer known as Richter's syndrome. Carter now decided that the United States could not in good conscience refuse the shah access to our superior medical treatment and admitted him into the country. The Iranians did not believe the story and concluded that the United States was planning a coup in Iran and would then re-install the shah at the head of a new government. Thousands of Iranians protested in the streets, demanding that the United States turn the shah over to the Iranian government for trial.

On October 26, a group of students in Iran met and formulated a plan to capture the American Embassy and demand the shah's return. On November 4, the embassy was stormed and captured. Of the approximately 90 people inside, 52 would remain in captivity until the end of the crisis. None of the embassy employees or the nine U.S. Marines on duty resisted, figuring that would only exacerbate the situation. No one in the embassy expected a long-term situation, but this was the beginning of an ordeal that would last 444 days.

All of Iran watched with excitement and fascination. The Americans had been humiliated and humbled by a small group of university students. For many in Iran, it was a wonder to behold. In the United States, public opinion was aghast that the U.S. could not protect its own citizens. Still not fully recovered from the humiliation of Vietnam, the impulse to act was overpowering. The media in the United States was not a calming influence. *ABC News* showed American viewers a howling mob of Iranians in front of the U.S. Embassy burning an American flag. Men with black beards and women shrouded in chadors cheered with delight as the American flag went up in flames.

The story of the hostage-taking headlined almost every newspaper around the world. Responses were by no means uniform, though many anxiously pondered the effect of American actions on the already precarious global oil market. In Paris, a *Le Figaro* editorial spoke for many: "What is important in this affair is the uncertainty over oil supplies. With the risk of a new price increase, a military raid must be excluded." The Japanese Foreign Ministry concurred; stating that oil exports must be maintained and that Japan would not tamper with its relationship with Iran despite the unfortunate difficulties.

The United States sent a two-man delegation to Iran, but Khomeini refused to see them. The situation became more explosive when a number of Iranian students living in the United States decided to hold rallies siding with their comrades in Iran, and demanding that Carter return the shah to Iran. Under no circumstances was Jimmy Carter going to send the shah back to Iran to be executed. That option was not on the table. Everything Carter had learned about Khomeini over the past few months increased his concerns about the hostage situation. In his diary, Carter expressed his fears about negotiating with Iran's spiritual leader: "It's almost impossible to deal with a crazy man."

Attorney General Benjamin Civiletti, on orders from the White House, ordered all Iranian students in the United States, some 50,000 (many of whom did not support Khomeini), to report to immigration officials to have their visas checked. Students with visa irregularities were immediately deported. Several congressmen got into the act by introducing resolutions calling for all Iranian students to be thrown out of the United States. Some American citizens decided to take matters into their own hands. In Los Angeles, a mob used baseball bats on Iranian student demonstrators, sending several to the hospital. On city streets any young man who looked vaguely Iranian, and that was not a clear image for most Americans, stood an excellent chance of receiving angry epithets from passing motorists and pedestrians.

Within days of the hostage takeover, Americans demonstrated a nationalistic and emotional bond to their fellow Americans held captive in Iran. Longshoremen refused to load any cargo bound for Iran. At the widely publicized request of the hostages' families, millions of people kept their car headlights on during the day to show their solidarity. Church bells rang at mid-day to honor the captives. At the urging of church leaders, labor union officials, civic groups, and political leaders, many of whom were coordinating the effort with the White House, hundreds of thousands of

Americans wrote letters to the Iranian Embassy and the Iranian U.N. delegation. Daytime radio and television talk shows competed with one another to interview hostage family members.

Six weeks into the hostage crisis, the *Washington Post* ran a short article about Penne Laingen, the wife of the senior American official who was still a hostage. She told the *Post* reporter that she tied a yellow ribbon around the oak tree in her yard. "So I'm standing and waiting and praying, and one of these days my husband Bruce is going to untie that yellow ribbon. The yellow ribbon is going to be out there until he returns." As word of her action spread through the mass media, Americans began to follow her example and tie yellow ribbons around trees, telephone poles, street lamps, car radio antennas, and numerous other inanimate objects. Americans pinned little yellow ribbons to their clothes and pasted yellow-ribbon bumper stickers to their cars. On Super Bowl Sunday in January 1980, a stupendously long yellow ribbon was wrapped around the entire stadium.

The Ayatollah Khomeini had his own ideas about how to demonstrate the morality of the hostage-taking to the American people and others around the world. Two weeks after the hostages were seized; Khomeini ordered the release of the women and all the black Americans. Blacks, he observed, were themselves victims of American injustice and, thus, were not to blame for their government's policies. Islam, he further noted, always treated women with respect and decency.

Thirteen hostages, five white women and eight black men were released, but not before Khomeini milked it for all its propaganda value. Three of the hostages were selected by their captors to hold a press conference. Indicative of the magnitude of the story, some two hundred reporters from around the world attended. The woman hostage, Kathy Gross, a twenty-two-year-old Farsi-speaking embassy secretary, gave a statement sympathetic to the Iranian revolution: "If the American people were put in touch with the developments in the third world and America's interference in the internal affairs of these countries, they would certainly protest as well."

A twenty-four-year-old black U.S. Marine sergeant, William Quarles, was even more outspoken. He praised the Iranian revolutionaries, noting, "Freedom isn't just handed to you on a silver platter." And then, in explicit terms, he condemned American policy: "I think the American people have a lot to look at. Having been kept hostage here for two weeks, I got a chance to look at American imperialist practices. I'd like to, if I could, tell the American government to reevaluate their foreign policies. A lot of our policies are terribly wrong and a lot of people are suffering because of a few American leaders at the top."

Khomeini explained his actions to his closest associates. "This action has many benefits. The Americans do not want to see the Islamic Revolution taking root. As long as we hold the hostages our opponents dare not act against us. We can put the Islamic constitution to the people's vote without interference, and carry out the presidential and parliamentary elections. When we have finished with all these jobs, we can let the hostages go." Obviously, Khomeini had no interest in negotiating a quick end to the hostage crisis.

In the face of growing criticism about the shah's continued presence in the United States, Carter met privately with select congressional leaders and laid it on the line: "If you will excuse my expression, I don't give a damn whether you like or do not like the shah. I don't care whether you think he is a thief or not. I don't care whether you think I was wise or not wise in accepting the shah as one of our allies. The issue," Carter lectured, "is that American hostages are being held by kidnappers, radical and irresponsible kidnappers, with the encouragement and support of the Iranian government. I cannot abide Americans confusing the issue by starting to decide whether the history of Iran before the shah left was decent or indecent, was proper or improper. I don't care about that." It was a powerful and compelling unscripted talk, an emotional side of Jimmy Carter that the American public rarely, if ever, saw.

Through the first two months of the hostage crisis, the American people rallied around the president. Carter's standing in public opinion polls skyrocketed. But, Carter told the congressional leadership, "The patience of the American people is not a characteristic of America. People are inclined to be impatient here."

Although the United States was importing an average of 700,000 barrels a day of Iranian oil, it terminated all oil imports from Iran. Next, it froze all Iranian assets; nearly $12 billion on deposit in American banks either located in the U.S. or Europe. The most controversial aspect of the freeze order was its application to Iranian deposits in branches of U.S. banks outside the United States. In effect, this provision asserted that foreign branches of U.S. banks were subject to U.S. law rather than the laws of the nations in which they were created. The freeze order was quickly challenged by Iran in the courts of Great Britain, France, Germany, and the other nations where the banks were located. When the assets were ultimately unfrozen as part of the hostage release settlement, none of the court cases had come to judgment.

Influencing events at this time was David Rockefeller, chairman of Chase Manhattan Bank. Rockefeller met with Secretary of the Treasury William Miller, an old friend from the corporate establishment. Rockefeller's predicament was that if billions of dollars in Iranian loans to Chase had to be written off, it would seriously affect the earnings and stock price of Chase Manhattan Bank. Rockefeller had a plan to avoid this, having to do with an interest payment of $500 million that was coming due. Rockefeller sold his idea to Miller who in turn convinced Carter.

Carter's freeze announcement was made one day before Iran's interest payment to Chase Manhattan Bank was due to be paid. With all its assets frozen in the U.S., Iran was unable to make the interest payment. Chase Manhattan immediately declared Iran in default on the entire loan. Chase then used "cross-default" clauses in the loan agreement to declare all of Iran's other loans in default and seized Iran's cash deposits to pay off every loan in full. When the dust cleared, Chase no longer had any Iranian debt on its books.

From that moment, the entire hostage crisis was complexly entangled with America's bankers and their legal teams. In the end, the resolution of the crisis clearly benefited the American banking community. The banks emerged from the hostage crisis with compensation for all their major claims against Iran. Some banks had the use of Iran's frozen assets for fourteen months interest-free and made a whopping profit on the hostage crisis.

The threat of physical danger to the hostages was compounded by a bizarre combination of events elsewhere in the Arab world. On November 20, the Great Mosque in Mecca (Saudi Arabia) was taken over by a group of armed militant Islamics. This sudden attack, affecting one of the most sacred Muslim shrines sent shock waves throughout the Islamic world. Within hours, wild rumors began to circulate, including one particularly absurd story that the assault was the work of Israel with the assistance of the United States. That story was picked up by a radio station in Pakistan, where a mob invaded the U.S. Embassy. A U.S. Marine guard and an Army warrant officer were killed, and the embassy was almost burned to the ground. Secretary of State Vance feared that an anti-U.S. wave was sweeping the entire Islamic world. He ordered all nonessential U.S. personnel throughout the region to evacuate; some 900 U.S. dependents and officials returned to the United States over the following weeks.

President Carter suddenly had another crisis on his hands when the Soviet military, with some 85,000 troops, invaded Afghanistan, killed Prime Minister Hafizullah Amin, and hastily installed Babrak Karmal as their 'puppet' replacement. The Soviet government stated that its purpose was to safeguard the region against a growing Islamic revolutionary threat. This was the first Soviet use of military force outside its own satellite empire since World War II, and the invasion dramatically transformed the entire security balance of the Persian Gulf region.

The CIA should have foreseen the Soviet thrust into Afghanistan, but they were asleep at the switch. The blatant Soviet aggression was proof that the Soviet government had become emboldened by the Carter administration's relative timidity. It was feared that the Afghan move was only the first step in a Soviet campaign to insert itself into the Persian Gulf region. From this position, the Soviets could threaten the rest of the industrial world's oil supply.

President Carter harshly condemned the Soviet invasion and instituted economic sanctions against Russia, including a grain embargo (infuriating U.S. farmers) and a boycott of the 1980 Summer Olympics in Moscow. The American people responded positively to their president's leadership, which is almost always the case at a time of perceived crisis. On January 23, 1980, President Carter gave his State of the Union Address and warned the American people that the Soviet invasion of Afghanistan was not only an outrage against the Afghan people; it was a deliberate threatening move by the Soviets into the Persian Gulf region. "Let our position be absolutely clear," he told the American people. "An attempt by any outside force to gain control of the Persian Gulf region will be regarded as an assault on the vital interests of the United States of America, and such an assault will be repelled by any means necessary, including military force."

Carter did not ignore the Iran hostage crisis in his State of the Union speech. While warning the Iranian government that it would be held responsible for any harm done to the hostages, Carter also tried to shift the focus, stating that the American government must somehow demonstrate to "the Iranian leaders that the real danger to their nation lies in the north from the Soviet troops now in Afghanistan, and that the unwarranted Iranian quarrel with the United States hampers their response to this far greater danger to them."

The hostage episode remained a colossal media event. Republicans used the crisis to depict Carter as weak and indecisive. With each passing day the American public became more outraged and they demanded action. The pressure mounted on Carter with every drop in his popularity in the polls and he buckled to the pressure for action. Succumbing to public opinion, he turned his attention to a proposed military rescue mission. It was a giant mistake. He was about to make an emotional response to the crisis when what was needed was cool rational leadership. At stake were the lives of fifty-two Americans, but without being cavalier about the understandable concern for welfare of the hostages, these were harden diplomats who understood the risks of serving in an embassy inside a foreign hostile country.

In terms of our national security this was no crisis – our pride was hurt and we were embarrassed – but the situation did not call for military action. Instead, Carter should have adopted what some call "creative inattention," and allowed diplomacy to continue. Iran could only benefit from further world attention and that is what any rescue attempt would bring. Iran would have released the hostages when the situation was no longer in the news. It was not in their interest to keep the hostages indefinitely. They certainly did not want harm to come to any of them - the military consequences and the wrath of world opinion would have been enormous.

Nonetheless, President Carter decided to act with a show of strength to prove to his critics that he had the resolute backbone. On April 11, he gave his approval to rescue the hostages and now everything was in the hands of the military.

Some five months earlier an elite team of American fighting men, Delta Force, led by Colonel Charlie Beckwith, had begun training to rescue the hostages. Delta Force had been specifically created as the U.S. military's first counter-terrorist unit. Chosen personally by Colonel Beckwith after an extraordinarily rigorous and competitive process, the men of Delta Force trained relentlessly to neutralize the hostage-takers. The meaning of "neutralize" was made clear by a sign Beckwith kept on his desk: "Kill 'em all. Let God sort them out."

The rescue plan – code named *Eagle Claw* – sounded as if it was taken from the plot of a spy novel or Hollywood movie. Using eight helicopters, an assault force of 118 men would make their way from the naval aircraft carrier *U.S.S. Nimitz* in the Gulf of Oman to a desert location in Iran, 200 miles from Tehran. There, they would refuel their huge RH-53D Sea Stallion helicopters from C-130 fuel-carrying transport planes that flew into Iran from a base in Egypt. Then, through a several-step process, aided by CIA operatives clandestinely in place in Tehran, the team would stealthily make their way to the U.S. Embassy. The Delta Force commandos would enter the embassy compound, kill every armed guard they encountered, free the hostages, and the helicopters would fly in and pick up team members and hostages, and return home safely. Everybody understood that each phase of the operation entailed risks and nobody thought it would be easy.

Task Force Commander General James Vaught and Colonel Beckwith briefed President Carter on the overall operation just a few days before it was to be launched. Carter listened with his usual intensity. Colonel Beckwith then specifically explained to the president how his people would rescue the hostages. The president asked the colonel how many casualties he anticipated. General Vaught replied for Beckwith. No one could answer that question, he said, but suggested that maybe six or seven Delta Force men might be wounded and perhaps two or three of the hostages. Warren Christopher, with his usual careful deliberation asked what would happen to the guards. Beckwith replied that his men would "take the guards out." Christopher wanted to make sure that the president understood: "What do you mean? Will you shoot them in the shoulder or what?" Beckwith clarified his statement: "No, sir. We're going to shoot each of them twice, right between the eyes."

The rescue mission failed long before it arrived at the embassy walls. In the early evening of April 24, eight helicopters took off from the carrier *Nimitz* in the Arabian Sea. Some two hours into the flight, after entering Iranian territory, helicopter number 6 of the formation began receiving warning signals in the cockpit of a possible impending rotor blade failure. The pilot landed and abandoned his craft. The crew was picked up by one of the other helicopters and the mission continued.

Shortly after this event, the remaining helicopters unexpectedly encountered a cloud of suspended dust, making visual observation extremely difficult. Since the helicopters were maintaining strict radio silence and were unable to maintain contact visually, they became separated. The helicopters broke out of the dust cloud, only to encounter another dust storm that was denser than the first. Because of the thick swirling dust, the helicopters were forced to rely almost entirely on their internal navigation equipment and instruments. Approximately four hours into the flight, helicopter number 5 began to experience malfunction. The pilot reversed course, flew back for more than two hours through the dust and returned safely to the carrier. Because of radio silence, the crew of helicopter number 5 was unaware that at the moment they decided to turn back they were only 25 minutes from their rendezvous site.

At approximately the same moment that helicopter 5 reversed course, helicopter 2 was beginning to experience hydraulic problems. Number 2 continued on to the rendezvous site and arrived safely. However, inspection after arrival revealed that the helicopter would have to be abandoned. At this point the mission commander was faced with a critical situation. The helicopters had arrived eighty-five minutes late; dawn was fast approaching and he only had five workable helicopters. It had been determined in advance that a minimum of six helicopters were required to conduct the assault mission. As a consequence, Colonel Beckwith, the mission commander at the site, concluded that the operation should be aborted. This decision was relayed to the White House, where President Carter concurred, and the force prepared to withdraw.

The situation got worse. After the abort order was issued, a helicopter lifted off in the dust storm and collided with a refueling plane. An explosion tore apart the helicopter and the C-130; flames shot three to four hundred feet into the night sky. Eight Americans were instantly killed. There was nothing to do but get the survivors out on the remaining C-130 aircraft and leave the five helicopters and the dead bodies behind as macabre trophies for the Iranian revolutionaries. The mission had gone from unlucky failure to tragic disaster.

Word of the catastrophe reached the White House just before the force left the ground in retreat. The president was in his study, surrounded by his advisers, still absorbing the shock of the abort decision when he received the call. As President Carter listened he closed his eyes and his face went pale. "Are there any dead?" Carter asked. The room was silent. Finally the president said softly, "I understand," and hung up the phone. He calmly explained to the others what had happened. The men took in the awful news quietly. Then Secretary of State Cyrus Vance, who had submitted his resignation earlier that day because he objected to the mission, said, "Mr. President, I'm very, very sorry." America's elite rescue force had lost eight men, seven helicopters, and a C-130, and had not even made contact with the enemy. It was a debacle.

Amid the fallout from the embarrassing and horrible disaster, some in Congress criticized Carter for ordering the high-risk mission without consulting with them ahead of time as required under the War Powers Resolution. But, Carter argued that consultation had not been required because the rescue mission depended on total secrecy and this was not a combat mission. His answer did not satisfy the critics, but Congress made no move to sanction him.

After the humiliating rescue failure, most Americans were hungry for new leadership. That summer the Republican Party nominated Ronald Reagan, who accepted his party's nomination with these words: "I will not stand by and watch this great country destroy itself under mediocre leadership that drifts from one crisis to the next, eroding our national will and purpose."

During the election campaign the hostage crisis dragged on. That July, a hostage who had been suffering from multiple sclerosis was released. The other American hostages were scattered to various places inside Iran. Then on September 22, 1980, catastrophically for the people of Iran, a major war broke out between Iraq and Iran. After a series of border skirmishes and troop escalations, Iraq invaded Iran's Khuzistan province, hoping to take advantage of Iran's political disarray and instability. Many Iranians blamed the United States for the bloody confrontation. They believed Saddam Hussein and the United States were working together – which they were.

President Carter worked desperately to free the hostages and gain a last-minute electoral boost. But, Reagan's election team, with future CIA director William Casey in the lead, was not going to let that happen. Casey flew to Madrid in July and August where he met with high level Iranian representatives and arranged a secret deal. If the hostages were not released until after the U.S. election, the newly elected President Reagan would guarantee vital arms shipments to Iran for use against Iraq's invasion forces. The arms would arrive secretly; either from the United States or via

Israel. In addition, Casey pledged $40 million to the personal bank accounts of the ayatollahs. The money was to be laundered through a number of Swiss banks before ending up in Tehran. At no time was the Carter administration aware of these secret dealings. It never occurred to Carter that a political party out of power would attempt to undercut an important negotiation affecting the lives of American hostages. The actions by Reagan and Casey were not only illegal; they were treasonous.

Despite the advantages of incumbency, Carter suffered a crushing defeat. Reagan carried all but four states and won the popular vote by well over eight million. It was a landslide victory and a portent of things to come.

In accordance with the secret deal made with Khomeini, the hostages were released minutes after President Reagan took the oath of office. On the day of President Reagan's inauguration, the United States released almost $8 billion in Iranian assets. Almost immediately thereafter, the flow of arms to Iran began. The secret deal with Iran stated that the United States would not in any way attempt to overthrow the revolutionary Iranian government or intercede in Iranian internal affairs.

In the end, the hostages were released because the Khomeini government no longer had any use for them. In Tehran, the newspaper headlines read: "America Bows to the Nation's Conditions: Hostages Released." While the headline was not literally true in all regards, from the Iranian perspective it was true enough. They had defeated the "Great Satan."

CHAPTER TWENTY ONE

IRAN-CONTRA

"The United States has to realize it does not own Central America or any other part of the world. People have a right to shape their own destiny and to choose the type of government they want. We did not lose Cuba or Nicaragua because they were never ours to lose."

Sister Ita Ford

"After seeing 'Rambo' last night, I know what to do the next time this happens."

President Ronald Reagan

Jimmy Carter had morality, integrity, honesty and intelligence, but lacked political savvy; Ronald Reagan had political savvy but none of the other qualities. If there ever was a president who should have been impeached for constitutional wrong-doing, or removed from office because of physical and mental disability – it was Ronald Reagan.

For more than forty years Reagan had been Hollywood's version of the genial boy next door, the all-American nice guy. Cocky without arrogance, wisecracking and fun-loving, he appeared to embody what the country identified as American virtues: informality, humor, and patriotism. He played the part so well so many times that it was hard for him to separate role from reality.

Ronald Reagan was recruited, managed and coaxed onward and upward by a group of West Coast businessmen, known as

"Reagan's Kitchen Cabinet." They trained and coached Reagan like a race horse. Reagan had two unique qualities: he could loyally follow orders and he read his lines flawlessly. "I like trade unions," he would quip, "if they're in Poland." With the country fed up with Jimmy Carter's mishandling of the Iran hostage crisis, Reagan was propelled from the governorship of California to the presidency of the United States.

Upon arriving in the White House, Reagan was dismayed to learn that there was no 'War Room.' "But I distinctly remember seeing it in the movie *Dr. Strangelove*," the baffled new president replied. When asked about the plight of the homeless and the poor in this country, he replied, "We are told that 17 million Americans go to bed hungry each night. Well, that is probably true. They are all on a diet." His stories about his youth and background were delusions actually taken from old movies.

Reagan believed that the United States was infinitely virtuous, and the Soviet Union infinitely wicked. The world struggle, according to Reagan was "Between right and wrong and good and evil; and we are enjoined by scripture and the Lord Jesus to oppose the communist evil with all our might." He ascribed to the view that the Soviet Union was personally responsible for the world's manifold ills. "Let us not delude ourselves. The Soviet Union underlies all the unrest that is going on. Once they acquire the proper margin of numerical superiority in warheads, we should expect them to launch a surprise nuclear attack on the United States. Safety lies only in the establishment of American military dominance. If this means a nuclear arms race, then the fault lies in Moscow not Washington, because America's heart is pure." Marxist-Leninism, according to our new president, "was first proclaimed by the serpent in the Garden of Evil when Adam and Eve were tempted to disobey God." And so began the Reagan era.

Ronald Reagan's first inaugural address served to recite various conservative bromides. "For decades we have piled deficit upon deficit, mortgaging our future and the future of our children for the temporary convenience of the present. To continue this long trend is to guarantee tremendous social, cultural, political, and economic upheavals." He vowed to put America's economic house in order. "You and I, as individuals, can, by borrowing, live beyond our means, but for only a limited period of time. Why, then, should we think that collectively, as a nation, we're not bound by that same limitation?" Reagan reiterated an oft-made promise "to check and reverse the growth of government."

Reagan would do none of these things. In each case, in fact, he did just the opposite. During the Carter years, the federal deficit averaged $54.5 billion annually. During the Reagan era, deficits skyrocketed, averaging $210.6 billion over the course of Reagan's two terms in office. Overall federal spending nearly doubled, from $590.9 billion in 1980 to $1.14 trillion in 1989. The federal government did not shrink. Instead, the bureaucracy grew by nearly 5 percent while Reagan occupied the White House. Although he promised to shut down extraneous government programs and agencies, that turned out to be just another political untruth.

To call Reagan a phony or a hypocrite is to miss the point. The Reagan 'revolution' over which he presided was never about fiscal responsibility or small government. The object of the exercise was to give the American people what they wanted to hear. Far more accurately than Jimmy Carter, Reagan understood what made Americans tick; they wanted self-gratification, not self-denial. Although always careful to embroider his speeches with inspirational homilies and testimonials to old-fashioned virtues, Reagan mainly indulged American self-indulgence.

Reagan's two terms in office became an era of gaudy prosperity and excess. Tax cuts and the largest increase to date in peacetime military spending formed the twin centerpieces of Reagan's economic policy; the former was justified by theories of supply-side economics, the latter as the response to perceived Soviet arms buildup and adventurism. Declaring that "defense is not a budget item," Reagan severed the connection between military spending and all other fiscal or political considerations - a proposition revived by George W. Bush after September 2001.

On March 23, 1983, Reagan announced his Strategic Defense Initiative - a futuristic "impenetrable anti-missile shield intended to make nuclear weapons impotent and obsolete." Critics derisively dubbed his proposal "Star Wars," a label the president embraced. Yet embedded in Reagan's remarks were two decidedly radical propositions: first, that the minimum requirements of U.S. security now required the United States to achieve a status akin to invulnerability; and second, that modern technology was bringing this seemingly utopian goal within reach. *Star Wars*, in short, introduced into mainstream politics the proposition that Americans could be truly safe if the United States enjoyed something akin to permanent global military supremacy - that military power offered an antidote to the uncertainties and anxieties of living in a world not run entirely in accordance with American preferences.

Whereas President Carter had summoned Americans to mend their ways, which implied a need for critical self-awareness, President Reagan obviated any need for soul-searching by simply telling Americans to carry on. For Carter, ending American dependence on foreign oil meant promoting moral renewal at home. Reagan mimicked Carter in bemoaning the nation's growing energy dependence, but did nothing to curtail that dependence. Instead, Reagan wielded U.S. military power to ensure access to oil, thereby prolonging America's dependence. Carter had portrayed the American preoccupation with "piling up material goods" as fundamentally at odds with authentic freedom. Reagan's view was the complete opposite – he believed that availability of cheap credit combined with cheap oil could sustain such a consumer economy indefinitely.

When skeptics and nuclear strategists worried that the pursuit of *Star Wars* might prove "destabilizing" - Reagan offered categorical assurances. "The defense policy of the United States is based on a simple premise: The United States does not start fights. We will never be an aggressor. We maintain our strength in order to deter and defend against aggression - to preserve freedom and peace." According to Reagan, the employment of U.S. forces for anything but defensive purposes was simply inconceivable. "Every item in our defense program - our ships, our tanks, our planes, our funds for training and spare parts - is intended for one all-important purpose: to keep the peace."

Illusions about military power, first fostered by Reagan, outlived his presidency. Unambiguous global military supremacy became a standing aspiration. For the Pentagon, anything less than unquestioned dominance now qualified as dangerously inadequate. A new national security consensus emerged based on the conviction that the United States military and advanced technology could dominate the planet. In Washington, confidence escalated that a high-quality military establishment, dexterously employed, could organize the world to our liking. By the time Reagan retired from office, this had become the basis for our national security strategy.

One thing that Ronald Reagan excelled at was a complete disregard for the law. He illegally supplied arms, including chemical and biological weapons, to Iraq in its war with Iran; and then, in an act of unbelievable imperial hubris, he supplied arms to Iran against our Iraqi ally. He supplied both sides with military intelligence enabling them to easily kill each other. He supported the Contra war in Nicaragua in direct violation of a specific congressional amendment not to do so. His actions in Latin America left 200,000 dead.

But first, Reagan ordered the invasion of Grenada, a small nation of 100,000 people and about 133 square miles near Barbados and Trinidad. The action was undertaken without warning, without congressional authorization, and in violation of the charters of the United Nations and the Organization of American States. The pretext for the invasion was the rescue of American citizens because Russia and Cuba were building an airport there in order to invade the United States.

Grenada was not simply attacked; it was overrun in a miniature D-day invasion: an air, ground, and sea assault that overthrew the existing government of Bernard Coard, a Castro admirer. A group of businessmen then formed a new government under American tutelage.

Neo-conservative spokesman, Irving Kristol, would later explain the Grenada invasion this way, "The reason we gave for the intervention – the risk to American medical students there was phony, but the reaction of the American people was absolutely and overwhelmingly favorable. They had no idea what was going on, but they backed the president. They always will."

After the invasion of this tiny island, Reagan had the audacity to address the nation and proudly proclaim, "Our days of weakness are over. Our military forces are back on their feet and standing tall." Reagan's explanation to the American public has to rank with one of the most incredible lies of all time. Reagan believed he could get away with any lie as long as he came across sincere and smiled – and he almost did.

Ronald Reagan's relationship to the truth was always a problematic issue. His own official biographer, Edmund Morris, called him "an apparent airhead." The late Clark Clifford stirred up a minor hornet's nest in the early years of Reagan's presidency by applying the term "amiable dunce." The editors of national news magazines appeared to prefer the more polite term: "disengaged." What the public did not know was that his Alzheimer's disease was progressing rapidly, causing his mental "lapses" to come more frequently and last for longer periods of time.

Members of his cabinet met privately to discuss having him removed for not being able to discharge his duties, but nobody was willing to take that step – it might look like a "coup" and that would mean political death for the participants. Instead, the country ambled along with the man at the top presiding over this nuclear age without all his mental faculties intact. It was almost as if the entire political system agreed to pretend that Reagan was stable and engaged because the truth was somehow too frightening to contemplate.

His "disengagement" episodes were truly startling. He told Israeli Prime Minister Yitzhak Shamir and Nazi hunter Simon Wiesenthal, in separate Oval Office visits, that as a young soldier in the U.S. Army Signal Corps during World War II, he filmed the liberation of Nazi death camps, but he never served in Europe! He entertained a strange fascination with the apocalyptic "End of Days" and was even known to speculate that they might take place during his presidency. He invented what he called "a verbal message" from the Pope in support of his Central American policies, which was news to everyone at the Vatican. He announced that South

Africa - though still ruled by the vicious apartheid regime of P.W. Botha - had "eliminated the segregation that we once had in our own country."

Such strange pronouncements by the President of the United States eventually grew to be considered so routine that rarely did anyone in the White House ever bother to correct them. One former senior adviser admitted that the president simply had a penchant to "build these little worlds and live in them." One of his own children added, "He makes things up and believes them." What is more astounding is that he convinced the vast majority of Americans to also believe them.

While Reagan may have believed his own inventions, his advisers - men such as Caspar Weinberger, William Casey, Alexander Haig, George Shultz, and Robert McFarlane – should not have stood by silently. Their silence was tantamount to participation in Reagan's deceptions. They placed personal self-interest and blind loyalty ahead of their responsibility to the truth and the well-being of the nation.

Reagan inherited many potentially explosive global situations. Although the hostages were free, Iran was financing international terrorism, particularly Hezbollah in Lebanon and Hamas in Palestine. Iraq and Iran were at war and we were concerned about the stability of our oil supplies from that region. The Soviet Union had invaded Afghanistan and we were secretly engaging in covert operations there. As if the Middle East wasn't a big enough problem, Latin America was politically veering to the "left" - endangering American corporate interests. Castro was still in power in Cuba and was as strongly anti-American and opinionated as ever; and Daniel Ortega was the new "leftist" hero in Nicaragua.

Iran-Contra was Ronald Reagan's legacy to the world of lies and deceits. Iran-Contra was not one affair; it was two separate and distinctly different operations. Both operations were managed by the same few officials and intersected at particular points, but that did not make them one and the same; it merely made the whole affair that much more bizarre and clandestine.

Iran-Contra had many independent pieces. It involved the Iran-Iraq war and the illegal sale of weapons to both sides; the utter disregard of congressional mandates regarding the Contras; the kidnapping of Americans in Lebanon; negotiating with terrorists; and Israel becoming a covert U.S. surrogate. Moreover, putting the Iran affair first reverses the chain of events. The armed support of the Contra opposition to the legitimate Sandinista regime in Nicaragua came first and had its own independent origins.

Reagan came into office just as the popular struggle against oppressive regimes in Central America reached a critical stage. More than two-thirds of the region's people had been made desperately poor by an American sponsored economic plan in which each Latin American country could only concentrate on the production of a single crop. This arrangement made five percent of the population extremely wealthy, while the rest languished in poverty. When vast numbers of dispossessed people showed signs of throwing off this system, the major beneficiaries of the system, American companies such as United Fruit, Domino Sugar, and Gulf & Western, realized they had a major problem.

Without delving into our entire history with Nicaragua, a few facts are pertinent. In the 1920s, in an effort to orient Nicaragua's economy in our direction and to protect our corporate interests there, U.S. Marines occupied Nicaragua. During that period, Augusto Sandino, a Nicaraguan general waged a guerrilla campaign against our military forces, but he was unsuccessful. When we finally left Nicaragua in 1933, we organized a U.S. trained and supported National Guard that was headed by Anastasio Somoza Garcia. Somoza came to control the government and his rule was oppressive. In the 1970s, that governing style was continued by his son, Anastasio Somoza Debayle. During this period, Guatemala and El Salvador were also ruled by corrupt pro-American dictatorships.

In the 1970s, a broad revolutionary movement in Nicaragua, opposed to Somoza, sought to overthrow him. It called itself *Sandinista*, named after the legendary Augusto Sandino. On July 17, 1979, toward the end of the Carter administration, the forty-two-year-old Somoza dictatorship collapsed. The new leadership was based on a mixture of socialist and Christian ideology. Three of the eight members of the ruling junta were Catholic priests, one was a hardcore Marxist, and the others were left-wing nationalists.

Carter was ambivalent about the Sandinistas, but he decided to treat the new regime with a show of respect and goodwill. Nicaragua quickly received $39 million in emergency food aid from the United States and then another $60 million in economic assistance. During the Cold War politics of the era, it was not unusual for Third World countries to play the United States and the Soviet Union against one another in an effort to receive aid from each. In March 1980, a Sandinista delegation went to Moscow and signed economic, technical, scientific, and cultural agreements with the Soviet Union.

The first official action taken by the new Sandinista government was to correct the environmental damage done under Somoza, which had permitted commercial interests to dump toxic wastes in the country's lakes. The Sandinistas then launched a literacy campaign to teach every Nicaraguan to read and write, and they set out to build 2,500 clinics so the people would have access to some kind of medical treatment. The government also expropriated the lands of Somoza, his family, and those who fled Nicaragua. These lands were turned over to the people in the form of cooperatives so that the poor could profit from the land they worked on. Four years after the revolution, Nicaragua had the greatest rate of economic growth of any Latin American country.

President Reagan viewed what was happening in Nicaragua in the most simplistic terms – it was a Moscow-sponsored thrust into 'our' Western Hemisphere. Reagan used classic Cold War rationale: communism in our backyard endangered our national security and the Sandinistas were Marxists. Reagan feared that Nicaragua was the new Cuba and he urged action. Secretary of State Alexander Haig told Reagan at a National Security Council meeting, "you give me the word and I'll turn that fucking place into a parking lot." When Reagan procrastinated, Haig explained that Central America's very insignificance made it the perfect antidote to Vietnam. "Mr. President, this is one you can win."

That was the clincher – Reagan was convinced. From that moment, Reagan made support for anti-Sandinista counter-revolutionaries, known as the Contras, a top priority. It was a perfect scenario in which to earn accolades: a covert U.S. operation against a weak adversary.

In 1981, CIA training bases for the Contras were set up in Florida, Texas, and California. Under the cover of military exercises, U.S. Army engineers built command posts for the Contras in Honduras and Costa Rica. Everything was organized, controlled, and paid for by the CIA.

The public is not lied to and misled by chance – it takes a coordinated effort. Recent declassified presidential files and tapes reveals that discussions with Reagan in the Oval Office pertaining to this subterfuge and deception, included CIA Director Casey, Secretary of State Schultz, National Security Advisor McFarlane, Secretary of Defense Weinberger, and Chief of Staff James Baker. They all agreed that the U.S. should finance the rebel Contras, and to lie about the plight of the Nicaraguan people and its new leaders. According to Reagan, the Contras were "the moral equivalent of our Founding Fathers and the brave men and women of the French Resistance."

In 1982, news reporters found out that the Contras were a CIA operation, and a congressional committee called in CIA Director William Casey to explain. Casey, who once told the president, "We will know that we have succeeded when everything the public believes is false," now told the committee that, yes, the CIA was aiding the Contras, but the aim was only to stop arms shipments from Nicaragua to insurgents in El Salvador where a civil war was in progress. Casey denied that we were trying to bring down the Nicaraguan government or put the Somoza forces back in power. Other administration officials, however, confirmed in closed session that our express aim was overthrowing Nicaragua's government.

An outraged Congress passed the Boland Amendment as part a foreign appropriations bill: the House vote was 411-0 and the Senate adopted the resolution 84-12. The amendment specifically stated that "none of the funds provided in this Act may be used by the CIA or the Department of Defense to furnish military equipment, military training or advice, or other support for military activities, to any group or individual for the purpose of overthrowing the government of Nicaragua." Since the Boland Amendmentand was attached to the Defense Appropriations Act, it had to be renewed annually.

Reagan completely disregarded Congress and the Boland Amendment, and instructed National Security Advisor Robert McFarlane that he wanted the Sandinista regime overthrown. McFarlane's orders were to keep the Contras going "body and soul." The Contras, with CIA support, terrorized villages and the atrocities that followed included castration, rape, and mutilation - all documented and condemned by the World Court.

President Reagan kept insisting these Nicaraguan death squads were "freedom fighters." To a joint session of Congress he declared: "Let us be clear as to the American attitude toward the government of Nicaragua. We do not seek its overthrow." At the very moment that Reagan was lying to Congress, the CIA was circumventing the Boland Amendment by appropriating funds from the U.S. Defense Department budget that had been earmarked for our armed services. To insure the secrecy of what we were doing, guns and supplies were flown into Nicaragua by the CIA's privately owned airline fleet.

On January 7, 1984, the CIA, with the approval of President Reagan, began placing magnetic mines in three Nicaraguan harbors in order to discourage supplies from reaching the government. The mining attracted little immediate attention because the Contras - at the instigation of the CIA - claimed credit for mining the harbors. However, on April 6, the *Wall Street Journal* revealed that the CIA and not the Contras was responsible for the mines, and that the mining resulted in damage to several ships, including a Soviet oil tanker. International law defined such an act as "a direct act of aggression against a sovereign state," and was clearly prohibited by international treaties. The mining raised the question of who in the American government authorized an act of war. When outraged senators complained, the CIA blandly promised not to do it again.

When Nicaragua prepared to make a formal complaint to the International Court of Justice, the Reagan administration announced peremptorily that it would no longer accept the World Court's jurisdiction over "disputes with any Central American state or arising out of or related to events in Central America." The United States thus arbitrarily set aside a treaty obligation that the Senate had ratified back in 1946.

Nevertheless, the World Court heard Nicaragua's case, and ruled that the United States had violated "general principles of humanitarian law" in mining harbors, bombing oil installations, arming the Contras, and distributing guerrilla-warfare manuals that encouraged the violent intimidation of Nicaraguan citizens. This was the first time in history that a world tribunal ever found the United States in violation of international law.

The reaction in Congress was wrathful. As a result, Congress passed a second Boland Amendment that was more drastic than the previous one. Known as Boland II, it prohibited any military or paramilitary support for the Nicaraguan Contras. Republican right-wingers had no difficulty grasping the scope and intent of the amendment. Representative Dick Cheney of Wyoming went so far as to characterize it as a "killer amendment," designed to force the Contras "to lay down their arms."

However, Reagan was not interested in what Congress had to say. He was fully committed to the Contras at all costs. The problem was how to get around the Boland II amendment. In February 1986, King Abdul-Aziz of Saudi Arabia visited President Reagan in Washington and secretly agreed to furnish $24 million to the Contras. Prince Bandar, the Saudi ambassador to the United States followed with his own $8 million contribution to the Contras. All of this was subterfuge to get around Boland II. But, the Saudi funds were not enough to effect regime change in Nicaragua. Something bigger and more sinister was needed.

The second part of the Iran-Contra affair had to do with Lebanon, Iraq, Iran and Israel. The new Iranian regime had already cancelled all its contracts with U.S. oil companies. A new ally was needed in the Middle East to ensure American access to oil. Iraq, with the second largest oil reserves in the world after Saudi Arabia, became our next best option. The United States was hoping to make Iraq "our new Iran."

Iran at the time was weak and still in transition from its revolution. The shah's army had been dismantled and its military leadership purged. The timing was perfect for the United States to "pay back" Iran for the overthrow of the shah, the hostage humiliation, and to insure that the Iranian Revolution did not spread to our other vital oil interests in the area. What we needed was a surrogate to do the fighting and dying. Saddam Hussein became that man.

Saddam Hussein was born in 1937 into an illiterate peasant family. At the age of ten, he fled from an abusive stepfather to live with his uncle, an army officer residing in Baghdad. There, Saddam entered school for the first time. Overage and untutored, he was a poor student, but fierce determination propelled him ahead. Like many young Iraqis, he soon found himself swept up in a world of political action and intrigue.

In 1956, he participated in an abortive coup against the monarchy. The next year, at the age of twenty, he joined the revolutionary Ba'th Party. The Ba'th was a minuscule movement at the time, dedicated to Arab unity and social egalitarianism, and it was anti-Western and anti-Communist. They believed that all existing Arab regimes had to be united and all borders eliminated. The culmination of this policy would be a single powerful Arab union that would no longer be at the mercy of the Western powers. The movement had great appeal to young radicals like Saddam, and to numerous intellectuals and dissident army officers chafing under the inefficiency of the old regime.

In 1958, at the age of twenty-one, Saddam was briefly imprisoned for the murder of his uncle's Communist rival in a local election, a man that also happened to be his own brother-in-law. Other terrorist assignments followed as he quickly developed a reputation among the Ba'th as a meticulous and daring assassin. The following year, he was chosen by party leaders to head a hit-squad against Iraqi strongman Abdul Karim Qassim, apparently in collusion with the Egyptian government of Colonel Abdel Nasser and the CIA.

When the assassins bungled the job, Saddam fled briefly to Syria and then to Egypt. In 1963, after a second and this time successful attempt on Qassim's life, Saddam returned to Iraq and soon emerged as the major Ba'th enforcer. He rose quickly through party ranks by intimidating or eliminating his rivals, and helped organize the Party's takeover of the government in 1968. Ostensibly second in command to Ahmad Hassan al-Bakr, Saddam was the real power in the Ba'th Party. On July 16, 1979, when President Bakr resigned, Saddam officially replaced him as President of the Republic and commander-in-chief of the armed forces.

To his credit, Saddam forged a single nation out of the patchwork of diverse and often antagonistic ethnic groups. Iraq's population of 17 million is divided among Sunni and Shiite Arabs, Kurds, and Bedouin tribes living in the sparsely populated western desert. The Sunnis dominate politically, but constitute only 20 percent of the population. For years, Saddam was able to retain the support of the majority Shiites (60 percent), and to keep the Kurds nominally pacified, while he extended his authority in Baghdad.

Geographically, Iraq borders Iran, which made Saddam Hussein the perfect partner for the United States. The ambitious Saddam was very receptive to our proposal, which would extend Iraqi influence into Iran. If Saddam could combine Iran's oil reserves with his own, it would enable him to emerge as the leader of the Arab world. Secondarily, he feared that the Iranian Revolution might engulf his country, since Iraq, like Iran, was predominately Shiite.

President Reagan sent Donald Rumsfeld as his special Middle East envoy to meet with Saddam and strike a deal. Urged on by promised military support from the United States, Iraq invaded Iran on September 22, 1980. U.S. space satellites monitored Iran's every move and sent Saddam reports about Iranian troop movements. Over the next seven years, the United States sold Saddam $200 million worth of weaponry. Washington also gave him $5 billion in agricultural credits and a $684 million loan to build an oil pipeline to Jordan, a project Saddam awarded to the California-based Bechtel Corporation.

Saddam envisioned a quick victory and a heroic triumph. As it turned out, Iran proved to be less of a pushover than expected.

The war would last eight years and end in a stalemate, taking one million lives from each side.

In June 1982, despite the ongoing war, Iran sent a thousand of its elite Revolutionary Guards to Lebanon. Israel had just invaded Lebanon in order to push Palestinian guerrillas beyond Israel's border. But, the Israelis were more successful than they planned; they received little resistance and continued driving into the center of Lebanon.

In August 1982, the United States, France and Italy dispatched troops to Lebanon to oversee the withdrawal of the PLO, hoping that would end Israel's occupation. But, when Lebanon's president-elect Bashir Gemayel was assassinated, Israel refused to leave.

On April 18, 1983, a suicide bomber crashed into the U.S. Embassy in West Beirut killing 63 Americans and Lebanese, including nine CIA officers and a member of the ultra-secret American Delta Force. On October 23, 1983, a young Shiite extremist drove his explosion filled truck into the main airport where American troops were housed. The explosion killed 241 American Marine and Navy personnel. In early November 1983, another suicide bomber rammed a truck into the facility that was occupied by the Israeli forces, killing 29 Israelis and more than 30 Lebanese and Palestinian prisoners.

In 1984, seven Americans were kidnapped from the streets of Beirut by masked gunmen from pro-Iranian Shiite groups. The captured Americans were: Jeremy Levin, Beirut chief for *Cable News*; William Buckley, the CIA's chief of station in Beirut; the Reverend Benjamin Weir; Father Lawrence Martin Jenco, director of Catholic Relief Services in Beirut; Terry Anderson, chief Middle East correspondent for *Associated Press*; David Jacobsen, director of the American University Hospital in Beirut; and Thomas Sutherland, acting dean of agriculture at the American University in Beirut.

U.S. policy had always been: "The United States gives terrorists no rewards. We make no concessions. We make no deals." The fate of William Buckley was a matter of particular concern to CIA Director Casey. If, as was believed, the hostage captors were linked to or controlled by Iran, freedom for the hostages was more likely to come about through dealings with Iran rather than any efforts in Lebanon. The administration had the choice of changing its policy to get back the hostages or resigning itself to their captivity in order to keep faith with its policy. Instead of either option, the Reagan administration stumbled onto a new policy.

In August 1985, President Reagan authorized the first shipment of American-made anti-tank missiles to Iran via Israel in what was supposed to be an exchange for the release of all the American hostages in Lebanon. But, not a single hostage was released. Nevertheless, another arms shipment was made the following month. After two shipments totaling over 500 missiles, Benjamin Weir was the only hostage released. The American public was not told about the arms shipments to Iran.

On September 16, 1985, Lt. Colonel Oliver North, on behalf of President Reagan, was waiting to greet Benjamin Weir upon his arrival at the Washington airport. North warned Weir that any indiscreet disclosures would be detrimental to the Reagan administration. "What happens to those left behind in Lebanon depends totally on you. Your greatest Christian task may be in the next few days ahead. Revelations regarding your release will only accelerate competition for holding others and result in killings and new seizures."

Over the next fifteen months of secret contacts between Iran, Israel, and the United States, at least 2,000 anti-tank missiles and some 235 ground-to-air missiles were transferred to Iran. Israel delivered weapons from its own stockpile, with the assurance that they would be replenished by the United States. This secret arrangement violated the Arms Export Control Act, which prohibited the transfer of U.S. arms to any recipient without the express permission of the president and notice to Congress. President Reagan authorized the transfers, but he deliberately did not notify Congress.

In November, the Israeli arms shipment included HAWK anti-aircraft missiles. Again, no hostages were released. While all this was going on, the funding for the Contras in Nicaragua was running out. Oliver North and his colleagues within the administration decided to combine the illegal activities in Iran with the illegal activities in Nicaragua. The proceeds from the sale of the weapons to Iran were secretly diverted to private Swiss bank accounts. From there the funds were funneled to the Contras in Nicaragua. The enormity of the illegality defied historical precedent.

In January 1986, despite the strong dissent of both Secretary of Defense Weinberger and Secretary of State Shultz, President Reagan authorized direct U.S. sales to Iran without the Israelis as an intermediary. Still, no hostages were released. In May, more arms were sent including HAWK spare parts. Two months later, Father Jenco was released. Iran was playing a game with the United States by reluctantly releasing one hostage at a time. They intended to use the hostages to their maximum advantage.

CIA Director William Casey decided the Iranians needed to be taught a lesson. He sent a message to Saddam Hussein via Vice President Bush that Iraq should step up its bombing attacks on Iran. To help in that effort, the CIA provided Saddam with satellite photographs of the best bombing targets. Two days following Bush's meeting with Saddam, the Iraqi air force flew 359 missions deep into Iranian territory. The United States hoped that Iran would get the message and release all the hostages.

Around the same time, our illegal Contra activities in Nicaragua began to unravel. An American plane piloted by Eugene Hasenfus, and carrying ammunition and AK-47 weapons to the Contras, was shot down over Nicaragua. Hasenfus was taken prisoner by the Nicaraguan government forces. Hasenfus was a former U.S. Marine who was now being paid $3,000 a month by the CIA to make periodic flights into Nicaragua. He was told that the operation "was being run directly out of the White House." After making about sixty drops, Hasenfus ran out of luck. He spent two-and-a-half months in confinement and was released on December 17. By that time the Contra affair had been fully exposed.

On November 2, David Jacobsen, the director of the American University Hospital became the third hostage released. The next day the Lebanese weekly *Al-Shiraa* broke the arms-for-hostages story, publishing an expose of U.S.-Iran dealings. American newspapers picked up the story and it exploded into front page headlines. All of Reagan's illegal activities were now exposed in print. It was all quite convoluted, but the American public and Congress became more enraged with each retelling.

On November 10, President Reagan called a meeting of his cabinet in the Oval Office. Vice President Bush, Chief of Staff Regan, Secretary of State Shultz, Secretary of Defense Weinberger, CIA Director Casey, Attorney General Meese, Poindexter of the NSC, and Lt. Colonel Oliver North were all there. This was the first official meeting to discuss the legal and political implications of Iran-Contra.

CIA chief Casey told Oliver North that he should get a criminal lawyer. Attorney General Meese advised the group that, "Our position is that we did not sell any weapons. Israel sold the weapons. Our hands are clean." President Reagan said that the administration had to issue a statement, but it should not say too much. "We must keep insisting that we have not dealt directly with terrorists. There has been no bargaining and no ransom," Reagan repeated several times. Twice he told the group, "We must not talk about specifics; avoid specifics."

"But, it is ransom," Secretary of State Shultz responded, annoying the president. Schultz warned the president of the dire consequences if their illegal activities were revealed. He explained that Iran-Contra involved a deliberate decision by the executive branch to reject congressional mandates regarding foreign policy and to secretly conduct its own illegal activities. Schultz wanted everyone to realize the seriousness and that these "were impeachable offenses."

Reagan quipped, "They can impeach me if they want; visiting day is on Wednesdays." The meeting ended with the president laying out the administration's official response: "Our policy of not making concessions to terrorists remains intact." Reagan decided to go on television the next night.

> "I know you have been reading, seeing, and hearing a lot of stories the past several days from unnamed sources. Well, now you are going to hear the facts from a White House source, and you know my name.

> The charge has been made that the United States has shipped weapons to Iran as ransom payment for the release of American hostages in Lebanon; that the United States secretly violated American policy against trafficking with terrorists. Those charges are utterly false. The United States has not made concessions to those who hold our people captive in Lebanon, and we will not. All these reports are quite exciting, but not one of them is true.
>
> For eighteen months now we have been pursing a secret diplomatic initiative to Iran. During the course of our secret discussions, I authorized the transfer of small amounts of defensive weapons and spare parts for defensive systems to Iran. My purpose was to convince Tehran that our negotiators were acting with my authority. These modest deliveries, taken together, could easily fit into a small single cargo plane."

Reagan's speech before the nation that night was the height of presidential hubris. Everything he said was a complete fabrication. This time Reagan's charm and Hollywood smile did not work. The first national poll after the speech reported that only twenty-two percent of respondents approved of sending arms to Iran, and worse, Americans believed the president was lying. Nixon telephoned Reagan and told him to admit the whole thing and say it was a mistake. This advice, coming from Richard Nixon, was like 'the pot calling the kettle black.'

Time magazine's lead story was that Reagan was lying. "It is not credible that Ollie North, a 43 year-old Marine and member of the NSC staff could have operated out of an office across the street from the White House, arranged the Contra scam without the knowledge of the State Department, the CIA, the Joint Chiefs of Staff, the White House Chief of Staff, or his boss, National Security adviser John Poindexter. This disaster throws a pitiless light on the way the president does his job, confirming the worst fears of both his friends and his critics." An editorial in the *Philadelphia*

Daily News said: "Reagan has surrounded himself with second-rate minds; his own second-rate mind is at least fronted by a first-rate presentation."

The president announced the appointment of a "special Review Board," to look into the role and performance of the National Security Council. The chairman was John Tower, a former Republican senator from Texas. The other two members were Senator Edmund Muskie, a Democrat, and General Brent Scowcroft, who had served as NSC director under President Ford. The board officially became known as the Tower Commission.

On December 10, in full Marine dress uniform complete with ribbons and medals, Oliver North appeared before the first public session of the House committee investigating Iran-Contra. On advice of counsel, Oliver North declined to answer any questions. On December 15, the front page of the *New York Times* reported that Oliver North personally controlled Swiss bank accounts and was diverting some of the funds into campaigns of congressmen who supported the Contras. On December 19, the investigation took a new turn when Lawrence Walsh was appointed as "independent counsel" and charged with unraveling the arm trades, cash diversions, and lies upon lies.

The day before Reagan's State of the Union speech, the president met for the first time with the Tower Commission to answer questions. The secret session lasted more than seventy minutes. The questions focused on whether Reagan had authorized arms shipments from Israel to Iran. He insisted he had trouble remembering details like that, but finally answered, "Yes."

On January 29, 1987, a U.S. Senate report on Iran-Contra concluded that the Iran operation was a straightforward arms-for-hostages deal. It stated that President Reagan had indeed approved every significant step of this illegal operation. The report also revealed for the first time that the United States provided military intelligence not only to Iraq, but also to the Iranian government, including satellite photographs of Iraqi positions.

The report said it could trace only part of the money involved, although it did identify numbered bank accounts in Switzerland and the Cayman Islands, and reported that significant amounts were controlled by Richard Secord, a retired Air Force general who was working with Oliver North to handle the delivery of weapons to Iran. Three days after the report was issued, William Casey resigned as CIA Director. Five days later, Robert McFarlane attempted suicide.

In early February 1987, the president asked for a second meeting with the Tower Commission. Reagan wanted to change his story. It was embarrassing for the three members of the commission to see Reagan so vague and confused. No recording or official note-taking was allowed, but news of the president's shifting testimony leaked to the press within an hour after the seventy-five minute session. Reagan also used the meeting to try to influence the language of the forthcoming Tower report.

As the Tower Commission's investigation was nearing its end, National Security advisor John Poindexter and Oliver North were destroying all relevant e-mail correspondence. The commission discovered the existence of the e-mails two weeks before the report was due. By then, Poindexter had deleted 5,012 of his 5,062 messages and North had deleted 750 of 758. Some, but not all of that correspondence was recovered from the mainframe computer. The e-mails that were recovered showed convincingly that Poindexter, North, and McFarlane, saw themselves as a secret cell within the Reagan administration.

On February 25, the three members of the Tower Commission came to the Oval Office to give the president a preview of their conclusions. Reagan protested their findings. He then slumped in his chair saying he just could not remember the details, but that the Commission was probably right. The Tower report was released the next day. The *New York Times* devoted its entire front page and eleven inside pages to the report. Its banner headline read: "Inquiry Finds Reagan and Chief Advisers Responsible For Iran Arms Deals." The secondary headline read: "Tower Panel Portrays the President as Remote and Confused."

One week later, President Reagan gave a twelve minute televised speech about the Tower Commission report. He admitted for the first time that what he did was a mistake. It did not help Reagan's cause when it was reported that his rich friends from the "Kitchen

Cabinet" had just bought him a $2.5 million home in Bel Air for when his term expired.

The televised congressional Iran-Contra hearing – conducted by fifteen senators and eleven representatives from the House, began on May 5. Staffers of the joint committee had already conducted 300 interviews, issued 140 subpoenas, and scrutinized more than 100,000 documents.

The big story of the televised 'show' was Lt. Colonel Oliver North. North used his months of public silence to negotiate some surprisingly generous ground rules. He was granted "immunity," which meant that his public testimony could not be used against him in criminal prosecutions. He was also accorded two other significant privileges. He could interrupt questioning and statements by committee members and attorneys, and more importantly, he could not be interrupted. The concessions gave him the chance to actually control the interrogation, deflecting lines of questioning that he did not like with long patriotic speeches on duty, honor, and country. He did that often and well. Television viewers were drawn to his stories of good-guys versus bad-guys out there in the jungles of evil.

"First of all, I'm not in the habit of questioning my superiors," he testified at one point. "I salute smartly and charge up the hill. That is what a Lt. Colonel is supposed to do. I have no problem doing that."

It was hard, that first day, to resist North's medals; two Silver Stars and a Purple Heart, his boyish grin, and his delight in his own use of candor as a substitute for the truth. He spoke about his service and dedication to his country. He quoted the Bible and spoke about liberty and justice. Asked about the lies he told in negotiating with the Iranians, he said: "There is great deception practiced in the conduct of covert operations. We make every effort to deceive the enemy. Yes, we regularly tell bald-faced lies. I would have done or said anything to get the American hostages home."

When the chief counsel to the committee characterized North as "lying to elected representatives of the people," the colonel snapped back: "President Reagan was elected by the people, too."

Then he asserted his job was advancing the president's agenda. North said: "I want you to know that lying does not come easy to me, but we have to weigh the difference between lies and lives." Right-wing America cheered their new hero – a confessed liar. President Reagan praised Oliver North as "a national hero."

That night, anchor Tom Brokaw began the NBC *Nightly News* program by saying: "The most popular soap opera on television this week is the Iran-Contra inquiry starring Lt. Colonel Oliver North." Daytime television viewing was up 10 percent. "He is a star, a new national folk hero," said Brokaw. On the CBS *Evening News*, correspondent Bob Schieffer reported an "Ollie North craze," with T-shirts and other memorabilia featuring pictures of him. *Newsweek* and *Time* put him on their covers. *Newsweek* compared him to Jimmy Stewart in the film *Mr. Smith Goes to Washington*. *Time* reported that its polling showed that 84 percent of respondents said they believed that North's activities had been sanctioned by higher-ups and applauded his patriotism.

Empty rooms in the Capitol were being filled with flowers and telegrams sent to North from all over the country. Capitol guards were trying to turn away people who came with personal checks they wanted delivered to an Oliver North defense fund. "Olliemania Sweeps USA" was the front-page headline of *USA Today*. The newspaper also published results of a special "Hot Line" it set up for popular comment: 52,804 callers said North was an honest man who should be given a medal; 1,572 called him a liar who should be in jail.

North testified that he was shredding documents in his office on November 22, 1986, even as Justice Department lawyers were examining other documents right outside his office. North admitted that he shredded the documents to prevent the disclosure of politically damaging evidence. When North was asked how he was able to shred documents when investigators were only ten feet away, he said: "They were working on their projects; I was working on mine. The shredder was right outside my office. I just walked out and shredded documents. Even if they didn't see me, they could hear the shredder." Asked if he considered the shredding of important government documents illegal or wrong, he smiled boyishly and said: "That's why the Government of the United States gave me a shredder."

Eleanor Clift of *Newsweek*, appearing on *The McLaughlin Group* news show described North as follows: "He's Rocky, Rambo, Patton and the boy next door all wrapped up in one." On Monday morning, the fifth day of the hearings, North offered a final surprise. He said that Manucher Ghorbanifar, the first middleman in the Iranian initiative, had offered him personally $1 million to speed up deliveries of weapons to Iran, but he rejected the bribe offer.

Oliver North's six-day miniseries ended with House chairman, Lee Hamilton, saying in closing: "It is depressing that you were part of a policy that was driven by a series of lies: lies to the Iranians, lies to the U.S. Congress, and lies to the American people." Oliver North was eventually convicted. He had to pay a fine of $150,000 and serve 1,200 hours of community service. In July 1990, a panel of judges voided his conviction.

In a bizarre series of events, President Reagan was called to testify in John Poindexter's criminal trial. Reagan was on the witness stand for two days – ten full hours. Reading the transcript of Reagan's under oath testimony reveals the total disregard the man had for the truth and the principles underlying the Constitution. The number of blatant lies is almost beyond belief; coming from the President of the United States it is such an immense embarrassment as to make any American cringe with shame.

Poindexter was convicted on April 7, 1990 for conspiracy, obstruction of justice, perjury, defrauding the government, and the alteration and destruction of evidence pertaining to the Iran-Contra affair. The convictions were reversed in 1991 on technical grounds. The prosecution was not able to re-try the case.

In a speech to the nation, the humiliated Reagan tried simultaneously to accept responsibility and to plead ignorance of any wrongdoing:

> "First let me say that I take full responsibility for my own actions and for those of my own administration. As angry as I may be about activities undertaken

without my knowledge, I am still accountable for those activities. As disappointed as I may be in some who served me, I am still the one who must answer to the American people for this behavior. And as personally distasteful as I find secret bank accounts and diverted funds - well, as the U.S. Navy would say, this happened on my watch. A few months ago, I told the American people I did not trade arms for hostages. My heart and my best intentions still tell me that it was true, but the facts and evidence tell me that it was not."

It was a strange explanation. In effect, Reagan assumed responsibility for irresponsibility. The most admired man in America, the President of the United States, was suddenly seen as a buffoon at best, a villain at worst.

The last two weeks of the hearings were taken up with a parade of cabinet members complaining that they had been lied to for more than a year by the White House, the NSC, the CIA, and each other. When it was over, Senator Daniel Inouye of Hawaii summed it up best:

"The story has now been told. It is a chilling story of deceit and duplicity and the arrogant disregard of the role of law. People with power ran a government outside of government. They conducted a secret foreign policy and concealed it through a concerted campaign of dishonesty and deception. And when the affair began to unravel, they attempted to cover over their deeds. This is a story of how a great nation betrayed the principles that made it great."

CHAPTER TWENTY TWO

THE GULF WAR

"I will never apologize for the United States.
I don't care what the facts are."

President George H.W. Bush

"To be a great president, you have to have a war.
All great presidents have had their wars."

Admiral William J. Crowe

It is often assumed that the greatest failure of American policy during the Cold War was its defeat in Vietnam. Yet, the loss of Vietnam proved to be strategically unimportant. It was politically embarrassing and the United States lost 58,168 precious American lives, but it was the people of Vietnam and Cambodia who paid the horrific price of American failure. Americans were able to walk away and leave the wreckage behind. The reality, which dawned only slowly on policy makers in Washington, was that Vietnam did not really matter.

On mature reflection, Cuba also did not matter, which was why the United States quietly abandoned the idea of toppling the Castro regime. Whether it was Hanoi or Havana, communists in the developing countries proved to be relatively harmless from the point of view of American national security. Cuba might make all kinds of mischief in other peripheral theaters: witness Castro's energetic participation in the Angolan and Ethiopian civil wars, but it was scarcely significant. There was only one region of the world that America could not possibly afford to lose and that was the Middle East.

Oil is the world's critical resource. By 1955, the United States was consuming more than a third of all energy produced in the world; six times more than any other nation. We were using that energy to produce more goods and wealth, to be sure, but Americans were also using more energy to heat their homes, cool their offices, and above all, drive their cars. This kind of consumption could not be sustained by America's domestic production of seven million barrels a day. Middle East sources of oil became critical and that meant Saudi Arabia, Kuwait, Iran, Iraq, and stability between Israel and her Arab neighbors.

Neo-conservatism sprang up in the 1970s out of a perception that the liberals were dismantling our intelligence capabilities, destroying our military, and were soft on communism. The neo-cons believed that the United States was the greatest force for good in the world, and as such, we had to do everything we could to spread democracy and freedom throughout the world. This new political group was disgusted with our defeat in Vietnam and switched their foreign policy thinking from 'containment' to a more aggressive use of unilateral military power.

Leading neo-cons were Dick Cheney, Jane Kirkpatrick, Donald Rumsfeld, Paul Wolfowitz, William Kristol, and Richard Perle. Neo-con 'think tanks' included the Heritage Foundation and the Hoover Institute. Leading journalists who supported this philosophy were Max Boot (LA Times); David Brooks (NY Times); and Charles Krauthammer and Robert Kagan (Washington Post).

Neo-cons believed that military power, not diplomacy, would save the world from tyrants bent on destruction. As such, they were against treaties that hampered America from pursuing its best economic interests. They believed that the only way to insure a stable peace was for the United States to control the 'hot spot' regions around the world. Their remedy was to overthrow non-cooperative governments in troubled areas and install 'friendly' new rulers. If necessary, military preemption should be available, but always couched in the rhetoric of spreading democracy. Existing U.S. civil liberties had to be curtailed because they were a hindrance to the new plan. Hence, they favored wiretaps and electronic eavesdropping without legal constraints, and secret

Lies and Deceits

prisons in foreign lands where the rules about torture to gather information were non-existent.

The first test for the neo-cons was Afghanistan. For centuries, the name "Afghanistan" has conjured up images of isolation and remoteness. It is a forbidding place, locked in the Asian land-mass, cut off from the world by towering mountain ranges and governed more by tribal tradition than by law. During the nineteenth century, Russia and Britain jousted for influence over Afghanistan in a high-stakes rivalry that became known as the "Great Game." Rivalries like this usually break out when a poor country has a resource that rich countries covet. Afghanistan has no oil, no mineral wealth, and little fertile land, but it does have one asset that has always attracted outsiders: location. It lies astride routes to India, Iran, Central Asia, and China; all strategic prizes.

True to its independent tradition, Afghanistan remained neutral in both World Wars. In the postwar years, its leaders sought with considerable success to remain outside the Cold War confrontation, but in 1979 a new Afghan regime entered into an alliance with the Soviet Union. Muslim fundamentalist protests ensued and grew to alarming proportions. This upheaval came while the region was still experiencing the shock of the Islamic revolution in Iran.

America feared that the Soviets would take advantage of the chaotic upheaval that was going on in the region and perhaps attempt to use Afghanistan as a base for a thrust toward the Persian Gulf oil fields. The Soviets, on the other hand, were concerned that the area's instability might encourage Islamic fundamentalism to spill over the Afghan border and into Russia. At an emergency meeting of the Soviet Politburo on March 17, 1979, Yuri Andropov, the KGB director who would later become the country's leader, urged his comrades to take a hard line. "Under no circumstances can we lose Afghanistan," he told them. On December 25, 1979, Soviet troops entered Afghanistan. They would remain there until February 15, 1989.

In the early 1980s, President Reagan and the CIA believed that with enough money and weapons, Afghan guerrillas could turn Afghanistan into "the Russian Vietnam." The CIA was convinced, based on its past success, that they could effectuate "regime change" at will; all that was needed was a strong U.S. commitment from the president and the necessary funds.

Pakistan's border with Afghanistan twists and turns for more than one thousand miles; it is the logical crossing point into Afghanistan. It was the perfect place for the CIA to set up rebel training camps before sending them into Afghanistan to fight the Russian invaders. To help pay for this costly campaign the United States recruited Saudi Arabia. The Saudis agreed to match all American aid to the Afghan rebels on a dollar-for-dollar basis.

In 1986, the CIA gave Afghan guerrillas $470 million and the next year $630 million - all of it matched by the Saudis. Despite the huge amounts of money involved, the United States was not in a position to decide which rebels should receive our gifts: that was left to the discretion of our Pakistan ally. However, Pakistan's objectives were far different from ours. We were concerned with "bleeding" the Russians in Afghanistan. Pakistan's sights were riveted on the type of Muslim world that would be left after the Americans left Afghanistan. With this in mind, Pakistan used the U.S. millions to support seven Afghan factions, all of them religious fundamentalists and anti-Western.

At these CIA-sponsored camps inside Pakistan, jihadis were trained in modern techniques of sabotage, ambush, and assault, and in the use of advanced weaponry and time-delayed bomb detonators. Eager for victory over the Soviets, the U.S. never weighed the potential long-term consequences of its actions. "For God's sake," one secular Afghan warned the Americans during this period, "you are financing your own assassins!"

Osama bin Laden was born in Saudi Arabia in 1957. His father, Muhammad Awad bid Laden, became a wealthy businessman because of his strong ties to the royal family. The elder bin Laden was married 22 times and fathered 55 children; Osama was his seventeenth son.

Osama was raised as a devout Sunni Muslim, but attended secular schools. He graduated from the top university in Saudi Arabia where he majored in civil engineering, economics, and business administration. Instead of joining his father's billion dollar construction business, he rushed to join the jihad in Afghanistan. After several months as a guerrilla fighter, he became responsible for welcoming foreign militants and channeling them to the various CIA training camps. It was an ideal post for someone eager to meet jihadis from around the world.

Slowly, the Muslim rebel insurgency grew stronger. Eventually it reached the point where it could seriously challenge the Red Army. In 1986, the new Soviet leader, Mikhail Gorbachev, told the Politburo that this war had to be ended. Later that year, he announced that 8,000 Soviet troops were being called home. Finally, he withdrew them all. On February 15, 1989, the last Red Army units crossed back into Soviet territory.

For the Soviets, this Afghanistan adventure had been an unmitigated disaster. It cost them, by their own account, nearly $100 million and the lives of 15,000 soldiers. They also lost incalculable amounts of international prestige and strategic power. Within a few years, the Soviet Union collapsed. The defeat it suffered in Afghanistan played a key role in speeding its demise.

In what must be considered the most bizarre series of events, the Cold War was finally over after forty-five years, leaving the United States as the world's only superpower. The CIA and our neo-con leadership gloated about our victory. This time they did not topple some weak Third World government – they defeated the mighty Soviet Union. But nobody was quite sure what we had won. With the Soviet Union bankrupt and out of the picture, we expected to "rule the world" with a free hand. However, in light of subsequent events, what seemed at first like a victory now looks more like a catastrophe. We planted, trained, equipped, and encouraged a terrorist movement that is out of control and more dangerous than anything we ever had to deal with.

If anyone lost more from this war than the Soviets, it was certainly the Afghan people. They were liberated from occupation by a foreign power, but at a staggering cost. One million Afghans were killed during the 1980s; three million were maimed; five million fled to refugee camps in neighboring countries. No war ever fought in Afghanistan left such a devastating physical and spiritual legacy.

One of the great absurdities of the Cold War was the incredible amount of money each side felt compelled to spend in a frantic effort to build a monster arsenal of nuclear weapons, to deter or if necessary, to fight the other. Trillions of dollars and rubles were expended on unnecessary weaponry while millions of young men were pulled out of productive roles in the economy. At the peak of the arms race, the United States and the Soviet Union held about 70,000 nuclear weapons. Both sides refused to accept the fact that a direct confrontation was never a sensible option. Russia never wanted to occupy the United States; it was merely paranoid about protecting its borders. The United States certainly had no designs on occupying the vast Soviet Union. It was all a dangerous game that fortunately did not erupt into a nuclear conflagration.

The United States "won" the Cold War in the sense that the other side gave up the fight. The transformation was sudden and momentous. It had more to do with Russia's Mikhail Gorbachev than anything else. Gorbachev, an incorrigible optimist, set out to reform the Soviet system without destroying it, what he called *perestroika*, and to permit more openness, *glasnost*, without going all the way to democracy. In foreign policy, he was determined to close what he called the "bleeding wound" in Afghanistan, shift to eastern European communist leaders the responsibility for their own survival, ease Cold War tensions in order to divert precious resources to domestic needs, secure desperately needed technology from the West, and reduce the risk of nuclear war. It was a unique and extraordinary moment in U.S.-Soviet relations.

The collapse of Communism left the neo-cons momentarily adrift. With the Cold War officially over, Democratic Senator Daniel Patrick Moynihan proposed to abolish the CIA and fold its secret operations into the State Department or the Pentagon where they might be more accountable to political oversight. "We have become a national-security state," Moynihan said, "a country mobilized for war on a permanent basis, where everything is secret. Can we recover the memory of what we were before we became what we are now? Can we rediscover a sense of proportion? The task of purging the Cold War from our institutions is enormous. It will require a sustained and determined effort."

The neo-cons, however, were not about to relinquish their preeminence even if the 'red menace' was gone. They turned their attention to the Middle East and oil. To do otherwise, they would have had to give up their plans for a new world order based on American military might. A return to a peacetime economy would require Americans to reduce their dependency on foreign oil, conserve energy, and redirect funds from the military industry. The neo-cons were not about to let that happen. They believed that a true empire should not have to radically alter its lifestyle as long as it had the military power to make the rules.

The neo-cons continued their rise to political power when George H. W. Bush came into office in early 1989. They were determined to eradicate the "Vietnam syndrome" and the reluctance of Americans to go to war. The key was to find easy targets; get in quickly, punish the victim, and get out quickly. Bush and the neo-cons found their first easy target in Panama; a perfect example of U.S. military power exerting itself on a foreign country that is completely defenseless and at our mercy. Naturally, American business interests played a paramount role in choosing Panama.

Our involvement with Panama dates back to 1885. Upon gaining its independence from Spain in 1821, Panama became part of the Republic of Gran Colombia, which was composed of territories from the present countries of Colombia, Venezuela and Ecuador. In 1885, we invaded that area to secure American economic interests. A French crew had tried to build a canal there in the 1880s, but they were decimated by malaria and gave up. The United States now wanted to take up that project. To obtain the right to build the canal, we first negotiated with Columbia, but they called the proposed treaty a giveaway and refused. Undaunted, the U.S. now took matters into its own hands and wrested Panama away from Columbia.

On November 3, 1903, Panama, with U.S. backing, seceded from Colombia and became an independent nation. The U.S. Navy arrived on the scene to prevent any Colombian military interference, and we immediately signed the Hay-Bunau Varilla Treaty with the new government, giving us the exclusive rights to build and administer indefinitely a canal in Panama that would allow our ships to pass directly through the Americas, instead of having to go all the way around the southern tip of South America. The canal, completed in 1914, also provided the United States with toll revenue and the right to exclude any other nation from using it.

The United States had a complete monopoly over the Panama Canal for the next 85 years; however, the Hay-Bunau Varilla Treaty became a contentious diplomatic issue between the two countries. In the 1976 presidential campaign of Ronald Reagan, he declared, "the Panama Canal Zone is sovereign U.S. territory just as much as Alaska or the territories carved from the Louisiana Territory – and we intend to keep it." However, after Jimmy Carter was elected president, the process of returning the Canal to Panama began.

Manuel Noriega came up through the military ranks to become the head of Panama's secret police. Noriega became a CIA asset in the early 1970s when George H.W. Bush was Director of the CIA. Noriega's well-paid functions were to advance U.S. interests in Central America, notably in sabotaging the communist Sandinistas in Nicaragua and aiding pro-USA revolutionaries in El Salvador. During the late 1980s, when the Iran-Contra affair exploded into public view, Noriega became concerned that he was going to become the fall guy and he stopped all cooperation with the United States. President Reagan, concerned that Noriega knew too much about our covert activities, demanded that the uncooperative Noriega step down and 'disappear.' Noriega refused.

George Herbert Walker Bush easily won the presidency over Democrat Michael Dukakis in 1988. Bush was the son of a wealthy and prominent Connecticut family, a decorated navy pilot in World War II, educated at Andover and Yale, and strongly believed in the Protestant ethos of hard work, modesty, competition, and public service. After graduation, he left for Texas and the oil business. Later he would become Nixon's ambassador to the United Nations, chairman of the Republican National Committee, ambassador to China, Director of the CIA, and vice-president under Ronald Reagan. By his own admission, he lacked "the vision thing." He was a doer rather than a thinker – and his views were thoroughly establishment oriented and pandered to the increasingly hawkish right wing of the Republican Party.

Bush's first act as president was to pardon six Reagan administration officials involved in the Iran-Contra affair. He knew that the public spotlight on Iran-Contra had made Nicaragua off-limits, so, instead he shifted his attention to Panama and the defiant posture of Noriega. Noriega's regime was always corrupt, brutal and authoritarian, but as long as he was on our team we overlooked what was going on. Now that Noriega's usefulness was over, his knowledge about U.S. illegal activities could prove extremely embarrassing. A decision was made to replace him with someone we could control. Noriega became a convenient target for an administration that wanted to prove that the United States was still a power in our hemisphere.

The United States started by imposing harsh economic sanctions on Panama. In the months that followed, Bush ordered 2,000 more U.S. troops into Panama "to protect Americans in the Panama Canal Zone." U.S. forces began conducting regular military maneuvers and operations, which was a violation of the Panama Canal Treaty. The message to Noriega was clear. By late summer, Bush began comparing Noriega to Adolf Hitler, declaring that "this form of aggression must be brought to an end."

The elections of May 1989 in Panama were surrounded by controversy. Most of the opposition banded behind a unified ticket of Guillermo Endara, Ricardo Arias Calderón, and Guillermo Ford. Noriega nullified the election results and maintained power by force. He claimed that CIA involvement in the election had unfairly affected the results.

The CIA met with Panamanian military leaders and offered them huge "rewards" to overthrow Noriega. When the CIA coup to oust Noriega failed in 1989, the United States invaded with 26,000 U.S. troops and high-tech attack aircraft. It was a quick and decisive victory against a hapless foe. A few hours after the invasion, a new president friendly to the United States was installed and sworn in at our naval base in Panama.

Virtually all U.S. newspapers supported the administration's decision to go to war to eliminate Noriega – America's new demonic enemy. The American public, confused about the issues, overwhelmingly backed the president. Many liberal Democrats, anxious to show that foreign policy was bipartisan, supported our military action. The U.S. Congress passed a resolution approving President Bush's actions, but urged him not to use this as a pretext to invade Mexico or the remainder of Latin America.

Our invasion of Panama, dubbed *Operation Just Cause*, was the largest U.S. invasion ever to be targeted exclusively at one man. Bush justified the action as "a war on drugs." The war was over in three weeks. The U.S. lost 23 soldiers and 325 were wounded. There was considerable controversy over the number of Panamanian casualties; best estimates put the number of Panamanian military dead at 314, along with 2,000 to 5,000 civilians. Some $1.5 billion in property was destroyed and about 20,000 people lost their homes and became refugees. One notorious after-effect of the invasion was widespread looting and lawlessness, a contingency which the United States military indicated it had not anticipated.

On December 22, the Organization of American States passed a resolution deploring the invasion and called for the withdrawal of U.S. troops. While six countries abstained, twenty nations severely criticized the United States for the invasion. The only vote against the resolution came from the United States. At the U.N. Security Council, a draft resolution demanding the immediate withdrawal of United States forces from Panama was vetoed by three of the permanent members of the Security Council: France, Britain, and the United States. On December 29, the General Assembly voted 75–20, with 40 abstentions, to condemn the invasion as a "flagrant violation of international law."

Noriega remained at large for several days, but realizing he had few options in the face of a massive manhunt and a $1 million dollar U.S. reward on his head, he sought political asylum in the Vatican diplomatic mission. However, after extensive political pressure was put on the Vatican by the United States, Noriega finally surrendered to the U.S. military. He was immediately put on a military transport plane and illegally extradited to the United

States where he was tried on eight counts of drug trafficking, racketeering, and money laundering. Noriega was found guilty and sentenced to 40 years in prison. His sentence was reduced to 30 years in 1999. There is still an ongoing legal battle being waged to decide Noriega's fate.

On the first anniversary of the invasion, President Bush addressed the American nation and declared, "One year ago today the people of Panama lived in fear under the thumb of a dictator; today democracy is restored. Panama is now free." The truth was somewhat different. Since Noriega's ouster, Panama has had three presidential elections with candidates from opposing parties succeeding each other. Panama's press is still subject to numerous restrictions, its poverty and unemployment has continued, and the removal of Noriega has failed to stanch the flow of illicit narcotics.

Noriega's downfall was also America's tragedy. While neo-cons engaged in self-congratulation, satisfied that American force was again righting wrongs and furthering democracy - it was a misplaced celebration. The use of massive U.S. military force that ended Noriega's rule was final proof of the failure of American foreign policy in Panama. Our invasion was the last resort of a policy that envisioned success at far less cost and trouble. Even more, it was an indictment of our thirty-year affair with Noriega.

The U.S. military 'victory' in Panama was too small to really accomplish what the Bush administration badly wanted, which was to overcome our post-Vietnam abhorrence for foreign military intervention. The Bush administration would have to wait another year for another opportunity - but Panama served as a warm-up exercise for our military to test its new volunteer army concept and advanced high-tech weapons.

The neo-cons in the Bush administration looked around impatiently for another victim, but that was not easy to find. With the Soviet Union no longer a threat, how were we going to justify our military-industrial spending without some evil threat? Fortunately for the neo-cons, Saddam Hussein came to the rescue. On August 1, 1990, Saddam's army crossed the border into Kuwait and rescued the military-industrial complex from the jaws of oblivion.

Before the oil boom, Kuwait was one of the poorest nations in the world with per capita income averaging around $35 a year. Its population of desert-dwelling Bedouins lived in desolate sand-swept land that offered nothing but hardship. Temperatures in the country frequently hovered over 115 degrees for months at a time.

However, by the 1980s Kuwait's wealth had become legendary. By then it was the world's sixth largest producer of petroleum and its assets abroad totaled $100 billion. Their revenues from investments actually surpassed their oil revenues by some $6 billion annually. Thus, unlike Iraq, the Kuwaitis had little incentive to increase oil prices because such increases would have depressed the stock, bond, and currency markets that had become Kuwait's main source of income.

After Iraq's eight-year war with Iran, Saddam Hussein was financially strapped and deeply in debt. One of Iraq's biggest obligations, somewhere around $12-14 billion, was to Kuwait. Relations between the two countries had always been strained owing to a border dispute that went back to the breakup of the Ottoman Empire. In an attempt to settle that dispute, Kuwait put financial pressure on Iraq by exceeding its OPEC oil quota. This flooded the oil market and drove prices down. By 1990, the price of oil had dropped from $18 to $11 a barrel, and as a result Iraq was losing $20 million a day. Saddam decided the time was ripe to teach his neighboring sheiks a lesson about power. A successful invasion would wipe out his debts to Kuwait, steal their enormous gold reserves, control their vast oil fields, and raise the price of each barrel of Iraq's oil production.

The United States supported Saddam when he attacked Iran nearly a decade before. Iraq and the United States were still allies, but Saddam wanted to be certain about America's position before he embarked on an invasion of Kuwait. He summoned April Glaspie, the American ambassador in Baghdad, for what he called "comprehensive political discussions."

Glaspie was a career foreign service officer who had been born in the Middle East. She had ascended step-by-step through the ranks at a time when diplomacy was a man's preserve, but she made it her life. She had been posted in Amman, Kuwait City, Beirut, Cairo, Tunis, and Damascus and had headed the State Department's office of Arabian Peninsula Affairs before taking up her current ambassadorial post. She was fluent in Arabic and a whole-hearted supporter of the Bush administration. Unmarried, she lived quietly in Baghdad with her mother and dog.

Saddam explained to Ambassador Glaspie that Iraq's border dispute with Kuwait had gone unresolved for too many years and that he intended to take action now. "Our patience has run out," he told her. Saddam's words were not difficult to decipher; he was planning to attack Kuwait. The day before this meeting, a State Department cable signed by Secretary of State James Baker provided guidance to Glaspie on the increasing Iraq-Kuwait tensions. "The United States has no opinion on Arab-Arab conflicts like Iraq's border disagreement with Kuwait."

This is what Glaspie told Saddam. With all our CIA intelligence in the area, including satellite surveillance, it is hard to understand how we could have misread Saddam's words or the military build-up that was taking place on the Kuwait border. A clear warning and a show of force by the U.S. would have kept the entire invasion from starting. Knowing our duplicitous history, maybe we wanted Saddam to commit an act of folly. Whatever our reasons, Saddam surely took Glaspie's words as a green light to invade Kuwait.

On August 2, 1990, the Iraqi army rolled into Kuwait, easily subdued the country, and announced that Kuwait had now become Iraq's nineteenth province. In Baghdad, motorists honked their horns and flashed their lights to celebrate the invasion. Radio and television stations broadcast patriotic songs and mobilization orders for the military. Most Iraqis thought the attack was justified. There was widespread support for Saddam and relief that victory had come so quickly.

To Saddam's great surprise, President Bush reacted with outrage. What Saddam did not realize was that his invasion of Kuwait provided the neo-cons with a perfect 'defining moment.'

Hussein suddenly was portrayed as another Hitler, and his army a massive military threat to world stability. Dick Cheney sounded the alarm and proclaimed that Saddam's invasion of Kuwait was the same threat to the world as Hitler's invasion of Poland in 1939. Actually, Saddam's invasion was more like our invasion of Panama.

Kuwait contains 10 percent of the world's oil reserves and is a key supplier to the United States. The neo-cons feared that if Saddam succeeded in Kuwait his next target would be the Saudi oil fields, which contains one-quarter of the world's oil reserves. Traditionally the United States' relationship with Saudi Arabia has been characterized as an undocumented agreement of "oil for security." Back in 1938, Standard Oil struck oil in Saudi Arabia and transformed the desperately poor kingdom into one of the richest and most important countries in the world. "Do you know what the United States will find when they reach Mars?" King Abdel Aziz asked his new American oil partners after he heard a radio report predicting that men would someday travel to the distant planet. He then answered his own question: "They will find Americans already on Mars hunting for oil."

The royal Saudi family was shocked by the Iraqi invasion of Kuwait. After years of paying billions of dollars to cultivate the friendship of neighboring countries, the royal family was stunned to discover how isolated they were in the Arab world. The Palestinians, Sudanese, Algerians, Libyans, Tunisians, Yemenis, and even the Jordanians openly supported Saddam Hussein. Osama bin Laden wrote a letter to the Saudi king beseeching him not to call upon the Americans for protection. The royal family itself was divided about the best course of action.

Colin Powell, Chairman Joint Chiefs of Staff, did not think Kuwait was worth a war, but the neo-cons led by Secretary of Defense Dick Cheney were already committed. Cheney flew to Saudi Arabia with a team of advisers, including General Norman Schwarzkopf, to persuade the Saudi king to accept American troops to defend his country. Schwarzkopf showed the King satellite images of three armored Iraqi divisions inside Kuwait - far more manpower than was needed to occupy such a small country as

Kuwait. Cheney handed the royal family a specially prepared CIA report attesting that there were 250,000 Iraqi troops deployed close to the Saudi border, ready to attack. It was all a lie; there were no Iraqi troops anywhere near the Saudi border.

Crown Prince Abdullah argued against the Americans entering Saudi Arabia for fear they would never depart. Cheney pledged, in the name of the President of the United States, that American troops would leave as soon as the threat was over, or whenever the King wanted them to go. That promise decided the matter. "Come with all you can bring," the King implored. "Come as fast as you can."

Weeks after American forces began arriving in Saudi Arabia, Osama bin Laden met with Prince Sultan, the Saudi minister of defense. Bin Laden brought his own maps of the region and presented a detailed plan of attack, with diagrams and charts, indicating trenches and sand traps along the border to be constructed with his family's extensive inventory of earth-moving equipment. Added to this, he would create an army made up of his colleagues from the Afghan jihad and unemployed Saudi youth. "I am ready to prepare 100,000 fighters with good combat capability within three months," bin Laden promised. "You don't need Americans. You don't need any other non-Muslim troops. We will be enough."

"There are no caves in Kuwait like you had in Afghanistan," the prince responded. "What will you do when Saddam lobs missiles at you with chemical and biological weapons?"

"We will fight him with faith," bin Laden responded. The Saudis rejected bin Laden's proposal.

Within weeks, 500,000 American soldiers streamed into Saudi Arabia. Although the Americans were stationed mainly out of view, Saudis were mortified by the need to turn to Christians and Jews to defend the holy land of Islam. That many of these foreign soldiers were women only added to their embarrassment. The weakness of the Saudi state and its abject dependence on the West for protection was paraded before the world, thanks to the 1,500 foreign journalists who descended on Saudi Arabia to report on the buildup to the war. For such a private and intensely religious people, the scrutiny by the foreign press was disorienting, creating a combustible atmosphere of fear, outrage, and humiliation.

Can a U.S. president just send American troops to a foreign land without congressional approval? The War Powers Resolution, which had been passed over President Nixon's veto in 1973, proclaimed that the president can only send U.S. armed forces into action abroad only by authorization of Congress or if the United States is already under attack or if there is a serious threat of attack. The resolution requires that the president must notify Congress within 48 hours of committing armed forces to military action and forbids armed forces from remaining for more than 60 days without a direct authorization from Congress or a formal declaration of war. The resolution reflected Congress' belated opposition to the war in Vietnam and its main thrust was that the president had to consult with Congress before sending American forces into combat.

But, the War Powers Resolution faced tough sledding from the day it was passed. All chief executives since Richard Nixon have asserted that the measure represented an unwarranted infringement on the president's authority as commander-in-chief, and, in varying degrees, all presidents have ignored its provisions. In twenty-three incidents involving the use of military force since the passage of the resolution, only once - at the time of the evacuation of Saigon in 1975 - did a president consult with Congress before deploying troops. On that occasion, Gerald Ford vainly sought congressional approval beforehand. When Congress failed to act, Ford went ahead on his own authority anyway.

Major operations such as the attempted rescue of the hostages in Tehran by President Carter, were undertaken without consultation with Congress. The Reagan administration ignored the Act altogether. In 1982, he deployed the Marines in Lebanon; invaded Grenada in 1983; and dispatched U.S. naval forces in 1987 to protect shipping in the Persian Gulf. In Bush's invasion of Panama in 1989, the congressional leadership was informed of the action only after the troops were on the way. In effect, every administration from Nixon to Bush has ignored the War Powers

Resolution and the U.S. Supreme Court has never ruled directly on the point.

With American troops now in position in Saudi Arabia, the Bush administration began selling the idea of going to war to Congress and the American public. A young Kuwaiti woman named Nayira appeared before a congressional committee and testified that she saw "Iraqi troops pulling sickly infants out of incubators and dumping them on the floor to die." As witnesses go, Nayira was terrific. She was tearful, but not weepy; distressed, but not hysterical; articulate and direct. Nayira was in fact, the 15-year old daughter of the Kuwaiti ambassador to the United States. She had rehearsed her testimony under the tutelage of Washington's biggest lobbying firm, whose major client was the government of Kuwait.

President Bush presented the issue in apocalyptic terms, declaring that our goal in the Persian Gulf had to be "maintaining access to energy resources. At stake is our jobs, our way of life, our freedom, and the freedom of friendly countries around the world." Rejecting any possibility of negotiating with Iraq to end its occupation of Kuwait, the Bush administration got the approval of Congress to go to war. The joint resolution passed in the House 250-183. In the Senate the vote was much closer, 52-47. Six senators spoke of how deeply they were affected by Nayira's testimony and how it convinced them to vote for war. Without those six votes, Bush would have lost in the Senate. The country was duped into going to war once again.

In a nationally televised address on August 8, President Bush announced his decision to use military force in the Gulf, "the sovereign independence of Kuwait and Saudi Arabia is vital to the interests of the United States." On the same day, Secretary of Defense Richard Cheney gave a more pointed statement to the Senate Armed Services Committee. "Once Saddam acquires Kuwait," Cheney said, "he would be in a position to dictate the future of worldwide energy policy, and that would give him a stranglehold on our economy." According to Cheney, America had to go to war to protect its supply of oil. Madeline Albright, one of the strong supporters of the war, was more caustic, "What is the point of spending all this money for high-tech weapons if you do not use them?"

A deadline of January 15 was set for the removal of Iraqi forces from Kuwait. As the deadline approached, U.S. troops were poised to strike from Saudi Arabia. Russia's Mikhail Gorbachev pleaded with Bush not to launch this war. He believed that the power of diplomacy, sanctions, and containment could diffuse the situation. A military threat is most successful, Gorbachev argued, when it is not carried out. The Soviet leader was certain that Saddam would bend to continued economic and diplomatic pressures, and that outright war would put the world on a dangerous new course. He proposed a peace plan that would get Saddam out of Kuwait, but by this time Bush was determined to have 'his' war, especially since the polls at home showed that two-thirds of Americans supported our military intervention.

Gorbachev was right; Saddam offered to pull out his forces, but in return he wanted the removal of sanctions, guarantees of an Iraqi route to the Persian Gulf, and control of the Kuwait border oil field that occasioned the dispute. Negotiations on such matters were going on when the bombardment of Baghdad began on January 16, 1991. The war started with a prolonged air campaign that made for great television and low American casualties. The ground offensive came six weeks later. The Gulf War was over quickly; it pitted two very unequal military machines. In spite of Saddam Hussein's orders that the Iraqi army was to stand and fight the Americans to the last man, his forces treated this absurd order with contempt and they fled back to Iraq.

The Gulf War was a war without precedent in the annals of warfare. It was the dawn of a new era in which high technology supplanted the rifle and bayonet. The war lasted 43 days; the actual land combat only took four days. Our entire military incursion was conducted by an elite volunteer army, thereby touching relatively few American homes.

The United States deployed 540,000 troops; our allies added another 200,000. Our pilots dropped 142,000 tons of bombs on Iraq and Kuwait. Fifty-seven U.S. planes and helicopters were lost. Not one American tank was destroyed. Our government was proud to announce that 100,000 Iraqis were killed, while only 148 Americans lost their lives – 35 by friendly fire. What was concealed from the American public was that 200,000 U.S. veterans filed claims for injuries and illness, and 160,000 were granted disability – most from Gulf War syndrome, the name given to an illness that included immune system disorders and birth defects.

"Tonight in Iraq, Saddam walks amidst ruin," President Bush proudly boasted on March 6. "Saddam's war machine is crushed. His ability to threaten mass destruction is destroyed." Although Saddam remained in power, the president was exultant. With this lightning victory, American hegemony was now undisputed.

The Gulf War was publicized as a great victory of "Good" triumphing over "Evil" - but the reality was a bit different. Kuwait was no thriving democracy. It was a country where only 65,000 out of 2.0 million had the privilege to vote and women had no rights. We accused Saddam of committing terrible atrocities in Kuwait, but that was proven false after the war. Our claim that Iraq had 250,000 troops in Kuwait was a lie – all they had was a 'phantom army' closer to 50,000; and our assertions that Iraq was about to use chemical and biological warfare never happened.

There was also no real threat to Saudi Arabia. Dick Cheney's satellite photos of Iraqi troops massed on the Saudi border was a lie. To this day, the Pentagon's photos of the so-called Iraqi troop buildup remains classified. The purpose of the phony photographs was to persuade Saudi Arabia that it was in mortal danger. Our troops were flown in and stayed for twelve years.

The reasons for the Gulf War were never made clear to the American public. Instead, the government embarked on a public relations campaign with empty patriotic platitudes that no loyal American could refute: "Support our troops and wear patriotic ribbons," we were told. All attention was diverted away from the real questions: Why are we at war? How come we supported Saddam Hussein for ten years and now he is suddenly a Hitler? Why did we give Saddam the chemical and biological weapons in the first place? Why didn't Saddam use these 'weapons of mass destruction' against our forces in Kuwait? Patriotism is more than hanging out an American flag or wearing a yellow ribbon – it is asking the right questions and demanding the truth.

Sadly, the American public loved the war. Like children at the video arcade, Americans stared at their television screens in amazement as the precision bombs hit their target. "Smart bombs" found their way down ventilator shafts of Iraqi strongholds; but there was never a picture, and scarcely a mention, of human beings being killed. The tremendous damage our planes wrecked on the Iraqis fleeing Kuwait showed mile after mile of wrecked vehicles – but no bodies. Andy Rooney of the CBS television program *60 Minutes* praised the Gulf War as "the best war in history."

Washington in June 1991 became the scene of an extraordinary victory celebration as 8,000 Gulf War veterans poured into the nation's capital for a military parade down Constitution Avenue. Americans who served in Vietnam had endured the ugliness of a public that shunned them; these Gulf War warriors by contrast were bathed in adulation. Eighty warplanes roared over the parade route and an estimated 800,000 people jammed the streets to cheer the returning heroes. At the Tomb of the Unknown Soldier at Arlington National Cemetery, Bush said: "There is a new and wonderful feeling in America." Turning to his advisers, Bush quipped: "Do you think the American people are going to vote for a Democrat now?"

The Gulf War cost American taxpayers $40 billion. We were told repeatedly that America only paid $10 billion; that the balance of $30 billion was paid by Kuwait and Saudi Arabia. But, that was an evasion of the truth. What really happened was that the price of oil went from $15 to $42 a barrel, generating an extra $60 billion in revenue for the oil producing countries, principally Saudi Arabia and Kuwait. They share this revenue 'fifty-fifty' with the American oil companies. Saudi and Kuwait kept $30 billion and Exxon, Shell, and Mobil got the other $30 billion. In effect, nobody got hurt financially by the war, except the consumers who paid extra every time they filled their gas tanks. As usual, ordinary Americans paid for the war; big business pocketed the profits.

With the war won, we expected the rest of the Islamic world to be grateful. We had ousted a secular dictator and protected an Islamic nation. As hard as we tried, the rest of the Islamic world was not 'buying' into our story. No matter how much we tried to convince them of the righteousness of our cause, the fact remained that a Christian nation had intervened militarily in a Muslim conflict. That posed a greater calamity than Saddam's invasion of Kuwait. Muslims viewed the Iraq invasion of Kuwait as a family affair to be settled within the Islamic family. They believed that the U.S. intervention in the name of some grand theory of international justice was a lie – America acted to protect its own interests, and President Bush's frequent rhetorical invocations of God on behalf of the United States reinforced Arab perceptions that this was a 'religious war' reeking of mercenary attacks by seventh century Christian crusaders.

Certain things did not change: Saddam Hussein was still in power and the Kuwait emirs were back in their fiefdoms. President Bush called for the overthrow of Saddam, and a revolt was started with CIA support, but it was crushed when no U.S. help followed. Saddam then ruthlessly leveled Shiite towns and holy shrines, and executed thousands - all with attack helicopters and weapons supplied to him by the United States during his war with Iran.

In order to drive Saddam out of power, the United States instituted a decade of economic sanctions and kept up a military campaign of focused bombing to harass and intimidate the Iraqi regime. In effect, the U.S. never stopped waging war against Iraq even after the Gulf War formally ended. One way or another, the United States was determined to punish Saddam and destroy his threat to Middle East oil stability. Washington hoped that the hardships of the sanctions would become so unbearable that with the help of the CIA, Saddam would be toppled. Just the reverse happened.

The sanctions that devastated the Iraqi civilian population forced them to rely on Saddam even more for their survival. Nobody knows precisely how many innocent Iraqis died because of these sanctions; a 1999 U.N. report concluded that "the gravity of the humanitarian situation of the Iraqi people cannot be overstated." There was inadequate food and medical supplies as well as breakdowns in sewage sanitation systems and the electrical power needed to run them. In 2002, the Iraqi government stated that 1.7 million of its people died from disease or malnutrition since the imposition of U.S. sanctions.

Before the Gulf War, the United States had few troops in the Middle East, preferring to keep its forces "over the horizon." Now, the United States became in the eyes of many Muslims, an occupying force. Instead of withdrawing U.S. forces from the Middle East, there was a tripling of the U.S. military commitment to the region. The frightened Saudi regime placed orders for more than $25 billion with U.S. armaments manufacturers. Disgusted by the Saudi reliance on American protection, Osama bin Laden left Saudi Arabia in April 1991 and set up an al-Qaeda base in Sudan.

American neo-cons were exasperated; Saddam was still in power and the Iraqi army was virtually intact. They believed that Bush had "wimped out" from ousting Saddam – after all, didn't we declare to the world that Saddam was the new Adolf Hitler? Now Saddam was more popular than ever. He had survived a war with the United States and still ruled. To fevered minds, Saddam's mere survival was an unendurable insult to U.S. hegemonic power. The neo-cons were discouraged, but still committed. All they needed was an opportunity and a president who was not afraid to act. Their time would come with September 11.

CHAPTER TWENTY THREE

GLOBALIZATION

> "Globalization as defined by rich people like us is a very nice thing."
>
> Jimmy Carter

> "Globalization is nothing more than a new and sophisticated form of plundering."
>
> Fidel Castro

Globalization has always been one of those vague benevolent terms that sounds good, but masks its real meaning; an American empire based on corporate colonization. Most people associate it with communications – the Internet, cell phones, and satellite television. However, for America's corporate elites it serves as a euphemism for the purest form of capitalism – seeking out the cheapest form of labor in order to increase each unit's profitability - and viewing the world as nothing more than billions of consumers.

It does not matter whether people in these new foreign markets need our products; advertising creates the demand by emphasizing cultural change and the adoption of modern lifestyles. What is needed is to get every Indonesian to switch from water or tea to Coke; from sandals to Nike sneakers; and from rice to Chicken McNuggets. When Coca Cola looks at Africa, it does not see endless poverty, rampant AIDS, and authoritative regimes – it sees 568 million potential soft drink consumers. Democracy is not the issue. People in repressive regimes are just consumers just like everyone else; making a profit knows no nationality or system of government.

Bill Clinton will always be remembered for his classic quote: "I did not have sex with that woman." Outside of his philandering behavior that besmirched the presidency, he is best known as the only Democratic president to have destroyed the unions and the voter base within his own party. The dismantling of the unions began with Ronald Reagan, but for reasons that still defy a satisfactory explanation, Clinton hammered the last nail into the coffin.

The key element in this globalized movement came with NAFTA (North American Free Trade Agreement), which took effect on January 1, 1994. NAFTA was the brain-child of the George H.W. Bush administration. It was pro-business and anti-labor, but NAFTA could not be rammed into law before Bush left office - that would have to wait for incoming President Bill Clinton. Labor and environmental groups strongly argued that NAFTA would launch a race-to-the-bottom in wages, destroy hundreds of thousands of good U.S. jobs, and threaten health, environmental and food safety standards. Despite these arguments, Clinton used every means at his disposal to cajole Congress into passing NAFTA.

Why did Clinton surrender the Democratic Party's liberal heritage and become a vigorous pro-business advocate? His answer was: "It's all about economics, stupid." As soon as Clinton signed the NAFTA Agreement, the big money began to roll in. He received $340 million from Corporate America for his re-election campaign; labor contributed a meager $52 million. Clinton was motivated by the same thing that drives virtually all politicians: power and money - you get money by being on the side of those who have the power.

NAFTA was camouflaged as a win-win situation for Mexico, Canada and the United States. However, only Corporate America won – American workers lost. The deal was supposed to eliminate tariffs on manufactured goods and agriculture, remove Mexican restrictions on foreign investment, and generally limit what Mexico could do to protect its own farms and businesses. NAFTA proponents predicted that increased U.S. investment in Mexico would raise Mexican wages, which in turn would reduce the incentive for Mexicans to emigrate to the U.S., and reduced tariffs would create demand for American-made products, which would increase U.S. jobs. Once again, Americans were sold a 'bill of goods' by a government controlled by powerful corporate interests.

The number of manufacturing jobs in the United States declined steadily every month; within two years, 4.4 million jobs were lost. One consulting firm predicts that another 1.4 million American jobs will soon move overseas and that the real wages of 80 percent of our population will fall. Unions have shrunk to seven percent of America's work force. The American worker no longer has any political, economic, or bargaining power. The balance that used to exist between labor and business is gone. Today's retirement plan for young workers is: "I'm going to work until I die." The American Dream is over for the American workingman.

Unwittingly, Americans contribute to the loss of their own jobs. Buying and consuming cheaper foreign products leads to more Third World manufacturing, which in turn results in more U.S. jobs being outsourced. Today's economy offers Americans a Faustian bargain – the more we consume the more jobs we lose. And, not only are we consuming foreign products, but twelve million illegal immigrants walked into this country undetected and are eroding America's already diminishing job base and undercutting wages. Worst of all, nobody knows how it happened and nobody knows what to do about it.

Out of necessity, the average American couple now works seven more weeks a year than they did in 1990, and the average American puts in 350 more hours than his or her European counterpart. Because of these work arrangements, parents spend less time with their children than they did three decades ago.

New jobs are created, but instead of high-paying ones in manufacturing they are in fast food, nursing homes, and day-care centers. Elderly parents are shuffled off to nursing homes because there is nobody at home to care for them. Young children are reared in day care centers because mom has to work. No one has the time to cook meals or sit around the dinner table as a family. It's just less of a hassle to eat fast food somewhere or bring in a pizza.

The United States no longer manufactures anything of value; everything has been outsourced. Outsourcing is not something new; it is as old as capitalism itself. It is nothing more than hiring another company to manufacture a component or to perform some service that is less costly than if we had to perform the function ourselves. It has long been used to boost efficiency, as companies replace small and perhaps inefficient in-house operations with high-quality purchased inputs. However, today's outsourcing has created something that is very new, something entirely outside our previous experience as a nation. Traditionally, companies that outsourced work tended to hire local suppliers, usually within a few miles of their main factory. In those circumstances, American workers were replaced by other American workers. However, American jobs that are outsourced today are lost forever – they are never returning to America.

Globalists admit that some Americans will be displaced as employment and production are transferred to Third World countries, but they claim these are merely growing pains, a passing phase subject to almost automatic self-correction. Globalization will, according to its proponents, generate an ultimate equilibrium, with the long-term benefits offsetting the initial hardships of the few.

One thing is certain; the benefits of globalization have been unevenly distributed. The wealthy are thriving on stock market profits (despite the 2008 crash) while more and more Americans are suffering from dislocation. Try explaining to a worker in Maine who has just lost his job to a Vietnamese worker that he "needs to be absorbed into the economy by learning a new trade because in the long run it is good for America." The term, "in the long run" can be a heartless phrase. In the short run, Americans need to feed their families. Ordinary people in America are beginning to ask, "Is globalization good for me?" and in a growing number of cases they are arriving at the conclusion that it is not.

Corporate America claims that globalization serves humanitarian purposes because it reduces poverty in Third World countries. Whenever capitalists start patting themselves on the back about their humanitarian motives you know they are not telling the truth. Capitalism is about profits – not about Christian virtues or American patriotism. The sanctity of profits overrides moral benevolence. If we were really interested in eradicating poverty in Third World countries we would insist on minimum wages for the people there – but that obviously would lower profits and stock market investors would take a dim view of such a gesture.

Capitalism and exploitation have always been synonymous – replacing the word capitalism with the more sanitized 'globalization' does not change anything. The 'game' is structured so that Corporate America reaps the major rewards; the poor in the Third World merely get some crumbs. So what, the global capitalists argue. Even if that is true, where is it written that the rich should share or take care of the poor? We are capitalists, they maintain. We do not believe in communism or socialism. Why should wealth be evenly distributed? Why should our Company or the United States be responsible for the world's poverty? Let each government lift up its own poor. The poor will benefit when the increased wealth we are developing 'trickles-down' to them; but all the evidence shows that the benefits of globalization mainly trickle up.

Globalization benefits Third World poverty the way slavery benefited African blacks in early America. Slavery was undeniably a terrible institution and an awful blight on an America that professed equality, liberty, and freedom. Africans were forcibly uprooted from their homes, torn away from their families, and transported against their will to a land where they were auctioned off as beasts of burden. Their survival depended on their ability to produce profits for their masters. If they were lazy or unproductive they were beaten, but never killed. The blacks were valuable chattels. The white owner needed to protect his investment so he took care of his property. The slaves were clothed, fed, housed, and given the best medical care. In order to insure their passivity and eliminate rebellious passions, they were Christianized and 'saved.'

Today, blacks are among the highest paid athletes and entertainers in the United States. They are Supreme Court justices and presidential candidates. People like Oprah and Shaq are household names, living in great splendor. Blacks attend the finest universities and teach at all the prestigious institutions. Most blacks still live at the lower economic scale, but they have come a long way from their slave status, which in terms of history is relatively short.

But, what would have happened had there been no slavery in America? Where would Oprah and Shaq be today had their ancestors not been dragged here in chains? Can it be perversely argued that slavery, seen from its long-term effects, was a humanitarian endeavor; that without the slave trade, people like Oprah and Shaq would be wallowing in abject poverty back in Africa? That is the argument of globalization to justify that Third World countries benefit from our 'humanitarian' global policies.

True, globalization today is not slavery, but it is not too far removed. The differences are cosmetic - we no longer have to uproot and transport slaves to America – instead we transport our industries to the 'slaves.' We pay the Third World worker a higher wage than he would earn without globalization, but it is still a pittance, and we do not have to provide housing, food, clothing, medical care, union benefits, retirement plans, or ecology safeguards – and if our new 'slaves' get 'uppity' and begin to make demands, we can move the industry to some other Third World country and get new 'slaves.'

There are thousands of examples of Third World slavery, from Liz Claiborne jeans to Wal-Mart brands to ecological disasters created by Coca-Cola. In Indonesia, a pair of Nike $150 sneakers now costs $5 to make, yet the price did not decrease when production was outsourced from the United States. Is it any wonder that Nike founder and CEO Philip Knight is the fifth-richest man in America with a net worth of $5.2 billion, while his Indonesian worker makes thirty-one cents an hour? And Philip Knight has never set foot in Indonesia, let alone in one of his 'slave' factories.

Globalization is today's sanitized form of exploitation. The statistics bear this out - 20 percent of the world population consumes 83 percent of global resources and the richest one percent receives as much income as the top 57 percent combined, yet, more than a billion people live on less than a dollar a day and lack access to clean water; 826 million suffer from malnutrition; 10 million die each year for lack of the most basic health care.

For Americans, globalization can be either good or bad. When American jobs are outsourced to cheaper foreign markets, that makes millions of American workers poorer, but cheaper imports makes those Americans who already have money, richer because their dollars can buy more. Some Americans win, but most lose. In a truly patriotic society, no American should benefit when it hurts a fellow American.

Corporate advertising and public relations is great at distorting the truth through language. Proposals that contain the word "Free" are particularly effective. Free trade and free markets are not 'free' and they have nothing to do with freedom - they are a means for American multinational corporations to obtain cheap labor without government regulations and environmental restrictions. Free trade is a euphemism for transferring jobs from high hourly wage Americans to cheap overseas labor sources, but calling it 'free' sounds so much better than the truth. Free trade is based on the idea that the nations of the earth are one instead of separate; that what is in the interest of one country is in the interest of all countries. That is a false premise.

Another flagrant violation of so-called 'free trade' is when we decide to embargo and forbid shipments of food or medicine to uncooperative countries. In those instances 'free trade' principles are discarded - we unilaterally determine that they do not apply. In September 2005, the World Health Organization warned that a new 'free trade' agreement between the United States and Bolivia, Columbia, El Salvador, and Venezuela would restrict local manufacture of generic medicines in favor of drugs produced by global pharmaceutical companies, thereby raising the price of medicines in these countries by 200 percent. The report warned that the price increase would make the medicines inaccessible to those poor people in need. No matter, when humanitarianism conflicts with profits – profit wins out every time.

The U.S. pharmaceutical companies are one of the worst examples of lies, deceits and American greed. These companies terrify our citizens - telling them that cheap foreign drugs are going to kill them. Meanwhile, their drugs are manufactured in the same cheap overseas markets and shipped back to the United States under the guise of 'free trade.' Once the drugs are back in the United States, the pharmaceutical company slaps on their label and charges the American consumer four times what he or she should be paying. It is all an unconscionable rip-off.

The power and greed of the drug companies extends beyond our borders. India, for example, is now our biggest foreign source of pharmaceuticals. A just-published study shows that the drugs being shipped out of India leave behind a toxic mess. Effluents discharged into streams and rivers in one Indian region show concentrations of antibiotics at thousand times the levels considered safe. Health surveys show higher rates of cancer and other illnesses in villages around this "special economic pharmaceutical zone" than in more distant villages. So while it's true that some people in the Third World benefit with jobs, others die.

Globalization did not become America's dominant worldview all at once – it represents the triumph of five decades of American foreign policy. During the Cold War the United States and the Soviet vied for the attention of the non-aligned nations. Foreign aid was a bribe to get a country to support capitalism rather than communism. With the end of the Cold War, we became the only 'game' in town so we changed the rules. Globalization emerged as a disguised form of foreign aid. Instead of huge handouts, we could control countries through economic programs that would also provide U.S. industries with cheap labor, weaken the unions in America, and eliminate regulations that were expensive and onerous in the United States. If the 'target' foreign country cooperated, they got our dollars and their people got our jobs. Part of the deal was that they had to recycle a major portion of their new U.S. dollars to fund our dangerously increasing debt, otherwise no deal.

At the center of this new global economy is the World Bank. The World Bank is another one of those disguised designations that is really a misnomer. The World Bank is really an American financial institution that finances our global interests and works hand-in-hand with our foreign policy. Since its inception in

1946, every president of the World Bank has hailed from the United States and each has been a foreign policy strategist. The International Monetary Fund (IMF) is another such misnomer; it is not some international humanitarian agency. Instead, it is run and controlled by American interests. Both agencies were created in response to the chaos after the Second World War. The World Bank makes long-term loans to Third World countries that are willing to advance our corporate interests. If that country develops a financial crisis, the IMF leaps in with stabilizing grants and loans. Both institutions are located in Washington, D.C.

The fact that Paul Wolfowitz was chosen to recently head the World Bank says volumes about our arrogance and intentions. Wolfowitz was one of President Bush's leading neo-con war hawks. He favored the economic sanctions that starved Iraqis for over a decade and caused the death of almost 500,000 Iraqi children. Wolfowitz was also a leading proponent of our disastrous invasion of Iraq. In 2003, he told a Congressional panel that our new oil revenues from Iraq would pay for the invasion and reconstruction. He was wrong about everything. To get him out of the administration, Bush shipped him to off to head the World Bank. After serving two tumultuous years, he resigned when his sexual liaison with a fellow employee became public knowledge.

John Perkins, author of *Confessions of an Economic Hit Man*, worked for years as chief economist at an international consulting firm in Boston. His job was to persuade countries that are strategically important to the U.S. to accept enormous loans for infrastructure development and then make sure that the lucrative projects are contracted to U.S. corporations. Saddled with huge debts they could not possibly repay, these countries came under the control of the World Bank and other U.S. dominated aid agencies that act like loan sharks, dictating repayment terms and bullying foreign governments into submission. Perkins describes how the process works.

> "We go to a Third World country and arrange a huge loan; usually the World Bank leads that process. One of the conditions of the loan is that roughly 90 percent comes back to big U.S. corporations such

as Bechtel or Halliburton. These corporations then build large infrastructure projects that basically serve the very rich. The poor people in these countries never benefit from the loans or projects. In fact, often their social services have to be severely curtailed in order to pay off the debt.

We then go back to these countries and say something like - look, you borrowed all this money from us and you can't repay your debts. In return for a postponement or concession, give our oil companies your oil at very cheap prices. That's what we're doing today around the world."

Examples of callous American business practices in Third World countries are too numerous to list in detail. A few examples will suffice. When school buses are deemed no longer safe for American children they are routinely sold to Latin America countries; the safety of children in foreign lands is not our concern. Exporting cancer to the Third World keeps U.S. tobacco companies profitable. When the Thai government banned the importation of American cigarettes for health reasons, the U.S. forced them to rescind the order. Corporate America has increased world trade in banned pesticides, leaded gasoline, asbestos, and other products restricted in the United States. We dictate the terms and conditions of a globalized economy; not with gunboats, but with power and money.

When Lawrence Summers was the chief economist for the World Bank, he wrote the following internal memo that proposed sending toxic waste from the United States to the Third World. The memo can be considered a working thesis for all our shameful global economic policies.

DATE: December 12, 1991

TO: Distribution

FROM: Lawrence H. Summers

Subject: Dirty Industries

Just between you and me, shouldn't the World Bank be encouraging MORE migration of dirty industries to the LDCs (Less Developed Countries)? I can think of three reasons for doing this:

1. The economic logic behind dumping a load of toxic waste in the lowest wage country is impeccable and we should face up to that.

2. Countries in Africa are vastly under-polluted compared to a populated city like Los Angeles. Polluting Africa rather than some Western industrial city just makes sense.

3. The concern over a toxic waste agent that causes prostrate cancer, for example, is obviously going to be much higher in a country where people live long enough to get prostrate cancer than in a Third World country where the under five-years of age mortality is so high anyway.

Summers' solution to toxic waste was simple and pragmatic - the people in the Third World are going to die young due to poverty and AIDS. It made sense, according to Summers, to dump all our toxic waste on them because they would die before the visible effects of cancer took effect.

After the memo became public in February 1992, Jose Lutzenburger, Brazil's Secretary of the Environment, wrote to Summers: "Your reasoning is perfectly logical, but totally insane.

Your thoughts provide a concrete example of the unbelievable alienation, social ruthlessness, and arrogant ignorance of many concerning the nature of the world we live in. If the World Bank keeps you as vice-president it will lose all credibility. To me it confirms what I often said - the best thing that could happen would be for the World Bank to disappear."

Oil is what makes globalization work; control of the world's oil supplies has become America's number one foreign policy objective. Third World countries now need huge amounts of oil to keep pace with American globalization quotas. In the past, U.S. manufacturing served the needs of millions of Americans, now, with billions of new consumers, the Third World needs the oil to keep up with America's outsourced needs. From an ecological view, can you imagine what the earth's atmosphere is going to be like when all those billions of people in China, India, and Africa, start driving automobiles? The more oil the rest of the world needs, the less oil will be available to Americans back home. Countries like Saudi Arabia, Iran, Iraq, Kuwait, and Venezuela, have already become the power brokers in this new world, but if oil scarcity becomes a crisis in the United States, watch how fast the American military goes into action.

According to former national security advisor Zbigniew Brzezinski, globalization has the backing of three powerful constituencies: the right-wing neo-conservatives, America's business elite, and our U.S. military. Once new markets and sources of cheap labor are established, our investments in these far-away lands have to be protected. If these industries were in the United States, our police force would provide law and order. But, the only way our foreign interests can be protected is through strategically placed U.S. military forces, which is why the U.S. presently maintains over 700 military bases in 132 different countries. In addition to these worldwide military bases, some thirteen naval task forces dominate the oceans and seas, and U.S. intelligence and space satellites monitor what people are saying and doing. In the past, empires conquered by force and took the riches back home for its citizens to enjoy. Globalization is still the subjugation of the poor to the powerful, but unlike traditional imperialism, we do not invade, conquer, and occupy. Instead, we control and monitor.

Our intention is not to wage war, but to show that force is available if needed to protect our interests. Our military power is not intended to be unleashed; instead, it is to be doled out in precisely measured increments against carefully selected targets that have little or no capacity to retaliate. Empire may not be the traditional word to describe what we are doing all over the globe, but it is closer than any other term in common usage.

The term "empire" derives from the Latin word *imperium* and refers to the control by a dominant country of weaker countries – politically, militarily, and economically. Empire has always been about economics backed by a strong military. Empires of the past wanted trade routes and the spoils of conquest, but governing some faraway land was always a nuisance filled with problems. When we speak of empire today we no longer mean the likes of Genghis Kahn, or Roman legions handsomely marching through the streets of Jerusalem, or the British sipping tea in colonial India. The United States certainly does not wish to rule or occupy countries like China, India, or Russia - that would be an impossible task - there are just too many people to control. Instead, we seek to control them through globalization.

Thomas Friedman, a major proponent of globalization, puts it this way: "The United States must enforce the capitalist global order with force. The hidden hand of the market will never work without a hidden fist – and the hidden fist that keeps the world safe for America's technologies and business interests is called the United States Army, Air Force, Navy, and Marine Corps." Friedman wrote a book about globalization called *The World Is Flat*, but the world is not really flat. The shape of global power is decidedly pyramidal - with the United States alone at the top.

No republic in history has lasted longer than three hundred years, but we think we are history's exception. Every prior empire deceived itself and followed the same downward path. These empires did not collapse suddenly; there was imperceptible erosion. The people were busily patting themselves on the back, overindulging, and believing their way of life would go on indefinitely. The truth was there for all to see, but nobody wanted to deal with it. If there is one maxim that is universal in all fallen empires it is, "fewer have more."

America's empire is no different. We are an empire that is constantly shocked that our 'good intentions' arouse resentment abroad. We refuse to acknowledge that our rhetoric about spreading democracy and human rights to the world are lies. We ignore the atrocities of Saddam Hussein when it suits our purpose and then overthrow him when he stands in the way of our global plans. We ignore the torture chambers in Egypt because they are torturing suspects at our request. We ignore the genocide in Darfur because we have no economic interest there. We are an empire untrue to our democratic ideals; we are an empire based on personal profit and greed.

Nearly two centuries ago, Alexander Hamilton defended the existence of the power elite this way, "All communities divide themselves into the few and the many. The first are the rich and well-born; the other, the masses of people." Nothing much has changed since then. That there is such a governing class in this country is America's worst-kept secret.

The Duquesne Club of Pittsburgh is just one example of American elitism and power. It is no different than the Somerset, the Knickerbocker, the Philadelphia or the Baltimore – its members are the aristocracy of America. The Duquesne is a private club wholly supported by large corporations who pay the membership and dining entertainment costs of their executives. Osborn Elliott, in his book, *Men at the Top*, describes the power politics of the club back in 1960, but it is as illustrative today as it was then.

> "It is when you go upstairs in the Duquesne that you begin to enter the sub-stratosphere of executive power. On the second floor there are no fewer than five dining rooms, and in each of these, day after day, the same people sit at the same tables. As you enter the main dining room, the Gulf Oil table is across the way. Gulf's chairman, David Proctor, sits facing the door surrounded by his senior vice-presidents. In the corner over to the right is the Koppers table,

populated by most of the top men in that company, and next to it is the U.S. Steel table, where vice-presidents break bread together. In a smaller room nearby, Pittsburgh Coke & Chemical's president and his vice-presidents gather daily. In still another room, Pittsburgh Plate Glass has a central spot, while Alcoa's executive committee chairman, Roy Hunt, holds forth in the corner next to Jack Heinz's table. Here the corporate elite get together and exchange ideas. There are daily exposures of people to people that are of the same ilk and the same mold."

C. Wright Mills, in his exhaustive study, *The Power Elite*, describes how the corporate elites, the military echelon, and our top political leaders run America while the rest of us follow along aimlessly. This claim cannot be denied; in America some men have enormous power denied to everyone else. Corporate funding elects politicians, the Pentagon awards billions in contracts to the military-industrial complex, and corporations in turn provide high-ranking jobs to politicians and the military once their careers are over. The cycle is continuous. The only ones left out of the 'loop' are the ordinary Americans.

Wealth is not the criteria necessary to belong to this power elite. "Old money" is what counts – the nouveau rich and wealthy minorities are excluded. One needs to be white and Protestant, and have the upper-class values that include a certain breeding exemplified by the best prep school traditions of St. Paul's, Groton, and Hotchkins. Being accepted into prestigious prep schools is followed by being 'Skull and Bones Men' of Yale, 'Ivy Men' of Princeton, and members of the best 'private' clubs in New York. Going to Harvard or Yale or Princeton is not enough. The prep school determines which of the two Harvard's you attend. There is the Harvard of the elites; and then there is the Harvard for the brainy nerds and minorities. The point is not Harvard, but which Harvard? Those who are members of the 'club' do not associate with the ordinariness of humanity except when absolutely essential. J.P.

Morgan described it best: "I can do business with anyone, but I only sail with a gentleman."

There is no official aristocracy in America, but this elite class comes pretty close. They are raised from childbirth to ascend to positions of power. Their enemy is socialism, taxation of the rich, and laws made for the poor. Understanding who the "elites" are is an interesting undertaking. It requires a through in-depth study of those in power. The history of the post-World War II era provides excellent examples.

Averill Harriman was the son of a railroad magnate multi-millionaire. At Groton, an elite prep school, he excelled in squash; at Yale he was immediately chosen for 'Skull and Bones.' His greatest achievement at Yale was as a member of the rowing team. Later, he would become our ambassador to Russia during the tumultuous years of the Cold War when nuclear war hinged on every decision. Robert Lovett, who became secretary of defense, was Averill Harriman's closest playmate during childhood and also a member of 'Skull and Bones.' Dean Acheson, secretary of state under Truman, attended Groton before embarking on an undistinguished career at Yale. Charles Bolen served in many high government capacities. He was expelled from St. Paul's, but was accepted into Harvard because of family connections. These were the men who determined American foreign policy during that era. They all possessed a similar background and experience, and a common liking for old wines, squash and polo, and proper English Savile Row clothing.

Today's examples are no different. Dick Cheney left his government position as secretary of defense to go directly to the Halliburton Corporation where he made hundreds of millions of dollars before returning as George W. Bush's vice-president. Donald Rumsfeld left government in 1977 to become CEO and Chairman of the huge pharmaceutical firm G.D. Searle. After being rewarded handsomely for his government connections in getting FDA approval for several of Searle's "suspect" drugs, he returned as Bush's secretary of defense. George W. Bush was born rich, attended the proper secondary schools, was a member of 'Skull and Bones' while attending Yale without distinction, and knew all the 'right' people. Those were his qualifications to be President of the United States.

Corporate America is always well represented at the highest levels of government. Bush's chief of staff, Andrew Card, was the chief lobbyist for General Motors. Secretary of State Condoleezza Rice was on the board of directors of Chevron and Transamerica. Secretary of the Treasury Paul O'Neill was chairman of Alcoa and a director of Lucent Technologies. Secretary of Commerce Donald Evans was CEO and chairman of Kellogg. Secretary of Labor Elaine Chao came from Citicorp and Bank of America. To show how powerful Corporate America is - no one from labor has been secretary of labor since Arthur Goldberg in 1961.

Not everyone in our nation's upper class knows everyone else, but everyone knows somebody who knows someone, thanks to a common school experience, a summer at the same resort, membership in the same social club, or being a member on the same board of directors. Lockheed Martin, the nation's largest defense contractor, had more connections to the George W. Bush administration than any other major defense contractor - eight Bush policy makers had direct or indirect ties to Lockheed. Northrop Grumman, the nation's third largest defense contractor, followed closely behind with seven former officials. To say that there is a power elite that directs the affairs of state is not to suggest the existence of some dark conspiracy. It is simply to acknowledge the way Washington actually works.

Americans look with pride and amazement at our country's accomplishments in space, but nobody asks what are we doing up there? Why are we spending billions in space instead of on our citizens here at home? What does ownership of space mean? Air Force General Thomas D. White explains it this way: "Whoever controls outer space will likewise possess the capability to exert control of the surface of the Earth." We are putting platforms in space for highly destructive nuclear and laser weapons that can be launched without warning to anywhere in the world. Over 250 U.S. satellites are now operating in space, representing an investment of over a $100 billion and the speculation is that another 1,800 satellites will be added in the near future.

To insure that our high-tech weapons hit the right target takes lots of expensive research and development. The Pentagon does not do R & D; it contracts the job to some major corporation like General Electric. It takes years to get it right, but all the costs are paid for by the American taxpayer. When the project is finished, the Pentagon gets its laser-controlled weapon and GE gets all future commercial applications from its research. General Electric makes billions from related new products that was fully funded by the government, in effect, by the U.S. taxpayer. That is how the Internet, computers, satellites, fiber optics, solar energy, and all kinds of automation got started. The American taxpayer provides the R&D funding and Corporate America gets a free ride and all the benefits. In a truly competitive capitalist society nobody is supposed to get a free ride – but in America, corporate elites enjoy a special status.

The enormity of our military-industrial complex starts with the Pentagon. With an annual budget of $310 billion, the Pentagon remains America's largest company: 5.1 million employees, 600 facilities nationwide, more than 40,000 properties and 18 million acres of land. Indeed, the Pentagon spends more on military research and development than the combined spending of two-thirds of the entire world.

To maintain and justify this military-industrial complex we must be in a constant state of war. There must always be an enemy of the moment that represents absolute evil – whether it is Iraq, Iran, North Korea, al-Qaeda, Afghanistan, Pakistan, Venezuela, Russia, or Cuba. Americans have been frightened into believing that our national security is constantly at risk. Questioning the propriety of spending these billions every year, as well as surrendering our civil liberties, is labeled unpatriotic and foolhardy.

FDR once said that we have nothing to fear but fear itself, but the Bush-Cheney administration took the opposite approach. Fear became the driving force behind the "war on terror." The choice, according to our leaders was "victory or holocaust." What does victory mean in a war on terror? Must we kill every Muslim to insure there are no terrorists or potential terrorists left? Can anyone define when this "war" will be won, or is it a never-ending program to control our lives and direct our nation's resources to the military-industrial arena?

There are two governments in the United States today. One is visible - the one we see on *CNN* and *Fox News* or read about in the newspapers. The other is invisible - it is the interlocking hidden machinery that carries out the policies of the visible government. This second government gathers intelligence, conducts espionage, and plans and executes secret operations all over the globe. This invisible government consists of formal bodies like the Central Intelligence Agency and the National Security Agency (NSA), and other loose amorphous grouping of individuals and agencies drawn from many parts of the visible government.

The American people know virtually nothing about the activities of these agencies. Their employment rolls and documents are classified, their activities are top-secret, and their budget is concealed in other appropriations. Congress provides money for their operations without knowing how much it has appropriated or how it is being spent. A handful of congressmen are supposed to be kept informed on its activities, but they know relatively little about what this invisible government does or how it operates. Our nation's leaders believe this invisible government is necessary; that certain decisions must be made in secret and without popular consent. The CIA is only accountable to the president. The NSA is so secretive that insiders joke that its initials stand for "No Such Agency."

After our defeat in Vietnam, the Pentagon decided to substitute its regular army of troublesome conscripts with an all-volunteer army. Members of this new professional force received extensive indoctrination designed to separate them from civilian society; to imbue them with a warrior ethic that emphasized loyalty to the military as their primary value. This indoctrination was designed to immunize them against possible contagion from anti-war and defeatist sentiments that might spring up in civilian America. However, this type of military created "two cultures" in the United States. In 1956, for example, 450 of 750 Princeton graduates served in the military. The figure for the class of 2004 was eight out of 1,100. All four Kennedy brothers – Joe, John, Bobby, and Ted –

served in the military, but not one of the thirty Kennedy cousins has spent a day in military service. Our military today bears no resemblance to the rest of our population.

The preponderance of our military personnel is comprised of southerners and Hispanics. Rich white Americans do not volunteer for military service. The values of loyalty, duty, and dedication come from our 'blue collar' society. Ironically, the poor protects the interests of the rich, while life back home goes on uninterrupted. It was not always this way. Millions of young men used to put in their time as members of the army because citizenship included a responsibility to contribute to the nation's welfare. When called upon, millions fought for the same reason. If everyone had to serve today, our war policies would receive far greater scrutiny. Our government would not rush into war or 'police actions' if every family had a son or daughter in harm's way.

The Roman Empire supplemented its elite legions with a mercenary army. Our empire is no different. Organizations like Blackwater provide military mercenaries on a contract basis to the defense department. Blackwater is a private army controlled by one person: Erik Prince, a radical right-wing mega-millionaire who has served as a major financier not only of ulltra-conservative Republican candidates, but of the broader Christian-right agenda. His mercenaries are given six-figure salaries in contrast to our active-duty soldiers. This may seem extravagant, but Blackwater bills the defense department after tacking on a profit, and everything ends up being paid for by the American taxpayer.

When our government tells the public how many troops we have in Iraq, it conveniently omits these 'hired guns' who are not subject to our military code of conduct and can kill indiscriminately without fear of reprisal or punishment. The media refers to these shadowy forces as "civilian contractors" as though they were engineers, construction workers, humanitarians, or water specialists. The term "mercenary" is almost never used to describe them. That is no accident. Indeed, it is part of a very sophisticated deceptive campaign by our decision makers in Washington.

What is the role of our media in all this? Americans are supposedly the best informed people in the world, but our information is filtered through corporate self-interest groups. In the 1970s – fifty corporations controlled virtually all the media. Today, the number has been reduced to nine. CBS is owned by Westinghouse; NBC by GE; both corporations are major members of the military-industrial complex. ABC is owned by Disney, a major corporation with a right-wing agenda. Rupert Murdoch owns *Fox News* along with a multitude of other television stations and newspapers. With each of Murdoch's media purchases, the editorial content switches radically to the right. Corporate advertisers pay $170 billion a year enabling them to control the content of what Americans view; even public television is now corporate funded. More and more, the news we get is being controlled by a handful of elites.

Today, capitalism stands tall while communism and socialism have proven to be abject failures. But, let us not forget that history is ongoing and the last chapter has yet to be written. The lasting effect of our current economic crisis remains uncertain. Whatever the outcome, one thing is certain: if capitalist greed remains unchecked and poverty gaps widen into intense class dissatisfaction, the stability of our society will be in danger. Revolutions are caused by such conditions. To think that it "cannot happen here" has always been the delusion of people in power.

Chalmers Johnson, a former Cold War consultant to the CIA and currently emeritus professor at the University of California, argues that we have already entered the "last days" of our republic. One reason for Johnson's end-of-days gloom is that he sees no power 'center' capable of resisting the forces that currently drive American foreign policy. He claims that because of the costliness of election campaigns and the insidious influence of congressional lobbyists, "the legislative branch of our government is broken." An elected body that owes its incumbency to Corporate America cannot reasonably be expected to swivel around and eliminate the influence that nourishes it. In Johnson's words, "our political system may no longer be capable of saving the United States as we know it." These are provocative words coming from a very distinguished scholar.

CHAPTER TWENTY FOUR

SEPTEMBER 11

"Every day I ask myself the same question. How can this be happening in America? How can people like this be in charge of our country? If I didn't see it with my own eyes, I'd think it was a hallucination."

Philip Roth
The Plot Against America

"I'm the commander in chief-in-chief. I don't need to explain why I say things. That's the interesting thing about being president. I don't owe anybody an explanation."

President George W. Bush

"It is the oldest story in the history of American government – the failure to tell the truth."

Bob Woodward
State of Denial

The war hawk neo-conservatives from Reagan's Iran-Contra and Bush's Gulf War were riding high until George H. W. Bush got booted out of office by William Jefferson Clinton. On January 26, 1998, the leading Republican neo-conservatives addressed a letter to President Clinton that stated in part:

We are writing to you because we are convinced that current American policy toward Iraq is not succeeding, and that we may soon face a threat in the Middle East more serious than any we have known since the end of the Cold War. We urge you to seize that opportunity, and to enunciate a new strategy that would secure the interests of the U.S. and our friends and allies around the world. That strategy should aim, above all, at the removal of Saddam Hussein's regime from power. Saddam Hussein has a seriously destabilizing effect on the entire Middle East. It hardly needs to be added that if he acquires the capability to deliver weapons of mass destruction, as he is almost certain to do if we continue along the present course, the safety of American troops in the region, of our friends and allies like Israel and the moderate Arab states, and a significant portion of the world's supply of oil will all be put at hazard. The security of the world in the first part of the 21st century will be determined largely by how we handle this threat.

Given the magnitude of the threat, our current policy is dangerously inadequate. The only acceptable strategy is one that eliminates Saddam Hussein and his regime from power. That now needs to become the aim of American foreign policy. Although we are fully aware of the dangers and difficulties in implementing this policy, we believe the dangers of failing to do so are far greater. We believe the U.S. has the authority under existing U.N. resolutions to take the necessary steps, including military steps, to protect our vital interests in the Gulf. In any case, American policy cannot continue to be crippled by a misguided insistence on unanimity in the U.N. Security Council.

What Bill Clinton would have done had he not been embroiled in severe personal issues that would lead to impeachment is pure conjecture. The neo-conservatives would just have to wait and bide their time, but they did not have to wait long. On December 12, 2000, the U.S. Supreme Court handed George W. Bush the presidency. Now it was just a matter of time and timing.

September 11, 2001 was a dramatic and shocking moment in American history. However, it should not have come as a big surprise to our government since it was merely the latest in a series of terrorist attacks against the U.S. that began much earlier.

On February 26, 1993, a truck bomb exploded in the B-2 level garage of the World Trade Center, killing six people and wounding another 1,000. On June 26, 1996, terrorists detonated a truck bomb at a U.S. military apartment complex in Dhahran, Saudi Arabia. Nineteen U.S. servicemen and one Saudi were killed; 372 others were wounded. On August 7, 1998, al-Qaeda terrorists bombed the U.S. embassies in Kenya and Tanzania. The attacks killed 12 Americans and over 200 others; more than 4,000 were injured. On October 12, 2000, the *U.S.S. Cole*, a billion-dollar guided-missile destroyer was 'attacked' by a fiberglass fishing boat filled with explosives. Seventeen American sailors perished and 39 were wounded. On August 6, 2001, one month before 9/11, the CIA sent a warning memo to President Bush – "Bin Laden Determined to Strike in U.S." President Bush did not seem concerned.

The terrorist attack on September 11, 2001 took years of preparation and was performed by nineteen men affiliated with al-Qaeda. Lucky or brilliant, equipped with nothing more than fake explosives and plastic knives, they hijacked four commercial passenger jet airliners between the morning hours of 7:45 and 8:10. In each instance the plan worked to perfection. The attack was methodically executed by people of such deep conviction that they were willing to give their lives to achieve the success of their mission. It is a level of commitment and depth few of us can imagine. The only modem equivalent is the Japanese kamikaze pilots of World War II when more than 4,000 of them flew to their certain deaths.

Terry McDermott, in his book, *Perfect Soldiers*, did an in-depth study of the 9/11 hijackers. These terrorists were not born to be soldiers - none seem to have come from a military background - and there was little in their early lives to suggest that they would become suicidal terrorists. The pilot of the first plane to hit the World Trade Center, Mohamed Atta, came from an ambitious, overtly religious middle-class household in Egypt. He led "a sheltered life" until he arrived in Germany in 1992 to do graduate study in architecture. The pilot of the second plane, Marwan al-Shehhi, was an amiable, "laid-back" fellow from the United Arab Emirates who joined the army for the money so he could further his education. Hani Hanjour, the Saudi pilot who flew the American Airlines plane into the Pentagon, lived in the United States off and on throughout the 1990s, mostly in Arizona. He was, in the view of one of his flight instructors, "intelligent, friendly, very courteous and formal, a nice enough fellow, but a terrible pilot." As for Ziad Jarrah, the pilot of the plane that crashed in Pennsylvania, he came from an industrious, middle-class secular family from Beirut; he also was a university student in Germany. For all of them, radical Islam and jihad soon became obsessions, eclipsing everything else. University studies were abandoned, families ignored, and the outer world became non-existent as they plunged themselves into their fanatical version of faith.

Many Americans are still bewildered by how this small group could breach U.S. security without detection and inflict such a terrible blow on our nation. Could this tragedy have been averted? Were we asleep at the switch? Conspiracy theories filled the airwaves. As recent as 2006, an Ohio University poll found that 36 percent of Americans believed that federal officials assisted in the attacks or knowingly let them happen so that the U.S. could go to war in the Middle East.

History may view the collapse of the World Trade Center as the moment the American empire began its decline from the summit. The collapse of those two superstructures testified to the tenuousness and fragility of our civilization. Who will ever forget the look on President Bush's face when he was informed of the terrorist attack? It was the perplexed look of a child who in time of crisis is lost without his parents. Sitting in that Florida elementary school class, he was paralyzed by the dreadful news. Without a script to follow or the intellect to act, he sat there waiting for Dick Cheney to rescue him. That was as disturbing as the attack itself.

By the time Bush returned to Washington, Dick Cheney had already set America's response in motion, defining the trajectory it would follow for the next seven years. In doing so, he was unleashing the impulses of his neo-conservative beliefs that had crystallized over the past three decades of his career. When President Bush finally addressed the nation, he declared war not against the attackers, but against unspecified "enemies of freedom." We should not panic or be morose he told the American public; instead we should leave everything to him. Bush defined the impending war on terror as a crusade, "a monumental struggle between good and evil, but good will prevail." However, he added a new dimension to those patriotic "buzz" words – he claimed he was a special envoy of God who instinctively was making the wisest of decisions. This moral interpretation of the conflict closed off any attempt to analyze its causes.

Predictably, the level of military spending after 9/11 more than doubled, reaching $700 billion. By 2006, our annual trade imbalance reached a whopping $818 billion. The following year, total public debt topped $9 trillion, or nearly 70 percent of our gross national product. But, even as the United States embarked on a global conflict expected to last decades, President Bush made a point of reducing taxes. "War costs money," Franklin D. Roosevelt had reminded his countrymen after Pearl Harbor, "that means taxes and bonds and bonds and taxes. It means cutting luxuries and other non-essentials." George W. Bush, however, had a different approach; instead of asking Americans to trim their appetite for luxuries, he told them to carry on as if nothing had occurred. "Get on board. Do your business around the country. Fly and enjoy America's great destination spots. Get down to Disney World in Florida. I encourage you all to go shopping more."

There is nothing like a 'splendid little war' to unite the country behind its president. The close election of 2000 did not provide a mandate for George W. Bush, but 9/11 corrected that. The attack evoked an enormous surge of patriotism. Overnight, American flags sprouted everywhere, but young men and women did not rush to enlist in this war on terror. Few parents were eager to offer up their sons and daughters for a cause they did not understand. Most Americans subscribed to a limited version of patriotism, one that emphasized the display of bumper stickers. Apart from expressions of national unity, the primary responsibility of the average citizen for the duration of the emergency remained what it had been in more peaceful times: to be an engine of consumption.

The story of modern day Islamic terrorism begins with Sayyid Qutb, the Egyptian intellectual father of the movement. A sojourn in America in the late 1940's radicalized the Egyptian educator. After being thrown in prison by the Egyptian regime, his writings and eventual execution in 1966 made him a martyr and hero to a fledgling revolutionary movement. While this was happening, Osama bin Laden, the heir to one of Saudi Arabia's great fortunes, grew from a shy boy who loved American television into a solemn religious adolescent. During this period, Ayman al-Zawahri, an Egyptian doctor whom Osama bin Laden got to know in the 1980's emerged as Osama's evil mentor, drawing a tight noose of influence over the young and impressionable bin Laden.

The continuing presence of American troops in Saudi Arabia after the first Gulf War continued to gnaw at bin Laden. He was not opposed to the United States because of its culture or ideas; only because of its political and military actions in the Islamic world. He and Zawahri drew up a plan of action to lure America into the same trap the Soviets had fallen into in Afghanistan - continually bait the U.S. forces to invade; then the *mujahideen* would bleed them until the entire American empire fell from its wounds. It happened to Great Britain and the Soviet Union – bin Laden and Zawahri were certain history would be repeated with America. When bombing American embassies or the *U.S.S Cole* was not enough to provoke a massive retaliation, bin Laden decided "he would have to create an irresistible outrage." That outrage, of course, was September 11. With this one act, bin Laden became the 'Robin Hood' of the Muslim world, hitting out against the bad Sheriff of Nottingham and then disappearing into Sherwood Forest, only to reappear again when least expected.

From Paul Nitze's NSC directive No. 68 to the present day, members of the power elite have shown an almost pathological tendency to misinterpret reality and inflate threats. September 11 was no exception. Declaring a "war on Al Qaeda and the elusive Osama bin Laden" was too narrow an agenda for Bush-Cheney. Instead, 9/11 became a 'War on Terror' - a false metaphor where the enemy is everywhere and nowhere – a perpetual war based on the fear that a second attack was imminent. What became known as the Bush Doctrine was accepted without debate – U.S. preemptive action became a necessary element of preventive war. According to Dick Cheney, "If there is a one percent chance of a threat, we have to treat it as a certainty in terms of our response."

On Friday, September 14, President Bush went before Congress to ask for special wartime powers. For months, Dick Cheney and administration lawyers had been incubating theories about how to expand presidential power. The language of the proposed resolution authorized the president "to use all necessary and appropriate force against those nations, organizations, or persons he determines planned, authorized, committed, or aided the terrorist attacks that occurred on September 11." The resolution passed in the Senate by a vote of 98 to 0 and in the House by a vote of 420 to 1. The lone dissenter in the House was Representative Barbara Lee of California. She pleaded: "However difficult this vote may be, some of us must urge the use of restraint. Our country is in a state of mourning. Some of us must say, let's step back for a moment, let's just pause for a minute and think through the implications of our actions today so that this does not spiral out of control. As we act let us not become the evil that we deplore."

The pledge from Bush and his top advisers to do everything in their power to stop another attack was a strong tonic for an American public anxious for redemption. It would spur the largest mobilization of law enforcement resources in the country's history, and it would lead Congress, just five weeks after the attacks, to pass a dense, 342-page package of sweeping counter-terrorism measures known as the USA Patriot Act, a smorgasbord of a bill pushed so urgently by the administration that few lawmakers who voted for it had time to read its fundamental reworking of the law, much less understand it. The use of the word "Patriot" should have been a warning; the legislation should have been more properly called, "The Erosion of American Civil Liberties Act." Americans were told these new constitutional infringements were necessary to protect our national security; objections were labeled unpatriotic.

A disaster, any disaster, where the population is in shock, is an unbelievable opportunity for a government to act with dictatorial-like authority and institute legislation that would not ordinarily be possible during peaceful times; fear and turmoil does not lend itself to a rational debate of the issues. September 11 became such a golden opportunity for the neo-conservatives. The American public, fearing that its security was threatened, was willing to acquiesce in incursions of its civil liberties as a trade-off to gain a sense of greater personal safety. Benjamin Franklin once said "Those who would give up essential liberty to purchase a little temporary safety deserve neither liberty nor safety."

With the shackles now off, agents at home and abroad looked for the faintest whiff of terrorism in an effort to stop the terrorists before they could hit again. Racial profiling approached World War II levels; 80,000 Arab and Muslim immigrants were subjected to fingerprinting and registration, and more than 5,000 foreign nationals were imprisoned. Hundreds of thousands of e-mails and phone calls were secretly tapped, but no convictions resulted.

The American public was bombarded with color coded warnings about the oncoming next attack. They were urged to stock up on duct tape and plastic sheeting to seal their homes from chemical and biological attack. Instead of calm rational leadership, Bush-Cheney kept the country on a war alert in a deliberate attempt to further their agenda. Bush's executive orders were not confined to the national security area. With public attention focused on the next terrorist threat, the administration rolled back expensive business regulations imposed for the safety of workers, did away with the requirement to hire only union work crews on federally funded projects, and killed all efforts about global warming and the environment, claiming this was no time to inflict 'unnecessary' costs on our economy.

On December 13, 2001, President Bush, flanked by Secretary of Defense Donald Rumsfeld and Secretary of State Colin Powell, invoked what he felt was his legal executive powers by revoking the thirty-year-old Anti-Ballistic Treaty with Russia. His justification was to allow the United States "to develop ways to protect our people from future terrorist missile attacks." This treaty, like all treaties, was initially approved by Congress. By unilaterally scrapping the ABM treaty, Bush seized for the presidency the power to pull the United States out of any treaty without first obtaining the consent of Congress. Constitutional precedent was now being discarded. Yale Law School professor Bruce Ackerman tried to sound the alarm about the serious implications of Bush's actions. "Presidents cannot just terminate statutes they don't like. They must get Congress to repeal; otherwise there is no constitutional guarantee of separation of powers."

When Donald Rumsfeld joined the Bush administration as secretary of defense, many wondered why he would want it. He was sixty-eight years old, had five grandchildren, and a personal fortune estimated at $250 million - and he had already held the same post in the Gerald Ford administration. Rumsfeld, however, had no desire to be a traditional defense secretary; he had greater ambitions than that - his personal mission was to reinvent warfare. Much has been written about Rumsfeld's controversial "transformation" project, which prompted eight retired generals to call for his resignation and eventually force him to step down after the 2006 mid-term elections.

Beneath all the jargon, Rumsfeld's program was simply an attempt to bring outsourcing from the corporate world into the heart of the U.S. military. Rumsfeld saw the army shedding large numbers of full-time troops in favor of a small core propped up by paid mercenaries from private firms whose costs were hidden from congressional view. Rumsfeld's plan was to shift his 'budget savings' to the latest satellite technology and 'smart bombs.' Not surprisingly, the generals soon became deeply hostile to his vision of a hollow military. After a little more than seven months in office, it was rumored that Rumsfeld's days were numbered, but 9/11 came along to save him – temporarily.

Donald Rumsfeld reacted to the World Trade Center attacks by declaring to Bush's cabinet that the United States should immediately attack Iraq. National Security Advisor Condoleezza Rice told her staff "to think about how we can capitalize on these opportunities." The neo-conservatives were ecstatic; September 11 provided them with the perfect opportunity to implement their ideological agenda about preemptive war and unilateral action, and Iraq was the perfect target. After ten years of economic sanctions against Iraq, a war against Saddam Hussein would be "a piece of cake."

When Bush took office, the number one item on his agenda was to find a way to invade Iraq and oust Saddam. None of this was outlined in his campaign rhetoric – election campaigns promise tax cuts, not war. Bush considered the 1991 Gulf War a failure because Saddam was still alive, but he intended to rectify his father's mistake. "I'm going to bring down the guy who wanted to kill my dad," our cowboy president told his cabinet. The administration decided on a two-part plan of action. The first part was to oust al-Qaeda from its Afghanistan refuge and destroy the Taliban regime. The second phase would be Iraq.

Afghanistan was definitely a haven for al-Qaeda terrorists. After the Soviet Union withdrew from Afghanistan in 1989, America immediately lost interest in that country. Afghan President Mohammad Najibullah publicly warned the United States that if they left Afghanistan, "it will be turned into a center for terrorism." Peter Thomsen, the U.S. State Department envoy to the newly victorious rebels, sent reports to Washington that if secular-oriented commanders were left without support, Islamic fundamentalists would regroup and crush them. No one took these arguments seriously, especially when the United States shifted its focus to the Gulf War in Kuwait. Sure enough, civil war erupted in Afghanistan.

The Taliban were primarily Afghan refugees raised in Pakistan. Most attended religious schools known as madrasas, in which they were indoctrinated in an extremely austere interpretation of Islam. The word 'talib' means religious student, so they called their movement the Taliban. By 1994, they had 20,000 fanatical idealists and plenty of U.S. weapons left over from the campaign against the Soviets. Once back in Afghanistan, they set about bringing order to the country by imposing strict Islamic law. They received strong backing from the Pakistan government, which saw the Taliban as a useful instrument for extending Pakistan's influence in the region.

On September 27, 1996, Taliban forces rolled triumphantly into the capital city of Kabul. Former president Najibullah was hanged in the public square. The Taliban forces were now completely in charge. Many Afghans welcomed them back despite their excesses, hoping they would finally bring a measure of peace to the country, but it was a peace enforced by amputations, floggings, and public executions.

Later that year, Osama bin Laden returned to Afghanistan after several years in Sudan and brought his al-Qaeda terror group with him. The Taliban and Osama bin Laden were an ideal match. Mullah Mohammed Omar, the Taliban leader, wanted to bring Afghanistan under pure Islamic rule and bin Laden had the same ambition for the entire Muslim world. Both seethed with hatred for the West. Soon they were running Afghanistan together and turning it into the world's most active breeding ground for terrorism.

Despite this, the United States maintained good relations with the Taliban. The reason, as usual, was economics. An American oil company, Unocal, wanted to build a $2 billion pipeline to carry natural gas from the rich fields of Turkmenistan to booming Pakistan and perhaps on to India. The pipeline would have to run across Afghanistan and Unocal was eager to see a government in Kabul - any kind of government - that could pacify the country. American journalist Steve Coll wrote, "American tolerance of the Taliban was publicly and inextricably linked to the financial goals of Unocal."

After September 11, 2001, everything changed. It was now time for the United States to go back into Afghanistan, hunt down Osama bin Laden and eliminate him. The American public was never told that our thrust into Afghanistan was also important because of Tajikistan, Uzbekistan, Kazakhstan, Kyrgyzstan, and Turkmenistan. Each of these countries had recently been satellites of the Soviet Union, but they were now independent. Located in the Eurasian region directly north of Afghanistan, their oil and natural gas reserves made them politically and economically significant. Kazakhstan, for example, borders China and Russia, and shares the Caspian Sea with Iran to the south. It produces a million barrels of oil a day, but that is expected to jump to three million barrels a day by 2015.

All of our initiatives with the countries in this region were well under way before September 11, but they gained added momentum in the months that followed. Within days of the 9/11 attacks, Kazakhstan agreed to provide logistic support for our flights into Afghanistan. Kyrgyzstan and Uzbekistan allowed American forces to establish bases on their territory. The Bush administration put fresh emphasis on our ties with the Caspian states by stating, "Our country is now linked with this region in ways we could never have imagined before September 11." To show our appreciation, the Bush administration increased military and economic aid to these countries by $1.5 billion. Our temporary military bases in these countries are now permanent installations.

In order to prepare the way for the arrival of U.S. Special Forces, CIA teams flew into Afghanistan, established contact with hundreds of Afghan tribes, and gained their support by spreading around millions of dollars in cash bribes. Targeted bombings commenced in early October. A few thousand U.S. troops arrived and were guided by the CIA agents already on the ground. The plan seemed to succeed. The Americans routed the Taliban, but Osama bin Laden eluded capture. It is hard to believe that bin Laden still remains free and alive despite all our high-tech surveillance and the $25 million reward we placed on his head.

On May 1, 2003, President Bush proudly proclaimed that the Taliban no longer posed a threat. "The bulk of Afghanistan is secure and stable," he assured the American public. Over the next six years we increased our troop level in Afghanistan to over 60,000, but the 'war' continues amid chaos and ruin. The Russians learned that nobody conquers Afghanistan – now it was our turn to learn about Afghan history.

While the Bush administration was assuring our nation of a quick victory in Afghanistan, the American public began asking disturbing questions about 9/11. How could these unsophisticated Muslims have pulled off such a successful attack from the remote caves of Afghanistan? How could they simultaneously hijack four commercial airliners and convince everyone they had real weapons? How could ill-trained pilots hit their exact targets? How could a modern structure like the World Trade Center just crumble and become dust? Why were there only four U.S. military jets guarding our entire nation at the time and why did two of them get lost?

In November 2002, a ten-member bipartisan commission was given a mandate to investigate all aspects of the attack, but not to assign blame. The goal was to provide the American people with the fullest possible account of the "facts and circumstances relating to the terrorist attack of September 11." All agencies, including the CIA, were to give the commission their fullest co-operation. From the start, Bush-Cheney tried to block any outside review, warning that an airing of intelligence errors would undermine our war against terror and damage our struggle to capture bin Laden and destroy al-Qaeda. Bush reluctantly provided the commission with an insultingly small budget - $3 million over eighteen months. The administration also imposed strict limits on the commission's powers to subpoena documents and witnesses.

On July 22, 2004, the 9/11 Commission released its final report. They had reviewed more than 2.5 million pages of documents and interviewed more than 1,200 individuals in ten countries, including nearly every senior official that had responsibility for topics covered in the commission's mandate. The commission held 19 days of hearings and took public testimony from 160 witnesses. The public was impressed, but not satisfied. The victim's families especially wanted to know why the White House, FBI, CIA, NSA, Pentagon, and other agencies had all missed the clues that could have prevented the tragedy.

Many of the puzzling questions were only partially answered. The commission was not allowed to directly question those being held in custody and who supposedly played key roles in the plot. White House Counsel Alberto Gonzales, at the direction of Bush-Cheney, refused to turn over essential documents or help the commission arrange interviews. CIA Director George Tenet made it clear to the commission that, "You are not going to get access to these detainees." The decision had less to do with the security of the detainees than with the fact that many of them were still being tortured in secret foreign prisons. The commission decided to appeal the CIA's refusal to produce the suspects, but again Gonzales refused to cooperate. In December 2007, it was revealed that the CIA deliberately destroyed hundreds of hours of video-taped interrogations of al-Qaeda operatives that should have been supplied to the commission.

When the commission requested President Bush to appear before the committee, he insisted that Vice President Cheney accompany him, a move that led many skeptics to believe that Cheney wanted to insure that Bush properly followed the correct script. Bush insisted on secrecy, so whatever was said in that room has never been disclosed.

During the course of the investigation, the commission became convinced that a number of sympathetic Saudi officials knew that al-Qaeda terrorists were planning some sort of attack on U.S. soil. It was even believed that these Saudi officials were providing assistance to the 9/11 terrorists. Twenty-eight pages in the commission's report relating to Saudi involvement have remained secret on national security grounds. Maybe in fifty years we will finally get the truth; by that time nobody will be interested and it will be too late for accountability.

It is hard to defend going to war under most circumstances, but the Iraq War was based on the most flagrant lies and deceits. Iraq was never a threat to anyone in the region. Israel, our military surrogate in the Middle East is loaded with nuclear capability, and countries like Kuwait and Saudi Arabia have almost 50 percent more weaponry (sold to them by the U.S. military-industrial complex) than Iraq. Many consider our determination to go to war with Iraq the greatest single strategic blunder by a leader of a Western democracy.

It is embarrassing to recall all the lies about Iraq's 'weapons of mass destruction' (WMD) and Saddam Hussein's non-existent ties to al-Qaeda. It is embarrassing to recall our president lying to the world about the necessity of going to war against such an inferior foe. It is embarrassing to remember all the lies told by Dick Cheney, Donald Rumsfeld, and Paul Wolfowitz. It is embarrassing to remember Colin Powell at the U.N. pointing to bogus photographs and claiming they were authentic proof that Iraq had WMD and that America was on a righteous mission. It is embarrassing to remember CIA Director George Tenet declaring that the war in Iraq was going to be a "slam dunk." It is embarrassing that General Tommy Franks was so inept at securing Iraq after the invasion, or that we completely botched the occupation. The entire affair was a colossal embarrassment.

President Bush led the rhetoric: "We fight for the principle of self-determination. People everywhere should be able to choose their own form of government without terror and without fear." Secretary of Defense Rumsfeld explained democracy in Iraq this way, "We will impose our reality on them."

What we really wanted was another presence in the Middle East to counteract Iran and protect our oil interests in Saudi Arabia and Kuwait. Bringing a true democracy to Iraq would mean the Iraqi people would be free to choose their own direction, even an alignment with Iran if that is what they wanted. That kind of democracy the United States would never tolerate. We would only allow a government in Iraq that was pro-USA; where we could control the decisions and the oil reserves. That is not democracy – it is called imperialism.

The neo-conservative plan went something like this. A U.S. controlled Iraq would leave Iran isolated and Syria intimidated. The Palestinians would then be more willing to negotiate seriously with Israel, and Saudi Arabia would have less leverage over American policymakers. Removing Saddam Hussein from power presented a genuine opportunity "to transform the political landscape of the Middle East." The only thing needed was a plausible excuse to attack. September 11 provided that justification.

Richard Clarke, a member of the National Security Council found the idea criminally irresponsible. "Having been attacked by al-Qaeda," he told Secretary of State Colin Powell, "for us to now go bombing Iraq in response to 9/11 would be like invading Mexico after the Japanese attacked Pearl Harbor." When Clarke wrote a report showing there was no Iraq link to 9/11, Condi Rice's office sent it back, saying: "Wrong answer – do it again." Treasury Secretary Paul O'Neill was perplexed about all this talk about invading Iraq. "Why Saddam, why now, and why is this central to U.S. interests?" O'Neill was shortly asked to resign. Bush's demand for 100 percent support from his inner circle precluded any dissent. What Bush failed to realize was that dissent does not mean disloyalty – it is often quite the opposite.

Not satisfied with the vast network of CIA intelligence, Cheney and Rumsfeld set up intelligence units that only reported to them. The purpose was to produce evidence to support the attack. Retired Air Force Lt. Col. Karen Kwiatkowski made the following assessment about these new intelligence units. "It was not intelligence; it was propaganda. They would take a little bit of intelligence, 'cherry-pick' it by taking it out of context, and then juxtaposition the two pieces of information that did not belong together."

Gregory Thielmann, a senior State Department intelligence official accused the Cheney-Rumsfeld intelligence units of "distorting information that we provided to make it seem more alarmist and dangerous. I thought there were limits to how far our government would go to twist things – I was wrong." One U.S. government source with two decades of experience in intelligence said: "This administration is capable of any lie in order to advance its war goal. Iraq never posed any threat to anyone in the region, let alone the United States. To argue otherwise is dishonest."

Paul Wolfowitz, speaking in Singapore in the summer of 2003, was asked why Iraq was invaded rather than North Korea. Wolfowitz gave one of the administration's few truthful answers, "Let's look at it simply. The most important difference between North Korea and Iraq is economics. Iraq swims on a sea of oil." Dick Cheney explained U.S. involvement this way: "The good Lord didn't see fit to put oil and gas only where there are democratically elected regimes friendly to the United States. Occasionally we have to operate in places where, all things considered, one would not normally choose to go. But, we go where the business is."

The only thing left was for Bush-Cheney to give their war plans credibility by supplying the U.S. media with bogus information. Like clockwork, the *New York Times* published a major story under the stark headline, "U.S. Says Hussein Intensifies Quest for A-Bomb Parts." Written by veteran reporters Judith Miller and Michael Gordon, the story quoted an unnamed administration official: "Iraq has stepped up its quest for nuclear weapons and has embarked on a worldwide hunt for materials to make an atomic bomb. The closer Saddam Hussein gets to a nuclear weapon, the harder he will be to deal with." The proof, according to the article, was the Iraqi leader's alleged attempted purchase of "specially designed aluminum tubes that are intended as components of centrifuges to enrich uranium."

The entire news story had been scripted and staged by the Bush administration. They deliberately planted the story to appear in the Sunday edition of the *New York Times*. Days earlier, all the administration's top officials made arrangements to appear on different Sunday morning talk shows. It was a perfect scheme - leak the lies the night before so you can give credence to them the next morning. "It is now public," said Dick Cheney during his appearance on *Meet the Press*, "that Saddam Hussein has been seeking to acquire the kind of tubes needed to build an atomic bomb. There is no doubt that he now has weapons of mass destruction and will use them against our friends, against our allies, and against us. Time is running out for America to remove this threat."

Condoleezza Rice on CNN's *Late Edition* that Sunday told Wolf Blitzer, "We do not want the smoking gun to become a mushroom cloud." On *Fox News*, Colin Powell talked of the "specialized aluminum tubing that we saw in the *New York Times* just this morning." And on CBS's *Face the Nation*, Donald Rumsfeld tied it all to September 11. "Imagine a September 11 with weapons of mass destruction that would kill tens of thousands of innocent men, women, and children."

Over and over the American public was bombarded about Iraq's threat to our national security. The CIA was under enormous pressure from Cheney to produce the justification for going to war. At a high-level CIA meeting regarding Iraq, officials were told in no uncertain terms, "if Bush wants to go to war, it is your job to give him a reason to do so." One CIA official later said, "The fact that someone could say that in the Agency and get away with it was just disgusting. It was criminal the way we were implicitly deceiving people." Another high-ranking CIA officer said, "The administration pressured us and we caved in."

The American public depends on the media for truthful information. Instead, the media aired and printed the lies they were fed. *Fox News* called the evidence that Saddam Hussein had WMD, "irrefutable, undeniable, and incontrovertible." When broadcaster Phil Donahue questioned the claims of the administration, he was fired. MSNBC was afraid of losing advertising revenue if Donahue was perceived as being anti-patriotic. Newscaster Peter Arnett was likewise fired from NBC for criticizing America's war plans. CNN telecasters were instructed from corporate headquarters that the American public must always be reminded that this war was a reprisal for 9/11. Bill O'Reilly of *Fox News* led the fight against criticism: "Once the war begins, we expect every American to support our military effort and if they can't do that they can shut up."

On November 8, the U.N. Security Council passed Resolution 1441 warning of "serious consequences" if Iraq did not take a "final opportunity to comply with its disarmament obligations." In response, Iraq submitted a 12,000 page report listing all its weapons. The United States deemed this report potentially embarrassing since it would expose U.S. complicity in arming Iraq during its war with Iran. The report listed twenty-four U.S. corporations and four agencies of the U.S. government that had illegally helped Iraq build its weapons program. The United States was concerned that these disclosures would dampen global enthusiasm for its planned invasion. The twelve-member Security Council wanted copies of Iraq's report, but Secretary of State Colin Powell 'persuaded' the president of the Security Council to first let the United States examine the original copy. When the Security Council members finally received their copies, the massive report had shrunk to 3,500 pages; the missing 8,500 pages were never made public.

During the ensuing U.N. debates regarding Iraq, our NSA eavesdropped on all the delegates. By listening in as the delegates communicated back to their home countries, the United States was able to discover which way they might vote, which positions they favored or opposed, what their negotiating positions would be, and indications of what "deals" could be made in return for their support. Hans Blix, the chief U.N. weapons inspector, was constantly monitored by the NSA, including his 'secure' faxes, his mobile phone, and his headquarters in Baghdad's Canal Hotel.

George Kennan, America's preeminent Cold War strategist, warned the United States not to rush into Iraq. "War has a momentum of its own, and it carries you away from all thoughtful intentions once you get into it. Today, if we go into Iraq, like the president would like us to do, you know where you begin, but you never know where you are going to end." Truer words were never spoken.

Bush's decision to invade Iraq may ultimately come to be seen as one of the most reckless acts in the history of American foreign policy. The consequences will not be clear for decades, but it is already abundantly apparent that it was the over-reach of an empire that does not understand limits and does not care. It was a textbook case of aggression – invading a country that is too weak to defend itself - and it almost worked, except the aftermath of the invasion fell apart.

Members of Congress fell into line – to do otherwise would have been political suicide. In October 2002, both houses of Congress voted overwhelmingly to authorize the use of military force against Iraq. Twenty-three senators objected to the president's usurpation of their constitutional power to declare war, but they could not prevent Congress from passing the resolution. West Virginia Senator Robert Byrd, then eighty-five years old, was an impassioned opponent of the measure. He remarked disgustedly that his colleagues might as well hang a "gone fishing" sign on the Capital and close up shop. He then quoted Hitler's formula for seducing a country into war: promote the idea that the country will be attacked and that all who oppose its defense are traitors.

With congressional approval in his pocket, Bush moved ahead with invasion preparations. At the same time, he went through the motions of seeking U.N. approval of an international coalition under the command of American generals, a move that would require Security Council approval. Knowing that France would veto the proposal, Bush nevertheless dispatched Secretary of State Powell to Manhattan on February 5, 2003. The highlights of Powell's show-and-tell presentation were aerial surveillance photographs of supposed chemical weapons facilities. "Our conservative estimate," Powell stated, "is that Iraq today has a

Lies and Deceits

stockpile of between 100 and 500 tons of chemical weapons and enough chemical agents to fill 16,000 battlefield rockets." When Powell left the United Nations without a supporting resolution, no one was surprised. Only the British offered any substantial commitment of troops.

On March 20, 2003, the United States attacked Iraq in what was patriotically labeled, *Operation Iraqi Freedom*. Clichés like freedom and democracy are great inspirational slogans to use when going to war. However, we soon learned that democracy cannot be exported like Coca-Cola. The war phase went according to plan. We bombed Iraq into submission – by April 30 it was all over. Over 9,200 Iraqi combatants were killed along with 7,300 civilians. We lost 139 military personnel.

On May 1, President Bush was dramatically flown by fighter jet and landed on the aircraft carrier *U.S.S. Abraham Lincoln*. Most Americans thought he landed somewhere near Iraq, but the ship was stationed a few miles off the coast of San Diego. The whole trip took a matter of minutes. The visit was climaxed with President Bush jumping out of the plane's cockpit and strutting up to the podium in his Air Force jump-suit, proclaiming, "Mission accomplished" as if he was Tom Cruise in the movie *Top Gun*. It was a cheap Hollywood publicity stunt using our fighting men and women as background props. Of all the embarrassments about this war, this may well have been the most distasteful.

To the cheers of our fighting men aboard the ship and to a nation of television viewers, President Bush boasted, "I'm driven by a mission from God. God told me, George, go and fight those terrorists in Afghanistan and I did. And then God told me, George, go and end tyranny in Iraq – and I did." *Operation Iraqi Freedom* was a quick and resounding success. All that remained was to mop-up, establish control, give out reconstruction contracts to American business firms, and begin pumping oil. Alas, God did not tell al-Qaeda this was the way it was supposed to work.

It is hard to believe that the Iraq invasion took only 21 days to accomplish and is still going on seven years later - almost twice as long as our involvement in World War II. Considering all our expertise with war and the billions we spend on weapons, training, tactics, and intelligence, it is mind-boggling that we could fail so miserably. In response to Tim Russert's query on *Meet the Press*, Dick Cheney at the beginning of the war assured the American public that "there is no question that we will be welcomed by the Iraqis as liberators." Unlike the American liberation of France in World War II – the Iraqi people did not throw flowers - they threw bombs and looted and burned everything in sight. Donald Rumsfeld, watching from his secure office in the Pentagon shrugged his shoulders and said, "Stuff happens."

There were many heroic patriotic stories to come out of Iraq, but many were propaganda lies to bolster public opinion at home. U.S. Army Sgt. Jessica Lynch was captured by the Iraqis and her rescue by U.S. Special Forces was one of the most stunning pieces of news management yet conceived. Lynch's unit was ambushed and several of her comrades were killed in the fracas. Lynch's jeep crashed and turned over, and she was taken to an Iraqi hospital. Eight days later, the U.S. military staged a successful rescue operation. A military cameraman came along to shoot the video footage of the rescue. Then it became a race against time for the video to be edited. Within a few hours of the rescue, the five-minute film was beamed back to viewers in the United States. It was the perfect reality TV that American armchair viewers love to watch.

The Pentagon portrayed Jessica as a "Rambo from West Virginia." General Vincent Brooks, the U.S. spokesman declared: "Some brave souls put their lives on the line to make this happen, loyal to a creed that we never leave a fallen comrade behind." The only thing wrong was that the Lynch rescue never really happened that way. Iraqi doctors and nurses had completed treating Jessica's broken bones and wanted to turn her over to the U.S. forces, but we were committed to the rescue mission. All the eyewitnesses at the hospital say the Iraqi guards had already fled. When the U.S. Special Forces arrived, there was no resistance; the hospital doors were wide open and we walked right in. The dramatic rescue was entirely faked. After all the hoopla and awards, Jessica Lynch appeared before a congressional committee. She heroically accused the U.S. government of a massive fabrication of the story as part of a propaganda effort to manipulate American and global public opinion into accepting and sympathizing with the Iraq invasion.

Then there was the story of army ranger and former NFL football player Pat Tillman. When Tillman lost his life in Afghanistan, his chain-of-command concocted a fictionalized account of what happened. According to the Pentagon, there had been a fierce firefight in which Tillman had performed with great valor; but ultimately fell to enemy fire. His commanders hastily awarded Tillman a posthumous Silver Star for gallantry. The result was a triumph of public relations. Soon the tale unraveled. The truth turned out to be that Tillman's own comrades killed him in a friendly-fire incident.

The calculated exploitation of Jessica Lynch and the effort to mislead Pat Tillman's parents regarding the cause of their son's death do not speak well of an institution that purports to care above all about our soldiers and their families. These are not isolated examples – the truth is that the American public is fed a continuous stream of disinformation and lies.

The United States quickly held elections in Iraq to show the world how easily American-style democracy could be implemented, but the result was utter chaos. The Iraqis were not interested in democracy – all they wanted was a restoration of water and electricity and some security. Seven years have gone by and the Iraqis are still afraid to come out of their homes. A million children no longer go to school because their parents fear they may not return home. Over 1.6 million Iraqis have fled the country. It is hard to picture another instance in history where a world power could not establish law and order over a defeated people with relative ease.

Bush's guarantee that the cost of the war and reconstruction would be paid for with Iraqi oil was an illusion. The result was perhaps the worst war plan in American history. Instead of altering the politics of a crucial region, we united all those who hate us. Worst of all, there was no accountability. A Pentagon file clerk who misplaces a classified document faces stiffer penalties than a defense secretary whose arrogant recklessness consumes thousands of lives. As Secretary of State Condoleezza Rice explained, "Look, some things went right and some things went wrong. And I will have a chance to reflect on that when I have a chance to write my book."

For a year prior to the invasion, sixteen groups of Iraqi exiles prepared a 1,000 page report on problems to be encountered in postwar Iraq. They stressed that post-invasion control of their country would be more difficult than the military victory itself. Paul Wolfowitz, speaking on behalf of the administration, refuted the report: "How can we possibly need more troops for the occupation than for the invasion itself?"

To make matters worse, our American administrator, Paul Bremer, was way over his head. Bremer was a Yale buddy of George W. Bush and a fellow 'Skull and Bones' man – qualifications that endeared him to our president. Bremer disbanded the Iraqi army and banned thousands of Ba'th Party officials from returning to their government jobs. This left the country without a government or a security force. What were 500,000 Iraqi soldiers with weapons supposed to do to support their families? Iraq quickly became a training camp for a new generation of terrorists.

According to the U.S. Army War College's Strategic Studies Group, the Iraq War "was not integral" to the global war on terrorism; instead it was a costly "detour from it." No military conflict in modern times has divided Americans more along partisan lines. The Democrats blamed the Republicans; the Republicans blamed the CIA. Democrats in Congress say they were lied to and would never have voted for the war had they been told the truth. The Republicans claim the intelligence was flawed, but the cause was just. Whether we should have gone into Iraq or not is for history to decide. What is certain is that the war was predicated on lies and deceits and our occupation was a disaster.

But, 'we' got Saddam. On December 13, 2003, Saddam Hussein was captured. He was found holed up in a tiny underground bunker like a desperate rat. It was embarrassing even for those who thought the worst of him. His trial began before the Iraqi Special Tribunal on October 19, 2005. On November 5, 2006, Hussein was sentenced to death by hanging. None of the trial was shown in the United States.

In April 2004, journalist Seymour Hersh rocked the American public with an expose, complete with photographs, of the abuses committed by U.S. military personnel at Abu Ghraib prison in Baghdad – a jail once used by Saddam Hussein as a center for torture and execution. The picture of a hooded man hooked up to electrodes became an American symbol worldwide, representing the hypocrisy of U.S. war aims. Another picture was of Al-Jamadi, a suspect who died while being tortured by the CIA. U.S. military pathologists classified Al-Jamadi's death as a respiratory condition. Later, it was confirmed that death was caused by the combination of broken ribs and the painful position of hanging him upside down. He died from asphyxia – as in crucifixion. The CIA refused to comment.

The abuses at Abu Ghraib were not limited to the actions of the CIA. Gloating American soldiers photographed the humiliation of prisoners; a pyramid made of naked Muslims stacked like cordwood one on top of another; a naked prisoner cringing before a snarling police dog; captives led around on dog leashes and forced to simulate fellatio and to masturbate in front of a cigarette-smoking female soldier while she gave a high-five salute of approval. Muslim male detainees were threatened with rape, beaten repeatedly, and forced to wear women's underwear. Such pictures of abuse became gruesome symbols of our occupation. The Muslim world had to wonder if Abu Ghraib is what we mean by humanitarianism and exporting democracy!

Rather than risk another Abu Ghraib incident, the CIA secretly transported detained suspects to foreign prisons where they could be tortured by non-U.S. monsters. President Bush on April 28, 2005 responded to a question from the press about our program of sending suspects to foreign prisons to be tortured: "Torture is never acceptable, nor do we hand over people to countries that do torture." His statement was a lie.

Robert Baer, a former CIA operative in the Middle East, explained how it all works. "We pick up a suspect and place him aboard a civilian or CIA transport and off he goes to some country of our choosing, where, let's make no bones about it, the suspect is tortured. If you want a good interrogation, you send someone to

Jordan. If you want them to be killed after interrogation, you send them to Egypt or Syria. Either way, the U.S. cannot be blamed because we are not doing the dirty work."

The war was a disaster for everyone except American business interests. Halliburton was awarded billions in no-bid contracts for projects ranging from rebuilding Iraq's oil refineries to constructing jails for war prisoners. Two other behemoths, Bechtel and the Carlyle Group, also profited handsomely. Boeing, Lockheed Martin, and McDonnell-Douglas were awarded $41 billion in contracts for more missiles, combat jets, and other weapons of war. Even before the Iraq War, British journalist George Monbiot predicted, "If the U.S. were not preparing to attack Iraq, it would be preparing to attack some other nation. The U.S. will go to war because it needs to go to war."

It took six years to finally come to a reckoning over how much the Bush administration knowingly twisted and hyped intelligence to justify the invasion. On June 5, 2008 - after years of Republican stonewalling - a report by the Senate Intelligence Committee gave us as good a set of answers as we are likely to get. The 170-page report accused Bush-Cheney of repeatedly overstating the Iraqi threat in the emotional aftermath of the attacks of September 11. The report showed clearly that Saddam Hussein had long abandoned his nuclear, biological and chemical weapons programs. He was not training terrorists or colluding with Al-Qaeda. The only real threat Saddam posed was to his own countrymen.

What a mess we are in today. An old Chinese proverb warned: "If you are out for vengeance – dig two graves." Iraq and Afghanistan have ignited all the slumbering frustrations of poor but proud Muslims. A holy crusade gave them a new purpose in life. They thronged to join the jihad against us. Meanwhile, we have killed thousands of innocents, which has only served to inflame the situation. No doubt several top al-Qaeda operatives have also been killed, but Osama bin Laden still lives and his basic strategy remains the same - "provoke and bait" the United States into "bleeding wars" throughout the Islamic world. Once the bankrupt and demoralized "far enemy" goes home, his al-Qaeda network can focus on destroying its "near enemies" - Israel and the "corrupt" regimes of Egypt, Jordan, Pakistan, and Saudi Arabia.

The U.S. occupation in Iraq and Afghanistan has helped move bin Laden's plan along. Nothing would suit his strategy more than triggering an even bigger war between the United States and Iran. Meanwhile, thousands of al-Qaeda networks within our society wait for a signal from some innocuous web site. While everyone waits to see what happens next, our government has reduced our civil liberties to a shambles. Another attack on our shore will certainly result in even more unprecedented executive power. The question for America is where is this all headed?

When George W. Bush was elected president, many wondered, how much damage could one man do? Now we know. The Clinton surplus has been spent on massive tax cuts for the rich, who in turn put the money into stocks and real estate in order to enhance their wealth even more. Now those markets have collapsed and for many the riches are gone. The country's debt and deficits are out of control. The financial markets needed a trillion dollar bailout from the government. General Motors is on the verge of bankruptcy. Homeowners cannot pay their subprime mortgages. Unemployment is steadily increasing. Suddenly, capitalism is tottering on the brink of collapse, pleading for the government to replace laissez-faire policies with corporate welfare. Osama bin Laden in his command headquarters must be laughing his head off.

The Bush-Cheney administration is now finally over. In eight short years, the damage to our country has been incalculable. I think back to the *Daily Mirror* headline in Britain the morning after Bush's election in 2000: "How Could 59,054,087 Americans Be So Dumb?" Even die-hard Republicans today cannot believe they elected this man, not just once, but twice. Bush's place in history will depend not on whether he lied to the American people - every president, arguably, has succumbed to that temptation. Put bluntly, posterity will judge George W. Bush on whether he ever recognized what the truth actually was.

CHAPTER TWENTY FIVE

TODAY AND TOMORROW

"Political language is designed to make lies sound truthful and murder respectable."

George Orwell

"Men never do evil so completely and cheerfully as when they do it from religious conviction."

Blaise Pascal

Pulitzer winning author Sinclair Lewis once said: "When fascism comes to America it will be wrapped in the American flag and carrying the Christian cross." Nothing could better describe the dangerous rise of the Religious Right as a political force in this country.

Historically, fundamentalist Protestants were not particularly active in national politics. This changed in the late 1970s as part of a calculated effort by conservative Republicans; they recognized that as long as their Party was primarily identified with the wealthy, they would forever remain a minority. They needed a new base and a new message. By adopting ultra-conservative positions on highly-charged social issues, Republican strategists were able to bring millions of fundamentalist Christians of lower-than-average income into the Republican Party.

Who exactly are these 80 million evangelical Protestants, 50 million of whom openly admit to being members of the Religious Right? What is their agenda and how do they affect the rest of our society?

Even religious pundits are not fully agreed on what sets the Religious Right apart from mainstream Christianity. However, almost all would agree that this group believes incontrovertibly that the Bible is the word of God and the sole authority for everything. They believe that to know God cannot be achieved through a discursive intellectual reasoning process; it must come by way of a sudden emotional illumination, a radical change of heart, a complete spiritual conversion. In effect, the person must be "born again." There is nothing wrong with such beliefs as long as they are not mandated on others or imposed on our nation as a whole. That is where the problem lies.

The mission of the Religious Right is to make America ready for the imminent coming of Christ. They are encased in a tightly sealed world, relying exclusively on Christian fundamentalist broadcasters for their news, health, entertainment, and devotional programs. They believe that a dark satanic force is undermining the stability of the American family and its values, and that evil is secularism. Their goal is to "save" our nation by political activism - capture the presidency, a majority of Congress and the Supreme Court, and return America to Christ.

The 1859 publication of Charles Darwin's *On the Origin of Species*, detailing the theory of evolution by natural selection, was by implication a direct attack on the literal interpretation and authenticity of the Bible. Future scientific research proved Darwin to be right, but the consequences for Christian fundamentalism were enormous. If man truly evolved from a lower form of animal rather than the *Genesis* account of Creation, what else in the Bible was not true? Could the Jesus story also be untrue? Was the resurrection scientifically unsustainable? Were the tenets of Christianity nothing more than fables and myths? The political implications went far beyond evolution: if evolution was true, then scientific positions on global warming, stem cell research and many other scientific issues might also be true.

President George W. Bush was the only Western leader that did not believe in evolution, and probably the only American president to publicly be in direct opposition to contemporary scientific thinking. "The jury is still out," was his official position. He vigorously advocated teaching both evolution and 'intelligent design' in the schools. Predictably, the Religious Right cheered

Bush's position, arguing that since local taxes pay teacher's salaries, local school boards should be able to control the content of what is taught in their neighborhood schools. And that is what is happening in school district after school district throughout our county – even though it is contrary to Supreme Court decisions.

Our Supreme Court has said that in keeping with the principle that church and state must be separate, biblical literacy has no place in our public schools. In 2001, PBS produced an eight-part documentary, accompanied by materials designed for use in the public schools, boldly entitled *Evolution*. The Religious Right went berserk, labeling the series anti-religious propaganda and succeeded in keeping the supplementary educational material out of most American schools. Furthermore, the evolution series prompted the Bush administration to begin monitoring all PBS productions for "liberal bias."

In 2005, Federal District Court Judge John E. Jones handed down a decision prohibiting the teaching of 'intelligent design' as an alternative to evolution in the public schools of Dover, Pennsylvania. Judge Jones stated unequivocally that 'intelligent design' was an attempt to introduce religion in the public schools and that violated the First Amendment. "To be sure, Darwin's theory of evolution is imperfect," Jones concluded, "however, the fact that a scientific theory cannot yet render an explanation on every point should not be used as a pretext to thrust an untested alternative hypothesis grounded in religion into the science classroom or to misrepresent well-established scientific propositions." Undeterred, the Religious Right continues to dominate local school boards to make sure the school curriculum reflects their views.

The Religious Right currently represents the largest voting bloc in the Republican Party. With such a concentration of strength they expect politicians to pay attention to their agenda. Christian fundamentalists now hold a political majority in 18 states along with large minorities elsewhere. Forty-five senators and 186 members of the House earned approval ratings of 80 to 100 percent from the three most influential Religious Right advocacy groups. As the *Washington Post* observed in 2004, "For the first time since religious conservatives became a modern political movement, the

President of the United States (George W. Bush) has become the movement's defacto leader." In 2008, had the Republican McCain-Palin ticket won, a Religious Right vice-president would have been a heartbeat away from the presidency. Certainly, this movement will be primed for a run at the White House in 2012, and they will have plenty of potential candidates pandering to them.

Those who say that the Religious Right is not a danger to our traditional form of government do not understand the power of mass movements in a society where there is an apathetic or fearful general citizenry. The Nazi Party in Germany started with seven members in 1919. By 1928, they represented 2.6 percent of the vote, 18.3 percent in 1930, and 37.4 percent in July 1932. The Hitler Youth movement started with a cadre of 5,000 and grew to 2.3 million. The story in Russia was similar. In 1918, there were 200,000 Communist Party members; by 1933 there were 3.5 million and by 1986, 19 million members. The growth of fanatically dedicated movements is like a farmer watching corn grow in the field – it is imperceptible until one day it is over your head!

Ralph Reed, executive director of the Christian Coalition, states his position clearly: "The Christian community got it backwards in the 1980s. We tried to change Washington when we should have been focusing on the local school boards, city councils, and state legislatures. What we Christians have to do is take back this country, one precinct at a time, one neighborhood at a time, and one state at a time. When that is in place, capturing Washington will be easy." Quietly, Reed is accomplishing his objectives. His organization received tax-exempt status from the Bush administration and he is keeping a low profile while recruiting members and amassing huge funds. "Our objective right now is to fly below the radar," he said.

Patrick Henry College, known as God's Harvard, was founded as a private Christian college specifically to train evangelical home-schooled students for jobs in government. Their agenda promotes political activism for Religious Right causes; they have strong ties to the Republican Party and hundreds of their students served as interns in the Bush White House, congressional offices, and Washington think-tanks. They are active in local and national politics, and work exhaustively for the election of Republican conservatives as well as lobbying extensively for conservative issues at the federal and state levels.

Regent University and Bob Jones University are two other institutions dedicated to the principles of the Religious Right. One hundred and fifty recent Regent University graduates held positions in the Bush administration. Bob Jones University has the reputation for being the most conservative religious school in the United States. Shortly after George W. Bush won re-election in 2004, Bob Jones III sent him a congratulatory letter asserting that the president had "been given a mandate" and urged him to put his "agenda on the front burner and let it boil. You owe the liberals nothing. They despise you because they despise your Christ."

The Religious Right believes that capitalism is God's ordained economic system - almost as if Adam Smith, Milton Friedman, and Alan Greenspan were biblical figures on a par with Isaiah, Jeremiah, and Ezekiel. Accordingly, they argue that a Christian has a responsibility to create material wealth, and belittle secular environmentalists who see America's natural resources as limited and global warming as a threat to our planet. They accuse these environmentalists of lacking faith in God's perfect world.

In 1990, 300,000 evangelical children were home-schooled. Today, 2.4 million children have been pulled out of the public schools. Special textbooks indoctrinate these young minds to their political agenda. Students are not confronted with scientific research that conflicts with their Christian teaching. Evolution, obviously, is not taught, and global warming is debunked as a myth. Females are taught to find their life's fulfillment through the accomplishments of their husband. Music, movies, and books are carefully selected. What they read is a fundamentalist series like *Left Behind* that has already sold over 100 million copies. The series describes how those who have not accepted Jesus will be "left behind" to be slaughtered after Jesus returns to earth for the Last Judgment. There is no questioning or dissent. These young people are brainwashed to die for Jesus just as fanatically as the young Muslim is willing to blow himself up for Allah. With fanatics poised on both sides, it is a scary future.

The past 300 years have seen momentous changes in America. From a land that was virtually uninhabitable, it has become the mightiest, richest, and most dynamic civilization in history. Yet, for all our greatness, America is a disappointment. Instead of thirteen independent colonies, we now have 50 states, each with its own self-interests; red states, blue states, southern states, northern states, and industrial and farming states. We have never achieved a sense of community. We live in millions of isolated communities. The rich in our society fill their lives with material abundance and impatiently await the new upgrades in their high-tech toys, while their children are glued additively to expensive video games. The plight of those less fortunate are not their concern.

Corporate America chases short-term profits over long-term investments. We now spend more time manipulating numbers than actually making things. Americans consume too much and save too little. Our nation has become corrupted by excessive debt, reckless speculation, and fleeting profits. Corporate greed, insider trading, stock market and banking abuses, the prevalence of special interests in politics, the ever-increasing gap between the rich and the poor, the continuing racial strife, the constant wars, the arrogance of power, the lies and deceits - all point to the undeniable fact that we can do better.

America has never been attacked on its shores, no country has ever declared war on us, yet we are always going off to war. We accept our government's lies like naive innocents; by now we should know better, but that is not the case. We are told that every new enemy is the reincarnation of Adolf Hitler and we believe it. We speak about peace and democracy as we bomb, kill, and maim millions of innocent victims - and nobody seems to care. Not only does our government "sell" war to our people, we hype withdrawal as unpatriotic. "We must stay the course," was our mantra in Korea, Vietnam, and now Iraq and Afghanistan.

The mandate from George Washington was to avoid foreign entanglements. He warned against "pretended patriotism." Our other great general turned president, Dwight David Eisenhower, understood George Washington's fears, but the military-industrial complex that Eisenhower warned against was unstoppable.

Eisenhower predicted exactly what has come to pass: U.S. military bases ready to strike throughout the world. Despite the collapse of the Soviet Union and the end of the Cold War, we continue to plow billions into the military-industrial complex for highly sophisticated weapons that can never stop a single suicide bomber or change the attitudes of those who hate us.

September 11 was a devastating blow to our national pride, but it was not an act of war in the traditional sense. Al-Qaeda is certainly not interested in taking over America. Their plan is to force us out of the Middle East so they can concentrate on establishing Islamic fundamentalist regimes throughout the Arab world. We, on the other hand, are committed to remain in that area because of oil. If they pull off a nuclear version of 9/11, we stand ready to retaliate by killing millions and leaving the Arab world in ruin. The future will be spent restoring the devastation.

While we wait for al-Qaeda's next move, there is serious trouble at home. Our entire financial structure is on the verge of collapse. Warren Buffett, a conservative billionaire not given to hysterics, said in March 2009 that the United States economy had "fallen off a cliff." Icons of American capitalism: General Motors, AIG and Citigroup are on their knees begging for government bailouts in order to avoid bankruptcy. The reasons for this collapse are complex, but capitalist greed is the root cause.

Yet, a year after the crash, the financial giants (JP Morgan, Goldman Sachs, etc.) are back paying million-dollar bonuses, while every month, hundreds of thousands of ordinary Americans face foreclosure or unemployment because of a crisis caused by a few Wall Street behemoths. And the rules are different for small debtors as against big debtors. If you lose your job and fall behind on your $1,500 monthly mortgage payment, no one is going to bail you out. But, Citigroup can lose $27.7 billion (as it did in 2008) and count on the federal government to hand it $45 billion. Worst of all, there is no public outcry about the unfairness.

If the current deep recession continues, the economic disparity in this country will grow even wider and certainly social unrest will turn ugly. History is clear: it behooves the rich to alleviate the problem, if not for humanitarian reasons, then for their own self-interest. John F. Kennedy, in his 1961 inaugural address probably said it best: "If a free society cannot help the many who are poor, it cannot save the few who are rich." Our Founding Fathers understood the problem very well; they wrote a constitution to protect the security of the affluent because in a class conflict the affluent are severely outnumbered.

Since the year 2000, there are 32 percent more Americans living below the federal poverty level and 57 million others not very far behind. But, it was a different story for affluent Americans. A booming stock market during the last decade played havoc with our traditional American values. A country that once adhered to the Puritan ethic of delayed gratification became reveled in instant pleasures. Luxury spending in the United States grew to obscene proportions. Hotel suites costing $3,000 a night were booked months in advance. World tours went for $50,000 per person. Designer wristwatches sold for $50,000. Luxury yachts were bought for $20 million and corporate jets for $50 million, and everything was back-ordered. Elective cosmetic surgery became the rage for women over fifty. Homes were purchased for millions and leveled to make way for new 'trophy' residences. Driving a Bentley or a Rolls Royce defined status. The wealthy sat around watching the ticker tape go up all day and then ordered more luxury toys. How could this be a healthy state of affairs for America?

Allan Sloan, the top economist for *Newsweek* said back in 2007 that the government was lying about the state of our economy. "Washington's math," Sloan said, "is not real-world math. Things are not getting better; they were getting worse." Nobody was listening, but how could employment figures be good when millions of jobs were being outsourced? What the government did not tell us was that high-paying skilled manufacturing jobs were being replaced by low-paying unskilled ones and wages and salaries were at all-time lows as a percentage of national wealth. Americans now had to work two and three jobs in order to make ends meet. Over sixty percent of married mothers of preschool children entered the job market and placed their children in expensive day care centers. With nobody in the house, aged parents were shuffled off to nursing homes where they were 'cared' for by aides who could barely speak English. With no time available for home-cooking and family togetherness, everyone grabbed fast food on the run.

Artificially low interest rates created construction jobs, a housing boom, and a rising stock market, but along with that came subprime mortgages and a search for reckless higher-yielding investments. Americans were oblivious to any downturn and just kept consuming; nobody was saving for that rainy day. At the same time, college tuition has become becoming increasingly unaffordable. On average, a year at a public four-year university now costs 31 percent of a family's income, but if you are in the bottom fifth of the income curve it is 73 percent of your annual income. What this means is that the rich can afford to send their kids to college while the poor cannot. This perpetuates the class disparity in this country. The same situation prevails in health care, justice in our courts, decent housing, and endless social issues. For too many of our citizens, the 'American Dream' has become the impossible dream.

When President George W. Bush cut taxes for the rich, the net worth of the "Forbes 400" richest men in the country tripled. In the 1990s, the wealth of the 500 corporations in the Standard and Poor's index increased by 335 percent. The Dow Jones average of stock prices went up 400 percent between 1980 and 1995, while the average wage of workers declined in purchasing power by 15 percent. In 2004, our so-called 'healthy' economy grew 4.2 percent, while real median family income - the purchasing power of the typical family actually fell. In short, it was a great economy if you were affluent, but for most other Americans, economic growth was a spectator sport.

It is criminal what has happened to our Social Security system. A full expose on how our government dipped into these retirement trust funds to pay for other projects will one day become the biggest scandal in U.S. history. When the problem became apparent, Bill Clinton, in his 1998 State of the Union address had a solution. "What should we do with this $200 billion surplus?" he asked. "I have a simple four word answer: Save Social Security first. Tonight, I propose that we reserve 100 percent of the surplus – that's every penny – until we have taken all the necessary measures to strengthen the Social Security system for the 21st century." Instead, George W. Bush gave the surplus to rich Americans in the form of massive tax cuts and created astronomical deficits. It does not take a genius to realize that we squandered our nation's surplus to benefit the rich.

Some lies are scarier than others, but Bush's claim that privatizing Social Security would be a boom to retirees was a whopper; its real purpose was to throw billions of new funds into the stock market in order to reinforce the stock gains of the wealthy. Can you imagine the horrible consequences had Social Security been privatized? After the stock market crash in 2008, retirees would be in a panic. There probably will be a Social Security actuarial problem in the year 2042, but that is 33 years away – and there are far safer solutions to the problem than the stock market.

Despite Obama's election, race in this country is still a major issue. Black Americans are three times more likely to live in poverty than white Americans and twice as likely to be unemployed. Black children are almost twice as likely to die before the age of four as white children, and young black women die from breast cancer in greater numbers than their white counterparts. Average mortality rates are higher for blacks and have actually increased since 1960. Our prisons are filled disproportionately with black men. While whites use illegal drugs at substantially higher percentages than blacks, black men are sent to prison on drug charges at 13 times the rate of white men. As of mid-2008, 4.7 percent of black men were in prison compared to less than one percent of white men. This is not a situation that any American can be proud of.

If you had to explain America's economic success with one word, that word would be "education." In the 19th century, America led the way in universal basic education. Then, as other nations followed suit, the "high school revolution" of the early 20th century took us to a whole new level. Then, in the years after World War II, America established a commanding position in higher education. But, that was then.

A recent study on higher education found that the United States now ranks seventh among developed nations in college degrees and is in the lower half for college completions. The study concluded that "perhaps for the first time in our history, the next generation of Americans will be less educated." Out of 38 countries, we rank 24th in mathematics, 19th in science, 12th in reading, and 26th in problem solving. In another study of 17 countries, we ranked last in biology, 11th in chemistry and 9th in physics. In 2004, China graduated 600,000 engineers, India 350,000, and the United States 70,000. We are falling behind in everything. We used to take pride in being number one; now we are racing to the bottom.

One of the biggest lies in America is that the 1954 *Brown v. Board of Education* Supreme Court decision ended segregation and integrated our nation's schools, thereby providing everyone with an equal opportunity. The truth is that our schools are more segregated now than ever before. The statistics are staggering. In Chicago, 90 percent of public school enrollment is black; in Washington, D.C., 94 percent is black; in St. Louis it is 82 percent; in Philadelphia and Cleveland 78 percent, in Los Angeles 84 percent, in Detroit 95 percent, in Baltimore 88 percent. In New York City, nearly three quarters of public school students are black or Hispanic.

Where are all the white kids? If their parents are part of the Religious Right they are being home-schooled; if they are affluent they go private schools; if they are upper middle-class they live in white suburban neighborhoods and go to predominantly white neighborhood schools. The era of integration is over – we are now in the process of re-segregation. It's no longer a southern problem – the four most segregated states in the U.S. are New York, Michigan, Illinois, and California. Jonathan Kozol, arguably America's leading education advocate, relates his conversation with a sixteen-year-old black girl. "Think of it this way," the young girl said. "If people in New York woke up one day and learned that all the blacks were gone, or that we had simply died or left for somewhere else, they would be relieved." As much as her statement may sadden many, its truth hits home with devastating force.

Residential segregation contributes to the problem. In suburban Roosevelt on Long Island, nearly 100 percent of the students are black or Hispanic. Take a twenty-minute drive to Plainview High, and black and Hispanic students make up only one percent of the enrollment. The disrepair and overcrowding of schools in the South Bronx would never be allowed in Scarsdale. The present per-pupil spending level in the New York City schools is $11,700 compared to $22,000 in the well-to-do suburban district of Manhasset. In 1997, the median salary of teachers in New York City was $43,000, as compared with $77,000 in Manhasset and $81,000 in Scarsdale – both suburbs are only 11 miles from Manhattan.

The elite prep schools operate in a different world from even the best suburban schools and it is all about money. St. Paul's, Hotchkiss, and Groton have endowments in the hundreds of millions of dollars, all from contributions made by their wealthy elite alumni. The endowment at Phillips Exeter Academy has now topped the $1.0 billion mark. What we have is a perpetuation of a privileged upper-class society that starkly resembles the aristocracies of France and Russia before their revolutions.

Our political and corporate elites insist that we must not talk about class; only Marxists do that. They prefer to have us believe that we are all one big happy family – you and me and Exxon; the children of the CEOs who live in luxury and the children of the restaurant workers who live in slums. We are all Americans, they say. Nobody wants to acknowledge that we send the poor off to war to fight while the rich go shopping and our corporations reap in the profits. After all the arms and legs have been blown off, our "patriots" return home with no jobs, inadequate medical care, and ruined lives.

The rich in America shrug their shoulders about these problems. Their kids get the best education and if anyone in the family gets seriously ill they receive the finest high-tech medical care. For those who are not rich, health care means waiting for hours in the emergency room or being unable to afford the drugs that are needed. The few with money live in multi-million dollar homes in gated communities while the poor cannot afford decent low-cost housing, and worst of all, this seems perfectly normal to everybody.

Between 1992 and 2004, household indebtedness in this country has doubled. Average credit card debt among young adults

(25-34) increased by 55 percent while younger adults (18-24) saw a sharp rise of 104 percent in their credit card debt. Instead of targeting the financially astute who can pay off their debts, credit card companies found they could make more money off the young and vulnerable. Fifty-six percent of students in their final year of college carried four or more credit cards. Not even personal bankruptcy stands in the way of the credit card industry's single-minded ambition to empower shoppers. Ninety-six percent of those who declared personal bankruptcy received offers for credit cards, car loans, and mortgages in the same year that their debts were discharged. One-half of those got more than ten offers a month. Spending and consumption has replaced saving and prudence as the American way.

The Chinese fill our homes with flat-panel TV screens, MP3 players, and computerized refrigerators, while they fill their bank accounts with money and U.S. Treasury bonds. In essence, the Chinese manufacture our products and save, and we borrow to consume more of their products. They get jobs – we get debt. The U.S. saving rate is 0.2 percent, while the savings rate in China is roughly 40 percent. With the current economic downturn now in its second year and more than 13 million Americans unemployed, few have any safety net to fall back on.

Even our tax system favors the rich. Warren Buffett, America's second wealthiest man, paid a 17.7 percent tax on his $46 million of income in 2006, while his secretary's tax rate was 30 percent. There are effectively two tax systems in America: one for the very rich and one for the rest of America. Hedge fund management fees and income from stock dividends and capital gains, are taxed at 15 percent, while wages, the bulk of what the rest of America earns, is taxed at up to 35 percent. Wealthy individuals hire expensive tax lawyers and accountants to find loopholes in the law to shelter their income from taxation. Large corporations have an assortment of ways to hide income or shift it to outside of the country. Corporate perks are outrageous abuses - first-class travel, expensive restaurants, fully paid vacations, and hundreds of other "freebies" are not available to the ordinary wage earner. No matter how you try to explain away these inequities, something is drastically wrong with the system - but beware - when you hear proposals for a new "fair" tax system you can bet that the middle-class is being conned once again.

Somewhere in the Middle East right now a half-dozen young Muslims are dressed in American jeans, wearing Nike sneakers, drinking Coca-Cola, and listening to rap music on their Walkman headphones. But, between their praying sessions they are putting together bombs to blow up Americans. They may like our movies and music, but they hate us. Somewhere in Latin America the story is similar, but not as explosively violent because it is not fueled by the fanaticism of religious fundamentalism. There, little by little, countries are moving to the political 'left' and away from the American capitalist umbrella. Cuba, Venezuela, Nicaragua, and Bolivia, have all elected leftist leaders. Traditionally, America has claimed this hemisphere as its own. But, Castro, Chavez, Ortega, and Morales, are spearheading a new Latin America. It remains to be seen how the United States will react to this new independence.

In the weeks after 9/11, public opinion was overwhelmingly sympathetic to the United States. Within two years, a far different picture emerged. In Indonesia, the most populous Muslim state, the attitude toward America plunged from 75 percent favorable to 85 percent negative. In pivotal Pakistan, backing for the U.S. 'war on terror' fell to 16 percent. Levels of support elsewhere remained disturbingly low: 12 percent in Jordan, 17 percent in Turkey, 31 percent in Lebanon. Majorities in Egypt, Morocco, and Saudi Arabia see the United States as a greater threat to the world order than Osama bin Laden. Meanwhile, many unstable countries have nuclear capabilities and other erratic regimes are rapidly joining the club. Pakistan is a potential nuclear nightmare if the pro-U.S. regime is ever ousted from power, and who knows what Israel might do if "push comes to shove."

Undaunted by the reality of current events, the Bush administration claimed that we were winning the war on terror; that God has anointed us to spread capitalism, democracy, freedom, and Christianity to the entire world. We believe that in every instance we are righteous and we are dismayed when these 'others' reject our offering and fight to maintain their own beliefs. We cannot understand why they do not submit to our will knowing that 'God is on our side.' And we cannot understand why they are not terrified of our awesome nuclear capability. Unfortunately, they know that our advanced military technology is useless against terrorists; you cannot swat a mosquito with an atomic bomb.

It is easy to fool ourselves into thinking that history is something ancient and unrelated to our present lives. Actually, history is continuous. Our wars follow a classic pattern – there is an impassioned debate in Congress followed by passage of a war resolution with a presidential commitment to consult periodically with congressional leaders. Widely told lies are believed. The information that comes out later is too late to prevent the unspeakable. We are told to support our troops and put patriotic stickers on our cars. No matter how much we follow the news, we rarely know the truth or the human consequences. Unhappiness festers and grows only when the war is not wrapped up in weeks or months.

America also exempts itself from all the rules. There is one set of rules for us and another set for the rest of the world. This is *not* a double standard – the great economist Adam Smith called it the single standard: "the vile maxim of the masters of mankind" - all for us and the rest of the world be damned. The United States refuses to be a party to the Kyoto Treaty that calls for the reduction of pollution because President Bush said it would hurt our economy and be too costly to implement – even though it endangers the planet and the lives of millions. We refuse to join the International Court of Justice because we would be bound by their decisions, yet we espouse slogans like "justice and liberty for all." Imperialists throughout history have behaved this way, from the Romans to the British, always telling themselves they were driven by a noble purpose - even as they wreaked havoc for material gain.

The United States used to be the beacon to the world; the admiration of all. Something happened. Today, everyone hates us because our rhetoric is at odds with our actions. We have overthrown governments on every continent. We pay lip service to procedural democracy while doing all we can to rig the outcome of foreign elections. When citizens elect Hamas, Hezbollah, Chavez, Castro or Ahmadinejad, we refuse to accept the democratic verdict of their people. On the other hand, we support any dictatorial regime abroad that is amenable to our economic interests or global plan.

Americans do not like to believe that our nation's actions are motivated by empire and self-interest, so our leaders present our overseas adventures as motivated by benevolence, Christian charity, and a noble desire to liberate the oppressed. The blessings of freedom that President McKinley claimed to bestow on the Cubans and the Filipinos; that President William Howard Taft claimed the United States was bringing to Central America; and that later presidents claimed they were spreading from Iran to Grenada, are the same ones that we used to justify our invasion of Iraq.

Our enemies have run the gambit since the end of World War II – Khrushchev, Mao, Sukarno, Castro, Qaddafi, Khomeini, and Saddam. Today it is Ahmadinejad, Kim Jong II, and Hugo Chavez; we never seem to run out of enemies to justify our military expenditures. We are fighting wars in Afghanistan and Iraq from our bases in Saudi Arabia, Pakistan, Somalia, Yemen, and Ethiopia. We are planning to take on Iran and Syria – all to revenge the diabolical work of nineteen clever suicide terrorists. We are told that unless we win this 'war on terror' we will face certain nuclear devastation. It is the same story we were told during the Cold War. It was not true then – it may or may not be true today - but it hard to envision a safer America by bombing thousands of Muslims who had nothing to do with 9/11.

We have been lied to so often by experts that is hard to know what the truth is. Donald Rumsfeld has now retired to sulk in private life. Dick Cheney, who was our de-facto commander-in-chief for the eight years of the Bush administration, is a man with so much bravado that he can convince people he is completely right even when he is completely wrong. He was certain that we were winning in Iraq and Afghanistan, when in fact we were losing. He explained that "staying the course" was our only option and if you disagreed with him it was because you had no backbone or lacked the requisite mentality to understand the situation. He spoke to the nation as if we were dummies that he had to begrudgingly take care of. According to Cheney, the enemy is everywhere.

We all know that losing 3,000 American lives in 9/11 was a great tragedy. Yet, over 500,000 Americans die from cancer each year and there is no public outcry. The death rate for cancer has barely changed since 1950, but our technology created the Internet, iphones, and "smart" bombs. When America wanted to put a man on the moon all it took was funds and commitment – the same could be true of curing cancer if we were not diverted elsewhere. Each year there are fewer patients enrolled in clinical cancer trials because there is not enough money. Fewer clinical trials mean fewer new treatments. U.S. funding for cancer is 60 percent of what the tobacco industry spends on encouraging teenagers to smoke. Does this make any sense? Are new weapons more important than cancer cures?

To find out the truth about what is going on in the world today it is important to view the economic implications. It is rare that American capitalism is not at the bottom of every major news story; it just takes some sorting out to get the connection. The key is not to believe everything you read or hear. David Halberstam, one of America's most respected journalists, put it this way:

"If there is one thing you must learn above all else it is to be skeptical of official accounts, to always stay on guard against the lies, fabrications, half-truths, misrepresentations, exaggerations and all other manifestations of falsehood that are fired at us like machine-gun bullets by government officials and others in high places, often with lethal results. You have to keep digging, keep asking questions, otherwise you will be seduced into believing the lies they are feeding you."

If there is one truism about capitalism it is that compassion has no place on its balance sheet or profit and loss statement. Capitalist greed is as infectious as the plague, ravishing the mindset of Wall Street tycoons and highly-paid corporate executives, as well as small business entrepreneurs. Human lives divorced from the profit motive become irrelevant. America's vital issues, such as outsourcing jobs, health care, and education – are determined by how it affects corporate or our own self-interest.

Common sense should tell us that such a system that benefits the few to the disadvantage of the many is not sustainable and must eventually self-destruct. This is not to suggest that capitalism needs to be replaced, but it certainly needs to be tempered with a heavy dose of compassion and patriotic pride. A few examples should suffice.

During the 1970s, the Ford Pinto was one of the best-selling subcompact cars in the United States. Unfortunately, its fuel tank was prone to explode when another car collided with it from the rear. More than five hundred people died when their Pintos burst into flames, and many more suffered severe burn injuries.

When one of the burn victims sued Ford Motor Company for the faulty design, evidence emerged at the trial that Ford engineers had been aware of the danger posed by the gas tank. But company executives had conducted a cost-benefit analysis and determined that the benefits in fixing the problem (lives saved and injuries prevented) were not worth the eleven dollars per car it would cost to equip each car with a device to make the gas tank safer.

To calculate the benefits to be gained by a safer gas tank, Ford estimated that another 180 deaths and 180 burn injuries would result if no changes were made. It then placed a monetary value on each life lost and injury suffered - $200,000 per life, and $67,000 per injury. It added to these amounts the number and value of the Pintos likely to go up in flames, and calculated that the overall benefit of the safety improvement would be $49.5 million. But the cost of adding this $11 device to 12.5 million vehicles would be $137.5 million. So the company concluded that the cost of fixing the fuel tank was not worth the benefits of a safer car. Is it any wonder that the U.S. auto industry eventually self-destructed?

Philip Morris, the tobacco company, does big business in the Czech Republic where cigarette smoking remains popular and is socially acceptable. Worried about the rising health care costs of smoking, the Czech government recently considered raising taxes on cigarettes. In hopes of fending off the tax increase, Philip Morris commissioned a cost-benefit analysis of the effects of smoking on the Czech national budget. The study found that the government actually gains more money than it loses from smoking. The reason: although smokers impose higher medical costs on the budget while they are alive, they die early and so save the government considerable sums in health care, pensions, and housing for the elderly. According to the study, once the "positive effects" of smoking are taken into account – the savings due to the premature deaths of smokers - the net gain to the treasury is $147 million per year.

Philip Morris illustrates the moral folly of capitalist thinking: bottom-line profits takes precedence over human lives. Philip Morris is in the business of making money, not in moralizing or considering the consequences of public health and human well-being. The Czech government finally agreed with Philip Morris and discarded the proposed tax increase. Everyone was now happy; the Czech citizens continued puffing away on their cancer-producing cigarettes, the Czech treasury would be more solvent in the long run, and Philip Morris continued making huge profits from its death-inducing product.

In the summer of 2004, Hurricane Charley roared out of the Gulf of Mexico and swept across Florida. The storm claimed twenty-two lives and caused $11 billion in damage. It also left in its wake a debate about price gouging. At a gas station in Orlando, they were selling two-dollar bags of ice for ten dollars. Lacking power for refrigerators or air-conditioning in the middle of August, many people had little choice but to pay up. Downed trees heightened demand for chain saws and roof repairs. Contractors offered to clear two trees off a homeowner's roof for $ 23,000. Stores that normally sold small household generators for $250 were now asking $2,000. A seventy-seven-year-old woman fleeing the hurricane with her elderly husband and handicapped daughter was charged $160 per night for a motel room that normally goes for $40.

Many Floridians were angered by the inflated prices. "After the Storm Come the Vultures," read a headline in *USA Today*. One resident told the news media that it would cost $10,500 to remove a fallen tree from his roof, and said that it was wrong for people to "try to capitalize on other people's hardship and misery." Charlie Crist, Florida's attorney-general at the time, agreed: "It is astounding to me, the level of greed that someone must have in their soul to be willing to take advantage of someone suffering in the wake of a hurricane."

But many economists disagreed. They argued that the public outrage was misconceived. In capitalist societies, prices are set by supply and demand. There is no such thing as a "just price." If ice fetches ten dollars a bag when Floridians are facing power outages in the August heat, ice manufacturers will find it worth their while to produce and ship more ice. There is nothing unjust about these prices, the economists explained; they simply reflect the value that buyers and sellers choose to place on the things they exchange. That is what a "free" market economy is all about – charging whatever the market will bear.

Economics aside – can this kind of philosophy be morally right? Are these the lessons we want taught to our children – that when an emergency strikes it is an opportunity to make a few extra bucks?

Let's bring capitalist greed up-to-date and examine the financial crisis of 2008-2009. For years, stock prices and real estate values climbed to record heights. The reckoning came when the housing bubble burst. Wall Street banks and financial institutions had made billions of dollars on complex investments backed by mortgages whose value now plunged, and once proud Wall Street firms teetered on the edge of collapse. The stock market tanked, devastating not only big investors, but also ordinary Americans whose retirement accounts lost much of their value.

In October 2008, President George W. Bush asked Congress for $700 billion to bail out the nation's big banks and financial firms. It didn't seem fair that Wall Street had enjoyed huge profits during the good times and was now asking taxpayers to foot the bill when things had gone bad. But there seemed no alternative. The banks and financial firms had grown so vast and so entwined with every aspect of the economy that their collapse might bring down the entire financial system. They were "too big to fail."

No one claimed that the banks and investment houses deserved the money. Their reckless bets (enabled by inadequate government regulation) had created the crisis. But here was a case where the welfare of the economy as a whole seemed to outweigh considerations of fairness. Congress reluctantly appropriated the bailout funds.

Shortly after the bailout money began to flow, news accounts revealed that some of these very same companies were awarding millions of dollars in bonuses to their executives. The most egregious case involved the American International Group, an insurance giant brought to ruin by the risky investments of its financial products unit. Despite having been rescued with massive infusions of government funds (totaling $173 billion), the company paid $165 million in bonuses to executives in the very division that had precipitated the crisis. Seventy-three employees received bonuses of $1 million or more.

This time the outrageous behavior was not about ten-dollar bags of ice or overpriced motel rooms. It was about lavish rewards subsidized with taxpayer funds to members of a division that had helped bring the global financial system to near meltdown. Something is drastically wrong with this picture. At the heart of all these outrages is a sense of injustice. The bonuses were rewarding greed. And it was not only the bonuses; the bailout as a whole seemed, perversely, to reward greedy behavior rather than punish it. The derivatives traders had landed their company, and the country, in dire financial peril - by making reckless investments in pursuit of ever-greater profits. Having pocketed the profits when times were good, they saw nothing wrong with receiving million-dollar bonuses even after their investments had come to ruin.

When we view America's economic decline over the past few decades we cannot ignore that the capitalist system that brought America to the summit, is now responsible for "pushing us over the cliff," as Warren Buffet aptly put it. We can ignore the truth if we choose, or we can wake up before we find our democratic society in the hands of extremists on the 'right' or the 'left.'

In the movie *A Few Good Men*, Colonel Jessep played by Jack Nicholson is asked on the witness stand to tell the truth about the cover-up killing of a young Marine. His answer was, "You want the truth? You can't handle the truth." This is a question each of us must honestly confront. Maybe we really do not want to know the truth. Maybe we want to follow along aimlessly like sheep. In another movie, *Network*, a television newscaster named Howard Keal is fed up with all our nation's lies and deceits. He gets all his viewers to stand up, open their windows and shout to the outside world, "I'm mad as hell and I'm not going to take it anymore." Unfortunately, Howard Keal gets fired for creating a fuss and Corporate America goes on as before. That's the way our system usually works. The strong do what they have the power to do and the weak accept the results.

I am reminded of the following statement:

> "Naturally, the common people don't want war; but after all, it is the leaders of a country who determine the policy, and it is always a simple matter to drag people along whether it is a democracy, or a fascist government, or a parliament, or a communist dictatorship. Voice or no voice, the people can always be brought to the bidding of the leaders. This is easy. All you have to do is tell them they are being attacked and denounce the pacifists for lack of patriotism and exposing the country to danger: It works the same in every country."

That was Hermann Goering describing the rise of Nazi Germany.

George Santayana, the famous Spanish philosopher, essayist, poet and novelist, prophetically said: "Those who cannot remember the past are condemned to repeat it." We Americans have a special tendency to ignore history. We remember only what is pleasant. Joseph Goebbels, the infamous Nazi minister for propaganda, explained how Nazism took over a civilized democratic nation like Germany: "The masses do not want to be burdened with problems. They desire only one thing: to be led by a great leader." For America to avoid such a fate requires a sense of the past and a herculean involvement from all its citizens. That is what democracy is truly all about.

EPILOGUE

On Tuesday, November 4, 2008, Barak Hussein Obama was elected President of the United States and suddenly everything seemed different. Americans went to the polls and voted in record numbers, and when the election results were tallied, nobody could really believe that a black man was president. Only 130 years ago blacks were still slaves; 50 years ago education facilities were still segregated; and less than 40 years ago a black could not sit next to a white person at a lunch counter, and now a black man was sitting in the Oval Office. Suddenly all the rhetoric about the 'American Dream' seemed possible. All over our great land, Americans shouted for joy and danced in the streets. Throughout the world people who hated us for various reasons, looked at America once again with wonder and awe. It was a proud moment to be an American.

Obama takes over a nation that has been crippled by eight years of executive-power plays and constitutional abuses. We are still fighting wars in Iraq and Afghanistan that costs our nation billions of dollars and hundreds of American lives. Iran continues to loom as a major threat and our relations with Russia have turned sour. Al-Qaeda terrorism continues to pose a menacing threat. Our economy is experiencing an unprecedented meltdown as the public tries to understand the meaning of derivatives, swaps, subprime, and our catastrophic national debt.

There have been many awful mistakes made in this country, but maybe now we have another chance. Barak Obama has inherited a mess and has a tough road ahead. Whether he is up to the task only history will judge. At Coretta Scott King's funeral in early 2006, Ethel Kennedy, the widow of Robert Kennedy, leaned over to the then Senator Obama and whispered, "The torch is being passed to you." Her words were prophetic. Many were reminded of one of Martin Luther King Jr's speeches, where he quoted a prayer from a preacher who was once a slave; it is an apt description of our past and present.

> Lord, we ain't what we want to be;
>
> We ain't what we ought to be;
>
> We ain't what we gonna be;
>
> But, thank God, we ain't what we was.

The story of America is like an epic drama. Act One describes its humble colonial beginnings. Act Two depicts its rise to greatness. In Act Three, America achieves economic and military supremacy, but the signs of decay are evident. The suspense mounts as we near the conclusion. How will it end? "Ah, that's the rub," Shakespeare would say.

BIBLIOGRAPHY

- Ackerman, Bruce – The Failure of the Founding Fathers
- Ahamed, Liaquat – Lords of Finance
- Alleged Assassination Attempts on Foreign Leaders
- Alperovitz, Gar – The Decision To Use The Atomic Bomb
- Alter, Jonathan – The Defining Moment
- Alterman, Eric – When Presidents Lie
- Amar, Akhil – America's Constitution
- Ambrose, Stephen – Nothing Like It In The World
- Anderson, Terry – Den of Lions
- Arendt, Hannah - The Origins of Totalitarianism
- Arnold, Thurman – The Folklore of Capitalism
- Bacevich, Andrew – American Empire
- Bacevich, Andrew – The New American Military
- Bacevich, Andrew – The Limits of Power
- Bamford, James – Body of Secrets
- Bamford, James – A Pretext for War
- Bamford, James – The Puzzle Palace
- Barber, Benjamin – Consumed
- Barber, Benjamin – Jihad vs. McWorld
- Barrow, Clyde – More Than A Historian
- Bauer, Yehuda – Jews for Sale?
- Beard, Charles – A Brief History of the United States
- Beard, Charles – A Century of Progress
- Beard, Charles – America Faces the Future
- Beard, Charles – America in Midpassage

- Beard, Charles – American Foreign Policy In the Making
- Beard, Charles – American Leviathan
- Beard, Charles – An Economic Interpretation of the Constitution
- Beard, Charles – Economic Origins of Jeffersonian Democracy
- Beard, Charles – President Roosevelt and the Coming of War
- Beard, Charles – Readings in American Government and Politics
- Beard, Charles – The American Spirit
- Beard, Charles – The Enduring Federalist
- Beard, Charles – The Idea of National Interest
- Beard, Charles – The Republic
- Beard, Charles – The Rise of American Civilization
- Beatty, Jack – Age of Betrayal
- Beeman, Richard – Plain, Honest Men
- Beran, Michael – Forge of Empires
- Berg, Scott - Goldwyn
- Berger, Suzanne – How We Compete
- Berman, Morris – Dark Ages America
- Bernstein, William – A Splendid Exchange
- Beschloss, Michael – Presidential Courage
- Bess, Michael – Choices Under Fire
- Bill, James – The Eagle and the Lion
- Bird, Kai – American Prometheus
- Black, Edwin – IBM and the Holocaust
- Black, Edwin – War Against the Weak
- Blackmon, Douglas – Slavery by Another Name
- Blight, David – Race and Reunion

- Bobbitt, Philip – Terror and Consent
- Bobbitt, Philip – The Shield of Achilles
- Bobrick, Benson – Angel in the Whirlwind
- Boorstin, Daniel – The Americans: the Colonial Experience
- Boorstin, Daniel – The Democratic Experience
- Boorstin, Daniel – The National Experience
- Borjesson, Kristina – Feet To The Fire
- Borning, Bernard – The Political and Social Thought of Charles A. Beard
- Boyer, Paul – Oxford Guide to U.S. History
- Branch, Taylor – Parting the Waters
- Branch, Taylor – At Canaan's Edge
- Brandt, Allan – The Cigarette Century
- Brewer, Susan - Why America Fights
- Brinkley, Douglas – Tour of Duty
- Briody, Dan – The Haliburton Agenda
- Briody, Dan – The Iron Triangle
- Bronson, Rachel – Thicker Than Oil
- Brown, Sherrod – Myths of Free Trade
- Browning, Christopher – Ordinary Men
- Brzezinski, Zbigniew – The Choice
- Brzezinski, Zbigniew – Second Chance
- Buchanan, Patrick - Churchill, Hitler, and the Unnecessary War
- Buchanan, Patrick – The Great Betrayal
- Buchanan, Patrick – State of Emergency
- Bugliosi, Vincent – Reclaiming History
- Burk, Kathleen – Old World, New World
- Burns, Stewart – To The Mountaintop

- Byrd, Robert – Losing America
- Caro, Robert – The Years of Lyndon Johnson
- Carroll, James – House of War
- Carter, Dan – The Politics of Rage
- Castro, Fidel – My Life
- Castro, Fidel – Nothing Can Stop the Course of History
- Chadwick, Bruce – 1858
- Chadwick, Bruce - Triumvirate
- Chandler, Alfred – Leviathans
- Chernow, Ron – Alexander Hamilton
- Chernow, Ron – The House of Morgan
- Chernow, Ron - Titan
- Childers, Thomas – Europe and Western Civilization
- Chomsky, Noam – Failed States
- Chomsky, Noam – Hegemony or Survival
- Chomsky, Noam – Media Control
- Chomsky, Noam – Understanding Power
- Christopher, Robert – Crashing the Gates
- Church, Forrester – God and Other Famous Liberals
- Chua, Amy – World on Fire
- Cleaver, Kathleen – Liberation, Imagination, and the Black Panther Party
- Cohan, William – House of Cards
- Cohen, Adam – Nothing To Fear
- Cooke, Alistair – America
- Cowley, Robert – What If?
- Crenson, Matthew – Presidential Power
- Culver, John – American Dreamer
- D'Souza, Dinesh - The End of Racism

- Dallek, Robert – Nixon and Kissinger
- Davis, David – Inhuman Bondage
- Davis, Devra – The Secret History of the War on Cancer
- Dershowitz, Alan – America On Trial
- Dershowitz, Alan – Finding Jefferson
- DiLorenzo, Thomas – How Capitalism Saved America
- Domhoff, G. William – Who Rules America?
- Domhoff, G. William – C. Wright Mills and The Power Elite
- Douglass, James – JFK and the Unspeakable
- Downey, Kirstin – The Woman Behind the New Deal
- Draper, Theodore – A Very Thin Line
- Drucker, Peter – The New Realities
- Dye, Thomas – Who's Running America?
- Eakin, Marshall – Conquest of the Americas
- Ebenstein, Alan – Today's Isms
- Edsforth, Ronald – The New Deal
- Ellis, Charles – The Partnership
- Ellis, Joseph – Founding Brothers
- Ellis, Joseph – His Excellency
- Ellsberg, Daniel - Secrets
- Emery, Fred – Watergate
- English, T.J. – Havana Nocturne
- Everest, Larry – Oil, Power, & Empire
- Exner, Judith – My Story
- Falk, Richard – The Declining World Order
- Farber, David – Taken Hostage
- Farrow, Anne – Complicity
- Faux, Jeff – The Global Class War
- Feingold, Henry – Bearing Witness

- Ferguson, Niall – The Ascent of Money
- Ferguson, Niall – The Cash Nexus
- Ferguson, Niall – The Pity of War
- Ferguson, Niall – Colossus
- Ferling, John – Adams v. Jefferson
- Ferling, John – A Leap in the Dark
- Fineman, Howard – The Thirteen American Arguments
- Foner, Eric – Reconstruction: America's Unfinished Revolution
- Fouskas, Vassilis – The New American Imperialism
- Frank, Robert – Luxury Fever
- Frank, Thomas – What's The Matter with Kansas?
- Freehling, William – The Road to Disunion – Volume I, II
- Frieden, Jeffrey – Global Capitalism
- Friedman, Benjamin – The Moral Consequences of Economic Growth
- Friedman, Thomas – Longitudes and Attitudes
- Friedman, Thomas – The Lexus and the Olive Branch
- Friedman, Thomas – The World Is Flat
- Fromm, Erich – The Anatomy of Human Destructiveness
- Fulbright, William – The Arrogance of Power
- Furiati, Claudia – ZR Rifle
- Gaddis, John – The U.S. and the Origins of the Cold War
- Gaddis, John – The Cold War: A New History
- Gaddis, John – We Now Know
- Galbraith, John - The Age of Uncertainty
- Garrison, Jim – America as Empire
- Garvey, Helen – Rebels With A Cause
- Gentry, Curt – J. Edgar Hoover

- Gerson, Joseph – With Hiroshima Eyes
- Giancana, Antoinette – JFK and Sam
- Giancana, Chuck – Double Cross
- Ginger, Ray – The Bending Cross
- Gladwell, Malcolm - Outliers
- Glantz, Stanton – The Cigarette Papers
- Gold, Philip – The Coming Draft
- Goldberg, Harvey – American Radicals
- Goldfarb, Ronald – Perfect Villains, Imperfect Heroes
- Goldhagen, Daniel – A Moral Reckoning
- Goldman, Emma – Living My Life
- Goldstein, Gordon – Lesson in Disaster
- Goodman, Amy – The Exception to the Rulers
- Goodwin, Doris – Team of Rivals
- Gordon, John Steele – An Empire of Wealth
- Gordon, John Steele – The Great Game
- Gottfried, Martin – Arthur Miller
- Graham, ELizabeth – The Real Ones
- Grandin, Greg – Empire's Workshop
- Grass, Gunter – Peeling the Onion
- Greenspan, Alan – The Age of Turbulence
- Greider, William – One World, Ready or Not
- Greider, William – Secrets of the Temple
- Greider, William – Who Will Tell the People?
- Grey, Stephen – Ghost Plane
- Gross, Jan - Neighbors
- Grossman, David – On Killing
- Guelzo, Allen – Lincoln's Emancipation Proclamation
- Hagedorn, Ann – Savage Peace

- Halberstram, David – War in a Time of Peace
- Hall, Kermit – Oxford Companion to American Law
- Hall, Kermit – Oxford Companion to the Supreme Court
- Hall, Kermit – Oxford Guide to Supreme Court Decisions
- Harris, Sam – Letter to a Christian Nation
- Hasegawa, Tsuyoshi – Racing the Enemy
- Hastings, Max - Retribution
- Hedges, Chris – American Fascists
- Herring, George – From Colony To Superpower
- Hersh, Burton – Bobby and J. Edgar
- Hersh, Seymour – The Dark Side of Camelot
- Hersh, Seymour – The Price of Power
- Hinckle, Warren – Deadly Secrets
- Hoffer, Eric – The True Believer
- Hook, Sidney – Out of Step
- Howe, Daniel – What Hath God Wrought
- Huntington, Samuel – The Clash of Civilizations
- Huntington, Samuel – Who Are We?
- Huq, Aziz – Unchecked and Unbalanced
- Irons, Peter – A People's History of the Supreme Court
- Irons, Peter – War Powers
- Isaacson, Walter – Benjamin Franklin
- Isaacson, Walter – Einstein
- Isaacson, Walter – The Wise Men
- Jacobson, Matthew - Whiteness
- Jacoby, Susan – The Age of American Unreason
- Jacoby, Susan – Alger Hiss and the Battle for History
- Jentleson, Bruce – With Friends Like These
- Johnson, Chalmers – Blowback

- Johnson, Chalmers – Nemesis
- Johnson, Paul – A History of the United States
- Johnston, David – Perfectly Legal
- Jones, Geoffrey – Multinationals and Global Capitalism
- Josephy, Alvin – 500 Nations
- Juhasz, Antonia – The Bush Agenda
- Kaiser, David – The Road to Dallas
- Kaplan, Robert – The Imperial Grunts
- Karp, Walter – The Politics Of War
- Katz, Fred – Ordinary People and Extraordinary Evil
- Kawashima, Yasuhide – Puritan Justice and the Indian
- Kelly, Cynthia – The Manhattan Project
- Kempe, Frederick – Divorcing the Dictator
- Kennedy, David – Freedom From Fear
- Kennedy, David – The American People in World War II
- Kennedy, Thomas – Charles Beard and American Foreign Policy
- Kershaw, Ian – Fateful Choices
- Kino Video – The Good Fight
- Kinzer, Stephen – Overthrow
- Klare, Michael – Blood and Oil
- Klein, Naomi – The Shock Doctrine
- Kleinknecht, William – The Man Who Sold The World
- Kluger, Richard – Ashes to Ashes
- Kluger, Richard – Seizing Destiny
- Kozol, Jonathan – The Shame of the Nation
- Krugman, Paul – The Great Unraveling
- Krugman, Paul – Peddling Prosperity
- Krugman, Paul – Conscience of a Liberal

- Langley, Monica – Tearing Down the Walls
- Lankford, Nelson – Cry Havoc!
- Lepore, Jill – New York Burning
- LeShan, Lawrence – The Psychology of War
- Levy, Leonard – The Establishment Clause
- Levy, Leonard – Original Intent
- Lewis, Michael – Liar's Poker
- Lipton, Robert – Hiroshima in America
- Liulevicius, Vejas – War, Peace, and Power
- Liulevicius, Vejas – Utopia and Terror
- Loewen, James – Lies My Teacher Told Me
- Lukas, J. Anthony – Big Trouble
- Lynn, Barry – End of the Line
- M.P.I. Home Video – Lifting the Fog
- Madaras, Larry – Taking Sides
- Mahler, Jonathan – The Challenge
- Maier, Charles – Among Empires
- Mailer, Norman – The Big Empty
- Mann, James – Rise of the Vulcans
- Marrs, Jim – Crossfire
- Martin, William – With God on Our Side
- Maumeister, Roy – Evil
- McCullough, David – 1776
- McCullough, David – John Adams
- McDermott, Terry – Perfect Soldiers
- McDougall, Walter – Freedom Just Around the Corner
- McKenna, George – The Puritan Origins of American Patriotism
- McKnight, Gerald – The Last Crusade

- McPherson, Myra – All Governments Lie!
- McPherson, James – Battle Cry for Freedom
- Meacham, John – American Lion
- Meacham, John – Franklin and Winston
- Mead, Walter Russell – God and Gold
- Means, Howard – The Avenger Takes His Place
- Middlekauff, Robert – The Glorious Cause
- Mills, C. Wright – The Power Elite
- Monk, Linda – The Words We Live By
- Morgan, Ted - Reds
- Morison, Samuel – The Growth Of The American Republic
- Morris, Roy – Fraud of the Century
- Mueller, John – Overblown
- Murphy, Cullen – Are We Rome?
- Nash, Gary – Forbidden Love
- Neiman, Susan – Moral Clarity
- Neufeld, Michael – The Bombing of Auschwitz
- North, Oliver – Under Fire
- Nye, Joseph – Bound To Lead
- Nye, Joseph – Must History Repeat the Great Conflicts?
- Nye, Joseph – Understanding International Conflicts
- O'Neill, John – Unfit For Command
- Oates, Stephen – Our Fiery Trial
- Oglesby, Carl – Ravens in the Storm
- Olson, Keith – Watergate
- Orwell, George - 1984
- PBS Home Video – The Civil War
- PBS Home Video - Reconstruction
- Patterson, James – Grand Expectations

- Patterson, James – Restless Giant
- Pendergrast, Mark – For God, Country, and Coca-Cola
- Pepper, William – An Act of State
- Perkins, John – Confessions of an Economic Hit Man
- Perlstein, Rick - Nixonland
- Perret, Geoffrey – Commander in Chief
- Perret, Geoffrey – Lincoln's War
- Peters, William – A More Perfect Union
- Phillips, Kevin – American Theocracy
- Phillips, Kevin – The Politics of Rich and Poor
- Phillips, Kevin – Wealth and Democracy
- Pietrusza, David – 1920
- Polenberg, Richard – Fighting Faiths
- Pollack, Kenneth – The Threatening Storm
- Pollack, Kenneth – The Persian Puzzle
- Porter, Bernard – Empire and Superempire
- Quigley, John – The Ruses of War
- Raab, Selwyn – Five Families
- Radcliff, Pamela – Interpreting the 20th Century
- Rakove, Jack – Original Meanings
- Ranelagh, John – The Agency
- Reeves, Richard – Ronald Reagan
- Rehnquist, William – All The Laws But One
- Reich, Robert - Supercapitalism
- Reynolds, David – From Munich to Pearl Harbor
- Reynolds, David – Summits
- Reynolds, David – Waking Giant
- Richardson, Heather – West from Appomattox
- Roberts, Paul – The End of Oil

- Robertson, Pat – The New World Order
- Rosecrance, Richard – The Rise of the Trading State
- Rosen, Jeffrey – The Supreme Court
- Rosin, Hanna – God's Harvard
- Russett, Bruce – No Clear and Present Danger
- Russo, Gus – Live By The Sword
- Ruttan, Vernon – Is War Necessary for Economic Growth?
- Safire, William – Lend Me Your Ears
- Sandel, Michael - Justice
- Savage, Charlie - Takeover
- Scahill, Jeremy – Blackwater
- Scalia, Antonin – Scalia Dissents
- Schecter, Barnet – The Devil's Own Work
- Schivelbusch, Wolfgang – Three New Deals
- Schlesinger, Arthur – The New Deal In Action
- Schlesinger, Arthur – The Crisis of the Old Order
- Schlesinger, Arthur – The Coming of the New Deal
- Schlesinger, Arthur – The Politics of Upheaval
- Schlesinger, Arthur – The Cycles of American History
- Schoor, Daniel – Come To Think Of It
- Shenon, Philip – The Commission
- Shiller, Robert – The Subprime Solution
- Shirer, William – The Nightmare Years
- Shirer, William – The Rise and Fall of the Third Reich
- Shogan, Robert – Backlash: The Killing of the New Deal
- Shulman, Alix – Red Emma Speaks
- Sick, Gary – All Fall Down
- Sick, Gary – October Surprise
- Simon, James - Lincoln and Chief Justice Taney

- Singer, Peter – Corporate Warriors
- Slaughter, Anne-Marie – The Idea That Is America
- Sloan, Cliff - The Great Decision
- Smith, J. Allen – The Spirit of American Government
- Solomon, Burt – FDR v. The Constitution
- Solomon, Norman – War Made Easy
- Sorensen, Ted – Counselor
- Speer, Albert - Memoirs
- Standiford, Les – Meet You In Hell
- Stauffer, John – Giants
- Stewart, David - Impeached
- Stinnett, Robert – Day of Deceit
- Stone, Geoffrey – Perilous Times
- Swearingen, Wesley – FBI Secrets
- Sweig, Julia – Friendly Fire
- Summers, Harry – On Strategy
- Szanto, Andras – What Orwell Didn't Know
- Takaki, Ronald – Hiroshima
- Talbot – Brothers
- Taylor, Nick – American Made
- Thomas, Gordon – Secrets & Lies
- Thompson, Nicholas – The Hawk and the Dove
- Timmerman, Kenneth – The Death Lobby
- Tirman, John – 100 Ways America Is Screwing Up The World
- Toland, John – Infamy
- Toobin, Jeffrey – The Nine
- Victor, George – The Pearl Harbor Myth
- Waldron, Lamar – Ultimate Sacrifice

- Walker, Samuel – In Defense of Civil Liberties
- Wallace, Max – The American Axis
- Walsh, Lawrence – Firewall
- Watkins, T.H. – The Hungry Years
- Watts, Steven – The People's Tycoon: Henry Ford
- Weiner, Tim – Legacy of Ashes
- Weinstein, Allen - Perjury
- Wessel, David - In Fed We Trust
- Wheelan, Charles – Naked Economics
- Wheelan, Joseph – Jefferson's Vendetta
- Williams, Edward – One Man's Freedom
- Williams, William – The Tragedy of American Diplomacy
- Wise, David – The Politics of Lying
- Wise, David – The Invisible Government
- Woods, Randall – LBJ
- Wright, Lawrence – The Looming Tower
- Wright, Robin – In the Name of God
- Wyman, David – The Abandonment of the Jews
- Wyman, David – The World Reacts to the Holocaust
- Yergin, Daniel – The Prize
- Zieger, Robert – American Workers, American Unions
- Zimbardo, Philip – The Psychology of Power and Evil
- Zimmermann, Warren – First Great Triumph
- Zinn, Howard – A People's History of the United States
- Zinn, Howard – A Power Government's Cannot Suppress
- Zinn, Howard -Postwar America: 1945-1971
- Zinn, Howard -The Politics of History
- Zinn, Howard – Voices of a People's History